The Complete Nyingma Tradition from Sutra to Tantra, Book 13

The Tsadra Foundation Series

published by Snow Lion, an imprint of Shambhala Publications

Tsadra Foundation is a U.S.-based nonprofit organization that contributes to the ongoing development of wisdom and compassion in Western minds by advancing the combined study and practice of Tibetan Buddhism.

Taking its inspiration from the nineteenth-century nonsectarian Tibetan scholar and meditation master Jamgön Kongtrül Lodrö Tayé, Tsadra Foundation is named after his hermitage in eastern Tibet, Tsadra Rinchen Drak. The Foundation's various program areas reflect his values of excellence in both scholarship and contemplative practice, and the recognition of their mutual complementarity.

Tsadra Foundation envisions a flourishing community of Western contemplatives and scholar-practitioners who are fully trained in the traditions of Tibetan Buddhism. It is our conviction that, grounded in wisdom and compassion, these individuals will actively enrich the world through their openness and excellence.

This publication is a part of the Tsadra Foundation's Translation Program, which aims to make authentic and authoritative texts from the Tibetan traditions available in English. The Foundation is honored to present the work of its fellows and grantees, individuals of confirmed contemplative and intellectual integrity; however, their views do not necessarily reflect those of the Foundation.

Tsadra Foundation is delighted to collaborate with Shambhala Publications in making these important texts available in the English language.

The Complete Nyingma Tradition from Sutra to Tantra, Book 13

Philosophical Systems and Lines of Transmission

Choying Tobden Dorje

TRANSLATED, INTRODUCED,
AND ANNOTATED BY
Gyurme Dorje

SNOW LION
BOULDER
2017

Snow Lion
An imprint of Shambhala Publications, Inc.
4720 Walnut Street
Boulder, Colorado 80301
www.shambhala.com

9 8 7 6 5 4 3 2 1

First Edition
Printed in the United States of America

♾ This edition is printed on acid-free paper that meets the American National Standards Institute z39.48 Standard.
♻ Shambhala makes every effort to print on recycled paper.
For more information please visit www.shambhala.com.

Distributed in the United States by Penguin Random House LLC
and in Canada by Random House of Canada Ltd

Designed by Gopa & Ted2, Inc.

LIBRARY OF CONGRESS CATALOGING-IN-PUBLICATION DATA

Chos-dbyiṅs-stobs-ldan-rdo-rje, Rdzogs-chen, 1785–1848, author.
[Mdo rgyud rin po che'i mdzod. English]
The complete Nyingma tradition from sutra to tantra / Choying Tobden Dorje;
translated by Gyurme Dorje.—First edition.
pages cm—(The Tsadra Foundation series)
Includes index.
ISBN 978-1-55939-435-2 (Books 1 to 10)
ISBN 978-1-55939-460-4 (Book 13)
ISBN 978-1-55939-459-8 (Book 14)
ISBN 978-1-55939-436-9 (Books 15 to 17)
1. Rñiṅ-ma-pa (Sect)—Doctrines. 2. Spiritual life—Rñiṅ-ma-pa (Sect). I. Title.
BQ7662.4.C468813 2014
294.3'923—dc23
2014007269

Contents

The author, Choying Tobden Dorje. Artist unknown.
Photo courtesy of Chenak Hūṃchen.

Preface to the 1986 Tibetan Publication of the Root Verses and Outline

This treatise entitled *The Precious Treasury of Sūtra and Tantra* [presented in translation here as *The Complete Nyingma Tradition from Sutra to Tantra*], a work that elucidates all vehicles of spiritual development, not only focuses on the field of Buddhist studies; it also contains a complete and error-free exposition of secular fields of knowledge, including Sanskrit grammar, logic, arts, and medicine. In clear and concise language, this text synthesizes the very vast and extremely profound essence of the five major subjects of Tibetan classical learning. Like a magical tree that grants all wishes, this book provides whatever information one might wish to know concerning those fields of knowledge.

On this occasion of the publication of the root verses and the outline, I will introduce this work in accordance with the widely accepted five-point model for initiating a discussion of treatises: What is the title of this text? For whom was it written? Who is the author? How long is this work? What is its purpose? In keeping with this formula, I will answer these questions with reference to this very treatise that is under discussion.

First, the title of this treatise, *The Precious Treasury of Sūtra and Tantra,* denotes the basic text or root verses. The synoptic outline that concisely elucidates the content of this treatise is entitled *Outline of the Text: A Creeping Plant That Brings Forth Wishes.*

Second, for which students or practitioners was this treatise composed? For persons interested in the extraordinary fields of Buddhist studies, this excellent text elucidates the enlightened intention of the buddhas; the pith instructions of learned and accomplished masters, awareness holders, and genuine spiritual teachers; and the exegeses of the major fields of Tibetan classical learning. It presents the structure of ground, path, and result in respect of the sūtra and mantra vehicles. It differentiates the view, meditation, and conduct in accordance with the path. It outlines the gradation of vows and commitments in accordance with the discipline of individual liberation, the training of bodhisattvas, and the conduct of secret mantra. It is an edifying text, which excellently establishes study, reflection, and meditation, based on the author's own authentic reasoning.

In 1838 (the earth dog year of the fourteenth sexagenary cycle), Longchen Choying Tobden Dorje wrote the root verses and their commentaries. The composition of the words and the meanings contained in his treatise is superb, a treasure resembling a precious gem that elucidates and eloquently explains the entire range of the vehicles of spiritual development, completely and without error. It has the complete three-part classical literary format of an introduction, main text, and conclusion. The content of the main text is elucidated by brief introductions and extensive exegeses, and its headings include main topics and subtopics. The root verses are concise and written in verse to facilitate memorization. The extensive commentary in prose facilitates understanding of the intended meanings. The authority provided by supportive quotations from scripture elicits the reader's confidence beyond any doubt. The concise commentary and the illustrated version render the subject matter of this treatise increasingly clear.

Third, who is the author? The author of the root verses entitled *The Precious Treasury of Sūtra and Tantra* and its commentaries is Longchen Choying Tobden Dorje Mapham Chokle Nampar Gyelwa. He was born in 1785 (the wood snake year of the thirteenth sexagenary cycle) in the region of Repkong, in Amdo. He began writing this treatise in his fifty-first year, in 1836 (the fire monkey year of the fourteenth sexagenary cycle), and completed it in his fifty-third year, in 1838 (the earth dog year). Apart from this minimal information, which is explicitly stated in the colophon of the text, no other account of his life has come into our hands. That being the case, at the time of this publication [1986], owing to the long distances involved, we have been unable to conduct any detailed research into his birthplace, his engagement in enlightened activities, his responsibilities, or even the place where he lived in Amdo. We are therefore unable to trace the present legacy of his major or minor acts, and we ask those who publish the supplementary portions of this treatise in the future to strive to fill these gaps in our knowledge.

Fourth, what is the extent of the root verses of *The Precious Treasury of Sūtra and Tantra*? In terms of its content, this work comprises 100 general topics and 2,179 subtopics, divided into twenty-five books that span the entire gradation of the vehicles of spiritual development, commencing from discipleship and ending with the establishment of the stages of fruitional, conclusive accomplishment. In terms of its words, the root verses of the treatise are ascertained to have three sections: an introduction that is "virtuous at the beginning," a main part that is "virtuous in the middle," and a conclusion that is "virtuous at the end." Among these, the introduction and the conclusion are composed in thirteen-syllable lines of verse, whereas the main part is composed in nine-syllable lines of verse. Altogether it comprises 984 verses. Apart from the root verses, the words of the outline, the concise commentary, the extensive commentary, and the illustrated version are structured in prose. The volumes containing the root verses and the commentaries definitely number thirteen.

Fifth, for what purpose was this work composed? It will prove useful for persons of supreme and inferior acumen; it will accomplish what they desire, both for the short and the long term. Study of this text leads to the resolution of outer misconceptions and the attainment of the rank of a learned person. Meditation on this text resolves inner misconceptions and leads to actualization of the spiritual goals to which each person aspires. Such is the purpose for which this work was composed.

We will gradually publish *The Precious Treasury of Sūtra and Tantra,* its root verses and commentaries, as well as the illustrated version. In doing so our purpose is to provide a comprehensive and multipurpose resource for those who are generally interested in definitive and quantitative knowledge, and more specifically for researchers in Tibetan culture. That said, this is not our only motivating concern: the entirety of the root verses and commentaries of this treatise had been previously carved in woodblocks in Amdo, yet that turned out not to be of great benefit for living beings, since in the midst of various turbulent events that later occurred in the Qinghai area, the woodblocks themselves disappeared without a trace. Therefore, nowadays it is certain that only one or two copies of the original treatise, comprising the root verses and its commentaries, have survived, and the continued existence of these texts is endangered. Thus it seems surely necessary to act swiftly to preserve these texts by publishing books that replicate exactly the content of their original manuscript. In the present case, we now publish the root verses and the outline, with the plan to gradually publish the entire series of texts in this collection. Zenkar Rinpoche Tubten Nyima, with the intention of preserving Tibetan culture, has gladly lent us the original copies of the texts. Further, he has graciously offered suggestions to assure the success of these publications. On this occasion of the first in the series, we must offer him our deepest gratitude.

Nordrang Orgyan, editor
August 15, 1986

Nordrang Orgyan is a renowned scholar who now lives in retirement. His magnum opus is the three-volume Compendium of Buddhist Numeric Terms, *published in 2008. Formerly he served as director of the Academy of Social Sciences of the Tibet Autonomous Region and the Rare Texts Publishing House.*

A Biography of the Author, Choying Tobden Dorje

THE SUPREME UNIVERSAL MONARCH, the learned and accomplished Longchen Choying Tobden Dorje Mapham Chokle Nampar Gyelwa Pelzangpo, was a reincarnation in human form of the lord among conquerors, Saroruhavajra [Guru Rinpoche]. He was born in 1785 (the wood snake year of the thirteenth sexagenary cycle) at Zhopong, in the Sermojong area of Repkong, in Amdo, Tibet, the Land of Snows. His father was named Rinchen and his mother, an emanation of Yeshe Tsogyal, named Jomo Yeshe Dolma, also known by the name of Gyelyum Ngodrub Dolma. Their child was initially known by the name Gongbo Yonten.

From the time of his infancy, he innately displayed the character of a holy person. Many local teachers, incarnate lamas, and spiritual mentors taught him to read and write. As he persevered in his study of the classical sciences and Buddhism, the vault of his talents overflowed.

As Kalden Gyatso, the incarnation of Avalokiteśvara, states:

> The illustrious Padmākara of Oḍḍiyāna
> Journeyed to the region of Tibet, Land of Snows.
> Here, in general, he inaugurated countless sites sacred to the *ḍākinī*s
> And specifically sent forth hundreds of emanations simultaneously.
> They opened the portals to hundreds of palaces of the *ḍākinī*s,
> Including the major sacred place of Nyagong Drakar in the east
> And the place known as Chuchik Shelgyi Gonpa,
> Where they bound [mundane] gods and demons under oath.
> In past times, during the earlier spread of Buddhism in Amdo,

> The fine names of Repkong's eight sacred sites of spiritual accomplishment
> Were as well known as the sun and moon.[1]

He again states:

> Moreover, one by the name of Kawa Dorje Wang,
> A supreme mantrin from Katok Monastery in the east,
> Arrived in this sacred place of Shelgon and attained the rainbow light body.[2]

As these eulogies mention, among Repkong's eight sacred sites of spiritual accomplishment appears one by the name of Shelgon Dechen Chokyi Podrang, generally known as Chuchik Shelgyi Gonpa. Choying Tobden Dorje joined the spiritual community living there, and, after gradually receiving the monastic vows, along with the bodhisattva vows and the commitments of the secret mantra, he studied, pondered, and experientially cultivated the profound and extensive oral teachings (*bka' ma*), spiritual revelations (*gter ma*), and pure visionary teachings (*dag snang*) of the ancient Nyingma tradition. Following this, he traveled to Rabgya Gon Ganden Tashi Jungne Shedrub Dargyeling, a supreme center of Kadampa learning, where he attended upon many spiritual mentors, headed by Shingza Paṇḍita Lobzang Dargye Gyatso. For a period of five years he assumed the lifestyle of an ordinary monk without family ties as he studied and reflected upon the three collections of Buddhist scripture and experientially cultivated the three aspects of training that constitute the spiritual path. At the end of this period, he left to practice meditation in mountain hermitages without settling down in a fixed residence. On one occasion, as he was inspired by a prophetic declaration given by deities and his teachers, there arose within him a firm determination that he should set out to find an extraordinary teacher, the lord of his enlightened family, in the manner of the bodhisattva Sadāprarudita who had sought Dharmodgata. His purpose above all was to request the profound instruction that would propel him in a single lifetime, in that very rebirth, to the level of Buddha Samantabhadra.

Choying Tobden Dorje traveled southward and arrived at such places as Dzogchen Monastery in Kham, where from Dzogchen Tulku IV Migyur Namkha Dorje and his nephew Pema Kundrol, among others, he received maturational empowerments and liberating guidance, based on the oceanic doctrines of sūtra and tantra.

Then, in particular, Choying Tobden Dorje traveled to the Buddhist encampment (*chos sgar*) of Dodrubchen Rinpoche Jigme Trinle Ozer, where he remained for a long time. It was Dodrubchen Rinpoche on whom he relied as his extraordinary teacher, the lord of his enlightened family, and whom he served with the three ways of pleasing the teacher. In that location, he was given the maturational empowerments, liberating guidance, and supporting transmissions for the profound doctrines of sūtra and mantra in general and the three classes of yoga according to the inner tantras in particular, so that he came to resemble a vase that has been filled to the brim. Consequently, his view of reality became spacious, and he actualized the pristine cognition that arises on the path of no-more-learning. Realizing that Choying Tobden Dorje would become illustrious among disciples of the future and had the good fortune to be associated with certain deities through his past actions, Dodrubchen Rinpoche, the supreme lord of his enlightened family, granted him the profound wrathful mantras of the ancient Nyingma tradition, including the crucial instructions of the four pulverizing rites (*thal 'byin rnam pa bzhi*) of Vajrakumāra, the cycles of Yamāntaka headed by the four wheels of Mañjuśrī (*'jam dpal 'khor lo rnam bzhi*), and the overturning of ominous signs by means of the imprecations of the *mātaraḥ* (*ma mo rbod gtong*), along with many profound instructions through which *mantrin*s may attain buddhahood on the basis of burnt offerings, combined with rites of suppression, incineration, and bombardment. Through his meditation on these, the dichotomy of subject and object and all the thoughts that arose in his mind were infinitely transformed as the display of pristine cognition, meditational deities, and mantras, and he grew confident that he had unimpededly mastered the enlightened activities of wrathful sorcery.

At that point, the venerable teacher Dodrubchen Rinpoche declared, "This dark *mantrin* from the north is the designated inheritor of an ocean of wrathful mantras. I name him Longchen Choying Tobden Dorje, Unvanquished Conqueror of All Directions." Praising him by means of this decree, he added many predictions of future events, saying, "Now the time has come for you to liberate your own mind through realization and compassionately liberate the minds of others. Therefore, you should return to your homeland, nurture students, and tend to the well-being of the Buddhist teachings and sentient beings. Your service to beings will continuously flourish."

As advised, Longchen Choying Tobden Dorje then returned home to Repkong in Amdo, where, through masterly attainments, his resources and entourage increased. In his homeland, he founded Ko'ude Gon Dzogchen Namgyeling, which has since been sustained by his series of reincarnations. At the present day, its ritual practices and so forth appear to follow the tradition of Orgyan Mindroling.

Further, there is a treasure text that makes the following prediction:

> In the east, a white conch shell will appear with the resounding voice of Brahmā.
> In the south will appear a mound of white rice, like a round fortress.
> In the west will appear one like a blossoming orange lotus.
> In the north will appear one with force and might like a planted ritual spike.[3]

Accordingly, among the four main disciples of Dodrubchen Rinpoche with the name Dorje, who were likened to supporting beams (*gdung bzhi*), Longchen Choying Tobden Dorje is renowned as the "supporting beam in the north," the thunder of his reputation resounding throughout the heavens. With the activity of a learned scholar in teaching, debate, and composition, and with the enlightened activity of an accomplished master, training each according to need through pacification, enrichment, subjugation, and wrath, he accepted countless disciples, establishing them on the path of maturational [empowerment] and liberating [guidance].

In general, his prodigious acts sustained the Buddhist teachings impartially, and in particular, he ensured that the precious teachings of the *Innermost Spirituality of Longchenpa* belonging to the Ancient Translation School would continue without deterioration, as far as the limits of time and space. The line of disciples issuing from this master and from Palchen Namkha Jigme are known as the "nineteen hundred dark *mantrins* from Repkong who bear the ritual spike." The continuity of their doctrine forms an incomparable rampart that manifestly continues to protect the teachings to the present day.

In 1841 (the iron ox year of the fourteenth sexagenary cycle), Zhabkar Tsokdruk Rangdrol sent a letter of request to Choying Tobden Dorje on the occasion of the lunar new year celebration. Choying Tobden Dorje sent a letter in reply, and during that year he extensively offered Zhabkar Rinpoche the reading transmission and guidance on *The Precious Treasury of Sūtra and Tantra,* its root verses and commentaries. This information is recorded in the *Autobiography of Zhabkar.* At that time, Choying Tobden Dorje was in his fifty-seventh year, and Zhabkar Rinpoche had reached his sixty-first.

The foregoing account, which is merely illustrative, is transcribed from relevant portions of the *Doctrinal History of Amdo* (*mDo smad chos 'byung*), the *Successive Hierarchs of Rongpo Gonchen* (*Rong po dgon chen gyi gdan rabs*), the *Autobiography of Zhabkar Tsokdruk Rangdrol* (*Zhabs dkar tshogs drug rang grol gyi rang rnam*), and the *Doctrinal History Derived from the Innermost Spirituality of Luminosity* (*'Od gsal snying thig gi chos 'byung*). Furthermore, I traveled to Ko'ude Monastery in Repkong to compile whatever I could see or hear in their records and the like that could be investigated. Nevertheless, I was unable to discover, apart from a mere outline, how long Choying Tobden Dorje lived in the perception of his disciples in this worldly realm, or even the seed of a full, detailed account of how he sustained his enlightened activities in teaching, meditation practice, and altruistic acts.

However, the activities and biography of this supreme individual can be essentially illustrated by the letter that Zhabkar Tsokdruk Rangdrol sent to Choying Tobden Dorje in 1841 (the iron ox year of the fourteenth sexagenary cycle). Therefore, I include the letter here in its entirety; the *Autobiography of Zhabkar Tsokdruk Rangdrol* states:

> Seeing the general eloquence of the composition of Kusho Dzogchen Rinpoche [Choying Tobden Dorje], in whom both learning and accomplishment are gathered, and in particular, his major treatise entitled *The Precious Treasury of Sūtra and Tantra,* a steadfast, inviolable faith arose. On New Year's Day, I offered him this letter:
>
> May the deities of longevity—
> Lord Amitāyus, White Tārā, and the rest—
> Who confer the supreme accomplishment of long life
> Bestow the spiritual accomplishment of immortal life!

Supreme reincarnation of venerable Orgyan, emanation of the mind
Of the buddhas of the ten directions and three times,
In whom both learning and spiritual accomplishment are gathered,
Please direct your enlightened intention toward me!
Lord protector, in times past you attained buddhahood,
Yet in later generations for the disciples you accept,
You demonstrate a life of spiritual liberation
Solely in order to show them how buddhahood should be won.

First you cast [the cares of] this life from your mind
And attended upon the lotus feet of many learned and accomplished masters.
You received pith instructions and guidance concerning sūtra and tantra
And resolved outer misconceptions through study and reflection.

Next, in secluded mountain hermitages,
You resolved inner misconceptions through meditation.
The vault of your experience, realization, and talent overflowed.

Finally, in accordance with the prophecies of spiritual teachers and deities,
And at the encouragement of your fortunate disciples,
You increased the spiritual and temporal well-being
Of the teaching and of living beings, day and night,
By your empowerments, transmissions, guidance, and so on,
And by teaching, debate, and composition.

Like a store of gems, this *Precious Treasury of Sūtra and Tantra*
Holds the content of oceans of vast discourses
And of the profound tantras
Which are the words of the infinite conquerors of the ten directions
Headed by Munīndra, lord of the teaching.

It contains the crucial points of all treatises written by many scholars,
Commenting on the enlightened intention of the Conqueror's words.
It contains the practical application and experiential guidance
Of the lineages deriving from all supreme individuals
Who maintain the teaching.
It contains the teaching styles and exegetical transmission of the learned;
The ground, path, and fruition of the sūtra and mantra vehicles;
The trio of the view, meditation, and conduct; the three levels of vows;
The five major and five minor subjects of classical learning;
And the clear meanings of all the vehicles—
It is a treasure of complete and error-free eloquence.

You have written this for the well-being of the teaching and of living beings in general,
And especially to help fortunate individuals
Of the present and of times yet to come.
How very kind you are!
Spiritual master imbued with great kindness,
To you I bow in utmost humility.

I present masses of offerings, real and imagined, to you.
I confess the negativity of faithlessness and wrong view.
I rejoice in your supreme liberating career.
I beseech you even now to turn the wheel of the sacred doctrine.
I pray that you live for a hundred years.
And I dedicate my store of virtuous acts
To ensure your lotus feet remain firmly upon this earth.

Spiritual master, may your health be excellent, splendidly bright.
May you live long in supreme well-being.
Spiritual master, may the renown of your goodness spread,

> And especially, may your intended goals meet with success.
> May the wealth of your teachings' sponsors flourish,
> And may your doctrine long remain in this world.
>
> When I meet you and all those around you, the event I wish for,
> May the auspicious circumstances arise for our repeated meeting.
> In the enjoyment of jubilant happiness,
> May we all encounter auspicious circumstances
> Conducive to the practice of the sacred doctrine!

> I offered this letter accompanied by a physical representation of my intentions—pills made at the conclusion of my practice of longevity—and a gift of divine silk embroidered with the deities of longevity (*tshe sku can gyi lha rdzas*).

So Zhabkar Rinpoche wrote.

Although it is reported that the collection of treatises written by Choying Tobden Dorje includes many texts such as the *Final Act of Suppression, the Dark Mount Sumeru* (*mNan pa'i las mtha' ri rab nag po*), which belongs to his cycle on the practical application of wrathful mantra, his magnum opus is the treatise entitled *The Precious Treasury of Sūtra and Tantra,* elucidating all vehicles of spiritual development. This work comprises thirteen large volumes. He began its composition in 1836 (the fire monkey year of the fourteenth sexagenary cycle) and successfully completed it in 1838 (the earth dog year of the fourteenth sexagenary cycle) when he was in his fifty-fourth year.

This treatise has five sections: (i) the root verses (*rtsa ba*); (ii) the outline (*bsdus don*); (iii) the concise commentary (*'bru 'grel*); (iv) the extensive commentary (*rgyas 'grel*); and (v) the illustrated version (*dpe ris*). The root verses are in metrical verse, while the other sections are written in prose or in the form of captions. Among the thirteen volumes, volume 1 (KA) contains the root verses and the outline. Volume 2 (KHA) contains the concise commentary. The next nine volumes from volume 3 (GA) to volume 11 (DA) contain the extensive commentary. Among them, the sūtra section comprises two volumes, the subjects of Indo-Tibetan classical learning comprise two volumes, the tantra section comprises two volumes, and the Dzogchen section comprises three volumes. The last two volumes, 12 (NA) and 13 (PA), both contain the drawings that illustrate the text.

Although woodblocks were prepared for this treatise, they were destroyed by fire in 1938 through the depredations of the warlord Ma [Bufang]. Later, Choktrul Tubten Nyima, who deeply values the classical texts of the Tibetan tradition, and others of like mind searched for, collected, and prepared this edition, which we are now able to publish.

Respectfully written by one called Nor-de, an invalid and an ignorant fool from the land of Golok.

May excellent virtue prevail!

This biography is included in the 2000 edition of The Precious Treasury of Sūtra and Tantra (DGD), *printed by the Sichuan Nationalities' Publishing House. Its author, Nor-de, is a well-known writer and editor who has served as head of the National People's Congress Bureau of Golok Prefecture, Qinghai Province.*

Foreword to the English Translation of *The Precious Treasury of Sūtra and Tantra*

Dzogchen Choying Tobden Dorje was one of the four spiritual heirs of Dodrubchen Jigme Trinle Ozer who are known as the "four supporting beams with the name Dorje." He is identified [in that prophetic verse] as the "one from the north who resembled a meteorite spike thrust into the ground." This great embodiment of splendid renown was born in the Ponru clan in 1785 (the wood snake year of the thirteenth sexagenary cycle) at Zhopong Lakha in the Repkong district of Amdo. His father was named Rinchen and his mother Ngodrub Dolma. From childhood he joined the spiritual community close to his birthplace, at Shelgon Dechen Chokyi Podrang. There, he learned without difficulty to write, read aloud, and spell the Tibetan alphabet (*yi ge'i phyi mo*), and so forth. Under Waka Tsering, secretary to Chogyel Ngagi Wangpo, the local potentate (*sa skyong chen mo*), he perfectly trained in the ordinary subjects of classical learning, exemplified by various scripts and history, and after attending upon Shingza Paṇḍita Lobzang Dargye Gyatso at Rabgya Ganden Tashi Jungne, he applied himself to training in the entire range of the ten fields of classical learning.

Then, after mentally rejecting the excellent phenomenal appearances of this worldly life, Choying Tobden Dorje met Drubwang Pema Rangdrol, who had journeyed to the Repkong area for the benefit of living beings. While Drubwang Pema Rangdrol devoted himself for a number of years to the essence of spiritual practice in retreat at Drakar Tsegyal in Tsanggo Dzong, Choying Tobden Dorje and Drubwang Kalden Rangdrol both acted as his attendants. The supreme Nyangkye Nangdze Dorje said that this was in accord with the following prediction that had been made [in former times] by the great awareness holder Palden Tashi:

From the hermitage of Drakar Tsegyal,
A mother bird and two offspring will take flight.

It was in those circumstances that Choying Tobden Dorje received from Drubwang Pema Rangdrol the entire corpus entitled *Further Secret: Wish-Fulfilling Gem of Hayagrīva and Vajravārāhī* (*Yang gsang rta phag yid bzhin nor bu*), a treasure doctrine that had been revealed by Kunzang Dechen Gyelpo. In particular, he perfectly studied, pondered, meditated on, and mastered profound guidance in the Great Perfection, from the initial mind training of the outer and inner preliminary practices to the main practice. In this way the enlightened intention of reality, [union] of awareness and emptiness, was born in Choying Tobden Dorje's mind. This period coincided with the lifetime of the third incarnation of Rigdzin Palden Tashi, king of secret mantra in Repkong; in his next lifetime that master would be reborn as the *mantrin* Dorje Namgyal, father of the learned scholar Gendun Chopel.

Choying Tobden Dorje then traveled to Dzogchen Orgyen Samten Choling in Kham, where, in the presence of many learned and accomplished masters, including Dzogchen Tulku Migyur Namkha Dorje and his nephew Pema Kundrol Namgyal, he studied and trained in the doctrinal traditions of sūtra and mantra in general and insatiably drank from the nectar stream of maturational [empowerment] and liberating [guidance] according to the transmitted precepts and treasures. In particular, at that time, from Dodrub Kunzang Zhenpen [Trinle Ozer] who was staying at the Rudam Shinje meditation cave, he received many tantras, transmissions, and pith instructions pertaining to the vehicle of indestructible reality, including the *Earlier and Later Innermost Spirituality* (*sNying thig gong 'og*). Later also, when Dodrubchen Rinpoche resided at Yarlung Pemako, Choying Tobden Dorje went there to see him repeatedly and received [instruction on] the *Secret Nucleus from the Net of Magical Emanation* (*sGyu 'phrul gsang ba'i snying po*), the *Trilogy of Rest* (*Ngal gso skor gsum*), *Unsurpassed Pristine Cognition* (*Ye shes bla ma*), and so forth.

In 1828 (the earth male tiger year of the fourteenth sexagenary cycle) at Ko'ude Valley in Repkong, Choying Tobden Dorje founded the monastery of Dzogchen Namgyeling and nurtured an infinite number of students, including those known as the twenty-one teachers of the Great Perfection: Shardakpa Rabjampa, Bongtak Marik Munsel, Rigdzin Hūṃnak Mebar, and so forth. Further, Dodrub Rinpoche had once remarked that the auspicious conditions existed for the preceptor, master, and religious king to converge in the same household. In accordance with that prediction, Choying Tobden Dorje accepted the *ḍākinī* Kunga Chodron as his consort (*rig ma*). To them were born two sons: the omniscient Tenpe Nyima, an emanation of the great preceptor Śāntarakṣita; and Togden Tenpe Gyeltsen, an emanation of the religious king Trisong Detsen. Choying Tobden Dorje himself was unmistakably an emanation of Guru Rinpoche. Likewise, based on the timely ripening of the superb aspirations of three masters—Choying Tobden Dorje, Dola Jigme Kalzang Choying Dorje, and Khamla Namkha Gyatso—the large community of awareness holders known as Repkong Longchen Ngagmang developed.

The Precious Treasury of Sūtra and Tantra [presented here in translation as *The Complete Nyingma Tradition from Sutra to Tantra*] is the magnum opus among Choying Tobden Dorje's compositions, which were said to have filled almost twenty volumes. These writings included an autobiography (*rang rnam*), a collection of his songs of spiritual realization (*mgur tshogs*), a cycle on the practical application of wrathful mantra (*drag sngags lag len gyi skor*), and a supporting cycle on the profound doctrine (*zab chos yang rgyab skor*). Nevertheless, some of those very important books vanished, with only their titles remaining, in the midst of turbulent times. Apart from *The Precious Treasury of Sūtra and Tantra,* his remaining extant works have been published by the Qinghai Ngagmang Research Institute in two volumes: the *Guide to the Great Perfection according to the Cycle of the Further Secret: Wish-Fulfilling Gem of Hayagrīva and Vajravārāhī* (*Yang gsang rta phag yid bzhin nor bu*) and *An Anthology of the Miscellaneous Writings of Dzogchen Choying Tobden Dorje* (*rDzogs chen chos dbyings stobs ldan rdo rje'i gsung thor phyogs bsgrigs*). These two were printed in 2006 and 2010, respectively, through the Beijing Nationalities' Publishing House.

The Precious Treasury of Sūtra and Tantra contains the essence of the enlightened intention expressed in oceans of discourses and tantras delivered by the conquerors of the ten directions; the commentaries on the enlightened intention of the words of the buddhas written by many learned and accomplished masters of India and Tibet who elucidate the teaching; the practical application and experiential guidance deriving from the lineages of accomplished masters who maintain the teaching; the exegetical traditions of various learned teaching styles; the structure of the ground, path, and result of the sūtra and mantra vehicles; an analysis of view, meditation, and conduct; the gradation of vows and commitments in accordance with [the distinctions between the vows of] individual liberation, bodhisattva, and secret mantra; and an exegesis of the five major fields of classical learning. In this work, nothing is lacking, and it is unprecedented. Concerning its supreme eloquence, the sublime elderly master Dodrub Rinpoche made this timely prophetic declaration:

> At first you cast the concerns of this mundane life from your mind and in seclusion applied yourself with intense diligence. Through the trio of study, reflection, and meditation on the sacred doctrine, you excellently refined your own mental continuum. Next, you brought the mental continuum of others to maturation and liberation through the trio of teaching, debate, and composition. Finally, through the trio of understanding, meditative experience, and realization, you have most extensively enhanced the spiritual and temporal well-being of the doctrine and sentient beings, for your own sake and for the sake of others. Now, for the sake of fortunate persons of the present and the time yet to come, you must prepare an auspicious text with words that describe those experiences, one that establishes by means of the view the abiding nature of all phenomena of cyclic existence, nirvāna, and the spiritual path; that may be experientially cultivated through meditation; that achieves success through conduct; and that is imbued with blessings.

At the time this prediction came true, Tendzin Chogyel Tsering Dondrub Pelzangpo, the Qosot ruler of Kokonor (Qinghai), encouraged Choying Tobden Dorje to compose the work, promising at that time to facilitate its printing and aid the precious Buddhist teaching. Due to this and other auspicious coincidences, Choying Tobden Dorje began writing in 1836 (the fire monkey year of the fourteenth sexagenary cycle), and fortunately completed the task in 1838 (the earth dog year).

The root text is in verse; the synoptic outline explains the framework of the treatise; the concise commentary is written in prose; the extensive commentary is accompanied by supportive citations from the scriptures; and the illustrated version is extremely vivid. Thus, the whole work has these five main sections, which are contained in thirteen precious volumes, with three parts: an introduction, a main text, and a conclusion. These volumes in turn comprise twenty-five books, 2,179 subtopics, and eighty separate chapters, a number equal to the Buddha's minor marks of physical perfection.

Another of the spiritual heirs of Dodrubchen Rinpoche who were known as the "four supporting beams with the name Dorje" was Jigme Kelzang Choying Dorje, who is [described in the aforementioned prophecy] as the "white conch shell of the east who appeared with a resounding Brahmā-like voice." His reincarnation Dzong-ngon Pema Tukchok Dorje, who lived in the Repkong area, later praised *The Precious Treasury of Sūtra and Tantra* with these words:

> Its root text in verse facilitates memorization.
> Through its authentic citations from the canon confidence undoubtedly arises.
> The clarity of its extensive commentary facilitates understanding of the intended meaning.
> Its framework distinguishes main topics and subtopics.
>
> This eloquent composition imbued with these four special qualities
> Gathers in their entirety the essential points of the commentaries
> On the enlightened intention of oceanic discourses and tantras in general.
> And in particular, it articulates the profundity
> Of the six million tantras of the path of Atiyoga, highest of the vehicles.
> The content of this precious treasury, with its many profundities,
> An unprecedented treatise sealed with the seven possessions of a universal monarch,
> Is resplendent, for it lacks nothing; it is error-free and unadulterated.

With these words he clearly elucidated the uncommon, special qualities of this treatise.

Subsequently [following his completion of this treatise], the Qosot ruler of Qinghai, Tsering Dondrub; Choying Tobden Dorje's mother, Ngodrub Dolma; his son, the omniscient Tenpe Nyima; his disciples Kunpang Gendun Palden, Atsok Lektsok Gyatso, Lama Marik Munsel, and Lama

Dorje Sherab; and, likewise, his faithful patrons with their entourage collected the funds necessary to sponsor the original carving of the woodblocks of the treatise. Over time these individuals fostered the continuity of its reading transmission, teaching, and study. Apart from that, the carving of the woodblocks for the sections of the extensive commentary (entitled *A Beauteous Ornament of the Aeon of Mighty Brahmā*) which concern the *Tantra of the Secret Nucleus* and the cycle of the Great Perfection was undertaken much later; for the words of aspiration contained in the colophon of the first imprint clearly indicate that the latter carving was completed in 1903 (the water hare year of the fifteenth sexagenary cycle). The complete set of woodblocks for the thirteen volumes of *The Precious Treasury of Sūtra and Tantra* was installed at the seat of Dzogchen Namgyeling. Then, thirty-five years later, in March 1938, through the depredations of the Qinghai warlord [Ma Bufang], those original woodblocks were consumed by the outer element, fire. Further, during the great calamity of the Cultural Revolution, even the transmission of guidance according to this treatise was interrupted in the Repkong area. These are extremely tragic matters.

In the 1980s, in accordance with the hopes of a few scholars, the Institute of Ancient Texts and the Nationalities Research Center, under the Committee of the Nationality Affairs of Sichuan Province, both began the process of searching out, collecting, and editing *The Precious Treasury of Sūtra and Tantra.* The Committee of the Nationality Affairs of China then initiated a nationwide project to restore rare ethnic texts, and they provided funding. Thus, as a result of sixteen years of painstaking labor, the original texts have been found, collected, and minutely collated and proofread. Consequently, in the year 2000, we were able to publish and distribute through the Sichuan Nationalities' Publishing House a modern edition of this treatise. That said, an original copy of the latter volume of the illustrated version, entitled *A Garland of Suns,* still eludes our search.

The great *mantrin* Tsedrub Tharchin, a native of Repkong living in the United States, regarded this unique jewel of sovereign power that is sufficient to gather and elucidate all the sūtras, tantras, and treatises as the beautifying adornment of the Repkong Ngagmang community. He single-mindedly applied himself to finding and restoring the continuity of its reading transmission and guidance. He kept two projects in mind: the translation of the entire *Precious Treasury of Sūtra and Tantra* into English so it could spread throughout the world, and the founding of a college based on *The Precious Treasury of Sūtra and Tantra* within the Repkong Ngagmang community. He felt that this would ensure that the resplendent wealth of his ancestors' heritage would be passed down to future generations. With this pure, insightful intention firmly in mind, his enlightened activity has been significant.

Now, the first of Repkong Lama Tharchin Rinpoche's aspirations has come true: *The Treasury of Sūtra and Tantra* has been translated into English and published under the title *The Complete Nyingma Tradition from Sutra to Tantra*. Its distribution will spread the precious teachings of the Buddha throughout this wide world. I consider this to be a wholly positive, meaningful event that will prove to be healing and beneficial in every way. To all who participated in this project, headed by Lama Tharchin Rinpoche—translators, editors, benefactors, and others—I offer my humble esteem again and again in great measure, and I send my aspirations for the auspicious success of all your projects.

Offered respectfully by Hūṃchen
March 2014

Chenak Hūṃchen is a yogin with a long family connection to the Repkong Ngagmang community, where he has been actively engaged in publishing their texts and preserving their traditions.

In Memoriam

The late Lama Tharchin Rinpoche undertook a thorough proofreading of the edition of *The Precious Treasury of Sūtra and Tantra* that had previously been published by the Sichuan Nationalities' Publishing House, and he provided a detailed list of errata. Furthermore, he intended to establish both a college and a retreat center based on *The Precious Treasury of Sūtra and Tantra* at the seat of its author, Choying Tobden Dorje. To facilitate studies and experiential cultivation in meditation at those institutions, he oversaw the making of a new electronic version of this text from which a new edition was to be printed. Likewise, in order that *The Precious Treasury of Sūtra and Tantra* might spread throughout the world, he planned for this work to be translated into English and also into Chinese. Indeed, many years ago, he asked the great translator and scholar Lodro Gyatso to translate the synoptic outline and other sections of this work into Chinese. Lama Tharchin Rinpoche's contribution concerning *The Precious Treasury of Sūtra and Tantra* is of the highest order.

In the midst of his activity in 2013, our merit was insufficient to restrain him, and he departed for another realm. Nevertheless, his wife Pema Dechen, his disciple Eric Colombel, and others are now having the entirety of *The Precious Treasury of Sūtra and Tantra* printed and distributed in accordance with his wishes. I rejoice in this and offer my heartfelt thanks.

Tubten Nyima
[Zenkar Rinpoche]
July 8, 2014

Zenkar Rinpoche Tubten Nyima is a lineage holder of the Nyingma and Sakya traditions. A preeminent lexicographer, library archivist, writer, editor, and publisher, he has been instrumental in preserving and disseminating the works of Tibetan literature in China and throughout the world. Since 1992 he has held research fellowships at the School of Oriental and African Studies in London and at Columbia University. Presently, Zenkar Rinpoche is director of the Paltseg Tibetan Rare Texts Research Center, a standing member of the China Buddhist Association, and board member of the China Association for Preservation and Development of Tibetan Culture.

Translator's Introduction

Choying Tobden Dorje was born in 1785 at Zho'ong in the Sermojong area of Repkong, within the Ponru clan. During his early, formative years, he joined the nearby spiritual community at Shelgon Dechen Chokyi Podrang (also known as Chuchik Shelgyi Gonpa), which is one of the eight renowned hermitages for spiritual practice in Repkong (*reb kong gi grub pa thob pa'i gnas brgyad*).[4] After gradually receiving monastic vows, along with the bodhisattva vows and the commitments of secret mantra, he studied, pondered, and experientially cultivated the profound and extensive oral teachings (*bka' ma*), spiritual revelations (*gter ma*), and pure visionary teachings (*dag snang*) of the ancient Nyingma tradition.

Then, traveling south into Golok, he studied for some five years as a simple monk at Rabgya Gonpa, on the banks of the Yellow River.[5] In that revered center of Kadampa learning, he attended upon many spiritual masters, headed by Shingza Paṇḍita Lobzang Dargye Gyatso, while studying and reflecting upon the canonical scriptures and cultivating the three trainings (*bslab pa gsum*).[6] Subsequently, he frequented mountain hermitages in unknown locations, where he practiced meditation. On one such occasion, as he was inspired by a prophetic declaration given by deities and his teachers, there arose within him a firm determination to set out to find an extraordinary teacher, in the manner of the proverbial bodhisattva Sadāprarudita who had sought Dharmodgata. His purpose above all was to receive profound instruction associated with the level of the primordial buddha Samantabhadra.

Journeying further south from Golok, he eventually arrived at Dzogchen Monastery in Dzachuka, where he received maturational empowerments and liberating guidance for the extensive sūtras and tantras from Dzogchen IV Migyur Namkha Dorje and Je'on Pema Kundrol, among others.[7] From there, he proceeded to the teaching encampment (*chos sgar*) of Dodrubchen Rinpoche Jigme Trinle Ozer at Yarlung Pemako in Sertar,[8] where he remained for some years. It was Dodrubchen Rinpoche whom he revered and served as his extraordinary root teacher. In that location, he was given the maturational empowerments, liberating guidance, and supporting transmissions for the profound doctrines of the sūtras and mantras in general, and the inner tantras of the Nyingma tradition in particular, so that he came to resemble a vase that has been filled to the brim. Consequently, his view of reality expanded and he actualized the pristine cognition associated with the path of no-more-learning. Realizing that he would become illustrious among disciples of the future and that he had good fortune, Dodrubchen Rinpoche granted him the profound wrathful mantras of the ancient Nyingma tradition, including the crucial points of the four pulverizing rites (*thal 'byin rnam pa bzhi*) of Vajrakumāra, the cycles of Yamāntaka headed by the four wheels of Mañjuśrī (*'jam dpal 'khor lo rnam bzhi*), and the imprecations of the *mātaraḥ,* along with many profound instructions through which *mantrin*s may attain buddhahood on the basis of burnt offerings, combined with rites of suppression, incineration, and bombardment. Consequently, all dualistic thoughts that arose in his mind were infinitely transformed as the display of pristine cognition, meditational deities, and mantra, and he grew confident that he had unimpededly mastered the enlightened activities of wrath.

At that point, Dodrubchen Rinpoche conferred upon him the name Longchen Choying Tobden Dorje, "Unvanquished Conqueror of All Directions, Holding the Descent of the Oceanic Wrathful Mantras," and made prophetic declarations, adding, "Now the time has come for you to liberate your own mind through realization and compassionately liberate the minds of others. Therefore, you should return to your native Repkong, nurture students, and care for the well-being of the Buddhist teachings and sentient beings."

Choying Tobden Dorje then returned home to Repkong in Amdo, where, in recognition of his masterly attainments, his resources and entourage increased. About eight kilometers southwest of Rongpo Gyakhar, near modern Chuku township, he established the monastery of Ko'ude Gon Dzogchen Namgyeling (Ch. Gude Si).[9] This institution had been affiliated with the Kadam lineage since the fourteenth century, but he was instrumental in transforming it into a center of learning for the traditions of Rigdzin Jigme Lingpa and Orgyan Mindroling. In this way, he ensured that the community of *mantrins* there, headed by his successive emanations, would maintain their allegiance to the Nyingma lineage.

Among the four main disciples of Dodrubchen Rinpoche with the name Dorje, who were likened to supporting beams (*gdung bzhi*), transmitting his teachings in the four cardinal directions, Choying Tobden Dorje is renowned as the "supporting beam in the north." By means of skilled teaching, debate, and composition, and the four rites of pacification, enrichment, subjugation, and wrath, training each according to need, he took innumerable students into his following and established them on the path of maturational empowerment and liberating guidance. At Ko'ude, he impartially promoted all the Buddhist teachings in general and the *Innermost Spirituality of Longchenpa* in particular, ensuring that these traditions would not decline. His followers became renowned as the "nineteen hundred lineage bearers of the ritual spike," and they have exerted great influence throughout Repkong. Consequently, following his death in 1848, his transmission has manifestly survived until the present day. Prior to its destruction in 1958, Ko'ude had eight incarnate lamas presiding over a community of 160 *mantrins*. Rebuilding has been taking place since the 1980s.[10]

The Precious Treasury of Sūtra and Tantra

Although there are other extant works by Choying Tobden Dorje concerning the application of wrathful mantras, his magnum opus is undoubtedly *The Precious Treasury of Sūtra and Tantra* (*mDo rgyud mdzod*)—presented in translation here as *The Complete Nyingma Tradition from Sutra to Tantra*—which elucidates the meaning of all the classical sciences and the Buddhist vehicles of spiritual development. He began writing and compiling this treatise in 1836 (fire monkey year) and completed it in 1838 (earth dog year) at the age of fifty-four. The *Autobiography of Zhabkar Tsokdruk Rangdrol* mentions that in 1841, at a festival commemorating the new year of the iron ox, Zhabkar (1781–1851) offered him a letter, along with a gift of long-life pills and sacramental substances. Following an exchange of correspondence, that same year, Choying Tobden Dorje, then aged fifty-seven, was invited to Gartse Monastery,[11] where he extensively bestowed the transmission and guidance of the root verses and commentary of his *Precious Treasury of Sūtra and Tantra* upon Zhabkar and others.

The Precious Treasury of Sūtra and Tantra is extant in thirteen large traditional volumes, although the woodblocks from which it was printed were destroyed by fire in 1938. The work is in six sections: (i) the contents entitled *The Golden Key* (*dKar chag gser gyi lde mig*); (ii) the actual root verses (*rtsa ba*) entitled *The Precious Treasury of Sūtra and Tantra*; (iii) the synoptic outline entitled *A Creeping Plant That Brings Forth Wishes* (*bsDus don dpag bsam 'khri shing*); (iv) the concise commentary entitled *A Noble Vase of Great Treasure* (*'Bru 'grel gter chen bum bzang*); (v) the extensive commentary entitled *A Beauteous Ornament of the Aeon of Mighty Brahmā* (*rGyas 'grel tshangs chen bskal pa'i mdzes rgyan*); and (vi) the illustrated version entitled *Garland of the Moon* (*dPe ris zla ba'i phreng ba*).[12] The golden key and the root verses are in metrical verse, while the other sections are written in prose or in the form of captions. The root verses themselves number 984, mainly in nine-syllable lines, with their introductory and concluding verses in thirteen-syllable lines. The synoptic outline sets the structure of the text within 100 main topics and 2,179 subtopics. The extensive commentary is drawn principally from the writings of celebrated Nyingma masters, such as Ngari Paṇchen and Longchen Rabjam, while the first four sections are Choying Tobden Dorje's particular arrangements and synopses of the same works.

Among the thirteen volumes, volume 1 (KA) contains the golden key, the root verses and the outline. Volume 2 (KHA) contains the concise commentary. The next nine volumes from 3 (GA) to 11 (DA) contain the extensive commentary. Among them, the sūtra section comprises two volumes; the subjects of Indo-Tibetan classical learning (*shes bya*) comprise two volumes; the tantra section comprises two volumes; and the Dzogchen section comprises three volumes. The last two volumes, 12 (NA) and 13 (PA), both contain the drawings that illustrate the text.

The content of each of the six sections is also subdivided according to twenty-five books (*skabs nyi shu lnga*). Of these, the first thirteen fall within the scope of the sūtras, covering topics such as the role of the spiritual teacher; the requisite changes of attitude from mundane to spiritual life; the taking of refuge; the ground, path, and result established through practice of the sūtras; and related themes such as cosmology, Indo-Tibetan classical learning, and the analysis of the Buddhist vehicles. The remaining twelve books concern the tantras—their general framework along with exegeses of the essential tantra texts of Mahāyoga, Anuyoga, and Atiyoga.

During the 1990s, Zenkar Rinpoche managed to retrieve the extant printed version from Repkong, which was then published in modern book form by the Sichuan Nationalities' Publishing House in 2000. Subsequently, scans of the original text were obtained and, with the support of the Tsadra Foundation, the late Tharchin Rinpoche in the United States prepared a digital version of the entire work, which was then edited by Zenkar Rinpoche. It is a long-term objective of the Tsadra Foundation to publish this entire work in traditional *dpe cha* format and in modern book form, alongside its English translation.

The 2000 edition comprises five volumes. Among them, the golden key, the root verses, the outline, and the concise commentary are all contained in volume 1, while the extensive commentary is found in volumes 2 to 4 and the illustrations in volume 5. Within the extensive commentary itself, the sūtra section, the subjects of Indo-Tibetan classical learning, and the section on Buddhist phenomenology are all found in volume 2, while the tantra section including Mahāyoga and Anuyoga is found in volume 3, and Atiyoga in volume 4.

The ordering of these sections is significant in that the author evidently conceived of *The Precious Treasury of Sūtra and Tantra* as an unfolding package, commencing with his own pithy golden key and root verses, continuing through the outline and concise commentary, and culminating in the elaborate extensive commentary and the illustrations. For the sake of the modern reader who may find this structure overly repetitive, the present translation series gives precedence to the extensive commentary, with the root verses, outline, and concise commentary placed after it.

The present volume contains an English translation of Book 13, which concerns the philosophical systems (*siddhānta, grub mtha'*) of India and Tibet, and their historical lines of transmission (*paramparā, brgyud pa*). The original Tibetan text may be found in DGD (Sichuan ed.)—the root verses in vol. 1, pp. 51–52, the concise commentary in vol. 1, pp. 276–86, the outline in vol. 1, pp. 111–14, and the extensive commentary in vol. 2, pp. 691–832.[13]

The term *siddhānta* implies the juxtaposition of different doctrinal traditions, inclusive of the texts concerning the ground, path, and fruition upheld from their respective standpoints, as well as the views and commentarial traditions based upon them that are elaborated through reason. Traditionally, both Buddhist and non-Buddhist philosophical perspectives (*grub mtha' smra ba gnyis*) are included, but more specifically the term denotes the four preeminent Buddhist philosophical systems (*grub mtha' smra ba bzhi*): Vaibhāṣika, Sauntrāntika, Cittamātra, and Madhyamaka.

Among the canonical sūtras, there are some sources that might be considered doxographical in content, most notably the *Sāmaññaphala Sutta,* contained in *The Long Discourses of the Buddha,* which outlines the eternalistic and nihilistic views reputedly held by six sophists who were contemporaries of Śākyamuni Buddha. The *Sūtra of the Net of Brahmā* additionally identifies sixty-two distinct speculations or notions with regard to the limits of past and future time. However, the Indian master Bhāvaviveka (c. 500–570) is reckoned to have been the first to formulate a comprehensive hierarchy of Indian philosophical systems.[14] In his treatises entitled *Heart of the Middle Way* and *Flame of Dialectics,* he differentiates 110 primary and 363 derivative philosophical views pertaining to the past, present, and future.[15] In particular, from a Madhyamaka perspective, he devotes entire individual chapters to the views attributed to pious attendants (*śrāvaka, nyan thos*) of the Hīnayāna persuasion, as well as to Yogācārins, and non-Buddhist schools such as Sāṃkhya, Vaiśeṣika, Vedānta, and Mīmāṃsika. Other commentators who elaborated extensively on this comparative approach include Avalokitavrata (fl. seventh century), Śāntarakṣita (725–783), Kamalaśīla (740–795), Vitapāda (fl. late ninth century), and Bodhibhadra (fl. 1000).

From the eighth century onward, the Indian Buddhist doxographical tradition began to take root in Tibet, initially in the writings of Kawa Peltsek and Zhang Yeshede, and later during the new wave of translations that flourished in Tibet from the eleventh century onward. Each of the main Tibetan schools gradually evolved its distinctive standpoints with regard to the aforementioned four recognized philosophical systems of Indian Buddhism. Among the Nyingmapa, this trend is exemplified by the writings of Rongzom Chokyi Zangpo (fl. eleventh century) and Longchen Rabjam (1308–1363). Two of the latter's seminal treatises—the *White Lotus* autocommentary on the *Wish-Fulfilling Treasury* and the *Precious Treasury of Philosophical Systems* (translated in Barron 2007)—are the principal sources for Choying Tobden Dorje's presentation of non-Buddhist and Buddhist systems in Book 13.

The first three parts of Book 13 effectively restate Longchen Rabjam's analysis of the views held respectively by (i) the established non-Buddhist Indian schools; (ii) the Vaibhāṣika, Sautrāntika, Cittamātra, and Madhyamaka, who exemplify the "causal" approach of the sūtras; and (iii) the outer and inner classes of fruitional tantra, comprising the tantras of action (*kriyā*), conduct (*caryā*), union (*yoga*), great union (*mahāyoga*), subsequent union (*anuyoga*), and highest union (*atiyoga*). Although Choying Tobden Dorje draws extensively on the presentation of Longchen Rabjam, probably for lack of space, he purposefully omits the nuanced refutations of those manifold perspectives that are detailed by his illustrious predecessor.

Part 1, entitled "Mundane Approaches," begins by exploring the difference between those following non-Buddhist spiritual paths who are said to have no understanding of the nature of reality but who nonetheless progress through the various god realms of form and formlessness on the basis of their meditative capacity and ethical conduct, and those of wrong understanding who fail to progress owing to their eternalist or nihilist views. The latter include the views attributed to the sophistic teachers who were contemporaries of Śākyamuni Buddha, the twenty false views about the perishable composites of phenomena known as the five psycho-physical aggregates, the sixty-two speculations or notions concerning the limits of past and future time, the 363 false views outlined by Bhāvaviveka, including those of ancient Vedic lore and the views of his near contemporaries, and the eleven specific categories of heretical notions concerning the present. There then follows a discussion of the purported views of the five well-defined non-Buddhist philosophies: Sāṃkhya phenomenology, Vaiśeṣika categorization (with Shaivism), Mīmāṃsaka ritual (with Vaisnavism), Nirgrantha Jainism, and Bārhaspatya nihilism or hedonism.

Part 2, entitled "The Philosophical Systems of the Causal Vehicles," begins by outlining the superiority of pious attendants (*śrāvaka, nyan thos*) and hermit buddhas (*pratyekabuddha, rang rgyal*) to non-Buddhists in terms of their refuge, view, meditative experience, conduct, and goal. The tenets accepted in common by pious attendants include the four noble truths, the positing of ultimate reality, the denials of substratum consciousness, the great vehicle and the ten bodhisattva levels, and the assertion that buddhas have an individual mental continuum.

The distinctive philosophical schools espoused by pious attendants are then analyzed in turn. Among them, the Vaibhāṣika analysis concerns the five basic categories of phenomena (matter, mind, mental states, disassociated formative predispositions, and unconditioned phenomena), the positing of decay as a separate entity, the positing of the substantial existence of the three times, the positing of an inexpressible self, the denial of intrinsic or objective awareness on the part of consciousness, the distinction between defining characteristics and exemplars, and the existence of unexhausted substances.

The Sautrāntika analysis concerns causality with its four conditions (causal, immediate, referential and predominant), the notion that appearances are mind, that objects are covert, that atomic particles have no intervening spaces, that the sense organs are causally effective, that disassociated formative predispositions are imaginary, and that nirvāṇa is a nonentity.

This discussion on the lesser vehicle (*hīnayāna, theg dman*) ends with a brief presentation of the vehicle of the hermit buddhas in terms of their focus, classes, view, and meditation based on dependent origination and its reversal, as well as their conduct and goal.

The great vehicle (*mahāyāna, theg chen*) is subsequently introduced with a paragraph concerning the superiority of bodhisattvas to pious attendants and hermit buddhas. Its philosophical trends are then discussed in turn. The Cittamātrin ("mind-only") system is generally presented according to its tenets, focus, and classes, and on the basis of the distinctions made between the three natures, substantial existents and imputed existents, and relative and ultimate truth, as well as its understanding of the enlightened intention of the buddhas, selflessness, conduct, and goal. More specifically, the Cittamātrins holding sensa to be veridical include some who claim that consciousness and sensa are distinct, others who hold that there are as many sensa as instances of consciousness, and yet others who assert that sensa are diverse and that consciousness is without duality. By contrast, those holding sensa to be false may claim that consciousness is tainted or immaculate.

The presentation of Madhyamaka ("middle way"), the culmination of the causal vehicles, includes a general introduction to those employing independent syllogisms—both the lower and higher Svātantrika—and a detailed presentation of the Prāsaṅgika. The latter are renowned for employing the consequential reasoning of the five axioms (absence of the singular and the multiple, vajra fragments, absence of production from existence and nonexistence, refutation of efficacious objects, and supreme relativity), along with subsidiary axioms that concern permanence and imperishability, change and nonchange, and the attributes of birth, aging, duration, and cessation. The Prāsaṅgika refutation of conceptual elaboration and nonrefutation of conventional appearances are then contrasted. In terms of praxis, the middle way of the ground emphasizes the two truths, the middle way of the path emphasizes the two provisions of merit and pristine cognition, and the middle way of the result emphasizes the two buddha bodies of reality and form. The chapter ends with a discussion on the validity of acceptance and nonacceptance, and their synthesis.

Part 3, entitled "The Philosophical Systems of the Fruitional Vehicles," begins by examining the distinctions between the ways of sūtra and mantra. The three outer classes of tantra—action (*kriyātantra, bya ba'i rgyud*), conduct (*caryātantra, spyod pa'i rgyud*), and union (*yogatantra, rnal 'byor gyi rgyud*) are then presented, followed by a brief account of the distinctions between the outer and inner mantras, and between the father tantras, mother tantras, and nondual tantras.

Following Longchen Rabjam, the author then moves swiftly to the main subject matter—the detailed presentation of the tantras of highest union (*atiyoga*), the Great Perfection. There are some preliminary remarks concerning the superiority of the Great Perfection to the generation and perfection stages of meditation as practiced in the tantras of great union (*mahāyoga*) and subsequent union (*anuyoga*), but the main emphasis is on the three classes of the Great Perfection (*rdzogs chen sde gsum*), which comprise the class of mind, the class of space, and the class of esoteric instruction.

There are seven perspectives that characterize the class of mind (*sems sde*). Respectively, these (i) hold the fruition to be the mind's point of origin; (ii) determine deviations and obscuration; (iii) shatter the authenticity of conventional appearances by means of rational axioms; (iv) avoid descending into partiality or bias; (v) observe dogmatic philosophical systems with disinterest; (vi) transcend dogmatism about that which is free from the intellect; and (vii) speak in terms of things being perspectives of mind.

There are four aspects that characterize the class of space (*klong sde*); namely, the black, variegated, white, and infinite spaces. Furthermore, there are three aspects of the class of esoteric instruction (*man ngag sde*), when the teachings of this class are presented in the context of miscellaneous instructions, informal advice, and formal instructions of the seventeen tantra texts. The last category includes both an aural lineage and an exegetical lineage, the latter in turn comprising four distinct cycles of teachings—outer, inner, secret, and unsurpassed secret.

Part 4, entitled "The Philosophical Systems of Tibet: Lines of Transmission," follows on from the aforementioned presentation of the non-Buddhist and Buddhist philosophical perspectives, by turning to indigenous Tibetan developments. It begins with a brief description of the geographical extent of the Tibetan plateau that accords with Konchok Tenpa Rabgye's *Doctrinal History of Amdo*. There then follows a listing of the royal dynasties of Tibet and a summary of the Bon religion, which both derive from the *Five Injunctions* of Yarje Orgyan Lingpa (1323–1360). A brief account of the origins of the medical and divinatory traditions is then followed by a detailed presentation of the foundation, establishment, and spread of Buddhism in Tibet during the imperial period. The long citations in this section derive from Orgyan Lingpa's *Injunctions of Padma*. There is a particular emphasis on the translation and transmission of the three inner classes of tantra in terms of both the distant lineage of the transmitted teachings (*ring brgyud bka' ma*) and the close lineages of spiritual revelations (*nye brgyud gter ma*).

Having completed his exegesis of the Nyingma transmission in Tibet, Choying Tobden Dorje then recounts the translations that were undertaken during the later phase of Buddhist propagation from the tenth century onward. Among the texts discussed here are father tantras such as the *Tantra of the Secret Assembly* and the *Tantra of the Slayer of Death,* and mother tantras such as the *Tantra of the Four Indestructible Seats, Mahāmāyā, Buddhakapāla, Cakrasaṃvara, Hevajra,* and *Kālacakra.* In conclusion, the author outlines the Tibetan evolution of the New Translation Schools—Kadampa, Kagyupa, Shangpa Kagyu, Pacification and Severance, Sakyapa, Gedenpa, and so forth, emphasizing in particular how each of these distinctive lineages and their branches had been foreordained in the prophetic declarations of Padmasambhava and Yeshe Tsogyal. The principal sources here are Ratna Lingpa's revelation entitled *Prophetic Declarations* (along with its derivatives) and Takzham Nuden Dorje's revelation entitled *Biography of Tsogyal* (translated in Padmakara Translation Group 1999).

Part 5, entitled "Dialectical Writings of Buddhist Phenomenology," introduces the reader to the complexities of consequential reasoning in the context of the first chapter of Vasubandhu's *Treasury of Phenomenology.* The subject matter predictably concerns the nature of conditioned and unconditioned phenomena, the sensory elements, sense faculties and sense fields, the hierarchy of the psycho-physical aggregates, the nature of vision, and so forth, but the approach is distinctive, as those successive themes are examined through "garlands" or series of consequential reasoning, taken verbatim from the Fifth Dalai Lama's *Precious Chariot Steering the Treasury of Phenomenology.*

Acknowledgments

In preparing this translation, I benefited from the insights of Herbert Guenther (1971) and Richard Barron (2007), whose works faithfully interpret Longchen Rabjam's presentation of the classical philosophical systems. Christian Lindtner's (2001a) edition of Bhāvaviveka's *Heart of the Middle Way* has also been instructive on the non-Buddhist systems of Bhāvaviveka. Over recent months, I had an opportunity to discuss obscurities in Choying Tobden Dorje's summary of Bon with Dan Martin, Donatella Rossi, and Samten Karmay; Sanskrit derivations with Peter Verhagen; and some complexities in the consequential reasoning of the Fifth Dalai Lama with Tom Tillemans. Their contributions and expertise are greatly appreciated—any errors in the translation are mine alone. My wife, Xiaohong, organized the entries contained in the concordance of technical terms and the lists of personal and place names. Dr. Martin Boord undertook the task of reading the translation and back matter prior to the submission of the manuscript, during the spring of 2016.

Again I would like to express my gratitude to Eric Colombel and all at Tsadra Foundation who have generously continued to support my work on the *Complete Nyingma Tradition from Sutra to Tantra* over the last two years. Finally, thanks are due to Nikko Odiseos of Shambhala Publications, and to our series editor, Michael Wakoff.

Gyurme Dorje
Crieff
May 2016

The Extensive Commentary: Book 13

A Beauteous Ornament of the Aeon of Mighty Brahmā

Book 13, Part 1
Mundane Approaches

Herein is contained Book 13, Part 1 (ki) from *The Extensive Commentary of the Precious Treasury of Sūtra and Tantra, concerning Mundane Approaches.*

The Golden Key

In order that one might become skilled in mundane approaches,
This book contains an exposition of the ways of gods and humans,
And of the approaches espoused by eternalists and nihilists.

Verses of Homage

Homage to Yamāntaka of mighty power,
Along with his terrifying female consort,
Who, assuming a most terrifying and awesome form,
Terrifies all the terrified hosts, without exception.[16]

The Content of Book 13, Parts 1–5

Book 13 offers an extensive exegesis of the philosophical systems associated with the entire gradation of the vehicles. It contains six main topics:

The first main topic [**Book 13, Part 1**] explains mundane approaches, including the basic ways of gods and humans who have no understanding [of the nature of reality], along with the approaches of [non-Buddhist] philosophical extremists who misunderstand [the nature of reality], propounding eternalism and nihilism.

The second and third main topics [**Book 13, Part 2**] explain the supramundane approaches [based on the Buddhist sūtras], comprising the vehicles of the śrāvakas ("pious attendants") who are of lesser acumen, the pratyekabuddhas ("hermit buddhas") who are of average acumen, and the bodhisattvas ("beings set on enlightenment") who are of superior acumen. The last of these includes an explanation of Cittamātra ("mind only") and Madhyamaka ("middle way").

The fourth main topic [**Book 13, Part 3**] concerns the approaches of vajrayāna (the "vehicle of indestructible reality"), comprising an explanation of the outer tantras of action (*kriyā*), conduct (*caryā*), and union (*yoga*), and of the inner tantras of great union (*mahāyoga*), subsequent union (*anuyoga*), and highest union (*atiyoga*).

The fifth main topic [**Book 13, Part 4**] explains the gradation [and lines of transmission] of the philosophical systems that were propagated in Tibet, Land of Snows.

Finally, the sixth main topic [**Book 13, Part 5**] offers a dialectical explanation based on the [first part of the] *Treasury of Phenomenology,* with an arrangement in the form of a "garland of consequential reasoning" (*thal phreng*).

These six main topics comprise three hundred fifty-one subtopics.[17]

Mundane Approaches

The Exegesis of Mundane Approaches [13.1]

The first main topic [the exegesis of mundane approaches] comprises (i) the basic ways of gods and humans who have no understanding [of the nature of reality] (13.1.1) and (ii) the approaches of [non-Buddhist] philosophical extremists who misunderstand [the nature of reality], propounding eternalism and nihilism (13.1.2).

The Basic Ways of Gods and Humans Who Have No Understanding [of the Nature of Reality] [13.1.1]

The former [comments on the verse]:

> **Having refined the fields of classical learning in the above manner**
> **[as expounded in Books 11 and 12],**
> **The [diverse] philosophical systems [are to be understood].**
> **There are those holding that one is born**
> **As a human being or as a god inhabiting the world system of desire**
> **By having practiced the ten virtuous actions,**
> **And that one is born in the [world systems of form and formlessness]**
> **By means of the four meditative concentrations and the four**
> **formless [absorptions].**

Having refined the major and minor fields of classical learning in the above manner [in Books 11 and 12], the [diverse] philosophical systems are to be understood. At the outset, there are those holding that by having practiced the esteemed ten virtuous actions, even though lacking meditative stability, the fruit is that one will come to abide on the [advantageous] level of gods and humans inhabiting the world system of desire. As is said in the *Tantra of Supreme Secret Conduct:*[18]

> By practicing the ten virtuous actions and forsaking nonvirtue,
> [One acquires] the causes of rebirth among gods and humans
> Inhabiting the world system of desire.

Then, by having practiced those ten virtuous actions in conjunction with the four meditative concentrations, one will attain the levels commensurate with the meditative concentration that one's mind has acquired. Projection into those [Brahmā levels] is brought about by the force of the ten virtuous actions. As is said in the same text:

> Projected by means of the ten virtuous actions,
> Through the four kinds of meditative concentration,
> One will attain the four [Brahmā] abodes
> With a physical form imbued with meditative concentration.

Then, by having practiced the four formless absorptions, projected by the ten virtuous actions, one will be born in the abodes of the four formless realms. In this regard, it says in the same text:

> Projected by means of the ten virtuous actions,
> Through the four kinds of formless meditative stability,
> One will traverse the four [formless realms]—
> Infinite space and so forth.

Eternalistic and Nihilistic Extremists

Approaches of the Eternalistic and Nihilistic Extremists Who Misunderstand [the Nature of Reality] [13.1.2]

The latter concerns the approaches of the eternalistic and nihilistic extremists who misunderstand [the nature of reality]. This discussion has six aspects, which respectively concern (i) the six sophistic teachers (13.1.2.1); (ii) the twenty false views about perishable composites (13.1.2.2); (iii) the sixty-two false views (13.1.2.3); (iv) the three hundred sixty false views (13.1.2.4); (v) the eleven specific categories [of false views] (13.1.2.5); and the five modes of sophistry in which all the aforementioned are subsumed (13.1.2.6).[19]

The Six Sophistic Teachers [13.1.2.1]

As to the first, [this comments on the verse:]

> **There are six [sophistic] teachers**
> **Associated with the main extremist traditions.**

Among these six teachers:

(i) Purāṇakāśyapa, the Ājīvika, held that there are no past and future worlds, that actions have no cause or effect, that there is no attainment of arhatship, and that there are no miraculous births.[20]

(ii) The wandering mendicant Maskarī Gośālaputravaruṇa held that afflicted mental states and purification occur naturally, without causes or conditions.[21]

(iii) Sañjayavairaḍīputra held that both virtuous and negative actions are nonexistent.[22]

(iv) Ajitakeśakambalin held that all things are the functions of destiny. As is said in the *Ocean of Texts:*

> Destined elements ripen,
> Destined sleep awakens,
> Destined living creatures take form.
> It is hard to go beyond destiny.[23]

This teacher therefore held that the joys and sorrows of all sentient beings come about through the power of destiny and emerge in a timely manner. Having been conceived with the mental continuum of a human being, god, animal and the like, by the power of destiny, that sole cause brings about change [of its own volition], without reference to positive or negative actions. Other than that, [experiences of] joy and sorrow arise from its perception. The rebirth process itself commences from the time of initial conception and lasts until eighty-four thousand aeons have elapsed, whereupon, whether they are foolish or wise, all beings are brought to liberation itself, in accordance with their destined release.[24]

(v) Kakudakatyāyana said, "When you ask me if other worlds exist, if I were to respond that they do exist [and I do not], I would have to consider all four sides of the argument, questioning also whether they do not exist, whether they both exist and do not exist, and whether they neither exist nor do not exist. Similarly, concerning the self, I would respond with all four sides of the argument, questioning whether it is permanent, impermanent, both, or neither. Also, with regard to the nature of a tathāgata prior to his physical death, I would respond with all four sides of the argument, questioning whether this constitutes a self, not-self, both, or neither; and with regard to [the relationship between] body and soul, I would respond with all four sides of the argument, questioning whether these are identical, different, both, or neither.[25]

(vi) Nirgranthajñātiputra held that all things are corporeal. Happiness emerges through the actions of previous austerities, and suffering emerges in this world through negative past actions. New actions are never efficacious in the present. Rather, happiness and suffering are experienced because the impact of past actions is actualized in the present. One should therefore persevere in training with regard to austerities and so forth. If [new actions] were efficacious in the present, it follows that when someone who is dumb practices austerities and so forth, he or she would actually know how to speak. That position should be rejected because it is untenable. Therefore it is said that once the contaminants that arise through past actions have been gradually exhausted, eventually no residue at all will be left behind, in the manner of a ripening harvest.[26]

The Twenty False Views about Perishable Composites [13.1.2.2]

Second, there are twenty false views about perishable composites. [This comments on the verse:]

> **And there are twenty summits of false view about perishable composites.**

Twenty false views are enumerated in that each of the five aggregates—physical forms, feelings, perceptions, formative predispositions, and consciousness—may be identified with the self, or the self may be posited as abiding within each of them, or the aggregates—physical forms and so forth—may originate on the basis of self, or else they may be controlled by the self. These are called the twenty summits of false view about perishable composites.[27]

The Sixty-Two False Views [13.1.2.3]

Third, there are sixty-two false views, [which comments on the verse:]

> **There are the sixty-two false views.**

Those who rely on the sixty-two false views perpetually roam through cyclic existence, so these are of no use for attaining release from that state. What, you may ask, do they comprise? There are eighteen speculations dependent on the past (13.1.2.3.1) and forty-four speculations dependent on the future (13.1.2.3.2).[28]

Eighteen Speculations Dependent on the Past [13.1.2.3.1]

Among these, the former are known to have five categories, comprising (i) the group of four that propound eternalism (13.1.2.3.1.1); (ii) the group of four that propound partial eternalism (13.1.2.3.1.2); (iii) the group of four that propound finitude or infinity (13.1.2.3.1.3); (iv) the group of four that propound endless equivocation (13.1.2.3.1.4); and (v) the two that propound fortuitous origination (13.1.2.3.1.5).

The Group of Four That Propound Eternalism [13.1.2.3.1.1]

With regard to the first group of four: (i) There are some who have renounced the household life and cultivated meditative concentrations during the initial aeon of time, and who have arrived at their speculations after recollecting through extrasensory power up to thirty intervening aeons. Since they can observe forward and backward in time, they propound that the self and all worlds are eternal, considering that the limits of past and future time are infinite.

Similarly, there are those propounding eternalism who have arrived at their speculations after recollecting (ii) sixty or (iii) ninety intervening aeons, and those who have done so (iv) after observing successions of rebirth, as they passed from one household life to another household life. Such is the [first] group of four.

The Group of Four That Propound Partial Eternalism [13.1.2.3.1.2]

Alternatively: (i) There are some mendicants who have arrived at their speculations after observing through extrasensory power that they themselves have passed away from the Brahmā realms but even now retain the sense faculties of Brahmā, and who propound that the Mahābrahmā realm is eternal whereas other gods and worlds are not eternal. (ii) There are some who have died after displaying anger toward other gods of the Trayastriṃśa realm, but who have speculated that all those other gods [of the Brahmā realms] still exist, on the basis of which they then propound that the gods of the world system of desire who are troubled are not eternal, whereas the others are eternal. (iii) There are some who have formed their speculations after observing that they forgot to eat and then passed away, having been distracted by the spectacle of the Trayastriṃśa realm. They therefore propound that those gods of the world system of desire who are deceived by amusements are not eternal, whereas the others are eternal. (iv) There are some who have refuted the existence of the four material elements in the context of the world system of formlessness and arrived at their speculations after observing that mind, mental states, and so forth, do occur therein. They then propound that the four material elements are not eternal, whereas mind and mental states are eternal.

These four views all observe eternal deities as a state of release and aspire to attain the level of those eternal deities.

The Group of Four That Propound Finitude or Infinity [13.1.2.3.1.3]

As for the four who propound finitude or infinity: (i) There are some who propound that the self and the world are finite, considering that there is nothing beyond this world because they do not observe through their extrasensory power anything other than [this world system], extending from the hells to the four meditative concentrations. (ii) There are some who, although they do not observe all levels, do perceive the boundaries of the finite, and therefore propound that the self and the world are infinite, speculating that the beyond does indeed exist. (iii) There are some who, although they observe the finitude of the human world, propound the extreme view of both finitude and infinity because they do not perceive the finitude of the worlds of Brahmā. (iv) There are some who, although they do observe the worlds of Brahmā, have arrived at their speculations after perceiving that limits cannot be appraised in terms of existence and nonexistence, and who have then propounded the extreme view that the self and the world are neither finite nor infinite.

The Group of Four That Propound Endless Equivocation [13.1.2.3.1.4]

The four who propound endless equivocation have made the following pledge: "When others criticize us with regard to a certain aspect of the past or future, we should equivocate, without abandoning our views." Consequently they make distinctions on the basis of the following four intellectual standpoints: (i) There are those propounding equivocation who are of feeble intelligence and do not know anything else when questioned about their view. (ii) There are those propounding equivocation who have not refined their minds in philosophy and who, on being questioned, do not know anything else. (iii) There are those who propound equivocation because, even though they have refined [their minds], they are still uncertain. (iv) There are those who propound equivocation, considering that even when individuals with pride in their clear realization are questioned, none of them can reply.

The Two That Propound Fortuitous Origination [13.1.2.3.1.5]

As for the two views that propound fortuitous origination, these may be formed on the basis of (i) meditative concentration or (ii) reason.

In the first case, there are some who in the past had been sentient beings devoid of perception, who, having died and transmigrated, cannot perceive any [residue from the past] on the basis of the subtle substratum but only perceive things that arise on the basis of their own six modes of sensory consciousness. They thereupon propound the fortuitous origination of all worlds. They do so, considering that the atoms derived from the indivisible atomic particles of the material world are not seen and are therefore of fortuitous origination, and also considering that the inhabitants of the physical world are of fortuitous origination because their minds had [formerly][29] been nonexistent.

In the latter case, which is based on reason, they propound fortuitous origination, speculating simply that clouds appear suddenly in the sky and that wind is also sudden in its appearance.

Forty-Four Speculations Dependent on the Future [13.1.2.3.2]

The forty-four speculations concerning the future fall into five categories: (i) sixteen speculations concerning percipient immortality (13.1.2.3.2.1); (ii) eight speculations concerning nonpercipient immortality (13.1.2.3.2.2); (iii) eight speculations concerning neither percipient nor nonpercipient immortality (13.1.2.3.2.3); (iv) seven speculations concerning annihilationism (13.1.2.3.2.4); and (v) five speculations concerning the immediate attainment of nirvāṇa in the present life (13.1.2.3.2.5).

Sixteen Speculations concerning Percipient Immortality [13.1.2.3.2.1]

These are divided into four groups of four, the first of which comprises four speculations, namely, that (i) the self is material and percipient; (ii) it is immaterial and percipient; (iii) it is both [material and immaterial] and percipient; and (iv) it is neither material nor immaterial and percipient.

The next group comprises four speculations, namely, that (i) the self is finite and percipient; (ii) the self is infinite and percipient; (iii) the self is both finite and infinite and percipient; and (iv) the self is neither finite nor infinite, and percipient.

The next group comprises four speculations, namely, that (i) the self is imbued with happiness; (ii) the self is imbued with suffering; (iii) the self is imbued with both happiness and suffering; and (iv) the self is imbued with neither happiness nor suffering.

The last group comprises four speculations, namely, that (i) the self is uniform; (ii) it is diversified; (iii) it is small; and (iv) it is extensive.

Thus there are four groups of four, making sixteen speculations concerning the self, which may all be subsumed under the following four headings: (i) the self is material and percipient; (ii) the self is finite and percipient; (iii) the self is imbued with happiness or suffering and percipient; and (iv) the self is uniform or diversified[30] and percipient.

"Uniform," in the last group of four, suggests that there is a single self pervading everything. "Diversified" suggests that there is a distinct self present in each human being. "Small" suggests the opinion that the self is present in the world system of desire. "Extensive" suggests the opinion that the self is present in the world system of form.

Eight Speculations concerning Nonpercipient Immortality [13.1.2.3.2.2]

The eight speculations concerning nonpercipient immortality comprise two groups of four.

The former explores four parameters according to which (i) the self is material and nonpercipient in the manner of hair and nail; (ii) the self is immaterial and nonpercipient in the manner of space; (iii) the self is both material and immaterial, and nonpercipient; and (iv) the self is neither material nor nonmaterial, and nonpercipient. The latter explores four parameters (v–viii) according to which the self is finite and nonpercipient, and so forth.

Eight Speculations concerning Neither Percipient nor Nonpercipient Immortality [13.1.2.3.2.3]

The eight speculations concerning neither percipient nor nonpercipient immortality also comprise two groups of four.

The former explores four parameters according to which (i) the self is material and neither percipient nor nonpercipient; (ii) the self is immaterial and neither percipient nor nonpercipient; (iii) the self is both material and immaterial and neither percipient nor nonpercipient; and (iv) the self is neither material nor immaterial and neither percipient nor nonpercipient.

The latter explores four parameters according to which (i) the self is finite and neither percipient nor nonpercipient; (ii) infinite and neither percipient nor nonpercipient; (iii) both finite and infinite and neither percipient nor nonpercipient; and (iv) neither finite nor infinite and neither percipient nor nonpercipient.

Seven Speculations concerning Annihilationism [13.1.2.3.2.4]

As for the seven speculations concerning annihilationism, it may be maintained that suffering exists among (i) the humans of the world system of desire; (ii) the gods of the world system of desire; (iii) the gods of the world system of form; (iv) the gods of [infinite] space; (v) the gods of [infinite] consciousness; (vi) the gods of nothing-at-all; and (vii) the gods of the summit of existence; and that happiness ensues at the time of death when all these are annihilated. Consequently, it is held that actions have no results pertaining to past and future lives.

Five Speculations concerning the Immediate Attainment of Nirvāṇa in the Present Life [13.1.2.3.2.5]

As for the five speculations concerning the immediate attainment of nirvāṇa in the present life, (i) there are those propounding the immediate attainment of nirvāṇa in the present life when gods and humans[31] of the world system of desire revel intensely in the desirable attributes of the senses here and now. Also, there are those propounding the immediate attainment of nirvāṇa in the present life when meditative stability is intensely cultivated, respectively, by means of the (ii) first; (iii) second; (iv) third; and (v) fourth meditative concentrations. They also hold that past and future lives are nonexistent.

The Three Hundred Sixty False Views [13.1.2.4]

Fourth, with regard to the three hundred sixty false views, [it says in the root verses:]

> **[There are] the three hundred sixty false views on which beings are fixated.**

There were one hundred twenty teachers who appeared in the past, including Rāṇāyana, and equal numbers of one hundred twenty who are alive here and now, and who will appear in the future. Combined together, they total three hundred sixty.[32] They never have attained, never do attain, and never will attain release [from cyclic existence] by means of a [genuine] path because they have been, are, and will be submerged in the torrents of eternalism and nihilism.

What, you may ask, are the names [of the adherents] of these teachers? They begin with the following ten: (i) the Jaiminīya; (ii) the Alaukika (nonworldly or without standpoint); (iii) the Ājīvika; (iv) the Rāṇāyanīya; (v) the Śrotriya (brahmins observing pure rituals); (vi) the Vaiṣṇava; (vii) the Vāsudevaka (holding Viṣṇu as a living being); (viii) the Tridaṇḍaka (possessing only the three staffs of ascetic restraint); (ix) the Śākalya; and (x) the Talavakāra.[33]

The Eleven Specific Categories [13.1.2.5]

Fifth, the three hundred sixty sorts of heretical texts and their teachers may also be presented in terms of eleven categories. On this [it says in the root verses:]

> **And [there are] the eleven specific categories of heretical texts.**

In this regard, there are three hundred notions concerning the limits of present time, starting with the ten imitations, which, along with the [aforementioned] eighteen notions concerning the limits of past time and the forty-two notions concerning the limits of future time, add up to three hundred sixty.

Among them, the notions concerning the limits of present time [may be subsumed in the following eleven categories]:

1. The ten imitations that include (i) conventional extremists who imitate the pious attendants; (ii) consumers who imitate the hermit buddhas; (iii) subtle practitioners who imitate the Cittamātrins; (iv) most subtle practitioners who imitate the Mādhyamika; (v) the ritualist class that imitates the tantras of action; (vi) the practitioner class that imitates the tantras of conduct; (vii) the yogin class that imitates the tantras of union; (viii) practitioners of intense ascetic discipline who imitate the father tantras; (ix) appraisers of spiritual triumph who imitate the mother tantras; and (x) acquirers of spiritual triumph who imitate the nondual tantras.

   These [imitations] are held to number one hundred when subdivided according to the five material elements and the sensory elements associated with the five quiddities.[34]
2. The nine propounding coherent eternalism that include (i) those upholding things in general to be eternal; and in particular, (ii) those holding chance and mighty Īśvara to be an eternal creator; (iii) those holding the words of the Vedas to be eternal; (iv) those holding an inexpressible soul to be eternal; (v) those holding objects of knowledge to be eternal; (vi) those holding attributes to be eternal; (vii) those holding primal matter and the soul to be eternal; (viii) those holding the nine categories [of phenom-

ena] to be eternal; and (ix) those holding classical learning to be eternal.

These may also number one hundred one when each of the nine is appraised in terms of the following eleven aspects: (i) the soul that is of eternal nature; (ii) primal matter; (iii–v) the three modifications [of motility, dullness, and lightness]; (vi) the cognized; (vii) the cognizer; (viii) the objects of cognition; (ix) conduct; (x) interaction; and (xi) the force of their combined impact.[35]

3. The six propounding irrationality that include (i) the followers of Jaimini who would establish silence as a reason for the proof of omniscient beings; (ii) the Naiyāyika who would establish that the attributes of the soul, including happiness and suffering, are apprehensible in all things in order to prove that the soul is present in all things; (iii) the Mīmāṃsika who would establish that sound is uncreated in order to prove that it is eternal; (iv) the Digambara who, in order to prove that wood is animate, would establish that leaves die during the night and that peeled bark will wither; (v) the Sāṃkhya who would establish the dying of peeled bark as a reason in order to prove that matter is animate; and (vi) the Vaiśeṣika who would establish that living beings possess life in order to prove that the body of living beings is endowed with a soul.

   These may number eighteen since, in terms of the understanding of compatible factors, each of the six seeks to prove that their (i) premise; (ii) reason; and (iii) example are discernible.[36]

4. The seven with faith in meditative concentration, including (i) the Bārhaspatya who meditate that even relative appearances are nonexistent; (ii) the Sāṃkhya who meditate on emptiness [of primal matter], devoid of modifications; (iii) the Saura who meditate on emptiness in which light is rejected; (iv) the followers of Jayadhara who meditate with one-pointed nonconceptualization, regarding the six modes of consciousness and their sense objects as defective; (v) the Vaiśeṣika who meditate with one-pointed nonrecollection, regarding recollection as defective; (vi) the Śaiva who meditate without distraction on the nature of mind, considering that all things are mind; and (vii) the Vaidika, who meditate in a manner similar to space, having rejected all [dichotomies of] happiness and suffering, or of conceptualization and nonconceptualization.

   These may also number twenty-eight, since each of the seven

may be considered in terms of (i) the essential nature of their focus on meditative stability; (ii) their categories; (iii) their experiences; and (iv) their fruits.[37]

5. The six teachers propounding nihilism who are the aforementioned sophistic teachers, starting with Purāṇakāśyapa.

Their tenets are also held to number thirty-two since they hold that there is a self devoid of (i) past and future lives; (ii) actions, causes, and results; (iii) release and liberation; and (iv) invisible beings, and they come to this understanding by means of (i) a single sensory gate that is cognitive; (ii–iv) three examples; and (v–viii) four modalities.

The "single sensory gate" implies that [this cognition] excludes the intrinsic observations of the perceptual range of [the five] sense faculties.

The "three examples" comprise (i) the example of noncausation, which is the bursting forth of mushrooms on the grasslands; (ii) the example of nonfruition, which is the scattering of dust by the wind; and (iii) the example of natural emergence, which corresponds to the verse "sunrise, waterfalls, peas that are round, thorns with tips that are long and sharp, princesses who are lovely to behold—all these appear naturally, uncreated by anyone!"[38]

The "four modalities" comprise (i) the modality through which happiness, suffering, and so forth, exist here in the present life, although there are no past or future lives; (ii) the modality through which suddenly arising corporeal forms are naturally present of their own accord when they take shape, even though the soul and primal matter are [supposed to be] unchanging through past and future lives; (iii) the modality through which living beings are formed from the suddenly arising material compositions of the five material elements, including earth, that enable awareness to develop;[39] and (iv) the modality through which, when one understands the fact that there is no cause and effect, since beings are not released through the austerities of refining the path but are released naturally, there will be no need to rely on hardships in this life, and so the textual tradition of the Lokāyatika will not be rendered meaningless—when beings pass away, they all abide in an identical state of release. Accordingly, various sources assert:

In accordance with three examples and four modalities,
All things are definitively established
To have a single sensory gate.
Since entities are entirely without cause,
How could the release or liberation be possible![40]

6. The six ministers including the masters: (i) Abhayaprāpta; (ii) Somabhāskarakīrti; (iii) Sāraprāpta; (iv) Satyaprāpta; (v) Jñānavāda; and (vi) Maṅgalaprāpta.[41] They claim that whatever is active and present in the world is true, contrary to the Buddhists and the [aforementioned] extremists. For this reason, they esteem six repositories of knowledge; namely, planets, constellations, seasons, gods, topics of scrutiny, and ritual observance, and they emphasize positive and negative ideas with regard to the present alone. In terms of their practical application, these six fields [of knowledge] may be reduced to three. That is to say, there are astrologers who disclose the positive and negative impacts of the planets, constellations, and calendar days; kings who protect their subjects by knowing the laws that derive from the lineage of universal monarchs and so forth and who maintain the righteousness of the gods; merchants who engage in distinctive topics of scrutiny, of horses, elephants, oceans, and so forth; priests who differentiate matters of state, such as [the prospects for] victory and defeat; and ordinary citizens who engage in their seasonal livelihood. But these may be subsumed in the three categories of kings, scientists, and citizens, so that the priests,[42] merchants, and ordinary citizens are rolled into one. Their fields of knowledge may also number thirty-six since there are six common [fields of knowledge], and then these six may be [differently] understood by kings, ministers [or priests], scientists, merchants, and ordinary citizens.[43]
7. The four types of incidental extremists, including (i) the aspirant; (ii) the attached; (iii) the distracted; and (iv) the perceptive who are prone to distraction. They all hold that by indulging in the happiness of this life they will attain liberation. They are four in number because they, respectively, aspire to the desirable attributes of the senses, are attached to them, have been distracted by them, and are being distracted by them.

8. There are six exponents of sophistry—namely, (i) those whose [rambling or equivocating reasoning resembles] a breeze driving a donkey; (ii) those whose [putrid reasoning resembles] a wall of skin and meat; (iii) those who wear foxes' heads [as hats and perversely kill] each one they see; (iv) those who are materialists; (v) those who always deny causality; and (vi) those who espouse meaningless apathy. These six derive from their [common belief in] the nonexistence of causes.[44]
9. The four false views regarding causes—namely, (i) the false view of nature as a cause; (ii) the false view of a creator [Brahmā divinity] as a cause; (iii) the false view of Īśvara as a cause; and (iv) the false view of time as a cause. These four are established as such because they derive from the false view of eternalism.
10. The two [preeminent] preceptors [propagating such views]—namely, Śaṅkara, the master of the eternalists, and Bṛhaspati, the master of the nihilists. These two are respectively the primary [exponents] of eternalism and nihilism.
11. The Vedāntaupaniṣadika who are included among the Mīmāṃsika.

So it is that there are one hundred imitative philosophical systems, one hundred one eternalist views, eighteen irrational views, twenty-eight false views of meditators, thirty-six false views of [nihilistic] ministers, four incidental false views, six exponents of sophistry, four false views regarding causes, two [primary] preceptors, and the Aupaniṣadika. Together these comprise the three hundred [false views] that depend on the limit of present time.[45]

In addition there are the [aforementioned] eighteen false views about the limits of past time, which comprise (i) four notions of partial eternalism with regard to the self and the world; (ii) four notions of eternalism; (iii) four notions of finitude; and (iv) four propounding endless equivocation, and two propounding fortuitous origination. The [aforementioned] forty-four false notions about the limits of future time comprise sixteen notions concerning percipient immortality; (ii) eight notions concerning nonpercipient immortality; (iii) eight notions concerning neither percipient nor nonpercipient immortality; (iv) seven notions concerning annihilationism; and (v) five notions propounding the immediate attainment of nirvāṇa.[46]

Five Modes of Sophistry

Presentation of the Five Modes of Sophistry [13.1.2.6]

Sixth, the presentation of the five modes of sophistry in which all the aforementioned are subsumed [comments on the verse]:

> **Then there are [the established non-Buddhist systems]**
> **Of Sāṃkhya, Vaiśeṣika, Mīmāṃsika,**
> **Nirgrantha, and Bārhaspatya.**

Although there are an infinite number of distinct classifications of the established non-Buddhist systems, if these are subsumed according to their main categories, they comprise (i) Sāṃkhya (13.1.2.6.1); (ii) Vaiśeṣika (13.1.2.6.2); (iii) Mīmāṃsika (13.1.2.6.3); (iv) Nirgrantha (13.1.2.6.4); and (v) Bārhaspatya (13.1.2.6.5). The first four of these uphold the texts that propound eternalism, and the last establishes the school of nihilism.

Sāṃkhya

Sāṃkhya [13.1.2.6.1]

First among them is the Sāṃkhya, whose texts are the oldest of those of the past professing philosophy. They understand that there are three [main categories of reality] comprising the self, primal matter, and modifications, and they propound that, through meditation, liberation will be attained. Buddhists have interjected that since this premise is false, the compilers [of the Sāṃkhya] never acquire liberation because they persist in the contradiction that release and nature are different.[47]

If the distinctions [of the Sāṃkhya] are explained more extensively, their tenets may be presented as follows: The teacher, a hermit sage named Kapila who had acquired ordinary learning associated with the path of austerity, appeared in the Himavat region during the reign of King Rāṣṭrapāla, in the era when human beings had a life span of twenty thousand years. The texts associated with him included the *Stanzas on Sāṃkhya* by Īśvarakṛṣṇa, the *Sixty Chapter Tantra,* and the *Fifty Defining Characteristics.* There are those among them who maintain that Īśvara was a god and others who hold him to have been human.

As far as their philosophical system is concerned, they hold that there are twenty-five categories of reality that can be known. In order to ascertain these, there are three aspects: (i) the essential nature of each of these categories; (ii) their distinctions; and (iii) the manner in which liberation is acquired by understanding them.

As to the first, the twenty-five categories of reality are enumerated as follows: (1) primal matter; (2) great principle; (3) ego; (4–14) the eleven sense faculties; (15–19) the five quiddities or subtle potentials of the sense objects; (20–24) the five elements; and (25) the soul.

Among these, the eleven sense faculties include the five mental sense faculties of the ear, eye, nose, tongue, and skin; along with the five physical faculties or motor organs of the head, the arms, the legs, the rectum, and the urethra [which respectively activate speech, handling, walking, excretion, and reproduction]; and the mental faculty that is common to all [the other sense faculties].[48] The five sense objects include sights, sounds, odors, tastes, and tangibles; and the five elements include earth, water, fire, wind, and space.

Primal matter is the natural state in which the three attributes—motility, dullness, and lightness, denoting suffering, delusion, and happiness, respectively, are combined in equilibrium. But when these three are imbalanced, rebirth ensues among the six classes of living beings. If suffering is predominant, it is said that rebirth will take place among the denizens of the hells and the anguished spirits, and if delusion is predominant, rebirth will take place among animals, whereas beings who have a predominance of happiness will be born among gods and humans. The *Stanzas on Sāṃkhya* by Īśvarakṛṣṇa teaches:

> When motility, dullness, and lightness—
> The attributes associated with activities—are in equilibrium,
> This is called primal matter.
> When they are imbalanced,
> It is said there are living beings.[49]

Primal matter also has five defining characteristics: it is inanimate, it is permanent, it is singular, it is the creator of living beings, and it is covert because it is invisible. "Inanimate" means that primal matter is demonstrated to be without cognizance and unseen by anyone because the Sāṃkhya also deny that it has physical form. "Permanent" means that it abides from the beginningless past until the unending future. "Singular" means that there is nothing but a single state of primal matter that exclusively permeates all knowable phenomena. "The creator of living beings" implies that all habitats and inhabitants have emerged from primal matter. "Invisible" means that primal matter cannot be seen by others except those such as Kapila who have acquired the eye of meditative concentration. It is also said that even though the eye of meditative concentration can see that primal matter abides in a state of permanence and singularity, it is not physically seen by anyone at all because it cannot be perceived by the eye [of flesh], which resembles a water bubble, even in the case of Kapila and so forth. Indeed, there are two facets because primal matter can be seen by the eye of meditative concentration, but it cannot be seen by the eye [of flesh] which resembles a water bubble. They seek to prove that this primal matter does not exist as a substantial entity because it is free from all that is extraneous, but that it does permeate all things because happiness, suffering, and neutrality are pervasive. This point is explained [in the *Stanzas on Sāṃkhya*] by Īśvarakṛṣṇa:

> When aversion, torment, sorrow, and anger repeatedly manifest,
> These are held to be the signs of motility.
> When dimness, delusion, carelessness,
> and distraction repeatedly manifest,
> These are the attributes of dullness.
> When rejoicing, joy, pleasure, happiness,
> And calm states of mind repeatedly manifest,
> These are the attributes of lightness.[50]

Modifications [of primal matter] occur due to the imbalance of these three attributes. Among them, the modification of intelligence, here designated as the "great principle," has three characteristics in that it is inanimate, it is endowed with sensa, and it engages with sense objects. "Inanimate" means that intelligence is nonsentient and nonphysical. "Endowed with sensa" means that it is the locus in which physical appearances arise. That is to say, externally there are the reflections of sights, sounds, odors, tastes, and tangibles and internally there are reflections of the self, all of which arise in this glass house of intelligence. When these two sorts of reflection interact, this is described as "the soul engaging with sense objects." However, it is not held that the actual soul or mind engages with the intrinsic characteristics of seeing sights, hearing [sounds], and so forth. This is why they say that the sensa arising within intelligence are ascertained by the soul. Although all appearances without exception are the interactions of the reflections of mind and physical objects in this intelligence, that which appears as awareness is not mind and that which appears as a vase and so forth is not an object. Indeed both objects and awareness[51] are covert [to the senses], as is said in the aforementioned [text]:

> Generating lightness in the mental faculty,
> And causing the physical attributes[52] of the soul to emerge,
> Or similarly to be modified,
> This intelligence reinforces sensory engagement.[53]

From intelligence, ego then arises in its three aspects—imbued with the modifications of suffering, imbued with modifications of sensa and imbued with dullness, and yet these are all regarded as a single ego. It is from ego imbued with the modifications of suffering that the eleven sense faculties emerge. It is from ego imbued with the modifications of sensa that the five quiddities of subtle potential emerge; and it is from these five quiddities in turn that the five elements emerge. [Specifically,] space emerges from the subtle potential of sounds, fire from the subtle potential of sights, earth from the subtle potential of odors, water from the subtle potential of tastes, and wind from the subtle potential of tangibles. Ego imbued with dullness assists in the production of these two, but it does not produce any separate effect.[54] It says [in the *Stanzas on Sāṃkhya*] by Īśvarakṛṣṇa:

> From nature there arises the great principle,[55]
> From that ego emerges,
> And from that sixteen[56] aspects emerge.
> Among these sixteen aspects, too,
> The quiddities emerge,
> And therefrom the five elements emerge.[57]

The Sāṃkhya deny entities that arise were formerly nonexistent and newly produced. Rather, they are primordially present in the natural state of primal matter, for which reason effects are said to abide within their causes. This is (i) because effects exclusively reinforce natural states that are present as causes; (ii) because they exclusively reinforce potencies; and (iii) because effects are produced from their causes. That is to say, effects do reinforce natural states that are present as causes, just as a blanket has the nature of wool and a golden vase has the nature of gold. Also, effects do reinforce potencies, such as the bitterness of gentian, the sweetness of molasses, and the shade offered by a metal vase and denied by a glass vase.

As for the reason that [effects] themselves are produced from their causes, they are indeed present [in their natural causes] but cannot newly arise when they are absent, just as the increment of the calendar days [of the month] is based on the roundness of the moon, and butter does not emerge from sand. They do not make the mistake[58] [of claiming that] even though a vase is produced from clay, there would be no need for a potter. For the vase that was formerly present when it was clay is rendered manifest, just as a vase shrouded in darkness is rendered manifest by the condition of a butter lamp. Nor do they make the mistake [of claiming that] the vase present in the clay would implicitly be visible because, even though such entities may be present, they will not be perceived since there are two [different] causes. It says in the *Sixty Chapter Tantra:*

> This may be due to remoteness, or due to proximity,
> Due to impairment of the sense faculties, due to absence of sense,
> Due to minuteness, due to obscuration,
> Due to outshining, and due to interaction.[59]

Two different causes will not manifestly be observed even though their respective conditions are present. Invisibility[60] due to remoteness is exemplified by the motion of the sun and moon. Invisibility due to extreme proximity is exemplified by things that are covert to the eyes. Invisibility due to impairment of the sense faculties is exemplified by forms as seen by a blind person. Invisibility due to absence of sense is exemplified by the perception of one's surroundings when one is asleep. Invisibility due to minuteness is exemplified by a particle of flour. Invisibility due to obscuration is exemplified by the entrails of the body. Invisibility due to outshining is exemplified by the stars during the day. Invisibility due to interaction is exemplified by particles of milk when water and milk are mixed together. Among these [examples], in this case of the vase present in a state of [unmodified] clay, the effect due to the potency of its cause is invisible because it is outshone [by the clay].

Perishable and manifest entities become nonmanifest due to their vanishing in an aeon of time or in primal matter. Like cattle that are steered into a barn, they do not perish but are invariably present. Briefly stated, it is not the case that entities that were not previously existent are newly produced, or that things that are always present can perish. Rather, there is a permanent natural state that is subject to provisional modifications. Entities emerge from primal matter and dissolve into primal matter. When the provisional state of a sheep, having been modified into wool, blankets, woolen cloth, dust, and atoms, is no longer manifest, it cannot be discerned because it becomes of a single savor in primal matter, just as in the beginning, atoms are in a state of great subtlety owing to the natural state of primal matter, and become manifestly visible due to provisional modifications. However, in the end there is no transformation from that original state into another.

The subject that engages with the twenty-four other categories, including the sense faculties, objects, and elements is designated as the self or soul. [It is cognizant.][61] It is eternal, it is singular, it is not a creator, and it is a consumer. With regard to that which possesses these five attributes, it says accordingly in the *Introduction* [*to the Middle Way*]:

> The extremists have determined that the self is a consumer and eternal,
> But not a creator, devoid of attributes and activities.
> With minor variations on this analysis,
> The extremists have differentiated their systems.[62]

In this regard, they hold that [the self] is cognizant because it is aware of objects, it is eternal because it does not change throughout the three times, and although its natural state is unchanging, it becomes happy and so forth due to provisional conditions. It is singular because each sentient being partakes of nothing but a single conscious awareness. Even in each of these individual cases, [the self] is without movement because it pervades everything. It is not a creator because it engages in nothing at all. Rather, all phenomenal existence is created by primal matter. However, the self is a consumer because it engages with the modifications emanated by primal matter.

In order to introduce this understanding, the Sāṃkhya hold that the clear and unimpeded consciousness that suddenly and lucidly arises, internally of its own accord, during the perception of sights and so forth, without forming conceptual notions about its sense object, is designated as the self and that those who acquire familiarity with this will attain liberation. This possessor of the [other] twenty-four categories of reality, such as the eyes, is of beneficial intent because these are compounded and accumulated, as, for example, in bedding and seats. They hold that there are no other knowable phenomena that exist apart from those twenty-five categories, and that while twenty-four of them may form the basis for disputation, this would not be appropriate for the soul, which is distinct from them.

The framework [of the twenty-five categories of reality] has three aspects: (i) the framework as presented on the basis of the inanimate and awareness;

(ii) the framework as presented on the basis of cause and effect; and (iii) the framework as presented on the basis of the relative and the ultimate.

As to the first, there are twenty-four categories of reality that are inanimate and one, the self, that is aware. The second [framework] is established owing to the designations of the natural state and its modifications, in which case there are four limits. Among these, (i) primal matter demarcates the limit of the natural state alone because it is uncreated by anyone at all; (ii) the ego, intelligence, and the five sense objects—these seven—demarcate the limit of both cause and effect because they arise from primal matter and because the five elements are produced from them; (iii) the eleven sense faculties and the five elements—these sixteen—[demarcate the limit of] modification alone because they arise from primal matter and do not produce anything else; and (iv) the self [demarcates the limit] of neither cause nor effect because it is not produced by anyone and does not produce anything else.

Nowadays, [in the time of Longchen Rabjam,] there are some who make a great assumption that this approach has been assimilated within our own school, which recognizes that the nature of mind is clear at the present moment, without conceptual notions, and entirely without cause and effect, and that since on that basis no cause or result at all is produced, one should become familiar with its disposition. However, those implying that this [view of the Great Perfection] is identical to the position of the Sāṃkhya have made a biased assumption.[63] For it says in the previous source:

> Primal matter is a natural state and not a modification.
> The seven beginning with the great principle
> Are both natural states and modifications.
> The sixteen [beginning with the sense faculties]
> Are themselves modifications.
> The soul is neither a natural state nor a modification.[64]

[As to the third,] when this framework is presented on the basis of the two truths, the inanimate primal matter and the self or soul that is conscious awareness are both ultimate, whereas the other twenty-three categories of reality are relative. It says in the same source:

> The supreme natural state endowed with the three attributes
> Is not within the scope of perception;

> Whatever is within the scope of perception
> Is extremely vacuous, like an illusion.[65]

Our own schools that accept that appearances are illusory are dissimilar to that; for, although appearances are not true, we do not accept that primal matter is true.

With regard to the liberation that ensues through the understanding of the meaning of these twenty-five categories of reality, when one has meditated having excellently understood their nature, it seems that this [liberation will ensue] whatever one's appearance. Even those with a pile of dreadlocks such as the Aiśvarya, those with hair fastened on the crown of their heads such as wandering mendicants, and those who grow hair on their heads such as the naked Nirgrantha Jains will themselves acquire liberation! It says [in the *Stanzas on Sāṃkhya*] by Īśvarakṛṣṇa:

> When one understands the twenty-five categories of reality,
> Those who have dreadlocks, or a topknot on their heads,
> Whatever their mode of dress,
> There is no doubt that they will attain liberation.[66]

Yogins who acquire the mind of meditative concentration become dissatisfied with all the attributes of the senses. Thinking "Alas, I have long been deceived by meaningless appearances," they examine from what source these modifications have emerged, and understanding them to have been emanated through primal matter, they come to behold primal matter and flee away [from them] in shame. Like a child in pursuit of its mother, the modifications also flee in pursuit of primal matter, so that, as if devoid of discriminative awareness,[67] the singular self comes to rest in that one-pointed nonconceptual state,[68] without being propelled toward the sense objects. They hold that this is called liberation.[69]

Vaiśeṣika

Vaiśeṣika [13.1.2.6.2]

Second, there is the description of the philosophical system of the Vaiśeṣika. The Vaiśeṣika extremists hold that liberation will be acquired after establishing all knowable phenomena in terms of six categories. However, this is not a genuine proposition because it succumbs to erroneous bias. Here, the philosophical system associated with their texts is presented as follows:[70]

The extremists who propound that spiritual accomplishment will be acquired by eating a single kernel of rice and propitiating Īśvara, hold Kaṇāda as their teacher and take Īśvara as their deity.

When those who follow the texts presented by him, including the *Tantras of Śiva* are classified, they comprise (i) the Aiśvarya; (ii) the Aulūkya; (iii) the Vaiśeṣika; and (iv) the Naiyāyika. Among these, the Aiśvarya are so called because they hold Īśvara as their deity. The Aulūkya are so called because they hold an [emanational] owl as their deity. It is said that after an owl alighted upon a stone *liṅgam* that Kaṇāda had been using to propitiate Īśvara, it was accepted as [an emanation of] Īśvara, and on being asked what constitutes the substantial existents, it turned its head in six directions, after which it flew away. The Vaiśeṣika are so called because they accept the distinctions [of the six categories], and the Naiyāyika are so called because they accept reasoning.[71]

The texts that they espouse suggest that the creator is Īśvara and that by making offerings to him, the blissful states of gods and humans will be acquired. They ascertain knowable phenomena in terms of the six categories and attain release on the basis of that understanding.

First, the defining characteristics, attributes, and proof statements pertaining to Īśvara will be considered. Among these, Īśvara is said to partake of the following five defining characteristics: (i) he is eternal; (ii) he is singular; (iii) he acts dynamically because his intelligence precedes all actions; (iv) he is subsumed in a divine state; and (v) he is pure and worthy of offerings. "Eternal" means that he exists, without birth and death, from beginning to end. "Singular" means that there is but a single Īśvara in the world. "Dynamic action" means that he creates all things—bondage, liberation, shapes, colors, and so forth.

When the world was in a state of vacuity, Īśvara had the thought that he wanted to emanate the world. At that time, he caused particles to be gathered by the wind, forming the maṇḍala of wind, and the mass of water and fire. Within this, [he emanated] the primal egg of Brahmā, inside of which resided the progenitor of all worlds—the four-faced Brahmā, with flowing locks of hair and lotus navel. As the sound of the *Four Vedas* resonated, the priestly class then emerged from his face,[72] the royal class from his shoulders, the mercantile class from his thighs, and the laboring class from the soles of his feet. In the same manner, all [phases of cyclical time]—the initial creation of the world, the intervening maintenance of the world, the terminal dissolution of the world, and the final state of vacuity—were generated by Īśvara.

"Subsumed in a divine state" means that he resides in the Paranirmitavaśavartin realm. "Pure and worthy of offerings" means that he does not delight in dog meat and so forth, and that when offerings are made with pure substances, he confers spiritual accomplishment. Accordingly, it says in the *Tantras of Śiva:*

> Paramaiśvara is the subtle and unique source of creation
> By whom all this [world] was created and destroyed,
> To whom divine offerings should be made.
> The quiescence that creates positive attributes should be obtained.[73]

And:

> Just as Pāṇini is the source of all grammar,
> Crystal is the source of all water,
> And the fig tree is the source of all branches,
> He is the source of all corporeal beings.[74]

As for the attributes [of Īśvara], they are eightfold, beginning with subtlety. It is said:

He manifoldly creates and destroys
By means of his arms, legs, eyes, complexion, and body.
Therefore [as Rudra] he is said to have subtlety.
He maintains space and wind,
Along with earth, water, and fire;
Absorbing them and causing them to expand.
Therefore [as Bhava] he is said to have agility.[75]
He controls all the elements,
Generating rest and motion, as he desires.
Therefore [as Īśāna] he is said to have supremacy.
As the lord with autonomy over gross corporeal forms,
Destroying some and others not,
He has dominion over all things.
Therefore [as Paśupati] he is said to have dominion.
Without resting, his mind pursues sense objects,
Food, delicacies, and all else that can be accumulated by the mind.
Therefore [as Bhīma] he is said to have the power
To move freely and obtain anything.
He is worshipped throughout the three worlds,
And[76] he is presented with offerings by all elemental spirits.
Therefore [as Śarva] he is worthy of offerings.
Transforming the three attributes—lightness, motility, and dullness—
He can create anything by merely opening his eyes.
Therefore [as Ugra] he is said to have irresistible willpower.
All the things that he himself desires whatsoever,
Be it release [from rebirth] or a divine body,
He will attain according to his desire.
Therefore [as Mahādeva] he is said to abide anywhere at will.[77]

As for the statements of proof pertaining to Īśvara: [it is held that] this inhabited world and its inhabitants have been created by Īśvara. This is (i) because he determines the size of cypress trees, large and small; (ii) because he determines [the qualities] of sharp thorns and the like; (iii) because he stays and moves, determining the seasons of summer and winter, and so forth; and (iv) because he creates [the disparities of] the rich, the poor, and so forth, and their dissimilar experiences.

If the fruits of past actions are true, it is incorrect that religious persons with a short life span would have killed living creatures in the past, because they are endowed with kindness. We [Buddhists] agree that one is endowed with kindness because one has not slain living creatures, but for them the life span is short due to the partiality of Īśvara. As it is said:

> Seeing acquisitive people who are rich,
> Virtuous people who are harmed by others,
> And irreligious people who are joyful—
> It is clear that all these are due to Īśvara.
> Seeing talented and rich people with short life spans,
> Evildoers with long life spans,
> [The disparities of] the rich and the poor—
> It is clear that all these were created by Īśvara.[78]

By making offerings to Īśvara, one acquires the blissful states [of gods and humans]. In this regard, when sentient beings excellently offer the flesh and blood of slain cattle to Īśvara alone, without engaging in other virtuous actions, they will attain the rank of gods and humans:

> Living creatures are not [innately] conscious.
> They have no control over the joys and sorrows
> That the soul experiences.
> At the dispensation of Īśvara
> They will proceed to higher or lower realms.[79]

[According to the Vaiśeṣika,] all knowable phenomena are subsumed within the following six categories, as it has been said:

> The six categories are (i) substances; (ii) attributes;
> (iii) actions; (iv) universals; (v) particulars; and (vi) inherence.[80]

When these are explained individually: substances have two modalities—permanent and impermanent. Permanent substances are of five types: (i) soul; (ii) time; (iii) mind;[81] (iv) direction; and (v) space.

The soul, according to the Naiyāyika, has an inanimate nature.[82] The sense objects in which the soul abides are cognized by the intellect, but this awareness is concomitant with the soul, just as visual consciousness is dependent on the eye that sees visual forms. Therefore it is said:

> Furthermore, as for the soul, here the soul is held
> To partake of attributes such as attachment and aversion;
> As a support [for sensory experience], as an all-pervasive consumer,
> The soul is essentially inanimate.[83]

Therefore, although the soul is eternal, the intellect undergoes transformation and differentiates its attributes. In this way, they hold that the soul does not perish and become a nonentity.

Although all entities can be incinerated by fire or crushed by a hammer, the atoms are merely dispersed—other than that, they cannot be destroyed. Even when the world is destroyed, when atomic particles begin to billow into space, they will be gathered in their appropriate classes by Īśvara, so that substances consisting of corporeal forms and so forth will reemerge.[84]

Space is endowed with five properties: (i) it is pervasive; (ii) it is permanent; (iii) it is accommodating; (iv) it transmits sound; and (v) it is an entity. The first three of these properties are largely accepted.

Impermanent substances include the four ancillary elements of earth, water, fire, and wind. Thus there are altogether nine types of substance.

[The second of the six categories,] the attributes, are twenty-four in number, the first group of six comprising (i) number; (ii) measure; (iii) connection; (iv) separation; (v) remoteness; and (vi) proximity.[85]

The next group of thirteen, occurring only with reference to the soul, comprise (i) intelligence of the eye; (ii) intelligence of the ear; (iii) intelligence of the nose; (iv) intelligence of the tongue; (v) intelligence of the body; (vi) happiness; (vii) suffering; (viii) attachment; (ix) aversion; (x) immorality; (xi) morality; (xii) effort; and (xiii) the impact of predispositions.

The last group comprises the five sense objects: (i) sights that are an attribute of heat; (ii) sounds that are an attribute of space; (iii) odors that are an attribute of earth; (iv) tastes that are an attribute of water; and (v) tangibles that are an attribute of wind.[86]

Sounds are said to abide permanently within space. Concealed by [the prevailing] raw wind, they are unheard, but when the syllable OṂ is uttered by human beings, the wind is dispersed and [sounds] are heard. Then, in their wake, when they vanish into the trail of the wind, [sounds] are [again] unheard.

[The third of the six categories] concerns actions, which are of five sorts: (i) expanding; (ii) contracting; (iii) rising; (iv) settling; and (v) moving.[87]

[The fourth of the six categories] concerns universals, which are of two sorts: (i) pervasive universals and (ii) ephemeral universals. The former are pervasive because they are present in all knowable phenomena. The latter include intermediate universals and lesser universals. Among these, the first is exemplified by the logical entailment that the term *vase* is applicable to all vases. The second is exemplified by the logical entailment that all limbs constitute the body.[88]

All universals also partake of three defining characteristics: (i) inclusion; (ii) permanence; and (iii) singularity. For example, [with regard to inclusion,] the term *vase* includes its own particulars, such as gold vases and clay vases, because it is logically entailed that a vase is present, whatever sort of vases there are, be they gold vases and the like. Their permanence is also discernible because [universals are perceived] to exist from before the time when particulars are formed until after they are destroyed. This is also why their singularity is established.[89]

In this regard, Vailuka, the student of Kaṇāda, held that those universals continue to exist even in an intervening vacuity when they are no longer discernible, saying that in the case of Īśvara, taking his corporeality as the subject for discussion, it is present as a universal even in the intervening vacuity when it is no longer discernible, because it is pervasive and eternal. On the other hand, the Naiyāyika teacher Vaira said that, taking the indiscernible intervening vacuity as the subject for discussion, it is not present as a universal because it is not perceptible.

[The fifth of the six categories,] particulars, include discernible and discrete phenomena, exemplified by a vase and a pillar.[90]

[The last of the six categories,] inherence has two aspects: differentiating and nondifferentiating. The former is exemplified by the two horns on the head [of a goat]. Nondifferentiating inherence is exemplified by a conch in which [the attributes] white and round are inherent.[91]

With regard to liberation that is attained through knowledge, once the six categories of reality have been understood, liberation will be attained when they have been cultivated. As it has been said:[92]

> Cyclic existence is indeed beginningless,
> But it is not unending.
> By understanding this reality alone,
> Human beings will finally attain liberation.[93]

When all conceptual notions of body and mind have been
  abandoned,
One will proceed to that utterly pure, immaculate state,
Like a fire of spent wood.[94]
The soul—intelligence and so forth—partakes of attributes.
The yogin is the one who has cultivated and brought these forth.
The Vaiśeṣika therefore have determined and understood
That the soul abides in the mental faculty.[95]

It is held that in the circumstances of release [from cyclic existence], the soul becomes free from all extremes of existence and nonexistence, eternalism and nihilism. This is said to accord with the following standpoint:[96]

Not existent, not nonexistent,
Not multiple, not singular,
Not minute, and not great,
This nonexistent state is not permanent,
Not impermanent, not self, and not other.[97]

Mīmāṃsika

Mīmāṃsika [13.1.2.6.3]

Third, the systems associated with the Mīmāṃsika are established as follows: They hold Viṣṇu as a deity and propound the authority of the Vedas, accepting ten tenets. However there is no liberation for those practicing extremists who seek release because they enter upon a mistaken pathway. It is as if they advance to the east, and veer to the west, while stepping forward.

Here, when their traditions are extensively analyzed, those who revere the priest Jaimini as their teacher and hold Viṣṇu as their deity comprise the following five classes: (i) Vaidika; (ii) Brāhmaṇa; (iii) Vaiṣṇava; (iv) Mīmāṃsika; and (v) Jaiminīya. They are so known because they respectively (i) hold the *Four Vedas* as an authority; (ii) hold the priestly class as supreme; (iii) hold Viṣṇu as their deity; (iv) hold that liberation will be attained merely by ritual conduct; and (v) follow the teacher Jaimini.

They adhere to [distinctive] philosophical texts, to schools (*śākhā, yan lag*) that espouse [distinctive] Vedic rituals (*kalpa, rtog pa*) and compilations (*saṃhitā, phan pa*), to the school of the [Kingly] Sage Janaka, to the sacrificial ceremony in which the [Brāhmaṇical] sacred thread (*yajñopavīta, nor bu skud pa*) is worn, to the [epic] anthology of *Bharata,* to the *Esoteric Verses of Rāṇāyana,* and so forth; and they accept the following ten tenets. They pledge that (i) Viṣṇu is their deity; (ii) the Vedas are their authority; (iii) purity comes through ablution; (iv) purity comes through sacred places; (v) purity comes through the protection of worldly existence; (vi) purity comes through the protection of war; (vii) purity comes through the protection of righteousness; (viii) purity comes through the protection of life; (ix) entities are without causation; and (x) there is no intrinsic awareness that comes through understanding.

As to the first [of these tenets]: All entities are emanations of Viṣṇu. It says in the [teachings of] the school of the [Kingly] Sage Janaka:

> This auspicious Vasudeva is omniscient and all-seeing,
> Conferring liberation and guiding all beings to the deity.
> Abiding as the essential nature of Vasudeva,
> Balabhadra, Amṛta, and so forth,
> The universal self is all-engaging and all-pervading.[98]

In order to discipline living beings, [Viṣṇu] assumed the following ten emanations: (i) Matsya the fish; (ii) Kūrma the turtle; (iii) Varāha the wild boar; (iv) Rāma, son of King Daśaratha; (v) Paraśurāma, the son of the hermit sage Jamadagni; (vi) Kṛṣṇa; (vii) Narasiṃha; (viii) Vamāna the dwarf; (ix) Śākyamuni; and [in the future] he will assume the emanation of (x) Kalkin, when the life span is ten years, and then, establishing all beings in release from the higher realms, he will empty cyclic existence. Previously, in an intervening age, while emanating as Varāha the wild boar, he is said to have been most gracious because he assumed the burden of compassion by supporting all worlds, liberating and discarding all [negative forces]. It says in the *Esoteric Verses of Rāṇāyana:*

> Matsya, Kūrma, Varāha,
> The two Rāma incarnations, Kṛṣṇa,
> Narasiṃha, Vamāna, Buddha, and Kalkin—
> These are his ten incarnations.[99]

Emanating in that manner, Viṣṇu is [identified with] the universal self, commencing from his first incarnation, as is said in the *Tantra of the Quiescence of Viṣṇu:*

> I am the consumer who grants boons.
> I am the food and the soul of all beings.
> Assuming the body of a priest,
> I consume and grant boons.
> It is revealed that those who have faith in,
> Or who would have faith in, other gods
> Are the sons of me—Kunda
> Because my rites have precedence.[100]

As to [the second tenet, whereby they accept] the Vedas as their authority, there are four great compilations of the Vedas, concerning sacrifices, legends, esoteric hymns, and worldly rites. Alternatively, it is held that the four Vedic compilations comprise (i) the *Ṛgveda*; (ii) the *Yajurveda*; (iii) the *Sāmaveda*; and (iv) the *Atharvaveda*.

Among them, the sacrifices [of the *Yajurveda*] include the making of offerings to the gods and the granting of gifts to sentient beings. Peaceful sacrifices are undertaken by avoiding the killing of living creatures, whereas wrathful sacrifices entail the ritual slaughter of cattle and so forth. It is held that there is a distinction between liberation and the fruit that is established according to provisional truth. It is also held that there are benefits for the animals that are slain, over and above the absolution of their sins, in that they will be guided by the gods to higher realms. So it is that beings of lower realms are established in higher realms. It says in the *Esoteric Verses:*

> The harmful [taking of life] that the Vedas teach
> Is reviled in other treatises,
> But they teach that [slain creatures] will be reborn elsewhere,
> Since they are without sins.[101]

The legends [based on the *Ṛgveda*] concern the genealogies associated with the incarnations of Viṣṇu, the abduction of Umādevī by Īśvara, and so forth. The esoteric hymns [of the *Sāmaveda*] teach that all things have come to pass in accordance with nature and so forth. The worldly rites [of the *Atharvaveda*] are [pointless] treatises of trivial pursuit, teaching the rituals of the priestly class. It says in the *Ocean of Texts:*

> Gautama! The woman [Ahalyā] is the fire itself.
> Her vagina is the hearth.
> The pubic hairs growing there[102] are the smoke.
> Its penetration is the coal.
> The sperm is the spark.
> In a fire such as this
> The offspring, the seed of the gods, is burnt,
> Out of this burnt offering, an offspring will arise.
> Born therein, he will live his life.[103]

These are called worldly rites because in that manner one's own worldly existence is secured and the family line is not interrupted. According to the tradition of those who engage in the practices of the priestly class, there is a treatise [stating that] after they have practiced chastity of up to sixty years, their family line may subsequently be extended, for which reason they may take a wife.

These *Four Vedas* are also endowed with three defining characteristics: (i) they are uncreated by human beings; (ii) they are eternal; and (iii) they possess true meaning. Are they not created, you may ask, because they were expressed by Brahmā? That is not the case. They are eternal, and although they were spoken from memory by Brahmā, they were not newly created. As it is said in the [*Heart Commentary on*] *the Eight Branches* [*of Medicine*]:

> Brahmā uttered the life-sustaining Vedas from memory,
> And explained them to Prajāpati.[104]

They maintain that if that were not the case, it would follow that "the expanse of reality that you Buddhists also hold to be uncreated would not be so, because it is enunciated by the buddhas." Rather, the words [of the Vedas], which exist eternally in space, were heard by Brahmā who recollected their meaning and spoke them from memory. They hold that all utterances are false but that the Vedas are true. It says in the *Esoteric Verses:*

> Since they are diminished by defects such as attachment,[105]
> The words of human beings are false,
> But the Vedas have not been created by human beings,
> For which reason they should be accepted as authentic.[106]

The sound of the Vedas, connected with its meaning, exists as an entity. As is said in the same text:

> Eternal words are elucidated by sound.
> They themselves are eternally associated with meaning,
> Those who understand their meaning,
> Will greatly develop their understanding.[107]

The expositors of the Vedas hold that Brahmā is true but that it is not possible for buddhas to be omniscient because "you Buddhists merely exaggerate and other than that in your own texts there are many contradictions." It says in the *Esoteric Verses:*[108]

> The speech of the buddhas is not authentic
> Because it refutes the threefold view [of the Vedas].
> Whatever they say, it is so,
> Just like the views of wandering naked ascetics.
> They lack understanding of all knowable phenomena,
> They do not arrive at another means of knowledge.
> One [person] cannot know all things, moving and unmoving.
> Because the Vedas cannot be recited by everyone,
> The human beings in the world
> And heretical practitioners too are not omniscient.[109]
> In order to subdue Devadatta
> Who could cast a slingshot,
> [The Buddha] acquired the strength of an elephant,
> But he did not understand future events.[110]

With regard to the permanence [of the Vedas], in general all sounds are themselves permanent because they facilitate communication, because they can be experienced, because they enable that which was formerly known to be subsequently known by others, and because they can be heard. Such is the general [description] of the nature of sound.

If sound were impermanent, it could not even be conveyed because, inasmuch as it were impermanent, it would subsequently cease and become nonexistent. Nor would it be capable of retaining words and so forth because [words] retained at the present moment would have been impermanent in the past, and therefore they would cease and become nonexistent. Nor could one's own understanding be explained to others because those former understandings would have ceased and been rendered entirely nonexistent. Nor could it even be heard because at the time when it is heard, former [sounds] would have ceased and become nonexistent. So it is because sound is permanent, that it can be known, retained, and heard. As the hermit sage Rāṇāyana has said:

> Because it can be conveyed on a single occasion,
> Because it can be repeatedly experienced,
> Because it can be recognized,

And similarly because it can be heard,
The nature of sound is such.
Sound should be known to be permanent.[111]

So it is that since Brahmā taught the entire import of the Vedas, they should be accepted because they are true. It is said in the [teachings of] the schools espousing rituals and Vedic compilations:

The Vedic rites are unspoken.
The Vedas are imperceptible.
Anything that can be expressed as nonexistent
Is not heard in the manner of the Vedas.[112]

[As for the third tenet,] concerning purity by means of ablution, in general purification may be achieved by all kinds of ablutions. This is because the mind will be immediately made clear and the body cleansed, while in the long term, negativity will be pacified. In particular, higher rebirth and release will be attained when ablutions are performed in the mighty waters that are the gateways of ablution: the Ganges, Kuśāvarta, Bilvakatīrtha, Nīlagiri, Kanaka, Candrabhāgā, Sārasvatī, Varāha, Śaravatī, Indus, Nairañjana, and Prayāgatīrtha, as explained in the *Gateways to Ablution* of the hermit sage [Uddalaka Aruni of] Pañcāla:

After performing ablutions at the gateways of the Ganges:
The fords of Kuśāvarta, Bilvakatīrtha, Nīlagiri, and Kanaka,
There will be no future rebirths.[113]
By virtue of these ablutions in the Ganges, the Candrabhāgā,
And similarly the Sārasvatī, Varāha, Śaravatī, and Indus,
Which flow into the oceans,
The souls who seek purity and perform ablutions,
Purified of negativity,
Will certainly attain the release of the higher realms.[114]

They hold that, having gone to those [bathing places] and weighed themselves, if they then become lighter, their negativity will have been reduced.

[As for the fourth tenet,] concerning purity through [contact with] sacred places, they hold that all those who are born in the place called Kurukṣetra and even, at the very least, all those who have come into contact with its dust will be reborn in the higher realms. It says in the [teachings of] the schools espousing Vedic rituals and compilations:

> If they are born in the land of Kuru
> And even if they are touched by the wind-borne dust of that land,
> Sentient beings who have committed evil acts
> Will be brought to superior realms of existence.[115]

[As to the fifth tenet,] concerning purity through the conservation of worldly existence, according to the established class system, it is held that those of the priestly class will be reborn in the higher realms. Women will certainly proceed to the lower realms, but on associating with a priest who has been celibate and then ceases to be celibate after the age of forty-two, they should give birth to sons. All women who have such sons will be reborn in the higher realms. Those who lack them will be reborn in the lower realms. Those who have many daughters or those who only have daughters will be born in the lower realms where it will indeed be hard for them to attain release. It says in the same text:

> Those who have sons will, on death,
> Proceed to states without sorrow.
> This path is indeed a path that leads to the god realms.
> Therefore [a priest] should cohabit with a woman.
> How could the world have evolved,
> Excellent in all respects
> From those who are without children,
> As those following a mundane path
> Have said when welcoming old age![116]

[As to the sixth tenet,] concerning purity through the protection of warfare, when destructive wars occur, negativity is purified by fighting without compassion, because there will be merit for those who strive to win for their own side. It says in the *Esoteric Verses:*

> If the warrior who is resolute, without play,
> Does not flee in the face of battle,
> But goes directly into battle,
> That one will, on dying, proceed to higher realms.[117]

[As to the seventh tenet,] concerning purity through the protection of righteousness, by slaying negative beings who inflict harm on the priestly class, the Vedas, and their teachers, negativity will be purified because [this action] will protect the supreme objective. It says in the same text:

In order to protect and enlighten living creatures
The thorns of the gods slay the antigods,
And yet they are without fault
Because they are protecting righteousness.[118]

[As to the eighth tenet,] concerning purity through the protection of life, when death is imminent due to the blight of famine, even though one steals something without being seen, there will be no crime, and in addition, negativity will be purified. This is because, by protecting one's own supreme life through common material things, great benefit will subsequently be achieved. It says in the *Esoteric Verses:*

When priests are aged,
Thieving is explained to be righteousness.
They should indeed steal the property of others without being seen.[119]

[As for the ninth tenet,] concerning entities that are without causation, it is held that all entities arise naturally and of their own volition, independent of causes and conditions, because even destruction and creation are without causation, and because clouds, hailstones, lightning, and so forth, emerge from an empty sky, just as the sun and moon naturally move from east to west. It says in the same text:

Sunrise, waterfalls, the sharpness of thorns,
And the patterns of peacock plumage have arisen naturally.[120]

[As for the tenth tenet, concerning their view that no intrinsic awareness comes about through cognition, they hold that this is because one does not engage in activity with respect to oneself, just as the eye itself does not perceive itself.][121]

Aupaniṣadika

Aupaniṣadika [13.1.2.6.3.1]

Among those who now uphold the Vedas as an authority, the school that emphasizes the tenets of the *Esoteric Words,* is the Aupaniṣadika. Their detailed explanation is as follows: Among the foregoing proponents of the Vedas who have just been explained, the subschool known as the Aupaniṣadika hold that the entire world is intellectually established to have the nature of form, endowed with a single soul—a nature that permeates all things and has nine distinctive attributes. Cyclic existence comes into being through the motion of a "surge of intelligence" at the summit of existence, which was not previously existent. This is described as astonishing because to scholars who disagree, that becomes an object of derision. As is said by Maitreya:

> I consider as astonishing
> That which is said to end obscuration,
> Revealing that extraneous phenomena are indeed existent
> And that they are also knowable.[122]

If the tradition of this [school] is analyzed in detail: The priests who hold Brahmā as their deity and emphasize the *Esoteric Verses* maintain, according to texts such as the *Cycle of Training That Effects Recollection,* that there is a soul endowed with nine distinctive attributes that permeates all knowable phenomena in the manner of space. That is to say, (i) [the soul] has an essential nature that is sentient; (ii) it is corporeal; (iii) it is pervasive; (iv) it is eternal; (v) it is singular; (vi) it is the support of things that originate and perish; (vii) it is untainted by corporeal faults and attributes; (viii) it is not within the perceptual range of the intellect; and (ix) it is not verbally expressible.[123]

With regard to the first [of these nine distinctive attributes]: although it appears as corporeal, [the soul's] essential nature is noncorporeal, and simply cognizant and perceptive.

With regard to [the second,] that it is corporeal: the entire zenith is [identified with] the head of the cosmic person, the entire nadir with the feet, space with the abdomen, the four directions with the limbs, the planets and constellations with the hair, Sumeru with the chest, the mountain chains with the bones, the rivers including the Ganges with the network of energy channels, the forests with the body hair and nails, the god and humans inhabiting the higher realms with the back, Brahmā with the forehead, morality with the right eyebrow, immorality with the left eyebrow, the lord of death with the frowns, the sun with the right eye, the moon with the left eye, the winds with the breath, the cliffs with teeth, the goddess Sārasvatī with the tongue, daylight with the opening of the eyes, the night with the closing of the eyes, the masculine with the right side, the feminine with the left side, foothills with the fingers and toes, mundane beings with the right nipple, supramundane beings with the left nipple, the two divine princes (*lha'i bu gnyis*) with the knees, the Aśvins (*tha skar*) with the forearms and shins, Divasa with the loins, Indra with the penis, Prajāpati with the natural expression of joy, Viṣṇu with the legs, and colors with the blood.[124]

Therefore, [the third of the nine distinctive attributes] is that [the soul] is said to permeate all knowable phenomena.

With regard to [the fourth of the nine distinctive attributes,] that [the soul] is eternal, this is because it is present from the beginning to the end. Therefore the notions that "it arose at this specific point in the past" or that "it will perish at this specific point in the future" are not applicable. It says in the *Cycle of Training That Effects Recollection:*

> Once the yogin has experienced
> The supreme abode of immortal Brahmā—
> Singular, all-pervasive, and eternal—
> That one will not take rebirth again.[125]

With regard to [the fifth of the nine distinctive attributes,] that [the soul] is singular, they hold that although to the bewildered it manifests in many [diverse] life forms, in all these [life forms] the soul has but a singular nature. As has previously been cited from the *Flame of Dialectics:*

Although there may be different vases,
There is no difference at all in their clay,
In the same way, although there may be different bodies,
There is no difference at all in the soul.[126]

With regard to [the sixth of the nine distinctive attributes,] that [the soul] is the support of things that originate and perish, although all corporeal things originate, they originate from the disposition of the soul, and although they are released [at the time of death], they are released into the disposition of the soul. It says in the previous text:

The diversity of worldly existence arises therefrom.
The skillful ones who dissolve therein
In the manner of the thread of a silkworm,
Will no longer be subject to rebirth.[127]

So it is that there is no profundity greater than this. As is said in the *Esoteric Verses:*

Since there is nothing else superior to this,
Nothing else more sacred than this,
And nothing else subtler than this,
Those diverse [life forms] partake of a single causal basis.[128]

Although there is but a single soul, it becomes bewildered and manifests in manifold life forms, just as when a hundred vases are made, the space they contain is a hundredfold.

With regard to those whose bewilderment has ceased, since they are absorbed in this great soul, they become indivisible, whether it is said that this refers to the past life or to the next life, just as when one or two vases and so forth are broken, the spaces they contain dissolve into the great space and then become indivisible. The same text says:

Just as when vases and so forth are broken,
The spaces contained within the vases and so forth
Are gathered in the great space,
In the same way, [individual] life forms are also absorbed into this soul.[129]

Actually, it is held that the imperishable and vacuous nature of knowable phenomena is [identified with] the soul and that, by experiencing this nonconceptually at the present moment, although one's body will disintegrate and life will cease at the time of death, apart from [the dissolution of] the elements into their four elemental parts, the vacuous mind will become indivisible with the vacuous disposition of all things, so that it will dissolve into the disposition of space and be liberated. Nowadays there are a great many who propound this [view]—it seems that their skulls are detached from their heads![130]

With regard to [the seventh of the nine distinctive attributes,] that [the soul] is untainted by corporeal faults and attributes, [they hold that the soul] is untainted by [dualities such as] good and evil, happiness and suffering, birth and death, joy and affliction, or virtue and negativity.[131] Although living beings appear wise and foolish, and social classes may appear good and bad, and so forth, these are nonexistent in the essential nature of the soul, just as a vase may appear large or small, and good or bad, but [such distinctions] are nonexistent in space. It says in the same text:

> Thereupon they see that all the elements are also gathered in the soul.
> The naive, the learned, the social outcastes,
> The priestly class, and so forth, are identical.[132]

In the same manner, the soul does not become happy though gods and humans experience happiness; nor does it change accordingly though the lower realms experience suffering, just as though the space contained within a single vase may increase and that contained within another may decrease, there is neither increase nor decrease in the overall vastness of space. It is said in the *Esoteric Verses:*

> Just as when the space contained within a single vase may be obscured by dust and smoke,
> But the entirety [of space] is not,
> In the same manner, happiness and so forth
> Are not present in the soul.[133]

Just as a vase may be fashioned or broken, but the space it contains is neither created nor ceases, so although corporeal forms appear to be born and to die, the soul is unchanging. It says in the same text:

> Just as a vase may arise and[134] perish,
> That is not the case for the soul that is the space it contains.
> Just as corporeal forms may arise and perish,
> These are not held to be the soul
> Because that [space] is the soul.[135]

Like certain deluded persons [holding in denial that] when a crime has been committed, even though punishment has been exacted, the ruler did not exact punishment for the crime, there are certain persons [who maintain that] even though one who has committed an evil act may be reborn in the hells, the soul will not be reborn there. It says in the *Esoteric Verses:*

> Though it abides in the body, it is unattached.
> Though it engages in conduct, it is untainted.
> Though it acts willfully, this king
> Does not inflict harm due to evil actions.[136]

With regard to [the eighth of the nine distinctive attributes,] that [the soul] is not within perceptual range of the intellect, this is because it cannot be comprehended by anyone in that there is nothing more profound and more subtle than it.

With regard to [the ninth of the nine distinctive attributes,] that [the soul] is not verbally expressible, [they hold that the soul] is ineffable in that we cannot conceive of the nature of this soul. The same text says:

> Those who have stolen through intellectual analysis
> That which is eternal, nonconceptual,
> And not within the perceptual range of anyone,
> Then attempt to verbalize it.[137]

They say that although [the soul] is actually inexpressible because the essential nature of knowable phenomena is vacuous and the natural expression of one's own mind transcends the objects of the intellect, explanations [of it] are simply opined on the basis of superimposition. This is identical to those claiming that nonconceptual meditation without wavering from a single point also settles into the disposition where external and internal emptiness, mother and child, converge.

Now when they formulate this as a statement of proof, [they assert that] this soul is pervasive in all things in the manner of space, because the attributes of the soul—happiness and suffering—are pervasive in all things. Also [they assert that] this soul is pervasive because it is eternal, and if it were not pervasive, it would be impermanent. This is because, if it were nonpervasive, it would [absurdly] remain efficacious and when certain people approach it, some would make contact with it while others [absurdly] would not make contact with it.

With regard to the liberation achieved through knowing this abiding modality, as long as the soul is unknown, bewilderment continues, just like a dream in which actions and their fruits appear to be experienced, and there are even attachments to these experiences. Apart from that, it appears that through the practice of the ten virtuous actions, one will achieve the higher realms, and through the practice of the ten nonvirtuous actions, one will be reborn in the lower realms. Therefore, it is necessary to take virtue and negativity into account as long as there is no understanding, because those who do not know and do not understand the soul are obliged to reject and accept dreamlike states of happiness and suffering. It says in the aforementioned text:

> One [who does not know or understand the soul]
> Engages in actions and their fruits,
> Which are virtuous and nonvirtuous,
> As if taking pride in the enjoyments of a dream.[138]

Then, just as on awakening from sleep, one knows that the circumstances of a dream are unreal bewilderment, so when one merely understands the soul, it is ascertained that both virtue and negativity are indeed the causes of cyclic existence, and liberation will be achieved without doing anything at all. As is said in the same text:

> One who sees and beholds
> The creator Īśvara, golden in color,
> Having transcended negativity and merit,
> Will attain the supreme quiescence.[139]

And in the *Esoteric Verses of Rāṇāyana:*

> Although present individually in life forms that are minute,
> It encompasses those that are vast.
> Having ascertained this soul,
> Which is the supreme primal matter, deity, and object of praise,
> One will proceed to extreme quiescence.[140]

Nowadays [i.e., in the time of Longchen Rabjam], there are those among the best of meditators, of high reputation and adorned with merits owing to their glory, who profess that although living beings do appear to have diverse perceptions, there is a single continuum of consciousness, identical in all those interacting perceptions and in their minds. [They further hold that] since nothing at all exists in the fundamental nature, nothing at all is achieved on the path. Cyclic existence arises through activity. The bewildering perceptions of sentient beings who do not understand these [perceptions], including the ten virtuous actions that are conditioned, achieve a mode of cyclic existence that is auspicious while those [indulging in] nonvirtuous actions achieve a mode of cyclic existence that is inauspicious. These [both] resemble the inner workings of a dream, and the yogin, as if awakening from sleep, is liberated by not doing anything at all, in a vacuous disposition, without the pith instructions of a master. Since one is a buddha at the present moment, there is nothing to be developed. Even without abandoning the illusory body, since mind and emptiness are indivisible, consciousness is absorbed into space and abides in the disposition of luminosity that is the buddha body of reality. This [they claim] is what they themselves experientially cultivate and also teach to others, so that their congregations of disciples have become as extensive as the constellations. But they have flourished in that manner having experientially cultivated the profound pith instructions of the masters of the Upaniṣads!

> O! The sun of the present-day teaching
> Indeed sets behind the hilltop to the west
> And the light of its sūtra and tantra rays are indeed rare,
> Apart from certain learned and accomplished masters.
> Those relying on [non-Buddhist] texts
> Will indeed be led astray by false friends!
> Behold the age when even perceptive beings are blind,[141]

And rejoice in the actions of the material elements—
The flourishing[142] of profane beings!

Such are the summarizing verses that describe the Aupaniṣadika.

So it is that the followers of the Upaniṣads revere their profound texts, stating that although the soul permeates all things, beings wander in cyclic existence because it is not understood, but having understood it at the present moment, they should meditate on the truth that there is nothing at all to be achieved.[143]

Nirgrantha

Nirgrantha [13.1.2.6.4]

Fourth, there are the philosophical systems related to the Nirgrantha, which are established as follows: Those who practice the ascetic discipline of nudity hold Brahmā as a deity or else they follow the teacher Vardhamāna Mahāvīra who hailed from the priestly class.[144] They classify all knowable phenomena into seven categories, and although appearances are infinite, the multiplicity of space, time, and number is subsumed in a single nature. Those who strive for liberation through this path enter into the unbearably dense forest of existence and at the time of their release they continue with their austerities.

When their texts are extensively classified, those holding Brahmā as a deity or Mahāvīra as their teacher maintain texts such as the Jaina Canon as an authority. Their subdivisions are known as (i) Nirgranthin; (ii) Tapasvin; (iii) Brāhmaṇa; (iv) Bhāsmāyana; (v) Digambara; (vi) Ājīvika; (vii) Jaina; [(viii) Jāyana;][145] and (ix) Parivrājika.

The Nirgrantha are so called because they go naked, without clothing. Since they dwell on the level where space is seen, without clothing, they are also called Ājīvika and Digambara.

The Tapasvin are so called because they undertake fasting and so forth. The Brāhmaṇa are so called because they hold Brahmā as their deity. The Jaina are so called because they hold the brahmanical Jina [Vardhamāna Mahāvīra] as their teacher. The Jāyana are so called because they rely upon the Jaina Canon. The Bhāsmāyana are so called because they smear ashes on their bodies. The Parivrājika are so called because they wander around, with no fixed abode.

According to their traditions, all things may be subsumed in the particular classification of knowable phenomena and in their common circumstances. The particular classification of knowable phenomena comprises the following seven topics: (i) austerities; (ii) commitments; (iii) afflictions; (iv) bondage; (v) release; (vi) animate substances; and (vii) inanimate substances. It says in the Jaina Canon:

> The Nirgrantha [espouse] the following seven topics:
> Austerities, commitments, afflictions,
> Bondage, and release,
> Along with both animate and inanimate substances.[146]

First, regarding austerities, these include fasting, nudity, reliance on the five fire rites, begging for alms, the ascetic discipline of grazing for grass, and pulling out the hair. Since the foremost causes of cyclic existence are the three attachments to food, clothing, and sexual intercourse, they hold that one should fast in order to emaciate the body, turning wind into food. It says in the same text:

> The person who undertakes fasting
> For one night, or three nights,
> Or for ever and a day,
> Will proceed to the higher realms.[147]

Since all clothing is artificial, one should go naked through town in order to destroy thoughts of frivolity and embarrassment. However they hold that in solitary retreat it is permissible to resort to clothing.

As for reliance on the five fire rites, they hold that during summer they should endure affliction by four fires [placed] in the four directions, with the sun overhead as the fifth [fire], and in winter they should endure affliction by cold water, and in the rainy season[148] they should do without a canopy. It says in the same text:

> Sitting in water during the winter,
> Relying on the five afflictions in the hot season,
> And sitting without a canopy in the summer [rainy] season,
> That priest practices severe austerities.[149]

It is said that begging for the acquisition of wealth, or for sustenance of one's precious life increases the contaminants of attachment and aversion, but those who have passed time in meditative concentration should go for alms. They should not accept the donations of the populace because their purity would be diminished, and if that were diminished, it is said that they would be reborn as an animal. Instead, after accepting donations given by those with a good family background, they should seek alms without offering service in return. It says in the Jaina Canon:

> They should subsist by going for alms,
> But they should not accept the donations of the populace
> Because these are impure.
> If a priest were to accept the donations of the populace,
> He would be reborn as a donkey.
> Why would that priest not consider
> The twelve rebirths as a donkey that he would take,
> The ten rebirths as a servant of ten townspeople,
> And the cogon grass of the groves
> Where he would pass ten rebirths as a sorrowful ungulate?[150]

And:

> If one who has attained the status of a priest
> Follows the injunctions of the royal class,
> That one will abandon the priestly state
> And be reborn in the laboring class.[151]

Similarly, [austerities may entail] eating grass and drinking, face downward, in the manner of cattle, and having an incestuous relationship even with one's own mother. It says in the same text:

> If they consume water and grass, facing downward,
> While maintaining an incestuous relationship
> With their own family, or with their mother or maternal relatives,
> And observe this ascetic discipline of grazing for one year,
> They will be triumphant over all.[152]

Similarly, they hold that by standing upright on one leg while looking at the sun, shaving the head and marking it with sandalwood dots, jumping over the point of a trident, and so forth, the sufferings associated with the next life will be conclusively experienced in this present life, and they will no longer be subject to rebirth.

[Second,] regarding commitments, they abandon the ten nonvirtuous actions. That is to say, fearing that an insect might go under the soles of their feet, they attach small bells to their ankles. Nor do they cut wood, and they do not take what is not given. On the road, even if they see water, they should remain thirsty if there is no one to dispense it. Since they forsake lies, they adopt the ascetic discipline of not speaking at all. They also observe fasting.

[Third,] regarding afflictions, these include attachment, aversion and delusion, and so forth.

[Fourth,] regarding bondage, this endures as long as the soul wanders within cyclic existence.

[Fifth,] regarding release, once the soul has been separated from all the faults of affliction, they hold that it assumes the resplendent and rounded form of a white colored [parasol], at the summit of existence. It says in the Jaina Canon:

> The Jina explains that
> Release resembles the shape of a white parasol,
> The color of snow, or sweet clover flower,
> The color of cow's curd, frost, or a pearl.[153]

[Sixth,] animate substances, being sentient, are of nine categories: (i) earth; (ii) water; (iii) fire; (iv) wind; (v) wood; (vi) animalcules with two sense faculties; (vii) ants with three sense faculties; (viii) bees with four sense faculties; and (ix) human beings with five sense faculties. The first four of these are sentient because they respectively grow, flow down, burn, and move while giving rise to sound. Wood is definitely sentient because flowers such as tamarind [or black walnut] contract during the night and extend their branches during the day, and close their petals. This is also because in the cold season [wood] withers and in the warm season it grows, and when its bark peels, it dies. It is similar to human beings in that it follows the course of time. Wood also has eyes because vines and so forth extend themselves, clinging on to other trees, and because medicinal plants face toward the sun. It has ears because when the rumbling of dense clouds occurs, the fruit of the plantain and so forth begins to fall to the ground. It has a nose because when the rotting corpse of a dog is placed at the roots of the madulungka plant, the stench causes it to bear many fruits. It has a tongue because when milk is poured on gooseberries and so forth, the fruits acquire a sweet taste. It also has a body because when samika [or arjuna] wood is pulverized, the hand sticks to it when it is merely touched, just like a centipede. It has a mental faculty because if an Aśoka tree does not grow flowers and fruits, it may become intoxicated by desire for a beautiful [yakṣiṇī] girl, entwining an anklet around her graceful leg, and when pressed with the sole of her foot smeared with a shellac solution, it will bring forth flowers and fruits. Also if a bulletwood tree has not blossomed, when a beautiful girl scatters a mouthful of molasses wine on it, flowers will bloom.

The Nirgrantha hold that animate substances with a single sense faculty include earth, water, fire, and wind, which all possess the faculty of touch. This is established because disease ensues when [earth] presses down, heat ensues when [fire] burns, and luck is dissipated when [water] pours. Those with two sense faculties include animalcules, conch, pearl, and so forth, which additionally have the sense faculty of taste because they can sense pleasant and unpleasant tastes. Those with three sense faculties include fireflies and ants, which possess the sense faculties of touch, taste, and smell. Those with four sense faculties include bees and mosquitos, which completely possess the four senses apart from sight, in that they can also hear sound. Those with five sense faculties include human beings and quadrupeds such as horses, birds, and ungulates, which completely possess the five senses, in that they can also see forms. Thus they hold that earth, water, fire, and wind have only a single[154] sense faculty, because they lack the others apart from touch. Wood [including plant life] completely possesses all the faculties and is similar to human beings. Other living creatures may possess two, three, four, or five sense faculties, as appropriate.

Inanimate substances, being nonsentient, include sounds, odors, tastes, lights, space, shadows, rainbows, and reflections.

As for the [aforementioned] "common circumstances," all knowable phenomena are said to subsume a multiplicity of place, time, and species, yet these are naturally identical. Multiplicity of place denotes this continent and the others. Multiplicity of time denotes the past and so on, through to the present year. Multiplicity of species denotes human beings, birds, ungulates, and so forth. Although all these do appear as multiplicities, they are naturally identical. Although a valuable agate may have many white and black markings, it remains nothing but a single valuable agate. The same goes for the feathers of a pigeon. Similarly, all modes of intellectual apprehension and epistemic standards [suggest that] these are naturally identical rather than a multiplicity of places, times, and species. It says in the Jaina Canon:[155]

> The multiplicities of place, time, and species
> Partake of a naturally identical state.
> For example, just as the color of a variegated [object]
> May be apprehended as one wishes,
> In the same way, because entities are diverse,
> They may be apprehended as entities of a dissimilar or similar kind,
> But one seeking to describe a multiplicity of entities
> In terms of their essential nature
> [Simply] maintains their essential nature.
> Apart from these two modes [of apprehension]—immediate and gradual—
> There are no other [possible] verbal actions.[156]

Bārhaspatya

Bārhaspatya [13.1.2.6.5]

Fifth, the nature of the philosophical system of the Bārhaspatya is established as follows: The Bārhaspatya who adhere to the hermit sage Bṛhaspati, teacher of the gods, hold seven tenets as authoritative, including their denial of past and future lives. Therefore they succumb to the bias of nihilism, holding that mind emerges from the vacuity of space. In terms of our own [Buddhist path] and the [non-Buddhist paths of] others, this is mundane deception, manifestly detrimental to this life. As is said in the [*Treasury of*] *Spiritual Songs:*

> Those who hold the mind to emerge from space,
> Assume the materiality of a noxious path,
> And deceive themselves that the self is going toward liberation.[157]

Here their texts will be ascertained as follows: In antiquity, during the legendary battles in the god realms with the antigods, when there was no one [among the gods] with an inclination to fight, because they held cause and effect to be authoritative, the hermit sage Bṛhaspati, teacher of the gods, composed a treatise entitled *Essence of the View That Refutes Everything,* and this was subsequently propagated in the human world by Vālmīki (*grog mkhar*). Holding Bṛhaspati as their teacher, and Śakra, along with the sun and moon, as their deities, they espouse texts such as the *Essence of the View,* and the *Six Tantras of Bṛhaspati.*

They are also called Lokāyatika because they reject past and future lives as "remote" and establish that there are advantages in this present life [alone]. They are called Kaivalya ("isolationists") because they hold that this life alone exists, denying the existence of past and future lives. They are called Nāstika ("nihilists") because they hold that there is no causality and there are no invisible beings. They are called Cārvāka ("hedonists") because they embellish any modes of happiness with respect to this present life. They are called Saura ("sun worshippers") because they hold the sun as their deity. They are called Cāndra ("moon worshippers") because they hold the moon as their deity. They are called Aindra ("worshippers of Indra") because they hold Indra as their deity, and they are called Bārhaspatya ("worshippers of Bṛhaspati") because they hold Bṛhaspati as their deity. Although there are differences owing to the deities [they espouse], their statements of proof in respect of the opinions that they hold in common propound an identical system of tenets.

These tenets are seven in number: (i) they hold that the four primary elements are ultimately real; (ii) they hold that body and mind are of a single material substance; (iii) they deny that there are past and future worlds; (iv) they deny that actions have causes and fruits; (v) they deny [the possibility of] release and omniscience; (vi) they deny the existence of invisible beings; and (vii) they do not accept valid cognition by means of inference.

With regard to the first [tenet], the four [elements], earth, water, fire, and wind ultimately exist.

[With regard to the second tenet,] mind is a corporeal substance because (i) it denotes the potency of the body that is inanimate in nature; (ii) the body is clearly formed from its luminosity;[158] and (iii) it emerges concurrently [with the body]. Mind acts in accordance with the happiness and suffering experienced by the body, because attachment and so forth fluctuate in accordance with the growth and decline of the physical body, and because the mind suffers pain when [the body] is wounded.

[With regard to the third[159] tenet,] they deny the existence of past and future worlds because body and mind are of a single substance, because dual and multiple [conditions] occur with reference to a single time frame, because [such past and future worlds] would contradict conventional experience, and because there are no subsequent rebirths.

Since the body decays into atomic particles, the mind too is not reborn elsewhere, nor do dualistic conditions of the body cause minds to emerge in an afterlife. Immediately after one is born, one is subsequently obliged to start learning, because one knows nothing at all. If there were a past, the past would not have to be relearned, just as when one awakens from sleep, one's previous consciousness is not forgotten. Since there are none who have returned from death, there are no past and future lives. They deny that the mind has past and future corporeal forms, because it is indivisible from the body and its material substance, like wine and the taste of wine. The taste of wine existed simultaneous with the grain at the time when it was prepared, and it is not the case that it came into existence and permeated the [wine] having been transferred from a former preexisting state of the wine.

Moreover, a [conceptualized] vase has two [applications of reasoning], because it may signify [the materiality of] any living person of the future, anywhere in the world, or else it may signify any actual vase whatsoever because it is [a material object] distinct from the lily [it contains], just as the wall [alongside which it rests is distinct from it].

To establish the premise that the vase is distinct from the lily, when a vase is placed alongside a wall, the logical entailment [of their difference] may be established by any means whatsoever. They also contradict [the assertion] that a [specific] vase and a generic [conceptualized] vase are [requisite] counterparts. On this basis, [they claim] it is incorrect to state that [a vase] is distinct from [the materiality of] a living person.[160]

Moreover, if a pile of meat, the size of Mount Sumeru, were heaped up, and if it then rained for seven days, so that the size of the pile of meat turned entirely into a mere pile of worms, they deny that the minds of those sentient beings would have died or returned from elsewhere in a single moment of time.

Since there are no past worlds, there is no conventional experience of them. Therefore children[161] must learn to communicate. Nor are there future worlds, because old persons who pass away do not return. So it is that all corporeal things suddenly assume physical form through the cohabiting of male and female, within being transferred from another domain, like mushrooms arising from meadows, and at that time the mind is formed from the luminosity[162] of its atomic particles. Also, when one dies, the primary elements subside and decay, like a butter lamp that dies having run out of oil, the four elements vanishing into their respective latent potencies and the mind into the expanse of space, so that no one at all will assume a future rebirth. It says in the *Esoteric Words of Vālmīki:*

> Act joyously, [good lady],
> While you are not dead,
> For nothing is not within death's range.
> Once your body has turned to ashes,
> How could there be future rebirths![163]

This verse has been cited in five contexts by Avalokitavrata.[164]

[Fourth,] they deny that actions also have causes and fruits. The fruits of past actions, such as the short life span acquired by those who have killed living creatures, or the beautiful form acquired by those who have cultivated loving-kindness, do not ripen in the present life—they are invisible and nonexistent in future lives. This modality of cause and fruit was deceitfully propounded by Buddhists in order that mendicants with shaved heads without sustenance could be sustained. As is said in the *Essence of the View:*

> When living creatures grow old, they do not die [and
>   transmigrate].
> There are no other past and future worlds.
> There are no fruits arising from merits and demerits.
> There are no causes and no such actions.
> These were spoken by the sons of Śākya for the sake of profit.
> Therefore, do not be moved by faith [in them]![165]

They also deny that benefits will accrue through sacrificial offerings originating from the Vedas, because the Vedas themselves secure the livelihood of certain debased people who act, confusing deceitful and pure [motives]. Certain persons, having dyed some of their robes and so forth [in sacred colors], have slain cattle, discarded their hearts, and deceitfully eaten them, offering sandalwood marks to their horns, hooves, hides, and so forth.

Homeless women, those using the residue of wood from a sacrificial offering, those binding their throats with thread, barbers, merchants, and cobblers— these six [sorts of inauspicious persons] the Vedas have mentioned.

As for the three sorts of [auspicious] people who are held to perform the burnt offerings utilizing fire:

> Those who possess the three staffs,
> Those who smear themselves with ashes,
> And those who are feeble in intellect and effort—
> Bṛhaspati says they all were designed for gaining a livelihood.[166]

[Fifth,] they deny [the possibility of] release and liberation because they do not see that release or omniscience is attained in this life by having cultivated a spiritual path, and because such release is nonapprehensible in future lives. This is because there is no one at all who has seen the future.

[Sixth, they deny the existence of invisible beings.] They accept that there are two kinds of living creatures—humans and animals, and that there are three kinds of birth—viviparous and oviparous birth, along with birth through heat and moisture. Other than these, there is no possibility of miraculous birth, because it cannot be seen:

> As many creatures as there are,
> They exist solely
> Within the range of the senses.
> Whatever the learned may say, Good Lady,
> Resembles the tracks of a [deceiving] wolf.[167]

[Seventh,] there is no valid cognition by means of inference, because that would turn [conceptualized] object universals into objects [of the senses], so that nonentities would be falsified as entities, like the water that is apprehended in a mirage.

In general, because they see the threefold axiomatic reasoning as mistaken, it would be like inferring [meaninglessly] that "a shining white thing visible to the rear is azure blue because it is the son of Devadatta."

In particular, because they hold that all the three axioms of reasoning are incorrect, there is no discernible cause that can be ascertained [through inference] as to whether fire has originated from firewood, flint, charcoal, or a meteor. This is because [among the three axioms], the axiom of identity may indeed discern a white and round conch as an indivisible identity, but otherwise it discerns differences.

Since [such inferences] are mistaken with regard to results, predicates or causes, and subjects or statements of proof, they hold that the [axiom of the] result is incorrect, because the cause and the subject are negated, and that the axiom of the absence of the objective referent is also incorrect, because it is mistaken with regard to the negation of the predicate.[168]

Epilogue

Just as there is nothing more precious to oneself than life,
One who cherishes others' lives should not kill.
Just as attachment to one's own wealth is great,
One should not steal the wealth of others.
One should renounce sexual misconduct due to desire
For dependents who lack independence.
One should renounce negative acts of speech, as if they were poison—
Obfuscation by means of lies, division by means of slander,
Distraction due to irresponsible chatter,
And one should not covet the glory of others.
One should renounce vindictiveness at all times,
Renouncing all wrong views holding
That happiness comes from engaging in negative acts,
Including the view that there is no cause and effect.
One should strive toward the paths of the ten virtuous actions,
Including devotion to the correct view.
As a result one will be born among gods
And humans of the higher realms,
And by connecting with the four meditative concentrations
And the four formless meditative stabilities,
One will be born in the world system of form
And the world system of formlessness.

In order that the basic ways of gods and humans should be known and that the erroneous ways of Māra, which are not the [Buddhist] path, might be abandoned, [this book] was compiled by Longchen Choying Tobden Dorje. May virtue prevail!

Book 13, Part 2
The Philosophical Systems of the Causal Vehicles

Herein is contained Book 13, Part 2 (KHI) from *The Extensive Commentary of the Precious Treasury of Sūtra and Tantra, concerning the Philosophical Systems of the Causal Vehicles.*

The Golden Key

In order that one might become skilled in the dialectical
vehicles,
This book contains an exposition of the philosophical systems
Espoused by pious attendants, by advocates of Cittamātra,
And by exponents of Madhyamaka
Who follow either independent or consequential reasoning.

Verse of Homage

Homage to those who uphold, maintain, and enhance the teaching of the causal vehicles, based on the transcendent perfections!

Exegesis of the Supramundane Approaches [13.2]

The second main topic (see above 5) concerns the exegesis of the supramundane approaches [of Buddhism]. It has three parts, comprising (i) an exegesis of their superiority over non-Buddhist systems (13.2.1); (ii) an exegesis of the philosophical systems of the pious attendants, which is for those of lesser acumen (13.2.2); and (iii) an exegesis of the vehicle of the hermit buddhas, which is for those of moderate acumen (13.2.3).

The Superiority of Buddhist over Non-Buddhist Systems

Exegesis of Their Superiority over Non-Buddhist Systems [13.2.1.1]

The first [concerning the superiority of Buddhist over non-Buddhist systems comments on the verse]:

> **[The superiority of the Buddhist systems is considered in terms of]**
> **The refuge and the four principles constituting the foundation**
> **[Of view,] meditation, conduct, and result.**

There are five aspects indicative of the superiority [of the Buddhist systems over non-Buddhist systems]: (i) the superiority of the refuge on which they rely (13.2.1.1.1); (ii) the superiority of the view that is their foundation (13.2.1.1.2); (iii) the superiority of the meditation that is their experience (13.2.1.1.3); (iv) the superiority of the conduct in which they engage (13.2.1.1.4); and (v) the superiority of the result that is to be attained (13.2.1.1.5).

As to the first, Buddhists are those who take refuge in the three precious jewels, whereas non-Buddhists are those who do not accept that and instead uphold other [refuges] such as Brahmā and Viṣṇu, as Candrakīrti has said:

> Those who have gone for refuge to the genuine buddhas
> Do not pay homage to other deities.[169]

As to the second, Buddhists are those who commonly accept four principles [indicative of the Buddhist teachings], and who uncommonly accept [that their view] is free from extremes, inconceivable, and indescribable.

Non-Buddhists do not accept these and instead fall into the extremes of eternalism and nihilism. It says in the *Pagoda of Precious Gems:*

> Those who enter with faith in the teaching of the buddhas,
> Having unfailingly seen that conditioned phenomena are impermanent,
> In order that suffering might be abandoned,
> Should earnestly focus on the objective
> That phenomena are without self and calm,
> In the manner of space.[170]

The four principles are therefore that (i) all conditioned phenomena are impermanent; (ii) all phenomena are without self; (iii) all corrupt phenomena are imbued with suffering; and (iv) nirvāṇa is calm.

With regard to [the third,] meditation, since they take the three precious jewels as a refuge, with release [from cyclic existence] as their objective, Buddhists are those who commonly meditate on selflessness in a graduated manner by means of the thirty-seven factors conducive to enlightenment, who uncommonly understand that all phenomena are of the intrinsic nature of space and who then meditate on that essential nature, which is one of emptiness and compassion. Non-Buddhists are those whose thoughts have simply been blocked without meditating or who fix their minds upon a mere state of partial bliss, radiance, and nonconceptualization. It says in the *Dispelling of Negative Views:*

> A yogin is one who strives toward enlightenment,
> Compassion, and emptiness without conceptual notions, just as it is.
> The opposite are explained to be alien doctrines.[171]

As for conduct, [the fourth,] Buddhists are those who seek to block pathways that naturally partake of attachment, aversion, and delusion, which are fixated on objects [of the senses] and that inflict harm on others. Non-Buddhists are those who do not seek [those objectives] but behave in a contrary manner. As is said in the *Seventy Verses on Going for Refuge:*

> Those who seek refuge in the sacred doctrine
> Do not harm [others] and they are without malice.[172]

As for the result, [the fifth,] Buddhists are those who actually attain any of the three modes of release by means of this very path,[173] whereas non-Buddhists are those who do not. As is said in the *Mother:*

> The transcendent perfection of discriminative awareness is established so that nirvāṇa might be attained. Even those who wish to attain nirvāṇa on the level of the pious attendants should train in the transcendent perfection of discriminative awareness. Even hermit buddhas who wish to attain final nirvāṇa on the level of the unsurpassed buddhas should train in the transcendent perfection of discriminative awareness.[174]

And:

> Other wandering mendicants either lack this path or else they lack the clear realization of this path.

The Philosophical Systems of the Pious Attendants

Exegesis of the Philosophical Systems of the Pious Attendants [13.2.2]

The second is the exegesis of the philosophical systems of the pious attendants for those of lesser acumen. This has three aspects: (i) ordinary tenets that all schools [of the pious attendants] commonly accept (13.2.2.1); (ii) the philosophical system of the Vaibhāṣika (13.2.2.2); and (iii) the philosophical system of the Sautrāntika (13.2.2.3).

Ordinary Tenets That All Schools of the Pious Attendants Commonly Accept [13.2.2.1]

The first [comments on the verse]:

> **There are seven tenets that [pious attendants] commonly accept, commencing with the four truths.**

The level of the pious attendants will be considered in terms of the seven tenets that they commonly accept and the detailed presentation of the characteristics of each of its systems.

As to the former, there are seven [commonly held tenets]: (i) their focus is the four truths (13.2.2.1.1); (ii) ultimate reality is posited (13.2.2.1.2); (iii) arhatship is conclusive (13.2.2.1.3); (iv) the substratum [consciousness] is nonexistent (13.2.2.1.4); (v) the great vehicle is nonexistent (13.2.2.1.5); (vi) the ten [bodhisattva] levels are nonexistent (13.2.2.1.6); and (vii) buddhas have an individual mental continuum (13.2.2.1.7).[175]

Their Focus Is the Four Truths [13.2.2.1.1]

As to the first [of these commonly held tenets], their focus is on the things that are to be accepted and rejected in accordance with the four truths; namely, suffering, its cause, its cessation, and the path [that leads to its cessation].

The first of these, suffering, characterizes the ripened[176] psycho-physical aggregates. It imbues both the births that sentient beings assume and their actual places of birth. Birth denotes the cyclic existence within which beings roam from one of the six realms to another. The actual places of birth are, as previously mentioned, the world systems forming this external environment. Therein[177] there are many modes of suffering, commencing from birth itself.

The cause of suffering comprises both actions and afflicted mental states. Afflicted mental states include desire and so forth. Actions are of two sorts: resolute and intentional; or else they are of three sorts: virtuous, nonvirtuous, and neutral. Therefore:

> It is held that "resolute" denotes actions of body and speech
> Whereas "intentional" denotes actions of mind.[178]

Nonvirtuous actions include the ten commencing with the killing of living creatures, the five inexpiable crimes beginning with patricide and matricide, the five subsidiary inexpiable crimes beginning with the killing of bodhisattvas, and infringements of the monastic disciplines. Virtuous actions include the ten commencing with abstention from killing living creatures, and the rest. Neutral actions include those that are satisfactory.

Cessation denotes the firmly established quiescence of suffering and its cause. Cessation may be characterized as (i) residual; (ii) nonresidual; (iii) cessation obtained through analytical means; and (iv) cessation obtained through nonanalytical means.

The path is the means of understanding suffering, renouncing the cause of suffering, and manifesting the cessation of suffering. Based on the circumstances of the path within the mental continuum [of sentient beings], five paths are differentiated; namely, the path of provisions, the path of connection, the path of insight, the path of cultivation, and the path of no-more-learning. As is said in the *Treasury* [*of Phenomenology*]:

The truths are explained to be four:
Namely, suffering and the cause of suffering.
Cessation and the path.
Their order is that in which they are clearly understood.[179]

Ultimate Reality Is Posited [13.2.2.1.2]

With regard to [the second commonly held tenet,] the positing of ultimate reality, the extreme state of gross materiality comprises indivisible atomic particles that cannot be smashed by a hammer and so forth; and the extreme state of consciousness comprises indivisible temporal moments that cannot be destroyed by the intellect. It says in the same source [*Treasury of Phenomenology*]:

Whatever, on its destruction or intellectual elimination,
Ceases to convey an idea, like water and a vase,
Is relatively existent; all else is ultimately real.[180]

This is because mountains and other material things may be measured according to "yoking distances," and then into "earshots," "double arm spans," "cubits," "finger-widths," "barley grains," "lice," "nits," "cow-hair particles," "goat-hair particles," "rabbit-hair particles," and "atomic particles." Atoms, approximately one forty-ninth[181] of a standard particle of solar rays are considered to be ultimate. Since these cannot be bisected by the intellect, even sublime beings do not perceive them as composites containing parts. This is because, even if they are cut by weapons and crushed in a mortar, they cannot be bisected.

The human life span and an aeon of time are both relative because they can be broken down into a multiplicity of years. Years themselves can be broken down into months, days, hours, minutes, and breaths. Even pulsations are not [ultimately] true because they can be broken down into sixty temporal moments. Instants of time, approximately one sixtieth of a single pulse of a healthy adult, are considered to be ultimate. This is because these are swift and instantaneous, even faster than a bullet, and so forth, and therefore they cannot be crushed or transformed.

It says, accordingly, in the same source [*Treasury of Phenomenology*]:

The confines of matter, words, and time
Are respectively atoms, syllables, and temporal instants.
As far as atoms and similarly [small particles] are concerned,
[Including "iron" particles, "water" particles, "rabbit-hair"
particles,
"Sheep-hair" particles, "cow-hair" particles,]
"Solar-ray" particles, "nits," ["lice" and "barley grains,"]
Which all derive from indivisible atomic particles,
And likewise, the "finger-width" measurement [of length],
Each of these is obtained
By multiplying the previous seven times.
Then, one "cubit" equals twenty-four "finger-widths."
One "bow" or "double arm span" equals four "cubits."
One "earshot" equals five hundred of these [arm spans],
And this is held to be the remote distance of a hermitage.
One "yoking distance" is said to equal "eight earshots."
[As far as time is concerned,]
One *tatkṣaṇa* equals one hundred twenty temporal instants.
One *lava* equals sixty of these.
Then, one *muhūrta,* one day, and one month
Are each obtained by multiplying the previous by thirty.
One year equals twelve months,
Plus the [six] omitted days.[182]

Nonfragmentary particles are stable, such that they cannot be torn asunder [even] by a hurricane. They cannot be torn asunder because they are said to be compounded by, or imbued with, the force of "generic action." Mountains are formed from multiple atomic particles, and it is through the continuity of temporal instants that mountains and so forth endure for a long period of time, but this appearance is the bewilderment of a naive and coarse intellect. Sublime beings know that they are reducible to atomic particles and temporal instants. It says in venerable Śrīlāta's *Seventy Stanzas on Particles:*

Just as human beings do not feel
A single strand of hair in the palm of the hand,
But the same [hair], in the eye, causes discomforts,
So, naive persons resembling the palm of the hand

Do not recognize the hair as suffering due to conditioning,[183]
Whereas sublime beings resembling the eye
Are absolutely distressed by it.[184]

Arhatship Is Conclusive [13.2.2.1.3]

With regard to [the third commonly held tenet] that arhatship is conclusive, there is nothing higher than arhatship because [arhats] do not regress into cyclic existence, and they have ended the causes of rebirth in the three world systems since they have abandoned the latent impulses associated with abandoning the path of insight and abandoning the path of cultivation. Nor is it possible for them to advance and attain buddhahood because they are fixed within the enlightened heritage of the pious attendants and it would therefore not be permissible for them to acquire the causal basis of buddhahood. In general, the emergence of the buddhas that is spoken of in the scriptures refers to the most saintly of beings, whereas they themselves admit that they cannot bear to endure suffering in cyclic existence for countless aeons. So they will not degenerate from their path; nor can they act for the benefit of irrepressibly cruel sentient beings.

The Substratum Is Nonexistent [13.2.2.1.4]

With regard to [the fourth commonly held tenet] that the substratum is nonexistent, [they claim that] the six modes of engaged consciousness, from visual consciousness to mental consciousness, exist in turn, but apart from these, the substratum consciousness does not exist because it is nonapprehensible. For them, when a[185] mind supported [within a body] is formed, it is actually identified with the self of individual persons.

The Great Vehicle Is Nonexistent [13.2.2.1.5]

With regard to [the fifth commonly held tenet] that the great vehicle is nonexistent, [they claim that] the texts of monastic discipline including the four scriptural transmissions with the *Vows of Individual Liberation,* and sūtras such as the *Diffusion from a Single Source,* and Abhidharma scriptures such as the *Seven Sections [of Phenomenology] on Designation,* [and so forth,] alone were spoken by the Buddha, and that apart from these, the *Transcendent Perfection of Discriminative Awareness in One Hundred*

Thousand Lines, the *Pagoda of Precious Gems,* the *Great Bounteousness* [*of the Buddhas*], and so forth, were not spoken by him. Rather these were fabricated after the Buddha had passed into nirvāṇa by Māra and heretical extremists in order that they might denigrate the Buddhist teaching. This is (i) because no [teachings] were received other than by pious attendants such as the elder Mahākāśyapa, who were always inseparably present, alongside the Teacher; (ii) because the [scriptures of the great vehicle] contradict the four principles [of the teachings]; (iii) because they contradict [the arrangement of] the three baskets; and (iv) because they contradict the principles of action, cause and effect.

As to their contradiction of the four principles: First, they contradict the principle that all conditioned things are impermanent, because the buddha body of perfect resource is revealed to be permanent. [Second,] they contradict the principle that phenomena are without self, because they teach that [beings] are imbued with the seed of buddha nature and that there is a substratum consciousness that is acquisitive. [Third,] they contradict the principle that all that is contaminated is suffering, because they hold that bodhisattvas progress from happiness to happiness. [Fourth,] they contradict the principle that nirvāṇa is peace, because pious attendants are foreordained to become buddhas and because they hold that buddhas never pass into nirvāṇa. They also contradict the three baskets, because they reveal that homage should be paid even to householders and because they reveal that laymen might even kill, steal, and so forth. They also contradict the principles of action, cause and effect, because they hold that even inexpiable crimes may be purified in this lifetime, on the basis of the following words:

> The actions of corporeal beings
> Are not squandered, even in a hundred aeons;
> When [these actions] have accrued and the time has arrived,
> Their very fruit will ripen.[186]

The Ten Levels Are Nonexistent [13.2.2.1.6]

With regard to [the sixth commonly held tenet] that the ten levels are nonexistent, they do not accept that those who are said to be on the tenth level perceive the truth and thereafter can remain in cyclic existence for many aeons. Rather, they hold that after accumulating the provisions for three countless aeons on the level of an ordinary person, until they acquire certitude [on the path of insight], they will actualize [their fruit], in a single night, in a single sitting.

Buddhas Have an Independent Mental Continuum [13.2.2.1.7]

With regard to [the seventh commonly held tenet] that buddhas have an independent mental continuum, they hold that the term *buddha* does not denote the buddha body of emanation but one who is subject to the residual ripening [of past actions], such that his body still bleeds, he feels pain in the back, and so forth. Nor is the Buddha always equipoised [in meditation] because in the scriptures it is said that he arose from meditative stability and went begging for alms. After passing into nirvāṇa, his work on behalf of living beings was interrupted.[187]

The Philosophical System of the Vaibhāṣika

The Philosophical System of the Vaibhāṣika [13.2.2.2]

The second, the philosophical system of the Vaibhāṣika [comments on the verse]:

> **The Vaibhāṣika have seven tenets, commencing with the five basic categories.**

Although there are many philosophical strands according to the Vaibhāṣika ("followers of the detailed exposition of phenomenology"), there are seven principal tenets that they espouse. These comprise (i) the five basic categories of knowable phenomena (13.2.2.2.1); (ii) decay as a separate entity (13.2.2.2.2); (iii) substantial existence of the three times (13.2.2.2.3); (iv) the inexpressible[188] self (13.2.2.2.4); (v) denial of intrinsic or objective awareness on the part of consciousness (13.2.2.2.5); (vi) the difference between defining characteristics and exemplars (13.2.2.2.6); and (vii) unexhausted substance (13.2.2.2.7).

The Five Basic Categories of Knowable Phenomena [13.2.2.2.1]

As to the first tenet, all knowable phenomena are ascertained in terms of five basic categories: (i) matter (13.2.2.2.1.1); (ii) mind (13.2.2.2.1.2); (iii) mental states (13.2.2.2.1.3); (iv) formative predispositions disassociated [from mind and mental states] (13.2.2.2.1.4); and (v) unconditioned states (13.2.2.2.1.5).

MATTER [13.2.2.2.1.1]

[First,] as for the basic category of matter, its defining characteristic is that it is physical. There are fifteen subdivisions, including four aspects of causal matter and eleven aspects of fruitional matter. As is said in the *Treasury* [*of Phenomenology*]:

> Matter comprises the five sense organs,
> The five sense objects, and nonapperceived form.[189]

The four aspects of causal matter are earth, water, fire, and wind. The eleven aspects of fruitional matter are the five sense organs of the eye, ear, nose, tongue, and body, along with the five [corresponding] sense objects: sights, sounds, odors, tastes, and tangibles, and nonapperceived form.

The last of these, [nonapperceived form,] is [classed as] unrevealed and unobstructed. It is determined[190] to be present during periods of distraction [from the apperception] of objects and also during nonconceptual meditative absorption, either arising in the form of discipline that provides continuity to virtuous actions, or nondiscipline that provides continuity to nonvirtuous actions, or in those forms that provide continuity to actions that are neutral in terms of virtue and nonvirtue. It says in the *Treasury* [*of Phenomenology*]:

> There is a serial continuity that may be virtuous or nonvirtuous,
> [Possessed by those who are distracted and those without
> mentation,]
> Contingent on the basis of the [primary] elements,
> And that is called nonapperceived [form][191]

And:

> Nonapperceived form is threefold:
> Disciplined, undisciplined, and neutral.[192]

MIND [13.2.2.2.1.2]

As for the basic category of mind, this is the awareness that apprehends mere objects and has six modes, commencing with visual consciousness.

The Vaibhāṣika do not, in the manner of the Sautrāntika, hold that objects are apprehended covertly but that objects such as a vase are directly perceived, and so forth. The apprehension of objects occurs remotely by means of the eye, the ear, and the mental faculty, but the apprehension [of sense objects] by means of the nose, tongue, and body occurs in close proximity, at which time, the particles of the sense object and the particles of the [relevant] sense organ are equal in number. It says in the same text:

> The eye, the ear, and the mental faculty—these three—
> Are not in close proximity with their objects,
> Whereas the other three, including the nose,
> Are held to apprehend sense objects in equal number.[193]

Mental States [13.2.2.2.1.3]

As for the basic category of mental states, this denotes the apprehension of the particular attributes of a sense object. When subdivided, they altogether number fifty-one, including the five ever-present mental states—namely, (i) contact; (ii) attention; (iii) feeling; (iv) perception; and (v) volition; the five object-determining mental states—namely, (i) will; (ii) resolve; (iii) mindfulness; (iv) meditative stability; and (v) discriminative awareness; the eleven virtuous mental states—namely, (i) faith; (ii) conscience; (iii) shame; (iv) nonattachment; (v) nonhatred; (vi) nondelusion; (vii) perseverance; (viii) refinement; (ix) vigilance; (x) equanimity; and (xi) nonviolence; the six primary afflicted mental states—namely, (i) desire; (ii) hostility; (iii) pride; (iv) ignorance; (v) wrong view; and (vi) doubt; the twenty subsidiary afflicted mental states—namely, (i) anger; (ii) enmity; (iii) hypocrisy; (iv) annoyance; (v) jealousy; (vi) miserliness; (vii) deceit; (viii) pretentiousness; (ix) self-satisfaction; (x) violence; (xi) lack of conscience; (xii) shamelessness; (xiii) dullness; (xiv) mental agitation; (xv) faithlessness; (xvi) indolence; (xvii) carelessness; (xviii) forgetfulness; (xix) distraction; and (xx) inattentiveness; and the four variable mental states—namely, (i) drowsiness; (ii) regret; (iii) ideation; and (iv) scrutiny. As is said [in the same source]:

> Feeling, volition, perception,
> Will, contact, mindfulness, discernment,
> Attention, resolve, and meditative stability

Coexist in all minds.
Faith, vigilance, refinement,
Equanimity, conscience, shame,
And the two basics—nonviolence and perseverance—
Always arise on the basis of virtuous actions.[194]

All these [mental states] are also substantially different from mind, and they follow mind on the basis of five concomitant factors—namely, (i) concomitance of location [or support]; (ii) concomitance of objective referent; (iii) concomitance of sensum; (iv) concomitance of time; and (v) concomitance of substance. [For example,] [visual] sensations and visual consciousness both arise dependent on an identical sense organ (the eye), they have an identical object of reference, such as a vase, they both [for example] also apprehend blueness, and they are equal in the number of substances [and the times] to which they refer. As is said in the *Treasury* [*of Phenomenology*]:

Mind, mental faculty, and consciousness
Denote a single object.
Mind and mental states also share five concomitant factors,
Including support, objective referent, and sensum.[195]

And:

Feelings entail the experience of sensations
And perceptions entail the apprehension of characteristics.
Formative predispositions are distinct from the other four
  aggregates.[196]

Formative Predispositions Disassociated from Mind [13.2.2.2.1.4]

As for the basic category of the formative predispositions that are disassociated from mind, these are twenty-three in number, comprising (i) acquisition; (ii) meditative absorption devoid of perception; (iii) meditative absorption of cessation; (iv) the state of nonperception; (v) the faculty of the life force; (vi) similarity of class or homogeneity; (vii) birth; (viii) aging; (ix) duration; (x) impermanence; (xi) nominal clusters; (xii) syllabic clusters; (xiii) phrasal clusters; (xiv) the status of an ordinary individual; (xv) engagement; (xvi) distinctive regularity; (xvii) connection; (xviii) rapidity; (xix) sequence; (xx) time; (xxi) location; (xxii) number; and (xxiii) grouping.[197] All these are substantially different from physical forms, mind, and mental states. In the manner of the palm of the hand and a fist, they are distinguishing counterparts in terms of their location, but substantially different.

Unconditioned Phenomena [13.2.2.2.1.5]

As for the basic category of unconditioned phenomena, which do not arise dependent on causes and conditions, these are three in number, comprising (i) space; (ii) cessation obtained through analytical means; and (iii) cessation obtained through nonanalytical means. It says in the same [*Treasury of Phenomenology*]:

> There are also three kinds of unconditioned phenomena,
> Comprising space and the two modes of cessation.[198]

These three are established to be substantially existent in the sense that they are permanent entities.

Decay as a Separate Entity [13.2.2.2.2]

[The second tenet of the Vaibhāṣika] is that decay is [regarded as] a separate entity. There are four defining characteristics indicative of conditioned phenomena, such as a vase—namely, (i) arising or production; (ii) aging; (iii) duration; and (iv) impermanence. These four also partake of four subsidiary defining characteristics indicative of conditioned phenomena—namely, the production of production, the aging of aging, the duration of duration, and the decay of decay. Thus there are four defining characteristics, four subsidiary defining characteristics, and eight substances[199] of the vase, totaling sixteen aspects altogether. Like sixteen people alongside each other, these are established to be substantially existent as different substances present in an identical time frame.

In this regard, when a vase is produced, it is the operational production of production that brings the realm of the future into the realm of the present. Therefore, the production of the eight attributes of [conditioned phenomena] such as a vase has as its power [an operational production] that is distinct from their production. That operational production is the power of production. Similarly, in the case of a vase that has not yet decayed, there is a distinct operational entity of decay that causes it to be relegated along with its associate [attributes] to the realm of the past.[200] It says in the *Treasury* [*of Phenomenology*]:

> The defining characteristics [of conditioned phenomena] are
> Production, aging, duration, and impermanence.
> These [have subsidiary defining characteristics]
> Such as the production of production.
> A conditioned phenomenon partakes of eight attributes,
> But it has a single [operational attribute].[201]

Substantial Existence of the Three Times [13.2.2.2.3]

[The third tenet of the Vaibhāṣika] is the substantial existence of the three times. Accordingly, past entities such as a broken vase exist permanently without ever being destroyed, and future entities such as seven suns, also exist permanently from past [immemorial]; but these are invisible, respectively, in the realms of past and future due to the [intervening] aeons of time and cannot be utilized.

If entities exist permanently, how, one might ask, would the three times be differentiated? Their respective fruits are that the past denotes the activity of production that has ceased, the future denotes the activity of production that has not taken effect, and the present denotes the activity of production that is taking effect.

That said, there are some differences between them and the Sāṃkhya regarding the existence of a future vase when in a state of [unmodified] clay, because [for the Vaibhāṣika] the realm of the present does not last more than an instant, and the causes and fruits of so many instants of time—the clay, the vase, the potsherds, and so forth, are all different. Therefore as long as the vase is not produced, until the instant of its production in the realm of the future, it yields to the realm of the past.

The Inexpressible Self [13.2.2.2.4]

[The fourth tenet of the Vaibhāṣika] is the inexpressible self. [Some Vaibhāṣika such as the Vātsīputrīya claim that] ordinary individuals must certainly have a self that engages in actions and experiences their fruits because, otherwise, it follows that if one were reborn among the gods after maintaining ethical discipline, one's deeds would be squandered because one would have interrupted the human aggregates that maintain ethical discipline, and instead encounter a state in which they no longer do so because the aggregates of the gods experience the fruit of not maintaining ethical discipline. Therefore, although a temporal continuum from one rebirth to another is rejected, there is a self that uniquely experiences the fruits of past actions. This is known because there is a scripture that says:

> When, on that occasion, I had been reborn as a brahmin child, I offered a flower to the tathāgata Ratnaketu, and on that basis, obtained the body of a god for five hundred lifetimes, and now, even though I have attained buddhahood, I have been adorned with that name.[202]

Insofar as this self has functioned as the accumulator of virtuous actions in the past, it will become their protector as the experiencer [of the fruits of those virtuous actions] in a future life. It says in the same scripture:

> The self is the protector of the self,
> But who is the protector of this self?
> The deeds enacted by the self
> Will be experienced by the self alone.[203]

[They claim that] a self such as this is not to be identified with the psycho-physical aggregates; nor is it separate from the psycho-physical aggregates. It cannot be expressed as eternal; nor can it be expressed as impermanent.

Denial of Intrinsic or Objective Awareness on the Part of Consciousness [13.2.2.2.5]

[The fifth tenet of the Vaibhāṣika] is that there is no intrinsic or objective awareness on the part of consciousness. The intellect is not intrinsically aware otherwise the object of that awareness and the subject of that awareness would be without duality. Rather [they hold that the intellect] is extraneously aware.

As far as the awareness of objects is concerned, it is not due to mind that awareness [of objects] occurs, because it follows that there would be awareness even when [objects] are obscured inasmuch as mind has no beginning. Rather, it is due to the sense organs that awareness [of objects] occurs. Moreover, it is not due to all the sense organs that awareness [of objects] occurs, but due to consciousness along with its supporting sense organ that awareness [of objects] occurs. It says in the *Treasury* [*of Phenomenology*]:[204]

> It is the eye that sees sights,
> When conjoined with the shared support [of visual
> consciousness],
> Not [the visual] consciousness that that [sense organ] supports.
> This is because obscured sights are not seen.[205]

Defining Characteristics and Exemplars Are Substantially Different [13.2.2.2.6]

[The sixth tenet of the Vaibhāṣika] is that there is a [substantial] difference between defining characteristics and their exemplars. While white and brown and dewlap all are indicative of a bull, these three attributes cannot be substantially identical [with the bull]. If the dewlap and the white and brown colors were [substantially] identical, defining characteristics could not be exemplified because the objects and the subject would be identical, and [in this case, these defining characteristics—dewlap, color, etc.] would be identical with the subject—the bull, [but this is not the case,] just as roasted grain, ground grain, and the grinder cannot be identical. Rather, these three [characteristics of the bull] are substantially different, just like three [distinct] people.

Unexhausted Substance [13.2.2.2.7]

[The seventh tenet of the Vaibhāṣika] is that there is an unexhausted substance. It is a distinctive feature of acquisition—[the first of] the formative predispositions disassociated from mind—that an action that has been carried out is not exhausted [but lingers,] in the manner of an outstanding bill.

As such [they claim that] this represents a nonspecific [or neutral] category of phenomena, [neither virtuous nor nonvirtuous, and substantially] different from [physical forms],[206] mind, and mental states; and that even when it has ceased, its fruit continues to be produced.

During the present life [this unexhausted substance] assumes different circumstances, and at the time of death it distills the virtuous and nonvirtuous actions accrued by beings in the world system of desire. Transmigration takes place once the unexhausted [residue of] the desire, form, or formlessness realms or else of the uncontaminated states has been integrated in a single substance. The ripening of past actions is not therefore exhausted but lingers as a residue, without ceasing, just like an outstanding bill pertaining to the formation of cyclic existence that has not yet been erased.

However, when the cessation [of cyclic existence] does occur and [the fruit of] being tied to a single rebirth has been attained, [it is said that] the unexhausted [substance] associated with beings on the level of entering the stream and so forth will cease, and that therefore those [lesser] fruits may indeed cease at the time of transmigration.

[Unexhausted substance] will also cease in the case of beings who have already achieved transcendence. That is to say, when those who have attained [the fruit] of no longer being subject to rebirth [in the world system of desire] are born into the world system of form or formlessness, any unexhausted [substance pertaining to the world system] of desire will simply cease.

In addition, when nonresidual [nirvāṇa] is attained, all [lesser] attainments will cease because one will then partake of a level that has transcended all of the three world systems. It says in the *Fundamental Stanzas of the Middle Way:*

> Like a debt recorded in a contract
> Actions are not exhausted.
> [Manifesting] in four ways, according to the world systems,
> Their intrinsic nature is nonspecific.
> They are not eliminated by renunciation,
> But through meditation they will be eliminated.[207]

And:

> Even after ripening, they linger.[208]

And:

> Since they have affinity with a given world system,
> There may be similarities and dissimilarities,
> But they all arise in a single modality
> When involuntary rebirth takes place.[209]

In brief, the Vaibhāṣika assert that all phenomena that cannot be expressed [in terms of the previous tenet][210] as different are permeated by a single substance.[211]

The Philosophical System of the Sautrāntika

The Philosophical System of the Sautrāntika [13.2.2.3]

The second, the philosophical system of the Sautrāntika, [comments on the verse:]

> **The Sautrāntika have seven tenets, commencing with the four conditions of causation.**

Those pious attendants who adhere to the Sautrāntika system hold the following seven tenets: (i) causation has four conditions (13.2.2.3.1); (ii) appearances are mind (13.2.2.3.2); (iii) objects are covert (13.2.2.3.3); (iv) atomic particles have no intervening spaces (13.2.2.3.4); (v) the sense organs are causally effective (13.2.2.3.5); (vi) formative predispositions disassociated from mind are imaginary (13.2.2.3.6); and (vii) nirvāṇa is a nonentity (13.2.2.3.7).

Causation Has Four Conditions [13.2.2.3.1]

As for the first [tenet of the Sautrāntika], all that arises does so dependent on four conditions: (i) the causal condition; (ii) the immediate and homogenous condition; (iii) the referential condition; and (iv) the predominant condition. The first of these generates the essence [of a given causal process]—the mere capacity to facilitate an effect. The second generates a subsequent cognition similar to the preceding one, immediately after the latter has ceased. The third denotes the object of this cognition. The fourth generates a particular effect and simply ensures that there are no impediments.

In this regard, there are also five kinds of cause—namely, (i) the concomitant cause; (ii) the all-pervasive cause; (iii) the homogenous cause; (iv) the efficient cause; and (v) the coemergent cause. As is said in the *Treasury* [*of Phenomenology*],

> There are said to be four conditions:
> Five causes constitute the causal condition.
> Mind and all mental states that have arisen
> With the exception of the last of these [at the attainment of arhatship]
> Constitute the immediate and homogenous condition.
> All phenomena constitute the referential condition.
> The efficient cause is explained to be the predominant condition.[212]

As far as the causal process is concerned, the mind and all mental states arise through all four conditions. In the case of visual consciousness, the causal condition is the seed of cognition present in a preceding cognition. The immediate condition is the cognition that immediately follows the cessation of a preceding cognition. The referential condition is the sight that is seen. The predominant condition is the eye.

The meditative absorption of cessation and the meditative absorption devoid of perception both arise from three [of the four] conditions, since the referential condition is absent. All the other formative predispositions that are disassociated from mind and all physical forms arise dependent on two conditions—the causal and predominant. In the case of a vase, for example, the causal condition is the clay and the predominant condition is the potter. This is why arising and enduring minds, on their cessation, no longer perceive signs, sounds, and so forth. It says in the *Treasury* [*of Phenomenology*]:

> Mind and mental states arise through four conditions,
> The two meditative absorptions arise through three conditions,
> And the other [formative predispositions] arise from two conditions.[213]

All appearances Are Mind [13.2.2.3.2]

[The second tenet of the Sautrāntika] is that all appearances are mind. In general, there are three kinds of objects that appear to cognition: (i) generic objects or object-universals such as [the visualizations] of deities during the generation stage [of meditation]; (ii) illusions such as double moons that may appear but are nonexistent; and (iii) [conceptualized] objects with independent characteristics such as a vase. [According to the Sautrāntika,] all appearances subsumed under these three types are actual cognition, so there is no difference between them and the [Cittamātrins] who hold sensa to be veridical.

Objects Are Covert [13.2.2.3.3]

[The third tenet of the Sautrāntika] is that objects are covert. Object-universals and things that appear, though nonexistent, are no different from this covert nature, because they are conceptual and nonconceptual appearances of bewilderment, respectively. All objects with independent characteristics that appear as unbewildered are actually termed *conceptual sensa.*[214] That which appears as a vase is not a vase but it is the mind. The vase exists covertly. It can never actually be seen by anyone—the appearance of the vase and its comprehension are not different. Similarly, the weapons that pierce a body and so forth exist covertly. Therefore the point of the statement "there is an awareness of objects on the part of consciousness" is not that cognition is nakedly and directly aware of actual objects; for in the second temporal instant after an object arises as a vase, to cognition there arises a sensum similar to the vase, and it is merely imputed that cognition apprehends a cognitive object, just as a child is said to recognize its father's face when a reflection of its father's face arises, even though the child cannot grasp its father's face. It says in the *Exposition of Valid Cognition:*

> Since there is a difference of time,
> How, you may ask, does [cognition] apprehend [an object]?
> Cognitive awareness cognizes as its object
> The very cause [with the capacity to establish a cognitive sensum].[215]

Therefore, all cognitions consist of both intrinsic experiences and extraneous referents, among which the extraneous referents merely resemble objects. It says in the [*Exposition of Valid Cognition*]:

> So it is that the referential and experiential aspects
> of all cognitions are different—
> Oneself clearly experiences referents that resemble objects.[216]

Atomic Particles Have No Intervening Spaces [13.2.2.3.4]

[The fourth tenet of the Sautrāntika] is that atomic particles have no intervening spaces. When atomic particles form a gross conglomerate, the atoms cannot touch one another because they would have six portions;[217] nor can they orbit with spaces between them because atoms of light and dark would then adhere and therefore they would have six portions. Rather they continue to adhere without touching; indeed they adhere without intervening spaces and do not touch one another because the portions of their surface do not touch.

The Sense Organs Are Causally Effective [13.2.2.3.5]

[The fifth tenet of the Sautrāntika is that the sense organs are causally effective.] The sense faculties are not covert substances, but they do have the capacity to generate consciousness through, [for example,] both the eyes and the patterns [they observe]. The sense faculties of others cannot manifestly determine that this is the case because, without actually seeing its effect, the capacity cannot be manifestly determined. When one's own sense faculties give rise to visual consciousness and so forth, [the capacity] is covert, but, at the time when the actual cognition arises, it may be determined through the impact of both the object-oriented cognition that grasps sense objects, and the intrinsic or reflexive awareness that apprehends visual consciousness.

Formative Predispositions Disassociated from Mind Are Imaginary [13.2.2.3.6]

[The sixth tenet of the Sautrāntika] is that formative predispositions disassociated from mind, such as birth and decay, are imaginary, just like the horns of a rabbit, in that they have been refuted simply because the notions that they are either identical with, or other than, physical forms, mind, and mental states, or that they are both [identical to them and other than them] are refuted. These are merely labels that have been applied because there are no objects apart from[218] those three [categories].

Nirvāṇa Is a Nonentity [13.2.2.3.7]

[The seventh tenet of the Sautrāntika is that nirvāṇa is a nonentity.] They hold, like the Vaibhāṣika, that after pious attendants, hermit buddhas, arhats, and buddhas have passed into nirvāṇa, the psycho-physical aggregates along with their seeds will be entirely nonexistent, like clouds vanishing in the sky or like ice melting on a lake, and that sense objects will be quiescent, because they will be indivisible from cessation in reality's expanse, so that not even the slightest particle or name will be left behind. However, [unlike the Vaibhāṣika,] they do not accept that all those substances that have attained the status of substances disassociated [from afflicted mental states in the context of the various fruits] are actually entities.[219]

The Vehicle of Hermit Buddhas

The Exegesis of the Vehicle of Hermit Buddhas [13.2.3]

The third part [of the second main topic, see above, p. 5] is the exegesis of the vehicle of the hermit buddhas, which is for those of moderate acumen. [This comments on the verse:]

> **The hermit buddhas [are considered] in terms of their focus—**
> **Class, view, and dependent origination—**
> **As well as their conduct and result.**

The hermit buddhas of moderate acumen who are the sharpest of the adherents of the lesser vehicle, and who attain buddhahood by means of the engaging and reversing modalities of dependent origination, are classed as lower than the [bodhisattva] adherents of the supreme vehicle because they do not abide on the conclusive level.

When classified here, their tenets are examined under the following three categories: (i) their focus (13.2.3.1); (ii) the gist of their conduct (13.2.3.2); and (iii) the fruits of their attainment (13.2.3.3).

The Focus of the Hermit Buddhas [13.2.3.1]

First, their focus will be considered in the contexts of (i) class (13.2.3.1.1); (ii) view (13.2.3.1.2); and (iii) dependent origination (13.2.3.1.3).

Class [13.2.3.1.1]

As far as their class is concerned, hermit buddhas are of moderate acumen because they belong neither among the pious attendants nor among the bodhisattvas. They constitute the middling category of those described in the *Compendium* [*of Phenomenology*] as the persons who follow the vehicle of pious attendants, the vehicle of hermit buddhas, and the great vehicle.[220]

View [13.2.3.1.2]

As far as their view is concerned, although hermit buddhas do not accept the notion of the self of an individual person or the notion of external objects that consist of atomic particles, they have not yet abandoned the notion of the momentary subjective cognition that apprehends falsely appearing objects. It says in the *Ornament of Clear Realization:*

> Because they have abandoned conceptions about apprehended
> objects,
> And because they do not abandon the apprehending subject,
> On that basis, the path of those rhino-like [hermit buddhas]
> Should be known to be perfectly summarized.[221]

Dependent Origination [13.2.3.1.3]

Dependent origination should be understood through its five aspects: (i) its classification (13.2.3.1.3.1); (ii) its essential nature (13.2.3.1.3.2); (iii) its structure (13.2.3.1.3.3); (iv) the completion [of the twelve links of the cycle] over specific lifetimes (13.2.3.1.3.4); and (v) its cultivation (13.2.3.1.3.5).

Classification [13.2.3.1.3.1]

The classification includes outer dependent origination and inner dependent origination. The outer modality includes the process through which shoots arise dependent on seeds, and the inner modality denotes the twelve links [of dependent origination] that arise dependent on fundamental ignorance, and extend as far as aging and death.

Essential Nature [13.2.3.1.3.2]

As for the essential nature of each [of the twelve links]:

(i) With regard to fundamental ignorance, although it is not cognized as an object of knowledge, in this context, when one is reborn in this life, the afflicted mental states of past lives are established as fundamental ignorance from the perspective of the present life.

(ii) With regard to formative predispositions, although they are generally produced through causes, in this context, they denote the actions of past lives that take effect in this life.

(iii) With regard to consciousness, although in general it denotes the awareness of sense objects alone, in this context, it denotes the five psycho-physical aggregates present when one initially enters the mother's womb.

(iv) With regard to name and form, although in general this comprises the four nominal aggregates and physical forms, in this context, it denotes the five psycho-physical aggregates from the time when one enters the womb until the mouth and eyes [of the embryo] are formed.

(v) With regard to the six sensory activity fields, although in general this simply includes the eyes and so forth, in this context, it denotes [the phase of embryonic development], from the formation of the mouth and eyes until one is able to apprehend odors, tastes, and tangibles.

(vi) With regard to sensory contact, although in general this signifies the simple convergence of sense objects, sense faculties, and cognition, in this context, it denotes the short period commencing from the [embryo's] apprehension of the causes and objects associated with happiness and suffering, and lasting until actual happiness and suffering arise.

(vii) With regard to sensation, although in general this denotes bare experience, in this context [of the embryo], it comprises happiness and suffering, commencing from the gross experience of happiness and suffering in the womb until there is a capacity to experience sexual union.

(viii) With regard to craving, although in general this denotes mere attachment, in this context, it indicates the short period, commencing from the [embryo's] capacity to experience sexual union until there is a longing for materiality and a searching for sexual union between a female and a male.

(ix) With regard to grasping, although in general it denotes mere longing and attachment, in this context, it indicates the period commencing from the [embryo's] search for the objects of craving and their acquisition.

(x) With regard to the rebirth process, although in general it denotes all activities, in this context, it indicates the period commencing from the acquisition and enjoyment of sense objects until one has gathered the actions commensurate with the next life and passed away.

(xi) With regard to birth, although in general it denotes all that arises from causes, in this context, it signifies the period immediately after one has entered the womb in the next life due to the capacity of those actions.

(xii) With regard to aging and death, although in general this denotes all things that are approaching cessation and all things that are ceasing, in this context, it signifies everything, commencing from the time when one has entered into that womb until the four links associated with the next life—namely, name and form, six sense fields, sensory contact, and sensation, have been perfected. From the link of the rebirth process in that life onward, there commences another cycle of dependent origination.

It says in the *Treasury* [*of Phenomenology*]:

> Fundamental ignorance and so forth pertain to a previous life.
> Formative predispositions and so forth
> Are associated with the actions of a previous life.
> Consciousness denotes the psycho-physical aggregates at
> conception.
> Name and form is the period from then
> Until the six sense fields are formed.
> The latter lasts until the three [aspects of sensory contact].
> Sensory contact lasts until there is a capacity
> To cognize the causes of happiness, suffering, and so forth.
> Sensation lasts until there is sexual union.
> Craving is associated with attachment
> To enjoyments and sexual union.
> Grasping is running around for the sake of obtaining enjoyment.
> The rebirth process is the performance of actions
> That bring about the future result of the rebirth process.
> Birth is involuntary reincarnation.
> Aging and death last as long as sensation.
> All this is [revealed] in order to reverse
> The delusion associated with past and future lives
> And the interval between them.[222]

Structure [13.2.3.1.3.3]

As far as the structure [of dependent origination is concerned], these twelve [links of dependent origination] are subsumed in actions, afflicted mental states, and suffering. That is to say, fundamental ignorance, craving, and grasping represent afflicted mental states. Formative predispositions and the rebirth process represent actions. The remaining seven, starting with consciousness, represent suffering.

Completion of the Twelve Links of the Cycle over Specific Lifetimes [13.2.3.1.3.4]

As far as the completion [of the twelve links of the cycle] over a single lifetime is concerned: with reference to speed, they will be completed over three [lifetimes]. It says in the same source [*Treasury of Phenomenology*]:

> The wheel of the rebirth process is beginningless.
> It comprises the twelve links of dependent origination,
> Which are divided into three phases[223]—
> Two are associated with the past life, two with the next life,
> And eight with the intervening [present] life.
> This is with reference to a completed cycle.[224]

Cultivation [13.2.3.1.3.5]

As far as the cultivation of dependent origination is concerned, hermit buddhas examine a skeleton in a charnel ground and accept that this has come about through death. They then realize the twelve links, commencing with the arising of death from aging and concluding with fundamental ignorance. With their minds they then cultivate the reverse modality [of dependent origination], commencing from the cessation of fundamental ignorance until [all links] have ceased, up to and including aging and death.

The Gist of Their Conduct [13.2.3.2]

As far as the gist of their conduct is concerned, while both pious attendants and hermit buddhas are engaged in the path of provisions, rather than listening to, and reflecting upon, [the teachings] of a spiritual mentor, the hermit buddhas have abandoned worldliness through the power of reasoning and they delight in solitude. Through cultivation [of the modes of dependent origination], they will attain individual enlightenment.

The Fruits of Their Attainment [13.2.3.3]

As far as the fruits that they attain are concerned, those of dull acumen and lesser attributes who engage in the accumulation of the provisions [of merit and so forth] in a group, like a flock of parrots, can indeed, through cultivation, attain the fruit within three lifetimes. As it is said [in the *Treasury of Phenomenology*]:

> They swiftly [reach their goal] at the end of three rebirths.[225]

Among them there are explained to be two sorts—those of greater and lesser conduct with respect to the provisions.

Then there are those who have sharp acumen and greater attributes, who dwell alone in solitude, in the manner of a rhinoceros, and who have amassed the provisions over a hundred aeons. They will also attain their fruit. As it is said [in the *Treasury of Phenomenology*]:

> Those rhino-like [solitary hermit buddhas] are endowed
> With the causal basis of a hundred aeons [of merit].[226]

When the latter have gathered the provisions, based on the path of provisions, they will actualize the five paths in a single sitting. For this reason, they are established to be of sharp acumen, whereas the former are of dull acumen because they have no such capacity. It says in the *Treasury* [*of Phenomenology*]:

> The teacher [i.e., the Buddha] and the hermit buddha,
> Similar to a [solitary] rhinoceros,
> All attain enlightenment in a single sitting,
> On the basis of the final meditative concentration.[227]

Both pious attendants who are arhats and hermit buddhas who are of dull acumen can see with their extrasensory powers as far as the dichiliocosm, while those who resemble a [solitary] rhinoceros can see the trichiliocosm, and the buddhas perceive countless [world systems]. It says in the same source [*Treasury of Phenomenology*]:

> Arhats, rhino-like [hermit buddhas], and buddhas
> Respectively perceive a dichiliocosm, a trichiliocosm, and
> countless worlds.[228]

Hermit buddhas manifest both during periods of progress [when a buddha is present] and of decline [when a buddha is not present]. During the interval after a buddha has passed away and while even no pious attendants are present, by achieving their former aspirations, realization naturally arises in their minds and they attain their fruit.[229] As is said in the *Fundamental Stanzas of the Middle Way Entitled Discriminative Awareness:*

> When perfect buddhas do not emerge,
> And even pious attendants have ceased to be,
> The pristine cognition of the hermit buddhas
> Naturally manifests without support.[230]

The Philosophical Systems of the Bodhisattvas

Exegesis of the Philosophical Systems of the Bodhisattvas [13.3]

The third main topic [see above, p. 5] is the exegesis of the philosophical systems of the bodhisattvas, which are for those of greater acumen. This has three parts: (i) an exegesis of their superiority over the lesser vehicle (13.3.1); (ii) an exegesis of the philosophical system of the adherents of Cittamātra (13.3.2); and (iii) an exegesis of the philosophical system of the adherents of Madhyamaka (13.3.3).

Their Superiority over the Lesser Vehicle [13.3.1]

The first of these, [the exegesis of their superiority over the lesser vehicle comments on the verse:]

> **[The great vehicle] is superior owing to its focus, attainment,**
> **Pristine cognition, perseverance, skillful means,**
> **accomplishment, and activity.**

In terms of its skillful means, conduct, and teaching approach, the great vehicle is likened to an oceanic glacial lake, whereas by comparison the lesser vehicle is regarded as the water contained in the footprint of an ox. This is because the former has seven attributes of greatness. That is to say, the great vehicle is superior for the following reasons:

(i) The greatness of focus indicates that [followers of the great vehicle] can apprehend the nature of reality, which is similar to space, whereas the lesser vehicle cannot.

(ii) The greatness of attainment indicates that [followers of the great vehicle] can, during the phases of the path and conduct, attain great benefit for themselves and others, whereas pious attendants and hermit buddhas can attain only their own benefit.

(iii) The greatness of pristine cognition indicates that [followers of the great vehicle] possess the pristine cognition integrating compassion and the reality that is empty of the two notions of selfhood, whereas the lesser vehicle does not.

(iv) The greatness of perseverance indicates that [followers of the great vehicle] can proliferate for the benefit of sentient beings over countless aeons, whereas pious attendants and hermit buddhas cannot.

(v) The greatness of skill in means indicates that [followers of the great vehicle] can achieve their purpose since they do not abide in the extremes of existence and quiescence, whereas pious attendants and hermit buddhas cannot.

(vi) The greatness of accomplishment[231] indicates that, having attained buddhahood, [followers of the great vehicle] act for the benefit of others and possess infinite enlightened attributes, such as the [ten] powers, whereas the followers of the lesser vehicle do not.

(vii) The greatness of activity indicates that [followers of the great vehicle] can act spontaneously for the benefit of others, as long as cyclic existence endures, whereas the pious attendants and hermit buddhas cannot.

It says in the *Ornament of the Sūtras [of the Great Vehicle]*:

> The great vehicle is so called
> Because it is endowed with the following seven attributes of greatness:
> The greatness of focus,
> And similarly the greatness of the twofold attainment,
> The greatness of pristine cognition, of the application of perseverance,
> Of skill in whatever means, and of genuine accomplishment,
> And the greatness of buddha activity.[232]

Among all these attributes, [the great vehicle] is particularly sublime on account of its skillful means and compassion. It says in the *Precious Garland:*

> Among [adherents of] the vehicle of the pious attendants

The aspiration, conduct, and dedication
Of the bodhisattvas are not explained.
How could that constitute the great vehicle![233]

In brief, [the great vehicle] attains the benefit of self and others and engenders spiritual and temporal well-being during the phase of the path through its sky-like vastness in respect of skillful means, discriminative awareness, and all aspects of liberation; and it also[234] engenders these [attributes] after buddhahood has been attained. It says in the *Verse Summation* [*of the Transcendent Perfection of Discriminative Awareness*]:

This vehicle is a large celestial mansion, immeasurable like space,
The supreme vehicle actualizing joy, felicity, and happiness,
Riding on which all sentient beings will pass into nirvāṇa.
For this reason, it is called the great vehicle.[235]

The Cittamātrins

Exegesis of the Philosophical System of the Adherents of Cittamātra [13.3.2]

The second part concerns the exegesis of the philosophical system of the adherents of Cittamātra. This comprises (i) a general presentation of the philosophical system of the Cittamātrins (13.3.2.1); (ii) a description of the particular philosophical system of Cittamātrins who hold sensa to be veridical (13.3.2.2); and (iii) a description of the philosophical system of Cittamātrins who hold sensa to be false (13.3.2.3).[236]

A General Presentation of the Philosophical System of the Cittamātrins [13.3.2.1]

The first of these has four topics: (i) a general exegesis (13.3.2.1.1); (ii) the tenets of Cittamātra (13.3.2.1.2); (iii) proof statements establishing the tenets of Cittamātra (13.3.2.1.3); and (iv) points to be established (13.3.2.1.4).

General Exegesis [13.3.2.1.1]

The first of these [comments on the verse]:

> **Generally compatible with the great vehicle,**
> **There are three [philosophical] approaches**
> **In which enlightened intention is directed.**

Although there is no [fundamental] difference between [all the schools of the great vehicle], because they concur that the essence of this great vehicle is the lack of inherent existence in respect of all phenomena, that the two provisions [of merit and pristine cognition] are accumulated on the path over countless aeons, and that the fruit is the emergence of enlightenment for the benefit of others, even so, on account of slight dissimilarities in their elucidations of the enlightened intention of the scriptures, the great masters who steer the supreme chariot of the unsurpassed scriptures are known as [the exponents] of Cittamātra and of Madhyamaka—the latter including both independent reasoning and consequential reasoning. In the purport of their respective treatises, they have all subsumed the enlightened intention of the buddhas.

First among these schools, the yogācārin adherents of Cittamātra will be described. Since the great master Vasubandhu and his followers spoke of the entire enlightened intention of the buddhas in terms of "mind only," it is held that the view [of this school] is not alien [to the Buddhist teachings]. As is said in the *Short Commentary:*

> For the benefit of living beings
> Vasubandhu, kinsman [of Asaṅga],
> Chiefly of his own volition,
> [Held that] knowable phenomena are internal,
> And that liberation is attained on that authentic basis.[237]

Tenets of Cittamātra [13.3.2.1.2]

The second, concerning their tenets, [comments on the verse:]

> **The [proponents of Cittamātra] hold that**
> **There is no subject-object dichotomy**
> **And that conscious awareness is ultimately real.**

They hold that there is no subject-object dichotomy but that cognition is ultimately real—a naturally radiant, intrinsic awareness. It says in the *Ascertainment of Valid Cognition:*

> The things experienced by the mind are not extraneous.
> Nor do their experiences exist extraneously.
> The mind is therefore naturally radiant,
> Since subject and object are without duality.[238]

And in the *Commentary on the Thirty Verses:*

> If there are those who claim that consciousness indeed exists relatively as an object of knowledge but is ultimately nonexistent, they are deficient in their reasoning, because even on the relative level it is without entity since there cannot be relative appearances without an [objective] support.[239]

Here there is no dichotomy between subject and object, in contrast to [the vehicle of] the hermit buddhas who hold that the subject exists while the object does not exist. Since they hold that both [subject and object] are nonexistent, are they, you may ask, identical to those who expound emptiness? Although objects such as physical forms and the mind that apprehends them are both nonexistent, they hold that there is a naturally radiant, intrinsic awareness that experiences this nonduality, and so they are dissimilar to both those who propound emptiness and to the hermit buddhas. However, since objects are false, the mind that apprehends them is also false and therefore nonexistent in ultimate reality. Accordingly it is said:

> When there is no apprehended object, there is no apprehending subject.[240]

Proof Statements Establishing the Tenets of Cittamātra [13.3.2.1.3]

The third, concerning their establishment [of those tenets], [comments on the verse:]

> **Appearances are not truly existent;**
> **[They derive from] the familiarity of minds,**
> **Bewildered due to past actions.**

External appearances and extraneous objects are not truly existent. Since even the single element water is perceived in accordance with the different apparitional modalities of the six classes of living beings, its mere appearance as such derives from the established familiarity of their respective minds, which are bewildered due to past actions and propensities. As it is said:

> Since the mental faculty that is a single entity
> Assumes different [appearances],
> Perception occurs although external objects are nonexistent.[241]

And in the *Sūtra of the Descent to Laṅkā:*

> Although there are no external objects,
> The nature of mind mistakenly perceives external objects.
> The dependent [nature] does exist,
> But the imaginary does not exist.
> Concepts are destroyed in the extremes
> Of exaggeration and deprecation![242]

And in the *Great Bounteousness of the Buddhas:*

> O Royal princes, these three world systems are only mind.[243]

The appearances of external objects, which manifest as external due to the cognition that has grown propensities, are established as dependently real, contingent on this internal cognition that is subjective. Therefore, external objects are not extraneously existent because they appear to develop on the basis of the differing aspects of consciousness. Also, the nature of the appearances that constitute the objective aspect, such as the color blue, is not an extraneous substance apart from the mind. This is because its objective referent is determined in coemergence with the apprehending cognition. It says in the *Ascertainment* [*of Valid Cognition*]:

> Blue and that [coemerging referent] are not different to the mind.[244]

The substratum does exist—when the six modes [of consciousness] cease, it is regenerated. This is because if there were no substratum, the six modes [of consciousness] would cease, and if there were no cognition apart from them, no regeneration could occur. The afflicted mental consciousness also exists because it is present as unadulterated ignorance, because it is present as the predominant condition of mental consciousness, and because it is invariably present in the sensa that constitute the [notional] self. The six modes of [engaged] consciousness that are commonly accepted are also established. So it is that consciousness has these eight aspects.

Points to Be Established [13.3.2.1.4]

The fourth concerning the points that are to be established has three parts: (i) focus (13.3.2.1.4.1); (ii) the gist of their conduct (13.3.2.1.4.2); and (iii) the fruits to be attained (13.3.2.1.4.3).

Focus [13.3.2.1.4.1]

The focus [of the Cittamātra] is threefold: (i) the classes that constitute the foundation of auspicious [practitioners] (13.3.2.1.4.1.1); (ii) the five basic categories that are the foundation of focusing through view (13.3.2.1.4.1.2);[245] and (iii) selflessness that is the foundation of focusing through meditation (13.3.2.1.4.1.3).[246]

The Classes That Constitute the Foundation of Auspicious [Practitioners] [13.3.2.1.4.1.1]

The first of these [comments on the verse]:

> **There are five classes: pious attendants, hermit buddhas,**
> **bodhisattvas, indeterminate beings, and cut-off beings.**

Sentient beings partake of five classes: the class of pious attendants, the class of hermit buddhas, the class of bodhisattvas, the class of indeterminate beings, and the class of cut-off beings.

The first of these includes sentient beings of dull acumen who from beginningless time have not studied under another but delight in swiftly attaining nirvāṇa.

The second include those who are naturally of moderate acumen, who delight in solitude and delight in swiftly attaining nirvāṇa, since they are intent on their own personal release.

The third include those of sharp acumen who have great compassion for all sentient beings, who have mastered the selflessness of phenomena, who are of great benefit to living beings, who are not afraid to hear of the supremely expansive conduct of bodhisattvas, and who rejoice in the practice of the six transcendent perfections. As is said in the *Ornament of the Sūtras* [*of the Great Vehicle*]:

From the start of their engagement [in practice],
Compassion, devotion, tolerance,
And virtuous conduct
Are assuredly explained to be the principles of this class.[247]

The fourth includes those beings in whom there arises an inclination toward the path where [the positive] conditions [of the great vehicle] are encountered. This is because even though pious attendants are held to assume the level of lesser receptiveness and below, when they are appraised by followers of the great vehicle, they will indeed become arhats.

The fifth includes those beings who, even though they may have heard, to some extent, of the benefits of the sacred doctrine and release [from cyclic existence], of the disadvantages of cyclic existence, of the praiseworthiness of the higher realms, and of the sufferings of the lower realms, their minds are obdurate, and even though they may have genuinely seen a spiritual mentor, the wondrous three receptacles [of buddha body, speech, and mind], and so forth, they are without the slightest faith, even to the extent of a sesame seed.

Whether or not the simple thought arises that they should engage with the [Buddhist] teaching, they become mendicants either with an exclusively harmful intention, or for the sake of their own sustenance and so forth. They are without faith and accrue deeds that abandon the sacred doctrine. Since, commencing from their initial training, their minds lack authenticity, whether they are attached or not, they will be worn out, so that their approach will be only shallow. In that regard, it is held that "such perverse individuals never acquire the attributes through which final nirvāṇa will be attained."[248] It says in the *Compendium* [*of Phenomenology*]:

> I regard those who always possess afflicted mental states as lacking the attributes through which final nirvāṇa will be attained, and as possessing great attachments. This is because they lack the basis and never will have the basis for release [from cyclic existence].[249]

The Five Basic Categories That Are the Foundation of Focusing through View [13.3.2.1.4.1.2]

The second topic comprises the five basic categories that are the foundation of focusing through view. It has three aspects: (i) the essence of each [category] (13.3.2.1.4.1.2.1); (ii) their systematic presentation (13.3.2.1.4.1.2.2); and (iii) the enlightened intention of the Sage (13.3.2.1.4.1.2.3).

The Essence of Each [Category] [13.3.2.1.4.1.2.1]

The first of these [comments on the verse]:

> **[The basic categories of phenomena] comprise matter,**
> **Mind, and its peripheral [mental states],**
> **Along with objective referents,**
> **And the seed of buddha nature, which is the genuine substratum.**

Matter does not essentially exist as inanimate things, but the appearance of matter is assumed owing to the maturation of the propensities of objective appearances within the substratum. The mind comprises eight aspects of consciousness—namely, the six modes of engaged consciousness, the substratum consciousness, and the afflicted mental consciousness. These constitute eight distinct substances.

Among them, the substratum is the ground of propensities, the awareness of the mere haecceity of objects. Its defining characteristic is that it is revealed as a series of multiple contiguous temporal instants. When analyzed, it comprises a maturational aspect and a germinal aspect. The substratum is unobscured by the force of virtuous and nonvirtuous actions, and remains nonspecific in terms of that dichotomy. Both [aspects of the substratum—maturational and germinal] have the capacity to generate fruits commensurate with the distribution of the propensities they have.

Peripheral to [the substratum consciousness] are the five ever-present mental states, such as contact, so that there are six substantial existents [including these and the propensities] from which it is never separated.

As far as the objective referent of the [substratum] is concerned, the substratum consciousness indistinctly apprehends the extent of the inhabited world and its sentient inhabitants. Therefore the seven [other] aspects [of consciousness] and their peripheral [mental states] do not arise from their own [discrete] continuum [of temporal instants], but are subsequently produced, similar in class to [the corresponding propensities within the substratum]. These propensities are distributed in the substratum, arising with each moment of the substratum, like the shadow of a vase.

Since it acts as the support for the formative predispositions of cyclic existence, along with virtuous, nonvirtuous, and nonspecific phenomena that are conditioned and the [other seven] aspects of consciousness, this is established as the "substratum of diverse propensities."

The seed of buddha nature is established as the "genuine substratum" because it arises coemergently with naturally pure nirvāṇa and unconditioned enlightened attributes. Through familiarity with virtuous attributes present within the substratum of propensities, in conformity with [the process of] release [from cyclic existence], the stains covering the seed of buddha nature are worn away, and the [regenerating] capacity of the substratum of propensities, which is their support, will be weakened.

It says in the *Sūtra of the Bounteous Array:*

> This seed [of buddha nature] has been expressed
> And it is indicated by the term *substratum*.[250]

In this context, the term is widely explained to denote the substratum of propensities, acting as the support for cyclic existence.

It is taught that the afflicted mental consciousness makes the assumption of simply conflating the substratum with the self. Accompanied by nine associated [mental states] such as the mistaken view of self,[251] it emerges in all [mundane] circumstances, except during the meditative equipoise of the sublime path and so on, up to and including the meditative absorption in cessation. These [nine] are in addition to the [standard enumeration of] fifty-one mental states, such as contact. That is to say, there are altogether sixty substantially existent [mental states] imbued with awareness and so forth that may be present in a single mental continuum, at a single time.

The central mind and its associated mental states do not apprehend each other because if they were to apprehend one another, it is implicit that they would do so in conjunction with themselves.

As far as formative predispositions disassociated from mind are concerned, these number twenty-three, including acquisition. These are merely imputed existents—imputed according to circumstances—and apart from that they have no substantial existence.

The unconditioned phenomena are six in number, comprising (i) the real nature of nonentities uncreated by causes and conditions; (ii) cessation obtained through [conscious] analytical means; (iii) cessation obtained through [unconscious] nonanalytical means; (iv) stable cessation; (v) cessation of perceptions and feelings; and (vi) space.

Among them, the real nature is the inalienable nature deriving simply from the cessation of [the notion of] self with respect to the psychophysical aggregates. They hold that although it is a substantial existent, it is neither identical in essence nor different from the mind.

Cessation obtained through [conscious] analytical means denotes the circumstances when, in the real nature, the entities to be abandoned are destroyed by an antidote and then no longer arise. Cessation obtained through [unconscious] nonanalytical means denotes the circumstances when, in the real nature, the conditions that give rise to conditioned phenomena do not arise because they are incomplete. Stable cessation denotes the circumstances when, in the real nature, the phenomena of the world system of desire do not arise. Cessation of perceptions and feelings denotes the circumstances when, in the real nature, the seven other modes of consciousness do not arise. Space denotes the circumstances when, in the real nature, there are no tangible phenomena causing obstruction.

The Systematic Presentation [13.3.2.1.4.1.2.2]

Second, their systematic presentation has three parts: (i) the presentation according to the three natures (13.3.2.1.4.1.2.2.1); (ii) the presentation according to substantial existents and imputed existents (13.3.2.1.4.1.2.2.2); and (iii) the presentation according to relative and ultimate truth (13.3.2.1.4.1.2.2.3).

The Presentation according to the Three Natures [13.3.2.1.4.1.2.2.1]

This first [comments on the verse]:

> **[As for the systematic presentation of the ground,]**
> **They hold that there are three [natures]—**
> **The imaginary, the dependent, and the consummate.**

The imaginary denotes phenomena that, apart from being merely imputed, have no defining characteristics of their own. The dependent denotes phenomena that arise contingent on causes and conditions. The consummate denotes phenomena that are present when the dependent is delimited[252] in the imaginary.

The imaginary has two aspects: (i) The imaginary nature of delimited characteristics denotes things that are intellectually imputed, such as the [notional] self of individual persons and the [notional] self of phenomena. As the lord of awareness [Asvabhāva] has said:

> Objects that are conceptually imputed
> Denote the imaginary nature.
> Conceptual thought denotes the dependent nature.
> The emptiness of that denotes the consummate nature.[253]

(ii) The nominal imaginary denotes things that appear to the mind although they are nonexistent, such as the appearance of a double moon. As is said [in Vasubandhu's *Exposition of the Three Natures*]:

> That which appears is the dependent [nature].
> How it appears is the imaginary.
> That which is the permanent absence
> Of how things that appear do appear
> Is known as the consummate nature
> [Because it is said not to be dependent].[254]

The [nominal imaginary] includes therefore the nature of reflections that appear although they are nonexistent and of [conceived] object-universals and of all designations. [Elements] such as earth, water, fire, and wind are established by the mind as the nominal [imaginary].

The dependent nature includes (i) the pure dependent nature, that is, the mind and mental states that are projected during postmeditation, and (ii) the impure dependent nature, that is, mundane mind and mental states. These appearances constitute the defining characteristics of the dependent nature because they are actually the bewildered mind.

The consummate includes (i) the unchanging consummate nature, which denotes absolute reality, and (ii) the incontrovertible consummate nature, which denotes the nonconceptual pristine cognition of pure mind. Thus there are said to be two modes of the consummate nature—unchanging and incontrovertible.

For example, physical forms are imaginary either since they appear although they are nonexistent, or since they are not produced through causes in that they do not exist as entities. Mind and mental states are dependent because they arise contingent on previous [mind and mental states] of a similar type. Formative predispositions disassociated from mind are classed as imaginary in that they are circumstances pertaining to physical forms, whereas the circumstances of mind and mental states are classed as dependent. The unconditioned absolute reality denotes the consummate nature, and its other [aspects] are classed as circumstances of the consummate nature. It says in the *Thirty Verses:*

> Because of whatever conceptual thought,
> Such and such an entity appears and is imagined,
> This is the imaginary nature.
> That nature does not exist.
> The dependent nature is conceptual thought, born of conditions.
> The consummate nature is the eternal nonexistence
> Of the former in respect of the latter.[255]

The Presentation according to Substantial Existents and Imputed Existents [13.3.2.1.4.1.2.2.2]

The second is the presentation according to substantial existents and imputed existents [that comments on the verse]:

> **That there are substantial existents and imputed existents,**

When phenomena are presented in terms of substantial existents and imputed existences, there are twenty-three mental states, commencing with contact, that are classed, along with [the unconditioned phenomenon] absolute reality, as substantial existents, and there are twenty-nine mental states, commencing with carefulness, that are classed, along with space and the four aspects of cessation,[256] as imputed existents. It says in the *Summation [of Ascertainment from the Yogacaryā Level]*:

> If you ask whether the absolute reality should be described as

a substantial existent or as an imputed existent, it should be described as a substantial existent.[257]

The Presentation according to Relative and Ultimate Truth [13.3.2.1.4.1.2.2.3]

The third is the presentation according to relative and ultimate truth [that comments on the verse]:

That there is an ultimate truth pertaining to the appearances of reality
And to actual reality, and that there is a relative truth.

When [the three natures] are presented in terms of relative and ultimate truth, the dependent nature denotes the ultimate truth pertaining to the appearances of reality, the consummate nature denotes the ultimate truth pertaining to actual reality, and the imaginary nature denotes the relative truth. This, one might think, seems to contradict the following passage from the *Commentary on the Distinction between the Middle and Extremes* that states:

> The consummate nature alone pertains to ultimate truth because both the dependent and imaginary natures cannot be ultimate.[258]

The response to that standpoint would be that these remarks are consistent, because it is said that the dependent nature, provisionally at least, does have an aspect that is causally effective and present in bare and lucid experience. In terms of entity, however, the first two [natures] are relative and [only] the last, [the consummate nature,] abides in ultimate truth.

The Enlightened Intention of the Sage [13.3.2.1.4.1.2.3]

Third [see above p. 121], when [this discussion] is conjoined with the enlightened intention of the Sage, [it comments on the verse:]

The enlightened intention denotes definitive meaning and provisional meaning, [absence of] defining characteristics, and essencelessness.

Since it is the enlightened intention of all the scriptures of the buddhas that mind and mental states are empty of self and phenomena, all those teachings that were delivered accordingly are classed as definitive in meaning, whereas all those that speak of self and physical form as existent, and which do not in the slightest speak of the authentic reality are classed as provisional in meaning. That is to say, all teachings stating that all phenomena are empty of essential nature intend that the imaginary indicates the absence of defining characteristics, the dependent indicates the absence of a self-arising essential nature, and the consummate indicates the absence of the essential nature of entities in ultimate truth.

Though they may say that consciousness is nonexistent, the intention is that consciousness partakes of the imaginary nature. Though they may say that there is no arising and no cessation, the intention is that things that do not independently arise and cease are not substantially existent. Though they may explain that dependent origination neither originates from the self nor from others and so forth, the intention is that it does not arise exclusively from individual[259] causes and conditions and that it does not abide atemporally in an amalgam [of causes and conditions].

Though they may profess that "things are naturally pure," the intention is that such things are without the defining characteristics of the imaginary. Though they may say that all things are inexpressible, the intention is that [the inexpressible] is within the range of the pristine cognition of the individual intrinsic awareness of sublime beings [which cannot be described], just as the dreams of a mute [cannot be verbalized], and that all the teachings that there are cannot express this directly to others, except through the mere superimposition of object-universals or concepts.

Though they may say that all things are without conceptual elaboration, [the intention is that] such things are not objects of sound and thought, because all sounds that are verbalized and all that appears as thought are the superimposition of object-universals or concepts, and apart from that, the nature of mind is actually without verbalization and without thoughts.

Though they may say that all things resemble a magical display, the intention is that such things are contingent on conditions and appear in terms of the subject-object dichotomy, but it would be totally incorrect [to describe] "nothing at all" as a magical display because it would not be contingent on conditions. Therefore, statements suggesting that "all things are emptiness" are correct in terms of apperception[260] alone. That is to say, the dependent nature comprising mind and mental states is empty because it is said to be extraneously empty of external objects such as a pillar, unlike intrinsically empty forms which are empty of themselves. As for the negandum of which [mind and mental states] are empty, they are empty of both aspects of the subject-object dichotomy—the [notional] self of individual persons and the [notional] self of phenomena. However the expression "nothing at all" cannot be described even in conventional terms as "empty" because it lacks the basis for negation.

Selflessness, the Foundation of Focusing through Meditation [13.3.2.1.4.1.3]

Third there is [selflessness], which is the foundation of focusing through meditation. [This comments on the verse:]

> **Since there is no self, one comes to rest in a nonreferential disposition.**

Since there is no self, even in terms of the dependent nature, one comes to rest in an entirely nonreferential disposition, without the mind relying on anything. It is said in the *Thirty Verses:*

> Setting anything whatsoever before one
> And objectifying it [as a meditation object],
> Saying, "this is the nature of apperception alone,"
> One does not even abide in [apperception] alone.[261]

The Gist of Their Conduct [13.3.2.1.4.2]

Second [see p. 119], there is the gist of their conduct, [which comments on the verse:]

> **The six transcendent perfections should be practiced for three "countless" aeons.**

One should practice the six transcendent perfections for three "countless" aeons for the benefit of others, apprehending inestimable beings, who comprise a mere series of mental instants, but are conceived as sentient beings.

The Fruits to Be Attained [13.3.2.1.4.3]

Third, there are the fruits to be attained, [which comments on the verse:]

> **The fruits comprise the inconceivable attributes of the buddhas.**

Although the classifications of the attributes of the buddhas are inconceivable, the nonconceptual pristine cognition that apprehends the pure reality alone is the incontrovertible consummate nature—the ultimate reality. The realization[262] that cognizes the world and its inhabitants and so forth during postmeditation, comprising the emanations that appear for the sake of others, the appearances of the ornamental array of the Akaniṣṭha field, and the appearances of the [buddha body of] perfect resource, constitute the pure dependent nature—that is, the relative truth. That is to say, along with the other four pristine cognitions, [this realization is] substantially different.

As explained above (p. 122), these objects are the fruits of the transformation of the substratum and its propensities in the mind. In this regard, the impure dependent nature, through transformation of objective appearances, becomes the pure dependent nature. Objects concomitant with the mind, through purification and transformation, become pristine cognition. The consciousness of the substratum, through transformation, becomes the mirror-like pristine cognition. The mental consciousness, through transformation, becomes the pristine cognition of sameness. The afflicted mental consciousness, through transformation, becomes the pristine cognition of discernment. The consciousnesses of the five sensory gates, through transformation, become the pristine cognition of accomplishment.

They hold that, once the supporting substratum [of cyclic existence], endowed with its diverse propensities, has been reversed, there remains the aspect that rests in the genuine substratum—obscurations are purified, so that the genuine reality is actualized, and the excellences of the enlightened activities, embodying all the attributes of nondual pristine cognition, are attained, and they emerge spontaneously, without effort, for the benefit of sentient beings, as long as cyclic existence endures.[263]

The Philosophical Systems of Cittamātra That Hold Sensa to Be Veridical [13.3.2.2]

Second [see p. 115], there is the description of those maintaining the philosophical systems of Cittamātra that hold sensa to be veridical. [This comments on the verse:]

> **Those holding sensa to be veridical [assert]**
> **That consciousness and its sensa [are distinct],**
> **That there are as many [instances of] consciousness as there are sensa,**
> **Or that [consciousness and sensa] are without duality.**

[Among Cittamātrins,] there are both those holding sensa to be veridical, who claim that diversely appearing external objects are instances of intrinsic consciousness appearing as distinct objects, and there are those holding sensa to be false, who claim that these are not consciousness but assume the appearance of supported propensities because they are false in terms of consciousness. However, since both are alien to the [perspective of] Madhyamaka, they are merely philosophical systems in which their respective opinions are imbued with deception.

First, with regard to the presentation of their tenets, both these schools of Cittamātra agree that external objects do not exist as entities with independent characteristics, that the internal mind does exist, and that intrinsic awareness is introverted, but they disagree as to whether appearances exist or do not exist as entities. Therefore, there are those such as the brahmin Śaṅkarānanda who say that phenomena cannot be nonentities because the objective aspect [of perception] consists simply of appearances or apparent things, while the subjective aspect is the bare essential nature, radiant and aware, like the diverse sensations of pleasure and pain. So they claim that all phenomena, being impermanent mental entities, exclusively constitute the dependent nature, while the imaginary nature denotes attachment to the idea that self is imputed in respect of these [phenomena].[264]

In this context, the traditions of those holding sensa to be veridical are threefold: (i) those holding that consciousness and its sensa are distinct (13.3.2.2.1); (ii) those holding that there are as many sensa as there are instances of consciousness (13.3.2.2.2); and (iii) those holding that sensa are diverse and that consciousness [and sensa] are without duality (13.3.2.2.3).

Those Holding That Consciousness and Its Sensa Are Distinct [13.3.2.2.1]

As to the first of these, there are some who hold that although the appearances of external objects such as mountains are indeed consciousness, they are substantially different from the consciousness that objectively appears. Thus, the appearance of blueness and the consciousness that apprehends blueness are both veridical in these two aspects [of perception] in a straightforward manner, just as when an egg has been hard boiled, the yellow part and the white part are distinctly present in a straightforward manner.

Those Holding That There Are as Many Sensa as There Are Instances of Consciousness [13.3.2.2.2]

As to the second, there are some who hold that just as a large number of sensa can be differentiated, so can the consciousness [that apprehends them]. Therefore it is impossible for two sensa to appear to a single consciousness. For example, the consciousness that apprehends the five fingers is veridical as five substances, but not veridical as a single substance.

Those Holding That Sensa Are Diverse and That Consciousness [and Sensa] are without Duality [13.3.2.2.3]

As to the third, there are those who hold that all sorts of diverse appearances such as blue and yellow or static and dynamic appear to a single consciousness, and that this essential nature is veridical, and indeed they hold that although an amalgam [of sensa] may manifoldly appear, these are the appearances of a single consciousness.[265]

The Philosophical System of Cittamātra That Holds Sensa to Be False [13.3.2.3]

Third, there is the description of the philosophical system of those holding sensa to be false, [which comments on the verse:]

Those claiming sensa to be false

Include some holding consciousness to be tainted
And others holding it to be immaculate.

The masters Dharmottara and so forth [hold that] all appearances within the range of extraneous awareness are not in any respect sense objects or consciousness, but the imaginary nature that appears corrupted due to fundamental ignorance.[266] It also says in the *Exposition of Valid Cognition:*

> The objects and subject of awareness and sensa are nonexistent,
> But, as hairs and so forth and consciousness are different,
> When, differentiated by the subject-object dichotomy,
> [Pure awareness] has corrupt characteristics of sensa
> Imposed upon it to the extent that these are seen through
> bewilderment,
> At that time it is indisputable
> That [pure awareness] assumes such characteristics
> Due to the dichotomy of subject and object.[267]

In their opinion, all that appears as sense objects, even in terms of relative truth, cannot be entities. There is not the slightest distinction between the diverse objects and appearances that arise in dreams and the objects that appear to direct perception. Rather, these appearances manifest ostensibly, not veridically, and last for a long or short time depending on propensities that may be stable or unstable. Accordingly they hold that external objects are false appearances and the subject that apprehends them is nonexistent, whereas the series of instances forming the self-luminous consciousness that realizes the subject-object dichotomy to be without duality does exist, even in ultimate truth.

They are divided into two schools: (i) those claiming that consciousness is tainted (13.3.2.3.1) and (ii) those claiming that it is immaculate (13.3.2.3.2). There are two distinctions between them; that is, distinctions during the causal phase and during the fruitional phase.

Those Claiming That Consciousness Is Tainted [13.3.2.3.1]

Among these, those claiming consciousness to be tainted hold that, in the context of sentient beings, consciousness exists in ultimate truth in its eight aspects, and they hold that the environment and its inhabitants distinctly appear in their entirety on the buddha level.

Those Claiming That Consciousness Is Immaculate [13.3.2.3.2]

Those claiming consciousness to be immaculate even in the context of sentient beings hold that the seven modes of consciousness that provisionally and adventitiously arise are relative, but that the substratum consciousness, here described as the "naturally innate consciousness," is ultimate because it is without increase or decrease and without disharmonious modes of apprehension. Even on the buddha level, when one has awoken from sleep and all bewildering appearances of sense objects have been interrupted, just as dreams are pacified, it is experienced that nothing at all appears and nothing at all is thought apart from mind. Abiding in this bare and naturally luminous intrinsic awareness, this is the buddha body of reality; and, through its blessings, although there are no entities, the entirety of the world and its inhabitants appears in the presence of those to be trained as the buddha body of form, which is omniscient, teaches the sacred doctrine, and manifests to act on their behalf.

Some of those claiming consciousness to be immaculate hold that all modes of conscious awareness distinct from that natural luminosity constitute relative truth.[268]

The Mādhyamika

Exegesis of the Philosophical Systems of the Mādhyamika [13.3.3]

The third [see above, p. 111] is the exegesis of the philosophical system of the Mādhyamika, which has two parts: (i) a general exegesis of the Svātantrika ("those employing independent syllogisms," 13.3.3.1) and a detailed exegesis of the Prāsaṅgika ("those employing consequential reasoning," 13.3.3.2).

A General Exegesis of the Svātantrika [13.3.3.1]

The former include (i) the lower Svātantrika (13.3.3.1.1) and (ii) the higher Svātantrika (13.3.3.1.2).

The Lower Svātantrika [13.3.3.1.1]

The former [comments on the verses]:

> **The lower sort [of Svātantrika] employing independent syllogisms**
> **Holds appearances to be empty in ultimate truth.**

The followers of Madhyamaka who employ independent reasoning bring an end to conceptual elaborations concerning existence and nonexistence by differentiating all knowable phenomena in terms of the two truths. Although they determine that ultimate truth is naturally pure and that phenomena resulting from past actions and so forth are not confused in relative truth, it is determined that they deviate from the thoroughly nonreferential

Madhyamaka of the real nature because they still remain attached to the advocacy that seeks to establish their own standpoints.

As far as the lower Svātantrika are concerned, although in general the Cittamātra ("mind only") position is known to the lower Svātantrika, they do not hold that knowable phenomena exist as intrinsic awareness[269] in ultimate truth.

When the texts [of the Svātantrika] are differentiated, there are two [perspectives], established as higher and lower, depending on whether they hold that in ultimate truth appearances are empty of inherent existence but with an apparitional nature, or whether they do not hold that standpoint. Therefore those who claim that the *Yogacaryā Level* is a Svātantrika text have not understood the point of this philosophical system.

According to the master Samudramegha and others, all phenomena are empty of inherent existence, and abide in an apparitional nature, in the essence of the two truths.[270] That is to say, the relative truth is nothing other than the amalgam of interdependent causes and conditions, deriving merely from conventional, causal effectiveness present in radiant [pure] appearances and in the essence of things as they appear to bewildering perception. Ultimate truth is empty of conceptual elaborations, including verbalizations concerning causes and conditions, or the absence of causes and conditions, and so forth, since the imputations of the relative are reversed. And yet, it is described as an apparition on the basis of its unimpeded radiance as dependent origination, in the manner of a reflection. Although the sense objects that manifest in meditative stability may assume the appearance of physical forms and so forth, these are mere appearances, arising in an apparitional manner, in which [distinctions of] identity and difference are quiescent. Therefore, once the apparitional goal of enlightenment has been attained by accumulating the two apparitional causal provisions, the perpetual abiding in this apparitional nature that ensues is [termed] meditative equipoise, and the apparitional enlightened activities that arise are then engaged for the benefit of apparitional sentient beings. If that were not the case, whether they are ultimately true or not at all, the path and liberation would come about without effort or attainment.

Although the lower Svātantrika do to some extent describe emptiness and so forth, it is just because the interdependent entities that appear do appear that all phenomena are true in a mere apparitional manner. From that perspective, it is appropriate that both the provisional and conclusive benefit of oneself and others is achieved through the gradation of renunciation and acceptance. It also says in the *Mother:*

> Although all phenomena pass into dreamlike and apparitional nirvāṇa, if there were anything superior to that dreamlike and apparitional nirvāṇa, I say that it too would be dreamlike and apparitional.[271]

And also in the *Sūtra of the King of Meditative Stability:*

> The skillful one who would enter accordingly
> Into ultimate truth that resembles a dream
> And into nirvāṇa that is similar to a dream,
> Is indeed said to be superior in mind control.[272]

And:

> Just as illusionists may emanate forms
> Before a crowd of ordinary people,
> Conjuring various horses, oxen, and wagons,
> While these diverse appearances are seen to be unreal,
> In the same way, all phenomena should be so known.[273]

And in the *Tantra of Hevajra:*

> Just as their intrinsic nature is originally nonarising,
> And is neither true nor false,
> All things are like the reflection of the moon in water,
> O Yoginīs, understand it as you will![274]

They hold that all things partake of two sorts of apparitional nature: (i) an impure apparitional nature that relatively appears but is inherently nonexistent in ultimate truth because it ceases when the path is concluded and (ii) a pure apparitional nature that comprises the appearances, without inherent existence, that are cultivated on the path and through which, in the result, the intrinsic essential nature of the indivisible buddha body of reality and the buddha body of form appear, without inherent existence, present in an apparitional manner in Akaniṣṭha, and from which apparitional emanations then emerge.

They also hold that, relatively, there is attachment to [the notion] that the apparitional interdependence of causes and conditions is true, whereas, ultimately, the apparitional and interdependent appearances are described as "the abiding nature that appears but is without conceptual elaboration or expression, liberated from the conceptual elaborations of the single and the multiple."[275]

The Higher Svātantrika [13.3.3.1.2]

Second, there is [the exegesis of] the higher Svātantrika, [which comments on the verse:]

> **The higher sort [of Svātantrika] employing independent syllogisms**
> **Holds that [ultimate truth] transcends existents, nonexistents,**
> **thought, and description.**

The masters Jñānagarbha, Śāntarakṣita, Kamalaśīla, and so forth, understood the enlightened intention of the Sage, establishing genuine reality as beyond extremes, and apparitional interdependent sensa, just as they abide, as the relative truth. They also investigated relative truth through valid cognition endowed with the threefold criteria,[276] which promotes independent reasoning, proving their own theses and refuting the theses of others. For example, when it is held that entities are permanent, they would say, "Taking entities as the subject for discussion, it follows that these are impermanent because they are created, as for example, a vase." After refuting [their opponents] in this way, they would then present the tenets consistent with their own independent reasoning, "Taking entities as the subject for discussion, they are impermanent because they are created, because they arise from causes and conditions."

As far as the two truths espoused by this tradition are concerned: They hold that that which accords with appearances is the relative truth, appearing diversely as mere interdependence and arising from extraneous [causes and conditions]. They agree with all the earlier Buddhist systems in holding that things arise from extraneous [causes and conditions]. The relative also includes the authentic relative truth in which appearances are causally effective, and the false relative truth in which appearances are not causally effective. It says in the [*Distinction between*] *the Two Truths:*

> Although correct and incorrect relative truth
> Are similar in appearance,
> They have been distinguished
> Because [the former] is causally effective
> And [the latter] is not causally effective.[277]

Since relative appearances are bewildering, they cannot be reversed until the pure level has been attained. Sublime beings call the latter "pure mundane [appearances]" since they are present in postmeditation, whereas for ordinary persons, [relative appearances] are present at all times. This is because, even when they are equipoised in the [paths of] provision and connection, the distinct appearances associated with the five gates of sensory consciousness are not interrupted. These diversely manifesting appearances are not [identified with] mind, in the manner of the Cittamātrins, nor are they [identified with] external objects, in the manner of the pious attendants, Rather, they appear to the mind as such, owing to bewildering propensities. Therefore, they hold that the defilements that are to be abandoned constitute the relative truth.

As far as ultimate truth is concerned, they hold that it cannot be established that [ultimate truth] is "not proven," as was previously the case when the nature of relative appearances was rationally[278] investigated, since there is no inherent existence of the single and the multiple and so it transcends objects of conceptual elaboration, description, and thought in respect of anything that could be existent or nonexistent, present or absent, proven or not proven, and so forth. It says in [Atiśa's *Introduction to*] *the Two Truths:*

> If one examines by reason
> How this relative truth appears,
> Nothing is found.
> This very finding of nothing constitutes ultimate truth,
> The reality that timelessly abides.[279]

And in the *Diamond Cutter:*

> Reality is not an object of knowledge.
> One cannot become conscious of it.[280]

And in the aforementioned [*Distinction between the Two Truths*]:

> The Omniscient One knows entities that exist
> And those that do not exist;
> Whatever he does not see[281]
> Should be examined very carefully
> As to what kind of entity[282] it is.[283]

Its mode of realization is as follows: Anything that is nonapprehensible consequent on analysis by means of discriminative awareness is ultimate. Realization ensues through the nonperception of anything at all by means of individual intrinsic awareness. It says in the *Mother:*

> Those who see through the nonperception of anything at all see the transcendent perfection of discriminative awareness.[284]

By knowing the two truths in this manner, after one has accumulated the two provisions—the provision of merit that is imbued with appearances in the context of relative truth, and the provision of pristine cognition, without appearances, in the context of ultimate truth—one will actualize the two buddha bodies: the buddha body of reality that is free from conceptual elaborations, for one's own benefit, and the apparitional buddha body of form, which appears for the benefit of others, and through which one acts for the benefit of others as long as cyclic existence endures.

They hold that while the buddha body acts by means of apparitional pristine cognition in postmeditative states, in ultimate truth, there is no buddhahood; nor is any act of benefit performed because the extreme of conceptual elaboration is transcended.

Whereas the lower Svātantrika hold that the ultimate is apparition and emptiness, here, they do not hold either [to be ultimate] because existence and nonexistence are transcended. The distinction is that rather than attributing truth to relative apparitions and entities, they say here that the very nature of that fiction, while being fictitious, is mere dependent origination, arising through causes and conditions.[285]

The Prāsaṅgika

Detailed Exegesis of the Prāsaṅgika [13.3.3.2]

The second is the detailed exegesis of the Prāsaṅgika ("those who employ consequential reasoning"). This comprises (i) a brief presentation (13.3.3.2.1) and (ii) an extensive exegesis (13.3.3.2.2).

Brief Presentation [13.3.3.2.1]

The former [comments on the verses]:

> **Those who employ consequential reasoning,**
> **In accordance with the conclusive enlightened intention,**
> **Are without tenets, in that all phenomena**
> **Constitute the emptiness of dependent origination—**
> **Beyond the extremes of the two truths,**
> **Where all conceptual elaborations cease.**

The tradition of consequential reasoning is established within Buddhism as the pinnacle of the [branch of the] great vehicle concerning defining characteristics. That is to say, the consequential reasoning of Madhyamaka ("middle way") incontrovertibly reveals the enlightened intention of the Sage, the transcendent lord [Buddha].

The original promulgator of this [tradition] was lord Nāgārjuna, who, as the Transcendent Lord had foreordained in the *Sūtra of the Great Drumbeat,* dispelled the obscuration of mistaken views by means of the immaculate sunlight of sublime discriminative awareness.

The commentators who elucidate the meaning contained in his texts, the sixfold *Collection of Reasoning,* include Āryadeva, Buddhapālita,

Bhāvaviveka, and Candrakīrti. Among them it was the sublime Candrakīrti, endowed with unbewildered discriminative awareness and compassion, who incontrovertibly comprehended the master's enlightened intention and then composed his commentary on the meaning of the *Fundamental Stanzas of the Middle Way,* entitled the *Introduction to the Middle Way,* and his commentary on the verses of that same text, entitled *Clear Word.* By generating the sunrise of the consequential reasoning of Madhyamaka, the conclusive enlightened intention of the buddhas throughout Jambudvīpa, he dispelled the obscurations of mistaken view.

Here I will present without error the summation of his texts: The essential disposition [of all things] is without inherent existence, and all standpoints professed by those who claim, in their own textual traditions, that [things] do inherently exist are contradictory in that they are fixated on the truth. All that is known within the texts of those who accept cogent evidence [for their standpoints] is refuted by this [method of consequential reasoning], but once the refutation has been established, the Prāsaṅgika do not, in the manner of those who employ independent reasoning, profess any definitive tenets. For it is understood that:

> If I were to maintain certain tenets,
> I would thereby be at fault,
> But since I am without tenets,
> I am absolutely without faults.[286]

The Extensive Exegesis [13.3.3.2.2]

The latter, the extensive exegesis [of those who employ consequential reasoning], comprises (i) a refutation of conceptual elaboration without accepting anything in the essential disposition [of reality] (13.3.3.2.2.1); (ii) a systematic presentation of the nonrefutation of conventional appearances (13.3.3.2.2.2); and (iii) a demonstration to others of the framework concerning acceptance and nonacceptance [of standpoints] (13.3.3.2.2.3).

A Refutation of Conceptual Elaboration without Accepting Anything in the Essential Disposition [of Reality] [13.3.3.2.2.1]

The first of these [comments on the verse]:

There are the five axioms of reasoning—namely,
The absence of the singular and the multiple,
The vajra fragments,
The absence of production from existence [and nonexistence],
The refutation of efficacious objects, and supreme relativity.
And there are three further axioms
Concerning permanence and imperishability,
Change and nonchange,
And the refutation of the four attributes [of birth, aging, duration, and cessation].

Since all things, from the moment of their appearance, whether they seem to change, arise, cease, or endure, and so forth, are without any inherent existence, in the manner of reflections; they are entirely divorced from premises concerning existence and nonexistence, and those who make them.

There are five great axioms (13.3.3.2.2.1.1) through which all the philosophical systems fixated on the truth, professed by those who propound entities, may be destroyed. These comprise (i) the axiom of the absence of the singular and the multiple (13.3.3.2.2.1.1.1); (ii) the axiom of the vajra fragments (13.3.3.2.2.1.1.2); (iii) the axiom of the absence of production from existence and nonexistence (13.3.3.2.2.1.1.3); (iv) the axiom of the refutation of efficacious objects (13.3.3.2.2.1.1.4); and (v) the axiom of supreme relativity (13.3.3.2.2.1.1.5).

There are also three further axioms (13.3.3.2.2.1.2)—namely, the axiom concerning permanence and imperishability (13.3.3.2.2.1.2.1); the axiom concerning change and nonchange (13.3.3.2.2.1.2.2); and the axiom that refutes the four attributes (13.3.3.2.2.1.2.3).

Five Great Axioms [13.3.3.2.2.1.1]

The Axiom of the Absence of the Singular and the Multiple [13.3.3.2.2.1.1.1]

According to the first axiom, taking that which appears as an object as the subject for discussion, it follows that it exists neither as an entity nor as a nonentity, owing to the absence of the singular and the multiple, just like the moon in water. This mode of absence resembles that which was previously described [in the section on Svātantrika]—the negandum is without independent defining characteristics because all things are indeed without inherent existence. However, in this context, it suffices merely to refute the superimposition of existence on that which does not exist. It says in the *Refutation of Disputed Topics:*

> Since the negandum is not at all existent,
> I do not refute anything at all.
> This is why the refutation takes effect.
> It is you who indulge in denigration.[287]

The Axiom of the Vajra Fragments [13.3.3.2.2.1.1.2]

According to the second axiom, taking anything as it appears as the subject for discussion, it follows that it is without substantial existence because there is an absence of production from causes, be they self, other, both, or neither, as in a dream. When a shoot is produced from a seed, due to [inherent] fallacy, it cannot be proven that substantial things are produced from causes that are both existent and nonexistent, and by implication, it is also invalid that production can take place from neither [existent nor nonexistent causes], because the extreme consequence of holding that things are produced without causes is that a lotus could implicitly arise from within the sky.

If there were production from an existent [cause], it could not be proven that things are produced from themselves, because [the notion of] a substantial thing that is both the object of production and the cause of production is contradictory. And if anything were produced from anything else, it is implicit that even darkness could be produced from flames, because they would be different [from each other].

If you then ask whether production occurs from extraneous things with an independent continuum, it is impossible for anything to be produced from a permanent cause, because it cannot be proven that a result is produced through a cause that does not change; and if [a result] is produced, the [posited] permanence would be untenable because [the cause] would have changed.

If anything were produced from an impermanent cause, since the cause would cease within an instant of time, no result could be produced because the cause would not be existent. Since even the encounter between cause and result is refuted, there is no encounter between them, and so the production [of results] from causes is nonexistent.

The Axiom of the Absence of Production from Existence and Nonexistence [13.3.3.2.2.1.1.3]

According to the third axiom, taking this diversity of things that appear as entities as the subject for discussion, it follows that they are not entities owing to the essential absence of production from existence and nonexistence. If a vase were produced at the time when it exists as a vase, we do not agree that there would be production, because the vase would already have come into existence. If it were produced at the time when it did not exist [as a vase], it is impossible for something that is existent to emerge from that which is nonexistent because such substances would be contradictory.

The Axiom of the Refutation of Efficacious Objects [13.3.3.2.2.1.1.4]

According to the fourth axiom, taking mere knowable phenomena as the subject for discussion, it follows that they do not exist as entities because they are not causally efficacious. At a given instant of time, [knowable phenomena] are not efficacious, because they will have ceased and become nonexistent at the time when they would start to be efficacious. As a series [of instants of time, knowable phenomena] would not be efficacious, because [the notions of] an instant of time and a continuum are contradictory.

The Axiom of Supreme Relativity [13.3.3.2.2.1.1.5]

As for the fifth axiom, taking mere appearances as the subject for discussion, it follows that they do not exist as entities, because they are interdependent, like a reflection. If entities had inherent existence, they would not emerge dependent on causes and conditions because they would already have existed as entities. This is logically entailed because anything that is interdependent is itself emptiness. Just as a horse or an elephant can appear, dependent on causes and conditions, when a wooden effigy and recitation of a spell coincide, but that [illusory] horse or elephant is empty, so whether things are coarse or subtle, when they appear in distinct forms dependent on each other, the former is empty and the latter is also empty because it has no inherent existence apart from the former. When a horse or elephant appears, it is empty because the forms—the wooden effigy and the spell—are nonexistent, and their essential nature is also empty in that the horse or elephant is nonexistent. It says in the *Fundamental Stanzas of the Middle Way:*

> There is nothing that is not dependently arisen,
> Therefore, there is nothing that is not empty.[288]

According to this approach, all things that diversely appear—mountains, mansions, men, and women—are empty because on a coarse level they do not exist apart from the amalgam of atomic particles, manifesting in and of themselves, and on a subtle level the intrinsic nature of indivisible time moments is empty of any continuum. Thus, things that are dependently arisen appear but are without inherent existence, and so one should know that they merely appear to be distinct. Things that appear to arise and so forth are of the intrinsic nature of emptiness. Nāgārjuna has said [in the *Fundamental Stanzas of the Middle Way*]:

> If there were the slightest thing not empty
> [How would it be empty!][289]

And:

> You have said that all that arises
> Resembles the emergence of a magical display.[290]

Things that appear to arise emerge in the manner of a dream, in that baseless sensa are distinctly apprehended. It says in the *Introduction to the Conduct of a Bodhisattva:*

> When entities do not exist,
> Their nonentity is clearly deceptive.
> Without contacting any entity to be investigated,
> Their nonentity cannot be apprehended,
> Just as when in a dream, a child has died,
> The thought that he is no more

Impedes the thought that he is alive,
But that [thought] is also deceptive.[291]

Three Further Axioms [13.3.3.2.2.1.2]

The Axiom concerning the Absence of Permanence and Imperishability [13.3.3.2.2.1.2.1]

As for [the first of the three further axioms]—the axiom concerning the absence of permanence and imperishability: taking mere appearances as the subject for discussion, these are nonexistent as entities because both perishable and imperishable things are nonexistent. Furthermore, if things were perishable, a vase would either be perishable at the time when it exists or perishable at the time when it does not exist. It cannot be perishable at the time when it exists because there is a contradiction in perishable existents becoming nonexistents; and it cannot be perishable at the time when it does not exist because it follows that it could not be established as perishable in that there is no possibility of a nonexistent substance. It is also nonexistent in terms of imperishability because it consists of indivisible time moments and atomic particles, and it appears as a flux of time. So it is that it cannot be established [as permanent and imperishable] because it is inconsistent for a single entity to be both existent and nonexistent. It says in the *Fundamental Stanzas of the Middle Way:*

For an entity that provisionally exists,
Cessation is not tenable.
For it is inconsistent[292] that in a single thing
Existence and nonexistence should coincide.
Neither is cessation tenable
For an entity that is nonexistent.[293]

The Axiom concerning Change and Nonchange [13.3.3.2.2.1.2.2]

As for the axiom concerning change and nonchange: taking mere appearances as the subject for discussion, it follows that they do not exist as entities because both change and nonchange are nonexistent. In that scenario, entities would either change or not change. If they did change, it follows that an old man could again become young because that would be a circumstance indicative of change. Also, it is established that permanent things do not change because that [premise] is refuted at the time when they become impermanent, so change is not proven. Nor indeed is there anything that could change—[any such thing] would be invalid when its details are investigated. And if they did not change, it follows that a young man could not become an old man. Change is also nonexistent because it is not proven that something becomes something else. It says in the *Fundamental Stanzas of the Middle Way:*

> Things do not change into something else,
> Nor do they even exist as something else.
> This is why young men do not become aged
> This is why aged men also do not become aged.[294]

Indeed, [such postulated changes] are not proven even when [one considers] oneself. A young man does not become aged because there is a material contradiction between [youth] and old age. Similarly, aged men do not age because there is a material contradiction in the time moments that constitute aging being causally effective, and because it would be pointless for one who has already grown old to age.

The Axiom That Refutes the Four Attributes [13.3.3.2.2.1.2.3]

As far as the refutation of the four attributes [of birth, aging, duration, and cessation] is concerned, this has already been explained in the section on the pious attendants (see above pp. 91–92).

So it is that all those who seek to prove substantialist premises are striving [pointlessly] to sustain a citadel that manifests in a dream—it would be much better for a fox not to kick against the jaws of a lion![295] The transcendent lord Buddha Śākyamuni praised as the most sublime among all exponents of Madhyamaka those who could pulverize the opinions of opponents by means of their respective arguments, whichever were appropriate. It says in the *Mother:*

> Subhūti! This reality is utterly profound. It should be known by those persons who are learned, lucid, and intelligent, but it is not within the range of sophists.[296]

And in the *Clear Word Commentary:*

> This should be elucidated by those who have been unagitated by the wind of well-crafted statements and sophistry.[297]

In this context, all those propounding substantialism are termed "sophists" because their standpoints are established on the basis of their respective notions.

The implementation of this approach [of consequential reasoning] is applicable in two contexts, when engaging in (i) the disputation of one another's philosophical systems (*phan tshun grub mtha' rnam par rtsod pa*) and when (ii) attaining liberation through the discriminative awareness of the path (*lam shes rab gyis grol ba*).

The Disputation of One Another's Philosophical Systems

When engaging in the disputation of philosophical systems, this is established by contradicting [the tenets] contained in the texts of the proponents of substantialism, without accepting any premise of one's own, and without having to prove any tenets or reject any criticism. As is said [in the above-cited verse from the *Refutation of Disputed Topics*]:

> If I were to maintain certain tenets,
> [I would thereby be at fault,
> But since I am without tenets,
> I am absolutely without faults.][298]

And also in the *Refutation of Disputed Topics:*

> If I were to apprehend certain things
> Through points of direct perception and so forth,
> Those proofs would be subject to refutation,
> But since I do not,
> I am without faults.[299]

Attaining Liberation through the Discriminative Awareness of the Path

When engaging, by means of the discriminative awareness of the path, in one's experiences of external objects that diversely appear, internal thoughts that diversely appear, thoughts of impermanence, meditative stabilities, and meditations and so forth, and in all [ordinary circumstances,] such as moving, sitting, eating, walking, liking, disliking, speaking, attending to morality, attending to immorality, lying down, sleeping, waking up, practicing the sacred doctrine, and so forth, one should analyze all things without activating them since one is without fixation on signs and without apprehension in all respects, and without making judgments and assumptions, such as "This is our philosophical system. This is another's philosophical system. This is cyclic existence. This is nirvāṇa. These are entities. These are nonentities. This is happiness and suffering. This is to be rejected and that is to be accepted. This is the sacred doctrine. This is not the sacred doctrine." Since the middle way is utterly without conceptual elaborations, akin to the meditative equipoise of the three kinds of sublime beings, this analysis is itself free from conceptual elaboration, like the nature of a reflection, or the nature of the moon in water, or a magical display. It says in the *Verse Summation* [*of the Transcendent Perfection of Discriminative Awareness*]:

> As when a carpenter or skilled craftsman has created
> A replica of a man or woman,
> And that [replica] can indeed perform all sorts of activities,
> Just so bodhisattvas who are skilled in practicing discriminative awareness
> Perform all sorts of activities through pristine cognition,
> Without conceptual thoughts.[300]

The Systematic Presentation of the Nonrefutation of Conventional Appearances [13.3.3.2.2.2]

The second part [of the extensive exegesis of those who employ consequential reasoning (see above p. 142)] is the systematic presentation of the nonrefutation of conventional appearances. This has three sections: (i) the middle way of the ground that concerns the two truths (13.3.3.2.2.2.1); (ii) the middle way of the path that concerns the two provisions (13.3.3.2.2.2.2); and (iii) the middle way of the result that concerns the two buddha bodies (13.3.3.2.2.2.3).

The Middle Way of the Ground concerning the Two Truths [13.3.3.2.2.2.1]

The first of these, concerning the essential nature and so forth of the two truths, [comments on the verse:]

> **The two truths [are considered in terms of] their essential nature,**
> **Etymology, defining characteristics, classification, and purpose.**

The essential nature is that all things are without inherent existence. The essential nature of the relative denotes objects conceived by the intellect and the sense faculties, and the essential nature of the ultimate denotes the objects of pristine cognition, particular intrinsic awareness, which are free from the extreme of conceptual elaboration, but both truths are without inherent existence.[301] It says in the *Introduction to the Middle Way:*

> Since both of the two truths are indeed without inherent existence, they are neither permanent [entities] nor nihilistic [voids].[302]

If one were to think that particular intrinsic awareness and the intellect are not identical, each [of these] may be true for one who is deluded with respect to symbols, however in this context it is the intellect that creates conceptual thoughts. As is said [in the *Introduction to the Conduct of a Bodhisattva*]:

> The intellect is held to demarcate the relative truth.[303]

Conceptual objects, sense faculties, and attentiveness constitute the relative, and these are exclusively bewilderment. Particular intrinsic awareness is the unbewildered pristine cognition, beyond speech, thought, and description. As is said in *Rāhula's Eulogy of the Mother* [contained in Ratnakīrti's *Eulogy to the Deities of Fourfold Union*]:

> Homage to the Transcendent Perfection of Discriminative Awareness,
> Beyond speech, thought, and description,
> The nonarising and unceasing essential nature of space,
> Within range of pristine cognition—particular, intrinsic awareness,
> Mother of the conquerors of the three times![304]

And in the *Litany of the Names* [*of Mañjuśrī*]:

> Your individual intrinsic awareness is unwavering;
> First in supreme [intrinsic awareness],
> You maintain the three buddha bodies.[305]

The analysis of the intellect and intrinsic awareness in terms of the [three] natures occurs in the context of Cittamātra. Here the context has been mistaken.[306]

As far as the etymology is concerned, the *relative* is defined as that which appears as a magical display but lacks inherent existence. This is said to be "truth" because the defining characteristic of its respective [appearances] is that they are provisionally unfailing in the face of bewilderment. It includes the diverse appearances that arise as objects of the intellect and all aspects of fixation on truth. As is said in the *Introduction* [*to the Middle Way*]:

> The relative [is so named] because the intrinsic nature
> is obscured by delusion.
> For this reason, the Sage has stated to be relatively true
> Any of its fabrications that seem to be true.[307]

Apparent objects are not proven to be true or false, bewildered or unbewildered, because they are without inherent existence. Rather, when fixation on the subject-object dichotomy occurs after thinking "This is the sense faculties; this is consciousness; this is phenomena," the apprehended or objective aspect [of this perception] is conceived as relative truth.

With regard to the etymology of the term *ultimate truth,* it is so termed because [the ultimate] is the goal toward which one strives, and the attributes of the path and the fruit are unfailingly true. It says in the *Mother:*

> The transcendent perfection of discriminative awareness should be realized and cultivated. Unsurpassed attributes are attained through its total cultivation. Therefore, the ultimate [goal] of the bodhisattvas is the transcendent perfection of discriminative awareness.[308]

As far as their defining characteristics are concerned, phenomena and reality have an essential nature of purity and sameness, beyond conceptual elaborations, devoid of intellect and signs. It says in the *Fundamental Stanzas of the Middle Way:*

> This is the peace that cannot be known extraneously
> And it cannot be elaborated by conceptual elaboration.
> Without conceptual thought and without differentiation,
> This is its defining characteristic.[309]

The defining characteristic of relative truth is that it cannot tolerate scrutiny of phenomena that do not transcend the objects of the intellect. The defining characteristic of ultimate truth is quiescence focusing on the reality that transcends the intellect. It is incorrect that it can withstand scrutiny, as has already been refuted above.[310]

As far as the classification is concerned, there are both the relative truth and the ultimate truth. It says in the *Sūtra of the Meeting of Father and Son:*

> There are two truths that understand the world. You should not listen to others! Look yourself![311]

According to the distinctions of truth and falsehood that are applied to relative appearances through mundane convention—aspects of semantics—there are authentic relative appearances, comprising sights, sounds, odors, tastes, tangibles, and mental phenomena that manifest as the apparent objects of those with the six kinds of unimpaired [sense perception], and there are false relative appearances, including the blurred vision and hairs that may appear to those disturbed by impaired [sense perception]. It says in the *Introduction [to the Middle Way]*:

> Any object of the six unimpaired sense faculties
> Is understood by the world to be true

From the perspective of the world itself,
And the remainder are held to be erroneous
From the perspective of the world itself.[312]

As far as the purpose is concerned, it says in the [*Distinction between*] *the Two Truths:*

Those who know the distinction between the two truths
Are undeluded with respect to the Sage's teaching.
Having gathered all provisions, without exception,
They will reach the excellent goal.[313]

The Middle Way of the Path concerning the Two Provisions [13.3.3.2.2.2.2]

The second [section of the systematic presentation of the nonrefutation of conventional appearances] is the middle way of the path concerning the two provisions. [It comments on the verse:]

Skillful means engage in the provision of merit,
And discriminative awareness engages in the provision of pristine cognition.

Dependent on the relative truth, skillful means engage in the experiential cultivation of the six transcendent perfections and so forth, which constitute the provision of merit, and dependent on the provision of pristine cognition, discriminative awareness engages in the cultivation of the meaning of luminosity, the ultimate pristine cognition. Luminosity denotes the inner awareness or pristine cognition free from conceptual elaborations, due to the pacification of the engagement of mind and its mental states. It says in the *Transcendent Perfection of Discriminative Awareness in Eight Thousand Lines:*

That mind is not the mind. The intrinsic nature of mind is luminosity.[314]

It is experientially cultivated in the following manner: Sitting cross-legged, on a comfortable seat, one should [recite the verses] of taking refuge and setting the mind [on enlightenment]. Then, in a state of total relaxation, wherever the mind falls, one should place the mind in an utterly nonconceptual state, clear, vibrant, undistracted, and free from ebbing and flowing in respect of anything whatsoever. In that mind that engages in cultivation, free from the subject-object dichotomy, devoid of external entities since there is no thought of external objects and devoid of internal entities since there is no thought of the internal mind, there is neither refutation nor proof. Since nothing is established other than that, it is therefore said that there is nothing apprehensible before the mind. This nature of awareness, present within the pristine cognition of individual intrinsic awareness without objective referent, is the focus of the following verses from the *Introduction to the Conduct of a Bodhisattva:*

> When neither entities nor nonentities
> Are present before the mind,
> At that time since there are no external sensa,
> Without apprehension, it will become calm.[315]

Afterward, with reference to appearances that manifest in the manner of a magical display and are without inherent existence, the dedication should be made for the sake of sentient beings who resemble a magical display.

When the session [of meditation] has been completed, without the slightest attachment or clinging in respect of the nature of these magical appearances, one should strive to accumulate the provision of merit in conjunction with acts of prostration, circumambulation, recitation of the discourses, the making of terra-cotta imprints, the offering of consecrated water, and so forth.

Once the mind that grasps entities and the ebbing and flowing of its thoughts have become calm due to meditative equipoise focused on reality, even the subjective apprehension of reality as an object to be cultivated will become calm. It says in the same text [*Introduction to the Conduct of a Bodhisattva*]:

> Through familiarity with the propensity for emptiness,
> The propensity for accepting entities will be relinquished.
> Through familiarity with the state of nothing-at-all,
> Even that [propensity for emptiness] will subsequently be
> relinquished.[316]

When [the mind] has been calmed by placing it in the disposition where notions of "I" and of entities do not arise, even the focus on reality, which is the antidote bringing about the abandoning [of the subject-object dichotomy], will become calm, so that one will arrive at the transcendent perfection of discriminative awareness and will no longer be fixed within the meditative concentration that cultivates this state. It says in the *Verse Summation* [*of the Transcendent Perfection of Discriminative Awareness*]:

> Once perceptions have been destroyed and relinquished, one will reach transcendence.[317]

During postmeditation, by striving in respect of the two provisions and their appearances, one will achieve provisional benefits and all conclusive wishes will be fulfilled.

The Middle Way of the Result concerning the Two Buddha Bodies [13.3.3.2.2.2.3]

The third [section of the systematic presentation of the nonrefutation of conventional appearances] is the middle way of the result concerning the two buddha bodies. [It comments on the verse:]

> **For one's own benefit the buddha body of reality [will be achieved],**
> **And for others' benefit, the buddha body of form [will be achieved].**

At the conclusion of the continuum of the ten levels when the causal basis of cyclic existence, comprising the engagement of mind and mental states along with their propensities, has been calmed and dissolves into the expanse of reality, then the buddha body of perfect resource and the genuine buddha body of reality are actualized, manifesting to ordinary persons through the volition of sentient beings and through the power that fulfills the former aspirations of the buddhas, like the moon in water. The buddha body of perfect resource then manifests to sublime bodhisattvas, so that enlightened deeds are spontaneously accomplished in the manner of the supreme vase of gems or the wish-fulfilling tree. This actualization of the buddha body of reality for one's own sake and the buddha body of form for the sake of others is the genuine result. It says in the *Introduction to the Middle Way:*

When the dry brushwood of all that is knowable is burnt,
The peace that results is the buddha body of reality of the
conquerors.
At that time there is neither arising nor ceasing.[318]

And:

The peaceful buddha bodies are radiant like the Wishing Tree.
They are nonconceptualizing in the manner of the Wish-Fulfilling
Gem.
Ever remaining to guide the world until beings have been
liberated,
They appear to those who are free from conceptual elaboration.[319]

The Demonstration to Others of the Frameworks for the Acceptance and Nonacceptance of Standpoints [13.3.3.2.2.3]

The third part [of the extensive exegesis of those who employ consequential reasoning] is the demonstration to others of the frameworks for the acceptance and nonacceptance [of standpoints]. This has three sections: (i) the framework for the nonacceptance [of standpoints] (13.3.3.2.2.3.1); (ii) the framework for the acceptance [of standpoints] (13.3.3.2.2.3.2); and (iii) the synthesis (13.3.3.2.2.3.3).

The Framework for the Nonacceptance of Standpoints [13.3.3.2.2.3.1]

The first of these is the framework for the nonacceptance [of standpoints, which comments on the verse]:

Through nonacceptance, one is free from any acceptance whatsoever.

For adherents of the Madhyamaka, there is nothing at all to be accepted because the [middle way] is the circumstance pertaining to the meditative equipoise of the three kinds of sublime beings and because it is without tenets. It is said that ultimately they follow the meditative equipoise of sublime beings and relatively they follow mundane [conventions], and on that basis they do not accept anything at all. However, that is incorrect.

Although there is no acceptance of any [standpoint] in Madhyamaka, adherents of the middle way indeed accept that their goal is appraisable, and they also accept meditative equipoise since they say that it resembles the circumstance of the three modes of meditative equipoise of sublime beings. In ultimately following the meditative equipoise of sublime beings, leaving aside the attributes of the path and fruit, the attributes of the ground are indeed unknown because they cannot be instantaneously appraised. However, you may ask, can they be instantaneously appraised by the mind of an omniscient being? Although it might seem that they can be appraised by the buddhas who manifest extraneously, this standpoint is precluded because the unappraisable would be extraneously manifest.

It is [also] incorrect [to say] that they follow mundane [conventions] during postmeditation. Mundane beings lack the practice of a spiritual path, and they lack the framework through which liberation is sought. Since it would enmesh in further bewilderment the bewilderment that is fixated on truth with regard to perceptions of attachment and aversion that freely arise if they were to pursue that [mundane convention], it very much follows that the middle way of the path and fruit would not emerge.

The Framework for the Acceptance of Standpoints [13.3.3.2.2.3.2]

The second is the framework for the acceptance [of standpoints, which comments on the verse]:

> **Ultimately nothing is proven,**
> **But relatively [the framework of phenomena] is accepted.**

It is also incorrect to say that ultimately they do not accept [standpoints] because nothing is proven but relatively they do accept the framework of phenomena as it has been described. If they were to seek and accept a standpoint, holding the contradiction that that which does not ultimately exist does conventionally exist, then anyone could accept that the ultimate is distinct from the conventional, and the higher [reality] distinct from lower [appearances]. Since there would be a substantial contradiction pertaining to existence and nonexistence, this ineffectual tenet does not accord with the tradition of Great Madhyamaka.

The Synthesis [13.3.3.2.2.3.3]

The third is the synthesis [that comments on the verse]:

> **Acceptance and nonacceptance pertain to the relative,**
> **But not to the ultimate.**

Those who do not see the partial consistency and the partial inconsistency in both of these positions have indeed not understood the meaning of the scriptures. Although flaws are present in both acceptance and nonacceptance and there is therefore no tenet that can be determined one-sidedly, here the matter should be understood as follows: Since, for the adherents of consequential reasoning, acceptance and nonacceptance are present in terms of the relative truth, and there is no analytical framework for acceptance and nonacceptance in ultimate truth, it should be understood that both acceptance and nonacceptance are provisionally applied due to distinctions made in the context of relative or conventional [appearances].

When in the course of debate the ultimate is apprehended, there is nothing to be accepted because it is not accepted that any appearance is present in the fundamental state, without inherent existence. But when conventional [reality] is apprehended in the context of the postmeditation of the path, as explained in the scriptures and their analyses, it should be personally examined and considered, having understood that its tenets are merely dreamlike or illusory.

By demonstrating this to others, after apprehending and differentiating things that are to be adopted and rejected, one should then enter upon the middle way of the path that concerns the two provisions and accomplish the two fruitional buddha bodies.

The first of these, the context of nonacceptance has indeed been described in the [aforementioned] verses [from the *Refutation of Disputed Topics*] that begin:

> If I were to maintain certain tenets . . .[320]

The second, [the context of] acceptance, has also been mentioned by the master Candrakīrti in the *Clear Word Commentary:*

> Like a vessel for those who desire water, at first the relative truth should be accepted unquestionably.[321]

And in his *Commentary on the Introduction* [*to the Middle Way*]:

> Learned persons have considered this point to be faultless and endowed with enlightened attributes. It should be accepted unquestionably.[322]

Since [scholars] of the past did not differentiate these two approaches, I [Longchen Rabjam] can perceive merits and defects in both—nonacceptance being pure[323] and acceptance resembling a peacock [of multicolored hue]. Therefore, I, to some extent, do not think that these [two one-sided standpoints] reflect the definitive meaning of the scriptures.

This [discussion] has clearly exposed meanings that are hidden and dispersed within the scriptures by means of the broad vision originating from analytical intelligence and inspection of most textual traditions. In the future, those who know how to establish such tenets will understand how to probe this text of mine.

These points conclude the exegesis of the approach of consequential reasoning, according to Great Madhyamaka. In sum, this completes my determination of the vehicle of causal characteristics.

Epilogue

The Vaibhāṣika among the pious attendants
Who follow the *Treasury of Detailed Exposition,*
The Sautrāntika who follow the discourses,
The hermit buddhas [who dwell in solitude] like a rhinoceros,
And all those who go about in groups, large and small,
Having abandoned the sufferings of cyclic existence,
Strive for the peace and happiness of release.
The Yogācārins and Cittamātrins,
Both those holding sensa to be veridical and false,
And the Mādhyamika who employ independent reasoning
And who employ consequential reasoning
Have all renounced their own benefit
And strive for the buddha level,
Exclusively for the benefit of others.
Since it makes the two provisions into the path
In order that buddhahood might be achieved,
The vehicle of the transcendent perfections,
Which is that of causal characteristics,
Comprises three aspects: lesser, middling, and greater.

This section was compiled by Longchen Choying Tobden Dorje in order that the four philosophical systems and so forth, which are associated with the vehicle of causal characteristics, might be ascertained. May virtue prevail!

BOOK 13, PART 3
The Philosophical Systems of the Fruitional Vehicles

Herein is contained Book 13, Part 3 (GI) from *The Extensive Commentary of the Precious Treasury of Sūtra and Tantra, concerning the Philosophical Systems of the Fruitional Vehicles.*

THE GOLDEN KEY

In order that one might become skilled in
the vehicles of mantra,
This book contains an elucidation of the distinctions
Between the four classes of outer and inner tantra.

VERSE OF HOMAGE

Homage to the eighty great accomplished masters of India, the twenty-five of Tibet including King [Trisong Detsen] and his subjects, and so forth, who possessed the accomplishments of the secret mantra![324]

The fourth main topic [see above, p. 5] concerns the vehicle of indestructible reality (13.4). This has three parts: (i) an exegesis of the distinctions between sūtra and mantra (13.4.1); (ii) an exegesis of the system of the three outer classes of tantra (13.4.2); and (iii) an exegesis of the system of the three classes of inner tantra (13.4.3).[325]

The Distinctions between Sūtra and Mantra

An Exegesis of the Distinctions between Sūtra and Mantra [13.4.1]

The first of these [comments on the verse]:

> **There are fifteen distinctions of mantra over sūtra,**
> **Concerning view, conduct,**
> **Meditative stability based on mental [focus],**
> **Cause, path, fruition, level, time, resources, yoga, benefit,**
> **Purpose, difficulty, and provisions.**
> **The attainment of the nucleus is the mystery**
> **Of buddha body, speech, and mind.**

It says in the *Tantra of the Inconceivable Rali Cakrasaṃvara:*

> In the lesser vehicle that includes the pious attendants,
> There are no pith instructions.
> The vehicle of the awareness holders is superior
> Owing to fifteen distinctive features:
> The distinctions of its view, conduct, and mental focus,
> Of its cause, fruition, path, and level,
> Of its time, resources, and yoga,
> Of its self- and other-oriented benefits, and its intention,
> Its renunciation of laborious extremes, and its ease,
> And its accumulation of the provisions.[326]

Distinction of View [13.4.1.1]

In the dialectical approach, the view is merely that of emptiness, free from conceptual elaboration, and apart from that, there is no realization of the indivisible truth that is primordially present in the nature of deity and mantra.[327] The mantra approach does realize this. That is to say, it realizes that the relative reality, where appearances are actually nonexistent and merely emanations, purified as deities, and the ultimate reality, which is the timeless expanse and pristine cognition without duality, are both indivisible in a disposition, originally without inherent existence. It says in the *Sequence of the Path of Magical Emanation:*

> In the great maṇḍala of sameness
> Where relative and ultimate realities are inseparable . . .[328]

Indeed, the five psycho-physical aggregates are pure as the [male] deities,[329] as is said in the *Tantra of the Presence of Pristine Cognition:*

> Physical forms are Vairocana,
> Feelings are Ratnasambhava,
> Perceptions are Amitābha,
> Formative predispositions are Amoghasiddhi,
> And consciousness is Akṣobhya.[330]

The five elements are also pure, as the [corresponding] female deities, as the same text says:

> The five elements are in actuality the five female deities.
> All psycho-physical aggregates, sense fields, and sensory elements,
> Owing to their total purity, constitute the buddha fields.[331]

And in the *Secret Nucleus* from the *Net of Magical Emanation:*

> The tathāgatas themselves knew all things to be primordial buddhahood.[332]

Distinction of Conduct [13.4.1.2]

Regarding conduct, in the dialectical approach, there is nothing but the dualistic acceptance [of virtuous actions] and rejection [of negative actions], whereas the mantra approach is superior because, based on the disposition of the deities and their celestial palace, which have an intrinsic nature of apparitional purity and sameness, there are rituals and so forth associated with the communion offerings and the protector deities, as explained in the context of each respective maṇḍala. Exemplified by these, there are [other modes of conduct] including offerings to the deities, as well as conduct that conforms to the nature of reality and conduct based on the purity of afflicted mental states.

Distinction of Meditative Stability Based on Mental Focus [13.4.1.3]

With regard to meditative stability based on mental focus, the dialectical approach requires perseverance with great hardship to focus the mind for long periods of time in order to achieve calm abiding and higher insight, whereas the mantra approach is superior because conceptual elaborations are pacified through the symbolic generation stage [of meditation] and then pristine cognition arises simply by refining the focal points of the energy channels and winds [within the subtle body] in the context of the nonsymbolic perfection stage.

Distinction of Cause [13.4.1.4]

With regard to cause, in the dialectical approach, it is held that ultimate reality is realized, having previously gone through [the causal processes] of relative reality, where generative causes give rise to generated results. The mantra approach is superior because it engages with the realization of ultimate truth at the present moment through the powerful introduction to the pristine cognition that intrinsically abides as the cause of purity or the cause of separation [from obscuration], and then through cultivating that [pristine cognition].

Distinction of Path [13.4.1.5]

With regard to the path, in the dialectical approach, the five paths will not be traversed for aeons because in the accumulation of the two provisions [of merit and pristine cognition], meditative equipoise and postmeditation alternate, whereas the mantra approach is superior because the path of pristine cognition in which these two are indivisible is swiftly traversed by those who enter upon it.

Distinction of Fruition [13.4.1.6]

With regard to the fruition, in the dialectical approach it is held that the goal will emerge in the future, after a long period of time, whereas the mantra approach is superior because it is held to abide spontaneously present, here and now.

Distinction of Level [13.4.1.7]

With regard to the levels [of spiritual realization], in the dialectical approach it is held that the levels number eleven, based on the differentiation between the successive factors to be eliminated and their respective antidotes, whereas the mantra approach is superior because there are three additional levels—namely, (i) the level of the indivisible essence on which the expanse and the real are spontaneously present; (ii) the level of the supreme pristine cognition of purity and sameness in which the two stages [of meditation] are genuine luminosity; and (iii) the level of the pure, supreme phenomenon of spontaneous presence that is the fruition of great purity. Alternatively, the mantra approach is superior because, over and above the [eleven] causal levels, there is the twelfth level named "unattached lotus endowed," the thirteenth level named "vajra holder," and so forth. The *Secret Nucleus* alludes to this in the following verses:

> The extraordinary levels, comprising the ten [causal levels]
> And the three [fruitional levels] . . . [333]

Distinction of Time [13.4.1.8]

With regard to time, through the dialectical approach, one will not attain accomplishment for three "countless" aeons[334] and the like, whereas the mantra approach is superior because, with perseverance and pure commitments, one can attain accomplishment in this lifetime. It says in the *Prophetic Declaration of Enlightened Intention:*

> Whatever the buddhas have come to know
> Over extremely long "countless" aeons,
> The *mantrins* [know] all at once.
> They may attain perfect enlightenment in a single lifetime.[335]

Distinction of Resources [13.4.1.9]

With regard to resources, in the dialectical approach attainment comes after the desirable attributes of the senses have been renounced, whereas their assistance is cultivated through the mantra approach. It says in the *Array of Indestructible Reality:*

> The five desirable attributes of the senses,
> Which are debasing and from which renunciation ensues,[336]
> Are of most excellent assistance to skilled *mantrins*.
> Fortunate ones should relish them to the utmost.[337]

Distinction of Yoga [13.4.1.10]

With regard to yoga, in the dialectical approach a nonreferential, sky-like emptiness is cultivated during meditative equipoise and in postmeditation the yoga of illusoriness is carried onto the path, whereas the mantra approach is superior because the inconceivable yoga in which these are indivisible is carried onto the path.

Distinction of Benefits That Are Self- and Other-Oriented [13.4.1.11]

With regard to the achievement of benefits that are self- and other-oriented, through the dialectical approach nothing more than provisional or slight benefit can be achieved, whereas the mantra approach is superior because it can benefit others by bringing good auspices to the environment, for example, alleviating famine by causing a downpour of rain, or, through the practice of yoga, causing a cascade of food, drink, and gemstones, healing diseases and calming disturbances. It can also benefit oneself as one's inner realization and meditative stability progress higher and higher, each moment, through the inconceivable two stages [of meditation].

Distinction of Intention [13.4.1.12]

With regard to intention, in the dialectical approach nothing is known apart from the mere causal vehicles, whereas in the mantra approach the great mystery of the fruition is ascertained. It says in the *Indestructible Peak:*

> The defining characteristic of all the mantras
> Is the mind of all the buddhas.
> Since they cause the nucleus of reality to be attained,
> They are genuinely endowed with reality's expanse.[338]

Distinctions of the Renunciation of Laborious Extremes, and of Ease [13.4.1.13–14]

With regard to the renunciation of laborious extremes due to the absence of difficulty, [the mantra approach] is superior to the dialectical approach because the great fruition will be achieved with little hardship, as has already been explained in the words:

> [The mantra approach has] many methods and is without difficulty.[339]

Distinction of the Accumulation of the Provisions [13.4.1.15]

With regard to the distinctions in their accumulation of the provisions, in the dialectical approach the ordinary provisions take a long time [to accumulate] because they entail nothing but the mere six transcendent perfections, including mere generosity and mere ethical discipline. On the other hand, the mantra approach is extensive because all things are understood to be buddha fields and so anything that is experienced may be included within the provisions. It is ennobling because material resources are understood to be nectar, it is supreme because the intrinsic nature [of all things] is realized to be one of purity and sameness, and the two provisions are swiftly gathered and perfected because afflicted mental states are naturally pure without having to be renounced. Therefore, liberation will be achieved through a single lifetime. Similarly, just as the skillful means [of the mantra approach] are superior, so the discriminative awareness established by these[340] skillful means is also known to be superior when one practices the path.

The causal vehicles are so-named because it is held that through the dialectical approach of the causal [vehicles] the "nucleus of the sugata" that is present as a mere seed of buddha nature will be enhanced through the condition of the two provisions and in this way buddhahood will be attained. This is because they hold that there is a temporal sequence of cause and result.[341] This nucleus [i.e., the seed of buddha nature], according to the mantra approach, is held to be naturally and spontaneously present in all sentient beings, fully endowed with extensive[342] enlightened attributes, as the ground of purification, exemplified by the sun. The object of this purification is the intrinsic nature of cyclic existence that has been obscured by the eight modes of consciousness including the substratum, as if by clouds. The means of purification include the empowerments and the generation and perfection stages [of meditation] through the cultivation of which provisional enlightened attributes will be attained by a process of gradual refinement, exemplified by the dispelling of clouds. The result of this purification is the actualization of the genuine substratum, radiant like the sun. Since at that time there are no preceding stains, the substratum and its propensities are nominally reversed, but it is clear that no actual temporal sequence is distinguished. Accordingly, it says in the *Two Part* [*Tantra of Hevajra*]:

> Sentient beings are themselves buddhas.
> However this has been obscured by adventitious stains.
> Once eliminated, they are themselves buddhas.[343]

And in the *Ornament of the Sūtras of the Great Vehicle:*

> There are indeed no distinctions of temporal sequence.
> The real nature is pure.[344]

Other Distinctions [13.4.1.16]

There are also other distinctions. Although [both approaches] are identical in their attainment of fruitional buddhahood, there is a distinction in terms of their means of attainment between one that is deluded and one that is not deluded. According to the dialectical approach, delusion persists with regard to awareness that arises through the reversal of attachment to the truth of external appearances, through the cultivation of [those appearances] as a magical display, and so forth. Delusion persists with regard to the abiding reality because the inner aggregates are not understood to be deities. Delusion persists with regard to the aspects of the path because it is not understood that the secret amalgam of ideation and afflicted mental states is pristine cognition; and delusion persists with regard to the view of realization because it is not understood that all things are the indivisible truth of purity and sameness. In the mantra approach, on the other hand, the five elements of external appearance are the five female buddhas, the [five] aggregates of internal appearance are the five male buddhas, and the amalgam of ideation comprises the five pristine cognitions, embodied in the bodhisattvas. This approach is indeed superior because the indivisible truth establishes the inhabited world and its inhabitants as a great buddha field of purity and sameness. It says in the [*Tantra of the Secret Nucleus,* from the cycle of the] *Net of Magical Emanation:*

> The aspects of the aggregate of indestructible reality
> Are known as the five perfect buddhas.
> All the manifold sense fields and sensory elements
> Are the nature of the maṇḍala[345] of bodhisattvas.
> Earth and water are Buddhalocanā and Māmakī.
> Fire and wind are Pāṇḍaravāsinī and Samayatārā.
> Space is Dhātvīśvarī.
> The three planes of existence are primordial buddha fields.[346]
> All things that there are without exception
> Are not extraneous to the buddhas themselves.
> Phenomena extraneous to the buddhas themselves
> Have not been found by the buddhas themselves.[347]

The Mysteries of Buddha Body, Speech, and Mind [13.4.1.17]

In brief, one should know that the mystery of buddha body is carried onto the path, the mystery of buddha speech is carried onto the path, and the mystery of buddha mind is carried onto the path. It says in the *Tantra of the Presence of Pristine Cognition:*

One should know that the supreme secret mantras
Are absolutely superior to the causal great vehicle,
Owing to the great mysteries of the paths
Of buddha body, speech, and mind.[348]

In the dialectical approach, buddha body denotes nothing but the intrinsic nature of illusory appearance and engagement in virtuous actions through ordinary physical activities. However, the mantra approach is superior because the mystery of buddha body denotes the perfection of appearances and existences as deities and their celestial palace, and of the ordinary body as a maṇḍala, while dynamic gestures of sealing, dance movements, and so forth, are also carried onto the path.

In the dialectical approach, buddha speech denotes emptiness, in the manner of an echo, and the engagement in virtuous actions through ordinary speech, either in the context of recitation or when it is controlled and interrupted [so that silence prevails]. However, the mantra approach is superior because the mystery of buddha speech denotes the understanding that sounds and melodies are the intrinsic nature of the Sanskrit vowels and consonants, causing a cascade of the sacred doctrine, while ordinary speech abides primordially as the maṇḍala of buddha speech, enabling sounds and words to arise naturally as mantra, and goals to be achieved through the unimpeded capacity of [mantra] recitation.

In the dialectical approach, buddha mind denotes the sealing [of the realization] that memories and thoughts are without inherent existence, while calm abiding and higher insight are achieved by reversing and deliberately blocking the ebbing and flowing thoughts of the ordinary mind. However, the mantra approach is superior because the memories and thoughts of buddha mind arise as the display of reality, and on that basis, ordinary mind arises as the naturally radiant and naturally present pristine cognition, achieving meditative stability in a continuous stream of yoga. Thus, buddha mind is spontaneously present in the maṇḍala, which arises nonconceptually.

The Three Outer Classes of Tantra

Exegesis of the System of the Three Outer Classes of Tantra [13.4.2]

The second part [of this fourth main topic] is the exegesis of the system of the three outer classes of tantra. This [comments on the verses]:

> **[The tantras of] action emphasize conduct,**
> **[The tantras of] conduct give equal weight**
> **To both [physical rites and mental meditation].**
> **[The tantras of] union emphasize meditation, with conduct as an aid.**

Tantra of Action [13.4.2.1]

As far as the sequence of the tantra of action is concerned: Tantra of action, *kriyā* [in Sanskrit], is grounded in the understanding that appearances and emptiness are the two truths. During the path, there are disciplines such as the habitual practice of bathing and ablution, partaking of the three dairy products, and changing the three kinds of attire.[349] On this basis, one should meditate on oneself in the form of [the visualized deity, i.e.,] the being of commitment as a servant, and on the deity such as Avalokiteśvara in front, as a noble master or king, and one should maintain [this practice] by means of mantra recitation, fasting rituals, and so forth. It is held that through this sequence [of the tantra of action], buddhahood will be actualized within sixteen lifetimes.

Tantra of Conduct [13.4.2.2]

As far as the tantra of conduct is concerned: In the tantra of conduct, alternatively rendered in Sanskrit as *ubhayatantra* ("tantra of both"), the view is that oneself and the deity are both of equal status. While visualizing oneself as the being of commitment and the deity in front as the being of pristine cognition,[350] the garland of mantra letters exits one's own mouth and enters into the mouth of the deity, before exiting from the navel [of the deity] and reentering through one's own navel in a cyclical movement. Then, after reciting [the mantra syllables], the being of pristine cognition departs and one should meditate on the ultimate reality, without conceptual elaboration.

This [tantra of conduct] is also known as the "vehicle of the tantra of both" because its conduct resembles that of the tantra of action and its engagement resembles that of the tantra of union.

Tantra of Union [13.4.2.3]

As far as the tantra of union is concerned: In the tantra of union, which is rendered as *yogatantra* in Sanskrit, the performance of ablutions is merely an aid, and, rather than that, the main practice emphasizes meditation on the deity as the nature of mind. After generating oneself as the being of commitment, one engages by means of the five awakenings[351] until the being of pristine cognition enters into [the visualized being of commitment]. That is to say, after taking refuge and setting the mind [on enlightenment], emerging from the disposition of emptiness, (i) the causal basis of accomplishing the excellence of buddha field and location is the awakening that derives from [visualizing the deity's] seat with its lotus and moon cushions; (ii) the causal basis of the excellence of the sacred doctrine is the awakening that derives from the [visualized] seed syllables of buddha speech; (iii) the causal basis of the excellence of time, which is permanent and inconceivable, is the awakening that derives from the [visualized] hand-held emblems of buddha mind; (iv) the causal basis of the excellence of retinue is the awakening that derives from the [visualization of] the complete buddha body [of the deity], along with its maṇḍala circle; and (v) the causal basis of the excellence of the essential nature of buddha body is the awakening that derives from [the visualization of] the deity as the being of pristine cognition. Once these five awakenings have been secured by means of the four seals—namely, the commitment seal, the doctrinal seal, the action seal, and the great seal, the rites[352] will be completed. After the being of pristine cognition has departed, the [visualized] being of commitment should be dissolved.

Having cultivated the generation [stage] by means of these three classes of outer tantra, one should cultivate the perfection stage [of meditation] as follows: Meditate on phenomenal appearances that constitute relative truth as the deity. Then, when that [visualization] has also settled into the nonreferential state, meditate on the ultimate truth that is without conceptual elaboration. The experiential cultivation should focus alternately on these two truths in a temporal sequence.

The Three Inner Classes of Tantra

Exegesis of the System of the Three Inner Classes of Tantra [13.4.3]

Third, there is the exegesis of the system of the three inner classes of tantra. This has three parts: (i) an explanation of the distinctions between the outer and inner mantras (13.4.3.1); (ii) a description of the father tantras, the mother tantras, and the nondual tantras (13.4.3.2); and (iii) a description of the pith instructions: the Great Perfection (13.4.3.3).

An Explanation of the Distinctions between the Outer and Inner Mantras [13.4.3.1]

The first of these [comments on the verse]:

> **The inner [classes of tantra] are distinguished**
> **From the outer [classes of tantra]**
> **In terms of their ground, path, fruition, food, clothing,**
> **Deities, [the ornaments] that are worn, their locale,**
> **And their [associated] rites.**

One should know that the intrinsic nature of the unsurpassed way of secret mantra that constitutes the inner class of mantra is superior to the outer class of mantra on the basis of three distinctions—namely, (i) the distinction of the ground comprising maturational empowerment (13.4.3.1.1); (ii) the distinction of the path comprising the generation and perfection stages [of meditation] with conduct as an aid (13.4.3.1.2); and (iii) the distinction of the fruition that is the time of liberation (13.4.3.1.3).

Distinction of the Ground Comprising Maturational Empowerment [13.4.3.1.1]

The outer [classes of tantra] place great emphasis on the vase empowerment, whereas the inner [classes of tantra] place great emphasis on the three other empowerments.[353] Those three [action, conduct, and union tantras] that are established as outer[354] because they are shown to be effective through the entrustment of awareness, permission ritual, and the vase empowerment are [collectively] called the "vehicle of the austere outer tantras" because they partly resemble the dialectical approach in their acceptance and rejection of certain things, and in their renunciation and antidotes. On the other hand, the vehicle of inner secret mantra is so called because the mental continuum is brought to maturity by means of four precious empowerments—namely, (i) the vase empowerment; (ii) the secret empowerment; (iii) the empowerment of discriminating pristine cognition; and (iv) the word empowerment, and because it can carry anything at all onto the path as skillful means, without acceptance or rejection.

Distinction of the Path Comprising the Generation and Perfection Stages [of Meditation] with Conduct as an Aid [13.4.3.1.2]

As for the distinction in their meditation on the path: When one meditates on the perfection [stage] alternating with the elaborate generation stage, that accords with the outer [class of tantra]. When the generation and perfection stages are integrated without conceptual elaboration, that accords with the inner [class of tantra]. The outer class is that which employs conduct as an aid or habitually practices bathing and ablution. The inner class is that which engages in sameness.

Distinction of the Fruition That Is the Time of Liberation [13.4.3.1.3]

So it is that followers of the outer classes do not swiftly attain liberation, even though they may strive over a long period of time. Each of the outer classes can attain their respective fruition, over sixteen lifetimes, through the [tantras of] action, over seven lifetimes, through [the tantras of] conduct, and over three lifetimes, through [the tantras of] union. They cannot, as in the inner [classes of tantra], attain [liberation] through extreme perseverance in a single lifetime, or during the intermediate state [after death]. It says in the *Presence of Pristine Cognition:*

> By ascetic discipline, fasting, control,
> And meditating on the form of a deity,
> Endowed with various hand-held emblems,
> The practitioner will not become accomplished.[355]

Other Distinctions [13.4.3.1.4]

Moreover, there is a distinction in the foods that they may enjoy. The followers of the outer classes of tantra are those who place great emphasis on the three dairy products and the three sweet things.[356] The inner classes are those that emphasize the five meats and the five nectars.[357]

There is a distinction in the clothing they wear. The followers of the outer classes of tantra are those who place great emphasis on new clothes, whereas the inner classes are those that emphasize the wearing of human hides, or nudity, without clothing.

There is a distinction between the activities in which they engage. The followers of the outer classes of tantra are those who place great emphasis on bathing and ablution, whereas the inner classes are unharmed by wear and tear, or by impurity.

There is a distinction in the deities of the maṇḍala. The followers of the outer classes of tantra do not meditate on the deities in union, whereas followers of the inner classes do meditate on the male and female consorts in union.

There is a distinction in the ornaments they wear. The followers of the outer classes of tantra are those who place great emphasis on silken and gemstone ornaments, whereas the inner classes emphasize bones and human skulls as ornaments.

There is a distinction in their locale. The followers of the outer classes of tantra are those who meditate in pure and isolated places, such as Mount Sumeru, whereas the followers of the inner classes are those who meditate in Oḍḍiyāna or in charnel grounds.

There is a distinction in their water-offering bowls. The followers of the outer classes of tantra conceive of them as containers of precious gems or as a basin of lotus flowers, whereas the inner classes emphasize skull cups.

There is a distinction in their rites of enlightened activity. The followers of the outer classes of tantra are those who emphasize the rites of pacification and enrichment, whereas the inner classes emphasize the rites of subjugation and wrath.

Father, Mother, and Nondual Tantras

Description of the father tantras, the mother tantras, and the nondual tantras [13.4.3.2]

Second, there is the description of the father tantras, the mother tantras, and the nondual tantras [that comments on the verses]:

> **There are father tantras of skillful means**
> **In which the generation stage [of meditation],**
> **[The refinement of] subtle winds,**
> **And the rites of wrath are emphasized.**
> **There are mother tantras of discriminative awareness**
> **In which the perfection stage [of meditation],**
> **[The refinement of] the generative essences,**
> **And the rites of subjugation [are emphasized].**
> **And there are nondual tantras**
> **In which the nonduality of the generation and perfection stages [is emphasized].**

The tantras that emphasize the generation stage [of meditation] and [the refinement of] subtle winds during the perfection stage, and extensively demonstrate the rites of sorcery and diverse [associated rites] are the father tantras. Those that emphasize the perfection stage [of meditation] and discriminative awareness dependent on [the refinement of] generative essences, and also emphasize the rites of subjugation are the mother tantras. In brief, the differentiation between father tantras and mother tantras is made on the basis of their respective [emphases on] skillful means and discriminative awareness, generation and perfection stages, and vastness and profundity; and it is also explained in human terms, that these tantras are twofold from the perspective of training on the basis of the twofold gradation of masculine and feminine. It says in the *Indestructible Tent:*

> In order to train those with masculine traits
> Endowed with skillful means,
> The father yogatantras are explained.
> In order to train those with feminine traits
> Endowed with discriminative awareness,
> The mother yogatantras are subsequently explained.[358]

Those that equally demonstrate the generation stage of skillful means and the perfection stage of discriminative awareness in order that the intrinsic nature of both [stages] might be experientially cultivated in like manner, and that emphasize that all things are, through their natural disposition, the pristine cognition endowed with luminosity are termed the "glorious nondual tantras."

In the *Glorious Secret Assembly, the Slayer of Death,* and other such [father tantras], it says that the essence of the path is the pristine cognition of nondual profundity and radiance. In the *Cakrasaṃvara,* the *Four Indestructible Seats,* and other such [mother tantras], it says that the essence of the path is the pristine cognition of coemergent bliss and radiance. In the *Wheel of Time* and the *Net of Magical Emanation* [and other such nondual tantras], it says that the essence of the path is the pristine cognition of nonconceptual luminosity.

The Great Perfection

Description of the Pith Instructions: The Great Perfection [13.4.3.3]

Third, there is a description of the pith instructions: the Great Perfection. This has four sections: (i) the superiority of the Great Perfection over the generation and perfection stages (13.4.3.3.1); (ii) the class of mind characterized by diversity (13.4.3.3.2); (iii) the class of space characterized by primordial liberation (13.4.3.3.3); and (iv) the particularly sublime class of esoteric instructions (13.4.3.3.4).

The Superiority of the Great Perfection over the Generation and Perfection Stages [13.4.3.3.1]

Among these, the first [comments on the verses]:

> **[The lower vehicles] are contrived and changeable,**
> **But [the Great Perfection] is not.**
> **The eight [lower] vehicles are themselves deviations and obscurations.**
> **There is a distinction in that [here there is no duality]**
> **Of view and conduct, or cause and result,**
> **And in that the three buddha bodies are naturally established.**
> **Mind's creations, excellent and perfect in all respects,**
> **Are subsumed in, arise from, and abide in [its natural disposition].**

Here it is held that the nature of mind, the expanse that is intrinsically pure, luminous, and spontaneously and timelessly present in a state of supreme natural abiding, is the ground, uncontrived and unchanging in naturally occurring pristine cognition.[359] In contrast, all the lower vehicles have obscured naturally occurring pristine cognition with the veil of hope and doubt because they engage in acceptance and rejection through their striving that is contrived and corrupt. They have no opportunity to reach the fundamental reality. It says in the *Tantra of the All-Accomplishing King, the Enlightened Mind, the View Equal to Space:*

> O Great Being, Listen!
> The three teachings of the three types of teachers within my retinue
> Are obscure owing to their deviations.
> If you ask how this is so,
> The six vehicles of definitive attainment
> Are shown to be deviations from the Great Perfection.
> If one asks how this is so,
> The sūtras of the bodhisattvas
> Posit the level of Universal Light.
> Through ideation and scrutiny concerning the two truths,
> They hold reality to be empty as space.
> The supreme bliss of Atiyoga, however,
> Is the enlightened mind transcending ideation and scrutiny.
> That which transcends ideation and scrutiny is obscured by the sūtras.
> Ideation and scrutiny, according to the Great Perfection,
> Are explained to be the deviation of the sūtras.
>
> Kriyātantra posits [the level of] the vajra holder.
> Having entered through the portal of the three purities,
> One abides in the purity of the subject-object dichotomy.
> The supreme bliss of Atiyoga, however,
> Is the enlightened mind transcending the subject-object dichotomy.
> That which transcends the subject-object dichotomy
> Is obscured by Kriyātantra.
> Engaging in the subject-object dichotomy, according to the Great Perfection,
> Is explained to be the deviation of Kriyātantra.
>
> Concerning the view and conduct of Ubhayatantra,
> Conduct is as in Kriyātantra

And attainment is as Yogatantra.
Since it is senseless to connect that view and that conduct,
One does not realize the nondual truth.
The supreme bliss of Atiyoga, however,
Is the enlightened mind without duality.
That which is free from dualism is obscured by Ubhayatantra.
That which engages in dualism, according to the Great Perfection,
Is explained to be the deviation of Ubhayatantra.

Yogatantra posits the Bounteous Array.
Having entered through the portal of symbolic and nonsymbolic [methods],
It emphasizes the four seals.
But it cannot enter that which is without acceptance and rejection.
The supreme bliss of Atiyoga, however,
Is the enlightened mind, without acceptance and rejection.
That which is without acceptance and rejection is obscured by Yogatantra.
Engaging in acceptance and rejection, according to the Great Perfection,
Is explained to be the deviation of Yogatantra.

Mahāyoga posits [the level of] Vajradhara.
Having entered through the portal of skillful means and discriminative awareness,
In the pure maṇḍala of one's own mind,
One achieves the four phases of the approach and attainment.
The supreme bliss of Atiyoga, however,
Is the enlightened mind beyond striving.
That which transcends striving is obscured by Mahāyoga.
Striving, according to the Great Perfection,
Is explained to be the deviation of Mahāyoga.

Anuyoga posits indivisibility.
Having entered through the portal of the expanse and pristine cognition,
One views phenomena, however they appear,
As the cause that is the pure expanse,

And one views the result as the maṇḍala of pristine cognition.
The supreme bliss of Atiyoga, however,
Is the enlightened mind transcending cause and result.
That which transcends cause and result is obscured by Anuyoga.
To behold a duality of cause and result, according to the Great
Perfection,
Is explained to be the deviation of Anuyoga.[360]

Natural Great Perfection, the essential nature of the luminous expanse, is the naturally occurring pristine cognition. Since it is devoid of produced results and productive causes, along with their conditions, it is atemporally present, like the intrinsic nature of space. This is also indicated in the following verses from the *Supreme Continuum of the Great Vehicle:*

Subsequently, just as it was before,
Is the unchanging reality.[361]

And:

Unconditioned and spontaneously present . . .[362]

Ultimate truth, the luminous expanse that is unchanging and empty like space, cannot be delimited as anything whatsoever, whether changeable, pure, or impure. Since it appears and its radiance is spontaneously present, this is not restricted,[363] but is comparable to [the vastness of] the solar and lunar discs. Since its essential nature is without cause and result, it cannot be delimited at all as cyclic existence or nirvāṇa. Since it is the ground of anything at all that arises, it is distinguished as the "expanse" or pristine cognition,[364] the source or support of all phenomena. This itself is the ground, but the lower vehicles have deviated from and obscured it by engaging in striving, attainment, rejection, and acceptance.

When it is said that the ground is made into the path, since the uncontrived and unchanging ground cannot be made into anything, the ground has not actually been made into the path; for that would entail a contradiction between ground and path. Under that scenario there would never be a time when the fruition is attained because the nature of mind that is like space and need not be contrived or modified would have become corrupted. It says in the *All-Accomplishing King:*

O Great Being!
The view and conduct of the Great Perfection
Are unlike achievements based on causes and results.
This enlightened mind, comprising view and conduct,
Has an intrinsic nature similar to space.
Space transcends ideation and scrutiny.
Those who engage in ideation and scrutiny
Will not achieve enlightenment, which is like space.
The emergence of both ideation and scrutiny
Is the deviation and obscuration [of the sūtras].[365]

Those who engage in the subject-object dichotomy
With respect to view and conduct,
Which are of the intrinsic nature of space,
Will not achieve enlightenment,[366] which is like space.
The emergence of both aspects of the subject-object
dichotomy
Is the deviation and obscuration [of Kriyātantra].

The dichotomy of view and conduct has emerged,
But just as space is without duality,
Enlightenment is without duality.
Those who engage in dualism
Will not achieve enlightenment,[367] which is like space.
The emergence of both view and conduct
Is the deviation and obscuration [of Ubhayatantra].

Enlightenment has an intrinsic nature similar to space.
In space there is no acceptance or rejection.
Those who engage in acceptance and rejection
Will not achieve enlightenment, which is like space.
[The emergence of both][368] acceptance and rejection
Is the deviation and obscuration [of Yogatantra].

Enlightenment has an intrinsic nature similar to space.
In space there is no striving or achievement.
Those who engage in striving or achievement
Will not achieve enlightenment, which is like space.

Striving and achievement are the deviation
And obscuration [of Mahāyoga].

Enlightenment has an intrinsic nature similar to space.
In space there is no cause or result.
Those who view the dichotomy of cause and result
Will not achieve enlightenment, which is like space.
The viewing of cause and result is the deviation
And obscuration [of Anuyoga].[369]

In ultimate reality, the expanse that is essentially pure, there are no causes and results; and yet, since all that is conditioned, including impure cyclic existence and [the attributes of] the path, is generated through causality and shown to perish on the basis of [various] conditions, it would seem important to take causality into account. However, it is revealed that fundamental reality is not contrived by the scriptural transmissions of any doctrine concerning causes and conditions, acceptance and rejection, or especially by the ten natural aspects of the outer and inner mantras. The same source (*All-Accomplishing King*) indeed says:

There is no view to be cultivated, no commitment to be guarded,
No level to be refined, no path to be traversed,
No enlightened activity to be vigorously pursued,
No empowerment to be conferred,
No efforts of body, speech, or mind,
No maṇḍala to be generated,
And as in space, there is no duality of cause and result.[370]

And:

Enlightened mind is timelessly unerring.
Being timeless, it is timelessly unerring.
Do not superimpose truth and falsehood upon that which is unerring.
This transcends all causes, conditions, results, striving, and achievements.
If without knowing that it has already been accomplished
And is beyond striving and achievement,

One were to regard it as something to be accomplished
By meditation that engages in striving and achievement,
There would be no greater obstacle to enlightenment than that.[371]

On the other hand, if buddhahood is not held to be attained once the stains covering the seeds [of buddha nature] have been refined through acceptance and rejection on the path, one might wonder how it does come about, and what is the difference between it and the ordinary [state of mind]? The naturally occurring pristine cognition, the Great Perfection itself, has no need to search elsewhere because the supreme attributes of primordial buddhahood are spontaneously present, and so the three buddha bodies are naturally complete in and of themselves. It is therefore revealed that [buddhahood] will itself be attained without wavering from that uncontrived state, just as it is. The same source (*All-Accomplishing King*) also says:

O Great being, listen!
The buddha body of reality is enlightened mind.
Apart from enlightened mind,
The buddha body of reality cannot in the slightest
be contrived by anyone.
Therefore, there is no buddhahood apart from the mind.
The buddha body of perfect resource is enlightened mind.
And the buddha body of perfect resource derives from
enlightened mind.
The forms that arise from mind have no other embodiment
Apart from the buddha body of perfect resource.
The buddha body of emanation is enlightened mind.
No acts of benefit for living beings are undertaken elsewhere
Apart from the emanations of enlightened mind.
All the buddhas of the three times, too,
Are none other than enlightened mind.
The buddhas of the past have previously seen and realized
This uncontrived natural mind.
The buddhas who are alive at present,
By realizing the uncontrived natural mind,
Just as it is, without contrivance,
Indeed perform acts of benefit for living beings, here and now.
The buddhas who will appear in the future

Are not foreordained [to attain] this natural mind,
The nature of enlightened mind,
As something that was once contrived.
Even now the mind is not contrived through meditative stability
But reached by entering into the uncontrived path.[372]

And in the *Secret Nucleus:*

From any of the four times and ten directions,
The perfect buddha will not be found
The nature of mind is the perfect buddha.
Do not search elsewhere for the buddha![373]

And:

Though sought, none is found by the conquerors.[374]

Therefore, the nature of mind, the unwavering buddha body of reality, the enlightened mind, is the intrinsic nature of the Great Perfection, beyond laborious striving. It says in the *All-Accomplishing King:*

Mind is the definitive essential nature.[375]
All phenomena are present in that real nature.
Do not contrive that definitive state!
Do not accomplish anything other than the essential nature!
If they were to search, the conquerors
Would not find anything else within the expanse.
Now there is no need to create that which has already been created.
Without trying to accomplish now
That which has already been accomplished,
Settle in equanimity, without conceptual thought,
And without intending anything![376]

Naturally occurring pristine cognition, free from conceptual elaborations, is the summit because the meanings of all vehicles are completely perfected therein, without restrictions or pitfalls. It says in the *All-Accomplishing King:*

> Perfect in one, perfect in two, perfect in mind.
> Perfect in one, it is perfection in mind's creations.
> Perfect in two, it is perfection in excellent attributes.
> Perfect in all, it is perfection in enlightened mind.[377]

In this regard, the term "mind's creations" denotes all phenomena subsumed in the aggregates, sensory elements, and sense fields that manifest as the inhabited world and its inhabitants—the apparitional and impure cyclic existence, as well as all attributes that are designated in terms of view, meditation, and conduct—the ground, path, and result associated with the [diverse] vehicles. All these propensities of mind are bewildering because they are adventitiously created by the artistry of the mind. Although they seem to be true since they arise at the present moment as the bewildering apprehension of bewildering appearances, they are actually without inherent existence and thus they are perfect because they do not deviate from the state of naturally occurring pristine cognition.

The term "perfection in excellent attributes" denotes the luminosity of naturally occurring pristine cognition. Its essence is the empty buddha body of reality, its natural expression is the buddha body of perfect resource, and its compassionate spirituality is the buddha body of emanation. These three buddha bodies are perfect because one does not need to strive and achieve them extraneously, in that they are fully present, timelessly and naturally.

The term "perfection in enlightened mind" denotes that all phenomena that manifest and exist, however pure or impure they appear, are subsumed in the disposition of fundamental, naturally occurring pristine cognition, they arise from that disposition, and they abide within that disposition, just as a person's sleep and the dissimilar images that appear in dreams are subsumed in the disposition of awareness, arise from that disposition, and abide dependent on that disposition. So it is that [all things] are perfect in the nature of mind, the enlightened mind.

The term "mind" denotes the thought patterns that arise from the substratum as the eight modes of consciousness, for which reason it is tainted and to be purified. However, it should be recognized that terms such as "enlightened mind," "nature of mind," "luminosity," "genuine aspect of mind," "nonconceptual pristine cognition," "expanse [of reality]," "buddha body of reality," "ultimate truth," "real nature," and "great perfection" denote the naturally occurring pristine cognition, the nucleus of enlightenment, which is the conclusive essence to be sought.

The Class of Mind

The Class of Mind Characterized by Diversity [13.4.3.3.2]

The second section [of the exegesis of the Great Perfection] concerns the class of mind characterized by diversity (13.4.3.3.2), propounding that the ground is penetrated. This has seven aspects: (i) the perspective of mind holding the fruition to be the mind's point of origin (13.4.3.3.2.1); (ii) the perspective of mind that has determined deviation and obscuration (13.4.3.3.2.2); (iii) the perspective of mind that shatters the authenticity [of conventional appearances] by means of rational axioms (13.4.3.3.2.3); (iv) the perspective of mind that does not descend into partiality or bias (13.4.3.3.2.4); (v) the perspective of mind concerning dogmatic philosophical systems (13.4.3.3.2.5); (vi) the perspective of mind transcending dogmatism about that which is free from the intellect (13.4.3.3.2.6); and (vii) the perspective of mind that speaks in terms of things being perspectives of mind (13.4.3.3.2.7).

The Perspective of Mind Holding the Fruition to Be the Mind's Point of Origin [13.4.3.3.2.1]

The first of these [comments on the verse]:

> **[According to the class of mind,]**
> **From the standpoint of their nonexistence,**
> **[Mind's creations] do not waver,**
> **And from the standpoint of their appearance,**
> **They have originated, abide, and will dissolve.**

Regarding the perspective of mind holding the fruition to be the mind's point of origin: The fruition is said to be the original expanse [of reality]. The nature of mind is without transition or change because reality is unchanging. Apparent phenomena that manifest as mental images are timelessly liberated and abide as spontaneously present manifestations of the ground of liberation. The entirety of the inhabited world and its inhabitants comprising the three world systems that are perceived in bewilderment do not actually exist and yet they do appear. From the standpoint of their nonexistence, they have not wavered, do not waver, and will not waver from the ground. Therefore they are devoid of the intrinsic characteristics of impurity. From the standpoint of their appearance, initially they originated from the expanse [of reality], presently they abide within that expanse, and finally they will dissolve into that expanse. In the manner of a miraculous event in the sky, they are said to be settled in the ground, spontaneously present without beginning or end. Since they are timelessly settled, they are not restored to an original state or liberated by means of an antidote. Since they are naturally settled, there are no actual antidotes. Since they do not require effort, they are held to be spontaneously present, in their diversity, free from limits and extremes.

The Perspective of Mind That Has Determined Deviation and Obscuration [13.4.3.3.2.2]

The second, the perspective of mind that has determined deviation and obscuration, [comments on the verse:]

> **It is determined that there is a single state of evenness**
> **In which causes, conditions, renunciations, and antidotes are groundless.**

The eight [lower] sequences [of the vehicle] are not established to be authentic because they have been designated by the intellect and they have deviated from[378] the ground. According to this perspective, naturally occurring pristine cognition, essentially free from the intellect, is the reality that has transcended causes and conditions, the great, primordial emptiness that is held to be without recollection, thought, or bias. Although the inhabited world and its inhabitants, comprising the entirety of phenomenal existence, manifests as if it were impure, initially they have not originated from anywhere—their source is groundless. Presently they do not abide anywhere—there is no abode and nothing that abides. Finally, they will not go anywhere—there is nowhere to go and nothing that goes. Therefore, even that which is called[379] "bewilderment" is nonexistent, apart from its mere name. In the fundamental state, the supreme liberation that is the ground of the three world systems, opinions concerning liberation, bewilderment, being, or nonbeing are nonexistent, and so there is held to be a single state of evenness, in which things to be renounced and antidotes to be applied are groundless.

The Perspective of Mind That Shatters the Authenticity [of Conventional Appearances] by Means of Rational Axioms [13.4.3.3.2.3]

The third, the perspective of mind that shatters the authenticity [of conventional appearances] by means of rational axioms, [comments on the verse:]

> **Apparent and imputed phenomena are primordially liberated,**
> **Their authenticity shattered.**

Since this mind, the ground, cannot be identified, there is no authenticity in the mind that imputes things that "originate from its disposition." There is nothing in the slightest that can be identified. All apparent and imputed phenomena,[380] manifest though nonexistent, are primordially liberated in a single state that shatters their authenticity. Therefore actions and propensities are without support. There is no creator of actions and propensities since even the mind that accrues them is not found, nor can the maturation and fruition of actions be established because whenever actions that have been accrued are indeed examined, no reason for their existence can be identified. Therefore, cyclic existence abides in great primordial liberation, where even its name is nonexistent. From the nonarising expanse that is the nature of mind or naturally occurring pristine cognition, pristine cognition openly arises in an unceasing display, giving rise to the conviction that there is nothing to reject, accept, refute, or establish. Since the rational axioms that reality is primordially empty and a great liberation from extremes intuitively arise from within, this is held to be liberation in a single pervasion throughout the extent of cyclic existence and nirvāṇa.

The Perspective of Mind That Does Not Descend into Partiality or Bias [13.4.3.3.2.4]

The fourth, the perspective of mind that does not descend into partiality or bias, [comments on the verse:]

> **Cyclic existence and nirvāṇa are not established**
> **As different or even indivisible.**

Since the essential nature of naturally occurring pristine cognition encompasses the extent of cyclic existence and nirvāṇa, all that diversely appears, pure or impure, originates as a display arising from pristine cognition. Although things actually appear as such owing to the unimpeded energy [of awareness], essentially cyclic existence and nirvāṇa cannot be established as different, identical, or even indivisible. They do manifest in our perception as different, but their intrinsic nature is pure. They do not fall outside the view of pervasive, primordial perfection, the churning of the depths of cyclic existence and nirvāṇa. It is held that since there is no descent into the partiality of existence and nonexistence, appearance and emptiness, this is the reality without activity, transcending happiness and suffering.

The Perspective of Mind concerning Dogmatic Philosophical Systems [13.4.3.3.2.5]

The fifth, the perspective of mind concerning dogmatic philosophical systems, [comments on the verse:]

> **This is nothing at all, but it manifests as the diversity of appearances.**

Since in the perspective of mind the essential nature is not perceived, it does not abide in any aspect of cyclic existence or nirvāṇa. It is the expanse [of reality], naturally occurring pristine cognition, in which nothing at all exists, and in which anything at all can arise. All that arises manifests as the display of mind. This presence is nothing at all, but it manifests as the diversity of appearances. It is held that all things—appearances and mind—have an intrinsic nature that is beyond laborious effort because they are primordially and naturally liberated without restrictions or partiality.

The Perspective of Mind Transcending Dogmatism about That Which Is Free from the Intellect [13.4.3.3.2.6]

The sixth, the perspective of mind transcending dogmatism about that which is free from the intellect, [comments on the verse:]

> **Free from the intellect, the things that appear are naturally free, transcending dogmatism.**

The naturally occurring pristine cognition that is free from the intellect does not exist as a real entity and since things that appear are naturally arising, the concepts present within the intellect are naturally free, transcending dogmatism. That is to say, things appear just as they appear, and it is held that they do not exist as truth or falsehood, but are a display of great liberation from the extremes of being and nonbeing.

The Perspective of Mind That Speaks in Terms of Things Being Perspectives of Mind [13.4.3.3.2.7]

The seventh is the perspective of mind that speaks in terms of things being perspectives of mind, [which comments on the verse:]

> **Phenomenal appearances are the essenceless display of mind.**

It is held that the world and its inhabitants manifesting as phenomenal appearances diversely appear because they are the display of mind, but the nature of mind is essenceless, and so its diverse manifestations are also essenceless. This therefore implies that phenomena,[381] whether manifest or imputed, are nonexistent. Although both the subjective mind that arises and its objective appearances that emerge seem to differ, they are actually indivisible in reality, the naturally occurring pristine cognition, where they are not anything at all; and so it is held that that which manifests as phenomena[382] is a display of the mind. The display of mind originates from the mind, manifests to the mind, and arises from the mind, and yet the nature of mind is essenceless; it is not held that this is either identical to, or different from, its display, but rather it is simply demonstrated that things appearing as external objects do not exist as external objects. For this reason, the distinctive feature of this perspective is that although everything arises as pure or impure, nirvāṇa or cyclic existence, depending on whether or not it is recognized to arise from naturally occurring pristine cognition, the locus [of mind] from which [the display] arises[383] and [the display] that arises are actually pure in the expanse [of reality].[384]

The Class of Space

The Class of Space, Propounding That the Fruition Is Primordial Liberation [13.4.3.3.3]

The third section [of the exegesis of the Great Perfection] concerns the class of space, propounding that the fruition is primordial liberation. This has two aspects: (i) [an exegesis of] its essential nature (13.4.3.3.3.1) and [an exegesis of] its subdivisions (13.4.3.3.3.2).

Exegesis of Its Essential Nature [13.4.3.3.3.1]

The former [comments on the verse]:

> **[According to the class of space,] pristine cognition,**
> **The essential nature [of mind], and all phenomena**
> **Are supreme primordial liberation.**

The naturally occurring pristine cognition and all things that arise from its disposition are the supreme natural purity of primordial liberation. That is to say, although things do exist, naturally arising as diversity, they do not exist in that they are primordially liberated in their primordially pure fruition. Therefore, it is not simply established [as in the class of mind] that there is mind and the display of mind. Within awareness that is a great freedom from perspectives concerning existence and nonexistence, one should let appearances manifest, let them arise, and let them vanish. Although one may have examined whether they are pure or impure, and so forth, from the moment when they manifest, their essential nature is a great panorama of primordial liberation, beyond existence, nonexistence, being, and nonbeing. Having determined that philosophical systems that impute rigid concepts can be appraised in diverse ways, and are inherently empty and bewildered, it is held that from the moment things appear or arise, there is an infinite evenness, limitless like space, in which all things are supremely equal.

Exegesis of Its Subdivisions [13.4.3.3.3.2]

The latter, the classification, comprises (i) the black space speaking in terms of the absence of causes (13.4.3.3.3.2.1); (ii) the variegated space speaking in terms of diversity (13.4.3.3.3.2.2); (iii) the white space speaking in terms of [the nature of] mind (13.4.3.3.3.2.3); and (iv) the infinite space determining causes and results (13.4.3.3.3.2.4).

The Black Space Speaking in Terms of the Absence of Causes [13.4.3.3.3.2.1]

The first of these [comments on the verse]:

> **The black space, when classified, comprises**
> **Enlightened deeds, compassionate spirituality, and emanation.**

The essential nature of the black space is naturally occurring pristine cognition that is unchanging and beyond causes and conditions in its natural perfection. Since it is not fragmented, it refers neither to apparent phenomena nor to their reality. When classified, it comprises (i) the black space of enlightened deeds (13.4.3.3.3.2.1.1); (ii) the black space of compassionate spirituality (13.4.3.3.3.2.1.2); and (iii) the black space of emanation (13.4.3.3.3.2.1.3).

The Black Space of Enlightened Deeds [13.4.3.3.3.2.1.1]

As to the first, [the black space of enlightened deeds,] when [emanational things] that arise diversely from within the expanse of naturally occurring pristine cognition have arisen, their manifestations that appear impartially are naturally empty, and therefore lack causes and conditions with independent characteristics. From the moment of their manifestation, they are liberated, so that cyclic existence and nirvāṇa are gathered together therein, their names no longer existing. Through the axiom of equanimity with regard to standpoints of being and nonbeing,[385] the Great Perfection is established as freedom from limits and extremes.

The Black Space of Compassionate Spirituality [13.4.3.3.3.2.1.2]

As to the second, [the black space of compassionate spirituality,] since [emanational things] that arise are pristine cognition, knowledge is not dependent on something else and because liberation is the nature of mind, this transcends causes and conditions. Since [emanational things] that arise and are liberated are present without duality, the fruition itself is present as primordial liberation. Through the axiom of natural purity with regard to common appearances,[386] the Great Perfection is held to be manifest and primordially liberated.

The Black Space of Emanation [13.4.3.3.3.2.1.3]

As to the third, [the black space of emanation,] from the moment when naturally occurring pristine cognition and all the phenomena that are its display manifest, they are free from fixed perspectives of being and nonbeing, and do not exist as a duality of self and other. They are present without cause in primordial purity and do not depend on being created or contrived. By means of the primordial sealing in primordial liberation of equanimity with regard to standpoints, the supreme pristine cognition that is naturally pure and nonabiding is primordially liberated and any basis on which it might depend is ended. Through the axiom that transcends the bewildered mind,[387] it is held that imputed phenomena are liberated right where they are.

The Variegated Space Speaking in Terms of Diversity [13.4.3.3.3.2.2]

The second is the variegated space speaking in terms of diversity [which comments on the verse]:

> **The variegated space, when classified, comprises**
> **One aspect in conformity with the class of mind,**

One in conformity with the natural position [of the class of space],
And one in conformity with the esoteric instructional class.

[The essential nature of the variegated space] is that the things that manifest as the display of naturally occurring pristine cognition are positively held to be the display of reality that appears as a naturally arisen diversity, and negatively held to be the display that arises all-pervasively, without direction, and beyond refutation and proof. When classified, it comprises (i) the variegated space that speaks in terms of being, in conformity with the class of mind (13.4.3.3.3.2.2.1); (ii) the variegated space that speaks in terms of nonbeing, in conformity with the natural position [of the class of space] (13.4.3.3.3.2.2.2); and (iii) the variegated space that speaks in terms of both being and nonbeing, in conformity with the esoteric instructional class (13.4.3.3.3.2.2.3).

The Variegated Space That Speaks in Terms of Being, in Conformity with the Class of Mind [13.4.3.3.3.2.2.1]

As to the first, [the variegated space that speaks in terms of being, in conformity with the mental class,] since naturally occurring pristine cognition has not been differentiated in any way whatsoever, as abiding or liberated, its essential nature is natural purity. Since it does not exist as a duality of refutation and proof, its natural expression is inner radiance; and its defining characteristic is nonduality.[388] So, it is held that natural liberation is subsumed in the nature of mind. Since this display arises unceasingly, liberation occurs in the nonduality of appearances and mind. It is held that through the axiom of the essential nature free from the intellect, the phenomena of cyclic existence and nirvāṇa, whether manifest or imputed, abide in primordial liberation right where they are.

The Variegated Space That Speaks in Terms of Nonbeing, in Conformity with the Natural Position [of the Class of Space] [13.4.3.3.3.2.2.2]

As to the second, [the variegated space that speaks in terms of nonbeing, in conformity with the natural position of the spatial class,] since the essential nature is that visible appearances are liberated right where they are, there is being in the sense that reality arises as diversity and nonbeing in the sense that appearances are liberated right where they are, transcending actions and their maturation. Through the axiom that change is empty and fading,[389] it is established that things that are manifest but nonexistent are naturally pure.

The Variegated Space That Speaks in Terms of Both Being and Nonbeing, in Conformity with the Esoteric Instructional Class [13.4.3.3.3.2.2.3]

As for the third, [the variegated space that speaks in terms of both being and nonbeing, in conformity with the esoteric instructional class,] the essential nature is that things abide in primordial emptiness and so they are primordially pure, without relying on cause and effect. Because appearances that manifest as conditioned phenomena, originating through circumstances, are empty in their manifestation, they are liberated from the constraints of cyclic existence and nirvāṇa. The axiom then arises that things that manifest or are imputed arise primordially empty, without wavering from the naturally occurring ground.

Therefore, since all things are primordially present, ineffable, and beyond the intellect, there are three crucial points: (i) the crucial point that there is nothing to behold and nothing to experience; (ii) the crucial point that the nature of mind is unchanging because it is liberated in the nonduality of its rest and motion; and (iii) the crucial point that since created phenomena adventitiously arise, the essence of those views and meditations based on conditioned speculation is a primordially liberated, nonconceptual state. Thereby, it is determined that cyclic existence and nirvāṇa are without effort or attainment.

The White Space, Speaking in Terms of [the Nature of] Mind [13.4.3.3.3.2.3]

The third is the white space speaking in terms of [the nature of] mind, [which comments on the verse:]

> **The white space, when classified, comprises both natural arising and nonduality.**
> **The former includes the greater and lesser [space of the] ocean,**

And the latter comprises [the space of] sun [and moon]
And [the space of] gemstones.

[The essential nature of the white space is that] everything that arises as outward appearance or inner awareness from the disposition of naturally occurring awareness is a display of mind. Appearances and conditions are pure from their basis, with nothing to be done, because they are naturally liberated; and there is nothing to be established in the abiding nature. When classified, it comprises (i) the white space of the supreme naturally arising ineffable state (13.4.3.3.3.2.3.1) and (ii) the white space of the nonduality of view and meditation (13.4.3.3.3.2.3.2).[390]

The White Space of the Supreme Naturally Arising Ineffable State [13.4.3.3.3.2.3.1]

As for the former: the essential nature is that mind and its objects are held to be without duality because the perceiver is directly liberated and what is perceived is naturally pure. When classified, it has two further subdivisions: (i) the space of the ocean (13.4.3.3.3.2.3.1.1) and (ii) the space of sky (13.4.3.3.3.2.3.1.2).

The Space of the Ocean [13.4.3.3.3.2.3.1.1]

As for the space of the ocean, the essential nature is that on the basis of primordial liberation one perceives the crucial point that there is nothing to be done, and so recollection and thought are naturally liberated. Since things arise in a primordial and completely free way, this knowledge decisively determines that things are without duality, beyond the intellect. When it is classified, there are two aspects: the greater space of the ocean and the lesser space of the ocean.

Among these, according to the greater [space of the ocean], the nature of mind is pure in respect of emptiness because mind is manifest in and of itself, empty and primordially liberated. That is to say, in the essential nature of naturally pure appearances and mind, all things are alike in the supreme primordially transcendent reality. Therefore everything is empty of arising, cessation, and duration, and owing to emptiness, it is held that nothing exists in any way whatsoever.

According to the lesser space [of the ocean], mind is untainted because its supporting ground has no inherent existence; and the circumstances of cyclic existence are naturally pure because the supporting [ground] permeates all phenomena, naturally radiant and without changing. This is held to be the supreme reversal of the tide of battle with cyclic existence.

The Space of Sky [13.4.3.3.3.2.3.1.2]

The essential nature of the space of sky is that because the nature of mind is uncontrived, the [ordinary] mind that arises from its disposition is naturally liberated. When classified, there are two further subdivisions: (i) the white space of the sun and moon and (ii) the space of gemstones. The essential nature of the white space of the sun and moon is the empty state of purity, naturally uncreated and primordially liberated. The essential nature of the space of gemstones is that enlightened attributes arise primordially and naturally perfect, so that causes and effects that entail strenuous effort and attainment are naturally pure. Since there is nothing to be done with respect to mind, it is held that reality itself is spontaneously present.

The Infinite Space Determining Causes and Results [13.4.3.3.3.2.4]

The fourth is the infinite space determining causes and results (13.4.3.3.3.2.4) [that comments on the verse]:

> **The infinite space, when classified, comprises outer, inner, secret, and real aspects.**

[As for the essential nature of the infinite space,] it is held that phenomena arising from the disposition of naturally occurring pristine cognition are known through mind inasmuch as they are apparent, and are known through the abiding nature inasmuch as they are not apparent. When classified, infinite space comprises (i) the outer infinity concerning freedom from activity (13.4.3.3.3.2.4.1); (ii) the inner infinity speaking of this system in its own terms (13.4.3.3.3.2.4.2); (iii) the secret infinity concerning the dispelling of obstacles (13.4.3.3.3.2.4.3); and (iv) the infinity of the real that unravels the crucial point (13.4.3.3.3.2.4.4).

The Outer Infinity concerning Freedom from Activity [13.4.3.3.3.2.4.1]

As for the first, [the outer infinity that concerns freedom from activity,] its essential nature comprises (i) the crucial point that since naturally occurring pristine cognition is without cause, it cannot be impeded; (ii) the crucial point that since it is without conditions, it cannot be affected by diversified appearances; and (iii) the crucial point that since it is without causes or conditions, it does not exist as anything whatsoever, whether of cyclic existence or nirvāṇa. Owing to these three crucial points, it is held that [naturally occurring pristine cognition] transcends laborious efforts to accept or reject anything. Since in the essential nature of mind there is nothing to be done, the crucial point is that buddhahood is not attained by means of conditioned phenomena. Since mind has no causal basis, it arises primordially, transcending identity and difference.

The Inner Infinity, Speaking of This System in Its Own Terms [13.4.3.3.3.2.4.2]

As for the second, [the inner infinity, speaking of this system in its own terms,] its essential nature is that naturally occurring pristine cognition is not dependent on the eight [lower] vehicles, and so anything that causes the intellect to deviate toward progressive efforts and prevents it from going beyond the dichotomy of cause and effect, the cage of cyclic existence, is eliminated. In that fundamental panoramic state where there is nothing to be done, even though there are diversified appearances, they are liberated in that single abiding nature, which is therefore termed "the naturally occurring transcendence of effort and attainment." By way of analogy, the shade of various trees is not itself various, and various kinds of wood can make a single fire. The abiding nature, the primordially perfect great perfection, arises as an all-pervasive, limitless diversity, and yet its enlightened intention is a state of being—one of primordial liberation and total rest; that is to say, it is held to be the intrinsic nature that is without limits or restrictions.

The Secret Infinity concerning the Dispelling of Obstacles [13.4.3.3.3.2.4.3]

As for the third, [the secret infinity concerning the dispelling of obstacles,] its essential nature is that in naturally occurring pristine cognition appearances and mind have never been known to exist, and the obstacle of mistaking the biased appearances of the intellect for mind is eliminated in the primordial purity of its own essence. Therefore, appearances and mind are perfect in the supreme state of natural liberation, without having to be renounced, and gathered within the single uniform space of nonduality. Since fleeting recollections and thoughts that impede the intellect are clearly and directly perceived, pure in their very essence, their ebb and flow arise within reality itself. That is to say, fleeting [recollections and thoughts] are gathered in the supreme state of pure emptiness. Sensory objects manifesting diversely on the outside and the awareness that is the intellect apprehending them on the inside seem to be mutually out of contact and disconnected, and yet they are all primordially present in reality itself. Dualistic fixation on the subject-object dichotomy, which occurs due to a lack of recognition [of this reality,] is gathered in the supreme state of natural purity and total rest.

The view [of this space] transcends words and conventional expressions because there is an absence of being, its meditation is without acceptance, rejection, refutation, or proof because there is an absence of nonbeing, its conduct liberates conditioned phenomena in reality because there is an absence of being and nonbeing, and its result is held to be self-established[391] and free from dependence because there is nothing to reject or attain.

The Infinity of the Real That Unravels the Crucial Point [13.4.3.3.3.2.4.4]

As for the fourth, [the infinity of the real that unravels the crucial point,] its essential nature is that the phenomena of cyclic existence and nirvāṇa, appearances and consciousness, arise as the buddha bodies and pristine cognition, and so it is held that in the supreme reality that cannot be divided at all into cyclic existence and nirvāṇa, from the present moment, whatever manifests as sensory objects and mind is indeed this [network of buddha body and pristine cognition], without addition or subtraction. Identifying this directly, one relaxes in this supreme state, open-eyed, with clarity and without distraction. Thus one is said to "hammer the nail of supreme unchanging spontaneous presence between the two polarities of the subject-object dichotomy." That is to say, one determines that the phenomena of cyclic existence that bewilderingly appear are the enlightened intention of Samantabhadra, the reality that, without laborious effort, does not have to be transformed and does not have to be renounced. By resting right where one is, mindful of the crucial point of directly perceiving one's own true nature, the innately pure essence of the thoughts that arise through conceptual elaboration is released into a state without [the duality of] outer and inner objects, and this is called "the attainment of buddhahood in the supreme state of total liberation, without supporting basis." This [awakening] is said to transcend the intellect because the restlessness of recollection and thought is absent, it transcends the sense objects because whatever manifests arises without supporting basis, it transcends the need to renounce anything or apply an antidote because anything that arises dissolves into that very state [of awakening], and it transcends laborious effort and cause and effect because things that appear or are imputed arise in a common savor.

Synopsis of the Class of Space

When all these subcategories [of the class of space] are subsumed, they may be gathered within the four spaces of display, adornment, reality, and freedom from activity.

Among them, the space of display is present because the display of the nature of mind does not waver or change into cyclic existence or nirvāṇa from the disposition in which it unimpededly arises; and it is absent because this display is without substantiality and is not apprehended as an extreme. Thus it is understood to be the enlightened intention that is open, in the manner of the sky.

As for the space of adornment: appearances primordially arise as the adornments of mind, the nature of mind primordially arises as the naturally occurring adornment, and the naturally occurring state primordially arises as the adornment of freedom from artificiality and corruption. Arising unimpededly, from that unborn disposition [of reality], appearances and mind are therefore neither denied nor affirmed. This is understood to be the enlightened intention that is a great natural rhythm, natural presence and natural radiance.

As for the space of reality: all things, whatever their source, neither come about, nor do they abide, and nor do they cease. These appearances, and their display or dynamic expression, are a wondrous manifestation that diversely appears from the disposition of reality, but, just as the changes undergone by the four elements do not stray from the underlying state or space element, they are held to rest in an infinite expanse, free from the emergence and engagement of the intellect and free from hope and doubt, in a disposition of supreme reality that is primordially empty, primordially liberated, and primordially present.

As for the space of freedom from activity: acceptance and rejection through strenuous efforts are not required with reference to anything whatsoever. It is held that one should understand everything to be unchanging, uncontrived, and uncorrupted like space because it is already primordially completed without having to be done, it is already primordially liberated without having to be liberated, it is already primordially purified without having to be purified, and it is already primordially attained without having to be accomplished.[392]

The Class of Esoteric Instructions

The Particularly Sublime Class of Esoteric Instructions [13.4.3.3.4]

The fourth section [of the exegesis of the Great Perfection] concerns the particularly sublime class of esoteric instructions (13.4.3.3.4), which speaks directly in terms of the path. This has three aspects: (i) its distinctions (13.4.3.3.4.1); (ii) its essential nature (13.4.3.3.4.2); and (iii) its subdivisions (13.4.3.3.4.3).

Its Distinctions [13.4.3.3.4.1]

The first of these [comments on the verse]:

> **[The class of esoteric instructions] naturally clarifies [the abiding nature]**
> **And surpasses [the classes of mind and space]**
> **That maintain speculation and adhere to reality.**

This class [of esoteric instructions] is superior to the [aforementioned] classes of mind and space, as is said in the *Great Array* [*of the Highest*]:

> O Vajra Holder!
> If this is not established
> One will be no different to those who cling to speculation.
> Therefore this definitive, secret nucleus,
> As a lamp in darkness,
> Or a bull among oxen,
> A lion among wild beasts,

Or a horseman among infantry,
Is superior to all others.

Followers of the class of esoteric instructions, inasmuch as the abiding nature of reality is naturally clarified therein, surpass those who resort to speculation, whether by speculating, in the context of the class of mind, about what the mind is, or by adhering, in the context of the class of space, to reality.

Its Essential Nature [13.4.3.3.4.2]

Second, as for the essential nature [of the class of esoteric instructions, this comments on the verse]:

It resembles moxibustion treatment,
Because the crucial point is reached,
Without languishing in speculation.

The essential nature is that [the esoteric instructions] resemble moxibustion treatment because they directly reach the crucial point, without languishing in conjecture and speculation.

Its Subdivisions [13.4.3.3.4.3]

Third, the subdivisions [of the class of esoteric instructions] comprise (i) an exegesis of miscellaneous instructions (13.4.3.3.4.3.1); (ii) an exegesis of informal advice (13.4.3.3.4.3.2); and (iii) formal instructions based on actual tantra texts (13.4.3.3.4.3.3).

An Exegesis of Miscellaneous Instructions [13.4.3.3.4.3.1]

As to the first, [this comments on the verse:]

The essence of the miscellaneous instructions
Denotes the path that establishes [the abiding nature of reality]
And the pure power of liberation.

[The essence of the miscellaneous instructions] is that naturally occurring pristine cognition that transcends the intellect instantaneously arises by relying upon the crucial points.

There are two subdivisions, the first of which comprises those esoteric instructions that determine the path by establishing [the abiding nature of reality]. In this context, the distinctive feature of the ground is that the ground of conceptual elaboration is without letters, transcending names or words, because it cannot be established through mere words. The distinctive feature of the path is that when one's true nature arises as the path in this manner, without conceptual elaboration, there is no laborious effort involved, and so the fruition is like reclaiming one's natural state, free from fluctuations in respect of [the nature of] reality. It is held that through these axioms that are without plans, actions, causes, or conditions, the depths of cyclic existence are churned, and one is liberated in nirvāṇa, the natural state.

The second are the esoteric instructions that disclose the path by the pure power of liberation. These are grounded in the fact that, from the abiding perspective of reality, mind is unchanging. When the three buddha bodies manifest on the path, there is nothing that is unliberated, and when one arrives at the crucial point, the fruition is held to be an encounter with one's own mother, reality itself.

An Exegesis of Informal Advice [13.4.3.3.4.3.2]

As to the second, [this comments on the verse:]

The essence of informal advice
Denotes advice that [dispenses with] all discourse
And informal advice that hits the mark, without [delay].

The essence [of informal advice] is that it is unbewildered and free from the intellect. Its natural expression is that it puts an end to the source of conceptualization. Its defining characteristic is that it is without duality and it cannot be specifically identified.

There are two subdivisions, among which [the first] comprises informal advice that dispenses with all discourse. This concerns the subtle energy within the focal points of the energy channels, for it is by means of the focal points of subtle energy that the mind subsides into natural quiescence, and that pristine cognition thereby becomes clear. Once the connection between body, speech, and mind has been determined, fluctuations are liberated in this natural state. So these are the esoteric instructions that put an end to talk about buddhas and sentient beings.

[The second comprises] informal advice that hits the mark without delay. This takes into account that the expanse [of reality] encompasses cyclic existence and nirvāṇa because, in respect of its vastness, there is nothing that it does not accommodate. It also takes into account that it gets to the essence because the expanse of reality is empty and cannot be specifically identified. Also, the expanse [of reality] is free from laborious effort. It is for these reasons that naturally occurring pristine cognition may be recognized.

Formal Instructions Based on the Actual Tantra Texts [13.4.3.3.4.3.3]

As to the third, formal instructions based on the actual tantra texts (13.4.3.3.4.3.3), [this comments on the verses:]

The essence of the actual tantra texts [of the Great Perfection]
Is that they encapsulate the view,
[Remove obstacles] like a blood-letting instrument,
Conceal [and disclose hidden meanings],
And give exegesis [in a naturally clear manner].
[The last of these, giving exegesis in a naturally clear manner,]
Is divided [between texts maintaining]
That bewilderment [is to be corralled],
That bewilderment [is to be reversed in] the ground,
And that the crucial point [of seminal importance has been reached].
The essence of [the last of these,] concerning the crucial point, includes the aural lineage and the exegetical lineage,
The latter being subdivided according to its four cycles.

In terms of their essential nature, [these formal instructions] are the source of all the words [of the buddhas]. In terms of their natural expression, they are effortless with regard to rejection and acceptance because they are free from cyclic existence and nirvāṇa, and in terms of their defining characteristics,[393] they are the emptiness that is free from all bases of disputation because they are soundless and wordless.

There are four subdivisions because these instructions are delivered in such a manner that they include (i) formal instructions encapsulating the enlightened intention of the view (13.4.3.3.4.3.3.1); (ii) formal instructions that remove obstacles like a blood-letting instrument (13.4.3.3.4.3.3.2); (iii) formal instructions that conceal and disclose (13.4.3.3.4.3.3.3); and (iv) formal instructions with exegeses that are naturally clear (13.4.3.3.4.3.3.4).

Formal Instructions Encapsulating the Enlightened Intention of the View [13.4.3.3.4.3.3.1]

According to the first method, [encapsulating the enlightened intention of the view,] the essence of this state permeates the ground free from conceptual elaborations, and so karma is neither positive nor negative and the three world systems arise totally liberated. The natural expression of this state manifests as [the union of] emptiness and radiance, and is therefore free from positive and negative actions that would bring benefit or harm, respectively; indeed there are neither buddhas nor sentient beings. Since it is devoid of nouns, words, and letters, buddhahood is not attained through the sacred doctrines of the diverse vehicles, but it is revealed that those with appropriate acumen are instantaneously liberated.

There are two subdivisions, among which [the first] is that there is nothing to be done in respect of apparent and imputed phenomena that constitute the view (13.4.3.3.4.3.3.1.1). The essence of this state is that even the name *buddha* is not found because phenomena are nonexistent. The natural expression of this state arises as dynamic energy so that [the realms of] cyclic existence manifest distinctly. The defining characteristic of this state is that the view and meditation are without limitation because it cannot be identified precisely.

The second is that the conceptual mind is encapsulated within the view (13.4.3.3.4.3.3.1.2). The essence of this state is pure in its nonarising, so that mental afflictions are liberated right where they are. The natural expression of this state arises unceasingly, so that there is no rejection, acceptance, refutation, or proof. The defining characteristic of this state is that it arises as primordial liberation, and so the paths associated with cyclic existence and nirvāṇa have been brought to an end.

Formal Instructions That Remove Obstacles like a Blood-Letting Instrument [13.4.3.3.4.3.3.2]

As for the second method, according to which the transmitted precepts remove obstacles like a blood-letting instrument, the essence of this state is revealed to be the fundamental nature of reality, demarcating the borderline between cyclic existence and nirvāṇa. The natural expression of this state is that since there is no room for error, there is no need to mingle the mother and child aspects of mind. The defining characteristic of this state is that since the ground is pure, bewilderment is directly eliminated.

It has two subdivisions: (i) the elimination of obstacles to authentic presence (13.4.3.3.4.3.3.2.1) and (ii) the elimination of obstacles blocking the warmth of the view and meditation (13.4.3.3.4.3.3.2.2). The essence of the first state is that since nothing is contrived, anything that manifests is liberated, in that it is mind. The natural expression of this state is that since there is no cause and no effect, the three world systems are vacuous, in that names do not exist. The defining characteristic of this state is that since there is no need for familiarization, it does not depend on anything extraneous that is to be known.

As for the second type, the warmth of the view merges both cyclic existence and nirvāṇa in a common savor. When the view is unstable, one should identify the reality of cyclic existence, as if trying to identify a poltergeist. When the view is acquired,[394] warmth is obtained with regard to body and speech, as if adding wood to a blazing fire. Then, when the view is stable, one distinguishes between cyclic existence and nirvāṇa, in the manner of a soldier who is victorious in battle. When meditation is unstable, one should acquire mastery over the subtle wind and mind, as if entering into the treasury of a wealthy person. When meditation is acquired, the mind is established on the path, like an elephant lying down on straw. Then, when meditation is stable, one finds the strength of awareness, and this resembles the crowning of a monarch. When conduct is unstable, the rigid focus of ordinary consciousness should still fade away, like the ravings of a madman. When [control over] conduct is acquired, bewildering perceptions are overcome and this resembles a garuḍa soaring in the sky. When conduct is stable, one has acquired [mastery of] the extent of warmth in relation to the three buddha bodies, and this resembles a brahmin girl who has completed her tasks.

Moreover, through conduct, obstacles concerning sensory appearances are eliminated so that the conditions giving rise to those appearances are supportive, and there is no place to go apart from reality. Through meditation, obstacles caused by the movement [of thought] are eliminated, so that recollection and thought have no place to go apart from meditative stability. Through the view, obstacles pertaining to reality are eliminated, so that even though one does not rely on the sacred doctrine, one has no place to go apart from buddhahood.

Formal Instructions That Conceal and Disclose [13.4.3.3.4.3.3.3]

As for the third way in which the transmitted precepts are delivered, through concealment and disclosure, the essence of this state is that there is nothing to be attained, and so one should not make assumptions about anything at all. The natural expression of this state is without bias, so that there is no clinging to the cycle of hope and doubt. The defining characteristic of this state is such that when it is examined, nothing is found, so that it is said that the root of cyclic existence and nirvāṇa has rotted away.

There are two subdivisions: (i) instructions concealing one aspect and disclosing two others (13.4.3.3.4.3.3.3.1) and (ii) instructions concealing two aspects and disclosing one other (13.4.3.3.4.3.3.3.2). Among them, as for the first: when both the view and conduct are disclosed and meditation is concealed, the essence of this state is a coalescence in which there is no beginning or end, and so [notions concerning] the beginning or end of cyclic existence and nirvāṇa are cut off. The natural expression of this state is that there is no differentiation, so that the vital essence is without external and internal aspects. The defining characteristic of this state is that there is no dependence, so that it is core penetrating and without cause.

Alternatively, when conduct is concealed and the view and meditation are disclosed, there is said to be "purity that is empty of emptiness." When the view is concealed and conduct and meditation are both disclosed, the nonapprehending consciousness arises without bias, so that one is said to be "liberated in objectless, nonreferential awareness."

As for the second, when meditation is disclosed and view and conduct are concealed, nonreferential awareness arises without dependence on anything at all, so that the fruition that is without cause is said to "abide within one." When conduct is disclosed and the view and meditation are concealed, it is said that "the body is cast into an abyss and the mind proceeds to reality." When the view is disclosed and both conduct and meditation are concealed, it is said that "the mind is escorted to emptiness, so that one reaches the crucial points of body and speech." There are a great many scriptural passages in the tantras in conformity with the latter method. In some, the view concerning the expanse [of reality] is emphasized and the other two [meditation and conduct] are revealed incidentally, as is the case in the [*Tantra of the*] *All-Accomplishing King.*

Formal Instructions with Exegeses That Are Naturally Clear [13.4.3.3.4.3.3.4]

As for the fourth way in which the transmitted precepts are delivered, exegeses that are naturally clear, the essence of this state is that it transcends sounds and words, so that it does not sit within any philosophical system. The natural expression of this state is that primordially pure reality arises naturally and without bias. The defining characteristic of this state is that it transcends the intellect, so that it is free from the ebb and flow of thoughts that generate movement.

There are three subdivisions: (i) formal instructions maintaining that bewilderment is like a cow to be herded (13.4.3.3.4.3.3.4.1); (ii) formal instructions reversing bewilderment in the ground (13.4.3.3.4.3.3.4.2); and (iii) formal instructions that reach the crucial point of seminal importance (13.4.3.3.4.3.3.4.3).

Formal Instructions Maintaining That Bewilderment Is like a Cow to Be Herded [13.4.3.3.4.3.3.4.1]

As to the first of these, the essence of this state is that fundamental ignorance is uprooted by pursuing bewilderment, the root of fundamental ignorance that lays the foundation of cyclic existence, back into its very ground. Intrinsic awareness arrives at its original ground; and this is irreversible. The natural expression of this state is that it arises in diverse ways, so that if the cow of causes and conditions is herded, doubts concerning one's perception will be cut off and this is said to be "supreme, primordial purity, in which the ground of bewilderment and cyclic existence has ended." The defining characteristic of this state is that bewilderment is naturally pure, so that the pathway of bewildered consciousness has ended.

Formal Instructions Reversing Bewilderment in the Ground [13.4.3.3.4.3.3.4.2]

This has three subdivisions, among which [the first] is the method [of instruction] that undermines the dichotomy of cyclic existence and nirvāṇa by eradicating bewilderment (13.4.3.3.4.3.3.4.2.1). The essence of this state is that the nature of fundamental ignorance, which is the root of bewilderment, is known to be naturally liberated, thereby affirming that bewilderment has never been experienced from beginningless time. That is to say, this state transcends both bewilderment and nonbewilderment. The natural expression of this state is that [phenomena] that are individually bewildered have been determined to be imaginary and adventitious. That is to say, they transcend the objects of the subject-object dichotomy. The defining characteristic of this state is that by recognizing the true nature of bewilderment, one has determined the warmth of unbewildered pristine cognition.

[The second] is the recognition[395] of unbewildered reality achieved by settling bewilderment in its natural state (13.4.3.3.4.3.3.4.2.2). The essence of this state is that from the beginning bewilderment has never been experienced, so that the causal basis[396] of fundamental ignorance is pure. At present it does not abide as bewilderment, so that karma and afflicted mental states are devoid of any basis, and in the future bewilderment will be impossible, so that positive and negative actions have also been eliminated. The natural expression of this state is that it is indivisible, so that in awareness cyclic existence and nirvāṇa have an identical ground—that is to say, bewilderment is naturally pure. The defining characteristic of this state is that there is no basis for bewilderment, and so the depths of the three world systems have been churned.

[The third] is the interruption of the machinations of bewilderment by subverting its basis (13.4.3.3.4.3.3.4.2.3). The essence of this state is that it is devoid of any basis for falling into cyclic existence, so that the ground in which nothing is found is established. The natural expression of this state is that it is beyond estimation, so that it cannot be proven to be either bewilderment or nonbewilderment. The defining characteristic of this state is that it is free from the intellect, whether bewildered or unbewildered.

Formal Instructions That Reach the Crucial Point of Seminal Importance [13.4.3.3.4.3.3.4.3]

[As to the third], the formal instructions that reach the crucial point of seminal importance, the intrinsic essence of this state is that it is uniquely free from conceptual elaboration, so that it is neither singular nor multiple. The natural expression of this state is that it is without duality, so that it transcends conventional terms. The defining characteristic of this state is that conviction is decisively acquired through being introduced to it.

There are two subdivisions: (i) the aural lineage (13.4.3.3.4.3.3.4.3.1) and (ii) the exegetical lineage [of the tantra texts] (13.4.3.3.4.3.3.4.3.2).

The Aural Lineage [13.4.3.3.4.3.3.4.3.1]

With regard to the aural lineage, the essence of this lineage is that it is close because a connection with it is established through direct transmission from one individual to another. The natural expression of this lineage is that nothing intervenes because the connection is established through one's faculty of hearing. The defining characteristic of this lineage is that it gives rise to trust and conviction because it is without error. When analyzed, this aural lineage comprises pith instructions of word and meaning that have been handed down, whether in written or unwritten form.

The Exegetical Lineage [of the Tantra Texts] [13.4.3.3.4.3.3.4.3.2]

With regard to the exegetical lineage, the essence of this lineage is that naturally occurring pristine cognition, the reality devoid of laborious effort, is without causal basis, and so there is no basis for counteracting it within the three world systems. The natural expression of this lineage is that it is immaculate inner radiance, enabling the defining characteristics of the five pristine cognitions to be known. The defining characteristic of this lineage is that it transcends ideas and scrutiny, so that the enlightened intention of the three buddha bodies and five pristine cognitions constantly abides.

There are four subdivisions: (i) the outer cycle (13.4.3.3.4.3.3.4.3.2.1); (ii) the inner cycle (13.4.3.3.4.3.3.4.3.2.2); (iii) the secret cycle (13.4.3.3.4.3.3.4.3.2.3); and (iv) the unsurpassed secret cycle (13.4.3.3.4.3.3.4.3.2.4).

The Outer Cycle [13.4.3.3.4.3.3.4.3.2.1]

First, with regard to the outer cycle, the essence of this state is that afflicted mental states are not to be abandoned, and so one abides by carrying the five poisons onto the path. The natural expression of this state is that whatever appears arises as reality because it entails no effort or attainment. The defining characteristic of this state is that emptiness cannot be divided into anything at all because it is unfragmented.

The Inner Cycle [13.4.3.3.4.3.3.4.3.2.2]

With regard to the inner cycle, the essence of this state is that it denotes the signless reality because it does not exist as an independent characteristic with material properties. The natural expression of this state is pristine cognition that constantly abides because it is without fluctuations. The defining characteristic of this state is that it resembles a root from the perspective of its penetration [of cyclic existence and nirvāṇa], it resembles a tree trunk from the perspective of its summation [of the intrinsic face of awareness], it resembles leaves from the perspective of its extension [on all sides], it resembles flowers from the perspective of its radiance, and it resembles fruits from the perspective of its maturation [of diversity].

The Secret Cycle [13.4.3.3.4.3.3.4.3.2.3]

With regard to the secret cycle, the essence of this state is that there is no dependence on study, reflection, and meditation because the introduction to it is simultaneous with the attainment of realization. The natural expression of this state is that there is no dependence on effort or the power of familiarization because the cessation of breathing [at death] is simultaneous with the attainment of buddhahood. The defining characteristic of this state is that there is no dependence on the perfection of the two provisions as a causal basis because the attainment of buddhahood is simultaneous with the emergence of compassionate spirituality.

The Unsurpassed Secret Cycle [13.4.3.3.4.3.3.4.3.2.4]

With regard to the unsurpassed secret cycle, the essence of this state is that there is no dependence on discriminative awareness that entails ideas and scrutiny because there is no reliance on words. The natural expression of this state is that one does not remain fixed in a view embracing speculation because it is known in direct experience. The defining characteristic of this state is that one reaches the full extent of four visionary appearances,[397] and so one can dispense with the hope that the fruition [will be attained] in the three buddha bodies and five pristine cognitions. This is because primordial spontaneous presence becomes manifest in this present lifetime.[398]

To establish confidence in the intrinsic nature of those [four cycles] on the basis of scriptural transmission, it says in the master Vimalamitra's *Illuminating Lamp:*

> The outer cycle is comparable to the body,
> And it extensively presents conventional descriptions.
> The inner cycle is comparable to the eyes,
> And its teachings employ symbols of visual perception.
> The secret cycle is comparable to the heart,
> And its teachings employ retention that facilitates recollection.
> But this [unsurpassed secret cycle] is comparable
> To a person with a completely perfect physique.[399]

Epilogue

On this occasion when we have in our practical experience
The good fortune to meet with the supreme and most secret
Vehicle of indestructible reality, the profound path,
Which crosses over to buddhahood in a single lifetime,
Having completely eschewed negative thoughts
Fixated upon the meaningless activities of this life,
We should be steadfast, without ever swerving
From the attainment of our constant aspiration.
Keeping all primary and subsidiary commitments,
Holding them dearer than one's own life,
The experiential cultivation of the crucial points
Of the generation and perfection stages [of meditation]
Over six sessions of practice, day and night,
Is of paramount importance, equal to life itself.

This [section of Book 13] was compiled by Longchen Choying Tobden Dorje in order that the distinguishing features and profound points of the outer and inner mantras, and of the generation and perfection stages, and the great perfection might be ascertained.

Book 13, Part 4

The Philosophical Systems of Tibet: Lines of Transmission

Herein is contained Book 13, Part 4 (NGI) from *The Extensive Commentary of the Precious Treasury of Sūtra and Tantra: A General Exegesis of [the Lines of Transmission] of the Philosophical Systems of Tibet, the Land of Snows.*

The Golden Key

In order to clarify the philosophical systems of Tibet,
This book summarizes the transmission of Bon,
medicine, and divination,
And details the propagation of the Buddhist teachings,
According to the ancient and new traditions.

Verse of Homage

Homage to those persons who upheld the Buddhist teachings,
having attained learning and accomplishment, and who have
appeared over time in Tibet, the Land of Snows!

The fifth main topic [**Book 13, Part 4**] explains the lines of transmission through which the [aforementioned] philosophical systems were specifically propagated in Tibet, the Land of Snows (13.5).

It has three parts, comprising (i) a general exegesis of the spread of Bon, medicine, and divination (13.5.1); (ii) a detailed exegesis of the [dissemination of] the sūtras and tantras during the early translation period (13.5.2); and (iii) a particular exegesis of the dissemination of the new translation schools of the way of secret mantra during the later translation period (13.5.3).

The Spread of Bon, Medicine, and Divination

A General Exegesis of the Spread of Bon, Medicine, and Divination [13.5.1]

The first of these [comments on the verse]:

In Tibet, Bon, medicine, and divination were propagated gradually.

The Land of Tibet [13.5.1.1]

The whole of Tibet includes the three highland districts of Ngari, which resemble a reservoir, the four moderately high "horns" of Utsang, which resemble an irrigation channel, and the six lower-lying ranges of Dokham, which form, as it were, an irrigated field.

In the highland region, the first district comprises the three enclaves of Purang, Mangyul, and Zangskar. The second district comprises the three enclaves of Khotan, Gilgit, and Baltistan. The third district comprises the three enclaves of Zhangzhung, Upper Khri-te, and Lower Khri-te. All these constitute the three highland districts of Ngari.[400]

In the moderately high part of the country, in U, there are the two "horns" of Uru and Yoru, while in Tsang there are the two "horns" of Yeru and Rulak. All these constitute the four moderately high "horns" of Utsang.[401]

The lower-lying parts of the country comprise three regions—namely, Dokham or Markham, Do-me or Yarmotang, and Tsongkha or Gyitang.[402] Alternatively, they comprise six upland ranges—namely, (i) Nguldza Zelmogang; (ii) Tsawagang; (iii) Markhamgang; (iv) Poborgang; (v) Mardzagang; and (vi) Minyak Rabgang.[403]

Among them, the highland and moderately high parts of the country are known as Tibet and the low-lying parts are known as Greater Tibet. To the east of the land of Tibet lie China and Manchuria, to the south are India and Kashmir, to the west are Tajikistan and Persia, and to the north are Turkestan and Tartary.[404] Tibet is surrounded on all sides by these eight countries.

The Royal Dynasties of Tibet

The Royal Dynasties of Tibet [13.5.1.2]

Commencing from Nyatri Tsenpo, the first of the Tibetan kings, there were [in succession] seven heavenly kings called Tri, two middling kings called Teng, six earthly kings called Lek, seven miscellaneous kings, five linking kings called Tsen, and thirteen kings in the auspicious [imperial] succession.[405]

The son of Nyatri Tsenpo (1) was Mutri Tsenpo (2). His son was Dingtri Tsenpo (3). His son was Sotri Tsenpo (4). His son was Metri Tsenpo (5). His son was Daktri Tsenpo (6). His son was Sibtri Tsenpo (7). All these comprise the seven kings of heavenly succession called Tri.[406]

The son of Sibtri Tsenpo was Drigum Tsenpo (8), and his son was Pude Gungyal (9). These are the two kings of intermediate succession called Teng.[407]

The last-mentioned's son was Esho Lek (10). His son was Desho Lek (11). His son was Drongzhi Lek (14). His son was Tisho Lek (12). His son was Guru Lek (13). [Drongzhi Lek's son was Isho Lek (15).] His son was Zanam Lek (16). All these comprise the six kings of earthly succession called Lek.[408]

The-last mentioned's son was De Trulnam Zhungtsen (17). His son was De Nol-be [also known as Senol Namde] (18). His son was De Nolya [also known as Se Nolpo De] (19). His son was Sornonam [also known as De Nolnam] (20). [His son was De Nolpo (21).] His son was Sotelek [also known as De Gyalpo] (22). His son was Trin Gyaltsen (23). His son was Tongri Tongtsen (24). All these comprise the seven kings of sundry succession.[409]

The last-mentioned's son was Tri Namtsen (25). His son was Tri Dra Pungtsen (26). His son was Tri Tokje Tsen (27). His son was Totori Nyentsen (28). His son was Trinyen Zhungtsen (29). All these comprise the five kings of connected succession called Tsen.[410]

The last-mentioned's son was Drong Nyenderu (30). His son was Takri Nyenzik (31). His son was Namri Songtsen (32). His son was Songtsen Gampo (33). His son was Mangsong Mangtsen (35). His son was Gungsong Gungtsen (34). His son was Lung Namtrulgyi Gyalpo [also known as Dusong Mangpoje] (36). His son was Tri-de Tsukten Me Agtsom (37). His son was Trisong Detsen (38). His three sons were Mune Tsenpo (39), Murum Tsenpo, and Mutri Tsenpo (40), among whom the son of Mune Tsenpo was Tri Relpachen (41). All these comprise the thirteen kings of the auspicious imperial succession.[411]

Mutri Tsenpo had five sons, among whom one was Lang Darma (42). His son was Osung. His son was Pelkhortsen. His son was Kyide Nyima Gon. His son was Tashi Gon. His son was Lha Lama Yeshe-o. The son of the latter's younger brother [Jangchub-o] was Lha-de.[412] His son was O-de, and his son was Tsen-de.[413]

Bon

Bon [13.5.1.3]

During the lifetime of [the first king] Nyatri Tsenpo, the ancient tales were widespread, but during the lifetime of King Drigum Tsenpo, the Bonpo of Takzik and Azha were invited and [new] ritual practices were propagated, including offerings to the gods for the sake of the living and the subjugation of spirits for the sake of the dead.[414]

According to the Bon tradition, Tonpa Shenrab appeared during the age when human beings had a life span of ten thousand years, and he then taught the eighty-four thousand approaches of Bon.[415]

In this regard, there are four causal modes of Bon, four fruitional modes of Bon—eight transmissions comprising four rivers and four streams[416]—and there are three modes of ritual activity that engage with the intention [of Tonpa Shenrab]. For, although one may enter by means of any of the nine vehicles, training in the austerity of the seals denotes the ritual activity of the body, training in the austerity of vital heart mantras denotes the ritual activity of speech, and training in the austerity of meditative stability denotes the ritual activity of mind.

The nine vehicles comprise (i) the way of the priests of prediction; (ii) the way of the priests of the visible world; (iii) the way of the priests of miraculous power; (iv) the way of the priests of the rebirth process; (v) the way of lay practitioners; (vi) the way of ordained hermit sages; (vii) the way of the white syllable A; (viii) the way of the primordial priests; and (ix) the way of the extraordinary [Great Perfection].[417]

Among them, the teaching associated with the priests of the visible world, which is entered by means of the four portals of ritual chanting, was established by Gyaltrim Narwa.[418]

The teaching associated with the priests of miraculous power, including the thirteen miraculous powers and the six great methods, was established by Wel-se Ngampa.[419]

The teaching associated with the priests of the rebirth process, including the three hundred sixty funerary rites and the four portals of the funeral rites, was established by Durshen Mawo.[420]

The teaching associated with lay practitioners, including the four delights, the two purities, and the three severities, was established by Yekhyen Trulgyam.[421]

The teaching associated with the [ordained] hermit sages, including the ten constraints, the two models, the two refinements, and the three attainments, was established by Yungdrung Chayi Gyalpo.[422]

The teaching associated with the way of the white syllable A, including the eighteen branches of attainment and the nine approaches of ritual service, was established by Sangwa Dupa.[423]

The teaching associated with the way of the primordial priests, including the four entrances, the sixty aspects of meditative stability, and the sixteen signs, was established by Yewang Gyalpo.[424]

The teaching associated with the extraordinary way [of the Great Perfection], including the three perspectives and the single absolute reality, was established by Tse-me Oden.[425] The priest Tse-me Oden attained liberation without leaving a residue of the psycho-physical aggregates behind, through having practiced austerities and meditated in the expanse of the sky. Trulshen Nangden also attained liberation, along with his consort and entourage, without leaving a residue of the psycho-physical aggregates behind, through having practiced austerities and meditated at the summit of Mount Sumeru.[426]

Medical Traditions

Medical Traditions [13.5.1.4]

With regard to the propagation of the medical traditions [in Tibet], during the lifetime of Lhatotori Nyentsen, the physicians Biji and Bilhama arrived from India. The princess Lhacham Yidkyi Rolcha was offered to Biji, and a son was born to them who would train in medicine and become known as the physician Dungi Torchokchen. The son lineage and the royal lineage gradually evolved thereafter.[427]

In particular, [this lineage included] Dreje Vajra. His son was Khyungpo Dorje, and his son, known as Yutok Yonten Gonpo [the Elder], actually became the king of physicians, who lived for one hundred twenty-five years and served as a teacher and physician to both Me'agtsom and Trisong Detsen. He was the supreme propagator of the teachings of the medical tradition.[428]

[During that time,] Vairotsana translated the *Four Medical Tantras* and concealed them as treasure, after which they were brought forth by Drapa Ngonshe and propagated.[429]

The son of Yonten Gonpo [the Elder] was Bumseng, who had five sons, including Drogon, all of them exclusively attaining spiritual accomplishment. So later, just as in the past [in the time of Biji], there was a lineage that descended from Dreje Vajra for five successive generations.[430]

Yonten Gonpo [the Younger] composed the *Eighteen Branches* [*of Medical Science*].[431]

Divination

Divination [13.5.1.5]

Divination was gradually propagated [in Tibet] during the lifetime of Songtsen [Gampo] through the twelve [translations] prepared by [Wencheng] Konjo and others in the early, middling, and later phases [of that reign], as has already been explained.[432]

It also says in the *Injunctions* [*of Padma*]:[433]

> In Jampel Ling at the eastern gate [of Samye],
> The texts of divination and medicine were translated.
> The Chinese master Hara Nagpo,
> The monks Mahāyāna, [Mahā]sūtra,
> Mahārāja, and Mahādeva,
> Along with four learned Tibetan translators,
> Including Birje Tsenpo Shila,
> Translated texts of elemental divination.
> The earlier translations were commissioned by the Chinese princess Konjo,
> And the remainder of the *Science of Pang-gyen Lama* was also translated.
> The later translations were the work of Tride Tsukten,
> On which Birje Tsenpo Shila was invited [to participate],
> And eighteen Chinese tracts were translated, and more besides.
> The translations that were undertaken in the intervening period
> Included the outer tantras, the inner tantras, the secret tantras,
> Along with the *Tantra of Utterly Secret Mind,*
> The *Tantra Comprising the Divisions*,

And all the other [divination tantras] that had not previously been translated.
Many works were also retranslated, including
The *Fivefold Mother and Child of Luminosity,*
The *Gathering of the Nine Branches,* the *Disclosure of the Hidden,*
And the *Gathering of Four Brahmā Divinations,*
As has been indicated in the thirty-fifth canto.[434]

The Early Translation Period

A Detailed Exegesis of the Dissemination of the Sūtras and Tantras during the Early Translation Period [13.5.2]

[This comments on the verses:]

The sacred doctrine of the early translation period had its inception [in the reign of Lhatotori],
Was formally introduced [in the reign of Songtsen Gampo],
And then disseminated and established [in the reign of Trisong Detsen].
[Samye] was constructed, [texts] were translated,
And [teachings of] exegesis and attainment were propagated.

The Reign of Lhatotori Nyentsen [13.5.2.1]

During the reign of Lhatotori Nyentsen, the fourth of the [five linking kings called] Tsen, a copy of the *Cornucopia of Avalokiteśvara's Attributes,* the *Sūtra of the Hundredfold Homage of Renunciation and Fulfillment,* a mold engraved with the *Dhāraṇī of the Wish-Fulfilling Gem,* and other objects fell down upon the roof of the Yumbu Lakhar palace, whereupon they were given the name "awesome secret" (*gnyan po gsang ba*), and they were then worshipped. Simply on the basis of this event, the foundation of the sacred doctrine [of Buddhism] was laid.[435]

The Reign of Songtsen Gampo [13.5.2.2]

During the lifetime of Songtsen Gampo, an emanation of Avalokiteśvara, in order to introduce the traditions of the sacred doctrine, Thonmi Sambhoṭa and his entourage traveled to India, where he perfectly mastered [indigenous] scripts and grammatical texts under the guidance of Devavidyāsiṃha and the brahmin Lijin. By subtracting and supplementing the fifty Indic letters, he devised thirty-four letters of the Tibetan script. He also composed eight grammatical treatises in conformity with the Tibetan language, equal in number to the eight great grammatical texts of India. It was on that basis that writing evolved in Tibet.[436]

The Indian master Kusara, the brahmin Śaṅkara, the Newar Śīlamañju, and others were invited [to Tibet], where, with Thonmi Sambhoṭa acting as translator, they translated twenty-one sūtra and tantra texts, including the *Sūtra of the Cloud of Precious Jewels* and the *Cornucopia of Avalokiteśvara's Attributes,* as well as the *Purification of All Lower Realms,* the *Indestructible Subjugator,* and other tantras.

Modeled on the Temple of Vikramaśīla in India, the Rasa Trulnang Temple was constructed, and two images of Śākyamuni in the form of a bodhisattva prince were brought from China and Nepal.[437] One hundred eight temples of the "district controlling" class, the "border taming" class, and the "further taming" class were also constructed.[438] A legal system based on the ten virtuous actions was implemented.[439]

In the presence of disciples who were worthy recipients, the king himself then emanated the maṇḍalas of the appropriate meditational deities and he conferred upon them the empowerments and pith instructions, so that there were many who attained spiritual accomplishment. He also composed the treatise entitled the *Collected Words of the King concerning the Mantra* OṂ MAṆI PADME HŪṂ.[440] In such ways he founded the tradition of the sacred doctrine.

The Reign of Trisong Detsen [13.5.2.3]

With regard to the spread and expansion of the sacred doctrine [of Buddhism in Tibet], during the lifetime of the religious king Trisong Detsen, who was an emanation of venerable Mañjughoṣa, one hundred eight paṇḍitas, headed by the monastic preceptor Śāntarakṣita, the great master Padmākara, Vimalamitra, and Buddhaguhya, and one hundred eight translators, headed by the translator Vairotsana, Ma Rinchen-chok, Nyak Jñānakumāra,

Kawa Peltsek, Chokrolui Gyaltsen, and Nyangben Tingdzin Zangpo, translated the entire sūtra division of the great and lesser vehicles contained in the Kangyur, with the exception of thirteen minor sūtras. As for the mantra division, they translated many tantras, including the three outer classes of tantra—namely, those of action, conduct, and union, and the three inner classes of tantra that concern the generation stage, the perfection stage, and the great perfection, respectively. They also translated the treatise commenting upon the enlightened intention of these [canonical works], along with the texts of medicine, divination, and all the [other] classical sciences.[441]

The temple of Samye Lhungyi Drubpa was also constructed, modeled on the temple [of Odantapurī near] Śrī Nālandā in India, which represented Mount Sumeru surrounded by the four continents.[442]

Transmission of the Tripiṭaka [13.5.2.3.1]

Among the two ways in which the teachings of the sūtras and tantras were propagated, first, with regard to the propagation of the sūtras (13.5.2.3.1), these comprise works concerning (i) monastic discipline; (ii) phenomenology; and (iii) the [actual] discourses.[443]

Monastic Discipline [13.5.2.3.1.1.1]

First, with regard to the spread of monastic discipline, which is the foundation of the [Buddhist] teaching: Arriving in Tibet at an advanced age exceeding nine hundred, Śāntarakṣita was appointed monastic preceptor. He had traveled from India with twelve monks, in order to test whether Tibetans were capable of receiving the renunciate ordination or not, and accordingly he conferred this renunciate ordination according to the tradition of the Sarvāstivādin order, upon Ba Trizik, Ba Selnang, Pagor Vairotsana, Ngenlam Gyalwa Choyang, Ma Rinchen-chok, Khon Luiwangpo Sungwa, and Lasum Gyalwa Jangchub. The names Śrīghoṣa and so forth were conferred upon them, and they subsequently received ordination as full-fledged monks. These seven became known as the "seven men who were tested" (*sad mi mi bdun*). Thereafter, approximately three hundred intelligent subjects were given the renunciant ordination.[444]

Kawa Peltsek, Chokrolui Gyaltsen, and others translated many works, including the four great canonical scriptures of monastic discipline, along with treatises such as the *Root Sūtra of Monastic Discipline* and its commentaries. They were the first of all to elucidate the transmission of the exposition and study of monastic discipline and all its practical applications [in Tibet].

From Śāntarakṣita, the line of transmission descended in succession through Pelyang (Śrīghoṣa), Nub Sañjayavairaḍīputra Sangye Yeshe, Kawa Ochok Drak, and the latter's three assistant preceptors named Mar Śākyamuni, Yo Gejung, and Tsang [Rabsel], who traveled to Achung Namdzong, and ordained Lachen Gongpa Rabsel. He in turn ordained as renunciants the ten men from Utsang, from whom the lowland Tibetan Vinaya lineage spread [once again throughout the central parts of Tibet].[445]

In To Ngari, Lha Lama Yeshe-o invited the paṇḍita Dharmapāla, and he ordained many as renunciants and full-fledged monks, including the "three Pālas." From them, the lineage known as the highland Vinaya gradually spread.

As for the exegetical transmission [of the Vinaya], Chokrolui Gyaltsen studied under the two paṇḍitas Dānaśīla and Jinamitra; and from him the transmission passed in succession through Mar Śākyamuni, Yo Gejung, and Tsang Rabsel, then Lachen Gongpa Rabsel, Drum Yeshe Gyaltsen, Lume Tsultrim [Sherab] Wangchuk, and Zu Dorje Gyaltsen. The last mentioned integrated this [lowland Vinaya transmission] with the exegetical transmission of the highland Vinaya lineage.

Furthermore, the transmission also descended from Jinamitra and Dānaśīla to Śākyasena and Dharmapāla, and thereafter to both Lub Lotsāwa and Kyok Duldzin, who were also met by Zu Dorje Gyaltsen—the one who integrated the exegetical transmissions of the highland and lowland Vinaya lineages.[446]

Among the treatises on monastic discipline, the foremost are the *Root Sūtra of Monastic Discipline* and its commentaries, which have been extensively propagated, commencing from the early spread of the [Buddhist] teachings, until the present. In this regard, there were many emanational translators who translated the manifold treatises on monastic discipline, which fill some eighteen volumes within the Tengyur.

PHENOMENOLOGY [13.5.2.3.1.1.2]

Second, with regard to the dissemination of the piṭaka of Abhidharma, which represents both the great and lesser vehicles: During the early promulgation of the [Buddhist] teachings, the paṇḍita Jinamitra, the translator Kawa Peltsek, and others translated and expounded the *Treatise on Designation,* which has three parts: *Designation of the Mundane, Designation of Causes,* and *Designation of Actions.* They also translated and expounded the texts of Asaṅga's *Compendium of Phenomenology according to the Great Vehicle* and Vasubandhu's *Treasury of Phenomenology,* along with its autocommentary, the commentary by Prince Yaśomitra, and so forth.[447]

Among the three [illustrious Tibetan exponents of phenomenology], Nanam Dawei Dorje, Lhalung Pelgyi Dorje, and Be Yeshe Gyalwa, the last mentioned traveled to Kham, where he expounded [phenomenology] to Drub Gyalwei Yeshe and others. Consequently the teaching and study of phenomenology has evolved extensively until the present day throughout [Tibet], this land of snow mountains. The treatises that were translated by many translators in early and later times comprise approximately two volumes on the higher phenomenology [of the *Compendium*] and nine volumes on the lower phenomenology [of the *Treasury*].[448]

Discourses [13.5.2.3.1.1.3]

Third, with regard to the dissemination of the discourses, there are three promulgations, among which the discourses included in the first turning of the wheel were largely untranslated [in Tibetan], except for the *Hundred Parables on Deeds* and so forth. Consequently, there has been no exegetical tradition of these [in Tibet].[449]

All the discourses of the *Transcendent Perfection of Discriminative Awareness* extant in India that constitute the intermediate turning of the wheel were translated in Tibet. During the early promulgation of the Buddhist teachings, Lang Khampa Gocha or Nyang Tingdzin Zangpo journeyed to India, and after retaining in mind the *Transcendent Perfection of Discriminative Awareness in One Hundred Thousand Lines* translated it into Tibetan.[450]

Out of great devotion to the sacred doctrine of the great vehicle, King Trisong Detsen is said to have mixed his own vermilion-red blood with the milk of a white goat and then had the text inscribed in four volumes, which were known as the "solitary red leopard." These he placed within an older brick stūpa in Lhasa.

Moreover, Be Mañjuśrī and Nyang Indabaro both brought a manuscript version from India and translated it. This was inscribed with ink compounded from the ash of the king's burnt hair and the milk of a white goat. There were reported to have been four volumes, which became known as the "solitary blue leopard."

Since both the "solitary blue leopard" and the "solitary red leopard" lacked all the extensive enumerative modulations [of the aggregates etc.], they were reedited by Pagor Vairotsana who added supplements for the missing refrains and so forth. The words were expanded, making the text easier to recite. At that time, the great translator [Vairotsana] himself inscribed the text. Known as the "Leather Pouch" *Transcendent Perfection of Discriminative Awareness in One Hundred Thousand Lines* (*'Bum sha sgro can*), after the container in which it is kept, this [manuscript] is nowadays preserved at Chimphu.[451]

So it was that the seventeen "mother and child" discourses forming the long, intermediate, and short versions of the *Transcendent Perfection of Discriminative Awareness* and so forth, were translated, along with the root verses and commentary of the *Ornament of Clear Realization,* the *Extensive Commentary on the Transcendent Perfection of Discriminative Awareness in One Hundred Thousand Lines* by Daṃṣṭrasena, the *Commentary on the Three Mothers Entitled Subduer of Harm* by Vasubandhu, the *Illuminating Commentary on the Transcendent Perfection of Discriminative Awareness in Twenty-Five Thousand Lines* [by Vimuktisena] (*Nyi khri snang ba*),[452] the *Great Commentary on the Transcendent Perfection of Discriminative Awareness in Eight Thousand Lines,* and so forth. The transmissions of their exegesis and experiential cultivation were extensively propagated.[453]

Since the exegesis and experiential cultivation of the sequential aspects of emptiness that form the actual presentation of the transcendent perfection of discriminative awareness are renowned in Madhyamaka, the *Fundamental Stanzas on the Middle Way Entitled Discriminative Awareness* and the text of its commentary entitled *Lamp of Discriminative Awareness* and so forth were translated, expounded, propagated, and developed by paṇḍita Jñānagarbha and Chokrolui Gyaltsen.

Moreover, the other five treatises contained in the *Collection of Reasoning of the Middle Way* were also translated, along with Aryadeva's *Four Hundred Verses of the Middle Way,* Buddhapālita's *Commentary on the Fundamental Stanzas of the Middle Way,* Candrakīrti's *Introduction to the Middle Way,* Kamalaśīla's *Lamp of the Middle Way,* and Śāntideva's *Introduction to the Conduct of a Bodhisattva* and his *Compendium of Lessons*; and the transmission of their exegesis and practice was extensively propagated. Within this corpus, the great transmission of the exegetical tradition of the philosophical exponents of independent reasoning had conclusively appeared [in India] but was not established.

As for the discourses of the final turning of the wheel, apart from those that were extant later in India, such as the *Great Bounteousness of the Buddhas,* the *Pagoda of Precious Gems,* and the *Descent to Laṅkā,* the majority were not completely translated. The treatises commenting on their enlightened intention, including the *Ornament of the Sūtras [of the Great Vehicle]*, the *Supreme Continuum of the Great Vehicle*, the *Distinction between Phenomena and Reality*, and the *Distinction between the Middle and Extremes* were extensively propagated along with their commentarial exegeses.

Based on the *Sūtra of the Buddhas of Medicine in Eight Hundred Verses*, the great monastic preceptor Śāntarakṣita composed the *Rite according to the Discourse of Bhaiṣajyaguru*.[454] Consequently [regular] offering ceremonies associated with [the recitation of] the discourses were implemented as a commitment of King [Trisong Detsen]. Large dialectical colleges were established in Lhasa and in Samye.

Transmission of the Tantras [13.5.2.3.1.2]

The second [of the two ways in which the teachings of the sūtras and tantras were propagated in Tibet] concerns the dissemination of the secret mantra, the vehicle of indestructible reality. In this regard, when [Padmākara,] the great master of Oḍḍiyāna, had reached the age of three thousand, he journeyed to Tibet and remained there for one hundred eleven years. It was he who bound the eight classes of Tibetan gods and demons under an oath of allegiance.[455] He expounded the four classes of tantras in accordance with the mantra approach, and in particular, the unsurpassed tantras. He also conferred their empowerments and pith instructions, so that the teaching of the secret mantra was established [as clear] as the light of day. Immeasurable treasures of the sacred doctrine and treasures of wealth were concealed [for the benefit of posterity].

Moreover, master Śāntigarbha, the *mantrin* Dharmakīrti, and others also translated tantras indicative of the mantra approach, and they conferred empowerments and established the exegeses of these tantras at Dudul Ngakpaling [in Samye]. King [Trisong Detsen] founded large meditation hermitages at Yerpa, Chimphu, Chuwori, and elsewhere; and there were one hundred eight saintly persons, including Yik Dorje Gyaltsen, Nub Namka Nyingpo, venerable Pelyang, Ngenlam Gyalwa Choyang, and Nyang Tingdzin Zangpo who attained spiritual accomplishment there. Foremost among them were the twenty-five comprising the king and his subjects.[456]

The master Buddhaguhya promoted the teaching and study of the tantras of action, conduct, and union, and he translated the tantras and treatises indicative of those three outer classes of tantra, including his own commentarial compositions, extensively propagating their exegesis and practice.

The eighteen tantras of Mahāyoga, which emphasizes the generation stage [of meditation], including the *Tantra of the Secret Assembly,* and among them [in particular] the root and commentarial tantras of the *Secret Nucleus: The Net of Magical Emanation* were initially translated by Vimalamitra and Ma Rinchen-chok, who propagated the transmissions of their exegesis, study, meditation, and practice. Among the eight classes of means for attainment, those pertaining to Hayagrīva, Vajrakīla, and so forth, as well as the three mundane classes were propagated by Padmasambhava. Similarly, Śāntigarbha propagated the cycle of Mañjuśrī indicative of buddha body, Hūṃkāra propagated the cycle of Viśuddha Heruka indicative of buddha mind, and Vimalamitra propagated the cycle of Vajrāmṛta indicative of buddha attributes, along with their respective empowerments and experiential cultivations.[457]

The tantras of Anuyoga, the supreme scriptures [emphasizing the perfection stage of meditation], and in particular the concise *Sūtra That Gathers All Enlightened Intentions* were translated and expounded by both the master Chetsenkye of Gilgit and Nub Sangye Yeshe. As for the esoteric instructions of the Great Perfection, [the tantras of] the class of mind and the class of space were translated, expounded, accomplished, propagated, and developed by both master Śrīsiṃha and Vairotsana. [The tantras belonging to] the class of the esoteric instructions were translated and established through exegesis and practice by Vimalamitra who journeyed to Tibet having reached the age of three hundred, along with Kawa Peltsek and others. The tantras of the Chiti (*spyi ti*) and Yangti (*yang ti*) classes were translated and so forth by the great master Padmākara himself, and others.[458]

So it was that during the lifetime of the religious king Trisong Detsen, the Kangyur and Tengyur were established, exegetical colleges and meditation hermitages were founded, and the [Buddhist] teachings became widespread. It says in the *Injunctions of Padma:*

> The king rejoiced and also founded seminaries.
> At Lhasa he established the festival of monastic discipline, in accordance with the sacred doctrine.
> At Tradruk he established the festivals of phenomenology and secret mantra.
> In each of the one hundred eight border-taming and further-taming temples
> He established timely festivals and spectacles of teaching and study.
> At Samye Chimphu and Yarlung Sheldrak,

At the Dawapuk in Yerpa and in other such places of attainment,
He established hermitages, offerings of spiritual attainment,
Expositions of the tantras, and tenth-day ceremonies.[459]
[In all he founded] one hundred eight meditation hermitages and five retreat centers.[460]

The Reign of Mutri Tsenpo [13.5.2.4]

Prince Mutri Tsenpo constructed the temple of Karchung Dorjeying. All the volumes of the Kangyur and Tengyur housed in the "pillarless" temple of Phangthang were established in terms of their verses, chapters, fascicles, and so forth, and the *Phangtangma Catalogue* was compiled.[461]

The reign of Relpachen [13.5.2.5]

The latter's son Ngadak Tri Relpachen, an emanation of Vajrapāṇi, constructed the temple of Onchangdo. He invited many Indian and Newar scholars, gathering the likes of Jinamitra, a preceptor from the borderlands, and translators such as Kawa Peltsek and Chokrolui Gyaltsen. They established the Kangyur and Tengyur in accordance with the revised orthography, ensuring that the doctrines translated during the time of his paternal ancestors, and those that had been translated from many languages including Oḍḍiyāna, Newari, and Chinese, and those passages that had been left in the original because they were hard to convey in Tibetan, were in conformity with the Indic manuscripts extant in Central Tibet. [Along with Songtsen Gampo and Trisong Detsen,] Relpachen is included in the trio renowned as the "three ancestral religious kings."[462]

Chronicles of the Ancient Translations [13.5.2.6]

The period prior to the arrival of Smṛtijñānakīrti in Tibet and his composition of the *Sword at the Gateway to Language* is known as the era of the "ancient translations" (*snga 'gyur rnying ma*).[463] Concerning the ways in which [the texts of] the sacred doctrine were translated, it says in the *Injunctions of Padma:*

Southwest of the three-tiered Utse, at Dragyurling,[464]
The translators and scholars translated all the scriptures.
The Indian preceptor Dānaśīla, Jinamitra, Śīlendrabodhi,

Pravarta, Dharmaśīla, Surendrabodhi, Dharmaśrī,[465]
Śākyaśrī, Samantaśrī, and Śrībaladhara—these ten took the primary role
While the translators Yeshe De, Kawa Peltsek, Chokrolui Gyaltsen,
Yudra Nyingpo, Konchok Jungne, Rakṣita, Śākyaprabhava,
Lhalung Peldor, Maitrīśrībhadra, and the translator Kichung—
those ten took the secondary role.
These twenty translators and scholars translated [the texts]
Pertaining to the three successive promulgations of the teachings.

As for the first of these promulgations,
They translated ten sūtras that demonstrate the provisional meaning.

As for the intermediate promulgation, they translated seventeen primary and secondary texts of definitive meaning,[466]
Combined with the eight sections of clear realization contained in the [*Sūtras of*] *the Transcendent Perfection* [*of Discriminative Awareness*] and their seventy subtopics, five paths, ten levels,
And one hundred eight modulations [concerning phenomenological structures].

As for the final promulgation, they translated texts such as the *Descent to Laṅkā,* the *Great Bounteousness of the Buddhas,* the *Pagoda of Precious Gems,* the *Elucidation of Enlightened Intention,* and the *Lion's Roar of Śrīmālādevī.*

The higher and lower transmissions of phenomenology are incomplete in terms of these threefold promulgations; for those texts that were no longer extant in India were not translated into Tibetan.
The *Fivefold Nectar of Kāśyapa/Viśvabhuk* was translated by Yeshe De,
The *Mirror of the Sacred Doctrine of Vipaśyin* was translated by Chokrolui Gyaltsen.
The *Distinction of Emptiness of Kāśyapa* was largely translated by Yeshe De, along with commentaries on the enlightened intention of the sūtras (*mdo chos*).

Vairotsana translated both Bon and Buddhist texts together.
Vairotsana translated texts of astrology and medicine together.
Vairotsana translated texts of sūtra and mantra together.
In the sūtra translations, he wrote under the name Yeshe De,
In the mantra translations, he wrote under the name Vairotsana,
In the Bon translations, he wrote under the name Ganjag Thangta,
In the astrological translations, he wrote under the name Indra Vairo,
And in the medical translations, he appended the name Chobar.

As for the texts translated jointly by the translators and scholars Bodhisattva [Śāntarakṣita], Balo Trizher, Balo Yeshe Wangpo, Ba Ratna, Bami Yeshe Jamyang, and Be Thirlen,
These included the *Ground Rules of Monastic Discipline,*[467]
The *Analyses of Monastic Discipline,* the *Supreme Scripture,*
And the *Minor Transmissions.*
So it was that these four great scriptures of monastic discipline were translated.
The *Ground Rules of Monastic Discipline*[468] demonstrates seventeen topics, including the first part that contains the ground rules concerning the habitation of a renunciant, and the second part that includes the ground rules of the confession ceremony.
The *Analyses of Monastic Discipline* demonstrates the precepts appropriate for fully ordained monks and nuns.
The *Supreme Scripture* explains the [aforementioned] *Ground Rules* and *Analyses* in detail.
And the *Minor Transmissions* supplements all their omissions.
Apart from those primary scriptures,
The *Vows of Individual Liberation for Monks,*
The *Vows of Individual Liberation for Nuns,*
And also the *Ordination Rite,*
The *Root Sūtra,* and the *Stanzas* [*on the Novitiate of the Mūlasarvāstivāda Order*] concerning their implementation,
And the *Ordination Rite and Questions concerning Age Applicable for Novices* were all translated and established by many scholars and translators,
Along with their commentarial exegeses and practical applications.

Padmākara, the great [master] of Oḍḍiyāna, and Vairotsana,
The skilled translator who knew twenty-one different languages,
Translated seven fruitional sūtras pertaining to the inner tantras of secret mantra.
That is to say, they translated the *Sūtra on the Nondistinction between the Five Buddha Bodies,*
The *Sūtra on the Distinct Details of the Five Aspects of Buddha Speech,*
The *Sūtra on the Five Gateways to Pure Pristine Cognition Forming the Five Aspects of Buddha Mind,*
The *Sūtra That Eliminates Mistaken Views concerning the Five Aspects of Buddha Attributes,*
The *Sūtra That Ascertains the Enumeration of the Five Aspects of Buddha Activities,*
The *Sūtra That Demonstrates the Roots of the Three Codes of Ethical Discipline,*
And the *Sūtra That Appoints the Executors of the Rites*—these seven were translated.
They also translated the ten general tantras pertaining to the *Gathering of the Transmitted Teachings,* which is the king of secret mantra,
Along with its twenty-one particular tantras and their instructions.
They translated the five general tantras pertaining to the *Root Tantra of the Gathering of the Sugatas,*
Along with its ten particular tantras, the five great transmissions, and so forth.
They also translated the *Tantra* [*That Gathers*] *Perfect Unsurpassed Meaning,* along with its commentary and pith instructions,
And they translated twenty-one great tantras of the secret innermost spirituality.
Vimalamitra, the great paṇḍita of Kashmir, and the translator Nyakchen Jñānakumāra
Translated the *Net of Magical Emanation of Vajrasattva,*
And tantras of *Viśuddha, Vajrakīla, Mātaraḥ,* and *Yamāntaka,* along with their commentaries,
As well as those pertaining to the classes of mind, space, and esoteric instructions, along with the innermost spirituality.

Buddhaguhya and Vairotsana translated the eight sections of the *Net of Magical Emanation,* the *Expanse of Indestructible Reality,* the *Gathering of Enlightened Intentions,*
Four sūtras of Anuyoga—five including the key
[*Sūtra That Gathers All Enlightened Intentions*],[469] and so forth.

The great paṇḍita Samantaśrī, Dharmaśrī, and the two translators Kawa Peltsek and Chokrolui Gyaltsen,
Along with Yeshe Nyingpo, Lekjin Nyima, and Luyiwang Chokyi Lhunpo and others
Translated the action tantras that emphasize physical conduct,
The conduct tantras that emphasize verbal conduct,
The union tantras that emphasize mental conduct,
The unsurpassed tantras that emphasize all three,
The three classes of father tantras,
And the five classes of mother tantras.

The Chinese monk Mahāyānasūtra, the Chinese scholar Saṃshaṃ and others,
Along with five translators including Rinchen-chok, a monk of the Ma [family],
Translated many texts, such as the Chinese version of the *Sūtra of the Hundredfold Homage of Renunciation and Fulfillment,*
The Chinese versions of the *Sūtra of Final Nirvāṇa,*
The *Great Bounteousness of the Buddhas,*
The *Sūtra of Supreme Golden Light,*
The mnemonic incantations pertaining to *sri* demons, and [rituals of] Tārā.

Dānaśīla, Dharmakīrti, Kawa Peltsek, Chokrolui Gyaltsen,
Luwang Sungwa, Yeshe De, and others
Translated many texts, such as the *Root Tantra of Mañjuśrī,*
The [*Eulogy to*] *Mañjuśrītīkṣṇa,*
The *Tantra of the Litany of the Names of Mañjuśrī,*
The *Root Tantra of Avalokiteśvara Entitled Lotus Net,*
And its *Exegetical Tantra Entitled Amoghapāśa,*
As well as the *Tantra of the Great Assembly of Vajrapāṇi* and so forth,
Along with the *Tantra of Tārā.*

Jinamitra, the master of Kashmir, along with Dānśīla, Surendrabodhi,
The great brahmin Ānanda of Gilgit,
And the three translators Kawa Peltsek, Chokrolui Gyaltsen, and Zhang [Yeshe De]
Translated sūtras largely belonging to the great vehicle,
Along with many texts translated from Kashmiri and from Burushaski,
Such as the *Sūtra of the King on Whom Oral Instructions Are Conferred,*
And *Various Recensions of the Inspection of Great Mystery.*

Śīlamañju—the great Newar paṇḍita, the Newar Vasudhara, and others,
Along with the renowned translator [Nub] Sangye Yeshe,
Translated many texts pertaining to Mātaraḥ, Yamāntaka, Piśācī, and Vajramantabhīru,
Including the *Tantra of Mañjuśrī Yamāntaka Entitled Dark Secret Moon,*
And the *Pact of the Nine Offspring of the Emaciating Black [Slayer of Death].*

Namka Nyingpo translated five tantras belonging to the sacred promulgation of the teachings,
The *Tantra of Ucchuṣmakrodha: Blazing Like Fire,*
The *Tantra of Secret Mañjuśrī,*
The Dark Amulet,
The *Tantra of the Secret Zombie [Marutse],*
And the *Tantra of the Secret [Enlightened] Mind [of the Mātaraḥ].*

The great preceptor Sarvajñādeva, along with the translators Kawa Peltsek and Rakṣita,
Translated texts such as the *Introduction to the Conduct of a Bodhisattva.*
The great paṇḍita Padmākarabhadra, Jñānagarbha, and Sarvajñādeva,
Along with the translators Kawa Peltsek, Chokrolui Gyaltsen, Yeshe De, and others,

Translated texts such as the sixfold *Collection of Reasoning of the Middle Way,*
And the commentaries on their enlightened intention.

Śākyasiṃha, Prajñāvarman, Jinamitra, Śīlendrabodhi,
And the great translator Yeshe De translated many treatises
Including the *Five Treatises of Maitreya* and their commentaries,
Along with the *Yogacaryā Level.*

Jinamitra, Śīlendrabodhi, the great preceptor Dānaśīla,
And the great editor and translator Vairotsana
Began to translate three hundred works
Such as the treatise entitled *Great Treasury of Detailed Exposition,*
But the remainder of that translation was left unfinished.
The actual Sanskrit manuscripts are preserved in the Utse temple at Samye,
Where translators and paṇḍitas are even now present,
And where those of posterity will come.

Owing to the rivalries between good and evil,
The *Great Treasury of Detailed Exposition* was left [untranslated].
Similarly, the *Five Hundred Thousand Verses of Hevajra,*
The *Hundred Thousand Verses of Cakrasaṃvara,*
The *Root Tantra of the Wheel of Time in Twelve Thousand Verses,*
The *Tantra of the Supreme Awareness of Vajrakīla in One Hundred Thousand Verses,*
And the *Three Hundred Rites of Vajrabhairava* were not translated.
The extensive and complete version of the [*Transcendent Perfection of Discriminative Awareness in*] *One Hundred Thousand Lines* was left in the domain of the nāgas.
The version of the *Sūtra of Final Nirvāṇa* was damaged by fire, so that it was translated without the title and conclusion.

On the other hand, there are also certain sūtra and mantra texts
That were lost in India but to some extent remained intact,
Having been translated into Tibetan.
Similarly, countless texts on astrology and medicine were translated.[470]

Moreover, it says in the same source:

> Then the master Padmākara,
> From the end of the ox year to the beginning of the tiger year,
> Taught the three outer classes of action and union tantras,
> According to the way of secret mantra,
> Which Chokrolui Gyaltsen had translated.
> He then taught the three classes of the inner union tantra
> According to the way of secret mantra,
> Which Vairocana had translated.
>
> They translated the ten sūtras of the king concerning the outer rites of fulfillment that sustain the physical body,
> That is to say, they translated the *Sūtra of the Profound View: The Heart of Discriminative Awareness,*
> The *Sūtra of the Cultivation of the Definitive Meaning of Pristine Cognition at the Moment of Death,*
> The *Sūtra of the Extensive Aspiration Prayer for Good Conduct,*
> The *Sūtra of Ablution through the Indestructible Subjugator,*
> The *Sūtra of the Confession of Obscurations from the Confession of Downfalls on the way to Enlightenment,*
> *The Sūtra of Reversal through Uṣṇīṣasitātapatrā,*
> *The Sūtra of Protection through the Blue Clad Lord of Secrets,*
> The *Sūtra That Prolongs Life through Lord Amitāyus,*
> *The Sūtra That Increases Resources through Vasudharā,*
> And the *Sūtra of the Essential Single Syllable.*
>
> Then, as for the translators' colophons
> Appended to the sacred texts representative of buddha speech:[471]
> First, according to the translators' colophons appended to texts espoused by pious attendants and hermit buddhas,
> They translated the following ten sūtras of provisional meaning:
> The *Sūtra Revealing Positive and Negative* [*Causes and Results*],
> The *Hundred Parables on Deeds,*
> The *Sūtra That Analyzes Past Actions,*
> The *Sūtra of the Gathering of All That is Woven,*
> The *Description of Transformations Due to Past Actions,*
> The *Hundred Narratives of Pūrṇa and so Forth,*

The *Sūtra of the Repayment of Kindness with Gratitude,*
The *Sūtra of the Wise and the Foolish,*
The *Sūtra of the Applications of Mindfulness,*
And the *Sūtra That Eradicates Immorality.*

An inestimable number of sūtras representing the lesser vehicle were also translated,
Along with the *Ground Rules of Monastic Discipline,*
The *Analyses* [*of Monastic Discipline*],
The *Supreme Scripture,* the *Minor Transmissions,*
And the two sūtras on the *Vows of Individual Liberation* [*for Monks and Nuns*].

According to the translators' colophons appended to texts of the intermediate promulgation espoused by bodhisattvas,
They translated the seventeen "mother and child" *Sūtras of the Transcendent Perfection* [*of Discriminative Awareness*],
Along with many [other] sūtras that emphasize the transcendent perfection of discriminative awareness and emptiness.
In terms of the sūtras of the final promulgation concerning the essential definitive meaning,
They translated an inestimable number of texts,
Including the *Sūtra of the Enlightened Attributes of Ten-Wheeled Kṣitigarbha,*
The *Great Bounteousness of the Buddhas,*
The *Pagoda of Precious Gems,* the *Descent to Laṅkā,*
The *White Lotus,* the *Sūtra of Final Nirvāṇa,*
The *Elucidation of Enlightened Intention,*
The *Bounteous Array,* and the *Supreme Golden Light.*

According to the translators' colophons appended to treatises corresponding to the sūtras,
[Which were composed] in order to comment on the enlightened intention of the three promulgations:
Numerous treatises of the vehicles of the pious attendants and hermit buddhas that concern the four truths were translated.
Including many textual commentaries on monastic discipline,
And commentaries on the corresponding sūtras.

The Sanskrit manuscript of the *Great Treasury of Detailed Exposition* was preserved [untranslated],
But an infinite number of translations were made,
Including the *Aggregates of the Sacred Doctrine* compiled by the elder Śāriputra,
The *Treatise on Designation* compiled by Maudgalyāyana,
The *Collection of Sensory Elements* compiled by the arhat Pūrṇa,
The *Collection of Consciousness* compiled by Devaśarman,
The *Enumeration of Classes* compiled by Mahākoṣṭhila,
The *Introduction to Knowledge* compiled by Katyāyanīputra,
[And the *Dissertation* by Vasumitra]—
These seven treatises of phenomenology,
Along with the five independently composed treatises by Vasubandhu,
Comprising the *Dissertation on the* [*Five*] *Aggregates,*
The *Dissertation in Twenty Verses,*
The *Dissertation in Thirty Verses,*
The *Dissertation on the Proof of Past Actions,*
And the *Rational System of Exposition,*
And textual commentaries including the [*Autocommentary on the*] *Treasury of Phenomenology.*
These are abbreviated [here] because if all of them were elaborated,
The list would be too verbose.

As for the treatises belonging to the vehicle of the bodhisattvas,
Many treatises of the great vehicle were translated,
Including the *Collection of Reasoning of the Middle Way,*
The *Collection of Eulogies* and the *Collection of Tales,*
Which were all composed by the illustrious lord Nāgārjuna,
As well as the *Four Hundred Verses* of Āryadeva,
The *Flame of Dialectics* of the master Bhavya,
The *Commentary* [*on the Fundamental Stanzas of the Middle Way*] of Buddhapālita,
The *Introduction to the Middle Way* of Candrakīrti,
The *Distinction between the Two Truths* of Jñānagarbha,
The *Ornament of the Middle Way* of Śāntarakṣita,[472]
The *Lamp of the Middle Way* of Kamalaśīla,
The *Garland of Birth Stories* [of Śūra],

And the *Epic Deeds* of Aśvaghoṣa,
The *Collection of Aphorisms* of the arhat Dharmatrāta,
The hundred eight dissertations of Dignāga,
The seven commentaries of Dharmakīrti, including the *Exposition [of Valid Cognition]*,
And the *Analytical Reasoning* of Indrasena,
As well as the *Introduction to the Conduct of a Bodhisattva,*
The *Compendium of Lessons* and other works of Śāntideva,
And the *Five Treatises of Maitreya,* which Asaṅga received,
The latter's *Five Sections of the [Yogacaryā] Level,*
The *Three Vows,*[473] and so forth.

As far as the commentarial exegeses of the sūtras of definitive meaning are concerned,
Many textual traditions of authoritative scholars were translated,
Including Vasubandhu's *Exegesis of the Ten Levels,*
[Pṛthivībandhu's] *Commentary on the White Lotus,*
[Vasubandhu's] root *Exegesis of the [Ten] Levels,*
Along with [Sūryasiddhi's] branch *Exegesis,*
And [Asaṅga's] *Commentary on the Elucidation of Enlightened Intention* in sixty fascicles.
So it was that a great many treatises were preserved.

Then, according to the translators' colophons appended to texts belonging to the vehicle of the secret mantra:[474]
They translated [tantras] such as
The *Wish-Fulfilling Gem: A Cornucopia Array,*
The *Jewel Crest of the Assembly,*
The *Five Protective Mnemonic Incantations,*
And one hundred eight lesser mnemonic incantations.

According to the translators' colophons of the tantras of action,
They translated six primary tantras—namely,
The *Tantra of Buddha Body: [Victorious] Protuberance,*
The *Tantra of Buddha Speech: Amoghapāśa,*
The *Tantra of Buddha Mind: Supreme Awareness,*
The *Exegetical Tantra Originating from the [Buddha's] Shoulders Entitled Subāhu,*

The *Tantra That Achieves Excellent Accomplishment, Originating from the* [*Buddha's*] *Navel,*
And the *Tantra of Acala, Which Derives from the* [*Buddha's*] *Knees.*

Among the general action tantras,
They translated the *Root Tantra of Mañjuśrī,*
And among the particular [tantras] they translated
The *Tantra That Minutely Reveals the Rites,*
The *Tantra of the Deities,* the *Long Mnemonic Incantation,*
The *Tantra Elucidating the Final Stage of Meditative Concentration,*
The *Tantra of the Diffusion of Light Rays,*
The *Tantra of the General Secrets,*
And the *Tantra of the King of Empowered Conception,* and so forth.

In terms of the three enlightened families [of the action tantras],
[With regard to the family of Mañjuśrī,] they translated:
The *Root Tantra of Mañjuśrī,*
The *Tantra of the Secrets of Mañjuśrī,*
The *Subsequent Tantra That Reveals the Secrets of Mañjuśrī,*
Ocean from the Exegetical Tantra Entitled Array of Letters,
The *Attainment of the Single Hero,*
The *Songs of Praise;* and so forth.

[With regard to the family of Avalokiteśvara,] they translated:
Twenty-one sūtras and tantras,
The *Lotus Net,* the *Amoghapāśa,*
The [*Mnemonic Incantation of the*] *Wish-Fulfilling Wheel,*
The Mnemonic Incantation of the Thousand-Armed and Thousand-Eyed One,
The *Tantra of Siṃhanāda,* the *Tantra of the Lotus Crown,*
The *Tantra of the Rites of Lokeśvara,* and so forth.

[With regard to the family of Vajrapāṇi,] they translated
The *Root Tantra of Fierce Vajrapāṇi,*
Along with its subsequent tantra and further subsequent tantra,
The *Tantra of Vajrapātāla,*

The *Tantra of the Indestructible Subduer of the Three Spheres of Existence,*
The *Tantra of Indestructible Wrathful Bliss,*
The *Tantra of the Indestructible Cobra Hood,*
The *Indestructible Nucleus,*
The *Descent of the Flames,* and so forth.
They also translated the *Root Tantra of the Indestructible Subjugator,*
And the *Indestructible Stacked Mansions of Sumeru,* and so forth.

Moreover, they translated the *Tantra of Tārā: Blazing with Splendor,*
The *Tantra of Cuṇḍa,* the *Tantra of the Black Slayer of Death,*
And an inconceivable number of mnemonic incantations of awareness.[475]

According to the translators' colophons of the tantras of conduct, also known as the tantras of both [physical and mental emphasis],
They translated the *Root Tantra of the Awakening of Vairocana,*
The great *Exegetical Tantra Entitled Splendor of the Sun*—
Its root tantra, subsequent tantra, and further subsequent tantra,
The *Tantra of Trailokyavijaya That Shines within the Child,*
The *Litany of the Names of Mañjuśrī in Sixty-Thousand Chapters,*
The *Burning Mass of Flames,*
The *Kingly Array of the Three Commitments,*
The *Tantra of the Empowerment of Vajrapāṇi,* and so forth.

According to the translators' colophons of the tantras of union,
They translated:
The great *Root Tantra Entitled Summation of the Real,*
The *Exegetical Tantra of That* [*Tantra of*] *Union Entitled Indestructible Peak,*
The blessed *Tantra of the Purification of All Lower Realms,*
The supplementary *Tantra of Paramādya,*
The *Tantra of Supreme Awareness,*
The *Victory over the Three World Systems,*
The *Net of the Magical Emanation of Mañjuśrī,*

The *Tantra of the Ornament of the Indestructible Nucleus,* and so forth.

They also translated an inestimable number of treatises corresponding to those tantras, including commentarial exegeses, means for attainment, empowerment rites, oral instructions, and practical implementations.
In brief, these [texts] are [all] renowned within the three tantra classes of action, conduct, and union.

According to the translators' colophons of the Mahāyoga texts, which emphasize the generation stage [of meditation], they translated:
The eighteen great primary root tantras,
The four sections of the *Net of Magical Emanation,* including *Vairocana,*
The eight sections of *Secret Vajrasattva,*
The general tantras and particular tantras pertaining to the *Gathering of the Transmitted Precepts of the Eight Classes of Means for Attainment,*
Six tantras belonging to the class of means for attainment,
Including the *Tantra of the Dark Secret Moon from the Mañjuśrī Class, Indicative of Buddha Body,*
The *Tantra of the Emanational Play of Aśvottama from the Lotus Class, Indicative of Buddha Speech,*
The *Tantra of Heruka Galpo from the Viśuddha Class, Indicative of Buddha Mind,*
The greater and lesser *Tantra of the Emanational Play of Nectar, from the Nectar Class Indicative of Buddha Attributes,*
The *Tantra of Supreme Awareness, from the Vajrakīla Class Indicative of Buddha Activity,*
And the *Hundred Thousand Marks of the Mātaraḥ,*
Along with the tantras pertaining to the [secret offerings of] union and liberation,
And [the inner offerings of] nectar, blood, and tormas.[476]

According to the translators' colophons of the scriptures of Anuyoga, which represent the inner transmission, they translated:

The *Root Tantra Entitled Sūtra of the Emanational Play of the Seal of Pristine Cognition,*
The *King of Empowerment,*
The *Sūtra of the Six Awareness Holders,*
The *Sūtra of Supreme Meditative Stability,*
The *Sūtra Elucidating the Secret Gate,*
The *Sūtra of Indestructible Reality, Free from Deviations*,
And the *Sūtra of the Mount of Tārā*—
These seven root sūtras were translated according to the translators' colophons.

The seven inner and primary sūtras belonging to this great scriptural transmission comprise
The *Sūtra That Gathers All Enlightened Intentions of All the Buddhas,*
The *Sūtra of All-Gathering Awareness,*
The *Sūtra of the Great Mind Transmission,*
The *Flash of the Splendor of Pristine Cognition,*
The *Sūtra of the Cuckoo's Emanational Play,*
The *Heruka Galpoche,*
And the *Sūtra of the Supramundane.*
These are the seven inner sūtras of the great scriptural transmission.

They also translated other texts including:
The *Tantra of the Aeon Blazing like Fire, Indicative of Supreme Buddha Body,*
The *Tantra of the Assembly of the Mighty Wrathful King, Indicative of Melodious Buddha Speech,*
The *Tantra of the Pure White Lotus, Indicative of Supreme Buddha Mind,*
The *Tantra of the Unerring Goddess, Indicative of Spontaneously Perfect Buddha Attributes,*
The *Tantra of the Six Points of Meditation, Indicative of Perfected Buddha Activities,*
And the *Tantra That Gathers Perfect Unsurpassed Meaning,*
As well as the *General Tantra Entitled Ornament of Emptiness,* and so forth.
[Among all these texts of Anuyoga,]

The *Sūtra That Gathers All Enlightened Intentions of All the Buddhas* is established as an exemplary model of all the transmitted precepts.

According to the translators' colophons of Atiyoga, the [Great] Perfection, many texts were translated. These included:
The five sections of the root tantras,
The seven sections of ancillary tantras,
Four exegetical tantras, with their ancillaries,
The eighteen lower tantras of the class of mind of the Great Perfection,
The mother and child cycles pertaining to the white, black, and variegated sections of the class of space,
And the oral teachings, revelations, and aural lineage of the class of esoteric instructions.
Each of the latter also comprises five [distinct] cycles—
The outer cycle, the inner cycle, the secret cycle, the unsurpassed cycle, and the cycle of the most secret vital essence.[477]
In all there were five texts classed as earlier translations, thirteen that were classed as later translations, eighteen that were classed as intermediate translations, and twenty that were classed as retranslations.
They translated seven fruitional sūtras pertaining to Chiti Yoga,
The *Tantra of the Gathering of the Transmitted Precepts of the Great Perfection* and so forth;
And they also translated their commentarial exegeses, practice manuals, and an inestimable number of corresponding treatises.

The King also had those masters bring forth through their miraculous powers
[Texts] that had been preserved at Nālandā Monastery and in the domains of the gods, nāgas, yakṣas, and ḍākinīs.
These have been preserved in the vaults of Samye until the present time.[478]

Transmissions of the Great Perfection [13.5.2.7]

As for the lineage that derives from the master Vairotsana, the promulgator of the [seven] perspectives of mind: Vairotsana first imparted the Great Perfection to King [Trisong Detsen]. In Tsawarong, he then taught Yudra Nyingpo and Sangton Yeshe Lama. At Drakmar Gondzong, he taught Pang Sangye Gonpo. In U, he taught Nyak [Jñānakumāra] and Liza Sherab Dronma; and then his physical body vanished into a mass of light at the Bhasing Forest in Nepal.[479]

Pang Sangye Gonpo taught Ngenlam Jangchub Gyaltsen and was then liberated in the body of light. The latter imparted the teachings to his disciple Zadam Rinchen Yik, and then, when he had reached the age of one hundred seventy-two, he was liberated in the body of light. The latter imparted the teachings to Khugyur Selwei Chok, and then when he reached the age of one hundred forty-four, he too was liberated in the body of light. The latter imparted the teachings to Jangchub Drak, and when he reached the age of one hundred seventy, he passed away in a mass of light. The latter granted the teachings to Nyang Sherab Jungne and then passed away in a mass of light. The latter granted the teachings to Bagom [Yeshe Jangchub] and then his physical body became translucent, like the colors of a rainbow. The latter [imparted the teachings] to his disciple Dzeng [Dharmabodhi] and passed away when he had reached the age of one hundred seventeen. The latter's student was Dzeng Jo-se, and his student was the master Kunzang.[480]

Now, as for the history of the Innermost Spirituality, whose lineage derives from the master Vimalamitra, a great promulgator of the esoteric instructional class: Vimala imparted the teachings to Nyang Tingdzin Zangpo and thereafter remained as an awareness holder with power over the life span at Wutai Shan.[481]

Nyang granted the teachings to the elder Dangma Lhundrub and then was liberated in the body of light. The latter granted the teachings to Chetsun the Great and was then liberated in the body of light. The latter granted the teachings to Zhangton and was then liberated in the body of light. The latter [granted the teachings] to his disciple and son Nyibum, he to Guru Jober, he to Trulzhik Senge Gyab, he to Drubchen Melong Dorje, he to Rigdzin Kumārādza, and he to his senior disciple, the supreme Gyalwa Longchen Rabjam, of whom the great master [Padmasambhava] has foreordained, "The princess in her last lives [will appear as] Pema Lendreltsel and as Drime Ozer, who will unravel the enlightened intention of the oral teachings and the treatises." Accordingly Longchen Rabjam undertook most extensive acts for the sake of the Buddhist teaching in general and [particularly] on behalf of the teaching of the most secret Great Perfection.[482]

Transmissions of the Oral Teachings [13.5.2.8]

The descent of the [oral] teachings [of the Nyingma tradition] concerning the *Sūtra* [*That Gathers All Enlightened Intentions*], the [*Net of*] *Magical Emanation*, and the *Mind* [*Class of the Great Perfection*], first descended to Nyak [Jñānakumāra].[483]

Next it descended to Nub Sangye Yeshe. The latter had four disciples who maintained [the transmission]. Among them, he explained the quintessence of the view to So Yeshe Wangchuk. He explained the texts combined with their commentaries to Pagor Lochen Phakpa. He explained [the instructions] given in the [remedial] manner of bloodletting to Den Yonten Chok. He eloquently explained their words and metric versification to Pu Lekpei Dronma. The one who [mastered] all four methods was Yonten Gyatso. The student of both Yonten Gyatso, father and son, and of So Yeshe Wangchuk was Nyang Sherab Chok. The latter [transmitted the oral teachings] to his disciple [Nyang] Yeshe Jungne.[484]

It was the latter's disciple Zurchen Śākya Jungne who, during the later dissemination of the Buddhist teachings, planted the foundations of the teaching of the ancient translations. [His nephew] Zurchung Sherab Drak nourished their branches, and Sangdak Drophukpa enabled their leaves and fruits to flourish. So these are collectively renowned as the "three ancestral Zurs" (*zur mes dpon rnam gsum*).[485]

[The transmission then passed] from the latter's disciple Cheton Gyanak, in succession through the great lama Yonten Zung, Upa Tonśāk, Upa Zhikpo, Zhikpo Dudtsi, Taton Jo-ye, the latter's younger brother Taton Jo-se, Taton Zijid, Zur Jampa Senge, Yungton, Tanak Drolmawa Samdrub Dorje, and so forth.[486]

As for the [oral transmission] that became renowned as the Kham tradition: Tsangton Drowei Gonpo was a disciple of Zur Sangdak Drophukpa. The latter's disciple was Kadampa Deshek, of whom it says in the *Biography of Tsogyal:*

> In the eastern direction from here,
> In a place called Katok,

The base of the teaching of Guru Senge Dradrok,
Where Padmākara conferred thirteen consecrations,
At the neck of that mountain resembling a yawning lion,
Potent and profound treasures have been concealed,
In the future when circumstances have become ripe,
The work of Padmākara and his consort,
For the sake of living beings, will flourish in that direction.
Dampa Gyaltsen, an emanation of me, Tsogyal,
Will maintain until the very end
The teaching of Ati, the way of secret mantra.[487]

Thus there was a most extensive flourishing [of the oral transmission] in this monastery [of Katok] since [it is reported that] a congregation of one hundred eighty thousand monks once gathered there.[488]

The Transmissions of Spiritual Revelation [13.5.2.9]

As for the appearance of the hundred revealers of the profound treasures (*zab mo'i gter ston brgya rtsa*) and so forth, the great master [Padmākara] had said:[489]

Sangye Lama, Drugu Yangwang,
Nyang[rel Nyima Ozer], Cho[kyi Wangchuk],
Gokyi Demtrulchen,
Dorje, Ratna, Pema, Karma Ling,
And others who are indeterminate,
The eleven authentic Lingpas,[490]
The five immaculate ones,[491]
Lords of living beings,
Will bring forth the profound treasures.
Their indestructible verses and translations from Sanskrit are unerring.
In each generation a worthy child will come forth, and
I, Orgyan, will nurture their propensities, without error.
All who have this connection will form an unbroken transmission
Of accomplished masters endowed with truth.
The final phase of the Buddhist teaching will be protected by my treasures.

In future times my teaching will flourish,
And all will pray to me.
Kunkyong Ling, the emanation of the translator Vairo[tsana],
Will establish many beings in happiness through the antidote of the Innermost Spirituality.
One called Melong Dorje, [an emanation of] Luyi Wangpo,
Will bring forth great [works] of the Great Perfection
From the Kharchu area.
At Shelkar Gon, one with the excellent name Kyikye Jangchubsem
Will practice the sacred doctrine concerning inner radiance.
The disciplined emanation of Namkei Nyingpo
Known as Tsāripa, will appear in the Khomting area.
The lord of living beings Gonpo Yeshe,
An emanation of Sangye Lodro, will benefit the teaching.
One called Rangjung Dorje, the emanation of myself, Orgyan,
Will appear as the lord of Tibet and Kham, a saint upholding the [Buddhist] teachings.
One called Ratna Lingpa, [the emanation of] Konchok Jungne,
Will master the treasure doctrines of the buddha mind of Padma.
Kṛṣṇacārin will have diverse, unreliable emanations,
But the reputation of the ascetic yogin named Urgyanpa
Will soar like the wind.
Tangtong Gyalpo, an emanation of myself, Orgyan, at the Chuwori hermitage, will bridge rivers with iron.
Paṇchen Tulku Pema Wangyal, an emanation of Mutik [Tsenpo],
Will appear in the Ngari area.
One named Tashi, an emanation of Ngadak [Relpachen],
Will appear in the Lato area, as a master of profound treasures.
One with the name Lekden, [emanating] as the natural light
Of the magical display of Dorje Dudjom,
Will appear as an accomplished master of wrathful mantras.
One named Mapham Gonpo Sonam will appear in Kongpo,
In the descent of the transmitted precepts of the Great Perfection.
One named Yonten Nātha, an emanation of myself, Orgyan,
And lamp of the Buddhist teachings,
Will construct a temple, symbolizing the three realms.
Dampa, a magical emanation of Tsogyal,
Will appear as a lamp of the Buddhist teachings in the Katok area.

Emanations of the three [translators]—
Kawa Peltsek, Chokrolui Gyaltsen, and Vairotsana
Who are partisans of the [early translations]
Will appear in Tsawarong.
One named Lodro, [an emanation of] Odren Pelgyi Wangchuk,
Will bring forth profound treasures from a secret location.
Dungtso Repa, an emanation of Tingdzin Zangpo,
Will bring forth profound treasures
And confer maturation and liberation on many living beings.[492]

In words such as these, many great individuals [of the future] were foreordained to maintain the Buddhist teachings.

The secret mantra texts that appeared during the early propagation of the Buddhist teachings [in Tibet] became renowned as the ancient translations of secret mantra. They include the empowerments, tantras, exegeses, and esoteric instructions pertaining to both the oral teachings and the treasure revelations of this tradition that have been widely disseminated until the present time.[493]

The Later Translation Period

A Particular Exegesis of the Dissemination of the New Translation Schools of the Way of Secret Mantra during the Later Translation Period [13.5.3]

The third [part of this chapter] is the particular exegesis of the dissemination of the new translation schools of the way of secret mantra during the later translation period. [It comments on the verse:]

> **The later translations include the *Secret Assembly,***
> **The *Slayer of Death,* the *Wheel of Bliss,***
> ***Hevajra,* and the *Wheel of Time.***
> **[And they are maintained by the lineages of]**
> **Kadam, Kagyu, Pacification, Sakya, and Geluk.**

Transmission of the Action and Conduct Tantras [13.5.3.1]

The texts of secret mantra that were translated from the time of Rinchen Zangpo are called the later translations or new traditions. In this regard, during the later dissemination of the Buddhist teachings [in Tibet], it is clear that there was no custom of explaining and studying the action tantras and conduct tantras, except for the oral transmission of the empowerments dependent on these two [classes of tantra], along with the permission rituals, the simple entrustment of awareness, the conferral of scriptural transmission, and so forth. Although one teacher is known to have explained the *Subāhu* and other such texts, his was merely an adroit exposition and it was not regarded as laying the foundation of an exegetical transmission.[494]

Transmission of the Union Tantras [13.5.3.2]

As far as the union (*yoga*) tantras are concerned, Lochen Rinchen Zangpo traveled to Kashmir, where he served many teachers. Having studied many tantras and oral instructions, he became extremely learned in the way of secret mantra in general and union [tantra] in particular. In Tibet he newly translated almost all of the union tantras that had been extant in the past, in conformity with their commentaries. He also translated the commentaries, such as the *Lamp of the Summation of the Real,* which is a commentary on the *Summation of the Real*, and he excellently established them through teaching and study, making their practical implementation precise. He conferred these on many disciples, the foremost of whom were the four heart sons, including Ngok Lekpei Sherab.[495]

Through teaching and study, many lineage holders appeared. Phodrang Zhiwei-o invited the paṇḍita Mantrakalāśa and others, and they undertook many translations. In particular, he explained the *Supplementary Fragment of the Paramādya* and the *Exegetical Tantra Entitled Indestructible Peak* to many students.[496]

Zangkar Lotsāwa also undertook an extensive study of the cycle of union [tantra] and completely translated three sections from the latter part of [Ānandagarbha's] *Commentary* [*Illuminating*] *the Summation of the Real.* He then explained this to others, including his renowned four disciples, so that these doctrines were disseminated. In the lineage that derived from them, Buton Rinpoche later perfectly received all the empowerments and all the exegeses of the tantras and their commentaries. He, as it were, restored the teaching of the union tantra from its foundation. However, nowadays the exegetical tradition and so forth of these tantras and commentaries is largely nonexistent, apart from merely the recited scriptural transmission of these tantras and certain oral transmissions of their empowerments.[497]

Transmission of the Unsurpassed Union Tantras [13.5.3.3]

Father Tantras: The *Secret Assembly* [13.5.3.3.1]

Among the unsurpassed union tantras, the foremost of the father tantra class is the *Tantra of the Secret Assembly.* This text was not originally translated [in this period] in that the later translation is not different to the version included among the earlier translations. However, there are two [distinct] traditions—the tradition of sublime [Nāgārjuna] and the tradition of Jñānapāda.[498]

With regard to the former, the great translator Rinchen Zangpo first translated the actual *Tantra of the* [*Secret*] *Assembly* and many greater and lesser commentarial texts, such as the *Clarifying Lamp*. The empowerments, exegeses, and so forth, of these texts were also completely studied. Moreover, in later times, there were many translators who studied the tradition of sublime [Nāgārjuna] and who undertook various translations and exegeses associated with it. The foremost among them are renowned as the two traditions of Marpa and Go.

As far as the tradition of Go is concerned, Go Khukpa Lhatse attended upon the masters Dīpaṃkara, Devākaracandra, Vīryābhadra, and so forth, and he received the empowerments, tantras, commentaries, and esoteric instructions concerning the *Secret Assembly*. He made many revisions to the tantras that belonged to the earlier phase of translation in Tibet and their lesser commentaries. On their dissemination, these became known as the tradition of Go.[499]

Marpa Lotsāwa Chokyi Lodro attended upon the masters Nāropā and Jñānagarbha and received from them the cycle of the [*Secret*] *Assembly*. Among the teachings he gave in Tibet, he completely conferred the cycle of the [*Secret*] *Assembly* on Tshurton Wang-nge, one of the "four great pillars" (*ka chen bzhi*) among his disciples. The latter conferred these teachings on Khampa Ronyam Dorje, and this became known as the tradition of Marpa.[500]

Jowoje Atiśa also taught Nagtsho, and the latter gave the exegesis to Rongpa Chaksorpa. The line of transmission from the latter and others became known as the tradition of Jowo.[501]

Also, Chak Choje Pel attended upon the paṇḍita Ravendrapa, and others, and he studied the [*Secret*] *Assembly*. Having explained it to Kungrab Lama Pel of Uyuk and others, their short lineage became known as the tradition of Chak.[502]

Also, Paṇchen [Śākyaśrī] of Kashmir imparted these teachings to Sakya Paṇḍita, Chel Chokyi Zangpo, and others, so that [their line of transmission] became known as the tradition of Paṇchen.[503] There were also some diverse transmissions of the exegetical tradition that were slightly dissimilar, but to write of these would be endless.

With regard to the latter tradition, that of Jñānapāda, Lochen Rinchen Zangpo first disseminated it to Kyangpo Cholo and others. Smṛtijñāna imparted this exegesis in Kham, and it became known as the tradition of

Kham. There is also a line of transmission from paṇḍita Puṇyaśrī and Nyen Lo, which was prevalent among the Sakyapa, and became known as the tradition of Sakya. Ra Lotsāwa studied under paṇḍita Puṇyaśrī and others and disseminated that which became known as the tradition of Ra. Also Nyo Lotsāwa attended upon Balimācārya and, after studying the [*Secret*] *Assembly*, his [line of transmission] became known as the tradition of Nyo.[504]

So it was that in both the earlier and later traditions, there have appeared an extremely large number of authors here in Tibet who composed commentaries, means for attainment, maṇḍala rites, manuals of esoteric instruction, and so forth.

Father Tantras: *Yamāri* [13.5.3.3.2]

Also included among the father tantras, is the cycle of *Yamāri*.[505] During the later propagation, Chokdru Lotsāwa Sherab Lama first translated the *Tantra of the Black Slayer of Death*, the *Seven Rites of Vajrabhairava*, the two [other] *Rites of the Tantra of Vajrabhairava*, the *Means for Attainment of the Forty-Nine Deity Vajrabhairava*, and so forth. He disseminated also the empowerments and exegeses of the three [related deities]: Yamāri, Ṣaḍānana, and Vajrabhairava.[506]

Nagtsho Lotsāwa also received [these teachings] from Jowo Atiśa and Samayavajra, and he translated commentaries on these tantras. He manifoldly propagated the rituals as well, including those of empowerment and exegesis of the tantras.[507]

Rongzom Chozang attended upon Upālaśrīmitra, and he translated the tantras of the *Black* [*Slayer of Death*] and *Vajrabhairava* and others, and also undertook their exegesis.[508]

Moreover, there were an extremely large number such as Nyo Lotsāwa, Ra Lotsāwa, and Shuke Lotsāwa who newly translated and revised preexisting translations of many tantra texts and esoteric instructions pertaining to [meditational deities] such as *Red Slayer of Death*, *Black Slayer of Death*, and *Vajrabhairava*. But in particular, the main progenitors of this tradition were the group of four headed by Chel Lotsāwa, the group of three comprising Ra, Kyo, and Zhang, and [lastly] Nyo, making eight altogether.[509]

With regard to the cycle of *Red Slayer of Death*, the first mentioned of those [translators], Chel Lotsāwa Chokyi Zangpo, received [this teaching] from Niṣkalaṅka and propagated it in Tibet. Dānaśīla also gave it to Sakya Paṇchen. Chak Lotsāwa also translated and expounded the texts of

Virūpa. Lobo Lotsāwa received it from Darpana Ācārya and others; and [these texts] were propagated. Among these tantras, the empowerments, guidance, and esoteric instructions of the cycle of the *Red Slayer of Death* are found.

As for Ra Lotsāwa, Ralo Dorje Drak attended upon both the Newar Baro Chakdum and Metsa Lingpa, and he received the empowerments, tantras, and esoteric instructions of *Vajrabhairava*. In particular, he completely received the cycle of the three [related meditational deities]: Yamāri, Ṣaḍānana, and Vajrabhairava, and others from the Newar Mahākāruṇika. In Tibet he undertook a great promulgation of the sacred doctrine. It is said that just the students to whom he imparted the cycle of Yamāri exceeded two thousand. The foremost of these included Ra Chorab. The dissemination [of these teachings] from them is indescribable.[510]

As for that which is known as the tradition of Kyo, Lama Kyo received the cycles of *Vajrabhairava* from Amoghavajra and others, and he undertook their propagation. As for the tradition of Zhang, the aforementioned Chokdru Lotsāwa received both the *Black* [*Slayer of Death*] and *Vajrabhairava* [tantras] from Devākaracandra. Consequently there exists a tradition associated with his close lineage.[511]

As for the tradition of Nyo, Nyo Lotsāwa received the three cycles of *Black* [*Yamāri*] from Balimācārya, and disseminated them.[512]

Mother Tantras: *The Four Indestructible Seats* [13.5.3.3.3]

Among the mother tantras, the empowerment, guidance, exegesis, and esoteric instructions of the *Tantra of the Four Indestructible Seats* appeared to some extent during the time of Lochen Rinchen Zangpo, but it was Gayadhara, Drokmi, and their disciples who translated and expounded this text. Marpa and Go [Khukpa Lhatse] both were important progenitors of its exegetical and practical transmission.[513]

Mother Tantras: *Great Magical Emanation* and *Buddhakapāla* [13.5.3.3.4]

The same goes for the *Great Magical Emanation*. Dawei Ozer and others translated and expounded the tantra and commentary of the *Buddhakapāla*, and this was also disseminated by Marpa, Go, and others.[514]

MOTHER TANTRAS: *CAKRASAṂVARA* [13.5.3.3.5]

As far as the cycle of *Cakrasaṃvara* is concerned, at the start of the later propagation, Jowoje [Atiśa] imparted this [tantra] to Lochen Rinchen Zangpo, Rongpa Gar-ge, and others. Attending on many paṇḍitas, Lochen, Go, and others translated numerous texts of the *Cakrasaṃvara* cycle, including the tantras, means for attainment, and commentaries. Later Jowo [Atiśa] granted and disseminated [these teachings] also to Nagtsho Lotsāwa and others.[515]

Lok-kya Sherab Tsek received the cycles of *Cakrasaṃvara* from the Phamtingwa brothers in Nepal, and he conferred them on Mel Lotsāwa and others. Mel Lotsāwa himself attended upon the Phamtingwa brothers and many others and received [the teachings directly from them]. Thus, he became learned in the cycle of *Cakrasaṃvara*. Sachen [Kunga Nyingpo] received [these teachings] from him, and from the latter and others it was greatly propagated in the lineages of the Sakyapa and their disciples.[516]

Marpa Lotsāwa received the unsurpassed, definitively secret [teachings] of the cycles of *Cakrasaṃvara* from Nāropā, and later in Tibet he granted the instructions to his disciples. Among these, many particular traditions of empowerment and guidance became widespread among the Kagyu orders of Marpa and Mila. In particular, Marpa Dopa attended upon many teachers including a disciple of Nāropā named Manakaśrī, and he received the empowerments, tantras, exegeses, and esoteric instructions of *Cakrasaṃvara* according to the tradition of Nāropā. He undertook many translations from the doctrinal cycle of *Cakrasaṃvara* and completely [transmitted] them to many students in Tibet. In particular, the learned scholar from Tsang, Gyendo Zewa Loden, and others carefully maintained the transmission of this doctrine. The exegetical traditions and the transmission of practice that diverged from him became extremely widespread.[517]

Again Purong Lochung and Nyo Lotsāwa received [these teachings] from the three Phamthingwa brothers, and various sorts of transmissions then arose. Among them in particular, the exegetical tradition associated with the lineage holders in the line from Purong Lochung endured for a long time.[518]

Furthermore, Sumbha Lotsāwa Dharma Yonten attended upon paṇḍita Jayasena. He received and indeed translated the *Tantra of the Ocean of Sky-Farers of Cakrasaṃvara,* along with its commentaries and ancillary texts. In Tibet the transmission of its empowerment and the transmission of its exegesis and so forth were greatly propagated.[519]

Also, with regard to the cycle of Vajravārāhī, which concerns the precepts of the female consort according to that [tantra cycle], the empowerment of the renowned thirty-seven deity [maṇḍala] and the transmission of its approach and attainment appear to have been somewhat widespread. In particular, with regard to the renowned *Six Texts of Vārāhī,* the Newar Virendrarucita received the six texts along with their blessings. Similarly, Ngok Lotsāwa Chenpo, Bubton, Khu Netso, and others also received [the texts], and the lineages that then derived from each of these greatly flourished. Ra Lotsāwa also propagated them, having received them from Abhiyugha. Again Mar Lotsāwa received them from Nāropā and others, and the tradition that he propagated is also extant.[520]

Mother Tantras: *Hevajra* [13.5.3.3.6]

With regard to the cycle of the male and female deities of glorious *Hevajra,* Drokmi Lotsāwa and others translated and expounded this tantra, along with its commentaries and ancillaries, and it flourished. Among them, in particular, Drokmi attended upon paṇḍita Gayadhara and others, and then he received the empowerments, tantras, exegeses, and esoteric instructions, forming a close lineage. This was greatly propagated among the venerable Sakyapa hierarchs and their disciples.

Go Lotsāwa also received it from the brahmin Kṛṣṇapāda and others, and his lineage flourished. In particular, Marpa Lotsāwa received it after attending upon Nāropā. The transmission of exegesis and attainment derived from both Me and Ngok (*mes rngog*) also flourished very greatly, and Petsa Sonam Gyaltsen received the tradition of Nāropā from Phamtingwa [Abhayakīrti] and propagated it, and so on.[521]

Kālacakra [13.5.3.3.7]

In particular, with regard to the glorious *Kālacakra,* which is the summit of all classes of tantra, initially the paṇḍita Śrībhadrabodhi and Gyijo Lotsāwa translated the tantra commentary, and then the lineage tradition of Gyijo evolved from Dro Lotsāwa, progenitor of the empowerments, exegeses, and esoteric instructions, and others.[522]

Dro Lotsāwa, having attended upon Somanātha of Kashmir, completely translated the tantra commentary, except for the chapter on the supreme unchanging nature, and he conferred the empowerments, exegeses, and esoteric instructions. Later, Paṇḍita Sa himself translated the [chapter on] the supreme unchanging nature. Paṇchen obtained it through his peripatetic studies in Phenyul, and he became both learned and accomplished in the *Kālacakra*. He explained it to Droton [Namla Tsek], and it flourished from his time onward, and so forth. He had the custom of explaining it on the basis of the Dro translation—hence the name "tradition of Dro."[523]

Tsami Sangye Drak received it from Kālacakrapāda and translated the *Great Commentary* [*Entitled Taintless Light*]. Then, he explained it to his disciples including [Palchen] Ga Lotsāwa [Namgyal Dorje]—hence the tradition of Tsami.[524]

Ra Chorab received the tantra commentary from paṇḍita Samantaśrī of Nepal, and he translated that, on the basis of which the tradition of Ra spread to Ra Yeshe Senge and others.[525]

Moreover, many other [strands of the lineage] appeared, including the tradition of Paṇchen, the tradition of Chak, and the esoteric instructions of Shawaripa.[526]

The foremost of the oral instructions [of the *Kālacakra*] comprise the six-limbed yoga (*sbyor ba yan lag drug pa*). Other mother tantras including *Hevajra* also have certain modes of guidance based on the six-limbed yoga, but these are not actually the same.[527]

So it was that the cycles of the glorious *Kālacakra* were very greatly elucidated in the snow mountain ranges [of Tibet]. Later still, this [tantra] was elucidated further by many learned and accomplished masters, including the omniscient Buton [Rinchendrub], [Karmapa] Rangjung Zhabs, and Jomonangpa [Dolpopa Sherab Gyaltsen].[528]

The foregoing explanation is an approximate introduction to the origins of the most important tantras. One should know that this is illustrative. Otherwise, it would be impossible to describe in detail all the tantras that were translated into Tibetan because, for the most part, including their empowerments, permission rituals, exegeses, and esoteric instructions, there were none that were not extant [in Tibet].

Kadam Lineage [13.5.3.3.8]

With regard to Jowo Atiśa and his disciples, who were masters of the teaching of Jowo Kadam, the great master [Padmasambhava] had predicted:

> There will be an emanation of mine named Atiśa,
> And an emanation of the sovereign named Gyalwa Jungne.

The Bodhisattva [too] will make Tibetans virtuous.
Their lineage holders will form the Kadampa order.[529]

And:

The great paṇḍitas who are my emanations,
Including Atiśa and Śākyaśrī,
Will emerge in succession,
And kindle the lamp of the sacred doctrine in Tibet.[530]

And Khandro Yeshe Tsogyal [says]:

A rebirth of Śāntarakṣita,
Emanation of the buddha speech of Orgyan
Named Atiśa will widely propagate the sūtra and mantra.
I, Tsogyal, will appear as his translator and attendant,
One named Jayākara, of the Drom family,
And increasingly promote the teaching
At a time when the life span is seventy years.
By explaining the way of sūtra and mantra,
They will permeate the world with virtue.[531]

Jowoje himself said, "These are the doctrines prevalent among the *mantrins* of the present day, which are associated with the time when I, assuming the form of master Padmākara, subdued the gods and demons of Tibet."[532]

Jowo [Atiśa] composed the *Lamp of the Path of Enlightenment.* The lineage was extensively propagated by his three [main] disciples, Khu[ton], Ngok [Lekpei Sherab], and Drom[ton Gyalwa Jungne], and others, who spread the teaching of the gradual path and mind training, as well as by the disciples of Drom[ton], including Putowa, Chengawa, and Puchungwa, who were renowned as the "three brethren."[533]

Kagyu Lineage [13.5.3.3.9]

With regard to the Kagyupa [lineage], it says in the *Biography of Tsogyal:*

An emanation of the buddha mind of Padmākara
Will appear from the southern gorges.

Named Marpa, he will promote the teaching of secret mantra.
I, Tsogyal, will be his wife and consort.
One named Mila will attain accomplishment after practicing austerities,
And an emanation of the buddha attributes of Padmākara
will appear in Dakpo.
The Dri[gung], Tak[lung], Kar[ma], and Druk[pa] orders
Will gush forth like the rivers of Mount Kailash,
Securing [beings] in the ocean of the teaching,
And guiding them to bliss.[534]

The great master [Padmākara] has also said:

One named Mila will appear in Gungtang.
A bodhisattva emanation, like a lily,
A master of the teachings, will appear as Dakpo Da'o.[535]

And, with regard to Dakpo Lharje:

I, Orgyan, will emanate as Lharje in lower Nyal.
A member of the Khu family will appear,
Meditating in Dakpo and meditating on the essential truth.
Inseparable from me, Orgyan,
He will liberate those who see and hear him.[536]

And, with regard to Phagmo Drupa Dorje Gyalpo:

I will appear as Padmarāja,
In the environs of Phagmodru.[537]

And, with regard to Drogon [Drigungpa]:

In a place called Dri, in the northern direction,
My emanation named Rinchen Pel
Will nurture a congregation of thirty-six thousand.[538]

Also:

> My emanation, named Jigten Sumgon, will appear.
> He will act on behalf of my teaching.
> This protector, Jigten Sumgon,
> And Padmākara are no different.
> He will tame living beings through his magnanimous conduct.[539]

And, with regard to Tsangpa Gya-re:

> I, bearing the name Gyalwa,
> Will plant the vital tree that demonstrates the lineage of attainment.[540]

And, with regard to Karmapa Dusum Khyenpa:

> An emanation of Maitreya, son upholding the teaching,
> Dusum Khyenpa will appear from the domain of Tshuphu.[541]

And:

> One named Gyama Gon, endowed with genuine connections,
> And Taklung Thangpa, an emanation of Avalokiteśvara, will appear.
> One named Yudrakpa, an emanation of myself, Orgyan,
> And the mighty yogin Lingje Repa will appear—
> An emanation of Saraha, gushing forth the great rivers of realization.
> At Gotsang in Lato, an emanation of Yudra [Nyingpo]
> With the name of Dorje will bring forth signs of accomplishment.
> An emanation of Tiphu, named Yang Gonpa, [will appear].
> One named Rangjung Dorje, an emanation of myself, Orgyan,
> Lord of Tibet and Kham
> And saintly upholder of the teachings, will appear.
> Avalokiteśvara, emanating in Tibet, in human form,
> Thirteen incarnations with the name Karma will appear.[542]

And so forth.

Marpa Lotsāwa attended upon Nāropā and others, and he received diverse empowerments, exegeses, and esoteric instructions associated with the tantras, and in particular, [the teachings of] the profound path known as the *Six Doctrines of Nāropā.* He conferred them on his foremost disciples, the "four great pillars," who extensively propagated his teachings—the exegetical lineage emerging from the other [three] and the lineage of attainment from Mila Repa.[543]

The disciple of Mila Repa was Dakpo Lharje, and the latter's disciples were the "three men from Kham." Among them was Drubtob U-se, that is, Dusum Khyenpa, from whom the tradition of the Karma Kamtsang developed. Another was Phagmodrupa, whose disciples included Lingje Repa, Drigung Kyura Rinchen Pel, Taklung Tashi Pel, and Trophu [Lotsāwa].[544]

The disciple of Lingje Repa was Tsangpa Gya-re Yeshe Dorje, the latter's disciples were Gotsangpa, Lorepa, and Won-re [Darma Senge], from whom the upper, lower, and middle branches of the Drukpa order [emerged].

In addition, many [other suborders] evolved, including the Drigungpa, the Taklung Thangwapa, the Barom Kagyu, and the Trophu Kagyu.[545]

Furthermore, there were many propagated teachings, such as the *Aural Lineage of Rechung,* which derived from the disciple of Mila Repa named Rechungpa, and the *Aural Lineage of Ngendzong,* which derived from Ngendzongpa, but these cannot be described [here].[546]

Shangpa Kagyu Lineage [13.5.3.3.10]

With regard to the Shangpa Kagyu, the great master [Padmākara predicted]:[547]

> Khyungpo Neljor, an emanation of Maitripa,
> And one named Mokchokpa, an emanation of Niguma, will appear.

Accordingly, Niguma, the wife of Nāropā, accepted Khyungpo Neljor [as a disciple], and [he compiled] the cycle of the Shangpa doctrines, including the *Six Doctrines of Niguma.* He built the monastery of Shang Zhongzhong (*shangs gzhong gzhong gi dgon pa*) and founded the order known as the Shangpa Kagyu. He had some eighty thousand disciples, headed by Lato Konchok Khar and Mokchokpa. The *Six Yogas of Esoteric Instruction* and other teachings were disseminated by Palchen Ga Lotsāwa

[Namgyal Dorje], the accomplished master Yumo and his disciples, and by Buton Rinchendrub and Dolpopa Sherab Gyaltsen, among others.[548]

Pacification and Severance Lineages [13.5.3.3.11]

With regard to the [lineage of] Pacification, the great master [Padmākara had predicted]:

> My actual disciple and lineage holder,
> An Indian named black Dampa,
> Will appear in [La]-to Dingri.
> An emanation of Tsogyal, perfect in conduct,
> Named Labkyi Dronma, will appear at Zangri Kharmar.
> One named Mawei Senge Thopa,
> According to the *Biography of Tsogyal,*
> Will appear as an emanation of the buddha speech of buddha body,
> Endowed with the signs of Tārā.[549]

And:

> Establishing the textual tradition
> That reveals the profound secret mantra,
> The teaching of Severance, perfected in the profound truth, will appear.
> Beings will be tamed by the four lion-like disciples,[550]
> Through whom these teachings descended.

Dampa Gyagarwa traveled five times to Tibet. The foremost of the doctrines he then revealed comprise the *Cycles of the Sacred Doctrine: Pacification of Suffering.* These were extensively propagated by his early, later, and middling lineage holders, and so forth. His instructions known as Severance descended from Machik Labdron. Both of these lineages were transmitted through the Sakyapa, forming the Tsang lineage. But there are also the lineage of Ensapa and the lineage of U that were transmitted within the Geluk tradition, and the lineage of Katok, which is known as the Kham tradition.[551]

Sakya Lineage [13.5.3.3.12]

With regard to the Sakyapa, the great master [Padmākara had predicted]:

> One with the name Dhara, an emanation of myself, Orgyan,
> Will extract the essence of Virūpa's buddha mind,
> And in the lineage derived from him,
> Drokmi Śākya Yeshe, Zhangton Chobar, Śākya Zhang, and others
> Will successively appear.
> They will dispel the defects of living creatures
> By means of the doctrine of the Path and its Fruit.[552]

And in the words of the [*Biography of*] *Tsogyal:*

> An emanation of the religious king named Sa will hold the teaching.
> When the royal line has failed,
> There will be a patron-priest relationship with the Horpas.
> An emanation of the body of Padmākara, named Drokmi,
> Will appear and propagate the Path and its Fruit.
> Establishing the textual tradition of sūtra and mantra,
> His coming will resemble the advent of peerless Śākyendra.[553]

And [in a prediction of] the great master [Padmākara]:[554]

> An emanation of Vairotsana, named Kunga Dorje,
> Will appear at Sakya, in the sevenfold lineage of Mañjughoṣa.[555]

Accordingly, Drokmi Lotsāwa received the tantras and Path and its Fruit from the great paṇḍita Gayadhara. He granted the most important of the exegeses of the tantras to Khon Konchok Gyalpo, and he conferred the oral instructions along with the Path and its Fruit on Seton Kunrig. Seton also received the exegetical cycles (*bshad skor*) from Konchok Gyalpo. He conferred the oral instructions completely on Zhangton Chobar, and for the most part on Zhama Chamsing, and others.

Sachen Kunga Nyingpo received the textual exegeses from Seton, and he also extensively received them from Gonpa. Through experiential cultivation, he became a mighty lord of spiritual accomplishment. His two revered sons were the venerable Sonam Tsemo, who passed away in the manner of the sky-farers, and the venerable Drakpa Gyaltsen. Together with the paṇḍita Kunga Gyaltsen and Drogon Chogyal Phakpa, who are known as the "religious lords, uncle and nephew," these are known as the five founding hierarchs [of Sakya].

In this snow land [of Tibet], the root and branches of the teaching known as the Glorious Sakyapa are supreme. Derived from that, the lineage of the tradition of public exegesis (*tshogs bshad*) at Ngor and Gongkar Dzong and the lineage of the uncommon tradition of esoteric exegesis (*slob bshad*) [that of Doringpa and Tshachen Losal Gyatso] at Kha'u Drakdzong and so forth were propagated extensively.[556]

Furthermore, with regard to the succession of others who maintained the scriptural transmissions, Orgyan Rinpoche [had predicted]:

> Zangkar Lotsāwa, [an emanation of] Yeshe Wangpo, will appear.
> Trophu Lotsāwa, an emanation of Vairotsana, will appear.
> Yagde Paṇchen, an emanation of Pelyang, will appear.
> Diverse but uncertain emanations of Kṛṣṇacārin [will appear],
> And one named Orgyanpa will soar like the wind.
> One named Ngok, an emanation of Trisher, will appear.
> One named Bodhisattva Bu, endowed with the twofold benefit,
> An emanation of Bodhisattva [Śāntarakṣita], will appear.
> I, Orgyan, will assume the form of a physician and,
> As a householder with the name Nātha,
> Will save sentient beings from sufferings and diseases.
> Tangtong Gyalpo, an emanation of myself, Orgyan,
> From the hermitage of Chuwori
> Will bridge rivers with iron.[557]

And:

> One named Jonang, an emanation of Nāgārjuna, will appear.[558]

And in the words of the [*Biography of*] *Tsogyal:*

> The emanations of the buddha activity of Padmākara,
> Will emanate as Karma,
> And spread the teaching throughout Tibet,
> Prolonging the duration of the teaching thirtyfold.

The entire kingdom will be filled with the sacred sound of Maṇi.[559]

Gedenpa Lineage [13.5.3.3.13]

With regard to the Gedenpa, the great master [Padmākara had predicted]:

> At that time a spiritual advisor of the sacred doctrine,
> Discipliner of living beings,
> An emanation of Mañjughoṣa, named Lobzang Drakpa, will appear.
> Having passed away in this field,
> He will depart into the presence of Maitreya.[560]

And in the *Book of Kadam*:

> Departing from here,
> Through a succession of other [births], without interruption,
> They should seize Tibet's unprotected land with compassion,
> And act as authentic kings in this Tibet.
> Assuming temporal power, they should protect Tibet with ease.
> Just as has been said of the land of Oḍḍiyāna,
> I too will go there to tame the gods and demons.
> One emanation will go to the valley of Nepal,
> One emanation will journey through the great sacred places of India,
> One emanation will go to lower Dokham.[561]

Thus it is absolutely certain that the immaculate great [master of] Oḍḍiyāna, the Newar Padmarāja, glorious Atiśa, and venerable Tsongkhapa the Great all partake of a single stream of buddha mind.

It says in the *Questions Posed by Lhodrak Lekyi Dorje to the Lord of Secrets:*

> Lobzang Drakpa, who is entirely peerless,
> Will set his mind on supreme enlightenment
> In the presence of the King of the Śākyas.
> In this field he will propagate the sūtra and mantra texts.
> Then, transmigrating from this world,
> He will depart for the Tuṣita abode.

This supreme son of Maitreya, the essence of Mañjuśrī,
Will swiftly attain buddhahood, and become a tathāgata.[562]

Accordingly, Gyalwa Lobzang Drakpa perfected the study, reflection, and meditation on the infinite textual traditions of sūtra and mantra; and he undertook extensive activities on behalf of the teaching through teaching, debate, and composition. He founded the monastery of Riwo Ganden. He established the Great Prayer Festival of Lhasa and the Great Ceremony of the Rites of Attainment at Ganden.[563] The senior disciples were Gyaltsab and Khedrub, from whom the succession of the "golden throneholders" [of Ganden] gradually emerged.[564]

Gyalwa Gendun Drub founded Tashilhunpo Monastery, and after him the succession of the Gyalwa [Rinpoches] including seven and so forth with the name Gyatso emerged. Jamyang Choje founded Drepung, and Jamchen Choje founded Sera Monastery. Khedrub Sherab Senge established the glorious upper and lower tantric colleges. Afterward, the incarnate line of Paṇchen Rinpoches, including Paṇchen Lobzang Chogyen, emerged in succession. Moreover, there were an inestimable number of saintly holders of this teaching who built an inconceivable number of monasteries in the three lands of China, Tibet, and Mongolia, and extensively propagated [the teachings].[565] It says in the *Biography of Tsogyal:*

Thirty years thereafter, the teaching of the Gedenpa will appear.
An actual emanation of Padmākara will come from the central region,
And the happiness of Tibet will resemble the god realms.
A descendant of the Zahor line will emerge, assuming temporal power,
And extend the teachings through U, Tsang, and Kham.[566]

This prediction refers to the omniscient Fifth [Dalai Lama].

Epilogue

In this kingdom of Tibet, the land of snows,
The sūtras and tantras were translated in earlier and later phases,
And established by means of teaching, study, and spiritual
attainment.
The spiritual and temporal well-being of the teaching and living
beings
Was enhanced by many congregations of saintly beings—
The actual buddhas who came forth.
The precious teachings of the Nyingma, Kadam, Kagyupa,
Zhiche, Sakya, Geluk, and so forth, were gradually propagated.
[Texts of] medicine, Bon, and divination were also translated.
Since it is certain that many sorts of philosophical system
Are included within the enlightened activity of the conquerors,
It is important to refine an impartial pure vision.

This was compiled by Longchen Choying Tobden Dorje in order that an impartial pure vision might be refined, without exaggeration or deprecation in respect of any philosophical system.

Book 13, Part 5
Dialectical Writings of Buddhist Phenomenology

Herein is contained Book 13, Part 5 (CI) from *The Extensive Commentary of the Precious Treasury of Sūtra and Tantra, concerning Dialectical Writings of Buddhist Phenomenology.*

The Golden Key

In order to eradicate opponents through debate,
This book concerns the treasury of lower phenomenology,
And its presentation within garlands of consequential reasoning.
Book 13, Part 5: Dialectical Writings of Buddhist Phenomenology

Verse of Homage

Homage to supreme Dignāga and Dharmakīrti who expounded valid cognition, a beautiful ornament of Jambudvīpa!

The sixth main topic [**Book 13, Part 5**] explains dialectics according to the [first part of the] *Treasury of Phenomenology,* with an arrangement in the form of a series of consequential reasoning (13.6). [It comments on the verse:]

> **Dialectics are engaged by means of reasoning,**
> **Elimination, and the basis of debate.**
> **There are afflicted phenomena that are contaminated,**
> **And purified phenomena that are uncontaminated.**
> **[The systematic presentation of] the aggregates, sensory elements, and sense fields**
> **Concerns the defining characteristics of all conditioned phenomena,**
> **The three aspects of phenomena,**
> **And it includes an analysis of the aspects of the sensory elements.**
> **Then the sense faculties that possess the sense objects are analyzed.**

The content of this text (13.6.1) includes (i) a brief description that accords with the entire corpus [of phenomenology] (13.6.1.1) and (ii) an extensive exegesis that accords with the branches [of phenomenology] (13.6.1.2).[567]

Brief Description according to the Entire Corpus of Phenomenology

A Brief Description That Accords with the Entire Corpus [of Phenomenology] [13.6.1.1]

The first of these, the brief description, includes (i) the reduction [of phenomena] to two modalities (13.6.1.1.1) and (ii) a short explanation [of this reduction] (13.6.1.1.2). The former includes (i) a definition of terms (13.6.1.1.1.1) and (ii) a logical examination (13.6.1.1.1.2).

Definition of Terms [13.6.1.1.1.1]

With regard to the first, taking "knowable phenomena" as the subject for discussion, there is a reason why, in this treatise, the explanation highlights the meanings of both contaminated and uncontaminated phenomena. It is because when all phenomena are subsumed, they are gathered into these two categories.

Logical Examination [13.6.1.1.1.2]

Second, with regard to the logical examination, some [opponents] may say that the defining characteristic of contaminated phenomena is that their contamination can be increased by means of either perception or the [five-fold] concomitance [of mental states]. [Reply:] In that case, taking the "sense organ of the eye of one with the mind of an arhat" as the subject for discussion, it would follow [absurdly] that it fulfills that defining characteristic [of increasing contamination in those two ways] because it fulfills that definiendum [of being a contaminated phenomenon].[568] That in turn follows because [contamination] is something to be abandoned through [the path of] cultivation. That in turn follows because it [the sense organ of the eye] is one of the ten material elements. There is a logical entailment here because it is logically entailed that the ten [material elements] and the five elements of consciousness[569] are things to be abandoned through cultivation. It follows that [there is such an entailment] because it says [in the *Treasury of Phenomenology*]:

> The ten [material elements] and also the five [sensory
> consciousnesses]
> Are abandoned through cultivation.[570]

If one accepts this basic [proposition that the sense organ of the eye of one with the mind of an arhat can increase contamination by means of perception and the concomitance of mental states], then it would follow that contamination could be increased by means of [the fivefold] concomitance [of mental states], for [the proposition] has been accepted. If one were to accept that [contamination could be increased through the concomitance of mental states], it would follow [absurdly] that there might be afflicted mental states that have concomitance with this subject under discussion [i.e., the eye of an arhat], for [the proposition] has been accepted. If one were to accept [that there might be afflicted mental states that have concomitance with the eye of an arhat], it would follow [absurdly] that there would be arhats who have afflicted minds, since that proposition is accepted.

Some may say that if there is a phenomenon that does give rise to contamination through either perception or the concomitance [of mental states], it is logically entailed that it would be a phenomenon the contamination of which could be increased by either of those means. [Reply:] In that case, taking "the two [truths of] cessation and the path" as the subject for discussion, it would follow [absurdly] that the latter is the case [i.e., that cessation and the path would be phenomena in which contamination could be increased through perception or concomitance] because the former is the case [i.e., they are phenomena that give rise to contamination through perception or concomitance]. That in turn follows because there are occasions where contamination might arise with reference to these two [truths]. That in turn follows because there are both afflictions to be abandoned by seeing [the truth of] cessation and afflictions to be abandoned by seeing [the truth of] the path.

If one accepts this basic [proposition that the truths of cessation and the path are phenomena that can increase contamination], it would follow [absurdly] that [the truths of cessation and the path] would be contaminated, since [the proposition] is accepted. This [absurd] logical entailment holds because it says [to the contrary] in the *Autocommentary* [*on the Treasury of Phenomenology*]:

> It does not follow that these two [cessation and the path] are contaminated because [contamination] will not increase with regard to these two.[571]

A Short Explanation [of This Reduction] [13.6.1.1.2]

As for the latter: conditioned phenomena, excluding the truth of the path, are contaminated. If you ask why, it is because contamination increases in them in all ways through apprehension or through any sort of concomitance [of mental states].

[On the other hand,] taking the "truth of the path and also the three unconditioned phenomena" as the subject for discussion, these are uncontaminated because they are phenomena in which contamination does not increase through apprehension or the [fivefold] concomitance [of mental states] as appropriate.

The three [unconditioned phenomena] comprise space and the two kinds of cessation through analytical means and through nonanalytical means.[572] Taking "unconditioned space" as the subject for discussion, it is said to be unobscured because it is a vacuity that, in its naturally present ground, does not impede the arising of extraneous material things.

Taking "cessation resulting from the abandonment of the obscuration of afflicted mental states in the mind of a sublime pious attendant" as the subject for discussion, this denotes the cessation obtained through [conscious] analytical means because [sublime pious attendants] are divorced from any intrinsic share of afflicted mental states, which have been renounced by means of the uncontaminated and unobstructed path.

Incidentally, the four aspects of renunciation—the fourfold renunciation commencing from renunciation through seeing [the truth of] suffering—partake of distinct substances because the substances of which they partake are indeed different.[573]

Taking "cessation in which lesser phenomena continue to arise, distinct from that which is always without impediment" as the subject for discussion, this denotes the cessation obtained through [unconscious] nonanalytical means because one's intrinsic share of things to be renounced by means of the uncontaminated and unobstructed path has not yet been renounced, and because the cessation temporarily impedes any sense objects on account of the insufficiency of their causal basis.[574]

Extensive Exegesis according to the Branches of Phenomenology

The Extensive Exegesis That Accords with the Branches [of Phenomenology] [13.6.1.2]

This comprises (i) recognition of the topics of phenomenology that are to be known (13.6.1.2.1) and (ii) their attributes that are to be known accordingly (13.6.1.2.2).[575]

Recognition of the Topics of Phenomenology That Are to Be Known [13.6.1.2.1]

The first of these includes both (i) the topics of phenomenology that are to be known (13.6.1.2.1.1) and (ii) the way in which these are ascertained (13.6.1.2.1.2).[576]

The Topics of Phenomenology That Are to Be Known [13.6.1.2.1.1]

The first of these has two parts: (i) the systematic presentation of sense objects, psycho-physical aggregates, sensory elements, and sense fields (13.6.1.2.1.1.1) and (ii) an analysis of the sense faculties that are the subject of sense perception (13.6.1.2.1.1.2).[577]

The Systematic Presentation of Sense Objects, Psycho-physical Aggregates, Sensory Elements, and Sense Fields [13.6.1.2.1.1.1]

The first of these has three parts: (i) the defining characteristics of all conditioned phenomena (13.6.1.2.1.1.1.1); (ii) a systematic presentation of the three aspects of phenomena (13.6.1.2.1.1.1.2); and (iii) an analysis of the sensory elements (13.6.1.2.1.1.1.3).

The Defining Characteristics of All Conditioned Phenomena [13.6.1.2.1.1.1.1]

The first of these includes (i) the classifications (13.6.1.2.1.1.1.1.1) and (ii) the synonyms (13.6.1.2.1.1.1.1.2).

The Classifications [13.6.1.2.1.1.1.1.1]

The first of these includes (i) the definition of terms (13.6.1.2.1.1.1.1.1.1) and (ii) their logical examination (13.6.1.2.1.1.1.1.1.2).

The Definition of Terms [13.6.1.2.1.1.1.1.1.1]

With regard to the first, taking "knowable phenomena" as the subject for discussion, when conditioned phenomena excluding the aforementioned truth of the path are analyzed, although they are infinite, when they are subsumed, they are gathered in the five psycho-physical aggregates. This is because, among them, material things are gathered in the aggregate of physical forms, the central mind and so forth are gathered in the aggregate of consciousness, the mental states are gathered in the aggregates of feelings and perceptions, and those mental states that are other than [feelings and perceptions] are gathered in the aggregate of formative predispositions, along with the formative predispositions that are disassociated from mind.[578]

Logical Examination [13.6.1.2.1.1.1.1.1.2]

As for the logical examination, some [opponents] may say that if there are material elements, this entails that they belong to the sensory element of sights. Taking "the sensory element of sound" as the subject for discussion, it would follow [absurdly] that the latter is the case [i.e., that there are material elements] because the former is the case [i.e., that they belong to the sensory element of sights], and that in turn would follow because they belong to the aggregate of physical forms. That in turn would follow because the subject for discussion is as stated. [Reply:] If this [proposition] is accepted, it [absurdly] follows that [sound] would be visibly revealed, for the proposition is accepted.[579] There is a logical entailment here because it is entailed that among the ten material elements, the sensory element of sights is revealed and the other sensory elements are not revealed. That follows because it is said [in the *Treasury of Phenomenology*]:

> Only sights are visibly revealed herein.[580]

Some [opponents] may say that if something is a material element, then this entails that it is one of the ten material elements. [Reply:] Then taking as the subject for discussion "the vows of individual liberation" [that derive from some of the primary elements],[581] it would follow [absurdly] that the latter is the case [i.e., that the vow would be one of the ten material elements], because the former is the case [i.e., it is a material element]. And that in turn would follow [i.e., it is a material element] because these [vows of individual liberation] are material and are the subject under discussion. If [opponents] accept the basic proposition [i.e., that the vows of individual liberation are one of the ten material elements], then it would follow [absurdly] that these [vows] would be one of the five sense organs, such as the eye and others, or one of the five sense objects, such as sights and so forth, for the [proposition] is accepted. There is a logical entailment here, because it is said [in the *Treasury of Phenomenology*]:

> These sense organs and sense objects are exclusively held to comprise ten sense fields or ten sensory elements.[582]

Some [opponents may say] that it follows that the eighteen sensory elements[583] are mutually contradictory with regard to their internal counterparts because if any of the five sense organs, such as the eye, is present, it must exclude the [corresponding] sensory element of sights that constitutes its subdivision. If this [proposition] is accepted, it follows that all eighteen individually would be mutually contradictory, since this proposition is accepted. [Reply:] If so, there is no logical entailment. It cannot be accepted because the sensory element of the mental faculty and the six sensory elements of consciousness are not individually contradictory. That follows because if any of the six [consciousnesses] are present, the sensory element of the mental faculty must also be present.

Some [opponents may say] that it follows that the mind of a being in the intermediate state [after death] possesses five sense faculties because the sense organ of the eye possessed by the mind of someone in deep sleep is a material form resembling the sense faculty with which it has a shared support.[584] If this [proposition] is accepted, it follows that the mind of a being in the intermediate state within the world system of form would possess all five sense organs, including the eye, since [that proposition] is accepted. If that is accepted, it follows that therein [i.e., in the world system of form] the five sense organs including the eye would be present, since [that proposition] is accepted. If that is accepted, it follows that therein [in the world system of form] the sense organ of the nose and the sense organ of the tongue would be present since [that proposition] is accepted. If that is accepted, it follows that the consciousnesses corresponding to those two [sense organs] would be present, since that proposition is accepted. [Reply:] If so, there is no logical entailment because (i) the other fourteen [sensory elements] are present therein, [in the world system of form,] with the exception of four comprising the sensory elements of smell and taste, and the two corresponding consciousnesses—olfactory and gustatory, because (ii) in the world system of desire, all eighteen are present, and because (iii) in the world system of formlessness, the sensory elements of the mental faculty and mental phenomena, and the sensory element of mental consciousness are present but, excluding these, the others are not present. This follows because it says [in the *Treasury of Phenomenology*]:

> All of them are present in the world system of desire.
> With the exception of odor and taste,
> Olfactory and gustatory consciousness.
> The other fourteen are present in the world system of form.
> [Three of them,] comprising the sensory elements
> Of the mental faculty, mental phenomena, and mental
> consciousness,
> Are present in the world system of formlessness.[585]

Some [opponents] may say that if there are sounds produced from primary elements that are organically retained [as a support by mind and mental states, such as human language], this entails that [sound] is an organically retained element.[586] It follows that this is incorrect because when there are sounds, there must [also] be [sounds derived from] organically unretained elements. That follows because [among the eighteen sensory elements] there are seven mental elements, mental states comprising half of the sensory element of mental phenomena,[587] and sound—altogether nine elements that are organically unretained, and nine material elements that may be either organically retained or unretained, as is said [in the *Treasury of Phenomenology*]:

> Nine are organically unretained—
> The aforementioned eight and sound.
> The other nine are of both sorts.[588]

[Some may say,] taking "the vows of individual liberation" as the subject for discussion, that it follows that these are visibly revealed sights or forms because they constitute the sensory element of sights. That in turn follows because any one of the eighteen sensory elements is not any of the remaining seventeen.

[Reply:] In this case, the final statement is not established because they [the vows of individual liberation] constitute the sensory element of mental phenomena. That follows because any form that is nonapperceived [such as the vows of individual liberation] entails the sensory element of mental phenomena.[589]

The first [of these statements] follows because the vows [of individual liberation] are [classed as] nonapperceived forms. That follows because they are of three sorts: [nonapperceived forms] that retain the vows, those that do not retain the vows, and those that are neutral [i.e., neither]. That follows because it is said [in the *Treasury of Phenomenology*]:

> It should be known that nonapperceived [forms] are of three sorts:
> Those that retain the vows,
> Those that do not retain the vows,
> And those that do neither.[590]

The second [of these statements] follows because the three middle aggregates [of feelings, perceptions, and formative predispositions], along with nonapperceived forms and unconditioned phenomena, these five, entail the sensory element of mental phenomena and the sense field of mental phenomena. This is because it is said [in the *Treasury of Phenomenology*]:

> These three [aggregates], along with nonapperceived [forms]
> And unconditioned phenomena,
> Are said to comprise the sense field of mental phenomena.[591]

Indeed, the basic [proposition] cannot be accepted because there are forms that are visibly unrevealed and unimpeded and because the subject for discussion [the vows of individual liberation] is such.

Some may say that if there are sense organs associated with the mind of someone inhabiting the world system of desire, it entails that they are subsumed within the level of the world system of desire. In this case, taking as the subject for discussion "the sense organ of the eyes associated with the mind of someone in the first meditative concentration and inhabiting that [world system of desire]," it would follow that the latter is the case [they are subsumed within the world system of desire] because the former is the case [the sense organs are associated with the mind of someone inhabiting the world system of desire], and that in turn would [absurdly] follow because there are [sense organs of the eye associated with the mind of someone in the first meditative concentration and inhabiting the world system of desire].

This is because, when someone whose physical frame is that of [the world system of] desire beholds the sights associated with the first meditative concentration, dependent on the eyes of the first meditative concentration, the supporting [physical frame], sense organs, sense objects, and aspects of consciousness are incomplete. That in turn follows because the physical frame is still subsumed in the level of [the world system of] desire, but the remaining [attributes] are subsumed in the level of the first meditative concentration. That follows because when one [abiding] in the first meditative concentration beholds sights associated with the second [meditative concentration], dependent on the eyes of the second meditative concentration, the physical frame and consciousness [of that person] are both subsumed in the level of the first meditative concentration, but the remaining two [attributes] are subsumed in the level of the second meditative concentration. That in turn follows because when one [abiding] in the third [meditative concentration] beholds sights associated with the second [meditation concentration], dependent on the eyes of the fourth meditative concentration, the sense organs are subsumed in the level of the fourth [meditative concentration], the physical frame is subsumed in the level of the third meditative concentration, the sense objects are subsumed in the level of the second [meditative concentration], and the consciousness is subsumed in the level of the first [meditative concentration].[592]

Synonyms [13.6.1.2.1.1.1.1.2]

The second part [of the defining characteristics of conditioned phenomena] concerns synonyms (13.6.1.2.1.1.1.1.2). This includes (i) synonyms of conditioned phenomena in general (13.6.1.2.1.1.1.1.2.1) and (ii) synonyms of contaminated phenomena (13.6.1.2.1.1.1.1.2.2).

Synonyms of Conditioned Phenomena in General [13.6.1.2.1.1.1.1.2.1]

As to the first, taking "the nature of conditioned phenomena" as the subject for discussion, they are called "conditioned"[593] because they are the ground upon which the three times are framed. That subject for discussion is said to be the "basis of conversation" because it is the ground upon which expressive conversations arise. That subject for discussion is said to be "emancipating" (*nges par 'byung ba*) because it is unquestionably "definitive" (*nges pa*) and "gives rise" (*'byung ba*) to nirvāṇa, so that you, after abandoning it, must actualize the nonresidual nirvāṇa. That subject for discussion is said to be "associated with the ground" because it is associated with efficient causes.[594]

Synonyms of Contaminated Phenomena [13.6.1.2.1.1.1.1.2.2]

As to the second, taking "any of the five contaminated aggregates" as the subject for discussion, they are described as acquisitive aggregates because (i) these [aggregates] have arisen from acquisitive afflicted mental states; (ii) they are dependent on those [afflicted mental states]; and (iii) acquisitive afflicted mental states have arisen from them as their intrinsic fruit. These three resemble, respectively, for example, the manner in which a fire that originates from grassland is called a "grassland fire," a person who is dependent on a king is called a "king's man," or a tree that produces flowers is called a "flowering tree."[595]

Taking "these contaminated aggregates" as the subject for discussion, they are also said to be "in conflict" because, dependent on these [aggregates], a physical and verbal conflict arises with reference to oneself and others. That same subject for discussion is said to be "imbued with suffering" because [the contaminated aggregates] may be associated with any of the three modes of suffering.[596]

That same subject for discussion is said to be "the cause of suffering" because [the contaminated aggregates] give rise to subsequent suffering. That same subject for discussion is said to be "mundane" because [the contaminated aggregates] are instantaneously destroyed and may also be destroyed by an antidote. That same subject for discussion is said to be "a locus of wrong views" because [the contaminated aggregates] are a locus for the arising of mistaken views. That same subject for discussion is said to partake of "the rebirth process" because [the contaminated aggregates] have been the causal basis for the recurring of subsequent rebirths from beginningless cyclic existence.[597]

The Systematic Presentation of the Three Aspects of Phenomena

The Systematic Presentation of the Three Aspects of Phenomena [13.6.1.2.1.1.1.2]

The second part [of the systematic presentation of sense objects, psycho-physical aggregates, sensory elements, and sense fields] is the systematic presentation of the three aspects of phenomena (13.6.1.2.1.1.1.2). This comprises (i) the nature of the three different aspects of phenomena (13.6.1.2.1.1.1.2.1); (ii) the distinctive attributes of the three aspects of phenomena (13.6.1.2.1.1.1.2.2); and (iii) summation in the extraneous three aspects of phenomena (13.6.1.2.1.1.1.2.3).

The Nature of the Three Different Aspects of Phenomena [13.6.1.2.1.1.1.2.1]

The first of these [the nature of the three different aspects of phenomena] includes (i) the three aspects of phenomena subsumed in matter (13.6.1.2.1.1.1.2.1.1); (ii) the three aspects of phenomena subsumed in aggregates other than physical forms and mind [consciousness] (13.6.1.2.1.1.1.2.1.2); and (iii) the three aspects of phenomena subsumed in mind [consciousness] (13.6.1.2.1.1.1.2.1.3).

The Three Aspects of Phenomena Subsumed in Matter [13.6.1.2.1.1.1.2.1.1]

The first of these, [the three aspects of phenomena subsumed in matter,] includes both (i) the nature of the aggregate of physical forms (13.6.1.2.1.1.1.2.1.1.1) and (ii) the establishment of the derivative sensory elements and sense fields (13.6.1.2.1.1.1.2.1.1.2).

The Nature of the Aggregate of Physical Forms [13.6.1.2.1.1.1.2.1.1.1]

The first of these includes both (i) a brief presentation (13.6.1.2.1.1.1.2.1.1.1.1) and (ii) an extensive exegesis (13.6.1.2.1.1.1.2.1.1.1.2).

Brief Presentation [13.6.1.2.1.1.1.2.1.1.1.1]

As to the first, [the brief presentation,] taking as the subject for discussion "the eleven sorts of matter, including the five sense organs, the five sense objects, and nonapperceived form," these constitute the aggregate of physical forms because they are [collectively] the materials that appear as the object of the intellect, in the manner of a conglomeration.[598]

Extensive Exegesis of the Aggregate of Physical Forms [13.6.1.2.1.1.1.2.1.1.1.2]

As to the second, [the extensive exegesis,] this concerns (i) the five sense organs (13.6.1.2.1.1.1.2.1.1.1.2.1); (ii) the five sense objects (13.6.1.2.1.1.1.2.1.1.1.2.2); and (iii) an exegesis of nonapperceived physical forms (13.6.1.2.1.1.1.2.1.1.1.2.3).

The Five Sense Organs [13.6.1.2.1.1.1.2.1.1.1.2.1]

With regard to the first, [the five sense organs]: taking "knowable phenomena" as the subject for discussion, the physical frame supporting visual consciousness and so forth has as its predominant condition the sense organ of the eyes and so forth. This is established because it includes the clear and sensitive matter [of the eyes], present as the seed giving rise to the uncommon predominant condition of the visual consciousness that apprehends sights, its own [specific] or intrinsic fruit. Adding the words "and so forth" to the subject for discussion is necessary because the intent is that the four additional sense organs [of the ears, nose, tongue, and body] can also be implicitly understood.[599]

The Five Sense Objects [13.6.1.2.1.1.1.2.1.1.1.2.2]

With regard to the second, [the five sense objects]: taking "knowable phenomena" as the subject for discussion, these include the defining characteristics of the sense field of sights because it is this external sense field that highlights sights, the object of the apprehending visual consciousness. Taking the "sense field of sights" as the subject for discussion, when a basic analysis is made, this has two aspects because these "sights" include the two aspects of color and shape. When a secondary analysis is made, these have twenty aspects because there are twelve colors and eight shapes. The former is established because there are four primary colors and eight secondary shades. The former are established because there are four [primary colors]: blue, yellow, red, and white. The latter are established because there are [eight secondary shades,] namely, cloud, smoke, dust, mist, light—including moonlight, starlight, firelight, herbal light and gemstone light—darkness, sunlight, and shadow. The second primary indication [of sights or visual forms] is established because there are [eight] shapes—namely, long, short, square, round, high, low, even, and uneven.

Taking "sound" as the subject for discussion, when a basic analysis is made, this [sound] has two aspects because it includes both sounds that are organically retained and sounds that are organically unretained. When a secondary analysis is made, this [sound] has eight aspects because each of those two [modes of sound] has four aspects. That follows because the first mode [organically retained sound] includes sound that denotes a sentient being [as its source], whether pleasant or unpleasant, and [sound] that does not denote [a sentient being as its source], whether pleasant or unpleasant. The second mode [organically unretained sound] also has these [four aspects].

The former [four aspects of organically retained sound] are established because they include, respectively, [pleasant] songs sung by a person, harsh words spoken by a person, the [pleasant] sound of instrumental music, and the [unpleasant, thumping] sound of a fist. The latter [four aspects of organically unretained sound] are established because they include, respectively, the [pleasant] teaching of the sacred doctrine by an emanational teacher, [unpleasant] roaring, the [pleasant] sound of a bell or chime, tinkling of its own accord, and the [unpleasant] sound of breaking rocks.

Taking "taste" as the subject for discussion, when an analysis is made, this [taste] has six aspects because there are sweet, sour, bitter, spicy, astringent, and salty tastes. Taking that as the subject for discussion, taste may have multiple subdivisions because, when a basic analysis is made into the six aspects [of each], commencing with the sweetness of sweetness, it comprises thirty-six aspects, and because it also comprises one hundred eight aspects; for when each [of the thirty-six] is savored by the sense organ of the tongue, it is a taste that facilitates gustatory consciousness, when each contributes to digestion, it is a taste that does not harm the body, and when digestion occurs, it is a taste that benefits both the body and the mind. There are also other [subdivisions of taste] because the number of tastes increases to sixty-three owing to the distinctions made when the six primary tastes interact. This is because it is said in the *Commentary on the Treasury of Phenomenology* by Yaśomitra:

> With reference to the six kinds [of taste], although they are explained as such, there are multiple divisions owing to distinctions made when the six [primary] tastes interact. The physician Caraka has said, "Derived from the interaction of one, two, three, four, five, and six tastes, it is revealed that there are sixty-three aspects of taste."[600]

Taking "odor" as the subject for discussion, when a basic analysis is made, this [odor] has two aspects because there are both fragrant and sharp odors. Taking that as the subject for discussion, when a secondary analysis is made, odor has four aspects because the first aspect [fragrance] may be even or uneven [in its distribution], and the latter [sharpness] may be even or uneven [in its distribution]. That follows because the odors of sweet clover, eaglewood, asafoetida, and garlic are respectively [fragrant and even, fragrant and uneven, sharp and even, and sharp and uneven].

Taking "tangibles" as the subject for discussion, these [tangibles] are divided into eleven types because there are four tangibles that comprise the four primary elements [earth, water, fire, and wind] and seven tangibles that are physical sensations deriving from these primary elements. The latter are established because they comprise softness, hardness, heaviness, lightness, hunger, thirst, and cold.[601]

An Exegesis of Nonapperceived Physical Forms [13.6.1.2.1.1.1.2.1.1.1.2.3]

With regard to the third, [the exegesis of nonapperceived physical forms,] this includes both (i) their essential nature (13.6.1.2.1.1.1.2.1.1.1.2.3.1) and (ii) incidental remarks (13.6.1.2.1.1.1.2.1.1.1.2.3.2).

Their Essential Nature [13.6.1.2.1.1.1.2.1.1.1.2.3.1]

As to the former, it is established that there are nonapperceived physical forms because these [nonapperceived forms] are recognized to include forms with four attributes that are unrevealed and unimpeded. Nonapperceived forms are said to have four attributes because the following four are present: occasionality, essentiality, serial continuity, and causal basis. The first of these [occasionality] is established because not only does [nonapperceived form] arise in periods of undistracted mentation, but it also arises in periods of distracted mentation and periods when the mind is absent. The second [essentiality] is established because [nonapperceived form] is subsumed in both virtuous and nonvirtuous activities. The third [serial continuity] is established because subsequent instances [of nonapperceived form] are connected serially with previous instances. The fourth [causal basis] is established because [nonapperceived form] is a fruitional form that has the four primary elements as its causal basis.[602]

Incidental Remarks [13.6.1.2.1.1.1.2.1.1.1.2.3.2]

As to the latter, [the incidental remarks concerning the primary elements,] this has four parts: (i) the classification of the elements (13.6.1.2.1.1.1.2.1.1.1.2.3.2.1); (ii) their functions (13.6.1.2.1.1.1.2.1.1.1.2.3.2.2); (iii) their intrinsic natures (13.6.1.2.1.1.1.2.1.1.1.2.3.2.3); and (iv) the ensuing resolution of doubts[603] (13.6.1.2.1.1.1.2.1.1.1.2.3.2.4).

With regard to the first, [the classification of the elements,] taking "knowable phenomena" as the subject for discussion, the primary elements, when classified, are four in number because they comprise the earth element, the water element, the fire element, and the wind element.

With regard to the second, [their functions,] taking "knowable phenomena" as the subject of the discussion, the four primary elements have functions because earth is supportive, water and so forth are cohesive, fire is maturing, and wind is expanding.

With regard to the third, [their intrinsic natures,] taking "knowable phenomena" as the subject for discussion, the primary elements have their intrinsic natures because their defining characteristics are that earth is solid and hard, water is moist and wet, fire has the nature of warmth, and wind is light and mobile.[604]

With regard to the [Sanskrit] root *ḍudhāñ,* [meaning] "to hold," as *ḍu* is a technical marker, according to the rule *de'i tshar pa la kṛ ma ka'o,* the prefix *ḍu* is elided;[605] and according to the rule *in dang / nya dang / ya dza sogs las gnyis ka'o,* the suffix *ñ* is elided.[606]

Following the root *dhā,* according to the rule *sita-nigami-masi-sacy-avi-dhāñ-kuśibhyas tun,*[607] the suffix *–tu* can be added. After elision of the aforementioned technical markers, this may result in the form *dhātu,* ["sensory element," translated as] *khams* [in Tibetan].

With regard to the root *ḍudhṛñ,* meaning "to hold," according to the rule *pacādibhyo 'c,*[608] the suffix *aC* indicative of moderate vowel strengthening can be applied, resulting in the form *dhara,* ["holding," translated as] *'dzin pa* [in Tibetan].

However Drungchen Ngodrub [in his *Exegesis of the Treasury of Phenomenology: Intelligence That Opens the Lotus of the Mind*], not understanding that these should be taken as two different stem-formations, states "to *dhātu* the suffix of *dhāra* can be applied."

As [this statement] appears to be a ridiculous fiction, which is not known anywhere in the eight great grammatical treatises of India, others have no choice but to emphasize that point. Apart from that, it would be excellent if there were a single exponent of dialectics who could establish this [derivation] out of concern for the conventional sciences.

With regard to the fourth, [the ensuing resolution of doubts,] taking "knowable phenomena" as the subject for discussion, there are classifications [of the elements] such as earth and such as the color of earth because, according to worldly convention, the colors and shapes of the four primary elements express the four primary elements. That follows because earth is yellow and square, water is white and round, fire is red and triangular, and also wind is said to be blue and circular—no matter how many gusts the wind comprises, they resemble the preceding [gusts] because they are the very same wind element.[609]

The Establishment of the Derivative Sensory Elements and Sense Fields [13.6.1.2.1.1.1.2.1.1.2]

The second part [of the three aspects of phenomena subsumed in matter] concerns the establishment of the derivative sensory elements and sense fields (13.6.1.2.1.1.1.2.1.1.2). This comprises (i) the definitions of the terms (13.6.1.2.1.1.1.2.1.1.2.1) and (ii) their logical examination (13.6.1.2.1.1.1.2.1.1.2.2).

Definitions of the Terms [13.6.1.2.1.1.1.2.1.1.2.1]

As to the first, [the definitions of the terms,] taking "knowable phenomena" as the subject for discussion, the [aforementioned] ten sense organs and sense objects are exclusively established within [the context of] the sense fields. This is because they are established as the ten material sense fields. Also, taking these ["knowable phenomena"] as the subject for discussion, the [sense organs and sense objects] are established within [the context of] the sensory elements because they constitute the ten material elements.

Logical Examination [13.6.1.2.1.1.1.2.1.1.2.2]

As to the second, [the logical examination:] some may say that the defining characteristic of the male organ is a person with an individual mental continuum exhibiting masculine characteristics and that the defining characteristic of the female organ is a person with an individual mental continuum exhibiting feminine characteristics. In that case, taking as the subject for discussion, the "male organ of a hermaphrodite," it follows that the former defining characteristic [a person with an individual mental continuum exhibiting masculine characteristics] is fulfilled because its definiendum [the male organ] is fulfilled. If that proposition is accepted, then taking as the subject for discussion the female organ of that same individual, it follows that the latter defining characteristic is also fulfilled because its definiendum [the female organ] is also fulfilled. If that proposition is accepted, it follows that the person [in question] is both male and female.[610]

Some may say that if there are sense organs with feelings of suffering, this entails that there are sense organs with feelings of suffering in which the feelings are divided into five types [corresponding to the five sense organs]. In that case, taking the "sense organs with the feeling of unhappiness" as the subject for discussion, it follows that the latter [sense organs with feelings of suffering in which feelings are divided into five types] is the case because the former [sense organs with feelings of suffering] is the case. That in turn would [absurdly] follow because there would be sense organs with feelings of suffering in which feelings are divided into three types—those of happiness, sorrow, and indifference. That in turn would follow because the subject for discussion [sense organs with feelings of unhappiness] is as stated. If this proposition were accepted, it would [absurdly] follow that the body would consist of feelings, since the proposition has been accepted. If this proposition were accepted, it would [absurdly] follow that external [phenomena] are feelings.

Some may say that if there are sense organs with feelings of happiness, this entails that there are sense organs with feelings of happiness in which the feelings are divided into five types [corresponding to the five sense organs]. In that case, taking the "sense organs with feelings of happiness" as the subject for discussion, it follows that the latter [sense organs with feelings of happiness divided into five types] is the case because the former [sense organs with feelings of happiness] is the case. That in turn would [absurdly] follow because there would be sense organs with feelings of happiness in which feelings are divided into three types. That would follow because the subject for discussion [sense organs with feelings of happiness] is as stated.[611]

Some may say that if there is a faculty of faith, this entails that there is a faculty of faith, which is a subdivision of the thirty-seven factors conducive to enlightenment. In that case, if that were so, it follows that this would entail that it belongs to the path. This is because certain authorities include within the path the faith that is among the thirty-seven factors conducive to enlightenment. If this proposition is accepted, then taking as the subject for discussion the "faculty of faith within the mental continuum of a person who has not entered the path," it would [absurdly] follow that the latter [i.e., the presence of the faculty of faith as a subdivision of the thirty-seven factors conducive to enlightenment] is the case because the former [the presence of the faculty of faith] is the case; and so the proposition cannot be accepted.[612]

The Three Aspects of Phenomena Subsumed in Aggregates Other Than Physical Forms and Mind [Consciousness] [13.6.1.2.1.1.1.2.1.2]

The second part [of the nature of the three different aspects of phenomena] concerns the three aspects of phenomena subsumed in aggregates other than physical forms and mind [or consciousness] (13.6.1.2.1.1.1.2.1.2). This comprises (i) their essential natures (13.6.1.2.1.1.1.2.1.2.1) and (ii) the establishment of their derivative sensory element and sense field (13.6.1.2.1.1.1.2.1.2.2).

Their Essential Natures [13.6.1.2.1.1.1.2.1.2.1]

As to the first, [their essential natures,] taking "knowable phenomena" as the subject for discussion, feelings do have defining characteristics because they are mental states experienced through their own power. Taking "feelings" as the subject for discussion, these do have categories because there is a division into five categories—happiness, and so forth.[613]

Taking "knowable phenomena" as the subject for discussion, perceptions do have defining characteristics because they are mental states embodying the apprehension of dissimilar signs [such as] the patterns on the fur [of animals], through their own power. Taking "perceptions" as the subject for discussion, these are of two sorts when classified because they comprise perceptions endowed with ideation and perceptions devoid of ideation.[614]

Taking "knowable phenomena" as the subject for discussion, formative predispositions do have defining characteristics because they are conditioned phenomena that have been transformed from the other four aggregates. Taking "formative predispositions" as the subject for discussion, these are of two sorts when classified because they comprise formative predispositions that are associated [with mind] and formative predispositions that are disassociated [from mind].[615]

The Establishment of Their Derivative Sensory Element and Sense Field [13.6.1.2.1.1.1.2.1.2.2]

As to the latter, [the establishment of their derivative sensory element and sense field,] taking "knowable phenomena" as the subject for discussion, it is determined that there are mental phenomena distinct from [the aggregates of] physical forms and mind [consciousness]—the sense field of mental phenomena and the sensory base of mental phenomena are indeed determined accordingly. This is because the three [just-mentioned aggregates of feelings, perceptions, and formative predispositions] along with unconditioned forms that are not apperceived are established as a [distinct] sense field and sensory element.[616]

The Three Aspects of Phenomena Subsumed in Mind [13.6.1.2.1.1.1.2.1.3]

The third part [of the nature of the three different aspects of phenomena] concerns the three aspects of phenomena subsumed in mind

(13.6.1.2.1.1.1.2.1.3). This comprises (i) the nature of the three aspects of phenomena (13.6.1.2.1.1.1.2.1.3.1); (ii) recognizing the foremost of the three aspects of phenomena (13.6.1.2.1.1.1.2.1.3.2); and, incidentally, (iii) the elimination of disputation concerning the precise number of sensory elements (13.6.1.2.1.1.1.2.1.3.3).

The Nature of the Three Aspects of Phenomena [13.6.1.2.1.1.1.2.1.3.1]

As to the first, [the nature of the three aspects of phenomena,] taking the "six modes of consciousness" as the subject for discussion, these do constitute the aggregate of consciousness because, as an object of the intellect, they appear as a conglomerate and because their essential nature is the central mind that apperceives distinct [sensa] through its own power.[617]

Taking "knowable phenomena" as the subject for discussion, the sense field of the mental faculty is also present because it is that very sixfold [conglomerate formed by the six aggregates of consciousness].[618]

Taking "knowable phenomena" as the subject for discussion, when these [modes of consciousness] are established within [the context of] the eighteen sensory elements, there are also held to be seven sensory elements of consciousness. This is because these include the six modes of consciousness and the seventh, the sensory element of the mental faculty. This sensory element of the mental faculty is not an object distinct from the six modes of consciousness because the sensory element of the mental faculty is that consciousness that continues uninterrupted by other modes of consciousness immediately after the six modes of consciousness have passed.[619]

Taking the "sensory element of the mental faculty" as the subject for discussion, there is a reason why it is mentioned separately from the six modes of consciousness. This is because it is mentioned in order that the uncommon physical frame supporting the sixth [mode], the consciousness of the mental faculty, might be well formed.[620]

Taking the "sensory elements" as the subject for discussion, these [sensory elements], when classified according to distinguishing counterparts, are held to number eighteen. This is because these [sensory elements] comprise six sensory elements that give rise to the predominant condition [of sense perception], six sensory elements that constitute referential objects, and six sensory elements that constitute fruitional consciousness. These eighteen may be reduced to twelve in accordance with their substance because the six modes of consciousness are subsumed in the sensory element of the mental faculty. When only slightly reduced, they comprise seventeen because the sensory element of the mental faculty is not [substantially] distinct from the six modes of consciousness.

Recognizing the Foremost of the Three Aspects of Phenomena [13.6.1.2.1.1.1.2.1.3.2]

As to the second, recognizing the foremost of the three aspects of phenomena, taking as the subject for discussion "only the following three aspects of phenomena—the aggregate of physical forms, the sense field of the mental faculty, and the sensory element of mental phenomena," these are the foremost of the three aspects of phenomena because these [three] subsume all things. That follows because phenomena consisting of matter are subsumed in the aggregate of physical forms, phenomena consisting of mind are subsumed in the sense field of the mental faculty, and phenomena distinct from matter and mind are subsumed in the sensory element of mental phenomena. With regard to the way in which the last of these three are subsumed, they are subsumed intrinsically because the phenomena subsumed in this class are not associated with the entities subsumed in the other categories [of matter and mind].[621]

The Elimination of Disputation concerning the Precise Number of Sensory Elements [13.6.1.2.1.1.1.2.1.3.3]

As for the third, the elimination of disputation concerning the precise number of sensory elements (13.6.1.2.1.1.1.2.1.3.3), some may say it follows that the number of sensory elements is not precisely eighteen because [the eyes] comprise the right and left eyes and so forth. In that case, taking "knowable phenomena" as the subject for discussion, one should not make the mistake of saying it follows that the number is imprecise because three [of the sense organs], including the eyes, ears, [and nostrils,] are twofold. This is because the right and left eyes are established as a single sensory element, inasmuch as (i) they are of a single class in [constituting the sense organ of] the eye; (ii) the perceptual ranges of both refer objectively to sights; and (iii) their fruit is that they appear to give rise to [visual] consciousness.

On the other hand, one might question why a single individual has those three types of sense organ, including the eyes, which are twofold and each is causally effective. In that case, taking "knowable phenomena" as the subject for discussion, the reason that persons have two eye sockets is to beautify the physical frame.[622]

Distinctive Attributes of the Three Aspects of Phenomena [13.6.1.2.1.1.1.2.2]

Second, the distinctive attributes of the three aspects of phenomena (13.6.1.2.1.1.1.2.2) comprise (i) the definition of the term "three aspects of phenomena" (13.6.1.2.1.1.1.2.2.1); (ii) the purpose for the teaching of the three aspects of phenomena (13.6.1.2.1.1.1.2.2.2); and (iii) the hierarchy of the three aspects of phenomena (13.6.1.2.1.1.1.2.2.3).

The Definition of the Term "Three Aspects of Phenomena" [13.6.1.2.1.1.1.2.2.1]

As to the first, [the meaning of the term "three aspects of phenomena,"] taking the "five aggregates" as the subject for discussion, the term "aggregate" (*phung po*) is employed because it indicates a conglomeration or cluster [of similar phenomena].

Taking the "twelve sense fields" as the subject for discussion, the term "sense field" (*skye mched*) is employed because it "gives rise to" (*skye*) "and extends" (*mched*) [sense perception outward to extraneous objects] from the sensory gates where consciousness arises.

Taking the "sensory elements" as the subject for discussion, the term "sensory element" (*khams*) is employed because it indicates a "species" or "natural class" [of sensory phenomena] that gives rise to a [compatible] result.[623]

The Purpose for the Teaching of the Three Aspects of Phenomena [13.6.1.2.1.1.1.2.2.2]

As to the second, [the purpose for the teaching of the three aspects of phenomena,] this includes (i) the actual purpose (13.6.1.2.1.1.1.2.2.2.1) and (ii) the resolution of doubts[624] (13.6.1.2.1.1.1.2.2.2.2).

The Actual Purpose [13.6.1.2.1.1.1.2.2.2.1]

First, there is a purpose for teaching the three aspects of phenomena, including the aggregates. This is because the purpose is to reverse the threefold delusion of beings who are entirely deluded with regard to mental states, entirely deluded with regard to matter, and entirely deluded with regard to both matter and mind.

Taking "knowable phenomena" as the subject for discussion, the first [of these] delusions can be reversed by the explanation of the five aggregates because in the context of the five aggregates, the aggregate of mental states is divided into three [i.e., the aggregates of feelings, perceptions, and formative predispositions].

Taking "knowable phenomena" as the subject for discussion, the second delusion can be reversed by the explanation of the twelve sense fields because, in that context, the sense field of sights or visual forms is divided into ten.

Taking "knowable phenomena" as the subject for discussion, the third delusion can be reversed by the explanation of the eighteen sensory elements because, in that context, the material sensory elements are explained to number ten and the sensory elements of consciousness to number seven.[625]

Taking "knowable phenomena" as the subject for discussion, there is also another purpose for the teaching of the three aspects of phenomena. This is because they are revealed appropriately, corresponding to three types of individual—those of sharp acumen who seek concise words [of explanation], those of average acumen who seek moderately long [explanations], and those of dull acumen who seek extensive [explanations]; and thereafter the purpose is that [those beings] will be favored [with the appropriate level of understanding].[626]

The Resolution of Doubts [13.6.1.2.1.1.1.2.2.2.2]

Second, [regarding the resolution of doubts,] there is a reason why feelings and perceptions are established as distinct aggregates, among all the mental states. It is because these two [feelings and perceptions] are the basis of disputation and so they cause living beings to transmigrate in cyclic existence. That follows because they are coarser than the other [mental states] and are the causal basis for the hierarchy of afflicted mental states.[627]

Taking as the subject for discussion, the "nonexplanation of unconditioned phenomena in the context of the aggregates," the reason for this is that they cannot be conglomerated [as aggregates].[628]

The Hierarchy of the Three Aspects of Phenomena [13.6.1.2.1.1.1.2.2.3]

As to the third, the hierarchy of [the three aspects of phenomena,] this comprises (i) the hierarchy of the aggregates (13.6.1.2.1.1.1.2.2.3.1); (ii) the hierarchy of the sensory elements and sense fields (13.6.1.2.1.1.1.2.2.3.2); and (iii) incidental remarks (13.6.1.2.1.1.1.2.2.3.3).

The Hierarchy of the Aggregates [13.6.1.2.1.1.1.2.2.3.1]

First, in this hierarchy of the five aggregates, the coarsest [the aggregate of physical forms] is revealed at the beginning and the subtlest [the aggregate of consciousness] at the end. This is because the subsequent [aggregates] are more subtle that those that precede them. There is a reason why a hierarchy such as this has been formulated. It is because, through seeing physical forms, afflicted mental states arise, after which feelings ensue, and then happiness is held to be obtained on the basis of feelings. Then erroneous perceptions ensue, followed by formative predispositions of attachment, aversion, and so forth. Thereafter consciousness arises as the essential nature of those afflicted mental states. So this [explanation] is compatible with the hierarchy in which all afflicted mental states arise.

The purpose of formulating [the aggregates] in this manner is that one should know physical forms to resemble a pot, feelings to resemble food, perceptions to resemble the seasoning, formative predispositions to resemble the cook, and consciousness to resemble the consumer. That follows because through [the analogy of] the pot and so forth, the sense objects and sensory elements are definitively ascertained. That follows, in turn, because feelings are supported by physical forms, just as food is supported by the pot. Feelings are then enjoyed by consciousness, just as the food that is to be enjoyed. Conventional notions of happiness and sufferings are then conceived by perceptions, just as the seasoning renders the food delicious. Formative predispositions then give rise to happiness and suffering with regard to the objects of consciousness, just as a cook prepares the food. Consciousness then experiences happiness and suffering, just as a person consumes the food.[629]

There is a purpose for this formulation because one should know why the world system of desire is analyzed on the basis of physical forms, the four meditative concentrations are analyzed on the basis of feelings, the first three of the world systems of formlessness are analyzed on the basis of perceptions, the summit of [mundane] existence is analyzed on the basis of formative predispositions, and consciousness is all-pervasive.[630]

The Hierarchy of the Sensory Elements and Sense Fields [13.6.1.2.1.1.1.2.2.3.2]

Second, [in the hierarchy of the sensory elements and sense fields,] there is a purpose for the five material sense organs being revealed in the beginning, and then for the sense organ of the mental faculty being subsequently revealed. This is because the first five [sense organs] engage exclusively with present sense objects, and the last one alone has the role of engaging with [objects] in all the three times. Then, among the five material sense organs, there is a purpose for the sense organ of the body being explained last. This is because the [other] four have objects that are exclusively derivative matter and the last alone engages with both primary and derivative matter.[631]

Also, among the two sense organs of the eyes and the ears, there is a purpose for the explanation of the former having precedence. This is because the sense organ of the eyes engages with sense objects that are more remote, and the other one [the sense organ of the ears] cannot hear such equivalent sounds. Among the two sense organs of the nose and tongue, there is a purpose for the explanation of the nose having precedence. This is because it engages swiftly with its sense objects before they have been tasted by the tongue. Alternatively, there is another purpose [behind this sequence] that has just been mentioned. This is because the foregoing hierarchy accords with the positioning of the sense organs within the physical body [from top to bottom].[632]

Incidental Remarks [13.6.1.2.1.1.1.2.2.3.3]

Third, [there are the following incidental remarks:] There is a purpose for the sense objects of the eyes exclusively being assigned to a single category, which is the sense field of visual forms or sights. It is because although in general all ten sorts of material [sense objects] are physical forms, in this context the general term ["physical forms"] is applied with a particular usage [confined to sense objects of the eyes, i.e., sights]. There is a purpose for the application [of this term] in this manner. This is because [sights] are the foremost of physical forms.[633]

There is a purpose for the objects of mental consciousness exclusively being assigned to a single category, which is termed the "sense field of mental phenomena." This is because although in general all conditioned and unconditioned things constitute phenomena, the multiplicity of phenomena of both sorts is subsumed by this mental consciousness within the supreme phenomenon, which is the object of nirvāṇa.[634]

Summation in the Extraneous Three Aspects of Phenomena [13.6.1.2.1.1.1.2.3]

The third part [of the systematic presentation of the three aspects of phenomena (13.6.1.2.1.1.1.2)] concerns the summation in the extraneous three aspects of phenomena (13.6.1.2.1.1.1.2.3). This comprises (i) the summation of the sacred doctrine in the aggregates (13.6.1.2.1.1.1.2.3.1) and (ii) the summation in the extraneous sensory elements and sense fields (13.6.1.2.1.1.1.2.3.2).

Summation of the Sacred Doctrine in the Aggregates [13.6.1.2.1.1.1.2.3.1]

The former includes both the actual [explanation] (13.6.1.2.1.1.1.2.3.1.1) and incidental remarks (13.6.1.2.1.1.1.2.3.1.2).

As to the first, [the actual explanation,] taking as the subject for discussion the "eighty-[four] thousand sections of the sacred doctrine that were taught in divisions of twenty thousand by Munīndra as the respective antidotes for [the aspects of] desire, hatred, delusion, and those three poisons in equal measure," these according to the Sautrāntika are gathered in the aggregate of physical forms because they comprise expressive words. Taking these as the subject for discussion, according to the Vaibhāṣika, they are gathered in the aggregate of formative predispositions because they are [classed as] "general nominal clusters," disassociated [from mind].[635]

As to the second, [the incidental remarks,] taking "knowable phenomena" as the subject for discussion, there are other opinions concerning the quantification of the sections of the sacred doctrine. This is because there are some who hold that the treatise entitled *Sections of the Sacred Doctrine,* which was composed in six thousand quatrains by Śāriputra, and certain [other works] have passages that perfectly present each of the categories, including the aggregates and sense fields. That follows because the eighty-[four] thousand sections of sacred doctrine are said to correspond as antidotes for engagement in the eighty-[four] thousand afflicted mental states.[636]

Summation in the Extraneous Sensory Elements and Sense Fields [13.6.1.2.1.1.1.2.3.2]

The latter concerns the summation in the extraneous sensory elements and sense fields (13.6.1.2.1.1.1.2.3.2): Taking "knowable phenomena" as the subject for discussion, just as the sections of the sacred doctrine are subsumed in the three aspects of phenomena, also the aggregates, sense fields, and sensory elements that are mentioned in all sorts of circumstances in the sūtras should be thoroughly examined in terms of their defining characteristics, and in this context [their content also] should be subsumed in the three aforementioned aspects of phenomena. This is because, among the [five superior] aggregates of ethical discipline, meditative stability, discriminative awareness, liberation, and the perception of liberating pristine cognition, the first is subsumed in the aggregate of physical forms, and the remainder in the aggregate of formative predispositions, and because apart from these there is nothing that is not gathered therein.[637]

The apertures formed by a container, a window, and so forth, are termed the "space element" because their intrinsic nature is one of light during the day and darkness during the night.

Taking "knowable phenomena" as the subject for discussion, the consciousness that is endowed with contamination is [termed] "the consciousness element," differentiated into six [distinct] elements. This is because it is the consciousness differentiated into the six elements that acts as the support for the rebirth process, whereas the consciousness that is free from contaminants does not do so.[638]

An Analysis of the Sensory Elements [13.6.1.2.1.1.1.3]

The third section [of the systematic presentation of sense objects, psychophysical aggregates, sensory elements, and sense fields (13.6.1.2.1.1.1)] comprises an analysis of the sensory elements (13.6.1.2.1.1.1.3). This has six parts: (i) an analysis on the basis of their defining characteristics

(13.6.1.2.1.1.1.3.1); (ii) an analysis on the basis of their threefold subdivisions (13.6.1.2.1.1.1.3.2); (iii) an analysis on the basis of whether they are fabricated or not (13.6.1.2.1.1.1.3.3); (iv) an analysis on the basis of combined forms (13.6.1.2.1.1.1.3.4); (v) an analysis on the basis of their occurrence and so forth (13.6.1.2.1.1.1.3.5); and an analysis on the basis of vision and so forth (13.6.1.2.1.1.1.3.6).

An Analysis on the Basis of Their Defining Characteristics [13.6.1.2.1.1.1.3.1]

As to the first, [the analysis on the basis of their defining characteristics,] taking as the subject for discussion the "sense field of sights alone," this is visibly revealed because it comprises the sights that are visibly revealed as the sense objects of the eyes. Taking "all ten material [sense objects]" as the subject for discussion, these are [classed as] resistant because the arising of other material forms is resisted in the locus where they themselves are present, and because they themselves resist other [material forms] in all ways.[639]

The first [of these propositions] is established because it concerns the sense field of sights. The second is established because taking "knowable phenomena that appear as such" as the subject for discussion, these do encounter resistance because resistance may occur in respect of (i) sense objects; (ii) mental objects; and (iii) impenetrable objects.[640]

The first of these three [reasons] is established because subjects [i.e., sense organs] resist sense objects. That follows because the sense organ of the eyes is such. That follows because [the sense organ of the eye] has eight parameters or limits. That is to say, there is a limit whereby it resists water but does not resist dryness, a limit whereby it resists dryness but does not resist water, a limit whereby it resists both, and a limit whereby it does not resist either; and there is [a limit whereby] it resists night but does not resist daylight, [a limit whereby] it resists daylight but does not resist night, [a limit whereby] it resists both, and a limit whereby it does not resist either. The first [of those limits] is established because the eyes of a fish are such. The second follows because the eyes of most human beings are such. The third follows because the eyes of crocodiles, sea creatures, and frogs are such. The fourth follows because the eyes of exceptions to those [three types] are such. The fifth follows because the eyes of human beings are such. The sixth follows because the eyes of bats and owls are such. The seventh follows because the eyes of leopards and cats are such. The eighth follows because the eyes of exceptions to those [three types] are such.[641]

The second of the [three] primary reasons [i.e., resistance in respect of mental objects] is established because the sensory consciousness to which a double moon may appear is such.[642]

The third reason [i.e., resistance in respect of impenetrable objects] follows because in situations where there is an interaction of forms [such as a hand on a rock], one [the hand] is counterstruck or impeded.[643]

An Analysis on the Basis of Their Threefold Subdivision [13.6.1.2.1.1.1.3.2]

As to the second, [the analysis on the basis of the threefold subdivision,] this includes (i) an analysis on the basis of three activities—virtuous and so forth (13.6.1.2.1.1.1.3.2.1) and (ii) an analysis on the basis of the three world systems (13.6.1.2.1.1.1.3.2.2).

An Analysis on the Basis of Three Activities—Virtuous and so Forth [13.6.1.2.1.1.1.3.2.1]

In the case of the first, [the analysis on the basis of three activities—virtuous and so forth,] taking as the subject for discussion the "eight sorts of matter excluding sights and sounds," these may be associated with any of the three activities—virtuous, nonvirtuous, or neutral, because they are consistently neutral.

Apart from those [eight], the two [remaining sorts of matter] comprising sights and sounds, along with the seven elements of consciousness and the element of mental phenomena—ten [elements] altogether—are associated with all of those three activities, including virtue, because sights such as the discipline [maintained by a monk] should be recognized as virtuous and sounds such as lies as nonvirtuous.[644]

An Analysis on the Basis of the Three World Systems [13.6.1.2.1.1.1.3.2.2]

In the case of the second, [the analysis on the basis of the three world systems,] taking "knowable phenomena" as the subject for discussion, a differentiation is made according to the three world systems because all the eighteen [elements] are present on the level of the [world system of] desire.

Taking "knowable phenomena" as the subject for discussion, there are fourteen elements present in the world system of form. This is because, with the exception of [four] elements—odors, tastes, olfactory consciousness and gustatory consciousness—all the remaining [fourteen] elements are present.

Taking "knowable phenomena" as the subject for discussion, there are three [elements] that are included on the level of the world system of formlessness because these three elements comprise the mental faculty, mental phenomena, and mental consciousness.[645]

An Analysis on the Basis of Whether the Elements Are Fabricated or Not [13.6.1.2.1.1.1.3.3]

As to the third, [the analysis on the basis of whether the elements are fabricated or not,] this comprises (i) an analysis on the basis of whether the elements are contaminated or not (13.6.1.2.1.1.1.3.3.1); (ii) an analysis on the basis of whether the elements are realized or not (13.6.1.2.1.1.1.3.3.2); and (iii) an analysis on the basis of whether the elements are endowed with apprehension or not (13.6.1.2.1.1.1.3.3.3).

An Analysis on the Basis of Whether the Elements Are Contaminated or Not [13.6.1.2.1.1.1.3.3.1]

Among these, concerning the first, [the analysis on the basis of whether the elements are contaminated or not,] taking "knowable phenomena" as the subject for discussion, the last three elements [comprising the mental faculty, mental phenomena, and mental consciousness] have two aspects in that they may be contaminated or uncontaminated. This is because the three elements comprising the mental faculty, mental phenomena, and mental consciousness include conditioned things that are contaminated and excluded from the truth of the path, though included in the first two [noble truths], as well as unconditioned things that are uncontaminated, and included within the truth of the path. Taking "knowable phenomena" as the subject for discussion, the remaining fifteen [elements] are contaminated because they are abandoned through [the path of] cultivation.[646]

An Analysis on the Basis of Whether the Elements Are Realized or Not [13.6.1.2.1.1.1.3.3.2]

Concerning the second, [the analysis on the basis of whether the elements are realized or not,] this comprises (i) the actual [analysis] (13.6.1.2.1.1.1.3.3.2.1) and (ii) the elimination of disputations (13.6.1.2.1.1.1.3.3.2.2).

As to the former, taking "knowable phenomena" as the subject for discussion, the five elements of consciousness associated with the five sensory gateways are indeed endowed with ideation and scrutiny since they pertain to beings with a mental continuum. This is because both ideation and scrutiny that are included among the four variable [mental states] arise within the periphery of the consciousnesses associated with the five sensory gates. As for the last three elements [comprising the mental faculty, mental phenomena, and mental consciousness], they (i) include both [ideation and scrutiny]; (ii) exclude the former [ideation] but include the latter [scrutiny]; and (iii) exclude both [ideation and scrutiny], respectively. This is because the first of these categories comprises the last three elements belonging to beings within the world system of desire and those who have acquired the ordinary foundation of the first meditative concentration. The second category comprises the last three elements of those who have acquired the extraordinary foundation of the first meditative concentration. [The third category] in which both [ideation and scrutiny] are excluded comprises the last three elements and all the remaining fifteen elements of beings who have acquired the [other] meditative concentrations, from the second upward.[647]

As to the latter, [the elimination of disputations,] some may say it follows that it is incorrect [to propose that] the consciousnesses associated with the five sensory gateways possess ideation because that would contradict the explanation found in the following [quotation from a] sūtra to the effect that the consciousnesses of the senses are without ideation:[648]

> O monks! Visual consciousness perceives the color blue but it does not think of the color blue.

In that case, taking "knowable phenomena" as the subject for discussion, the defect of faulty reasoning is not introduced because this "possession of ideation" denotes the presence of ideation, which is one of the [four] variable [mental states], whereas the "absence of ideation" mentioned in the sūtra is intended to imply the "absence of conceptual thought" through rectification and recollection. Among these, the essential nature of the first is that it is in association or concomitance with mental consciousness, it gives rise to distraction during postmeditation, and it essentially focuses on the discriminative awareness through which its own objects are understood in the manner of object-universals. The essential nature of the latter is that it is in concomitance with mental consciousness, it arises in all circumstances including meditative equipoise and postmeditation, and it essentially focuses on recollection or memory.[649]

An Analysis on the Basis of Whether the Elements Are Endowed with Apprehension or Not [13.6.1.2.1.1.1.3.3.3]

Concerning the third, the analysis on the basis of whether the elements are endowed with apprehension or not, taking as the subject for discussion the "seven mental elements," these are endowed with apprehension because they comprise the intellect that apprehends its own referents. Also taking as the subject for discussion the "mental states comprising half of the element of mental phenomena," these are endowed with apprehension because they comprise the intellect that apprehends its own referents.[650]

An Analysis on the Basis of Combined Forms [13.6.1.2.1.1.1.3.4]

As to the fourth, [the analysis on the basis of combined forms,] this comprises (i) an analysis on the basis of whether these are organically retained or not organically retained (13.6.1.2.1.1.1.3.4.1); (ii) an analysis on the basis of whether these are primary or derivative (13.6.1.2.1.1.1.3.4.2); (iii) an analysis on the basis of whether these are accumulated or not (13.6.1.2.1.1.1.3.4.3); and (iv) an analysis on the basis of whether they are passive or active (13.6.1.2.1.1.1.3.4.4).

An Analysis on the Basis of Whether These Are Organically Retained or Not Organically Retained [13.6.1.2.1.1.1.3.4.1]

With regard to the first, [the analysis on the basis of whether these are organically retained or not organically retained,] taking "knowable phenomena" as the subject for discussion, there is a distinction between [elements] that are organically retained and those that are not organically retained. This is because they are respectively established as being capable or incapable of producing feelings of happiness and suffering consequent on the interaction with matter.

Taking as the subject for discussion the "seven elements of consciousness that number eight with the inclusion of mental states, and nine with the inclusion of sound," these are termed "organically unretained" because they are incapable of producing feelings of happiness and suffering consequent on the interaction with matter.

Taking as the subject for discussion the "other nine material [elements]," these partake of both organically retained and organically unretained aspects for the reason that has previously been explained [see above, pp. 304–31].[651]

An Analysis on the Basis of Whether These Are Primary or Derivative [13.6.1.2.1.1.1.3.4.2]

With regard to the second, [the analysis on the basis of whether the elements are primary or derivative,] taking the "element of tangibles" as the subject for discussion, these [tangibles] are of two sorts, primary elements and derivative elements, because they include four primary elements such as earth and seven derivative elements such as smoothness and roughness.

Taking "knowable phenomena" as the subject for discussion, the derivative elements derive exclusively from the eighteen sensory elements. This is because the remaining nine material elements, one part of the element of mental phenomena, and nonapperceived forms are exclusively derivative.[652]

An Analysis on the Basis of Whether These Are Accumulated or Not [13.6.1.2.1.1.1.3.4.3]

With regard to the third, [the analysis on the basis of whether these are accumulated or not,] this includes (i) the definition of the terms (13.6.1.2.1.1.1.3.4.3.1) and the logical examination (13.6.1.2.1.1.1.3.4.3.2).

Definition of the Terms [13.6.1.2.1.1.1.3.4.3.1]

First, taking the "ten material elements" as the subject for discussion, these are accumulated because they are inert matter, composed of indivisible atomic particles.

Logical Examination [13.6.1.2.1.1.1.3.4.3.2]

Second, as for the logical examination, some may say that there is a distinction between atoms of substance (*dravyaparamāṇu, rdzas rdul*) and accumulated atoms or molecules (*saṃghātaparamāṇu, bsags rdul*) because atoms of substance are the smallest of physical forms and accumulated atoms are larger than them. In that case, it follows that [this proposition] is incorrect. Accumulated atoms are extremely subtle because they are the smallest of physical forms. That follows because it says in the *Autocommentary* [*on the Treasury of Phenomenology*]:

> The subtlest forms among all physical forms are called "accumulated atomic particles" because particles smaller than these do not manifest.[653]

Some may say it follows that these conglomerations composed of six or eight atoms of substance [in the world system of form and desire, respectively,] are accumulated atoms because when any accumulated atom that is a conglomeration of [at least] two atoms of substance arises, it does so simultaneously with those [six or] eight atoms of substance.[654] In this case, the proposition is not logically entailed because if that premise is accepted, it follows that those conglomerations that are composed of seven atoms of substance would also be accumulated atoms, since the proposition has been accepted. If this is accepted, it follows that those conglomerations composed of seven indivisible atomic particles would themselves be indivisible atomic particles, since the proposition has been accepted. If this is accepted, it follows that that is not the case because the atoms would be coarse, and that follows because atoms are [actually] subtle.

Some may say that in the world system of desire atoms consist of no more than eight substances on the grounds that therein there are no atoms of the sense organs or atoms of sound. In that case, it follows that the premise is incorrect because in the world system of desire both the atoms of the sense organs and the atoms of sound do exist. That follows because therein the sense organs and sound both [manifestly] exist.

This mode [of reasoning] can also be applied to the world system of form because [the *Pursuit of Defining Characteristics: An Exegetical Commentary on the Treasury of Phenomenology*] actually makes the same point when it says:

> In the world system of form atoms consist of [only] six substances
> Because they are without the sense organ [of the body]
> And they are without sound.
> In the case of beings who have the sense organ [of the body],
> [The atoms] have seven substances,
> And in the case of beings with the other sense organs,
> [The atoms] have eight substances.[655]

That citation is correct—it is so on account of the absence of odors and tastes in the world system of form.

An Analysis on the Basis of Whether the Elements Are Passive or Active [13.6.1.2.1.1.1.3.4.4]

With regard to the fourth, [the analysis on the basis of whether the elements are passive or active,] taking "knowable phenomena" as the subject for discussion, there is a distinction among the eighteen sensory elements between those that are active [or capable of cutting] (*gcod byed*) and those that are passive [or capable of being cut] (*gcad par bya ba*), because [this distinction] applies to the four external elements excluding sound; the former [active elements] resembling an axe [that cuts] and the latter [passive elements] resembling wood [that is cut].

Taking that as the subject for discussion, there is a distinction between those [elements] that can be burnt and those that have weight because, as previously explained, the distinction between wood that can be burnt and ounces that have weight is also made on the basis of all four [elements].

Taking "knowable phenomena" as the subject for discussion, there are incompatible ways of explaining [the distinction between elements] that burn and those that have weight. This is because there are some who hold that all four elements themselves both burn and have weight, and there are some who say that only fire burns and only weight has weight.[656]

An Analysis on the Basis of Their Occurrence and so Forth [13.6.1.2.1.1.1.3.5]

As to the fifth, [the analysis on the basis of their occurrence and so forth (13.6.1.2.1.1.1.3.5), this has four parts: (i) an analysis on the basis of whether they have occurred or not (13.6.1.2.1.1.1.3.5.1); (ii) an analysis on the basis of outer and inner distinctions (13.6.1.2.1.1.1.3.5.2); (iii) an analysis on the basis of their support and concomitance (13.6.1.2.1.1.1.3.5.3); and (iv) an analysis on the basis of whether there are things to be renounced or not (13.6.1.2.1.1.1.3.5.4).

An Analysis on the Basis of Whether They Have Occurred or Not [13.6.1.2.1.1.1.3.5.1]

The first of these, [the analysis on the basis of whether they have occurred or not,] comprises (i) a general description of occurrences (13.6.1.2.1.1.1.3.5.1.1); (ii) elimination based on nonoccurrence (13.6.1.2.1.1.1.3.5.1.2); and (iii) shared concomitance of the sense organs and consciousness (13.6.1.2.1.1.1.3.5.1.3).

A General Description of Occurrences [13.6.1.2.1.1.1.3.5.1.1]

The first of these, [the general description of occurrences,] in turn comprises (i) ripening causes (13.6.1.2.1.1.1.3.5.1.1.1); (ii) enriching causes (13.6.1.2.1.1.1.3.5.1.1.2); and (iii) conforming causes (13.6.1.2.1.1.1.3.5.1.1.3).

As to the first, [ripening causes,] the five inner sense faculties have arisen from ripening [causes] because the five sense organs of beings within the lower realms have arisen from nonvirtuous actions, and the five sense organs of beings within the blissful realms have arisen from virtuous actions that are contaminated [by cyclic existence].[657]

As to the second, [enriching causes,] taking the "five sense organs" as the subject for discussion, these have arisen from enriching causes because the five inner sense faculties are enriched through mouthfuls, food, sleep, good deeds, and so forth; and these have enriched the trunk that is the supporting frame of the sense organs.[658]

Taking "sound" as the subject for discussion, it arises from both enriching and conforming causes but does not arise from ripening [causes] because it has control over all that it wills.[659]

As to the third, [conforming causes,] taking as the subject for discussion "the seven consciousnesses that are not resisted and their mental states—eight," these have arisen from conforming causes and they produce ripening [results]. This is because things that have arisen from causes that are similar in type to themselves and things that have arisen from all-pervasive causes have arisen from conforming causes, and things that have arisen from ripening [causes] produce ripening [results].[660]

Taking as the subject for discussion the "four sense objects excluding sound," these have arisen from all three sorts of causes because of the foregoing proof.[661]

The Elimination Based on Nonoccurrence [13.6.1.2.1.1.1.3.5.1.2]

The second part [of the analysis on the basis of whether they have occurred or not] concerns the elimination based on nonoccurrence (13.6.1.2.1.1.1.3.5.1.2): Taking as the subject for discussion a [posited] "element of mental phenomena that is unique and endowed with permanent substance," this has not arisen from those three causes because it is the opposite of the aforementioned.

[Also,] the last three elements [among the eighteen elements] in respect of someone who has reached the essence of the first moment of the [truth of] suffering, receptive to the reality [that phenomena are nonarising], do not arise from conforming causes because they are not preceded by their corresponding uncontaminated elements.[662]

Concomitance of the Sense Organs and Consciousness [13.6.1.2.1.1.1.3.5.1.3]

The third part [of the analysis on the basis of whether they have occurred or not] concerns concomitance of the sense organs and consciousness (13.6.1.2.1.1.1.3.5.1.3). Taking "knowable phenomena" as the subject for discussion, there are [different] ways in which the sense organ of the eyes and the element of visual consciousness are acquired because they may be acquired individually or collectively. This follows because there are four parameters—namely, the parameters whereby consciousness is not newly acquired when the sense organ of the eyes is newly acquired and vice versa; and the parameters whereby both are acquired and neither is acquired.

The first follows because when beings are born into the fourth meditative concentration from the world system of formlessness both [the sense organ of the eyes and visual consciousness] are not present; for although the eyes are present in the case of those who are subsumed in the fourth meditative concentration, the visual consciousness is absent.

The second follows because when beings are born into the first meditative concentration from the fourth meditative concentration, although the eyes are present in the case of those who are subsumed in the fourth meditative concentration, the visual consciousness is absent. On the other hand, both are present in the case of those who are subsumed in the level of the first [meditative concentration].

The third follows because when beings are born into the first meditative concentration from the world system of formlessness, both [the eyes and visual consciousness] are absent in the case of those who are subsumed in the level of formlessness, and both are present in the case of those who are subsumed in the level of the first [meditative concentration].

The fourth follows because the foregoing reasons are applicable when beings are born from the first meditative concentration into [the world system of] formlessness.[663]

An Analysis on the Basis of Outer and Inner Distinctions [13.6.1.2.1.1.1.3.5.2]

The second part [of the analysis on the basis of their occurrence and so forth (13.6.1.2.1.1.1.3.5)] is an analysis on the basis of outer and inner distinctions (13.6.1.2.1.1.1.3.5.2): Taking the "inner sensory elements" as the subject for discussion, these [inner elements] are twelve in number because with the exception of the six elements of the sense objects, including sights, all the others are present.[664]

An Analysis on the Basis of Their Support and Concomitance [13.6.1.2.1.1.1.3.5.3]

The third part [of the analysis on the basis of their occurrence and so forth] is an analysis on the basis of their support and concomitance (13.6.1.2.1.1.1.3.5.3). Taking as the subject for discussion the "sensory element of mental phenomena," this is consistently endowed with a support because its own [distinctive] outcome would be impossible without it becoming the object of consciousness.

Taking "knowable phenomena" as the subject for discussion, in the case of the remaining [seventeen sensory elements], there is both a support and a concomitance because any sensory element is supportive when it performs its own [distinctive] function and it has a concomitance when it does not.[665]

An Analysis on the Basis of Whether There Are Things to Be Renounced or Not [13.6.1.2.1.1.1.3.5.4]

The fourth part [of the analysis on the basis of their occurrence and so forth] is an analysis on the basis of whether there are things to be renounced or not (13.6.1.2.1.1.1.3.5.4). Taking as the subject for discussion the "ten material elements," these are renounced through [the path of] cultivation because anything that is to be renounced is not to be renounced through [the path of] insight.

Taking as the subject for discussion the "five elements of consciousness," the [same] reasoning is clear, as previously [mentioned].

Taking as the subject for discussion the "three last sensory elements" [among the eighteen], there are three aspects here because they are respectively (i) renounced through [the path of] insight; (ii) renounced through [the path of] cultivation; and (iii) not to be renounced.

Taking as the subject for discussion "the status of an ordinary person," this is not [necessarily] renounced through [the path of] insight because it may also be disassociated from afflicted mental states.

Taking as the subject for discussion the "ten material elements," these are not renounced through [the path of] insight because they are physical forms.

Taking as the subject for discussion the "consciousnesses of the five sensory gates that arise from the predominant condition of the material sense organs, excluding mental consciousness which is the sixth," these are not renounced through [the path of] insight because [in that path] there is no mistaken superimposition made, suggesting that the sense objects are true.[666]

An Analysis on the Basis of Vision and so Forth [13.6.1.2.1.1.1.3.6]

As to the sixth, the analysis on the basis of vision and so forth (13.6.1.2.1.1.1.3.6), this has four parts: (i) an analysis on the basis of whether there is or is not vision (13.6.1.2.1.1.1.3.6.1); (ii) an analysis on the basis of the transformation of consciousness into objects (13.6.1.2.1.1.1.3.6.2); (iii) an analysis on the basis of whether things are permanent or impermanent (13.6.1.2.1.1.1.3.6.3); and (iv) an analysis on the basis of whether the sense organs exist or do not exist (13.6.1.2.1.1.1.3.6.4).

An Analysis on the Basis of Whether There Is or Is Not Vision [13.6.1.2.1.1.1.3.6.1]

The first of these, [the analysis on the basis of whether there is or is not vision,] comprises (i) a brief description of the distinctions of vision (13.6.1.2.1.1.1.3.6.1.1); (ii) the proof that the eyes have vision (13.6.1.2.1.1.1.3.6.1.2); and (iii) the distinctive attributes of the sense organs (13.6.1.2.1.1.1.3.6.1.3).

A Brief Description of the Distinctions of Vision [13.6.1.2.1.1.1.3.6.1.1]

As to the first, [the brief description of the distinctions of vision,] taking "knowable phenomena" as the subject for discussion, there is a distinction between having and not having vision because the [sensory element of] the eyes and one aspect of the sensory element of mental phenomena partake of eight sorts of vision, including the five erroneous views, the genuine view of mundane beings, and the two views associated with [the paths of] learning and no-more-learning, and because the remaining sixteen and a half [elements] do not.[667]

Taking as the subject for discussion the "afflicted discernment of the mind that is in association with the five consciousnesses of the five sensory gates," this lacks genuine vision because [these five modes of sensory consciousnesses] are without the conceptual thoughts that apprehend names and meanings definitively.[668]

The Proof That the Eyes Have Vision [13.6.1.2.1.1.1.3.6.1.2]

As to the second, [the proof that the eyes have vision,] taking the "eyes" as the subject for discussion, these do have vision because they see sights. Among the two [aspects of] support and concomitance, [the eyes] are not exclusively supportive [for there is a concomitance] because consciousness is definitely required in association with the eye that sees sights.

Taking "knowable phenomena" as the subject for discussion, it is not the case that consciousness alone sees dependent on that [support] because it would necessarily see sights that are obscured and these are not seen.

Taking "visible objects" as the subject for discussion, these are seen by both the eyes because they are clearly seen by both eyes rather than by one eye.[669]

The Distinctive Attributes of the Sense Organs [13.6.1.2.1.1.1.3.6.1.3]

As to the third, [the distinctive attributes of the sense organs,] this comprises (i) the apprehension of sense objects by the sense organs (13.6.1.2.1.1.1.3.6.1.3.1); (ii) the transformation of the sense organs into a support (13.6.1.2.1.1.1.3.6.1.3.2); and (iii) the levels in which they are included (13.6.1.2.1.1.1.3.6.1.3.3).

The Apprehension of Sense Objects by the Sense Organs [13.6.1.2.1.1.1.3.6.1.3.1]

In the case of the first of these, [the apprehension of sense objects by the sense organs,] taking as the subject for discussion "the eyes, the mental faculty, and the ears," apprehension takes place without coming into contact with the sense objects. This is because the first of these [the eyes] see sights from a distance, the third [the ears] hear sounds, and the second [the mental faculty] engages with objects throughout the three times.

Taking as the subject for discussion the "nose and the other sense organs," distinct from those [aforementioned], apprehension takes place in contact with the sense organs. This is because the three [remaining] sense organs including the nose are held to apprehend objects that share an equivalence. That follows because the sense organ of the tongue apprehends particles of taste that equal its own particles in number, and does not apprehend them differently. Such reasoning can be applied by analogy [to the other sense organs—the nose and the body].[670]

The Transformation of the Sense Organs into a Support [13.6.1.2.1.1.1.3.6.1.3.2]

In the case of the second, [the transformation of the sense organs into a support,] taking as the subject for discussion the "mental consciousness that is the final element," the three times are not present as the support for this [mental consciousness]. This is because when [mental consciousness] itself is present, it depends exclusively on a predominant condition that has passed.

Taking "knowable phenomena" as the subject for discussion, the predominant conditions of the five preceding [sensory] consciousnesses, when these are themselves present, are both in past and present time. This is because the [conditions] are coemergent with them.

These five supports, comprising the sense organ of the eyes and so forth, are the supports of the [corresponding] consciousnesses because the clarity of these consciousnesses derives subsequently from the clarity of these five sense organs, including the eyes. There is a reason why the names of these five supports indicate the [corresponding] supported visual consciousness and so forth. This is because the sense organ of the eyes is the predominant condition of visual consciousness and so on, up to and including the sense organ of the mental faculty [which is the predominant condition of mental consciousness].

There is a reason why the terms "visual consciousness" [and so forth] indicate that their consciousnesses depend on the sense organ of the eyes and so forth, but do not depend on sights [and the other external sense objects]. This is because sights are not the predominant condition of visual consciousness and because the sense organ of the eyes is its uncommon predominant condition.[671]

The Levels in Which They Are Included [13.6.1.2.1.1.1.3.6.1.3.3]

In the case of the third, [the levels in which they are included,] taking "knowable phenomena" as the subject for discussion, the eyes of a being of a lower level are not generated from the body of a being of a higher level because the eyes supported by the body of a being of a higher level are, in terms of one's own present level, superior to the eyes of a being of a lower level.

Taking "knowable phenomena" as the subject for discussion, the eyes of a being on a lower level do not see the physical forms of beings on a higher level because the eyes of beings of a lower level are inferior and the physical forms of beings in a higher level are superior.

Taking "knowable phenomena" as the subject for discussion, the eyes of a being of a lower level do not support the consciousness of beings of a higher level, as has been reasoned above.

The physical forms that are the sense objects of those beings are included within three levels—a lower level, one's own present level, and a higher level. This is because, when those with a form that sustains the first meditative concentration have attained the actual foundation of the fourth [meditative concentration] and then acquired the sense organ of the eyes that is subsumed by that [higher] level, they can see three kinds of sights—those subsumed in the first [meditative concentration], which is the present level of their supported consciousness, those subsumed in the world system of desire, which is the lower level, and those subsumed in the fourth [meditative concentration], which is the higher level.

Taking "knowable phenomena" as the subject for discussion, with respect to the body as well, sights and [visual] consciousness are both present in all three [levels]—one's present level, the lower level, and the higher level—because this can be reasoned by analogy in the aforementioned manner.

Similarly, this rightly applies also to the ears because words that are enunciated may be subject to change [based on the levels of hearing].

Taking "knowable phenomena" as the subject for discussion, as far as the three [other] modes of consciousness—gustatory, olfactory, and tactile are concerned, all of these, along with their supports, sense organs, and sense objects, are generally similar for beings on the same present level but, as a special case, the tactile consciousness also pertains to the lower level.

Taking "knowable phenomena" as the subject for discussion, these [consciousnesses of the senses] are included in one's own present level in the context of the world system of desire and in the first meditative concentration, but it is uncertain whether mental consciousness and its own objects are similarly [restricted] because it can objectify the sights and so forth of all higher and lower worlds.[672]

An Analysis on the Basis of the Transformation [of the Sense Felds] into the Objects of Consciousness [13.6.1.2.1.1.1.3.6.2]

The second part [of the analysis on the basis of vision and so forth concerns the analysis on the basis of the transformation of the sense fields into the objects of consciousness (13.6.1.2.1.1.1.3.6.2)]. Taking "knowable phenomena" as the subject for discussion, the five external sense fields each become the objects of two modes of consciousness because [the sense field of] sights becomes the object of visual consciousness and mental consciousness, and the others can be reasoned on the basis of that analogy.[673]

An Analysis on the Basis of Whether Things Are Permanent or Impermanent [13.6.1.2.1.1.1.3.6.3]

The third part [of the analysis on the basis of vision and so forth concerns the analysis on the basis of whether things are permanent or impermanent (13.6.1.2.1.1.1.3.6.3)]. Taking "knowable phenomena" as the subject for discussion, all unconditioned things are permanent because the things that are other than these are impermanent.[674]

An Analysis on the Basis of Whether the Sense Organs Exist or Do Not Exist [13.6.1.2.1.1.1.3.6.4]

The fourth part [of the analysis on the basis of vision and so forth concerns the analysis on the basis of whether the sense organs exist or do not exist (13.6.1.2.1.1.1.3.6.4)]. Taking "knowable phenomena" as the subject for discussion, there are different [enumerations] of the sense organs or faculties that exist and do not exist. This is because the aspects of the sensory element of mental phenomena, which includes the five feelings such as happiness, the five faculties such as faith, and the three powers of purification—thirteen altogether—may be [classed as] sense faculties, along with the [standard] twelve sensory elements that are explained to be the inner sensory elements.[675] [Attributes] other than these are not explained to be sense faculties.

Taking "knowable phenomena" as the subject for discussion, this completes the exegesis of the first part of the *Stanzas of the Treasury of Phenomenology*, which concerns the meaning of the terms and their logical examinations.

This completes Book 13 of the *Precious Treasury of Sūtra and Tantra,* elucidating the meaning of all vehicles, which is a commentary on Book [13] that extensively explains the differences between the philosophical systems.

The Root Verses: Book 13

The Precious Treasury of Sūtra and Tantra

Book 13: Philosophical Systems and Lines of Transmission

Having refined the fields of classical learning in the above manner
[as expounded in Books 11 and 12],
The [diverse] philosophical systems [are to be understood].

Mundane Approaches

There are those holding that one is born
As a human being or as a god inhabiting the world system of desire
By having practiced the ten virtuous actions,
And that one is born in the [world systems of form and formlessness]
By means of the four meditative concentrations and the four
formless [absorptions].

Philosophical Extremists

There are six [sophistic] teachers
Associated with the main extremist traditions,
And there are twenty summits of false view about perishable composites.
There are the sixty-two false views,
The three hundred sixty false views on which beings are fixated
And the eleven specific categories of heretical texts.
Then there are the [established non-Buddhist systems]
Of Sāṃkhya, Vaiśeṣika, Mīmāṃsika,
Nirgrantha, and Bārhaspatya.

Superiority of the Buddhist Systems

[The superiority of the Buddhist systems is considered in terms of]
The refuge and the four principles constituting the foundation
[Of view,] meditation, conduct, and result.

The Lesser Vehicle

There are seven tenets that [pious attendants] commonly accept, commencing with the four truths.
The Vaibhāṣika have seven tenets, commencing with the five basic categories.
The Sautrāntika have seven tenets, commencing with the four conditions of causation.
The hermit buddhas [are considered] in terms of their focus—
Class, view, and dependent origination—
As well as their conduct and result.

The Great Vehicle

[The great vehicle] is superior owing to its focus, attainment,
Pristine cognition, perseverance, skillful means,
Accomplishment, and activity.
Generally compatible with the great vehicle,
There are three [philosophical] approaches
In which enlightened intention is directed.

Cittamātra

The [proponents of Cittamātra] hold that
There is no subject-object dichotomy
And that conscious awareness is ultimately real.
Appearances are not truly existent;
[They derive from] the familiarity of minds,
Bewildered due to past actions.
There are five classes: pious attendants, hermit buddhas, bodhisattvas, indeterminate beings, and cut-off beings.
[The basic categories of phenomena] comprise matter,

Mind, and its peripheral [mental states],
Along with objective referents,
And the seed of buddha nature, which is the genuine substratum.
[As for the systematic presentation of the ground,]
They hold that there are three [natures]—
The imaginary, the dependent, and the consummate,
That there are substantial existents and imputed existents,
That there is an ultimate truth pertaining to the appearances of reality
And to actual reality, and that there is a relative truth.

The enlightened intention denotes definitive meaning and provisional meaning, [absence of] defining characteristics, and essencelessness.
Since there is no self, one comes to rest in a nonreferential disposition.
The six transcendent perfections should be practiced for three "countless" aeons.
The fruits comprise the inconceivable attributes of the buddhas.

Cittamātra Divisions

Those holding sensa to be veridical [assert]
That consciousness and its sensa [are distinct],
That there are as many [instances of] consciousness as there are sensa,
Or that [consciousness and sensa] are without duality.
Those claiming sensa to be false
Include some holding consciousness to be tainted
And others holding it to be immaculate.

Svātantrika

The lower sort [of Svātantrika] employing independent syllogisms
Holds appearances to be empty in ultimate truth.
The higher sort [of Svātantrika] employing independent syllogisms
Holds that [ultimate truth] transcends existents, nonexistents, thought, and description.

Prāsaṅgika

Those who employ consequential reasoning,
In accordance with the conclusive enlightened intention,
Are without tenets, in that all phenomena
Constitute the emptiness of dependent origination—
Beyond the extremes of the two truths,
Where all conceptual elaborations cease.
There are the five axioms of reasoning—namely,
The absence of the singular and the multiple,
The vajra fragments,
The absence of production from existence [and nonexistence],
The refutation of efficacious objects, and supreme relativity.
And there are three further axioms
Concerning permanence and imperishability,
Change and nonchange,
And the refutation of the four attributes [of birth, aging, duration, and cessation].

The two truths [are considered in terms of] their essential nature,
Etymology, defining characteristics, classification, and purpose.
Skillful means engage in the provision of merit,
And discriminative awareness engages in the provision of pristine cognition.
For one's own benefit the buddha body of reality [will be achieved],
And for others' benefit, the buddha body of form [will be achieved].

Through nonacceptance, one is free from any acceptance whatsoever.
Ultimately nothing is proven,
But relatively [the framework of phenomena] is accepted.
Acceptance and nonacceptance pertain to the relative,
But not to the ultimate.

Distinctions of the Fruitional Vehicles

There are fifteen distinctions of mantra over sūtra,
Concerning view, conduct,
Meditative stability based on mental [focus],

Cause, path, fruition, level, time, resources, yoga, benefit,
Purpose, difficulty, and provisions.
The attainment of the nucleus is the mystery
Of buddha body, speech, and mind.

The Outer Classes of Tantra

[The tantras of] action emphasize conduct,
[The tantras of] conduct give equal weight
To both [physical rites and mental meditation].
[The tantras of] union emphasize meditation, with conduct as an aid.

The Inner Classes of Tantra

The inner [classes of tantra] are distinguished
From the outer [classes of tantra]
In terms of their ground, path, fruition, food, clothing,
Deities, [the ornaments] that are worn, their locale,
And their [associated] rites.
There are father tantras of skillful means
In which the generation stage [of meditation],
[The refinement of] subtle winds,
And the rites of wrath are emphasized.
There are mother tantras of discriminative awareness
In which the perfection stage [of meditation],
[The refinement of] the generative essences,
And the rites of subjugation [are emphasized].
And there are nondual tantras
In which the nonduality of the generation and perfection stages [is emphasized].

Distinctions of the Great Perfection

[The lower vehicles] are contrived and changeable,
But [the Great Perfection] is not.
The eight [lower] vehicles are themselves deviations and obscurations.

There is a distinction in that [here there is no duality]
Of view and conduct, or cause and result,
And in that the three buddha bodies are naturally established.

The Class of Mind

Mind's creations, excellent and perfect in all respects,
Are subsumed in, arise from, and abide in [its natural disposition].
From the standpoint of their nonexistence,
[Mind's creations] do not waver,
And from the standpoint of their appearance,
They have originated, abide, and will dissolve.
It is determined that there is a single state of evenness
In which causes, conditions, renunciations, and antidotes are groundless.
Apparent and imputed phenomena are primordially liberated,
Their authenticity shattered.
Cyclic existence and nirvāṇa are not established
As different or even indivisible.
This is nothing at all, but it manifests as the diversity of appearances.
Free from the intellect, the things that appear are naturally free, transcending dogmatism.
Phenomenal appearances are the essenceless display of mind.

The Class of Space

[According to the class of space,] pristine cognition,
The essential nature [of mind], and all phenomena
Are supreme primordial liberation.
The black space, when classified, comprises
Enlightened deeds, compassionate spirituality, and emanation.
The variegated space, when classified, comprises
One aspect in conformity with the class of mind,
One in conformity with the natural position [of the class of space],
And one in conformity with the esoteric instructional class.
The white space, when classified, comprises both natural arising and nonduality.
The former includes the greater and lesser [space of the] ocean,

And the latter comprises [the space of] sun [and moon]
And [the space of] gemstones.
The infinite space, when classified, comprises outer, inner, secret, and real aspects.

The Class of Esoteric Instructions

[The class of esoteric instructions] naturally clarifies [the abiding nature]
And surpasses [the classes of mind and space]
That maintain speculation and adhere to reality.
It resembles moxibustion treatment,
Because the crucial point is reached,
Without languishing in speculation.

Miscellaneous Instructions

The essence of the miscellaneous instructions
Denotes the path that establishes [the abiding nature of reality]
And the pure power of liberation.

Informal Advice

The essence of informal advice
Denotes advice that [dispenses with] all discourse
And informal advice that hits the mark, without [delay].

Tantra Texts of the Class of Esoteric Instructions

The essence of the actual tantra texts [of the Great Perfection]
Is that they encapsulate the view,
[Remove obstacles] like a blood-letting instrument,
Conceal [and disclose hidden meanings],
And give exegesis [in a naturally clear manner].
[The last of these, giving exegesis in a naturally clear manner,]
Is divided [between texts maintaining]
That bewilderment [is to be corralled],
That bewilderment [is to be reversed in] the ground,

And that the crucial point [of seminal importance has been reached].
The essence of [the last of these,] concerning the crucial point, includes the aural lineage and the exegetical lineage,
The latter being subdivided according to its four cycles.

Early Transmissions

In Tibet, Bon, medicine, and divination were propagated gradually.
The sacred doctrine of the early translation period had its inception [in the reign of Lhatotori],
Was formally introduced [in the reign of Songtsen Gampo],
And then disseminated and established [in the reign of Trisong Detsen].
[Samye] was constructed, [texts] were translated,
And [teachings of] exegesis and attainment were propagated.

Later Transmissions

The later translations include the *Secret Assembly,*
The *Slayer of Death,* the *Wheel of Bliss,*
Hevajra, and the *Wheel of Time.*
[And they are maintained by the lineages of]
Kadam, Kagyu, Pacification, Sakya, and Geluk.

Dialectical Writings of Buddhist Phenomenology

Dialectics are engaged by means of reasoning,
Elimination and the basis of debate.
There are afflicted phenomena that are contaminated,
And purified phenomena that are uncontaminated.
[The systematic presentation of] the aggregates, sensory elements, and sense fields
Concerns the defining characteristics of all conditioned phenomena,
The three aspects of phenomena,
And it includes an analysis of the aspects of the sensory elements.
Then the sense faculties that possess the sense objects are analyzed.

The Concise Commentary: Book 13

A Noble Vase of Great Treasure

Book 13: An Extensive Exegesis of the Enumerations of the Vehicle

This book concerns the extensive exegesis of the philosophical systems associated with all the sequences of the vehicle. There are six main topics: The first explains the mundane approaches, including those of gods and humans and those adopted by philosophical extremists. The second explains the philosophical systems of the supramundane [vehicle of Buddhism], including those of the pious attendants and hermit buddhas. The third explains the philosophical systems associated with the great [vehicle], including those of the exponents of Cittamātra and of Madhyamaka. The fourth explains vajrayāna (the "vehicle of indestructible reality"), including the outer and inner classes of tantra. The fifth explains the philosophical systems that were propagated in Tibet, Land of Snows. The sixth explains dialectics according to the *Treasury of Phenomenology,* with an arrangement in the form of a garland of consequential reasoning.

Mundane Approaches

The first main topic [the exegesis of mundane approaches] has two parts, of which the first [is described as follows]: **Having refined the fields of classical learning in the above manner** [as expounded in Books 11–12], **the diverse philosophical systems** are then to be understood. Among them **there are those** basic approaches of gods and humans, **holding that one is born as a human being or as a god inhabiting the world system of desire by having practiced the ten virtuous actions, and that one is born into the**

realms [of form and formlessness] **by means of** cultivating **the four meditative concentrations and the four formless** [absorptions].

The second part [concerns the approaches of philosophical extremists]. This has six sections, of which the first concerns **the six** [sophistic] **teachers associated with the main extremist traditions,** namely: Purānakāśyapa, Maskarī Gośālaputra[varuṇa], Sañjayavairaḍīputra, Ajitakeśakambalin, Kakudakatyāyana, and Nirgranthajñātiputra.

The second concerns the **twenty summits of false view about perishable composites**—namely, the views that each of the five aggregates may be identified with the self, the views that the self abides within each of them, the views that they originate on the basis of the self, and the views that they are controlled by the self.

The third concerns **the sixty-two false views.** These include eighteen speculations dependent on the past, which are in five categories comprising (i) the group of four that propound total eternalism; (ii) the group of four that propound partial eternalism; (iii) the group of four that propound finitude or infinity; (iv) the group of four that propound endless equivocation; and (v) the two that propound fortuitous origination.

They also include forty-four speculations dependent on the future, which are in five categories, comprising (i) sixteen speculations concerning percipient immortality; (ii) eight speculations concerning nonpercipient immortality; (iii) eight speculations concerning neither percipient nor nonpercipient immortality; (iv) seven speculations concerning annihilationism; and (v) five speculations concerning the attainment of nirvāṇa.

The fourth concerns **the three hundred sixty false views** on which **beings are fixated.** These are tallied by adding together [the false views of] the one hundred twenty teachers who appeared in the past, including Rāṇāyana and the equal numbers of one hundred twenty [false views] held by those who are alive in the present, and those who will appear in the future.

The fifth concerns **the eleven specific categories of heretical texts.** Those among them that concern the limits of present time include the ten imitations, the nine propounding coherent eternalism, the six propounding irrationality, the seven with faith in meditative concentration and its multiple approaches, the six teachers propounding nihilism, the six ministers, the four types of incidental extremists, the six exponents of sophistry, the holders of four false views regarding causes, the two [preeminent] preceptors, and the Vedāntaupaniṣadika. There are also eighteen that concern the limits of past time and forty-two [or forty-four] sophistic notions that concern the limits of future time.

Then the sixth concerns the five [established non-Buddhist systems in which all the aforementioned are subsumed]—namely, the **Sāṃkhya,** the **Vaiśeṣika,** the **Mīmāṃsika,** the **Nirgrantha,** and the **Bārhaspatya.**

The texts of the Sāṃkhya included the *Stanzas on Sāṃkhya* by Īśvarakṛṣṇa, the *Sixty Chapter Tantra,* and the *Fifty Defining Characteristics.* There are those among them who maintain that Īśvara was a god and others who hold him to have been human. As far as their philosophical system is concerned, they hold that there are twenty-five categories of reality that can be known.

The texts that the Vaiśeṣika espouse suggest that the creator is Īśvara and that, by making offerings to him, blissful states will be acquired. They ascertain knowable phenomena in terms of six categories.

The Mīmāṃsika hold Viṣṇu as a deity and propound the authority of the Vedas, accepting ten principles.

The Nirgrantha hold Brahmā as a deity and follow the teacher Vardhamāna Mahāvīra. They classify all knowable phenomena into seven categories because all things may be subsumed in the particular classification of knowable phenomena and in their common circumstances.

The Bārhaspatya who follow the hermit sage Amaraguru (Bṛhaspati) hold seven tenets as authoritative, including their denial of past and future lives.

Superiority of the Buddhist Systems

The second main topic [explains the philosophical systems of the supramundane vehicles, including those of the pious attendants and hermit buddhas]. This has three parts, the first of which concerns the superiority [of the Buddhist philosophical systems] over non-Buddhist systems. It has five aspects: the superiority of **the refuge** on which they rely, the superiority of **the view** that is their **foundation,** the superiority of the **meditation** that is their experience, the superiority of the **conduct** in which they engage, **and** the superiority of the **result** that is to be attained. Among these, there are **four principles constituting** [the superiority of their view]—namely, that all conditioned things are impermanent, all phenomena are without self, all that is corrupt is suffering, and nirvāṇa is peace.

The Lesser Vehicle

The second part [concerns the philosophical systems of the pious attendants]. This has three aspects, [of which the first] concerns the **seven tenets**

that the pious attendants commonly accept, commencing with the four truths, which are their focus. These seven also include [the common tenets that] ultimate reality is posited, arhatship is conclusive, the substratum [consciousness] is denied, the great vehicle is denied, the ten [bodhisattva] levels are denied, and that buddhas have an individual mental continuum.

The second aspect [concerns the philosophical system of the Vaibhāṣika], with regard to which, **the Vaibhāṣika have seven tenets, commencing with the five basic categories** of knowable phenomena. Their tenets therefore comprise the five basic categories of knowable phenomena, [the positing of] decay as a separate entity, [the positing of] the substantial existence [of entities] throughout the three times, [the positing of] an inexpressible self, [the positing that] consciousness is not aware of objects intrinsically, [the positing that] there is a [substantial] difference between defining characteristics and exemplars, and [the positing] that substances have an impact that is not exhausted. [Among them, concerning the first of these tenets,] all knowable phenomena are ascertained in terms of five basic categories—namely, matter, mind, mental states, formative predispositions disassociated [from mind and mental states], and unconditioned phenomena.

The third aspect concerns the philosophical system [of the Sautrāntika], with regard to which **the Sautrāntika have seven tenets, commencing with the four conditions of causation.** These seven also include [the tenets that] appearances are mind, that objects are covert, that atomic particles have no intervening spaces, that the sense organs are causally effective, that formative predispositions disassociated from mind are imaginary, and that nirvāṇa is a nonentity. [Among them,] concerning the first [of these tenets], all that arises does so dependent on four sorts of conditions: the causal condition, the immediate and homogenous condition, the referential condition, and the predominant condition.

The third part concerns [the philosophical system of the hermit buddhas]. In this regard, **the hermit buddhas** [are considered] **in terms of their focus,** [the nature of] the self that engages in **conduct, and** the **result** of their attainment; and their focus [is considered in terms of] **class, view, and** [the links of] **dependent origination.**

The Great Vehicle

The third main topic [explaining the philosophical systems of the bodhisattvas] has three parts, the first of which concerns their superiority over the lesser vehicle. [The great vehicle] **is superior owing to** seven distinctions, in that it possesses the following seven attributes of greatness—namely, greatness of **its focus, greatness of attainment, greatness of pristine cognition, greatness of perseverance, greatness of skillful means, greatness of accomplishment, and greatness of activity.**

Cittamātra

The second part [concerns the philosophical system of Cittamātra]. This has three aspects [a general presentation, a description of the exponents of Cittamātra who hold sensa to be veridical, and a description of the exponents of Cittamātra who hold sensa to be false].

The first [of these] has four topics, among which the first is [the general preamble]: **Generally, with** respect to **the great vehicle,** the essential nature [of the ground] is identified as the lack of inherent existence in all phenomena, the two provisions [of merit and pristine cognition] are then accumulated on the path, and the fruit is the attainment of buddhahood followed by reemergence for the benefit of others.

Although they are **compatible** [with one another] owing to this intrinsic nature, **there are** [from the perspective of the great vehicle] known to be just **three philosophical approaches in which the enlightened intention** of the scriptures **is elucidated**—namely, that of the Cittamātrins, and those of Mādhyamika; the latter including those who advocate independent reasoning and those who advocate consequential reasoning.

The second [concerns their tenets]: **The** [Cittamātrins] **hold that there is no subject-object dichotomy and that** the naturally radiant, intrinsic **conscious awareness is ultimately real.**

The third [concerns the establishment of these tenets]: External **appearances** and extraneous objects **are not truly existent.** Since even the single element water is perceived in accordance with the different apparitional modalities of the six classes of living beings—its mere appearances as such **derive from the** established **familiarity of** their respective **minds** that are **bewildered due to past actions** and propensities.

The fourth [concerns the points to be established]. This has three parts, [namely, focus, conduct, and the fruit to be attained,] among which the first [the focus itself] also has three parts [the classes of practitioners, the ground, and selflessness]. With regard to the first of these, **there are five classes** of which sentient beings partake: the class of **pious attendants,** the class of **hermit buddhas,** the class of **bodhisattvas,** the class of **indeterminate beings, and** the class of **cut-off beings.**

With regard to the second, [the ground,] there are three aspects [essential nature, systematic presentation, and enlightened intention]. Among these, the first concerns the essential nature [of the ground] that comprises **matter, mind, and its peripheral** [mental states], **along with** the **objective referents** [of the world and its inhabitants] **and the seed of buddha nature that is the genuine substratum** on the basis of which stains are worn away.

The second [the systematic presentation of the ground] is in three parts [that concern, respectively, the three natures, substantial existents and imputed existents, and relative and ultimate truth]. As for the first, **they hold that there are three** [natures]—**the imaginary, the dependent, and the consummate.** As for the second, they hold **that there are substantial existents and imputed existents.** As for the third, they hold that the dependent nature denotes **ultimate truth pertaining to the appearances of reality,** whereas the consummate nature denotes ultimate truth pertaining **to actual reality, and** the imaginary nature denotes **relative truth.**

The third [is the enlightened intention]: It is **the enlightened intention** [of the Sage] that all scriptures teaching that mind and mental states are empty of self and phenomena are of **definitive meaning, and** all those that speak of self and matter as existent, without in the slightest speaking of the authentic reality, are of **provisional meaning.** That is to say, all teachings stating that all phenomena are empty, without essential nature, **denote the absence of defining characteristics** in the imaginary nature, the essencelessness of self-production in the dependent nature, **and**, ultimately, the **essencelessness** of entities in the consummate nature.

With regard to the third [selflessness]: **since there is no self,** even in terms of the dependent nature, **one comes to rest in an** entirely **nonreferential disposition,** without the mind relying on anything.

The second part [of the points to be established concerns conduct]: **the six transcendent perfections should be practiced for three "countless" aeons** for the benefit of others.

The third part [of the points to be established concerns the fruits to be attained]: **The fruits comprise the inconceivable attributes of the buddhas.** And yet, the nonconceptual pristine cognition that objectifies reality alone is the incontrovertible consummate nature—the ultimate reality. The cognizance[676] of the environment and its inhabitants and so forth that appear during postmeditation, comprising emanations that appear for the sake of others and appearances of the [buddha body of] perfect resource, constitutes the pure dependent nature—that is, the relative truth.

The second aspect [of the Cittamātra presentation] concerns the traditions of **those holding sensa to be veridical.** This has three parts: those holding **that consciousness and its sensa are distinct,** those holding **that there are as many sensa as there are instances of consciousness,** and those holding that sensa are diverse and **that** [consciousness and sensa] **are without duality.**

The third aspect [of Cittamātra presentation] concerns **those** claiming **sensa to be false.** They **include some holding consciousness to be tainted and others holding it to be immaculate.**

Madhyamaka

The third part [of the third main topic, the philosophical systems of the bodhisattvas, concerns the philosophical system of the middle way]. This has two sections [a general exegesis of those employing independent syllogisms and a detailed exegesis of those employing consequential reasoning].

Svātantrika

The former comprise both [lower Svātantrika employing independent syllogisms and higher Svātantrika employing independent syllogisms]. With regard to the first, **the lower sort [of Svātantrika] employing independent syllogisms holds appearances to be** of the essential nature of a magical display, **empty of inherent existence in ultimate truth,** and they conceive that phenomena pertaining to the results of past actions and so forth are not confused in relative truth.

With regard to the second, **the higher sort [of Svātantrika] employing independent syllogisms holds that,** as far as **ultimate truth** is concerned, when a rational investigation is made, there is no inherent existence of the single and the multiple, and so ultimate truth **transcends** objects of conceptual elaboration, **thought, and description** in respect of any things that could be construed as **existents** or **nonexistents,** present or absent, proven or not proven, and so forth. On the other hand, they assign dependently originated phenomena, manifesting as a magical display, to the relative truth, just as they are present.

Prāsaṅgika

The second section [on the philosophical system of the middle way concerns the Prāsaṅgika who employ consequential reasoning]. This comprises both [a brief presentation and an extensive exegesis]. As to the former: **those who employ consequential reasoning, in accordance with the conclusive enlightened intention, are without tenets, in that all phenomena constitute the emptiness of dependent origination—beyond the extremes of** thought and description with respect to **the two truths, where all conceptual elaborations cease.**

As to the latter [the extensive exegesis], this has three parts [a refutation of all conceptual elaboration, a systematic presentation of the nonrefutation of conventional appearances, and a demonstration to others of a suitable framework for the acceptance and nonacceptance of standpoints].

Among these, as to the first [the refutation of all conceptual elaboration]: since all things, from the moment of their appearance, whether they seem to arise, cease, or endure, and so forth, are without any inherent existence, in the manner of reflections, they are entirely devoid of premises concerning existence and nonexistence, and those who make them.

On this basis, there are five great axioms through which all philosophical systems fixated on truth and professed by those who propound [the existence of] entities may be destroyed. These **five axioms of reasoning** are—**namely, the** axiom of the **absence of the singular and the multiple, the** axiom of the **vajra fragments, the** axiom of the **absence of production from existence** [and nonexistence], **the** axiom of the **refutation of efficacious objects, and the** axiom of **supreme relativity.** There are also **three further axioms concerning** the absence of **permanence and imperishability, change and nonchange, and the refutation of the four attributes** [of birth, aging, duration, and cessation].

As to the second [the systematic presentation of the nonrefutation of conventional appearances], this has three sections: [the middle way of the ground, path, and result]. First, the ground entails that **the two truths** [are considered in terms of] **their essential nature, etymology, defining characteristics, classification, and purpose.**

Second [with regard to the middle way of the path], dependent on the relative truth, **skillful means engage in** the experiential cultivation of the five transcendent perfections and so forth, which constitutes **the provision of merit; and** dependent on **the provision of pristine cognition, discriminative awareness engages in** the cultivation of authentic luminosity, the ultimate pristine cognition.

Third, with regard to the [middle way of the] result, **for one's own benefit the buddha body of reality** will be achieved, **and for others' benefit, the buddha body of form** will be achieved.

As to the third [the demonstration to others of a suitable framework for the acceptance and nonacceptance of standpoints], this has three sections [comprising the nonacceptance of standpoints, the acceptance of standpoints, and their synthesis].

The first is as follows: **through nonacceptance, one is free from any acceptance whatsoever,** for it is said that ultimately one follows the meditative equipoise of sublime beings and relatively one follows mundane [conventions].

The second is as follows: **ultimately** no [standpoints] are accepted because **nothing is proven, but relatively** the systematic presentation of phenomena is accepted, as it has been described.

The third [their synthesis] is as follows: since, for the adherents of consequential reasoning, **acceptance and nonacceptance pertain to the relative** truth, **but** there is **not** any analytical framework for acceptance and nonacceptance in **the ultimate** truth, it should be understood that both acceptance and nonacceptance are provisionally differentiated due to distinctions made in the context of relative or conventional truth.

The Fruitional Vehicles

The fourth main topic [concerns the vehicle of indestructible reality]. This has three parts [exegeses of the distinctions between sūtra and mantra, of the philosophical systems of the three outer classes of tantra, and of the philosophical systems of the three classes of inner tantra].

Distinctions of the Fruitional Vehicles

Among these, with regard to the first, **there are fifteen distinctions of mantra over sūtra, concerning view, conduct, mental** [focus or] **meditative stability, cause, path, fruit, level, time, resources, yoga, benefit** [of self and others], **purpose,** [degree of] **difficulty, and** the accumulation of **provisions.**

Through the sūtras, **the nucleus** of the sugata is present as the seed of buddha nature, whereas according to the mantra approach, enlightened attributes are spontaneously present as the ground of purification, which is likened to the sun. The object of this purification, comprising the phenomena of cyclic existence, resembles clouds, the means of purification entails cultivation of the generation and perfection stages [of meditation, which is likened to the dispelling of clouds], and the result of this purification is the genuine substratum, radiant like the sun.

In terms of their modes of **attainment**, there are distinctions between the four delusions [of the sūtra approach concerning awareness, abiding reality, the aspects of the path, and the view of realization] and the four nondelusions [of the mantra approach]. In the dialectical approach, the three media [of body, speech, and mind] are merely without inherent existence, whereas in the mantra approach, the three media [of body, speech, and mind] are carried [onto the path] as **buddha body, speech, and mind.** So there **is** [also] a particular distinction concerning the **mystery of** skillful means.

The Outer Classes of Tantras

The second part [of the exegesis of the vehicle of indestructible reality concerns the outer classes of tantra]: among them, the [tantras of] **action emphasize** external **conduct** of body and speech, the [tantras of] **conduct give equal weight to both physical** [rites] **and mental** [meditation], **and** the [tantras of] **union emphasize meditation, with conduct as** a mere **aid.**

The Inner Classes of Tantras

The third part [of the exegesis of the vehicle of indestructible reality concerns the three classes of inner tantra]. This has three sections, among which the first [concerns the distinctions between the outer and inner classes]: the inner [classes of tantra] are distinguished from the outer [classes of tantra] in terms of their **ground, path, fruition, food, clothing, the deities** of the maṇḍala, the ornaments **that are worn, their locale,** their bowls, **and their** [associated] **rites.**

The second [concerns father tantras, mother tantras, and nondual tantras]: As for the first, **there are father tantras of skillful means in which the generation stage** [of meditation] and [the refinement of] **subtle winds** during the perfection stage are emphasized, **and the rites of wrath are also emphasized. There are mother tantras of discriminative awareness in which the perfection stage** [of meditation] and [the refinement of] discriminative awareness based on **the generative essences** are emphasized, **and the rites of subjugation** are also emphasized. And **there are nondual tantras in which** both **the generation and perfection stages** are experientially cultivated in like manner and **nonduality** is emphasized since all things are, through their natural disposition, the great pristine cognition of inner radiance.

Distinctions of the Great Perfection

The third [concerns the esoteric instructions of the Great Perfection]. This has four aspects: [the superiority of the Great Perfection to the generation and perfection stages, the class of mind characterized by diversity, the class of space characterized by primordial liberation, and the particularly sublime class of esoteric instructions.]

As for the first, the superiority of the Great Perfection to the generation and perfection stages [of meditation], there is a distinction between [the lower vehicles] that **are contrived, changeable, and** attained through striving and [the Great Perfection] that **is not. The eight** [lower] **vehicles are themselves deviations** from **and obscurations** of Ati[yoga]. There is a distinction in that [here in the Great Perfection] there is no duality **of view and conduct, or of cause and result.** Since **the three buddha bodies** are effortlessly complete, there is no need to search for them elsewhere. So **there is a distinction in that** these **are** attained without wavering from the disposition of this uncontrived reality, **naturally established,** just as it is. The expression "**mind's creations**" denotes the perfection of all attributes of cyclic existence, nirvāṇa, and the path. "**Excellent**" denotes the excellence of the three buddha bodies. "**Perfect in all respects**" indicates that all phenomena **are subsumed in** the disposition of naturally present pristine cognition, **arise from** its natural disposition, and **abide in** its natural disposition.

The Class of Mind

As for the second [the class of mind characterized by diversity], this has seven aspects [namely, the perspective of mind holding the fruition to be the mind's point of origin, the perspective of mind that has determined deviation and obscuration, the perspective of mind that shatters the authenticity of conventional appearances by means of rational axioms, the perspective of mind that does not descend into partiality or bias, the perspective of mind concerning dogmatic philosophical systems, the perspective of mind transcending dogmatism about that which is free from the intellect, and the perspective of mind that speaks in terms of things being perspectives of mind].

With regard to the first of these [the perspective of mind holding the fruition to be the mind's point of origin]: The entirety of the inhabited world and its inhabitants comprising the three world systems that are perceived in bewilderment do not actually exist. **From the standpoint of** emptiness or **their nonexistence, they** have not wavered, **do not waver,** and will not waver from the ground. Therefore they are empty of the intrinsic characteristics of impurity. **And from the standpoint of their appearance,** initially **they have originated** from the expanse [of reality], presently they **abide** within that expanse, and finally they **will dissolve** into that expanse.

With regard to the second [the perspective of mind that has determined deviation and obscuration]: **it is determined that** because naturally occurring pristine cognition is essentially free from the intellect, **there is a single state of evenness in which causes, conditions, renunciations, and antidotes are groundless.**

With regard to the third [the perspective of mind that shatters the authenticity of conventional appearances by means of rational axioms]: All **apparent and imputed phenomena,**[677] manifest though nonexistent, **are primordially liberated** in a single state, **their authenticity shattered.** Therefore actions and propensities are without support.

With regard to the fourth [the perspective of mind that does not descend into partiality or bias]: in the essential nature of naturally occurring pristine cognition, **cyclic existence and nirvāṇa are not established as different,** identical, **or even indivisible.**

With regard to the fifth [the perspective of mind concerning dogmatic philosophical systems]: Since in naturally occurring pristine cognition, there is nothing at all that exists, there is nothing at all that arises. **This is nothing at all, but it manifests as the diversity of appearances.**

With regard to the sixth [the perspective of mind transcending dogmatism about that which is free from the intellect]: since naturally occurring pristine cognition is **free from the intellect,** it does not exist as a real entity, and since **the things that appear** are naturally arising, the concepts present within the intellect **are naturally free, transcending dogmatism.**

With regard to the seventh [the perspective of mind that speaks in terms of things being perspectives of mind]: **phenomenal appearances** diversely appear because they are the **display of mind** but **are essenceless.**

The Class of Space

The third part [of the exegesis on the Great Perfection concerns the class of space, which is characterized by primordial liberation]. This has two aspects: [an exegesis of its essential nature and an exegesis of its subdivisions.] Among them, as to the former, [according to the class of space,] supreme **pristine cognition,** which is **the essential nature** of mind, **and all phenomena** that arise from its disposition **are the supreme** natural purity of **primordial liberation.**

The latter [concerning the subdivisions of the class of space] has four sections: [namely, the black space speaking in terms of the absence of causes, the variegated space speaking in terms of diversity, the white space speaking in terms of the nature of mind, and the infinite space determining causes and results.]

Among these, the first is **the black space,** which has three aspects **when classified.** For it **comprises** the class of the black space of **enlightened deeds,** the class of the black space of **compassionate spirituality, and** the class of the black space of **emanation.**

The second is **the variegated space** that, **when classified, comprises** one **aspect** that speaks in terms of being, **in conformity with the class of mind; one** that speaks in terms of nonbeing, **in conformity with the natural position** [of the class of space]; **and one** that speaks in terms of both being and nonbeing, **in conformity with the class of esoteric instructions.**

The third is **the white space** that, **when classified, comprises both** the white space of the supreme **naturally arising** ineffable state and the white space of the **nonduality** of view and meditation. The former includes both **the space of the ocean and the space of the sky.** The space of the ocean has **greater and lesser** aspects, **and** the space of the sky, when classified, **comprises** the space of **sun** and moon **and** the space of **gemstones.**

The fourth is **the infinite space** that, **when classified, comprises** the **outer** infinity concerning freedom from activity, the **inner** infinity speaking of this philosophical system in its own terms, the **secret** infinity concerning the dispelling of obstacles, and the infinity of the **real,** untying the crucial point.

The Class of Esoteric Instructions

The fourth part [of the exegesis on the Great Perfection concerns the class of esoteric instructions]. This has three sections [the exegeses of its superiority, its essential nature, and its subdivisions]. With regard to the first, the class of esoteric instructions **naturally clarifies** the abiding nature and therefore **surpasses** the class of mind **that maintains speculation** based on what the mind is **and** the class of space **that** resorts to speculation, **adhering to reality.**

With regard to the second [its essential nature], [the class of esoteric instructions] **resembles moxibustion treatment because the crucial point is** directly **reached, without languishing in** conjecture and **speculation.**

With regard to the third [its subdivisions], these are of three sorts: [miscellaneous instructions, informal advice, and formal instructions based on the actual tantra texts.] As to the first, **the essence of the miscellaneous instructions** is that naturally occurring pristine cognition, which transcends the intellect, instantaneously arises by relying upon the crucial points. When classified, this **includes** esoteric instructions determining **the path that establishes [the abiding nature of reality] and** esoteric instructions disclosing the path by **the pure power of liberation.**

As to the second [informal advice], **the essence of informal advice** is that it is unbewildered and free from the intellect. Its natural expression is that it puts an end to the source of conceptualization. Its defining characteristic is that it is without duality and it cannot be specifically identified. When classified, it **includes** informal **advice that dispenses with all discourse and informal advice that hits the mark, without delay.**

As to the third [formal instructions], **the essence of** the esoteric instructions enunciated in **the actual tantra texts is** the source of all the words [of the buddhas]. Their natural expression is effortless with regard to rejection and acceptance because they are free from cyclic existence and nirvāṇa. Their defining characteristic[678] is emptiness, free from all bases of disputation, because they are devoid of sounds and words.

When classified, there are four sorts: those that **encapsulate** the enlightened intention of **the view,** those that **remove obstacles like a blood-letting instrument,** those that **conceal** and disclose [hidden meanings], **and** those that **give exegesis** in a naturally clear manner. **The last of these** that gives exegesis [in a naturally clear manner] has three further subdivisions: for it **is divided** [between texts maintaining] **that bewilderment** is like a cow to be corralled, that **bewilderment is to be reversed** in the ground, and that **the crucial point** of the vital essence itself has been reached.

[The last of these,] **concerning** [the teaching that] **the crucial point** of the vital essence itself has been reached, is also considered in terms **of the** intrinsic **essence,** natural expression, and defining characteristic. When classified, it **includes** both **the aural lineage and the exegetical lineage** [of tantra texts]. The aural lineage has four aspects: essential nature, natural expression, defining characteristic, and classification. The exegetical lineage also has four aspects: essential nature, natural expression, defining characteristic, and classification. When classified, it is further **subdivided according to its four cycles**: the outer cycle, the inner cycle, the secret cycle, and the unsurpassed secret cycle, each of which includes its own essential nature, natural expression, and defining characteristic.

Lines of Transmission in Tibet

The fifth main topic [of Book 13 explains how philosophical systems were specifically propagated in Tibet]. It has three parts [a general exegesis of the spread of Bon, medicine, and divination; a detailed exegesis of the [spread of] the sūtras and tantras during the early translation period; and a particular exegesis of the spread of the new translation schools during the later translation period].

Early Transmissions

As for the first of these: **in** the land of **Tibet,** during the lifetime of [the first king] Nyatri Tsenpo, the telling of ancient tales became widespread. His dynasty is [known as] the seven heavenly kings called Tri, and [they were followed by] the two celestial kings called Teng. During the lifetime of Drigum Tsenpo, who was the first of these [two celestial kings], the Bonpo of Takzik and Azha were invited and then **Bon** ritual practices were propagated, including offerings to the gods for the sake of the living and the subjugation of spirits for the sake of the dead.

Drigum Tsenpo was followed by the six earthly kings called Lek, the seven kings of miscellaneous succession, and the five linking kings called Tsen. Among the last mentioned, the fourth was Lhatotori Nyentsen, in whose lifetime the physician Biji arrived from India. Princess Lhacham Yidkyi Rolcha was offered to him, and she gave birth to a son, the physician Dungi Torchokchen. It was in the latter son's lineage that the earlier and later Yutok Yonten Gonpo and so forth gradually appeared. Yutok the earlier served as a practitioner of **medicin**e over the successive reigns [of Me Agtsom and Trisong Detsen].

And then, among the thirteen kings in the auspicious dynastic succession, the third was Namri Songtsen. It was during his lifetime that [the texts of] elemental **divination were** translated and **propagated gradually** by

[Wencheng] Konjo and others in twelve periods [i.e., the early, intermediate, and later translations, each of which had four phases—initial, middling, later, and final].[679]

The second part [of the fifth main topic] concerns the spread of the sūtras and tantras during the **early translation period.** During the reign of Lhatotori Nyentsen, the fourth of the [five linking kings called] Tsen, a copy of the *Cornucopia of Avalokiteśvara's Attributes,* the *Sūtra of the Hundredfold Homage of Renunciation and Fulfillment,* and a mold engraved with the *Mnemonic Incantation of the Wish-Fulfilling Gem* fell down upon the palace roof, whereupon they were worshipped and given the name "awesome secret" (*gnyan po gsang ba*). In this way, **the sacred doctrine** [of Buddhism] **had its inception.**

During the lifetime of Songtsen Gampo, an emanation of Avalokiteśvara, Thonmi Sambhoṭa established the thirty-four letters of the Tibetan script by subtracting and supplementing the fifty Indic letters. He translated twenty sūtra and tantra texts, including the *Sūtra of the Cloud of Precious Jewels.* The king constructed the Rasa Trulnang Temple and one hundred eight temples of the "district controlling" class, the "border taming" class, and the "further taming" class. Then he brought the two [renowned] images of Śākyamuni in the form of a bodhisattva prince and so forth. In this way, the sacred doctrine [of Buddhism] **was formally introduced.**

During the lifetime of Trisong Detsen, who was an emanation of Mañjughoṣa, one hundred eight paṇḍitas, headed by the monastic preceptor Śāntarakṣita and one thousand eight translators, headed by Vairotsana, Kawa Peltsek, and Chokrolui Gyaltsen translated an inconceivable number of texts, including the sūtra and tantra divisions of the scriptures, and the treatises commenting upon the enlightened intention [of these canonical works], along with the texts of medicine, divination, and so forth, **and** he **established** them in order that they might be **disseminated** and propagated. The temple of **Samye** Lhungyi Drubpa **was** also **constructed.**

The great preceptor Śāntarakṣita was appointed abbot, and three hundred persons received the mendicant ordination, headed by the "seven men who were tested," and thereafter the transmission of the vows of monastic discipline gradually prevailed. Chokrolui Gyaltsen studied under Dānaśīla and Jinamitra and propagated the exegetical transmission of the four scriptural transmissions of monastic discipline, the *Root Sūtra of Monastic Discipline,* and so forth.

Jinamitra, Kawa Peltsek, and others translated and expounded the seven treatises of phenomenology, along with the *Treasury of Detailed Exposition,* the *Compendium of Phenomenology according to the Great Vehicle,* and the root verses and commentaries of the *Treasury of Phenomenology,* and so forth.

The discourses of the intermediate turning of the wheel, including the extensive, middling, and short versions of the *Transcendent Perfection of Discriminative Awareness,* which concern the absence of defining characteristics, were translated and established though teaching and study, as were the *Ornament of Clear Realization,* which concerns their covert meaning, and the *Fundamental Stanzas on the Middle Way Entitled Discriminative Awareness* and its *Autocommentary,* which concern their overt presentation. The discourses of the final turning of the wheel, such as the *Great Bounteousness of the Buddhas* and the *Pagoda of Precious Gems* were also translated and expounded, along with treatises commenting on their enlightened intention, such as the *Supreme Continuum of the Great Vehicle.*

The master Buddhaguhya translated and expounded the tantras of action, conduct, and union. The great master Padmākara conferred the empowerments, transmissions, exegeses, and pith instructions of the outer and inner classes of mantra, the eight transmitted precepts of attainment, the generation and perfection stages, and the Great Perfection on twenty-five disciples, including the king and his subjects. In such ways he secured the teaching of secret mantra. Inestimable treasures of doctrine and wealth were concealed, and the twenty-five disciples including the king and his subjects attained spiritual accomplishment. Texts were **translated** and expounded—the *Sūtra That Gathers All Enlightened Intentions* by Nub Sangye Yeshe, the *Secret Nucleus* from [the cycle of] the *Net of Magical Emanation* by Vimalamitra, the class of mind and the class of space according to the Great Perfection by Vairotsana, and the class of esoteric instructions by Vimalamitra. The Chiti and Yangti [classes of the Great Perfection] were themselves translated by the great master [Padmākara]. In Lhasa, Samye, Tradruk, and so forth, exegetical colleges were founded, maintaining the division of saffron[-robed monks,] and in places such as Yerpa, Chimphu, and Chuwori, meditation hermitages were founded, maintaining the division of white[-robed yogins] with matted hair. In ways such as these, the teachings of **exegesis and attainment were propagated.**

Mutri Tsenpo constructed the temple of Karchung Dorjeying. All the volumes of the Kangyur and Tengyur were established in terms of their verses, fascicles, and so forth, and the *Phangtangma Catalogue* was compiled.

During the lifetime of Tri Relpachen, who was an emanation of Vajrapāṇi, the sūtras, mantras, and their treatises were established in accordance with the revised orthography, and the temple of Onchangdo was constructed.

The texts that were translated up until the composition of the *Sword at the Gateway to Language* by paṇḍita Smṛti[jñānakīrti] are known as "Nyingma." The oral teachings of the ancient translations first descended to [Nyak Jñānakumāra] and So [Yeshe Wangchuk]. Next they descended to Nub Sangye Yeshe, and finally to the "three ancestral Zurs" and others, from whom the transmission gradually spread. The spiritual revelations were gradually brought forth by the hundred eight treasure finders, such as Ngadak Nyang, and then extensively propagated.

Later Transmissions

The third [part of the fifth main topic] concerns the new schools of the way of secret mantra that promoted **the later translations.** These are the texts that were translated from the time of Lochen Rinchen Zangpo onward. [Among them,] the tantras of union were extensively propagated by Lochen [Rinchen Zangpo], as well as by Phodrang Zhiwei-o, Zangkar Lotsāwa, Buton [Rinchendrub], and others.

As far as **the *Secret Assembly*** is concerned, the tradition of sublime [Nāgārjuna] includes the tradition of Jowo [Atiśa], the tradition of Lochen [Rinchen Zangpo], the tradition of Marpa, the tradition of Go [Khukpa Lhatse], the tradition of Chak [Lotsāwa], and the tradition of Paṇchen [Śākyaśrī]. On the other hand, there is also the tradition of Jñānapāda, which itself includes the tradition of Lochen, the tradition of Kham, the tradition of Sakya, the tradition of Ra [Lotsāwa], and the tradition of Nyo [Lotsāwa]. Such are the transmissions of exegesis and attainment associated with the [*Tantra of the Secret*] *Assembly.*

As for the cycle of **the *Slayer of Death*,** the texts were translated and expounded by Chokdru Lotsāwa, Nagtsho [Lotsāwa], Rongzom Chozang, Nyo [Lotsāwa], Ra Lotsāwa, Shuke Lotsāwa, and so forth.

The cycle of **the *Wheel of Bliss*** was conferred by Jowo [Atiśa] on Lochen [Rinchen Zangpo], and so forth; and it was propagated by Lok-kya Sherab Tsek, Mel Lotsāwa, Marpa Lotsāwa, Purong Lochung, Sumbha Lotsāwa, and others.

The cycle of ***Hevajra*** was propagated by Drokmi Lotsāwa, Go Lotsāwa, Marpa Lotsāwa, Petsa Sonam Gyaltsen, and others.

The *Wheel of Time* was extensively propagated by Gyijo Lotsāwa, Dro Lotsāwa, Tsami Sangye Drak, Ra Chorab, Buton [Rinchendrub], and others.

The Kadam Lineage

With regard to the **Kadam** tradition, Jowo Atiśa, who is said to have been a speech emanation of Orgyan, traveled to Tibet and translated many sūtra and mantra texts. He composed the *Lamp of the Path of Enlightenment.* His disciples in upper Ngari included Lhatsen Jangchub-o, Lochen [Rinchen Zangpo], and Nagtso Lotsāwa. In Tsang they included Drokmi Lotsāwa, Golang Lotsāwa, and Gar-ge. In Lhodrak they included Chak Trichok and Gekyong. In Kham they included Chakdar Tonpa; and in particular, in Central Tibet, they included his three [main] disciples, Khu[ton], Ngok [Lekpei Sherab], and Drom[ton Gyalwa Jungne]. The teaching was maintained, nurtured, and propagated by a multitude of spiritual advisors of the Kadam tradition, including Geshe Putowa, Chengawa, and Puchungwa, who were the disciples of Dromton Gyalwa Jungne, himself an emanation of [Yeshe] Tsogyal.

The Kagyu Lineage

With regard to the **Kagyu** [lineage], the disciples of Marpa Lotsāwa of Lhodrak, who was a mind emanation of Orgyan the Great, included the "four great pillars," and in particular, Mila Repa. The latter's disciples included Dakpo Lharje, who was an emanation of the attributes of Orgyan the Great, and also Rechungpa. Dakpo's disciples included Dakpo Gomtsul, Phakmodrupa, and Dusum Khyenpa. Dusum Khyenpa's disciples included Ling Repa, Drigung Kyura Rinchen Pel, Taklung Tashi Pel, and Tropu Lotsāwa. Ling Repa's disciples included Tsangpa Gya-re Yeshe Dorje. The latter's disciples included Gotsangpa, Lorepa, and Won-re, from whom the upper, lower, and middle branches of Druk evolved. Other lineages became widespread in the same manner, including the Drigungpa, Karmapa, Taklung Thangwapa, Barom Kagyu, and Tropu Kagyu.

The Shangpa Kagyu Lineage

With regard to the Shangpa Kagyu, Khyungpo Neljor built the monastery of Shang Zhongzhong. He had some eighty thousand disciples, including Mokchokpa.

The Lineage of the Six-Branch Yoga

The lineage of the Six-Branch Yoga was propagated by Palchen Ga Lotsāwa [Namgyal Dorje], the accomplished master Yumo and his disciples, and by Budo, among others.

The Lineages of Pacification and Severance

With regard to the [lineage of] **Pacification,** Phadampa Gyagar, an actual disciple of Orgyan the Great, traveled five times to Tibet, and he taught the sacred doctrine [of Pacification] in three phases—early, middling, and later. In particular, there are the lineages of Severance that derive from [his disciple] Machik Labdron, a speech emanation of [Yeshe] Tsogyal. These include the lineage of Tsang, the lineage of U, which is associated with the Geluk tradition, and the lineage of Katok, which belongs to the Kham tradition.

The Sakya Lineage

With regard to the lineage of **Sakya,** Sachen Kunga Nyingpo attained spiritual accomplishment through experientially cultivating the teachings of the Path and Its Fruit, which he received from Drokmi Lotsāwa, a body emanation of Orgyan. His two sons, Jetsun Sonam Tsemo and Jetsun Drakpa Gyaltsen, were known as the "two venerable siblings." Paṇḍita Kunga Gyaltsen and Drogon Chogyal Phakpa were known as the "lords of the sacred doctrine, uncle and nephew." Together, these are the five founding hierarchs [of Sakya]. From them, the tradition of public exegesis was extensively propagated at Ngor and Gongkar Dzong, and the [tradition] of private exegesis at Kha'u Drakdzong and so forth.

The Geluk Lineage

And with regard to the lineage of the **Geluk,** Jetsun Tsongkhapa the Great, who had been foreordained by the great master [Padmākara], composed many texts concerning the sūtra and mantra traditions. He established the Great Prayer Festival of Lhasa and founded the monastery of Riwo Ganden. His two senior disciples were Gyaltsab and Khedrub. Gyalwa Gendun Drub founded Tashilhunpo Monastery, Jamyang Choje founded Drepung, and Jamchen Choje founded Sera Monastery. Khedrub Sherab Senge established the glorious upper and lower tantric colleges and so forth. Their teachings were propagated in the three lands of China, Tibet, and Mongolia.

Dialectical Writings of Buddhist Phenomenology

The sixth main topic presents dialectics according to the *Treasury of Phenomenology,* with an arrangement in the form of a series of consequential reasons. **Dialectics are engaged by means of reasoning, elimination, and the basis of debate.** This comprises both a brief description and an extensive exegesis. The former refers to the reduction [of phenomena] into two modalities and a short explanation [of this reduction]. The first of these in turn includes both a definition of terms and a logical examination [of the two modalities].

With regard to the first [the definition of terms], taking "knowable phenomena" as the subject for discussion, there is a reason why, in this treatise, the explanation emphasizes the meanings of both **afflicted phenomena that are contaminated and purified phenomena that are uncontaminated.** It is because, when all phenomena are subsumed, they are gathered into these two categories.

The latter is the extensive exegesis, which has two parts: a recognition of knowable phenomena and the attributes comprising knowable phenomena. The first of these [the recognition] includes both knowable phenomena and the way in which these are ascertained.

The former [knowable phenomena] comprises both the systematic presentation of sense objects, psycho-physical **aggregates, sensory elements, and sense fields;** and an analysis of the sense faculties that possess the sense objects.

The first of these [the systematic presentation of sense objects, psycho-physical aggregates, sensory elements, and sense fields] has three parts. **These concern the defining characteristics of all conditioned phenomena;** they offer a systematic presentation of **the three aspects of phenomena, and** they **include an analysis of the aspects of the sensory elements.**

The first of these [the defining characteristics of conditioned phenomena] includes their classifications and their synonyms; and the first of these includes both the meaning of the terms and their logical examination.

As to the former [the meaning of terms], taking "all phenomena" as the subject for discussion, when conditioned phenomena excluding the aforementioned truth of the path are analyzed, although they are infinite, when they are subsumed, they are gathered in the five psycho-physical aggregates. This is because, among them, material things are gathered in the aggregate of physical forms, the central mind and so forth are gathered in the aggregate of consciousness, the mental states are gathered in the aggregates of feelings and perceptions, and mental states that are other than [feelings and perceptions] are gathered in the aggregate of formative predispositions, along with the formative predispositions that are disassociated from mind.

There **then** follows an extensive exegesis in which **the sense faculties that possess the sense objects are analyzed.**

This completes Book 13 of the *Precious Treasury of* Sūtra *and Tantra*, elucidating the meaning of all vehicles, which is a concise word commentary **on the section that extensively explains the differences between the philosophical systems.**

The Outline: Book 13

A Creeping Plant That Brings Forth Wishes

This outline derives from and is occasionally elaborated on the basis of the synopsis found in the Sichuan edition of the *mDo rgyud mdzod,* from which the original Tibetan table of contents has been extracted. Readers will note that there are three distinct categories of numbering. The numbers in the left-hand column represent the nested structure of this synoptic outline, with their initial two digits specifically denoting the book number (13). The boldface numbers in parentheses, immediately following the text, represent the calculation of the subtopics made by Choying Tobden Dorje for mnemonic purposes, following the sequence of their first occurrence in the original Tibetan, albeit with some modifications that have already been noted. The numbers in the final column denote the pagination of the various subtopics as they appear in the present publication.

Book 13: Extensive Exegesis of the Philosophical Systems associated with All the Sequences of the Vehicle—The Six Main Topics (*theg pa'i rim pa thams cad kyi grub mtha' rgya cher bshad pa'i le'u la spyi don drug*)

Book 13, Part 1: Mundane Approaches (*'jig rten pa'i theg pa*)

Book 13, Part 2: Exegesis of the Causal Vehicles of Dialectics (*mtshan nyid rgyu'i theg pa bshad pa*)

Book 13, Part 3: Philosophical Systems of the Fruitional Vehicles of Mantra (*'bras bu sngags kyi grub mtha'*)

Book 13, Part 4: General Exegesis of the Philosophical Systems of Tibet, the Land of Snows (*bod gangs can gyi grub mtha' spyi bshad*)

Book 13, Part 5: Dialectical Writings of Buddhist Phenomenology (*chos mngon pa'i rtsod yig*)

Concordance of Terminology

The following concordance gives precedence to the original Tibetan in the first column, with Sanskrit equivalents in the middle column and English translations or proper names in the third column.

Tibetan	Sanskrit	English
ka pā la	*kapāla*	skull cup
kun 'gro lnga	*pañcasarvatraga*	five ever-present mental states
kun [tu] 'gro [ba]'i rgyu	*sarvatragahetu*	all-pervasive cause
kun tu rgyu	*parivrājika*	Parivrājika, wandering mendicant (Jainism)
kun rtog	*saṃkalpa*	thought pattern
kun brtags	*parikalpita*	imaginary
kun 'byung	*samudaya*	cause or origin of suffering
kun rdzob	*samvṛti*	relative (appearances)
kun rdzob bden pa	*samvṛtisatya*	relative truth
kun gzhi	*ālaya*	substratum
kun gzhi'i rnam par shes pa	*ālayavijñāna*	substratum consciousness
klags lung	*āgama*	scriptural transmission
klu	*nāga*	serpentine water spirit
klong dkar po sems su smra ba		white space, speaking in terms of (the nature of) mind

TIBETAN	SANSKRIT	ENGLISH
klong khra bo sna tshogs su smra ba		variegated space, speaking in terms of diversity
klong nag po rgyu med du smra ba		black space, speaking in terms of the absence of causes
klong bzhi		four spaces
klong rab 'byams rgyu 'bras la bzla ba		infinite space determining causes and results
dka' thub	*tapas*	austerity
dka' thub pa	*tapasvin*	ascetic (Jainism)
dkar gsum		three dairy products
dkon mchog gsum	*triratna*	three precious jewels
dkor mdzod		vault
dkyil 'khor	*maṇḍala*	maṇḍala
rkyang pa	*kaivalya*	isolationist (Bārhaspatya)
rkyen	*pratyaya*	condition
skabs 'gro	*śaraṇagamana*	going for, or seeking, refuge
skad cig ma	*tatkṣaṇa, kṣana*	indivisible temporal moment, second (= 1.06 secs.)
skad gsar bcad		revised orthography
skal ba mnyam pa'i rgyu	*sabhāgahetu*	homogeneous cause
sku	*kāya*	buddha body
sku'i ngo bo phun sum tshogs pa		excellence of the essential nature of buddha body
sku'i gsang ba	*kāyaguhya*	mystery of buddha body
skye mched	*āyatana*	sense field
skye ba	*jāti*	birth, arising, production, operational production
skyed par byed pa'i rgyu	*janakahetu*	efficient cause

Tibetan	Sanskrit	English
skyed byed rkyen	*janakapratyaya*	efficient condition
skyes bu	*puruṣa*	soul, cosmic person (Sāṃkhya, Aupaniṣadika)
skra 'bal	*keśaluñcana*	pulling out the hair (Jainism)
brkyang pa	*prasāraṇa*	expanding (Vaiśeṣika)
bskal pa	*kalpa*	aeon
bskal pa dang po	*prathamakalpa*	initial aeon of time
bskum pa	*saṅkoca*	contracting (Vaiśeṣika)
bskyed rim	*utpattikrama*	generation stage (of meditation)
kha cig chad par smra ba'i rtog pa	*ekatyaśāśvatavāda*	notions propounding partial eternalism
kha gtam		informal advice
kha 'thor		miscellaneous instructions
khams	*dhātu*	sensory element, seed of buddha nature, world system
khams gsum	*tridhātu*	three world systems
khar phog dus med pa'i kha gtam		informal advice that hits the mark without delay
khas len	*abhyupagama*	acceptance
khog pa	*deha*	trunk (of the body)
khong khro	*pratigha*	hostility
khyad par dgu	*navaviśeṣa*	nine distinctive attributes (Aupaniṣadika)
khyad par chen po		extraordinary way (Bon)
khyab 'jug pa	*vaiṣṇava*	Vaiṣṇava
khyab pa'i spyi	*vyāptisāmānya*	pervasive universal (Vaiśeṣika)
khyab bya	*vyāpya*	predicate

Tibetan	Sanskrit	English
khyab byed	*vyāpaka*	subject
khyung	*garuḍa*	garuḍa
khru	*hasta*	cubit (= 18 inches)
khrus	*snāna*	bathing
khrel med pa	*anapatrāpya*	shamelessness
khrel yod	*apatrāpya*	shame
khro ba	*krodha*	anger
mkhan po	*upādhyāya*	monastic preceptor
mkhan bu		assistant monastic preceptor
mkha' 'gro ma	*ḍākinī*	ḍākinī
'khon du 'dzin pa	*upanāha*	enmity
'khor phun sum tshogs pa		excellence of retinue
'khor ba	*saṃsāra*	cyclic existence
'khrul pa ba ded du 'dod pa		formal instructions maintaining that bewilderment is like a cow to be herded
'khrul pa rtsad bcad pas 'khor 'das lto bzlog pa'i lugs		method that undermines the dichotomy of cyclic existence and nirvāṇa by eradicating bewilderment
'khrul pa rang so la bzhag pas ma 'khrul pa'i chos nyid ngos zin pa		recognition of unbewildered reality achieved by settling bewilderment in its natural state
'khrul gzhi khog bskor bas 'khrul 'khor rgyun chad pa		interruption of the machinations of bewilderment by subverting its basis
'khrul pa gzhi la bzlog pa		formal instructions reversing bewilderment in the ground
'khrul sems la bzla ba'i gtan tshigs		axiom that transcends the bewildered mind

TIBETAN	SANSKRIT	ENGLISH
gang zag gi bdag	*pudgalātma*	self of an individual person
gab pa mngon du phyung ba		formal instructions that conceal and disclose
gar	*nṛtya*	dance
gar yang phyin pa	*prāpti*	power to move freely and obtain anything (Aiśvarya)
gegs bsal ba gsang ba'i rab 'byams		secret infinity concerning the dispelling of obstacles
go rim	*anukrama*	sequence, hierarchy
gong bu	*piṇḍa*	conglomeration
gong ma lnga		five founding hierarchs (of Sakya)
gol sgrib la bzla ba'i sems phyogs pa		perspective of mind that has determined deviation and obscuration
gos gsum brje ba		three kinds of attire
gyer sgo bzhi		four portals of ritual chanting (Bon)
grangs	*saṃkhyā*	number, enumeration
grangs can pa	*sāṃkhya*	Sāṃkhya
grangs med bskal pa	*asaṃkhyeyakalpa*	"countless" aeon
grub mtha'	*siddhānta*	philosophical system
grub mtha' rang gzhung du smra ba nang gi rab 'byams		inner infinity, speaking of this system in its own terms
grub pa chen po		greatness of accomplishment
grol chen po	*mahāmokṣa*	supreme liberation
grol ba stobs dag pa lam mngon gyur gyi man ngag		esoteric instructions that disclose the path by the pure power of liberation

Tibetan	Sanskrit	English
grva bskor		peripatetic studies
glang rdul	*goraja*	cow-hair particle
gleng ba yongs la bor ba'i kha gtam		informal advice that dispenses with all discourse
glo bur gyi dri ma	*agantukamala*	adventitious stain
dga' ba bzhi	*caturānanda*	four delights
dgag bya	*pratiṣedhya*	negandum
dgag gzhi		basis for negation
dga' mgur gnas pa	*yatrakāmāvasāyitva*	abiding anywhere at will (Aiśvarya)
dge bcu'i khrims		legal system based on the ten virtuous actions
dge ba	*kuśala*	virtuous (action)
dge ba bcu	*daśakuśala*	ten virtuous actions
dge ba bcu gcig	*ekadaśakuśalacaitasika*	eleven virtuous mental states
dge gshen theg pa		way of lay practitioners (Bon)
dgongs pa	*abhisandhi*	enlightened intention
dgos	*ched*	purpose
dgra bcom pa	*arhat*	arhatship, arhat
mgo snyoms pa bcu		ten imitators
mgon po	*nātha*	protector deity (esp. Mahākāla class)
mgyogs pa	*java*	rapidity
'gog pa	*nirodha*	cessation
'gog pa bzhi		four aspects of cessation
'gog pa'i snyoms 'jug	*nirodhasamāpatti*	meditative absorption of cessation

TIBETAN	SANSKRIT	ENGLISH
'gyu bas tong yal gyi gtan tshigs		axiom that change is empty and fading
'gyur ba med pa'i yongs grub		unchanging consummate nature
'gyur mi 'gyur gyi gtan tshigs		axiom concerning change and nonchange
'gyur byang		translators' colophon
'gyod pa	*kaukṛtya*	regret
'grel bzhad	*vyākhyā*	commentarial exegesis
'gres rkang		enumerative modulation (of phenomenological structures)
'gres rkang brgya rtsa brgyad		one hundred eight modulations (concerning phenomenological structures)
'gro ba	*gati*	moving, living being
'gro ba rigs drug	*ṣaḍgati*	six classes of living beings
rga ba	*jarā*	aging
rga shi	*jarāmaraṇa*	aging and death
rgod pa	*auddhatya*	mental agitation
rgya chad phyogs lhung med pa		without limit or restriction, partiality, or bias
rgya chad phyogs lhung med pa'i sems phyogs pa		perspective of mind that does not descend into partiality or bias
rgya spos		sweet clover (*Melilotus suaveolens*)
rgya mtsho'i klong		space of the ocean
rgya mtsho'i klong chung ba		lesser space of the ocean
rgya mtsho'i klong che ba		greater space of the ocean

TIBETAN	SANSKRIT	ENGLISH
rgyags pa	*mada*	self-satisfaction
rgyang grags	*krośa*	earshot (= 1,829 m)
rgyang 'phen pa	*lokāyatika*	Lokāyatika
rgyan gyi klong		space of adornment
rgyal dpog pa	*jaimini*	Jaimini, followers of Jaimini
rgyal ba pa	*jaina*	Jains, Jaina
rgyal byed pa	*jāyana*	Jāyana
rgyas 'debs	*mudraṇa*	sealing
rgyas pa'i las	*pauṣṭikarma*	rite of enrichment
rgyas byung gi rgyu	*aupacāyikahetu*	enriching cause
rgyu	*hetu*	cause, reason, species, material
rgyu rkyen gyis ma byas pa'i dngos med de bzhin nyid		real nature of nonentities uncreated by causes and conditions
rgyu lnga	*pañcahetu*	five kinds of cause
rgyu mthun gyi rgyu	*niṣyandahetu*	conforming cause
rgyu 'bras gnyis ka ma yin gyi mu		limit of neither cause nor effect (Sāṃkhya)
rgyu 'bras gnyis ka'i mu		limit of both cause and effect (Sāṃkhya)
rgyu med par smra ba'i rtog pa	*ahetuvāda*	notions propounding fortuitous origination
rgyu'i rkyen	*hetupratyaya*	causal condition
rgyu'i theg pa	*hetuyāna*	causal vehicle
rgyu'i bon bzhi		four causal modes of Bon
rgyu'i gzugs bzhi		four aspects of causal matter
rgyud pa brgyad		eight transmissions (Bon)

Tibetan	**Sanskrit**	**English**
rgyud rang gzhung du gsung pa		formal instructions based on actual tantra texts
sgeg 'chos	*helā*	frivolity (Jainism)
sgo	*dvāra*	gate, sensory gate
sgog skya		garlic (*Allium sativum*)
sgom lam	*bhāvanāmārga*	path of cultivation
sgom pa	*bhāvanā*	meditation, cultivation
sgyu	*māyā*	deceit
sgyu 'phrul bcu gsum		thirteen miraculous powers (Bon)
sgyu ma	*māyā*	magical display
sgyu ma'i rnal 'byor	*māyāyoga*	yoga of illusoriness
sgra	*śabda*	sound(s)
sgra nam mkha'i yon tan	*ākāśaguṇaśabda*	sounds as an attribute of space (Vaiśeṣika)
sgra'i khams	*śabdadhātu*	sensory element of sound
sgrib	*āvaraṇa*	obscuration
sgrib la thogs pa	*āvaraṇapratighāta*	resistance in respect of impenetrable objects
sgrub grva		meditation hermitage
sgrub rgyun		transmission of practice
sgrub thabs	*sādhana*	means for attainment
sgrub pa chen po		greatness of attainment
sgrub pa gsum		three attainments (Bon)
sgrub pa'i yan lag bco brgyad		eighteen branches of attainment (Bon)
sgrub byed	*vidhi*	proof, proof statement
sgrub sde		class of means for attainment

TIBETAN	SANSKRIT	ENGLISH
sgrub sde brgyad		eight classes of means for attainment
sgrub yig		practice manual
sgro 'dogs	*adhyāropa*	superimposition
sgrol ba	*mokṣa*	liberation
brgyud pa	*paramparā*	lineage, line of transmission
nga rgyal	*māna*	pride
nga rgyal	*ahaṃkāra*	ego (Sāṃkhya)
ngag	*vāk*	speech
ngan 'gro'i dbang po lnga		five sense organs of beings within the lower realms
nges don	*nītārtha*	definitive meaning
nges par rtog pa	*avakalpanā*	rectification, precise thought process
nges par 'byung ba	*niḥsaraṇa*	emancipation
nges 'byed	*nirvedha*	certitude
nges tshig	*nirukta*	etymology
ngo bo	*svabhāva*	essence, essential nature
ngo bo nyid med pa	*niḥsvabhāvatā*	lack of inherent existence
ngo bo nyid gsum	*trisvabhāva*	three natures
ngo tsha med pa	*āhrikya*	lack of conscience
ngo tsha shes pa	*hrī*	conscience
dngos po	*bhava*	entity
dngos po 'dug tshul gyi gegs bsal ba		formal instructions that eliminate obstacles to authentic presence
dngos gzhi khyad par can		extraordinary foundation
dngos gzhi tsam po ba		ordinary foundation

TIBETAN	SANSKRIT	ENGLISH
mngar gsum		three sweet things
mngon rtogs brgyad	*aṣṭābhisamaya*	eight sections of clear realization
mngon pa gong 'og		higher and lower transmissions of phenomenology
mngon pa['i chos]	*abhidharma*	phenomenology
mngon byang lnga	*pañcābhisambodhi*	five awakenings
mngon spyod	*abhicāra*	rites of sorcery
mngon shes	*abhijñā*	extrasensory power
snga 'gyur		early translation period
snga 'gyur rnying ma		Nyingma ancient translations
sngags	*mantra*	mantra
sngags 'chang	*mantrin*	mantrin
sngags bzlas pa	*mantrajāpa*	mantra recitation
sngags phyi nang gi rang bzhin bcu		ten natural aspects of the outer and inner mantras
sngon gyi mtha' la brten pa'i rtog pa	*pūrvāntakalpika*	speculations dependent on the past
bsngo ba	*pariṇāma*	dedication
cer re		open-eyed
cog gzhag		total rest
gcig gab nas gnyis mngon du phyung ba		formal instructions concealing one aspect and disclosing two others
gcig dang du bral gyi gtan tshigs		axiom of the absence of the singular and the multiple
gcer bu pa	*nirgranthin*	Nirgranthin (Jainism)
bcings pa	*bandha*	bondage

TIBETAN	SANSKRIT	ENGLISH
bcud	*rasa*	inhabitants of the physical world, essence, juice
lcags rdul	*loharaja*	iron particle
lce	*jihva*	tongue
lce'i rnam par shes pa	*jihvavijñāna*	gustatory consciousness
lce'i blo	*jihvabuddhi*	intelligence of the tongue (Vaiśeṣika)
chad lta	*ucchedadṛṣṭi*	nihilism
chad pa'i khongs su gtogs pa'i rtog pa		speculations or notions concerning annihilationism
chad par smra ba	*uccedhavāda*	annihilationism, nihilism
chu	*ab*	water
chu rdul	*abraja*	water particle
chu'i khams	*abdhātu*	water element
chud mi za ba'i rdzas	*avipraṇāśadravya*	unexhausted substance
chen po	*mahat*	great principle (Sāṃkhya)
chen po bdun		seven attributes of greatness
chos	*dharma*	phenomenon, attribute, thing, doctrine, mental phenomena
chos	*dharma*	morality (Vaiśeṣika)
chos brgyad	*aṣṭadharma*	eight attributes (of conditioned phenomena)
chos kyi skye mched	*dharmāyatana*	sense field of mental phenomena
chos kyi khams	*dharmadhātu*	sensory element of mental phenomena
chos kyi 'khor lo'i bskor ba	*dharmacakrapravartaṇa*	promulgation of the doctrinal wheel
chos kyi bdag	*dharmātma*	self of phenomena

TIBETAN	SANSKRIT	ENGLISH
chos kyi bdag med	*dharmanairātmya*	selflessness of phenomena
chos kyi phyag rgya	*dharmamudrā*	doctrinal seal
chos kyi dbyings	*dharmadhātu*	expanse of reality
chos kyi dbyings kyi 'gog pa	*dharmadhātunirodha*	cessation in reality's expanse
chos kyi phung po/ chos phung	*dharmaskandha*	sections of the sacred doctrine
chos sku	*dharmakāya*	buddha body of reality
chos khams kyi phyed sems byung		mental states comprising half of the element of mental phenomena
chos can	*dharmin*	apparent phenomena or reality, subject for discussion
chos can don dam		ultimate truth pertaining to the appearances of reality
chos nyid	*dharmatā*	reality, actual reality
chos nyid kyi klong		space of reality
chos nyid don dam		ultimate truth pertaining to actual reality
chos phun sum tshogs pa		excellence of the sacred doctrine
chos ma yin pa	*adharma*	immorality (Vaiśeṣika)
chos bzhi 'gog pa		refutation of the four attributes (of birth, aging, duration, and cessation)
chos lugs	*nīti*	righteousness (Mīmāṃsika)
chos gsum		three aspects of phenomena
mchod par 'os pa	*pūjya*	worthy of offerings (Aiśvarya)
mchod sbyin	*yajña*	sacrifice (Mīmāṃsika)
'chab pa	*mrakṣa*	hypocrisy

TIBETAN	SANSKRIT	ENGLISH
'jig rten	*loka*	world
'jig rten pa	*laukika*	mundane
['jig rten pa'i] yang dag pa'i lta ba	*samyagdṛṣṭi*	genuine vision or view (of mundane beings)
'jig rten las 'das pa	*lokottara*	supramundane
'jig rten gsum	*triloka*	three worlds (Aiśvarya)
'jig tshogs la lta ba	*satkāyadṛṣṭi*	false view about perishable composites
'jug pa	*pravṛtti*	engagement, sensory engagement
'jug pa rnam pa bzhi		four entrances (Bon)
'jug pa'i rnam shes [tshogs] drug		six modes of engaged consciousness
'jog pa	*sthāpana*	settling (Vaiśeṣika)
rjes thob	*piṣṭhalabdha*	postmeditation, postmeditative state
rjes dran gyi rtog pa	*anusmaraṇakalpa*	recollection
rjes gnang	*anujñā*	permission ritual
rjes su 'brel ba	*anubandha*	technical marker
rjes su mthun pa'i mtshan nyid bzhi	*caturanulakṣaṇa*	four subsidiary defining characteristics (of conditioned phenomena)
rjes su rnal 'byor	*anuyoga*	Anuyoga, (tantras of) subsequent union
brjed ngas pa	*muṣitasmṛtitā*	forgetfulness
brjod med rang shar chen po'i klong dkar po		white space of the supreme naturally arising ineffable state
nyams len	*anuṣṭhāna*	experiential cultivation
nyi ma	*sūrya*	sun

TIBETAN	SANSKRIT	ENGLISH
nyi ma pa	*saura*	Saura, sun worshippers
nyi tshe ba'i spyi	*avāntarasāmānya*	ephemeral universal (Vaiśeṣika)
nyi zer rdul	*chidraraja*	solar-ray particle
nyi zla'i klong dkar po		white space of the sun and moon
nyi 'og	*bhūmyanantara*	borderland
nyin zhag	*dina*	day
nye gnas	*upastha*	vagina (metaphor) (Mīmāṃsika)
nye ba'i mtshams med lnga	*pañcopānantariya*	five subsidiary inexpiable crimes
nye ba'i nyon mongs pa	*upakleśa*	subsidiary afflicted mental state
nye bar brgyud pa		short lineage
nyer len gyi phung po	*upadānaskandha*	acquisitive aggregate
nyon [mongs can gyi] yid	*kliṣṭamanas*	afflicted mental consciousness
nyon mongs pa	*kleśa*	afflicted mental state, affliction
nyon yid kyi rnam par shes pa	*kliṣṭamanovijñāna*	afflicted mental consciousness
gnyan po gsum		three severities (Bon)
gnyid pa	*middha*	drowsiness
gnyis ka'i rgyud	*ubhayatantra*	tantra of both action and union
gnyis gab nas gcig mngon du phyung ba		formal instructions concealing two aspects and disclosing one other
gnyis med rgyud	*advayatantra*	nondual tantra
mnyam nyid	*samatā*	sameness

TIBETAN	SANSKRIT	ENGLISH
mnyam nyid kyi ye shes	*samatājñāna*	pristine cognition of sameness
mnyam bzhag	*samāpatti*	meditative equipoise
snyan brgyud	*karṇaparamparā*	aural lineage
snying rje	*karuṇā*	compassion
snying rje chen po	*mahākaruṇā*	great compassion
snying thig	*cittatilaka*	innermost spirituality
snying thig gsang ba	*guhyacittatilaka*	secret innermost spirituality
snying stobs	*sattva*	lightness (Sāṃkhya)
snyoms 'jug	*samāpatti*	formless absorption
snyoms 'jug bzhi	*catuḥsamāpatti*	four formless absorptions
bsnyen bsgrub	*sevāsādhana*	approach (of ritual service) and attainment
bsnyen bsgrub rnam bzhi		four phases of the approach and attainment
bsnyen pa'i sgo dgu		nine approaches of ritual service (Bon)
bsnyen par rdzogs	*upasampadā*	full monastic ordination
tarka sde lnga	*pañcatarkavarga*	five modes of sophistry
tarka sde drug		six exponents of sophistry
ting nge 'dzin	*samādhi*	meditative stability
ting 'dzin gyi phung po	*samādhiskandha*	aggregate of meditative stability
ting 'dzin yan lag drug cu		sixty aspects of meditative stability (Bon)
ting ti ka	*tintiḍa*	tamarind
tin du ka	*tinduka*	black walnut
gtan tshigs	*hetu*	axiom

TIBETAN	SANSKRIT	ENGLISH
gtan tshigs khong rdib pa'i sems phyogs pa		perspective of mind that shatters the authenticity (of conventional appearances) by means of rational axioms
gtan tshigs lnga	*pañcahetu*	five great axioms (of Madhyamaka)
gtam gzhi	*kathāvastu*	basis of conversation
gtar ga gegs sel		formal instructions that remove obstacles like a blood-letting instrument
gti mug	*moha*	delusion
gti mug med pa	*amoha*	nondelusion
gter ma	*nidhi*	treasure, spiritual revelation
btags yod	*prajñaptisat*	imputed existent
btang snyoms	*upekṣā*	equanimity
rtag dngos	*śāśvatabhava*	permanent entity
rtag chad	*dhruvoccheda*	partial eternalism, eternalism and nihilism
rtag 'jig med pa'i gtan tshigs		axiom concerning the absence of permanence and imperishability
rtag lta	*śāśvatadṛṣṭi*	eternalism
rtag pa	*śāśvata, nitya*	permanent, permanence
rtag pa ther zug	*kūṭasthanityatva*	coherent eternalism
rtags bcu drug		sixteen signs (Bon)
rtags gsum	*triliṅga*	three axioms of reasoning
rten bcas	*sāśraya*	endowed with a support
rten 'brel	*pratīyasamutpada*	dependent origination
rten 'brel chen po'i gtan tshigs		axiom of supreme relativity

TIBETAN	SANSKRIT	ENGLISH
rten 'brel 'jug ldog		engaging and reversing modalities of dependent origination
rten tshungs can	*samāśraya*	having a shared support
rtog ge ba	*tarka*	sophist
rtog bcas	*savitarka*	endowed with ideation
rtog pa	*kalpa*	ritual, Vedic rite
rtog pa	*vitarka*	ideation
rtog pa'i dpa' rlabs		surge of intelligence (Aupaniṣadika)
rtog med	*nirvitarka*	devoid of ideation
rtog tshogs		amalgam of ideation
lta sgom gnyis su med pa'i klong dkar po		white space of the nonduality of view and meditation
lta sgom drod tshad kyi gegs bsal ba		formal instructions that eliminate obstacles blocking (one's experience of) the extent of warmth of the view and meditation
lta gnas	*dṛṣṭisthāna*	locus of views
lta ba	*dṛṣṭi*	view, wrong view
lta ba dgongs dril ba		formal instructions encapsulating the enlightened intention of the view
lta ba lnga	*pañcadṛṣṭi*	five visions
lta ba log pa	*mithyādṛṣṭi*	false view
lta mi spong bar smra ba'i rtog pa	*amaravikṣepavāda*	notions propounding endless equivocation
lta gsum		three perspectives (Bon)
stong gnyis pa'i 'jig rten gyi khams	*dvisāhasralokadhātu*	dichiliocosm

TIBETAN	SANSKRIT	ENGLISH
stong pa nyid	*śūnyatā*	emptiness
stong gsum pa'i 'jig rten gyi khams	*trisāhasralokadhātu*	trichiliocosm
stod 'dul		Highland Vinaya Lineage
ston pa drug		six sophistic teachers
stobs	*bala*	power
brtag pa'i gnas	*parīkṣasthiti*	topic of scrutiny
brtul zhugs	*vrata*	ascetic discipline
brtul bzhugs can	*vratin*	ascetic yogin
bltar med goms pa'i med pa'i gnad		crucial point that there is nothing to behold and nothing to experience
bstan du med la thogs pa med pa	*anidarśanāpratigha*	unrevealed and unobstructed
bstan yod	*sanidarśana*	visibly revealed
tha snyad	*vyavahāra*	convention
tha snyad du snang tshul		conventional appearance
thang cig	*lava*	minute (= 1.6 mins.)
thabs	*upāya*	skillful means
thabs chen drug		six great methods (Bon)
thabs la mkhas pa chen po		greatness of skill in means
thams cad yod par smra ba'i sde	*sarvāstivādavarga*	Sarvāstivādin order
thar pa	*mokṣa*	release
thar pa gsum		three modes of release
thal 'gyur	*prasaṅga*	consequential reasoning
thal 'gyur ba	*prāsaṅgika*	those employing consequential reasoning

Tibetan	Sanskrit	English
thig le	*bindu*	vital essence
thig le rang gnad la phebs pa		formal instructions that reach the crucial point of seminal importance
thugs	*citta*	buddha mind
thugs kyi gsang ba	*cittaguhya*	mystery of buddha mind
thugs rje	*karuṇā*	compassion, responsiveness
thugs rje'i klong nag		black space of compassionate spirituality
the tshom	*vicikitsā*	doubt
theg pa	*yāna*	vehicle
theg pa gdu		nine ways (of Bon)
theg pa dman pa/chung ngu	*hīnayāna*	lesser vehicle
theg pa chen po	*mahāyāna*	great vehicle
thob pa	*prāpti*	acquisition
mtha' 'dul gyi lha khang		border taming temples
mtha' dpyad	*vicāraṇa*	logical examination
mthong bya'i yul	*dṛśya[viṣaya]*	visible object
mthong byed	*paśyaka*	perceiver
mthong lam	*darśanamārga*	path of insight
mthun snang rang dag gi gtan tshigs		axiom of natural purity with regard to common appearances
da ltar gyi mtha'	*pratyutpannānta*	limit of present time
dag pa	*śuddhi*	purity
dag pa gnyis		two purities (Bon)
dag pa gsum		three purities

Tibetan	Sanskrit	English
dag pa'i sgyu ma		pure apparitional nature
dag pa'i 'jig rten		pure land
dad pa	*śraddhā*	faith
dad pa'i dbang po	*śraddhendriya*	faculty of faith
dam bca' bcu	*daśapratijña*	ten tenets (Mīmāṃsika)
dam bca' ba	*pratijña*	tenet
dam pa'i chos	*saddharma*	sacred doctrine
dam tshig	*samaya*	commitment
dam tshig gi phyag rgya	*samayamudrā*	commitment seal
dam tshig sems dpa'	*samayasattva*	being of commitment
du ma spungs pa		conglomerate
dud 'gro	*tiryak*	animal(s), animal realm
dur khrod	*śmaśāna*	charnel ground
dus	*kāla*	time
dus	*niyata*	destiny
dus phun sum tshogs pa		excellence of time
dus mtshungs pa	*kālasamprayukta*	concomitance of time
dus gsum		three times
de kho na nyid kyi dbu ma		Madhyamaka of the real nature
de tsam nyi shu rtsa lnga	*pañcaviṃśatitattva*	twenty-five categories of reality (Sāṃkhya)
de tsam lnga	*pañcatanmātra*	five quiddities (Sāṃkhya)
de mtshungs		concomitance
de bzhin nyid	*tathatā*	real nature, absolute reality
de bzhin gshegs pa	*tathāgata*	tathāgata

TIBETAN	SANSKRIT	ENGLISH
don	*artha*	meaning, object, genuine
don gyi kun gzhi		genuine substratum
don lnga	*pañcārtha*	five sense objects
don dam pa gcig		single absolute reality (Bon)
don dam pa'i bden pa	*paramārthasatya*	ultimate truth
don rnam pa bdun		seven categories (Jainism)
don spyi	*arthasāmānya*	object-universal, generic object
don byed 'gog pa'i gtan tshigs		axiom of the refutation of efficacious objects
drag gi las	*krūrakarma*	rites of wrath
drang don	*neyārtha*	provisional meaning
drang srong theg pa		way of ordained hermit sages (Bon)
dran pa	*smṛti*	mindfulness
dran shes	*smārttajñāna*	recollection, memory
dran bsam		recollection and thought
dri [ma]	*gandha*	odor(s)
dri sa'i yon tan	*kṣitiguṇagandha*	odor, as an attribute of earth (Vaiśeṣika)
gdams ngag	*avavāda*	oral instruction
bdag	*ātma*	self
bdag nyid	*ātman*	self, soul, gist
bdag gnyis		two notions of selfhood
bdag pa'i rkyen	*adhipatipratyaya*	predominant condition
bdag por gyur pa	*īśitva*	supremacy (Aiśvarya)
bdag med	*nairātmya*	selflessness

TIBETAN	SANSKRIT	ENGLISH
bdud rtsi	*amṛta*	nectar
bdud rtsi lnga	*pañcāmṛta*	five nectars
bde 'gro	*sugati*	beings within the blissful realms
bde ba	*sukha*	bliss, happiness
bde gshegs snying po	*sugatagarbha*	seed of buddha nature
bden pa	*satya*	truth
bden pa gnyis	*satyadvaya*	two truths
bden pa dbyer med		indivisible truth
mdo sde	*sūtra*	discourse
'du ba	*samavāya*	inherence (Vaiśeṣika)
'du byed	*saṃskāra*	formative predispositions
'du byed pa'i shugs	*saṃskāravega*	impact of predispositions (Vaiśeṣika)
'du shes	*saṃjñā*	perceptions
'du shes can	*saṃjñī*	percipient
'du shes dang tshor ba 'gog pa	*saṃjñāvedanānirodha*	cessation of perceptions and feelings
'du shes med pa	*āsaṃjñika*	state of nonperception
'du shes med pa'i snyoms 'jug	*asaṃjñīsamāpatti*	meditative absorption devoid of perception
'du shes yod par smra ba'i rtog pa	*saṃjñāvāda*	speculations or notions concerning percipient immortality
'du shes yod med gnyis ka ma yin par smra ba'i rtog pa	*naivasaṃjñānāsaṃjñāvāda*	speculations or notions concerning neither percipient nor nonpercipient immortality
'dun pa	*chanda*	will
'dur sgo bzhi		four portals of the funerary rites (Bon)

TIBETAN	SANSKRIT	ENGLISH
'dul ba	*vinaya*	monastic discipline
'dus byas	*saṃskṛta*	conditioned phenomena
'dus byas dge bcu		ten virtuous actions that are conditioned (Aupaniṣadika)
'dus ma byas	*asaṃskṛta*	unconditioned state
'degs pa	*utkṣopaṇa*	rising (Vaiśeṣika)
'dod dgu ldan	*prākāmya*	irresistible willpower (Aiśvarya)
'dod chags	*rāga*	attachment, desire
'dod pa	*icchā*	attachment
'dod pa'i khams	*kāmadhātu*	world system of desire
'dod [pa'i] yon [tan]	*kāmaguṇa*	desirable attributes of the senses
'dod yon lnga	*pañcakāmaguṇa*	five desirable attributes of the senses
'dom	*dhanu*	double arm span (= 1.8 m)
'dre rkun		poltergeist
rdul	*rajas*	motility (Sāṃkhya)
rdul phra rab	*paramāṇu*	indivisible atomic particle
rdul phran	*aṇu*	atomic particle
rdo rje	*vajra*	indestructible reality, adamantine, vajra
rdo rje 'dzin pa	*vajradhṛk*	vajra holder
rdo rje 'dzin pa'i sa		level of the vajra holder
rdo rje'i theg pa	*vajrayāna*	vehicle of indestructible reality
ldugs pa, snod	*pātra, bhājana*	water offering bowl or container
ldog pa	*vyāvṛtti*	distinguishing counterpart

TIBETAN	SANSKRIT	ENGLISH
sdang ba	*dveṣa*	aversion
sdug bsngal	*duḥkha*	suffering
sdug bsngal chos bzod skad cig ma dang po		first moment of the (truth of) suffering, receptive to the reality (that phenomena are nonarising)
sdug bsngal gsum po	*triduḥkhatā*	three modes of suffering
sde snod gsum	*tripiṭaka*	three baskets
sdom pa	*saṃvara*	vow, discipline, principle, commitment
sdom bzhi	*catuḥsaṃyama*	four principles
sdom gsum	*trisaṃvara*	three vows
brda shes	*saṃketajñāna*	semantics
nag rtsis		elemental divination
nang skor		inner cycle
nang gi khams	*ādhyātmikadhātu*	inner sensory element
nang gi dbang po lnga		five inner sense faculties
nang gi gzugs dvangs pa	*ādhyātmikarūpa*	clear and sensitive matter
nang rgyud gsum		three classes of inner tantra
nang rten 'brel	*ādhyātmikapratītyasamut-pada*	inner dependent origination
nang pa gsang sngags kyi theg pa		vehicles of inner secret mantra
nam mkha'	*ākāśa*	space
nam mkha' mtha' yas	*ākāśānanta*	infinite space
nam mkha' mthong sar gnas		dwelling in view of space (Jainism)
nam mkha'i klong		space of sky
nam mkha'i khams	*ākāśadhātu*	space element

TIBETAN	SANSKRIT	ENGLISH
nam mkha'i gos can	*digambara*	Digambara
nam mkha'i gos can pa	*ājīvika*	Ājīvika
nas	*yava*	barley grain size
nor bu skud pa	*yajñopavīta*	sacred thread
gnad bkrol ba de kho na nyid kyi rab 'byams		infinity of the real that unravels the crucial point
gna' sgrung		ancient tales
gnas kyi ldog pa		distinguishing counterpart in terms of location
gnas 'gyu gnyis med du grol bas sems nyid 'pho ba 'gyur med pa'i gna		crucial point that the nature of mind is unchanging because it is liberated in the nonduality of its rest and motion
gnas pa	*sthiti*	duration
gnas pa'i don		abiding reality
gnas phun sum tshogs pa		excellence of location
gnas ma'i bu pa	*vātsīputrīya*	Vātsīputrīya
gnas mtshungs pa	*sthitisamprayukta*	concomitance of location or support
gnod sbyin	*yakṣa*	sylvan spirit
gnod med pa drug		six kinds of unimpaired (sense perception)
rna	*śrotra*	ear
rna ba'i rnam par shes pa	*śrotravijñāna*	auditory consciousness
rnal 'byor chen po	*mahāyoga*	(tantras of) great union
rnam 'gyur	*vikāra*	modification
rnam 'gyur kho na['i mu]		limit of modification alone (Sāṃkhya)

TIBETAN	SANSKRIT	ENGLISH
rnam grangs pa'i kun brtags	*paryāyaparikalpita*	nominal imaginary
rnam grol gyi phung po	*vimuktiskandha*	aggregate of liberation
rnam grol gyi ye shes gzigs pa'i phung po	*vimuktijñānadarśana-skandha*	aggregate of the perception of liberating pristine cognition
rnam pa mtshungs pa	*ākārasamprayukta*	concomitance of sensum
rnam par rtog pa	*vikalpa*	conception, conceptual thought
rnam par mi rtog pa	*nirvikalpa*	absence of conceptual thought
rnam par mi rtog pa'i ye shes	*nivikalpajñāna*	nonconceptual pristine cognition
rnam par 'tshe ba	*vihiṃsa*	violence
rnam par mi 'tshe ba	*ahiṃsa*	nonviolence
rnam par g.yeng ba	*vikṣepa*	distraction
rnam par shes pa	*vijñāna*	consciousness
rnam par shes pa'i khams	*vijñānadhātu*	element of consciousness
rnam byang gi dbang po gsum		three powers of purification
rnam smin gyi rgyu	*vipākahetu*	ripening cause
rnam smin gyi cha	*vipākabhāga*	maturational aspect
rnam rig byed min gyi gzugs	*avijñaptirūpa*	nonapperceived form
rnam shes sgo lnga	*pañcavijñānadvāra*	five gates of sensory consciousness
rnam shes tshogs drug	*ṣaḍvijñānakāya*	six modes of sensory consciousness
rna'i blo	*śrotrabuddhi*	intelligence of the ear (Vaiśeṣika)
rnal 'byor	*yoga*	yoga, union

TIBETAN	SANSKRIT	ENGLISH
rnal 'byor gyi rgyud	*yogatantra*	tantra of union
rnal 'byor pa	*yogin*	yogin
rnal 'byor spyod pa	*yogācārin*	practitioner of yoga
rnal ma'i don		fundamental reality
sna	*ghrāṇa*	nose
sna tshogs sems kyi sde		class of mind characterized by diversity
snang brtags lta bar 'dod pa byar med pa		formal instructions that there is nothing to be done in respect of apparent and imputed phenomena that constitute the view
snang ba bzhi		four visionary appearances
snang gzhen theg pa		way of the priests of the visible world (Bon)
snang srid		phenomenal appearances or existence
sna'i blo	*ghrāṇabuddhi*	intelligence of the nose (Vaiśeṣika)
sna'i rnam par shes pa	*ghrāṇavijñāna*	olfactory consciousness
pa ṇḍi ta	*paṇḍita*	scholar, paṇḍita
dpag tshad	*yojana*	yoking distance (= 7,315 m)
dpyad ra		analytical framework
dpyod pa	*vicāra*	scrutiny
spang ba bcu		ten renunciations (Bon)
spangs pa bzhi po		four aspects of renunciation
spyi	*sāmānya*	universal (Vaiśeṣika)
spyi chung ngu	*mṛdusāmānya*	lesser universal (Vaiśeṣika)
spyi ti		Chiti class of Great Perfection

Tibetan	Sanskrit	English
spyi mthun gyi las		generic action
spyod pa	*caryā*	conduct
spyod pa ba/po	*mīmāṃsika*	Mīmāṃsika
spyod pa'i rgyud	*caryātantra*	tantra of conduct
sprul pa'i klong nag		black space of emanation
sprul [pa'i] sku	*nirmāṇakāya*	buddha body of emanation
spros pa	*prapañca*	conceptual elaboration
pha rgyud	*pitṛtantra*	father tantra
pha rol tu phyin pa	*pāramitā*	transcendent perfection
pha rol tu phyin pa drug	*ṣaṭpāramitā*	six transcendent perfections
phan pa	*saṃhitā*	Vedic compilation
phan tshun 'gal ba	*parasparavirodha*	mutually contradictory
phung po	*skandha*	psycho-physical aggregate
phung po lnga	*pañcaskandha*	five aggregates
phun sum tshogs par rdzogs pa		perfection in excellent attributes
phur bu pa	*bārhaspatya*	Bārhaspatya, worshipper of Bṛhaspati
phyag rgya	*mudrā*	seal, gesture of sealing
phyag rgya chen po	*mahāmudrā*	great seal
phyag rgya bzhi	*caturmudrā*	four seals
phyag mtshan	*cihna*	handheld emblems
phyam gcig		single state of evenness
phyi skor		outer cycle
phyi 'gyur		later translations
phyi rgyud gsum		three outer classes of tantra

Tibetan	Sanskrit	English
phyi thub rgyud kyi theg pa		vehicles of the austere outer tantras
phyi ma'i mtha' la brten pa'i rtog pa	*aparantakalpika*	notions or speculations dependent on the future
phyin ci ma log pa'i yongs grub	*aviparyāsaparinispanna*	incontrovertible consummate nature
phyi'i skye mched	*bāhyāyatana*	external sense field
phyug gi brtul zhugs paśuvrata gocarī		ascetic discipline of grazing for grass (Jainism)
phye ba	*vibhāga*	separation (Vaiśeṣika)
phyogs	*dik*	direction (Vaiśeṣika)
phyogs kyi gos can	*digmukhin*	Digambara
phyogs gtad		fixed perspective
phyogs 'byam gcig tu grol ba		liberation in a single pervasion
phyogs 'dzin	*pakṣapāta*	dogmatism
phyogs 'dzin grub mtha'i sems phyogs pa		perspective of mind concerning dogmatic philosophical systems
phyogs yan		free from constraints, open
phra rgyas	*anuśaya*	latent impulse
phra ba	*sūkṣmatā*	subtlety (Aiśvarya)
phrag dog	*īrṣyā*	jealousy
'phags pa	*ārya*	sublime being
'phags pa rnam pa gsum		three kinds of sublime beings
'phrad pa	*saṃyoga*	connection (Vaiśeṣika)
'phrin las, las	*kārya, karma*	rite of enlightened activity
'phrin las chen po		greatness of activity

TIBETAN	SANSKRIT	ENGLISH
'phrul gshen theg pa		way of the priests of miraculous power (Bon)
ba ku la	*bakula*	bulletwood tree (*Mimusops elengi*)
bag chags	*vāsanā*	propensity
bag chags kyi gzhi		ground of propensities
bag chags sna tshogs pa'i kun gzhi		substratum of diverse propensities
bag med	*pramāda*	carelessness
bag yod	*apramāda*	vigilance
bam po	*kalāpa*	fascicle
bar gyi bskal pa	*antarakalpa*	intervening aeon of time
bar gyi spyi	*antarasāmānya*	intermediate universal (Vaiśeṣika)
bar 'gyur		intermediate translations
bar [ma] do['i srid pa]	*antarābhava*	intermediate state (after death)
bum pa de nyid		generic (conceptualized) vase
bum dbang	*kalaśābhiṣeka*	vase empowerment
bem po, bems po	*jaḍa*	inanimate, inert matter
bod kyi lha srin sde brgyad		eight classes of Tibetan gods and demons
bon		Bon
bon gyi sgo mo brgyad khri bzhi stong		eighty-four thousand approaches of Bon
bon po		Bonpo
bya ba grub pa'i ye shes	*kṛtyānusthānajñāna*	pristine cognition of accomplishment
bya ba dang bral ba'i klong		space of freedom from activity

TIBETAN	SANSKRIT	ENGLISH
bya ba dang bral ba phyi'i rab 'byams		outer infinity concerning freedom from activity
bya ba dang rtsol ba las 'das pa		beyond laborious effort
bya rtsol		laborious effort
bya ba'i rgyud	*kriyātantra*	tantra of action
bya gshen theg pa		way of the priests of prediction (Bon)
byang chub	*bodhi*	enlightenment
byang chub kyi sems	*bodhicitta*	enlightened or awakened mind
byang chub snying po	*bodhimaṇḍa*	nucleus of enlightenment
byang chub phyogs chos sum cu rtsa bdun	*saptatriṃśadbodhipakṣikadharma*	thirty-seven factors conducive to enlightenment
byang chub sems su rdzogs pa		perfection in enlightened mind
byang sems	*bodhicitta*	generative essence
byas chos glo bur du shar bas 'dus byas yid dpyod lta sgom gyi ngo bo ye grol mi rtog pa'i gnad		crucial point that since created phenomena adventitiously arise, the essence of those views and meditations based on conditioned speculation is a primordially liberated, nonconceptual state
bye brag	*viśeṣa*	particular
bye brag pa	*vaiśeṣika*	Vaiśeṣika (Vaiśeṣika)
byed pa'i rgyu	*kāraṇahetu*	efficient cause
bral rgyu	*visaṃyogahetu*	cause of separation (from obscuration)
bral ba'i rdzas	*visaṃyogadravya*	disassociated substance
bral lugs		mode of absence

Tibetan	Sanskrit	English
bla gab med pa		without clothing, exposed (Jainism)
bla ma	*guru*	spiritual mentor
blag sha	*plakṣa*	fig tree
blang dang dor byed pa	*heyopādeya*	acceptance and rejection
blo [gros]	*buddhi*	intellect, intelligence, discernment
blo rtog		concept present within the intellect
blo bral ngo bo nyid kyi gtan tshigs		axiom of the essential nature free from the intellect
blo bral phyogs 'dzin las 'das pa'i sems phyogs pa		perspective of mind transcending dogmatism about that which is free from the intellect
blo sbyong		mind training
blo rigs bzhi		four intellectual standpoints
blo'i dbang po lnga	*pañcāntarendriya*	five mental sense faculties (Sāṃkhya)
dbang bka'		oral transmission of empowerment
dbang bskur	*abhiṣeka*	empowerment
dbang gi las	*vaṣitākriyā*	rite of subjugation
dbang chog	*abhiṣekavidhi*	empowerment rite
dbang du gyur pa	*vaśitva*	dominion (Aiśvarya)
dbang don	*indriyārtha*	sense object
dbang po	*indriya*	sense organ or faculty
dbang po lnga	*pañcendriya*	five sense organs or faculties
dbang po bcu gcig	*ekadaśendriya*	eleven sense faculties (Sāṃkhya)

TIBETAN	SANSKRIT	ENGLISH
dbang po pa	*aindra*	Aindra, worshiper of Indra
dbang po'i rdul	*indriyaraja*	atom of the sense organs
dbang phyug pa	*aiśvarya*	Aiśvarya
dbang bzhi	*caturabhiṣeka*	four empowerments
dbyu gu gsum can	*tridaṇḍin*	possessing the three staffs (of ascetic restraint)
dbu ma	*madhyamaka*	Madhyamaka
dbu ma chen po	*mahāmadhyamaka*	Great Madhyamaka
dbu ma pa	*mādhyamika*	Mādhyamika
dbugs	*śvāsa*	breath
dbye ba	*vibheda*	classification
dbyer med ngo bo nyid kyi sa dbyings de bzhin nyid lhun gyis grub pa		level of indivisible essence on which the expanse and the real are spontaneously present
dbyings	*dhātu*	expanse (of reality)
'bad rtsol	*yatna*	strenuous effort
'byung po lnga	*pañcabhūta*	five elements
'byung ba bzhi	*caturbhūta*	four material elements
'byor 'brel ba	*yoga*	connection
'bras bu	*phala*	fruit, result, outcome
'bras bu ye grol du smra ba'i klong gi sde		class of space, propounding that the fruition is primordial liberation
'bras bu sems kyi byung sar 'dod pa'i sems phyogs pa		perspective of mind holding the fruition to be the mind's point of origin
'bras bu'i rtags	*kāryahetu*	axiom of the result
'bras bu'i phung po	*kāryaskandha*	mature psycho-physical aggregate

Tibetan	Sanskrit	English
'bras bu'i bon bzhi		four fruitional modes of Bon
'bras gzugs bcu gcig		eleven aspects of fruitional matter
sbyang bya	*śodhya*	object of purification
sbyang gzhi		ground of purification
sbyangs 'bras		result of purification
sbyong byed	*śodhaka*	means of purification
sbyor lam	*prayogamārga*	path of connection
sbyor sgrol		(rites or secret offerings of) union and liberation
ma rgyud	*mātṛtantra*	mother tantra
ma chags pa	*alobha*	nonattachment
ma chags padma can gyi sa		level of unattached lotus endowed
ma rtogs pa sor bzhag lha mi'i theg pa		basic ways of gods and humans of no understanding
ma dag pa'i sgyu ma		impure apparitional nature
ma dag pa'i gzhan dbang		impure dependent nature
ma dad pa	*aśraddhya*	faithlessness
ma dmigs pa'i rtags	*anupalambhanahetu*	axiom of the absence of the objective referent
ma rig pa	*avidyā*	fundamental ignorance
ma zin pa'i khams	*anupāttadhātu*	organically unretained element
man ngag gi sde	*upadeśavarga*	class of esoteric instructions
man ngag rdzogs pa chen po	*mahāsandhyupadeśa*	esoteric instructions: the Great Perfection
mi dge ba	*akuśala*	nonvirtuous (action)

TIBETAN	SANSKRIT	ENGLISH
mi ldan pa'i 'du byed	*viprayuktasaṃskāra*	formative predispositions disassociated (from mind and mental states)
mi rtag pa	*anitya*	impermanent
mi rtag pa	*anityatā*	impermanence
mi rtog pa	*nirvikalpa*	nonconceptualization
mi rtog pa'i ye shes	*nirvikalpajñāna*	nonconceptual pristine cognition
mi g.yo ba'i 'gog pa	*akopyanirodha*	stable cessation
mi slob pa'i lam	*aśaikṣamārga*	path of no-more-learning
mig	*cakṣuḥ*	eye
mig gi rnam par shes pa	*cakṣurvijñāna*	visual consciousness
mig gi blo	*cakṣurbuddhi*	intelligence of the eye (Vaiśeṣika)
mig gi dbang po	*cakṣurindriya*	sense organ of the eye
mig sgo		eye socket
ming gi rnam grangs	*nāmaparyāya*	synonym(s)
ming gi tshogs	*nāmakāya*	nominal cluster
ming bzhi'i phung po		four nominal aggregates
ming gzugs	*nāmarūpa*	name and form
min pa med pa		absence of nonbeing
mu brgyad	*aṣṭānta*	eight parameters or limits
mu stegs pa	*tīrthika*	heretical extremist
mu bzhi	*caturanta*	four limits or parameters
mun pa	*tamas*	dullness (Sāṃkhya)
me	*agni*	fire
me lnga bsten pa	*pañcāgnisevā*	five fire rites (Jainism)

TIBETAN	SANSKRIT	ENGLISH
me tog zla mdzes	*supuṣpacandra*	lily
me long lta bu'i ye shes	*ādarśajñāna*	mirror-like pristine cognition
med pa	*nāstika*	Nāstika, nihilist
med smra rang gnas dang mthun pa'i klong khra bo		variegated space that speaks in terms of nonbeing, in conformity with the natural position (of the class of space)
me'i khams	*tejodhātu*	fire element
mes po	*pitāmaha*	progenitor
mos pa	*adhimokṣa*	resolve
mya ngan las 'das pa	*nirvāṇa*	nirvāṇa
mya ngan las 'das par smra ba'i rtog pa		notions propounding immediate attainment of nirvāṇa
myung bar gnas pa'i cho ga		fasting ritual
dmigs pa	*upalabdhi*	apprehension, perception
dmigs pa chen po		greatness of focus
dmigs pa mtshungs pa	*ālambanasamprayukta*	concomitance of objective referent
dmigs pa la thogs pa	*ālambanapratighāta*	resistance in respect of mental objects
dmigs pa'i rkyen	*ālambanapratyaya*	referential condition
dmigs pa'i gdar sha		doubt concerning perception
dmigs su med pa	*anupalabdhya*	nonapprehensible
dmyal ba	*naraka*	hells
rmugs pa	*styāna*	dullness
smad 'dul		Lowland Tibetan Vinaya Lineage
sman	*bhaiṣajya*	medicine

TIBETAN	SANSKRIT	ENGLISH
sman rak gtor ma		(inner offerings of) nectar, blood, and tormas
gtsang sbra	*caukṣa or śauca*	ablution
gtso bo	*pradhāna*	primal matter (Sāṃkhya)
gtso bo sems		central mind
rtsa	*nāḍi*	energy channel, nerve, blood vessel
rtsa rgyud	*mūlatantra*	root tantra
rtsa nyon drug	*ṣaṇmūlakleśa*	six primary afflicted mental states
rtsa 'phar ba		pulsation
rtsa ba'i dam tshigs	*mūlasamaya*	primary commitment
rtsa rlung gi gnad		focal point of the energy channels and winds
rtsis	*gaṇana*	divination
rtsol sgrub		strenuous effort and attainment
brtson 'grus	*vīrya*	perseverance
brtson 'grus chen po		greatness of perseverance
tshangs pa ba	*brāhmaṇa*	Brāhmaṇa
tshad ma	*pramāṇa*	valid cognition
tshig	*pada*	word, term, phrase
tshig gi don drug	*ṣaṭpadārtha*	six categories (Vaiśeṣika)
tshig gi tshogs	*padakāya*	phrasal cluster
tshig don	*padārtha*	definition of terms
tshig dbang	*vāgabhiṣeka*	word empowerment
tshur rol mdzes pa	*cārvāka*	Cārvāka, hedonist
tshul khrims kyi phung po	*śīlaskandha*	aggregate of ethical discipline

TIBETAN	SANSKRIT	ENGLISH
tshul gsum	*trairūpya*	threefold criteria (of valid cognition)
tshul gsum pa'i rtags	*trirūpaliṅga*	threefold axiomatic reasoning
tshes bcu		tenth-day ceremony
tshogs	*sambhāra*	provision
tshogs [kyi 'khor lo]	*gaṇa[cakra]*	communion offering, feast offering
tshogs gnyis	*dvisambhāra*	two provisions (of merit and pristine cognition)
tshogs drug		six aspects (of consciousness)
tshogs pa	*sāmagrī*	grouping
tshogs lam	*sambhāramārga*	path of provisions
tshogs bshad		public exegesis
tshol khro		restlessness
tshor ba	*vedanā*	feelings, sensation
mtshan bcas bskyed rim	*sanimittotpattikrama*	symbolic generation stage (of meditation)
mtshan nyid	*lakṣaṇa*	defining characteristic
mtshan nyid kyi bshad grva		dialectical college
mtshan nyid bzhi	*caturlakṣaṇa*	four defining characteristics (of conditioned phenomena)
mtshan nyid su chad pa'i kun brtags	*paricchedaparikalpita*	imaginary nature of delimited characteristics
mtshan gnyis pa ba	*ubhayavyañjanavat*	hermaphrodite
mtshan ma	*nimitta*	mental image, sign
mtshan med rdzogs rim	*nirnimittasampannakrama*	nonsymbolic perfection stage
mtshams med lnga	*pañcānantarya*	five inexpiable crimes
mtshon pa gnyis		two models (Bon)

TIBETAN	SANSKRIT	ENGLISH
mtshon bya	*lakṣya*	definiendum
mtshungs ldan gyi rgyu	*saṃprayuktahetu*	concomitant cause
mtshungs pa de ma thag pa'i rkyen	*samanantarapratyaya*	immediate and homogenous condition
mtshungs pa lnga	*pañcasamprayukta*	five concomitant factors
'tshig pa	*pradāśa*	annoyance
mdzad pa'i klong nag		black space of enlightened deeds
dzā ya dha ri ba		follower of Jayadhara
rdzas	*dravya*	substance
rdzas 'gal ba		material contradiction
rdzas brgyad	*aṣṭadravya*	eight substances
rdzas drug	*ṣaḍdravya*	six substances or substantial existents
rdzas rdul	*dravyaraja/ dravyaparamāṇu*	primary atom of substance
rdzas mtshungs pa	*dravyasamprayukta*	concomitance of substance
rdzas yod	*dravyataḥ*	substantial existent
rdzun	*mṛṣā*	lie
rdzogs pa chen po	*mahāsandhi*	great perfection
zhi ba pa	*śaiva*	Śaiva, Shaivite
zhi ba'i las	*śāntikriyā*	rite of pacification
zhe sdang	*dveṣa*	aversion, hatred
zhe sdang med pa	*adveṣa*	nonhatred
gzhan	*paratva*	remoteness (Aiśvarya)
gzhan gyi don byed pa	*paropakaraṇa*	beneficial intent (Sāṃkhya)
gzhan 'gyur bzhi	*caturvikāra*	four variable mental states

TIBETAN	SANSKRIT	ENGLISH
gzhan dbang	*paratantra*	dependent (nature)
gzhan ma yin	*ananyathā*	proximity (Vaiśeṣika)
gzhal yas khang	*vimāṇa*	celestial palace
gzhi	*sthāna, ādhāra, āśraya*	ground, basis
gzhi gzhag		settled in the ground
gzhon nu rtse ba'i bstan bcos	*kumārakrīḍāśāstra*	treatise of trivial pursuit (Mīmāṃsika)
bzhag pa lam gyi mtha' gcod pa'i man ngag		esoteric instructions that determine the path by establishing (the abiding nature of reality)
za ba pa	*bhakṣaka*	consumer (Vaiṣṇava)
zag bcas kyi chos	*sāsravadharma*	contaminated phenomena
zag bcas kyi rnam shes	*sāsravavijñāna*	consciousness endowed with contamination
zag pa	*srava*	contaminant
zag med kyi chos	*anāsravadharma*	uncontaminated phenomena
zag med kyi rnam shes	*anāsravavijñāna*	consciousness free from contaminants
zang thal		core penetrating
zin pa'i khams	*upāttadhātu*	organically retained element
zin pa'i 'byung ba las gyur ba'i sgra	*upāttamahābhūtahetukaśabda*	organically retained sound
zla ba	*māsa*	month
zla ba pa	*cāndra*	Cāndra, moon worshipper
zlum gor		atom
gzugs	*rūpa*	physical forms or matter, sights or visual forms
gzugs kyi sku	*rūpakāya*	buddha body of form

TIBETAN	SANSKRIT	ENGLISH
gzugs kyi skye mched	*rūpāyatana*	sense field of visual forms or sights
gzugs kyi khams	*rūpadhātu*	sensory element of visual forms or sights, world system of form
gzugs can gyi khams	*rūpyadhātu*	material (sensory) element
gzugs can	*rūpya/rūpī*	material
gzugs can ma yin pa	*arūpī*	immaterial
gzugs med kyi khams	*ārūpyadhātu*	world system of formlessness
gzugs me'i yon tan	*tejoguṇarūpa*	sights, as an attribute of heat (Vaiśeṣika)
gzugs su rung ba	*rūpya*	physical, material
gzung 'dzin	*grāhyagrāhaka*	subject-object dichotomy
gzungs	*dhāraṇī*	mnemonic incantation, retention
gzungs phran brgya dang drug cu		one hundred sixty lesser mnemonic incantations
bzod pa	*kṣānti*	tolerance, receptiveness, acceptance
bzod pa chung ngu		level of lesser receptiveness
bzlas brjod	*japa*	recitation
'ug pa ba	*aulūkya*	Aulūkya
'od gsal	*prabhāsvara*	luminosity
yang 'gyur		retranslations
yang ba	*laghutva*	agility (Aiśvarya)
yang ti		Yangti class of Great Perfection
yang dag pa'i kun rdzob	*samyaksaṃvṛti*	authentic relative truth/ appearances

TIBETAN	SANSKRIT	ENGLISH
yang dag pa'i gzhan dbang	*samyakparatantra*	pure dependent nature
yang 'dul gyi lha khang		further taming temples
yan lag	*śākhā*	school of Vedic lore
yan lag gi rgyud	*aṅgatantra*	ancillary tantras
yan lag gi dam tshig	*aṅgasamaya*	subsidiary commitment
yab yum 'khril sbyor		male and female consorts in union
yi ge'i tshogs	*vyañjanakāya*	syllabic cluster
yi dvags	*preta*	anguished spirit
yig 'bru	*akṣara/varṇa*	seed syllable
yid	*manas*	mental faculty, mind
yid kyi skye mched	*manāyatana*	sense field of the mental faculty
yid kyi khams	*manodhātu*	sensory element of the mental faculty
yid kyi rnam par shes pa	*manovijñāna*	mental consciousness
yid la byed pa	*manaskāra*	attention, attentiveness
yin pa med pa		absence of being
yin min phyogs mnyam gyi gtan tshigs		axiom of equanimity with regard to standpoints of being and nonbeing
yin min med pa		absence of being and nonbeing
yud tsam pa	*muhūrta*	hour (= 48 mins.)
yum lnga		five female buddhas
yul	*viṣaya*	sense object
yul	*deśa*	location
yul gyi don		haecceity of objects

Tibetan	Sanskrit	English
yul nges lnga	*pañcaviṣayaniyata*	five object-determining mental states
yul lnga	*pañcaviṣaya*	five sense objects
yul la thogs pa	*viṣayapratighāta*	resistance in respect of sense objects
ye grol klong gi sde		class of space characterized by primordial liberation
ye gzhag		timelessly settled
ye gzhen theg pa		way of the primordial priests (Bon)
ye shes	*jñāna*	pristine cognition, knowledge
ye shes kyi tshogs	*jñānasambhāra*	provision of pristine cognition
ye shes chen po		greatness of pristine cognition
ye shes sems dpa'	*jñānasattva*	being of pristine cognition
yongs grub	*pariniṣpanna*	consummate (nature)
yongs gcod	*pariccheda*	delimited
yod med skye bral gyi gtan tshigs		axiom of the absence of production from existence and nonexistence
yod med man ngag dang mthun pa'i klong khra bo		variegated space that speaks in terms of both being and nonbeing, in conformity with the esoteric instructional class
yod med rdzas 'gal		material contradiction pertaining to existence and nonexistence
yod smra sems sde dang mthun pa'i klong khra bo		variegated space that speaks in terms of being, in conformity with the class of mind
yon tan	*guṇa*	enlightened attribute, attribute

TIBETAN	SANSKRIT	ENGLISH
yon tan gsum	*triguṇa*	three attributes (Sāṃkhya)
g.yo	*śāṭhya*	pretentiousness
rang 'gros		natural rhythm
rang rgyud	*svatantra*	independent reasoning
rang rgyud gong ma		higher Svātantrika
rang rgyud 'og ma		lower Svātantrika
rang rgyud pa	*svātantrika*	those employing independent syllogisms
rang dang mnyam pa		equivalence
rang byung ye shes	*svayambhūjñāna*	naturally occurring pristine cognition
rang 'bras	*svakārya*	own fruit, own outcome, own result
rang gzhag		natural presence, naturally settled
rang bzhin	*svabhāva*	natural expression
rang bzhin	*prakṛti*	nature, natural state (Sāṃkhya)
rang bzhin kho na'i mu		limit of the natural state alone (Sāṃkhya)
rang bzhin gyi rtags	*svabhāvahetu*	axiom of identity
rang bzhin gnyug ma'i shes pa		naturally innate consciousness
rang yod pa'i gzhi		naturally present ground
rang rig	*svasaṃvid*	intrinsic awareness
rang sa	*svabhūmi*	one's own present level
rang sems ma bcos		uncontrived natural mind
rang song		intuitively
rang gsal		natural radiance

TIBETAN	SANSKRIT	ENGLISH
rab [tu] byung [ba]	*pravrajika/pravrajyā*	mendicant, renunciate ordination
rab byung gnas mal gzhi	*pravajyāśayanāsanavastu*	ground rules concerning the habitation of a renunciant
ri bong rdul	*śaśaraja*	rabbit-hair particle
rig gnas	*vidyāsthāna*	field of classical learning
rig gtad		entrustment of awareness
rig pa	*vidyā*	awareness
rig pa can pa	*naiyāyika*	Naiyāyika
rig pa'i gzungs sngags	*vidyādhāraṇī*	mnemonic incantation of awareness
rig byed pa	*vaidika*	Vaidika
rigs	*gotra*	class
rigs	*kula*	enlightened heritage
rigs mthun pa	*nikāyasabhāga*	homogeneity
rigs byed kyi mtha' gsang ba pa	*vedāntaupaniṣadika*	Vedāntaupaniṣadika
rin po che'i klong dkar po		white space of gemstones
rim pa gnyis	*dvikrama*	two stages (of meditation)
ru gnon gyi lha khang		district controlling temples
reg bya	*spraṣṭavya*	tangible(s)
reg bya'i khams	*spraṣṭavyadhātu*	element of tangibles
reg pa	*sparśa*	(sensory) contact
reg rlung gi yon tan	*vāyuguṇasparśa*	tangibles, as an attribute of wind (Vaiśeṣika)
ro	*rasa*	taste
ro chu'i yon tan	*apaguṇarasa*	tastes, as an attribute of water (Vaiśeṣika)

TIBETAN	SANSKRIT	ENGLISH
rol pa'i klong		space of display
rlung	*vāyu or vata*	wind
rlung sems		subtle wind and mind
lag len	*prakriyā*	practical implementation
lam	*mārga, patha*	path
lam rim	*pathakrama*	gradual path
las	*karma*	action, impact of past actions
las ka rnam pa gsum		three modes of ritual activity (Bon)
las kyi phyag rgya	*karmamudrā*	action seal
lug rdul	*eḍakaraja*	sheep-hair particle
lung	*āgama*	scriptural transmission
lung ma bstan	*avyākṛta*	neutral (action)
lus	*kāya*	body
lus kyi rnam par shes pa	*kāyavijñāna*	tactile consciousness
lus kyi blo	*kāyabuddhi*	intelligence of the body (Vaiśeṣika)
lus kyi dbang po	*kāyendriya*	faculty of touch (Jainism)
lus kyi dbang po lnga	*pañcabāhyendriya*	five physical faculties or motor organs (Sāṃkhya)
le lo	*kausīdya*	indolence
len pa	*upādāna*	grasping
le'u	*pariccheda*	chapter
lo rgyus	*vṛttānta*	legend
lo tsā ba	*lokacakṣu*	translator
log pa'i kun rdzob	*mithyāsaṃvṛti*	false relative truth/ appearances

TIBETAN	SANSKRIT	ENGLISH
log par rtog pa mu stegs		philosophical extremists who misunderstand (the nature of reality)
longs spyod rdzogs pa'i sku	*sambhogakāya*	buddha body of perfect resource
sha lnga	*pañcamāṃsa*	five meats
shi thabs sum brgya drug cu		three hundred sixty funerary rites (Bon)
shig yūka		lice-size particle
shing	*kāṣṭha*	wood
shing mya ngan med	*aśokavṛkṣa*	Aśoka tree
shin kun	*hiṅgu*	asafoetida (*Ferula asafoetida*)
shin tu sbyangs pa	*praśrabdhi*	refinement
shes pa tshogs drug	*ṣaṭkāyajñāna*	six modes of (engaged) consciousness
shes bya	*jñeya*	knowable phenomena
shes bya'i rab tu dbye ba		classification of knowable phenomena (Jainism)
shes bzhin ma yin pa	*asaṃprajanya*	inattentiveness
shes rab	*prajñā*	discriminative awareness
shes rab kyi pha rol tu phyin pa	*prajñāpāramitā*	transcendent perfection of discriminative awareness
shes rab kyi phung po	*prajñāskandha*	aggregate of discriminative awareness
shes rab ye shes kyi dbang	*prajñājñānābhiṣeka*	empowerment of discriminating pristine cognition
shlo ka	*śloka*	quatrain, verse
gshis	*marma*	fundamental state, vital point or essence
gshis ngo		essential disposition (of reality)

TIBETAN	SANSKRIT	ENGLISH
bshad bka'		oral transmission of exegesis
bshad grva		exegetical college
bshad rgyud	*vyākhyātantra*	exegetical tantra
bshad brgyud		exegetical lineage
bshad nyan grva		seminary
bshad pa rang gsal		exegeses that are naturally clear
sa	*pṛthivī, bhūmi*	earth, level
sa gong ma	*urdhvabhūmi*	higher level
sa bcu	*daśabhūmi*	ten levels
sa bon gyi cha	*bījabhāga*	germinal aspect
sa mi ka	*samika*	arjuna wood
sa 'og ma	*adharabhūmi*	lower level
sangs rgyas	*buddha*	buddha
sangs rgyas nyid	*buddhatva*	buddhahood
sa'i khams	*pṛthivīdhātu*	earth element
sems	*citta*	mind
sems kyi khams bdun	*saptacittadhātu*	seven mental elements
sems kyi dam pa	*varacitta*	genuine aspect of mind
sems kyis byas pa		mind's creations
sems bskyed	*cittotpāda*	setting the mind (on enlightenment)
sems can	*sattva*	sentient being
sems nyid	*cittatva*	nature of mind
sems rtog lta bar dril ba		conceptual mind encapsulated within the view
sems pa	*cetanā*	volition

TIBETAN	SANSKRIT	ENGLISH
sems phyogs yin du smra ba'i sems phyogs pa		perspective of mind that speaks in terms of things being perspectives of mind
sems byung	*caitasika*	mental state
sems tsam	*cittamātra*	mind only school
sems tsam pa	*cittamātrin*	Cittamātrin
sems tsam rnam bden pa	*sākāravādin*	Cittamātrins holding sensa to be veridical
sems tsam rnam rdzun pa	*nirākāravādin*	Cittamātrins holding sensa to be false
sems bzung		mental focus
ser sna	*mātsarya*	miserliness
so thar gyi sdom pa	*prātimokṣa*	vows of individual liberation
so ma zin pa'i grub mtha'		ineffectual tenet
so so rang gi rig pa	*pratisaṃvid*	individual intrinsic awareness
so so'i skye bo	*pṛthagjana*	ordinary person or individual
so sor nges pa	*pratiniyama*	distinctive regularity
so sor brtags pa'i 'gog pa	*pratisaṃkhyānirodha*	cessation obtained through analytical means
so sor brtags min gyi 'gog pa	*apratisaṃkhyānirodha*	cessation obtained through nonanalytical means
sor	*aṅgulī*	finger-width
sor rtogs ye shes	*pratyavekṣanajñāna*	pristine cognition of discernment
sor bzhag lha mi'i theg pa		basic ways of gods and humans
srang		ounce
sri gzungs		mnemonic incantations pertaining to sri demons
srid pa	*bhava*	rebirth process

TIBETAN	SANSKRIT	ENGLISH
srid zhi		existence and quiescence
srid gshen theg pa		way of the priests of the rebirth process (Bon)
srid srungs/bsrung ba	*ātharvaṇa*	observance of worldly rites (Mīmāṃsika)
sred pa	*tṛṣṇā*	craving
sro ma	*likṣā*	nit-size particle
srog	*jīva*	animate substance (Jainism)
srog gi dbang po	*jīvitendriya*	faculty of the life force
srog min pa	*ajīva*	inanimate substance (Jainism)
gsang skor		secret cycle
gsang ba pa	*aupaniṣadika*	Aupaniṣadika
gsang ba bla na med pa'i skor		unsurpassed secret cycle
gsang dbang	*guhyābhiṣeka*	secret empowerment
gsang tshig	*upaniṣad*	esoteric hymn, Upaniṣad
gsal ba	*prabhā*	radiance
gsar ma		new traditions
gsung	*vāk*	buddha speech
gsung gi gsang ba	*vāgguhya*	mystery of buddha speech
gsung rab	*pravacana*	scripture
bsags rdul	*pracitāṇu/ saṃghātaparamāṇu*	accumulated atoms, molecules
bsags pa'i rdul phra rab	*pracitaparimāṇu*	accumulated atomic particles
bsam gtan	*dhyāna*	meditative concentration
bsam gtan bzhi	*caturdhyāna*	four meditative concentrations

TIBETAN	SANSKRIT	ENGLISH
bsam pa	*āśaya*	resolve
bsod nams	*puṇya*	merit
bse ru	*khaḍga*	rhinoceros
slob bshad		esoteric exegesis
bslab pa 'dral ba	*śikṣābhaṅga*	infringement of monastic discipline
lha	*deva/devatā*	deity, god
lha zhal sbyor		deities in union
lha ma yin	*asura*	antigod
lhag bcas 'gog pa	*sāvaśeṣanirodha*	residual cessation
lhag med 'gog pa	*niḥśeṣanirodha*	nonresidual cessation
lhag med myang 'das	*niḥśeṣanirvāṇa*	nonresidual nirvāṇa
lhan cig 'byung ba'i rgyu	*sahabhūhetu*	coemergent cause
lhan ner		with clarity
lhun grub	*anābhoga*	spontaneous presence
lhun grub chos mchog dag pa'i sa 'bras bu rnam dag chen po		level of the pure, supreme phenomenon of spontaneous presence that is the fruition of great purity
a ka ru	*agaru*	eaglewood (*Aquilarea agallocha*)
a dkar theg pa		way of the white syllable A (Bon)
ā li kā li	*ālikāli*	Sanskrit vowels and consonants

Concordance of Personal Names

The following concordance gives precedence to the romanized Sanskrit or simplified Tibetan phonetic spelling in the first column, and provides the formal Tibetan transliteration in the second column. Readers should note that the chronology of the Tibetan kings is tentative.

Phonetic	**Tibetan Transliteration**
Abhayaprāpta	'jigs med thob
Abhiyugha (fl. early 11th century)	a bhi yugha
Ajitakeśakambalin (fl. 6th century BCE)	mi pham skra'i la ba can
Amoghavajra (fl. late 11th to early 12th century)	a mo gha badzra
Amṛta (deity)	'chi med
Ānanda of Gilgit (fl. 9th century)	bru sha'i bram ze ā nanda
Āryadeva (fl. 2nd to 3rd century)	'phags pa lha
Asaṅga (late 4th to early 5th century)	thogs med
Aśvaghoṣa (ca. 80–150)	rta dbyangs
Aśvins (deities)	tha skar
Avalokiteśvara (deity)	spyan ras gzigs dbang phyug
Ba Ratna (fl. late 8th century)	sba ratna
Ba Selnang (fl. late 8th century)	rba gsal snang
Ba Trizik (fl. late 8th century)	rba khri gzigs

PHONETIC	TIBETAN TRANSLITERATION
Bagom (Yeshe Jangchub) (fl. 11th century)	sba sgom (ye shes byang chub)
Balabhadra (deity)	stobs bzang
Balimācārya (fl. 11th century)	ba ling ā tsārya
Balo Trizher (fl. late 8th century)	sba lo khri gzher
Balo Yeshe Wangpo (fl. late 8th century)	sba lo ye shes dbang po
Bami Yeshe Jamyang (fl. late 8th century)	sba mi ye shes 'jam dbyangs
Baro Chakdum (fl. early 11th century)	'ba' ro phyag rdum
Be Thirlen (fl. late 8th century)	sbas thir len
Be Yeshe Gyalwa (fl. 9th century)	dbas ye shes rgyal ba
Bhāvaviveka (c. 500–570)	legs ldan 'byed
Biji (fl. 5th century)	bi byi
Bilhama (fl. 5th century)	bi lha ma
Birje Tsenpo Shila (fl. early 8th century)	bi rje btsan po shi la
Brahmā (deity)	tshangs pa
Bṛhaspati/Suraguru (deity)	phur bu/lha'i bla ma
Bubton (fl. 11th century)	sbubs ston
Buddhaguhya (fl. 7th to 8th century)	sangs rgyas gsang ba
Buddhajñānapāda (fl. late 8th century)	(sangs rgyas) ye shes zhabs
Buddhapālita (fl. early 6th century)	sangs rgyas bskyang
Bumseng (fl. 8th century)	'bum seng
Buton Rinchendrub (1290–1364)	bu ston rin chen grub
Candrakīrti (fl. 7th century)	zla ba grags pa
Chak Choje Pel (1197–1263/64)	chag chos rje dpal

Phonetic	Tibetan Transliteration
Chel Lotsāwa Chokyi Zangpo (fl. 12th century)	dpyal lo tsā ba chos kyi bzang po
Chengawa (Tsultrim Bar) (1033–1103)	spyan snga ba (tshul khrims 'bar)
Cheton Gyanak (1094–1149)	lce ston rgya nag
Chetsenkye (fl. 9th century)	che btsan skyes
Chetsun Senge Wangchuk (fl. 11th century)	lce btsun seng ge dbang phyug
Chobar (fl. late 8th to early 9th century)	chos 'bar (also known as Vairotsana)
Chokdru Lotsāwa Sherab Lama (fl. 11th century)	cog gru lo tsā ba shes rab bla ma
Chokrolui Gyaltsen Chobar (fl. late 8th to early 9th century)	cog ro klu'i rgyal mtshan
Chokyi Wangchuk/Chowang (1212–1270)	chos kyi dbang phyug
Dakpo Lharje (also known as Gampopa, 1079–1153)	dvags po lha rje
Daktri Tsenpo (fl. 2nd century BCE)	gdags khri btsan po (6th king of Tibet)
Dampa Gyagarwa (also known as Phadampa Sangye, fl. 11th to 12th century)	dam pa rgya gar ba
Dānaśīla (fl. 9th century)	dā na shī la
Dānaśīla (fl. late 12th to early 13th century)	dā na shī la
Dangma Lhundrub (fl. 11th century)	ldang ma lhun grub
Darpana Ācārya (fl. 11th century)	darpana ā tsārya
Daśaratha, king (epic figure)	rgyal po shing rta bcu pa
De Nolbe (also known as Senol Namde, fl. 2nd to 3rd century)	lde rnol sbas (18th king of Tibet)
De Nolpo (fl. 3rd century)	lde rnol po (21st king of Tibet)
De Nolya (also known as Se Nolpo De, fl. early 3rd century)	lde rnol ya (19th king of Tibet)

Phonetic	Tibetan Transliteration
De Trulnam Zhungtsen (fl. 2nd century)	lde 'phrul nam gzhung btsan (17th king of Tibet)
Den Yonten Chok (fl. 9th to 10th century)	dan yon tan mchog
Desho Lek (fl. 1st century)	de sho legs (11th king of Tibet)
Devākaracandra (fl. 11th century)	de vā ka ra tsandra
Devaśarman (traditionally 3rd century BCE)	lha skyid
Devavidyāsiṃha (fl. 7th century)	lha rig pa'i seng ge
Dharmakīrti (fl. early 7th century)	chos kyi grags pa
Dharmakīrti, mantrin (fl. late 8th to early 9th century)	sngags pa chos grags
Dharmapāla (fl. 11th century)	chos skyong/dharma pā la
Dharmaśīla (fl. late 8th to early 9th century)	dharma shī la
Dharmaśrī (fl. late 8th to early 9th century)	dharma shrī
Dharmatrāta (fl. 1st century BCE to 1st century)	chos skyabs
Dharmottara (fl. 8th century)	chos mchog
Dignāga (fl. late 5th to mid-6th century)	phyogs kyi glang
Dingtri Tsenpo (fl. 3rd to 2nd century BCE)	ding khri btsan po (3rd king of Tibet)
Dīpaṃkara (also known as Atiśa, 982–1054)	dī paṃ ka ra
Divasa (deity)	nyin zhag
Dolpopa Sherab Gyaltsen (1292–1361)	dol po pa shes rab rgyal mtshan
Dorje Dudjom (fl. late 8th to early 9th century)	rdo rje bdud 'joms
Dorje Lingpa (1346–1405)	rdo rje gling pa

PHONETIC	TIBETAN TRANSLITERATION
Drakpa Gyaltsen (1147–1216)	grags pa rgyal mtshan
Drapa Ngonshe (1012–1090)	grva pa mngon shes
Dreje Vajra (fl. 7th century)	'dre rje badzra
Drigum Tsenpo (fl. 1st century BCE)	gri gum btsan po (8th king of Tibet)
Drigung Jigten Sumgon (1143–1217)	'bri gung 'jig rten gsum mgon
Drigung[pa Kyura] Rinchen Pal (see previous entry)	'bri gung [pa skyu ra] rin chen dpal
Drime Ozer (1308–1363)	dri med 'od zer (also known as Longchen Rabjam)
Dro Lotsāwa Sherab Drakpa (fl. 12th century)	'bro lo tsā ba [shes rab grags pa]
Drogon (fl. 8th to 9th century)	'gro mgon
Drogon Chogyal Phakpa (1235–1280)	'gro mgon chos rgyal 'phags pa
Drokmi Lotsāwa [Śākya Yeshe] (993–1050)	brog mi lo tsā ba
Dromton Gyelwa Jungne (1004–1064)	brom ston rgyal ba'i 'byung gnas
Drong Nyenderu (fl. 6th century)	'brong gnyan lde ru (30th king of Tibet)
Drongzhi Lek (fl. 1st century)	'brong zhi legs (14th king of Tibet)
Droton [Namla Tsek] (fl. 11th century)	sgro ston [gnam la brtsegs]
Drubchen Melong Dorje (1243–1303)	grub chen me long rdo rje
Drugu Yangwang (fl. 11th century)	gru gu yang dbang
Drum Yeshe Gyaltsen (fl. 10th century)	grum ye shes rgyal mtshan
Dungi Torchokchen (fl. 4th century)	dung gi thor cog can
Dungtso Repa (fl. 13th to 14th century)	dung mtsho ras pa
Durshen Mawo (Bon teacher)	'dur gshen rma bo
Dzeng Dharmabodhi (1052–1136)	'dzeng dharma bo dhi
Dzeng Jo-se (fl. 11th to 12th century)	'dzeng jo sras

Phonetic	Tibetan Transliteration
Esho Lek (fl. 1st century BCE)	e sho legs (10th king of Tibet)
Fifth Dalai Lama (1617–1682)	rgyal mchog lnga pa
Four-Faced Brahmā (deity)	tshangs pa gdong bzhi
Ga Lotsāwa [Namgyal Dorje] (1203–1282)	rga lo
Ganjag Thangta (fl. late 8th to early 9th century)	gan jag thang ta (also known as Vairotsana)
Gayadhara (fl. 11th century)	ga ya dha ra/sprin 'dzin
Go Khukpa Lhatse (fl. 11th century)	'gos khug pa lha btsas
Gokyi Demtrulchen (1337–1408)	rgod kyi sdem 'phrul chen
Gonpo Yeshe (fl. 14th century)	mgon po ye shes
Gotsangpa [Gonpo Dorje] (1189–1258)	rgod tshang pa
Gungsong Gungtsen (r. 641–646)	gung srong gung btsan (34th king of Tibet)
Guru Jober (1172–1231)	gu ru jo 'ber
Guru Lek (fl. 1st century)	gu ru legs (13th king of Tibet)
Guru Senge Dradrok (manifestation of Guru Padmākara)	gu ru seng ge sgra sgrogs
Gyaltrim Narwa (Bon teacher)	rgyal khrims snar ba
Gyaltsabje [Darma Rinchen] (1364–1432)	rgyal tshab rje
Gyalwa Gendun Drub [Dalai Lama I] (1391–1474)	rgyal ba dge 'dun grub
Gyama Gon	rgya ma mgon
Gyendo Zewa Loden (fl. 11th century)	rgyan mdo'i gze ba blo ldan
Gyijo Lotsāwa [Dawa Ozer] (fl. 11th century)	gyi jo lo tsā ba
Hara Nagpo (fl. late 8th to early 9th century)	ha ra nag po
Hayagrīva (deity)	rta mgrin

Phonetic	Tibetan Transliteration
Hūṃkāra (fl. 6th century)	hūṃ ka ra
Indra (deity)	dbang po
Indra Vairo (fl. late 8th to early 9th century)	indra bai ro (also known as Vairotsana)
Indrasena	dbang sde
Isho Lek (fl. late 1st century)	i sho legs (15th king of Tibet)
Īśvara (deity)	dbang phyug
Īśvarakṛṣṇa (fl. 4th century)	dbang phyug nag po
Jamadagni (hermit sage)	drang srong dza mā ag ne
Jamchen Choje Shākya Yeshe (1355–1435)	'jam chen chos rje shākya ye shes
Jamyang Choje Tashi Palden (1397–1449)	'jam dbangs chos rje bkra shis dpal ldan
Jangchub Drak (fl. 10th century)	byang chub grags
Jayanta (c. 883–902)	rgyal byed
Jayasena (fl. 11th century)	dza ya se na
Jinamitra (fl. early 9th century)	dzi na mi tra
Jñānagarbha (700–760)	ye shes snying po
Jñānavāda	shes par smra
Jomonangpa (also known as Dolpopa Sherab Gyaltsen)	jo mo nang pa
Jowoje Atiśa (982–1054)	jo bo rje a ti sha
Kakudakatyāyana (fl. 6th century BCE)	ka ta'i bu nog can
Kālacakrapāda (fl. 11th century)	dus zhabs
Kalkin (future emanation of Viṣṇu)	rta ngang pa
Kamalaśīla (740–795)	ka ma la shī la
Kaṇāda (5th to 4th century BCE)	gzegs can

PHONETIC	TIBETAN TRANSLITERATION
Kapila	ser skya
Karma Lingpa (fl. 14th century)	karma gling pa
Karmapa Dusum Khyenpa (1110–1193)	karma pa dus gsum mkhyen pa
Karmapa Rangjung Dorje (1284–1339)	karma pa rang byung rdo rje
Katokpa Dampa Deshek (1122–1192)	ka thog pa gdams pa bde gshegs
Katyāyanīputra (2nd century BCE)	kā tyā na'i bu
Kawa Ochok Drak (fl. early 9th century)	ska ba 'od mchog grags
Kawa Peltsek (fl. late 8th to early 9th century)	ska ba dpal brtsegs
Khampa Ronyam Dorje (fl. 12th century)	khams pa ro mnyam rdo rje
Khedrub Sherab Senge (1383–1445)	mkhas grub shes rab seng ge
Khedrubje [Gelek Pelzang] (1385–1438)	mkhas grub rje (Panchen Lama I)
Khon Konchok Gyalpo (1034–1102)	'khon dkon mchog rgyal po
Khon Luiwangpo Sungwa (fl. late 8th to early 9th century)	khon klu'i dbang po srungs ba
Khu Netso (fl. 12th century)	khu ne tso
Khugyur Selwei Chok (fl. 10th century)	khu 'gyur gsal ba'i mchog
Khuton [Tsondru Yungdrung] (1011–1075)	khu ston [brtson 'grus g.yung drung]
Khyungpo Dorje (late 7th to early 8th century)	khyung po rdo rje
Khyungpo Neljor [Tsultrim Gonpo] (990–1127)	khyung po rnal 'byor
Kichung (fl. late 8th to early 9th century)	ki chung
Konchok Jungne (fl. late 8th to early 9th century)	dkon cog 'byung gnas

Phonetic	Tibetan Transliteration
Kṛṣṇa (emanation of Viṣṇu)	nag po
Kṛṣṇacārin (fl. 10th century)	nag po spyod pa
Kṛṣṇapāda (also known as Kṛṣṇacārin)	nag po'i zhabs
Kumāralāta (fl. 2nd century)	(btsun pa) gzhon nu len
Kunga Gyaltsen [Sakya Paṇḍita] (1182–1251)	kun dga' rgyal mtshan
Kungrab Lama Pel of Uyuk (fl. 13th century)	'u yug kung rab bla ma dpal
Kunzang (fl. 12th century)	kun bzang
Kūrma (turtle emanation of Viṣṇu)	rus sbal
Kusara (fl. 7th century)	ku sa ra
Kyangpo Cholo (fl. 11th century)	skyang po chos blo
Kyide Nyima Gon (fl. early 10th century)	skyid lde nyi ma mgon (great-grandson of Lang Darma)
Kyikye Jangchubsem	skyid skye ba byang chub sems
Kyok Duldzin (fl. 11th century)	skyogs 'dul 'dzin
Lachen Gongpa Rabsel (c. 892–975)	bla chen dgongs pa rab gsal
Lama Kyo [Ojung] (fl. 12th century)	bla ma skyo ['od 'byung]
Lang Darma (r. 841–846)	glang dar ma (42nd king of Tibet)
Lang Khampa Gocha (fl. 9th century)	rlangs khams pa go cha
Lasum Gyalwa Jangchub (fl. late 8th to early 9th century)	la gsum rgyal ba byang chub
Lato Konchok Khar (fl. 11th to 12th century)	la stod dkon mchog mkhar
Lekden [Rigdzin II or Dorje Drak] (1488–1569)	legs ldan
Lekjin Nyima (fl. late 8th to early 9th century)	legs sbyin nyi ma
Lha Lama Yeshe-o (947–1024)	lha bla ma ye shes 'od (great-great-great-grandson of Lang Darma)

PHONETIC	TIBETAN TRANSLITERATION
Lhacham Yidkyi Rolcha (fl. 5th century)	lha lcam yid skyid rol cha
Lha-de (fl. 11th century)	lha lde
Lhalung Pelgyi Dorje (fl. 9th century)	lha lung dpal gyi rdo rje
Lhatotori Nyentsen (fl. late 4th to 5th century)	lha tho tho ri gnyan btsan (28th king of Tibet)
Li byin, brahmin (fl. 7th century)	bram ze li byin
Lingje Repa [Pema Dorje] (1128–1188)	gling rje ras pa [padma rdo rje]
Liza Sherab Dronma (fl. late 8th to early 9th century)	li bza' shes rab sgron ma
Lobo Lotsāwa [Sherab Rinchen] (fl. 13th century)	glo bo lo tsā ba [shes rab rin chen]
Lok-kya Sherab Tsek (fl. 11th to 12th century)	glog skya shes rab brtsegs
Longchen Rabjam (1308–1363)	klong chen rab 'byams
Lorepa [Wangchuk Tsondru] (1187–1250)	lo ras pa
Lub Lotsāwa (1169–1233)	klubs lo tsā ba
Lume Tsultrim [Sherab] Wangchuk (fl. 10th century)	klu mes tshul khrims [shes rab] dbang phyug
Lung Namtrulgyi Gyelpo (also known as Dusong Mangpoje, 676–704)	klung nam 'phrul gyi rgyal po (36th king of Tibet)
Luyiwang Chokyi Lhunpo (late 8th to early 9th century)	klu'i dbang chos kyi lhun po
Ma Rinchen-chok (late 8th to early 9th century)	rma rin chen mchog
Machik Labdron (tentatively 1055–1149)	ma cig lab sgron
Mahādeva (late 8th to early 9th century)	ma hā de ba
Mahākāśyapa (fl. 6th to 5th century BCE)	'od srung chen po

PHONETIC	TIBETAN TRANSLITERATION
Mahākoṣṭhila	gsus po che
Mahārāja (late 8th to early 9th century)	ma hā rā dza
Mahāsūtra (late 8th to early 9th century)	ma hā sūtra
Mahāyāna (late 8th to early 9th century)	ma hā yā na
Mahāyānasūtra (late 8th to early 9th century)	ma hā [yā na] sūtra
Maitreya (deity)	byams pa
Maitrīśrībhadra (late 8th to early 9th century)	mi tri shrī bha dra
Manakaśrī (fl. 11th century)	ma na ka shrī
Maṅgalaprāpta	bkra shis thob
Mangsong Mangtsen (r. 650–676)	mang srong mang btsan (35th king of Tibet)
Mañjughoṣa (deity)	'jam pa'i dbyangs
Mañjuśrī (deity)	'jam dpal
Mantrakalāśa, paṇḍita (fl. 11th century)	mantra ka lā sha
Mapham Gonpo Sonam (see Pang Sangye Gonpo)	ma pham mgon po bsod nams
Mar Śākyamuni (fl. 9th late century)	smar śākya mu ni
Marpa Dopa [Chokyi Wangchuk] (1042–1136)	mar pa do pa
Marpa Lotsāwa Chokyi Lodro (tentatively 1012–1097)	mar pa lo tsā ba chos kyi blo gros
Maskarī Gośālaputra[varuṇa] (fl. 6th century BCE)	gnag lhas kyi bu chu lha
Matsya (fish emanation of Viṣṇu)	nya'i 'jug pa
Maudgalyāyana (fl. 6th to 5th century BCE)	maudgal gyi bu
Mel Lotsāwa [Lodro Drakpa] (fl. 11th century)	mal lo tsā ba [blo gros grags pa]

PHONETIC	TIBETAN TRANSLITERATION
Metri Tsenpo (fl. 2nd century BCE)	me khri btsan po (5th king of Tibet)
Metsa Lingpa (fl. 11th century)	me tsa ling pa
Mila Repa (1052–1135)	mi la ras pa
Mokchokpa [Rinchen Tsondru] (1110–1170)	rmog cog ba
Mune Tsenpo (r. 797–804)	mu ne btsan po (39th king of Tibet)
Murum Tsenpo (fl. late 8th to early 9th century)	mu rum btsan po (prince)
Mutri Tsenpo (also known as Mutik Tsenpo, r. 804–815)	mu khri btsan po (40th king of Tibet)
Mutri Tsenpo (fl. 3rd century BCE)	mu khri btsan po (2nd king of Tibet)
Nāgārjuna (fl. 2nd century)	klu grub
Nagtsho Lotsāwa [Tsultrim Gyalwa] (1011–1064)	nag tsho lo tsā ba
Namka Nyingpo (fl. late 8th to early 9th century)	nam mkha' snying po
Namri Songtsen (d. 629)	gnam ri srong btsan (32nd king of Tibet)
Nanam Dawei Dorje (fl. late 8th to early 9th century)	sna nam zla ba'i rdo rje
Narasiṃha (man-lion emanation of Viṣṇu)	mi seng ge'i gdong
Nāropā (1016–1100)	nā ro pa
Ngari Panchen Pema Wangyal (1487–1543)	mnga' ris paṇ chen padma dbang rgyal
Ngendzongpa (fl. 11th century)	ngan rdzong pa
Ngenlam Gyelwa Choyang (fl. late 8th to early 9th century)	ngan lam rgyal ba mchog dbyangs
Ngenlam Jangchub Gyaltsen (fl. 9th century)	ngan lam byang chub rgyal mtshan
Ngok Lekpei Sherab (fl. 11th century)	rngog legs pa'i shes rab

PHONETIC	TIBETAN TRANSLITERATION
Ngok Lo Chenpo (1059–1109)	rngog lo chen po (also known as Ngok Loden Sherab)
Niguma (fl. 10th to 11th century)	ni gu ma
Nirgranthajñātiputra (fl. 6th century BCE)	gcer bu gnyan gyi bu
Niṣkalaṅka (fl. 12th century)	ni ṣka langka
Nub Namka Nyingpo (fl. late 8th to early 9th century)	gnubs nam mkha'i snying po
Nub Sangye Yeshe (fl. late 8th to late 9th century)	gnubs sangs rgyas ye shes
Nyak Jñānakumāra (fl. late 8th to early 9th century)	gnyags dznyāna ku mā ra
Nyang [ben] Tingdzin Zangpo (fl. 9th century)	nyang [ban] ting 'dzin bzang po
Nyang Sherab Chok (late 9th century)	nyang shes rab mchog
Nyang Sherab Jungne (fl. late 10th century)	nyang shes rab 'byung gnas
Nyang Yeshe Jungne (fl. early 11th century)	nyang ye shes 'byung gnas
Nyangrel Nyima Ozer (c. 1124–1192)	nyang ral nyi ma 'od zer
Nyatri Tsenpo (fl. 3rd century BCE)	gnya' khri btsan po (1st king of Tibet)
Nyen Lotsāwa [Darma Drak] (fl. 11th to 12th century)	gnyan lo tsā ba [dar ma grags]
Nyibum (1158–1213)	nyi 'bum
Nyo Lotsāwa [Jungpo Yontan Drak] (fl. 11th century)	gnyos lo tsā ba
O-de (995–1037)	'od lde
Odren Pelgyi Wangchuk (fl. late 8th to early 9th century)	'o bran dpal gyi dbang phyug
Osung (840–893)	'od srungs (son of Lang Darma)
Padmākara (fl. 8th to 9th century)	padma 'byung gnas

Phonetic	Tibetan Transliteration
Padmarāja (also known as Phagmo Drupa Dorje Gyalpo)	padma rgyal po
Padmasambhava (a manifestation of Padmākara)	padma sambha va
Pagor Lochen Phak (fl. 9th century)	pa gor blo chen 'phags
Pagor Vairotsana (fl. late 8th to early 9th century)	pa gor bai ro tsa na
Palchen Ga Lotsāwa [Namgyal Dorje] (1203–1282)	dpal chen rga lo tsā ba [rnam rgyal rdo rje]
Paṇchen Lobzang Chogyen [Panchen Lama IV] (1567–1662)	paṇ chen blo bzang chos rgyan
Pang Sangye Gonpo (fl. 9th century)	spang sangs rgyas mgon po
Paraśurāma (emanation of Viṣṇu)	dza mā ag ne'i bu rā ma
Paśupati (deity)	phyugs bdag
Pelkhortsen (881–910)	dpal 'khor btsan (grandson of Lang Darma)
Pelyang (fl. late 8th to early 9th century)	dpal dbyangs
Pema Lendreltsel (1292–1316)	padma las 'brel rtsal
Pema Lingpa (1460–1521)	padma gling pa
Petsa Sonam Gyaltsen (fl. 11th century)	pe tsa bsod nams rgyal mtshan
Phagmo Drupa Dorje Gyalpo (1110–1170)	phag mo gru pa rdo rje rgyal po
Phamtingwa brothers [Abhayakīrti and Vāgeśvara] (fl. 11th century)	pha mthing ba sku mched
Phodrang Zhiwei-o (fl. 11th century)	pho brang zhi ba 'od
Piśācī (deity)	sha za
Prajāpati (deity)	skyes dgu'i bdag po
Prajñāvarman (fl. early 9th century)	pradznyā varma
Pravarta (fl. late 8th to early 9th century)	pra varta

Phonetic	Tibetan Transliteration
Pu Lekpei Dronma (fl. 9th century)	spu legs pa'i sgron ma
Puchungwa [Zhonu Gyaltsen] (1031–1106)	phu chung ba [gzhon nu rgyal mtshan]
Pude Gungyal (fl. 1st century BCE)	spu de gung rgyal (9th king of Tibet)
Puṇyaśrī (fl. 11th century)	puṇ ya shrī
Purāṇakāśyapa (fl. 6th century BCE)	'od srung rdzogs byed
Pūrṇa (fl. 5th century BCE)	gang bo
Purong Lochung (fl. 11th century)	pu rong lo chung
Putowa [Rinchen Sel] (1027–1105)	pu to ba [rin chen gsal]
Ra Chorab (fl. 11th century)	rva chos rab
Ra Yeshe Senge (fl. late 11th to early 12th century)	rva ye shes seng ge
Rakṣita (fl. late 8th to early 9th century)	rakṣi ta
Ralo Dorje Drak (1016–1128)	rva lo rdo rje grags
Rāma (kingly emanation of Viṣṇu)	ra ma ṇa
Rāṣṭrapāla, king	rgyal po yul 'khor skyong/srung
Ratna Lingpa (1403–1479)	ratna gling pa
Ravendrapa, paṇḍita (fl. 13th century)	ra vendra ba
Rikdzin Kumārādza (1266–1343)	rig 'dzin ku mā rā dza
Rinchen Zangpo (958–1055)	rin chen bzang po
Rongpa Chaksorpa (fl. 11th century)	rong pa phyag sor pa
Rongpa Gar-ge (fl. 11th century)	rong pa mgar dge
Rongzom Chozang (1042–1136)	rong zom chos bzang
Rudra (deity)	drag po
Sachen Kunga Nyingpo (1092–1158)	sa chen kun dga' snying po
Śākyamuni Buddha (fl. 6th to 5th century BCE)	shākya thub pa

Phonetic	Tibetan Transliteration
Śākyaprabhava (fl. late 8th to early 9th century)	shākya pra bha va
Śākyasena (fl. 10th century)	shākya se na
Śākyasiṃha (an emanation of Guru Padmākara)	shākya seng ge
Śākyaśrī of Kashmir (1127–1225)	kha che paṇ chen shākya shrī
Samantaśrī (fl. 11th century)	sa manta shrī
Samayavajra (fl. 11th century)	dam tshig rdo rje
Saṃshaṃ (fl. late 8th to early 9th century)	saṃ shaṃ
Samudramegha	rgya mtsho sprin
Sangdak Drophukpa [Śākya Senge] (1074–1135)	gsang bdag sgro phug pa
Sangton Yeshe Lama (fl. 9th century)	sang ston ye shes bla ma
Sangwa Dupa (Bon teacher)	gsang ba 'dus pa
Sangye Lama (c. 990–1070)	sangs rgyas bla ma
Sangye Lodro	sangs rgyas blo gros
Sañjayavairaḍīputra (fl. 6th century BCE)	smra 'dod kyi bu yang dag rgyal ba can
Śaṅkara (advaitavedāntin, fl. 8th century)	shang ka ra
Śaṅkara (fl. 7th century)	dung 'dzin
Śaṅkarānanda, brahmin (fl. 13th century)	bram ze shang ka rā nanda
Śāntarakṣita (725–783)	zhi ba 'tsho
Śāntideva (fl. early 8th century)	zhi ba lha
Śāntigarbha (fl. late 8th to early 9th century)	zhi ba'i snying po
Saraha (fl. 8th to 9th century)	sa ra ha

Phonetic	Tibetan Transliteration
Sāraprāpta	snying po thob
Śāriputra (fl. 5th century BCE)	shā ri bu
Sarvajñādeva (fl. late 8th to early 9th century)	sarba dznyā de ba
Satyaprāpta	bden pa thob
Seton Kunrig (1029–1116)	se ston kun rig
Shuke Lotsāwa [Drakpa Gyaltsen] (fl. 13th century)	shud ke lo tsā ba [grags pa rgyal mtshan]
Sibtri Tsenpo (fl. 2nd to 1st century BCE)	sribs khri btsan po (7th king of Tibet)
Śīlamañju (fl. 7th century)	shī la manydzu
Śīlendrabodhi (fl. late 8th to early 9th century)	shī lendra bo dhi
Smṛtijñānakīrti (fl. late 9th century)	dran pa ye shes grags pa
So Yeshe Wangchuk (fl. 9th century)	so ye shes dbang phyug
Somabhāskarakīrti	nyi zla grags
Somanātha of Kashmir (fl. 12th century)	kha che'i zla ba mgon po
Sonam Tsemo (1142–1182)	bsod nams rtse mo
Songtsen Gampo (617–650)	srong btsan sgam po (33rd king of Tibet)
Sornonam (also known as De Nolnam, fl. 3rd century)	sor rno nam (20th king of Tibet)
Sotelek (also known as De Gyelpo, fl. 3rd century)	so ste legs (22nd king of Tibet)
Sotri Tsenpo (fl. 2nd century BCE)	so khri btsan po (4th king of Tibet)
Śrībaladhara (fl. late 8th to early 9th century)	shrī ba le dha ra
Śrībhadrabodhi (fl. 11th century)	shrī bha dra bodhi
Śrīghoṣa (fl. late 8th to early 9th century)	dpal dbyangs

Phonetic	Tibetan Transliteration
Śrīlāta (fl. mid-4th to early 5th century)	(btsun pa) dpal len
Sumbha Lotsāwa Dharma Yonten (fl. 11th century)	sumbha lo tsā dharma yon tan
Surendrabodhi (fl. late 8th to early 9th century)	su rendra [bo dhi]
Taklung Thangpa Tashi Pel (1142–1210/11)	stag lung thang pa bkra shis dpal
Takri Nyenzik (fl. 6th century)	stag ri gnyan gzigs (31st king of Tibet)
Tanak Drolmawa Samdrub Dorje (1295–1376)	rta nag sgrol ma ba bsam grub rdo rje
Tangtong Gyelpo (1361/65–1486)	thang stong rgyal po
Tashi Gon (fl. early 10th century)	bkra shis mgon (great-great-grandson of Lang Darma)
Taton Jo-se/so (1167–1197)	(gcung po) rta ston jo sras/bsod
Taton Jo-ye (1163–1230)	rta ston jo ye
Taton Zijid (fl. 12th century)	rta ston gzi brjid
Thonmi Sambhoṭa (fl. 7th century)	thon mi sambho ṭa
Tisho Lek (fl. 1st century)	thi sho legs (12th king of Tibet)
Tongri Tongtsen (fl. early 4th century)	stong ri stong btsan (24th king of Tibet)
Tonpa Shenrab (founder of Bon)	ston pa gshen rab
Tri Dra Pungtsen (fl. 4th century)	khri sgra dpung btsan (26th king of Tibet)
Tri Namtsen (fl. 4th century)	khri nam btsan (25th king of Tibet)
Tri Relpachen (r. 815–838 or 841)	khri ral pa chen (41st king of Tibet)
Tri Tokje Tsen (fl. late 4th century)	khri thog rje btsan (27th king of Tibet)
Tri-de Tsukten Me Agtsom (r. 704–755)	khri lde gtsug brtan me ag tshom (37th king of Tibet)
Trin Gyaltsen (fl. late 3rd century)	sprin rgyal btsan (23rd king of Tibet)
Trinyen Zhungtsen (fl. late 5th to early 6th century)	khri gnyan zung btsan (29th king of Tibet)

Phonetic	Tibetan Transliteration
Trisong Detsen (r. 755–797)	khri srong lde'u btsan (38th king of Tibet)
Trophu Lotsāwa [Jampa Pel] (1173–1236)	khro phu lo tsā ba
Trulshen Nangden (Bon teacher)	'phrul gshen snang ldan
Trulzhik Senge Gyab (fl. 13th century)	'khrul zhig seng ge rgyab
Tsami Sangye Drak (fl. 11th century)	rtsa mi sangs rgyas grags
Tsang Rabsel (fl. 9th century)	gtsang rab gsal
Tsangpa Gya-re Yeshe Dorje (1161–1211)	gtsang pa rgya ras ye shes rdo rje
Tsangton Drowei Gonpo (fl. early 12th century)	gstang ston 'gro ba'i mgon po
Tsāripa	tsā ri pa
Tse-me Oden (Bon teacher)	tshad med 'od ldan
Tsen-de (fl. 11th century)	btsan lde
Tshurton Wang-nge (fl. late 11th to early 12th century)	mtshur ston dbang nge
Tsongkhapa Lobzang Drakpa (1357–1419)	tsong kha pa blo bzang grags pa
Ugra (deity)	drag po
Umādevī (deity)	u ma de ba
Upa Tonśāk (fl. early 12th century)	dbus pa ston shāk
Upa Zhikpo (1125–1195)	dbus pa zhig po
Upālaśrīmitra (fl. 11th century)	u pā ya shrī mi tra
Urgyanpa [Rinchenpel] (1230–1309)	u rgyan pa rin chen dpal
Vairotsana (fl. late 8th to early 9th century)	bai ro tsa na
Vajrapāṇi (deity)	phyag na rdo rje
Vamāna (dwarf emanation of Viṣṇu)	mi'i thung

Phonetic	Tibetan Transliteration
Varāha (boar emanation of Viṣṇu)	phag rgod
Vardhamāna Mahāvīra (c. 599–527 BCE)	rgyal ba dam pa
Vasubandhu (fl. late 4th to early 5th century)	dbyig gnyen
Vasudeva (deity)	nor lha
Vasudhara (fl. early 9th century)	ba su dha ra
Vasumitra (fl. 2nd century)	ba su mi tra
Vimalamitra (fl. early 9th century)	bi ma la mi tra
Virendrarucita (fl. 11th century)	barendra ru tsi da
Virūpa (fl. 10th century)	bi rū pa
Vīryābhadra (fl. 11th century)	biryā bha dra
Viṣṇu (deity)	khyab 'jug
Wel-se Ngampa (Bon teacher)	dbal gsas rngam pa
Wencheng Konjo (fl. 7th century)	kong jo
Won-re [Darma Senge] (1177–1237)	dbon ras [dar ma seng ge]
Yagde Paṇchen [Tsondru Dargye] (1299–1378)	g.yag sde paṇ chen [brtson 'grus dar rgyas]
Yang Gonpa [Gyaltsen Pal] (1213–1258)	yang dgon pa [rgyal mtshan dpal]
Yekhyen Trulgyel (Bon teacher)	ye mkhyen 'phrul rgyal
Yeshe De (also known as Vairotsana, fl. late 8th to early 9th century)	ye shes sde
Yeshe Nyingpo (fl. late 8th to early 9th century)	ye shes snying po
Yeshe Tsogyal (fl. 8th to 9th century)	ye shes mtsho rgyal
Yewang Gyalpo (Bon teacher)	ye dbang rgyal po
Yik Dorje Gyaltsen (fl. late 8th to early 9th century)	dbyig rdo rje rgyal mtshan

Phonetic	Tibetan Transliteration
Yo Gejung (fl. early 9th century)	g.yo dge 'byung
Yonten Gyatso (fl. 9th century)	yon gtan rgya mtsho
Yonten Zung (1126–1195)	yon tan gzungs
Yudra Nyingpo (fl. late 8th to early 9th century)	g.yu sgra snying po
Yudrakpa [Tsondru Drakpa] (1123–1193)	g.yu brag pa [brtson 'grus grags pa]
Yumo[wa Mikyo Dorje] (fl. 11th century)	yu mo [ba mi bskyod rdo rje]
Yungdrung Chayi Gyalpo (Bon teacher)	g.yung drung phya'i rgyal po
Yungton[pa Dorjepel] (1284–1365)	g.yung ston [pa rdo rje dpal]
Yutok Yonten Gonpo (the elder, 708–833)	g.yu thog yon tan mgon po
Yutok Yonten Gonpo (the younger, 1126–1202)	g.yu thog yon tan mgon po
Zadam Rinchen Yik (fl. 10th century)	za dam rin chen dbyig
Zanam Lek (fl. early 1st century BCE)	za nam legs (16th king of Tibet)
Zangkar Lotsāwa [Phakpa Sherab] (fl. 11th century)	zangs dkar lo tsā ba
Zhama Chamsing (fl. 11th century)	zha ma lcam sring
Zhang Yeshe De (see Vairotsana)	zhang ye she sde
Zhangton [Tashi Dorje] (1097–1167)	zhang ston [bkra shis rdo rje]
Zhangton Chobar (1053–1135)	zhang chos 'bar
Zhikpo Dudtsi (1149–1199)	zhig po bdud rtsi
Zu Dorje Gyaltsen (fl. 11th century)	gzus rdo rje rgyal mtshan
Zur Jampa Senge (fl. 13th century)	zur 'byams pa seng ge
Zurchen Śākya Jungne (1002–1062)	zur chen shākya 'byung gnas
Zurchung Sherab Drak (1014–1074)	zur chung shes rab grags

Concordance of Place Names

The following concordance gives precedence to the romanized Sanskrit or simplified Tibetan phonetic spelling in the first column, and provides the formal Tibetan transliteration in the second column.

Phonetic	Tibetan Transliteration
Achung Namdzong	a chung nam rdzong
Akaniṣṭha	'og min
Baltistan	sbal te
Bilvakatīrtha	bil ba can
Bounteous Array or Ghanavyūha, realm	stug po bkod pa (also known as Akaniṣṭha)
Brahmakāyika, realm	tshangs ris
Candrabhāgā, river	zla ba'i rgya mtsho skal ba can
Chimphu	mchims phu
China	rgya nag
Chuwori	chu bo ri
Dakpo	dvags po
Dawapuk	zla ba phug (in Yerpa)
Dokham	mdo khams
Dokham, six ranges of	mdo khams sgang drug
Do-me	mdo smad

Phonetic	Tibetan Transliteration
Dragyurling	sgra 'gyur gling
Drakmar Gondzong	brag dmar dgon rdzong
Drepung	'bras spungs
Dudul Ngakpaling	bdud 'dul sngags pa gling
Utsang, four horns of	dbu gtsang ru bzhi
Ganges, river	chu bo gaṅgā
Gilgit	bru sha
Gongkar	gong dkar
Gotsang	rgod tshang
Greater Tibet	bod chen po
Gungtang	gung thang
Gyitang	gyi thang
Himavat	gangs ri
India	rgya gar
Indus, river	sindhu
Jampel Ling	'jam dpal gling
Kailash	gangs ti se/rin po che
Kanaka, river	ka na ka
Karchung Dorjeying	skar chung rdo rje dbyings
Kashmir	kha che
Katok	ka thog
Kharchu	mkhar chu
Kha'u Drakdzong	kha'u brag rdzong
Khomting	mkho mthing
Khotan	li [yul]
Kongpo	kong po

PHONETIC	TIBETAN TRANSLITERATION
Kurukṣetra	yul ku ru
Kuśāvarta, river	ku sha 'khyil
Lahul	khri te smad
Lato	la stod
La-to Dingri	la stod ding ri
Lower Tantric College	rgyud smad
Mahābrahmā, realm	tshang pa chen po
Manchuria/Khitan	khri ten
Mangyul	mang yul
Mardzagang	dmar rdza sgang
Markham	smar khams
Markhamgang	smar khams sgang
Minyak Rabgang	mi nyag rab sgang
Mongolia	sog po
Nairañjana, river	nai rañdza na
Nālandā	nā lendra
Ngari, three districts of	mnga' ris skor gsum
Ngor	ngor
Nguldza Zelmogang	dngul rdza zal mo sgang
Nīlagiri, river	sngon po'i ri
Nyal	gnyal
Oḍḍiyāna	o rgyan
Onchangdo Temple	'on cang rdo'i lha khang
Pañcāla	lnga len
Paranirmitavaśavartin, realm	gzhan 'phrul dbang byed
Persia	gzigs phan

Phonetic	Tibetan Transliteration
Phagmodru	phag mo gru
Phangthang	'phang thang
Poborgang	spo 'bor sgang
Prayāgatīrtha	pra ya dir ba
Purang	spu rangs
Rasa Trulnang	ra sa 'phrul snang
Riwo Ganden	ri bo dga' ldan
Rulak	ru lag
Sakya	sa skya
Samye Lhungyi Drubpa, temple	bsam yas lhun gyis grub pa'i gtsug lag khang
Sārasvatī, river	dbyangs can
Śaravatī, river	'dam pa/bu can
Sera Monastery	se ra'i chos sde
Shang Zhongzhong Gonpa	shangs gzhong gzhong gi dgon pa
Shelkar Gon	shal dkar dgon
Spiti	khri te stod
Sumeru	ri rab
Tajikistan	stag sde
Takzik Azha	stag gzigs 'a zha
Tartary	ge sar
Tashilhunpo	bkra shis lhun po
Tibet	bod
Tradruk	khra 'brug
Trayastriṃśa, realm	sum cu rtsa gsum
Tsang	gtsang
Tsawagang	tsha ba sgang

Phonetic	**Tibetan Transliteration**
Tsawarong	tsha ba rong
Tshuphu	mtshur phu
Tsongkha	gtsong kha
Turkestan	khrom
Tuṣita	dga' ldan
U	dbus
Upper Tantric College	rgyud stod
Uru	dbus ru
Utsang, four horns of	dbu gtsang ru bzhi
Utse	dbu rtse (at Samye)
Varāha, river	phag can
Vikramaśīla Temple	bi kra ma shī la'i gtsug lag khang
Wutai Shan	ri bo rtse lnga
Yarlung Sheldrak	yar lung shal brag
Yarmotang	dbyar mo thang
Yerpa	yer pa
Yeru	g.yas ru
Yoru	g.yo ru
Zangskar	zangs dkar
Zhangzhung	zhang zhung

Abbreviations

BDRC	Buddhist Digital Resource Center. Online catalog at www.tbrc.org.
DGD	Choying Tobden Dorje (1785–1848), *mDo rgyud mdzod* (*Precious Treasury of Sūtra and Tantra*). 5 vols. Chengdu: Sichuan mi rigs dpe skrun khang, 2000.
Dg.K	The Derge Kangyur (sDe dge bka' 'gyur) xylograph edition. 103 vols. Edited by Situ Chokyi Jungne. Freely accessible online at www.tbrc.org.
Dg. NGB	The Derge xylograph edition of the Collected Tantras of the Nyingmapa (rNying ma'i rgyud 'bum). 26 vols. Edited by Katok Getse Gyurme Tsewang Chokdrub. Catalog by Thubten Chodar. Beijing: Mi rigs dpe skrun khang, 2000.
Dg.T	The Derge Tengyur (sDe dge bstan 'gyur) xylograph edition. 213 vols. Edited by Zhuchen Tsultrim Rinchen. Freely accessible online at www.tbrc.org.
GDKT	*Rgyud sde kun btus.* Compiled by Jamyang Loter Wangpo. 33 vols. Kathmandu: Sachen International, 2014.
KPD	Comparative edition of the Tibetan Kangyur (bKa' 'gyur dpe bsdur ma), largely based on the Derge Kangyur, input with annotations and references to alternative woodblock versions. 108 vols. Beijing: Krung go'i bod rig pa'i dpe skrun khang, 2006–2009. The contents are now searchable online at www.tbrc.org.
mTshams brag NGB	The most extensive version of NGB (the Collected Tantras of the Nyingmapa) in 46 vols., produced at mTshams brag dgon in Bhutan. Thimphu: National Library of the Royal Government of Bhutan, 1982.
NA	Not available; used for works that are probably not extant at the present time
NK	The Collected Transmitted Teachings of the Nyingmapa (rNying ma'i bka' ma). Currently 120 vols. in the most extended edition (*shin tu rgyas pa*), compiled and published

	by Khenpo Munsel and Khenpo Jamyang of Katok. Chengdu: 1999.
NL	Not located; used for works that may be extant at the present time but have not yet been identified
P	*The Tibetan Tripiṭaka.* Peking edition. 168 vols. Tokyo-Kyoto: Suzuki Research Foundation, 1955–61.
PZ	Pekar Zangpo, *mDo sde spyi'i rnam bzhag.* Beijing: Mi rigs dpe skrun khang, 2006. A sixteenth-century Tibetan-language summary of all the sūtras preserved in the Kangyur.
RTD	Treasury of Revealed Teachings (*Rin chen gter mdzod*), compiled by Jamgon Kongtrul. Palpung xylographic edition in 72 vols., printed from xylographs housed in Sde dge spar khang.
Skt.	Sanskrit
T	H. Ui et al., *A Complete Catalogue of the Tibetan Buddhist Canons.* Tohoku University catalog of the Derge edition of the canon. Sendai: 1934.
Taisho	J. Takakusu, K. Watanabe, et al., Taisho shinshu daizokyo. Tokyo: Taisho Issaikyo Kanko Kai, 1924–32.
Tib.	Tibetan
Tingkye NGB	*rNying ma'i rgyud 'bum* (Collected Tantras of the Nyingmapa). 36 vols. Photo-offset edition, based on the gTing skyes rdzong ms. Thimphu, Bhutan: Dilgo Khyentse Rinpoche, 1973. Catalog by E. Kaneko, Tokyo: 1982.
TPD	Comparative edition of the Tibetan Tengyur (bsTan 'gyur dpe bsdur ma), largely based on the Derge Tengyur, input with supplements, annotations, and references to alternative woodblock versions. 120 vols. Beijing: Krung go'i bod rig pa'i dpe skrun khang, 1994–2008. The contents are now searchable online at www.tbrc.org.

Notes

1. Jigme Tekchok, *Successive Hierarchs of Rongpo Gonchen,* pp. 45–46.
2. Ibid., p. 46.
3. Tulku Thondup (1999, 160–61) notes that the four prophesied individuals were respectively Dola Jigme Kelzang Dorje (in the east), Repa Damtsig Dorje of Khyunglung (in the south), Gyelse Rigpei Dorje Zhenpen Thaye (in the west), and Choying Tobden Dorje (in the north).
4. These eight renowned places conducive to spiritual attainment in Repkong are enumerated in Dragon Konchok Tenpa Rabgye, *Doctrinal History of Amdo,* vol. 2, pp. 304–12. See also Chenak Hūṃchen and Yeshe Ozer Dolma, *An Historical Anthology of the Mantrin Communities of Repkong* (*Reb kong sngags mang gi lo rgyus phyogs bsgrigs*), pp. 2–25; and Ricard 1994, 602–3. Among them, Chuchik Shel is located in the northeast.
5. For an account of Rabgya Monastery in Golok, see Dorje 2009, 759–60, and Gruschke 2001, 75–78.
6. The three trainings (*triśikṣā, bslab pa gsum*) comprise ethical discipline (*śīla, tshul khrims*), discriminative awareness (*prajñā, shes rab*), and mental development, i.e., meditation (*citta, sems*).
7. On Dzogchen Monastery in Dzachuka, see Dorje 2009, 593–96. The life of Dzogchen Migyur Namka Dorje (1793–1870) is summarized in Barron 2005, 400–404.
8. An extensive account of the life of the first Dodrubchen Rinpoche Jigme Trinle Ozer (1745–1821) can be found in Thondup 1999, 136–62. See also Barron 2005, 319–22. For a description of Yarlung Pemako in Sertar, see Dorje 2009, 772.
9. A detailed history of Ko'ude Dzogchen Namgyeling can be found in Chenak Hūṃchen and Yeshe Ozer Dolma, *An Historical Anthology,* pp. 70–106. A very brief account in Chinese has also been published in Pu Wencheng 1993, 456.
10. Further information on the life of Choying Tobden Dorje, along with those of his successive incarnations Dzogchen II Tenpe Gyaltsen (1849–1936), Dzogchen III Tubten Chokyi Nyima (1937–1961), and Dzogchen IV Jigme Choying Rangdrol Dorje (b. 1978), can be found in Chenak Hūṃchen and

Yeshe Ozer Dolma, *An Historical Anthology,* pp. 73–83. Some references can also be gleaned from Dragon Konchok Tenpa Rabgye's *Doctrinal History of Amdo,* Jigme Tekchok's *Successive Hierarchs of Rongpo Gonchen,* and Zhabkar Tsokdruk Rangdrol's *Autobiography,* the last of which is translated in Ricard 1994. A brief summary of Choying Tobden Dorje's life, compiled by Nyoshul Khenpo, is also found in Barron 2005, 407–8.

11. Gartse is an impressively located monastery in northeast Amdo, situated below the watershed pass at Amnye Nyemri. See Dorje 2009, 725–26.
12. The second part of the illustrated version, entitled *Garland of the Sun* (*dPe ris nyi ma'i phreng ba*), is unfortunately no longer extant.
13. The reader should note that although the root verses are repeated throughout the extensive commentary, their wording most closely matches that of the concise commentary and sometimes varies markedly from that of the extensive commentary.
14. Āryadeva's *Four Hundred Verses* (Lang 1986) with its refutation of non-Buddhist views may well have offered a partial Buddhist model for Bhāvaviveka's tenet systems.
15. It is well known that Jain canonical texts identified 363 distinct heretical views centuries before Bhāvaviveka. On this, see, nn. 32–33.
16. *DGD* (p. 691) here includes an annotation, indicating that the same word—*'jigs pa* ("terrifying," "terrified," "terrifies") occurs at the start of each of the four verses in this quatrain. The verses suggest affinity with Vajrabhairava, a "terrifying" (*'jigs byed*) aspect of the wrathful meditational deity Yamāntaka, on whom see Jigme Chokyi Dorje, *Great Anthology of Buddhist Icons,* pp. 330–33.
17. *DGD* (p. 691) here specifies only eighty-three subtopics, omitting all those listed in Part 6 of Book 13, as well as many others interspersed throughout Parts 1–5. Here I have followed the precedent of the editors of the Sichuan edition, who to some extent expanded the subtopics in their table of contents.
18. The following three citations are extracted from Longchen Rabjam's *Treasury of Philosophical Systems,* p. 44. See the translation in Barron 2007, 53–54. The original source is as yet unidentified. Note that the title of the original text is given in the latter as *gSang ba mchog gi rgyud,* not *gSang ba spyod pa mchog gi rgyud.*
19. This categorization derives from Longchen Rabjam, *White Lotus,* vol. 1, pp. 341–42.
20. As indicated in Longchen Rabjam, *White Lotus,* vol. 1, p. 342, these views are presented below in the context of the Bārhaspatya system. According to the *Sāmaññaphala Sutta,* contained in Walshe 1987, 93–94, Purāṇakāśyapa is said to have espoused amoralism, denying rewards and punishments for good and bad actions, respectively. See also the summary in Basham 1951, 14.
21. Longchen Rabjam, *White Lotus,* vol. 1, p. 342, suggests that this view is akin to the perspective of the Mīmāṃsika (*spyod pa ba*), although Maskarī Gośālaputra

is well recognized as a preeminent teacher of the Ājīvikas. On his life and views in general, see Basham 1951. According to the *Sāmaññaphala Sutta,* contained in Walshe 1987, 94–95, Maskarī Gośālaputra is said to have espoused fatalism and the predestination of suffering. His perspective is summarized in Basham 1951, 13–14.

22. Longchen Rabjam, *White Lotus,* vol. 1, p. 342, attributes this view to the Bārhaspatya. According to the *Sāmaññaphala Sutta,* contained in Walshe 1987, 97, Sañjayavairaḍīputra is said to have espoused equivocation and agnosticism, uncertain whether to admit any of the four standpoints (advocating existence, nonexistence, both, or neither). See also the summary in Basham 1951, 16–17.
23. This source has not yet been identified, and it may possibly denote a corpus rather than a specific text. The citation is found with some variations in Āryadeva's *Autocommentary on the Forty Verses,* TPD, vol. 57, p. 831.
24. This statement purporting to represent the view of Ajitakeśakambalin is found, along with its refutation, in Longchen Rabjam, *White Lotus,* vol. 1, pp. 342–43. However, according to the *Sāmaññaphala Sutta,* contained in Walshe 1987, 95–96, Ajitakeśakambalin espoused gross materialism and the annihilation of all phenomena, physical and mental, at the time of death—a view restated in Basham 1951, 15. The same sources attribute the view of long-term predestination to Maskarī Gośālaputra.
25. This statement representing the four-aspected equivocating view of Kakudakatyāyana is found, along with its refutation, in Longchen Rabjam, *White Lotus,* vol. 1, pp. 343–44. However, according to the *Sāmaññaphala Sutta,* contained in Walshe 1987, 96, Kakudakatyāyana espoused eternalism—the view that the material elements, joy, sorrow, and life are all eternal, without interaction. See also Basham 1951, 16. These sources attribute the four-aspected equivocating view instead to Sañjayavairaḍīputra, as noted above.
26. This austere view of Nirgranthajñātiputra is presented, along with its detailed refutation, in Longchen Rabjam, *White Lotus,* vol. 1, pp. 344–47. According to the *Sāmaññaphala Sutta,* contained in Walshe 1987, 96–97, Nirgranthajñātiputra espoused restraint and avoidance of all negative actions. Cf. Basham 1951, 16.
27. This passage derives from Longchen Rabjam, *White Lotus,* vol. 1, pp. 347–48, where the twenty alternatives are presented along with their refutation. The term *perishable composites* (*satkāya, 'jigs tshogs*) specifically denotes the five psycho-physical aggregates.
28. This passage derives from Longchen Rabjam, *White Lotus,* vol. 1, pp. 348–54, where the sixty-two views are discussed along with their refutations. The classic source for this analysis is the *Sūtra of the Net of Brahmā,* which is the first discourse of the *Dīgha Nikāya* of the Pali Canon. See the translations in Walshe 1987, 67–90, also Bhikku Bodhi 1978. A parallel text can also be found in the Kangyur (T 352; mDo sde, AḤ, ff. 70b–86a).

29. See Longchen Rabjam, *White Lotus,* vol. 1, p. 350, which reads *sems snga na med,* not simply *sems med.*
30. This reading accords with Longchen Rabjam, *White Lotus,* vol. 1, p. 351, whereas *DGD* (p. 694) omits *gcig* ("uniform").
31. This follows Longchen Rabjam, *White Lotus,* vol. 1, p. 352, which reads *lha mis,* whereas *DGD* (p. 695) reads only *lhas* ("gods").
32. It has been speculated that this classification may have Jain antecedents in that the *Sūtrakṛtāṅga,* the second book of the Śvetambara Jain canon, and its commentarial literature identify 363 heretical views that fall into four groups: (1) those holding that emancipation comes through action (*kriyāvādana*), which has 180 subcategories; (2) those holding that emancipation comes through nonaction (*akriyāvādana*), whose subcategories number eighty-four; (3) those skeptical of all those standpoints (*ajñānavādana*), whose subcategories number sixty-seven; and (4) those holding that emancipation comes through disciplined conduct (*vainayikavādana*), which has thirty-two subcategories. The evolution of this classification is analyzed in depth in Folkert and Cort 1993, 229–343. Further research is required to determine whether Bhāvaviveka's delineation of 360 views is simply analogous to the Jain clasification, or more directly related to it.
33. This is the first group of ten among the 120 false views that are fully enumerated in Longchen Rabjam, *White Lotus,* vol. 1, pp. 354–56. The subsequent groups of ten are not enumerated by Choying Tobden Dorje. Unfortunately the listing in Sanskrit appears to be no longer extant. The primary source is the ninth chapter (on Mīṃāmsā) from Bhāvaviveka's classic work concerning the doxography of Buddhist and non-Buddhist philosophical systems entitled *Flame of Dialectics,* TPD, vol. 58, pp. 676–79. This text explicitly states (p. 679, line 3) that the list denotes 120 philosophical views rather than the names of their exponents, as Longchen Rabjam, *White Lotus,* at one point (p. 354, line 18) appears to suggest. There are some obvious discrepancies between the two lists. See also Nordrang Orgyan, *Compendium of Buddhist Numeric Terms,* vol. 3, pp. 3838–40. Among the first group of ten, the first, the Jaiminīya (*rgyal dpog pa*), according to both Longchen Rabjam, *White Lotus,* vol. 1, p. 354, and our text, *DGD* (p. 695), appears as "followers of Buddhism" (*sangs rgyas pa*) in the *Flame of Dialectics,* p. 676, while the second is attested as "those without any standpoint" (*'dzin pa med pa*) in both Longchen Rabjam, *White Lotus,* vol. 1, p. 354, and the *Flame of Dialectics,* p. 677, suggesting that the reading of "nonworldly" (*'jig rten med pa*) as found in *DGD* (p. 695) may be mistaken. The inclusion of "followers of Buddhism" in the *Flame of Dialectics* could perhaps point toward an early Jain influence.

 Among this group of ten, the Jaiminīya (*rgyal dpog pa*), Talavakāra (*mnyam par spyod pa*), and Rāṇāyanīya (*lo ma can*) represent schools or branches of the *Sāma Veda;* the Śākalya (*ko lpags can*) represent the dominant school or branch of the *Ṛg Veda;* the Alaukika (*'jig rten med pa*), Ājīvika (*'tsho ba pa*), and Tridaṇḍaka (*dbyu gu gsum pa*) represent the heterodox or *parivrājika* schools, the Śrotriya (*gtsang sbra can*) are brahmins observing pure rituals and ablutions, while Vaishnavism is represented here by both the Vaiṣṇava (*khyab 'jug pa*) and the Vāsudevaka (*khyab 'jug sems dpa'*) who revere Viṣṇu in the form of a living being, especially Kṛṣṇa. Some of these names are attested in the aforementioned Jain listing of skeptical standpoints (*ajñānavādana*). See Folkert and Cort 1993, 337. NB This identification of Rāṇāyanīya with *lo ma can* and Rāṇāyana with *lo ma* is rather tentative. The names Paila for *lo ma* and Pailīya for *lo ma can* have also been suggested, Paila being the disciple of Vyāsa who first received the *Ṛg Veda*. However, one of the quotations attributed below to *drang srong lo ma can* anachronistically pertains to the ten incarnations of Viṣṇu.

34. The source for this passage is Longchen Rabjam's *White Lotus,* vol. 1, p. 357. Our text reads *'byung ba lnga dang chen po lnga dang khams las phye ba,* but Longchen Rabjam, *White Lotus* offers the more accurate reading of *'byung ba lnga dang chen po lnga yi khams las phye ba.* That said, the expression *chen po lnga* surely implies the five quiddities (*de tsam lnga*), on which see below, p. 28.
35. The source for this passage is again Longchen Rabjam, *White Lotus,* vol. 1, pp. 357–58. Some of these key terms are discussed below, in the context of Sāṃkhya. See also Nordrang Orgyan, *Compendium of Buddhist Numeric Terms,* vol. 3, p. 3840. Note also that our text reads *'grel pa* for *'brel ba.*
36. See Longchen Rabjam, *White Lotus,* vol. 1, p. 358.
37. See ibid., pp. 358–59.
38. A similar quotation also occurs in Longchen Rabjam, *Treasury of Philosophical Systems,* p. 54, on which see Barron 2007, 65. Cf. also Longchen Rabjam, *Dispelling All Mental Darkness with the Light of Eloquence,* p. 30.
39. Our text appears to be corrupt in reading *la sogs* for *sa sogs,* and *grol ba grub pa'i tshul* for *'gro ba grub pa'i tshul.* See Longchen Rabjam, *White Lotus,* vol. 1, p. 359.
40. See ibid., pp. 359–60.
41. The Sanskrit names given here are all unattested reconstructions. On this passage, see ibid., p. 360.
42. *DGD* (p. 697) and Longchen Rabjam, *White Lotus,* vol. 1, p. 360, both read *blon po* ("ministers") for *mdun na 'don* ("priests") at this point.
43. This would engender an enumeration of thirty rather than thirty-six, unless the common fields of knowledge are also counted. Nordrang Orgyan, *Compendium of Buddhist Numeric Terms,* vol. 3, p. 3841, is similarly perplexed.
44. This tentative interpretation follows Khepei Deu's *Extensive Religious History of India and Tibet,* pp. 113, 238, highlighted by Dan Martin. These six may denote the six sophists mentioned above (pp. 9–11) with the exception of Nirgranthajñātiputra, who is replaced here by the Lokāyatika materialists. For the second, Cabezón 2013, 169 reads "bleached human skin," perhaps a reference to Ajitakeśakambalin.

45. This calculation of three hundred omits the fifth of the eleven categories, comprising the six teachers who espouse nihilism and their thirty-two views. That same group is also excluded from the list found in the source text, Longchen Rabjam, *White Lotus,* vol. 1, p. 361, presumably because the immediately following list of the thirty-six ministers is reckoned to subsume both.
46. See above, pp. 11–17. *DGD*, p. 698, misreads *bzhi bcu rtsa gnyis* ("forty-two"). The correct reading is found in Longchen Rabjam, *White Lotus*, vol. 1, p. 361.
47. The source for this entire section on Sāṃkhya is Longchen Rabjam, *White Lotus,* vol. 1, pp. 363–78.
48. *DGD* (p. 699) reads *yin* ("is") for *yid* ("mental faculty").
49. This verse appears not to be extant in the *Stanzas on Sāṃkhya* by Īśvarakṛṣṇa. On the relevant stanzas 12–14, see Radhakrishnan and Moore 1957, 428–29. The present wording of this verse concurs with Longchen Rabjam, *White Lotus,* vol. 1, pp. 364–65.
50. Again, this precise wording appears not to be found in the *Stanzas on Sāṃkhya* by Īśvarakṛṣṇa. The Tibetan derives from Longchen Rabjam, *White Lotus,* vol. 1, p. 365.
51. *DGD* (p. 700) reads *lus gnyis ni* ("two bodies") for *yul shes gnyis ni* ("both objects and awareness"). See Longchen Rabjam, *White Lotus,* vol. 1, p. 366, line 13.
52. Longchen Rabjam, *White Lotus,* p. 366 reads *gzugs brnyan* ("physical reflections").
53. This citation is found in Longchen Rabjam, *White Lotus,* vol. 1, p. 366. The Sanskrit source is Bhāvaviveka's *Heart of the Middle Way,* TPD, vol. 58, p. 57; also Lindtner 2001a, p. 72, v. 2.
54. *DGD* (p. 700) misreads *la sogs pa* ("etc.") for *logs pa* ("separate"). See Longchen Rabjam, *White Lotus,* vol. 1, p. 367, line 1.
55. *DGD* (p. 700) misreads *can* for *chen.* See Longchen Rabjam, *White Lotus,* vol. 1, p. 367, line 2.
56. *DGD* (p. 700) reads *bcu gcig* ("eleven") for *bcu drug* ("sixteen").
57. This is v. 22. See Radhakrishnan and Moore 1957, 434. The Tibetan derives from Longchen Rabjam, *White Lotus,* vol. 1, p. 367.
58. *DGD* (p. 700) reads *nges pa med de* ("they do not ascertain") for *nyes pa med de* ("they do not make the mistake"). See Longchen Rabjam, *White Lotus,* vol. 1, p. 367, line 16.
59. This quatrain is actually found in v. 7 of the *Stanzas on Sāṃkhya* by Īśvarakṛṣṇa, although it may have been derived from the nonextant *Ṣaṣtitantra,* as is suggested here. See Radhakrishnan and Moore 1957, 428.
60. *DGD* (p. 701) reads *mthong ba* ("visibility") for *mi mthong ba* ("invisibility"), but see Longchen Rabjam, *White Lotus,* vol. 1, p. 368, line 3.
61. This line is missing in our text, but found in Longchen Rabjam, *White Lotus,* vol. 1, p. 369, lines 1–2.
62. Candrakīrti, *Introduction to the Middle Way,* ch. 6, v. 121.
63. *DGD* (p. 702) reads *brlan no* for *brlam mo.*

64. This quatrain is found in v. 3 of the *Stanzas on Sāṃkhya* by Īśvarakṛṣṇa. See Radhakrishnan and Moore 1957, 427. The Tibetan derives from Longchen Rabjam, *White Lotus,* vol. 1, p. 370.
65. The original source for this quatrain has not yet been located. However, the Tibetan derives from Longchen Rabjam, *White Lotus,* vol. 1, pp. 370–71. The same stanza is also cited in his *Treasury of Philosophical Systems.* See the translation in Barron 2007, 58.
66. The Tibetan derives from Longchen Rabjam, *White Lotus,* vol. 1, p. 371. See also *Treasury of Philosophical Systems* and the translation in Barron 2007, 60.
67. Longchen Rabjam, *White Lotus,* vol. 1, p. 371, line 15, reads *shel ras dang bral ba* ltar ("as if without a face").
68. *DGD* (p. 703, line 6) adds the curious expression *tshe gcig tu* ("for the duration of one's life") here, but this may suggest a scribal error, following *rtse gcig tu.*
69. At this juncture, Longchen Rabjam, *White Lotus,* vol. 1, pp. 371–78, includes a detailed refutation of the Sāṃkhya position, which is omitted in our text.
70. This section on the Vaiśeṣika follows Longchen Rabjam, *White Lotus,* vol. 1, pp. 378–87.
71. *DGD* (p. 703) reads *rig pa* ("awareness") for *rigs* ("reasoning").
72. *DGD* (p. 703) reads *khams* ("seed") for *kha* ("face"), but see Longchen Rabjam, *White Lotus,* vol. 1, p. 380, line 3.
73. The original source is unlocated. The Tibetan derives from Longchen Rabjam, *White Lotus,* vol. 1, p. 380.
74. Ibid.
75. *DGD* (p. 704) reads *spang ba* ("renunciation") for *yang ba* ("agility").
76. *DGD* (p. 704) reads *kyang* for *cing.* See Longchen Rabjam, *White Lotus,* vol. 1, p. 381, line 4.
77. Longchen Rabjam, *White Lotus,* vol. 1, pp. 380–81.
78. Ibid., p. 381.
79. Ibid., p. 382. This quotation is also found in the *Treasury of Philosophical Systems.* See the translation in Barron 2007, 61.
80. See Radhakrishnan and Moore 1957, 387. The Tibetan derives from Longchen Rabjam, *White Lotus,* vol. 1, p. 382. Cf. *Treasury of Philosophical Systems* (Barron 2007, 61).
81. *DGD* (p. 705) reads *sdug bsngal* ("suffering") for *yid* ("mind"). See Radhakrishnan and Moore 1957, 398; also Barron 2007, 81. Note, however that Longchen Rabjam, *White Lotus,* vol. 1, p. 382, reads *rdul* ("atoms").
82. *DGD* (p. 705) reads *min pa* for *yin pa.* See Longchen Rabjam, *White Lotus,* vol. 1, p. 382.
83. The Tibetan derives from Longchen Rabjam, *White Lotus,* vol. 1, p. 382. It is also found in his *Treasury of Philosophical Systems.* See the translation in Barron 2007, 62.
84. This paragraph actually comments on the permanence of atomic particles. For the omitted lines, see Longchen Rabjam, *White Lotus,* vol. 1, p. 382, lines 17–19.

Our text also fails to comment on two other permanent substances—time and direction—although they are mentioned in Longchen Rabjam, *White Lotus.*

85. These six are all said to pertain to time and space. See Barron 2007, 61.
86. See this list as presented in Radhakrishnan and Moore 1957, 398, 410–18.
87. See ibid., 398 and 419.
88. These are also differentiated as unlimited and delimited universals. See ibid., 398–99; also 419–21.
89. Here I have followed the syntax of *White Lotus,* vol. 1, p. 384, lines 6–8, rather than the confusing version found in *DGD* (p. 706).
90. See Radhakrishnan and Moore 1957, 421–22.
91. See ibid., 422–23.
92. The Tibetan derives from Longchen Rabjam, *White Lotus,* vol. 1, pp. 384–85.
93. This quatrain appears as a prose passage in Bhāvaviveka, *Flame of Dialectics,* TPD, vol. 58, ch. 7, p. 594.
94. This quatrain is cited in ibid.
95. Cf. the variant reading of the last quatrain as found in Bhāvaviveka's *Heart of the Middle Way,* TPD, vol. 58, p. 62.
96. Cf. the slightly variant reading in ibid., p. 64. The Tibetan derives from Longchen Rabjam, *White Lotus,* vol. 1, p. 385.
97. *DGD* at this juncture omits the detailed refutation of the six categories posited by the Vaiśeṣika, for which readers will have to consult Longchen Rabjam, *White Lotus,* vol. 1, pp. 385–404.
98. This stanza is cited in Bhāvaviveka, *Flame of Dialectics,* TPD, vol. 58, pp. 727–28. The Tibetan version derives from Longchen Rabjam, *White Lotus,* p. 405. Janaka, the kingly sage of Videha, is a seminal figure mentioned in the *Bṛhadāraṇyaka Upaniṣad.*
99. Bhāvaviveka, *Flame of Dialectics,* TPD, vol. 58, p. 720. The Tibetan version derives from Longchen Rabjam, *White Lotus,* vol. 1, p. 405.
100. Avalokitavrata, *Extensive Commentary on the Lamp of Discriminative Awareness,* TPD, vol. 58, p. 1221. The Tibetan derives from Longchen Rabjam, *White Lotus,* vol. 1, p. 406.
101. Bhāvaviveka, *Flame of Dialectics,* TPD, vol. 58, p. 685. The Tibetan derives from Longchen Rabjam, *White Lotus,* vol. 1, p. 406.
102. According to the *Bṛhadāraṇyaka Upaniṣad,* vi.2.13 (Radhakrishnan 1953, 313), the pubic hairs (*lomāni*) symbolize the smoke. Our text and Longchen Rabjam, *White Lotus* both read *skyes bu,* which could be interpreted as the "male organ."
103. Bhāvaviveka, *Flame of Dialectics,* TPD, vol. 58, p. 662. The original source is the *Bṛhadāraṇyaka Upaniṣad,* vi.2.13, on which see Radhakrishnan 1953, 313. The Tibetan derives from Longchen Rabjam, *White Lotus,* vol. 1, pp. 406–7.
104. Candranandana, *Heart Commentary on the Eight Branches of Medical Science,* TPD, vol. 111, p. 143. The Tibetan version derives from Longchen Rabjam, *White Lotus,* vol. 1, p. 407.

105. *DGD* (p. 708) misreads *phyag* ("hand") for *chags* ("attachment").
106. Bhāvaviveka, *Heart of the Middle Way,* TPD, vol. 58, p. 74, v. 3. For the Sanskrit, see Lindtner 2001a, 92, v. 3, and the translation in Lindtner 2001b, 9.
107. Bhāvaviveka, *Heart of the Middle Way,* TPD, vol. 58, p. 74, v. 6. For the Sanskrit, see Lindtner 2001a, 92, v. 3, and the translation in Lindtner 2001b, 10.
108. Bhāvaviveka, *Heart of the Middle Way,* TPD, vol. 58, p. 75. For the Sanskrit, which reads somewhat differently, see Lindtner 2001a, 94, v. 17, and the translation in Lindtner 2001b, 13.
109. These two stanzas are cited in Avalokitavrata, *Extensive Commentary on the Lamp of Discriminative Awareness,* TPD, vol. 59, p. 1392. The Tibetan derives from Longchen Rabjam, *White Lotus,* vol. 1, p. 408.
110. Avalokitavrata, *Extensive Commentary on the Lamp of Discriminative Awareness,* TPD, vol. 59, p. 1393. The Tibetan derives from Longchen Rabjam, *White Lotus,* vol. 1, p. 408.
111. Bhāvaviveka, *Heart of the Middle Way,* TPD, vol. 58, p. 74. For the Sanskrit, see Lindtner 2001a, 93, v. 7, and the translation in Lindtner 2001b, 10.
112. Āryadeva, *Compendium of the Nucleus of Pristine Cognition,* TPD, vol. 57, p. 885. The Tibetan derives from Longchen Rabjam, *White Lotus,* vol. 1, p. 409.
113. Prajñākaragupta, *Ornament of the Exposition of Valid Cognition,* TPD, vol. 100, p. 440. The Tibetan derives from Longchen Rabjam, *White Lotus,* vol. 1, p. 409.
114. Bhāvaviveka, *Flame of Dialectics,* TPD, vol. 58, p. 744. The Tibetan derives from Longchen Rabjam, *White Lotus,* vol. 1, p. 409.
115. Bhāvaviveka, *Flame of Dialectics,* TPD, vol. 58, p. 744, although there are variant readings for the first line (e.g., *ku ru'i zhing ni rab tu bsngags*). The Tibetan is found in Longchen Rabjam, *White Lotus,* vol. 1, p. 410.
116. This stanza is cited in Bhāvaviveka, *Flame of Dialectics,* TPD, vol. 58, p. 751, although there are significant variations: *bu med pa las 'jig rten ni| bzang po ye med rgyas byed kyi| ci ltar gling lam can gyis ni| rgas kar bsus nas smras pa bzhin|*.
117. This stanza is cited, with minor variations, in Bhāvaviveka, *Flame of Dialectics,* TPD, vol. 58, p. 751. The Tibetan is found in Longchen Rabjam, *White Lotus,* vol. 1, p. 410.
118. Bhāvaviveka, *Heart of the Middle Way,* TPD, vol. 58, p. 81, v. 68. For the Sanskrit, see Lindtner 2001a, 99, v. 68, and the translation in Lindtner 2001b, 28.
119. This couplet is similar to the verse cited in Śūra, *Garland of Birth Stories,* TPD, vol. 94, p. 107. The Tibetan is found in Longchen Rabjam, *White Lotus,* vol. 1, p. 411.
120. Cf. n. 21.
121. This description of the tenth tenet has been omitted in *DGD* (p. 710), but see Longchen Rabjam, *White Lotus,* vol. 1, p. 411. Thereafter *White Lotus,* vol. 1, pp. 411–30, continues with the refutation of the foregoing Vaiṣṇava tenets.
122. This citation is found in a number of treatises. See, e.g., Vimuktisena's *Commentary on the Ornament of Emergent Realization,* TPD, vol. 49, pp. 406–7.

123. Note that *DGD* (p. 711) reads *rang gis brjod du med pa* ("it is not intrinsically expressible") for *ngag gis brjod du med pa* ("it is not verbally expressible"). See Longchen Rabjam, *White Lotus,* vol. 1, p. 431.
124. This anthropomorphic cosmic being is originally described in the *Puruṣasūkta* hymn of the Ṛgveda (10:90).
125. This stanza is cited in Bhāvaviveka, *Flame of Dialectics,* TPD, vol. 58, p. 619, albeit in a different context. The Tibetan is found in Longchen Rabjam, *White Lotus,* vol. 1, p. 432.
126. Bhāvaviveka, *Flame of Dialectics,* TPD, vol. 58, p. 617.
127. Bhāvaviveka, *Heart of the Middle Way,* TPD, vol. 58, p. 65. Cf. the Sanskrit version in Lindtner 2001a, 79, v. 5. The Tibetan is also found in Longchen Rabjam, *White Lotus,* vol. 1, p, 432.
128. Bhāvaviveka, *Heart of the Middle Way,* TPD, vol. 58, p. 65, v. 7. For the Sanskrit, see Lindtner 2001a, 80, v. 7.
129. Śāntarakṣita, *Autocommentary on the Ornament of the Middle Way,* TPD, vol. 62, p. 966. The Tibetan is found in Longchen Rabjam, *White Lotus,* vol. 1, p. 433.
130. Tib. *thod pa mgo mi 'brel bar sngang ngo.* Longchen Rabjam, *White Lotus,* vol. 1, p. 433, reads slightly differently, suggesting that "they seem to say the skull is not attached to the head." This comment is reminiscent of similar rebuttals made by Longchen Rabjam in other works.
131. See the correct reading in ibid. *DGD* (p. 712) inserts *shes nas* between *bde sdug* and *skye shi.*
132. Bhāvaviveka, *Heart of the Middle Way,* TPD, vol. 58, p. 65. For the Sanskrit, see Lindtner 2001a, 80, v. 9.
133. Bhāvaviveka, *Heart of the Middle Way,* TPD, vol. 58, p. 66. For the Sanskrit, see Lindtner 2001a, 80, v. 13.
134. *DGD* (p. 712) reads *'byung bzhi 'jig pa ltar* ("just as the four elements may perish") for *'byung zhing 'jig pa ltar* ("just as [a vase] may arise and perish"). See Longchen Rabjam, *White Lotus,* vol. 1, pp. 433–34.
135. Bhāvaviveka, *Heart of the Middle Way,* TPD, vol. 58, pp. 65–66. For the Sanskrit, see Lindtner 2001a, 80, v. 10.
136. Bhāvaviveka, *Heart of the Middle Way,* TPD, vol. 58, p. 66. For the Sanskrit, see Lindtner 2001a, 81, v. 15.
137. Bhāvaviveka, *Heart of the Middle Way,* TPD, vol. 58, p. 66. For the Sanskrit, see Lindtner 2001a, 81, v. 17.
138. Bhāvaviveka, *Heart of the Middle Way,* TPD, vol. 58, p. 66. For the Sanskrit, see Lindtner 2001a, 80, v. 14.
139. Bhāvaviveka, *Heart of the Middle Way,* TPD, vol. 58, p. 65. For the Sanskrit, see Lindtner 2001a, 79, v. 3.
140. Bhāvaviveka, *Flame of Dialectics,* TPD, vol. 58, p. 620. The Tibetan is found in Longchen Rabjam, *White Lotus,* vol. 1, p. 435.

141. *DGD* (p. 714) reads *dngos 'gyur* ("resort to entities") for *mdongs gyur* ("blind"). See Longchen Rabjam, *White Lotus,* vol. 1, p. 436.
142. *DGD* (p. 714) reads *rgyal* ("triumph") for *rgyas* ("flourishing"). See Longchen Rabjam, *White Lotus,* vol. 1, p. 436.
143. At this point, Longchen Rabjam, *White Lotus,* pp. 436–41, includes a refutation of the Aupaniṣadika, which has been omitted from *DGD.*
144. On the class controversy concerning the parentage of Mahāvīra, see Jaini 1979, 7–8.
145. This is omitted in *DGD* (p. 714), but see Longchen Rabjam, *White Lotus,* vol. 1, p. 441.

  Jāyana (*rgyal byed pa*), here, seems to refer to the adherents of the Jaina Canon (*gzhung rgyal byed*) in general, although the same Tibetan term also corresponds to Jayanta—the name of a renowned proponent of Śaivism and Nyāya (fl. 883–902), whose *Flower Cluster of Reason* (*Nyāyamañjarī*) is critical of both Buddhism and Jainism.

  The original source of the verses cited in this section have not been identified; for the most part, they are derogatory and polemical in content. Some of them are extant in Tibetan translations, including Bhāvaviveka's *Flame of Dialectics.*
146. Longchen Rabjam, *White Lotus,* vol. 1, p. 442.
147. Bhāvaviveka, *Flame of Dialectics,* TPD, vol. 58, p. 750. The Tibetan derives from Longchen Rabjam, *White Lotus,* vol. 1, p. 442.
148. *DGD* (p. 715) reads *tshad pa'i tshe* ("during the hot season"), but see Longchen Rabjam, *White Lotus,* vol. 1, p. 442, which reads *char babs pa'i tshe* ("during the rainy season").
149. Bhāvaviveka, *Flame of Dialectics,* TPD, vol. 58, pp. 750–51. The Tibetan derives from Longchen Rabjam, *White Lotus,* vol. 1, p. 442.
150. These verses are cited in Bhāvaviveka, *Flame of Dialectics,* TPD, vol. 58, p. 741, with the exception of the first three lines. The Tibetan derives from Longchen Rabjam, *White Lotus,* vol. 1, p. 443.
151. Bhāvaviveka, *Flame of Dialectics,* TPD, vol. 58, p. 741.
152. The original source of this polemical passage is as yet unidentified. The Tibetan derives from Longchen Rabjam, *White Lotus,* vol. 1, p. 443.
153. Bhāvaviveka, *Flame of Dialectics,* TPD, vol. 58, p. 224. The Tibetan is found in Longchen Rabjam, *White Lotus,* vol. 1, p. 444.
154. *DGD* (p. 715) reads *bzhi* ("four") for *gcig* ("one"). See Longchen Rabjam, *White Lotus,* vol. 1, p. 445.
155. All but the first two lines of this verse are cited in Śāntarakṣita, *Autocommentary on the Ornament of the Middle Way,* TPD, vol. 62, p. 924, although the last two quatrains are reversed. The Tibetan is found in Longchen Rabjam, *White Lotus,* vol. 1, p. 446.
156. Longchen Rabjam, *White Lotus,* vol. 1, pp. 446–58, has a long section on the refutations of the Nirgrantha-related systems, which has been ommited in *DGD.*

157. Saraha, *Treasury of Spiritual Songs,* TPD, vol. 26, p. 194. See the translation in Guenther 1993, 4.
158. *DGD* (p. 718) omits *dvangs pa* ("luminosity"). See Longchen Rabjam, *White Lotus,* vol. 1, p. 469.
159. *DGD* (p. 718) reads "second" (*gnyis pa ni*).
160. See Jamgon Kongtrul's brief restatement of this argument in Dorje 2012, 404. The point is that the Bārhaspatya are unlike other logicians who accept that a conceptualized vase and an actual vase are requisite counterparts or isolates, precluding the possibility of the conceptualized vase pertaining to some other material object, such as a living person.
161. *DGD* (p. 719) misreads *byas pa* for *byis pa.* See Longchen Rabjam, *White Lotus,* vol. 1, p. 461.
162. *DGD* (p. 718) misreads *bcas pa* for *dangs pa.* See Longchen Rabjam, *White Lotus,* vol. 1, p. 461.
163. Cited with slight variations in Bhāvaviveka, *Precious Lamp of the Middle Way,* TPD, vol. 57, p. 1526; also in Jayānanda, *Exegetical Commentary on the Introduction to the Middle Way,* TPD, vol. 61, p. 544. Cf. Radhakrishnan and Moore 1957, 228. The Tibetan is found in Longchen Rabjam, *White Lotus,* vol. 1, p. 461.
164. This would refer to Avalokitavrata, *Extensive Commentary on the Lamp of Discriminative Awareness.* The same verses with slight modifications are found therein (TPD, vol. 59, p. 838).
165. This stanza is cited in the *Jewel Crest of the Assembly,* KPD, vol. 56, pp. 515–16.
166. Cited in Radhakrishnan and Moore 1957, 230 and 233. The Tibetan is found in Longchen Rabjam, *White Lotus,* vol. 1, p. 462. In the second line, *DGD* (p. 719) misreads *sman* ("medicine") for *smad* ("feeble").
167. Candrakīrti, *Clear Word Commentary,* TPD, vol. 60, p. 285. The Tibetan is found in Longchen Rabjam, *White Lotus,* vol. 1, p. 362.
168. The refutation of these Bārhaspatya views is presented in Longchen Rabjam, *White Lotus,* vol. 1, pp. 463–67, but omitted in *DGD.*
169. The original source is as yet unidentified. The Tibetan derives from Longchen Rabjam, *White Lotus,* vol. 2, p. 1.
170. As yet unidentified. The Tibetan derives from Longchen Rabjam, *White Lotus,* vol. 2, p. 1.
171. Not located in Maitripa, *Dispelling of Negative Views,* TPD, vol. 26, pp. 288–302. The Tibetan derives from Longchen Rabjam, *White Lotus,* vol. 2, p. 2.
172. This citation is not found in Candrakīrti, *Seventy Verses on Going for Refuge,* TPD, vol. 65, pp. 685–91, but it is contained with the minor variant *skyabs gsol na* for *skyabs song bas* in Karo, *Compendium of Discourses on the Stages of Meditation,* TPD, vol. 64, p. 402. The Tibetan derives from Longchen Rabjam, *White Lotus,* vol. 2, p. 2.
173. The three modes of release (*thar pa gsum*) comprise release obtained by pious attendants, hermit buddhas, and bodhisattvas.

174. This and the immediately following citation have not yet been located. The Tibetan derives from Longchen Rabjam, *White Lotus,* vol. 2, p. 2.
175. This entire discussion derives from ibid., pp. 11–19.
176. *DGD* (p. 724) reads *'byung ba'i phung po* ("arising aggregates") for *'bras bu'i phung po* ("ripened aggregates"). See Longchen Rabjam, *White Lotus,* vol. 2, p. 11.
177. *DGD* (p. 724) reads *de nas* for *de na.* See Longchen Rabjam, *White Lotus,* vol. 2, p. 12.
178. Not yet located. The Tibetan derives from Longchen Rabjam, *White Lotus,* vol. 2, p. 12.
179. Vasubandhu, *Treasury of Phenomenology,* ch. 6, v. 2; TPD, vol. 79, p. 42. See the translation in Pruden 1988–90, 896–97.
180. Vasubandhu, *Treasury of Phenomenology,* ch. 6, v. 4; TPD, vol. 79, p. 43. Cf. Pruden 1988–90, 910–11.
181. *DGD* (p. 725) reads "one-nineteenth," but see Longchen Rabjam, *White Lotus,* vol. 2, p. 13, line 7 for the correct reading.
182. Vasubandhu, *Treasury of Phenomenology,* ch. 3, vv. 85b–89c; TPD, vol. 79, pp. 22–23. See the translation in Pruden 1988–90, 474–75.
183. *DGD* (p. 725) reads *'du byed rdul du* for *'du byed sdug bsngal.* See the reference in the following note.
184. Bhadanta Śrīlāta (*btsun pa dpal len,* 330–410) appears to have been one of the two most influential exponents of Sautrāntika, alongside Bhadanta Kumāralāta (*btsun pa gzhon nu len*). His works are no longer extant, although he reputedly authored a *Sautrāntikavibhāṣa.* The verses are cited in Vasubandhu, *Autocommentary on the Treasury of Phenomenology,* ch. 6; TPD, vol. 79, p. 685. See also Pruden 1988–90, 900. Other Indian authors who refer to this passage include Guṇapabha and Guṇamati. The title of the cited text, tentatively reconstructed as *Rajusaptati* (*rDul bdun cu pa*) appears to be unidentifiable. It is found in Longchen Rabjam, *White Lotus,* where the author's name is given as *btsun pa dpal legs.* There is a suggestion that the title may have been conflated with Kumāralāta, *Duḥkhasaptati* (*sDug bsngal bdun cu pa*) mentioned in the same section in Yaśomitra, *Commentary on the Treasury of Phenomenology* (TPD, vol. 80, p. 1207). Two contrasting Sautrāntika views on the suffering of conditioning, attributed to Kumāralāta and Śrīlāta are discussed in Śākya Chokden, *Exegesis on Difficult Points in the Treasury of Phenomenology* (*Collected Works,* vol. 21 (ZHA), pp. 74–76). Extant Indic references to both are collated in Kato 1980; on Śrīlāta specifically, see Sen 1983.
185. *DGD* (p. 728) reads *gzhi* for *shig.* See Longchen Rabjam, *White Lotus,* vol. 2, p. 15, line 3.
186. Cited in the *Hundred Narratives of Pūrṇa and so Forth,* KPD, vol. 75, p. 94. The Tibetan is found in Longchen Rabjam, *White Lotus,* vol. 2, p. 16.
187. At this juncture, Longchen Rabjam, *White Lotus,* vol. 2, pp. 16–34, includes

a detailed refutation of these seven commonly held tenets, which is excluded from our text.

188. *DGD* reads *bdag med* for *brjod med,* but see ibid., p. 34, last line.
189. Vasubandhu, *Treasury of Phenomenology,* ch. 1, v. 9a–b.
190. *DGD* (p. 727) reads *des g.yengs pa ste* instead of *nges pa ste*. See Longchen Rabjam, *White Lotus,* vol. 2, p. 35, line 13.
191. Vasubandhu, *Treasury of Phenomenology,* ch. 1, v. 11.
192. Ibid., ch. 4, v. 13a–b.
193. Ibid., ch. 1, vv. 43c–44a–b.
194. Ibid., ch. 2, vv. 24–25.
195. Ibid., ch. 2, v. 34.
196. Ibid., ch. 1, vv. 14c–15b.
197. This accords with the listing found in Asaṅga, *Compendium of Phenomenology,* on which, see Jamgon Kongtrul's presentation in Dorje 2012, 508–10.
198. Vasubandhu, *Treasury of Phenomenology,* ch. 1, v. 5b–c.
199. The eight substances (*rdzas brgyad*) comprise the four elements along with the four sense objects: sights, odors, tastes, and tangibles. See Nordrang Orgyan, *Compendium of Buddhist Numeric Terms,* p. 1903.
200. See Pruden 1988–90, 238–50. The eight attributes of production include the principal mind or mental state, along with the four defining characteristics and three of the four subsidiary defining characteristics. That is to say, they exclude the operational production of production that gives rise to the conditioned phenomenon itself, and which is distinct from it. Note that *DGD* (p. 729) reads "future" (*ma 'ongs pa'i sa*) rather than "past," but see Longchen Rabjam, *White Lotus,* vol. 2, p. 38, for the correct reading.
201. Vasubandhu, *Treasury of Phenomenology,* ch. 2, vv. 45c–46b.
202. The original source of this citation has not yet been identified. The Tibetan is found in Longchen Rabjam, *White Lotus,* vol. 2, p. 39.
203. The original source of this citation has not yet been identified. The Tibetan is found in ibid.
204. Vasubandhu, *Treasury of Phenomenology,* ch. 1, v. 42.
205. The implication is that if visual consciousness alone were to see objects, it would also see obscured objects in that it in itself is unimpeded.
206. Omitted in *DGD* (p. 730) but found in Longchen Rabjam, *White Lotus,* vol. 2, p. 40.
207. Nāgārjuna, *Fundamental Stanzas of the Middle Way,* ch. 17, vv. 14–15b.
208. Ibid., v. 18d.
209. Ibid., v. 17.
210. *DGD* (p. 731) reads *brjod du rung ba* ("can be verbally expressed") whereas Longchen Rabjam, *White Lotus,* vol. 2, p. 41, reads the opposite: *brjod du mi rung ba.*
211. At this point, our text excludes the detailed refutation of the Vaibhāṣika views, which can be found in Longchen Rabjam, *White Lotus,* vol. 2, pp. 41–56.

212. Vasubandhu, *Treasury of Phenomenology,* ch. 2, vv. 61c–62d.
213. Ibid., v. 64a–c.
214. *DGD* (p. 731) reads *rtog pa'i rnam pa* ("conceptual sensa") whereas Longchen Rabjam, *White Lotus,* p. 58, reads *gtad pa'i rnam pa* ("targeted sensa").
215. Dharmakīrti, *Exposition of Valid Cognition,* TPD, vol. 97, p. 548. *DGD* (p. 732) is corrupt. See Longchen Rabjam, *White Lotus,* vol. 2, p. 58.
216. This citation is not found in the *Ornament of the Middle Way,* as our text suggests, but in Dharmakīrti, *Exposition of Valid Cognition,* TPD, vol. 97, pp. 566–67. Note that the couplets are reversed here and that the second should read *don dang 'dra ba dmigs pa ste| rang nyid gsal ba bdag myong yin.*
217. In the cardinal directions, the zenith and the nadir.
218. *DGD* (p. 732) misreads *log* for *logs,* but see Longchen Rabjam, *White Lotus,* vol. 2, p. 59.
219. *DGD* at this juncture, omits the detailed refutation of the Sautrāntika tenets, as found in Longchen Rabjam, *White Lotus,* pp. 59–61.
220. See the translation of the relevant section of Asaṅga, *Compendium of Phenomenology* in Boin-Webb 2001, 196–200.
221. *Ornament of Clear Realization* (*Abhisamayālaṃkāra,* ch. 2, v. 82).
222. Vasubandhu, *Treasury of Phenomenology,* ch. 3, vv. 21a–25d.
223. *DGD* (p. 734) reads *cha mnyam pa,* but see Longchen Rabjam, *White Lotus,* vol. 2, p. 64.
224. Vasubandhu, *Treasury of Phenomenology,* ch. 3, vv. 19d–20c.
225. Ibid., ch. 6, v. 24d; TPD, vol. 79, p. 44. See the translation in Pruden 1988–90, 942.
226. Vasubandhu, *Treasury of Phenomenology,* ch. 3, v. 94d; TPD, vol. 79, p. 1082. Cf. Pruden 1988–90, 483.
227. Vasubandhu, *Treasury of Phenomenology,* ch. 6, v. 24a–b.
228. Ibid., ch. 7, v. 55a–b.
229. The refutation of the vehicle of the hermit buddhas, missing in our text, can be found in Longchen Rabjam, *White Lotus,* vol. 2, pp. 65–68.
230. Nāgārjuna, *Fundamental Stanzas of the Middle Way Entitled Discriminative Awareness,* ch. 18, v. 12.
231. *DGD* (p. 735) reads *thub pa chen po* ("greatness of capacity"), but see Longchen Rabjam, *White Lotus,* vol. 2, p. 69.
232. Maitreya, *Ornament of the Sūtras of the Great Vehicle,* ch. 20, vv. 61–62. See the translation in Jamspal et al. 2004, 310.
233. Nāgārjuna, *Precious Garland,* v. 390.
234. *DGD* (p. 736) omits *kyang* ("also"). See Longchen Rabjam, *White Lotus,* vol. 2, p. 70.
235. *Verse Summation of the Transcendent Perfection of Discriminative Awareness,* ch. 1. v. 21; KPD, vol. 34, p. 6. See the translation in Conze 1973, 11.
236. The following account of the Cittamātra system derives from Longchen Rabjam, *White Lotus,* vol. 2, pp. 71–100.

237. Haribhadra, *Commentary on the Ornament of Clear Realization,* TPD, vol. 52, p. 205.
238. Dharmakīrti, *Ascertainment of Valid Cognition,* TPD, vol. 97, p. 641.
239. Sthiramati, *Commentary on the Thirty Verses,* T 4064; TPD, vol. 77, p. 392.
240. This is similar to a line in Vasubandhu, *Thirty Verses,* TPD, vol, 77, p. 6: *gzung ba med pas de 'dzin med.* The verse is however cited in the present form *gzung ba med na der 'dzin med* in Haribhadra, *Light for the Ornament of Emergent Realization,* TPD, vol. 51, p. 1104.
241. Jñānabhadra, *Commentary on the Sūtra of the Descent to Laṅkā,* TPD, vol. 70, p. 111.
242. This passage has not been precisely identified in the *Sūtra of the Descent to Laṅkā,* although some of its verses do occur. See KPD, vol. 49, p. 268 and p. 404.
243. This citation is said to derive from the *Sūtra of the Ten Levels.* The same wording is found in Advayavajra, *Precious Garland of the Real Nature,* TPD, vol. 26, p. 340.
244. Dharmakīrti, *Ascertainment of Valid Cognition,* TPD, vol. 97, p. 645.
245. Tib. *lta bas dmigs pa'i gzhi gzhi lnga. DGD* (p. 737) reads *lta ba dang dmigs pa'i gzhi bzhi dang lnga.* See Longchen Rabjam, *White Lotus,* vol. 2, p. 73.
246. Tib. *sgom pas dmigs pa'i gzhi bdag med. DGD* (p. 737) reads *sgom pa dmigs pa'i gzhi bdag med* ("selflessness that is the foundation of focusing through meditation") but see Longchen Rabjam, *White Lotus,* vol. 2, p, 73, for the correct reading.
247. Maitreya, *Ornament of the Sūtras of the Great Vehicle,* TPD, vol. 70, p. 810, ch. 4, v. 5. See also the translation in Jamspal et al 2004, 26.
248. Longchen Rabjam, *White Lotus,* vol. 2, p. 74.
249. Asaṅga, *Compendium of Phenomenology,* TPD, vol. 76, p. 186.
250. The original citation has not yet been identified. The Tibetan derives from Longchen Rabjam, *White Lotus,* vol. 2, p. 75.
251. On the mistaken view of self and related aspects of wrong view, see Jamgon Kongtrul's explanation in Dorje 2012, 499–504. The ninefold enumeration mentioned here has not yet been identified, but may possibly be conflated with the nine aspects of pride (*nga rgyal rnam pa dgu*) listed in Nordrang Orgyan, *Compendium of Buddhist Numeric Terms,* p. 1963, or the egotistical aspects mentioned in Dorje 2012, 524.
252. Skt. *pariccheda,* Tib. *yongs gcod. DGD* (p. 740) reads *long spyod la grub pa,* but see Longchen Rabjam, *White Lotus,* vol. 2, p. 77, line 1.
253. Asvabhāva, *Combined Commentary on the Summary of the Greater Vehicle,* TPD, vol. 76, pp. 577–78.
254. Vasubandhu, *Exposition of the Three Natures,* TPD, vol. 77, p. 29. See Anacker 1984, 291.
255. These verses derive from Vasubandhu, *Thirty Verses,* vv. 20–21; TPD, vol. 77, p.

5, not the *Ascertainment of Valid Cognition,* as stated in *DGD* (p. 740) and in Longchen Rabjam, *White Lotus,* p. 78. See the translation in Cook 1999, 381.

256. The four aspects of cessation (*'gog pa bzhi*) comprise cessation (*nirodha, 'gog pa*), quiescence (*śānta, zhi ba*), excellence (*praṇita, gya nom pa*), and emancipation (*niḥsaraṇa, nges 'byung*). See Nordrang Orgyan, *Compendium of Buddhist Numeric Terms,* pp. 552–53.

257. Asaṅga, *Summation of Ascertainment from the Yogacaryā Level,* TPD, vol. 74, p. 698.

258. This precise wording does not appear in Vasubandhu, *Commentary on the Distinction between the Middle and Extremes,* on which see Anacker 1984, 211–86.

259. Tib. *re re* missing in *DGD* (p. 742) but found in Longchen Rabjam, *White Lotus,* vol. 2, p. 79.

260. *DGD* (p. 742) reads *rig pa* ("awareness"), whereas Longchen Rabjam, *White Lotus,* vol. 2, p. 80, reads *rnam rig* ("apperception").

261. Vasubandhu, *Thirty Verses,* v. 27, TPD, vol. 77, p. 5. This is not cited in Asaṅga, *Summation of Ascertainment from the Yogacaryā Level,* as stated in our text and in Longchen Rabjam, *White Lotus.*

262. *DGD* (p. 743) reads *ldog pa* ("counterpart"), whereas Longchen Rabjam, *White Lotus,* vol. 2, p. 80, reads *rtogs pa* ("realization").

263. At this point, Longchen Rabjam, *White Lotus,* vol. 2, pp. 81–91, includes a critique of the aforementioned general Cittamātra tenets, which has been omitted in our text.

264. This would appear to accord with the arguments presented in Śaṅkarānanda, *Proof of Elimination,* TPD, vol. 106, pp. 769–820; T 4256, although the exact words are not found therein.

265. At this point, Longchen Rabjam, *White Lotus,* vol. 2, pp. 93–97, includes the refutation of these specific tenets, which is omitted in our text.

266. There are eight extant works of the logician Dharmottara extant in Tibetan translation. The exact source of this attribution has not yet been located.

267. Dharmakīrti, *Exposition of Valid Cognition,* TPD, vol. 97, p. 555. *DGD* attributes this citation to the *Ascertainment of Valid Cognition.*

268. The refutation of this school, omitted in our text, is detailed in Longchen Rabjam, *White Lotus,* vol. 2, pp. 98–100.

269. Tib. *rang rig. DGD* (p. 745) reads *rang rgyud,* but see Longchen Rabjam, *White Lotus,* p. 101.

270. Samudramegha (*rgya mtsho sprin*) is the author of the *Exegesis of the Bodhisattva Level,* contained in TPD, vol. 75, pp. 609–1443, although the exact reference has not yet been located therein.

271. Not yet located. The Tibetan is found in Longchen Rabjam, *White Lotus,* vol. 2, p. 102.

272. *Sūtra of the King of Meditative Stability,* KPD, vol. 55, p. 388.

273. Ibid., p. 64. Note that the third line is different, reading *de la ji ltar snang ba gang yang med,* instead of *de la mi bden snang ba sna tshogs lta* (*DGD,* p. 746).

274. *Tantra of Hevajra,* pt. 2, ch. 3, v. 36.
275. The refutation of the lower Svātantrika is found in Longchen Rabjam, *White Lotus,* vol. 2, pp. 103–96.
276. The threefold criteria (*trairūpya, tshul gsum*) of valid cognition comprise the property of the thesis (*pakṣadharma, phyogs chos*), forward logical entailment (*anvayavyāpti, rjes khyab*), and counter logical entailment (*vyatirekavyāpti, ldog khyab*). See Dorje 2012, 159.
277. Jñānagarbha, *Distinction between the Two Truths,* v. 12.
278. *DGD* here reads *rig pa* for *rigs pa.* See Longchen Rabjam, *White Lotus,* vol. 2, p. 108.
279. Atiśa, *Introduction to the Two Truths,* v. 20; TPD, vol. 63, p. 1052. See the translation in Sherbourne 2000, 356–57.
280. *Diamond Cutter,* KPD, vol. 34, p. 354.
281. *DGD* (p. 747) reads *gang na gzigs,* but see Longchen Rabjam, *White Lotus,* vol. 2, p. 108 (*gang ma gzigs*).
282. *DGD* (p. 747) reads *dngos pos,* for *dngos po.* See Longchen Rabjam, *White Lotus,* vol. 2, p. 108.
283. Jñānagarbha, *Distinction between the Two Truths,* v. 7.
284. The precise citation has not yet been identified. The Tibetan is found in Longchen Rabjam, *White Lotus,* vol. 2, p. 108.
285. The refutation of the higher Svātantrika, omitted in our text, is found in ibid., pp. 109–13.
286. Nāgārjuna, *Refutation of Disputed Topics,* TPD, vol. 57, p. 77; also *dBu ma rigs tshogs drug,* Gansu ed., p. 49.
287. Nāgārjuna, *Refutation of Disputed Topics.* The first three lines are found in *dBu ma rigs tshogs drug,* Gansu ed., p. 52, where the final line instead reads *yang dag min te khyod kyis smras* ("it is you who say that it is incorrect").
288. Nāgārjuna, *Fundamental Stanzas of the Middle Way,* ch. 24, v. 19. Note the difference in wording here: *gang phyir rten 'byung ma yin pa'i . . . de phyir stong pa ma yin pa'i. . . .*
289. Ibid., ch. 13, v. 7. TPD, vol. 57, p. 19.
290. These verses are cited in Candrakīrti, *Autocommentary on the Introduction to the Middle Way,* TPD, vol. 60, p. 676.
291. Śāntideva, *Introduction to the Conduct of a Bodhisattva,* ch. 9, vv. 139–41. This is a corruption of the original verses, for which see TPD, vol. 61, p. 1029. Cf. the bilingual Sanskrit and Tibetan edition, pp. 221–22.
292. Longchen Rabjam, *White Lotus,* vol. 2, p. 118, reads *'thad pa gang* instead of *'thad pa med. DGD* (p. 750) reads *'thad pa dang.*
293. Nāgārjuna, *Fundamental Stanzas of the Middle Way,* ch. 7, vv. 30–31a.
294. Ibid., ch. 13, v. 5.
295. Tib. *seng ge'i so brag tu vas ma 'phras pa nyid chos dge ba yin no.*
296. The exact citation is not yet identified. The Tibetan is found in Longchen Rabjam, *White Lotus,* vol. 2, p. 119.

297. Candrakīrti, *Clear Word Commentary,* TPD, vol. 60, pp. 3–4.
298. See above n. 286.
299. Nāgārjuna, *Refutation of Disputed Topics,* TPD, vol. 57, p. 77; also *dBu ma rigs tshogs drug,* Gansu ed., p. 49.
300. *Verse Summation of the Transcendent Perfection of Discriminative Awareness,* ch. 26, v. 8, KPD, vol. 34, p. 35.
301. *DGD* (p. 752, line 10) adds *phyir,* which is missing in Longchen Rabjam, *White Lotus,* vol. 2, p. 121.
302. Candrakīrti, *Introduction to the Middle Way,* ch. 6, v. 38, contained in the Tibetan ed., p. 91.
303. Śāntideva, *Introduction to the Conduct of a Bodhisattva,* ch. 9, v. 2; TPD, vol. 61, p. 1017. Note that *DGD* here reads *'dod* for *brjod* in the final syllable.
304. Ratnakīrti, *Eulogy to the Deities of Fourfold Union,* TPD, vol. 1, p. 741.
305. *Litany of the Names of Mañjuśrī,* ch. 6, v. 17.
306. *DGD* (p. 752) reads *chod pa* for *'chol ba.* See Longchen Rabjam, *White Lotus,* vol. 2, p. 121.
307. Candrakīrti, *Introduction to the Middle Way,* ch. 6, v. 28, contained in Tibetan ed., p. 89.
308. The precise citation has not yet been identified. The Tibetan is found in Longchen Rabjam, *White Lotus,* vol. 2, p. 122.
309. Nāgārjuna, *Fundamental Stanzas of the Middle Way,* ch. 18, v. 9. Note that the order of these verses differs. See Padmakara 2016, 60.
310. This is an internal reference pertaining to the refutation sections of Longchen Rabjam, *White Lotus,* which are excluded from our text.
311. *Sūtra of the Meeting of Father and Son,* KPD, vol. 42, p. 150.
312. Candrakīrti, *Introduction to the Middle Way,* ch. 6, v. 25, contained in Tibetan ed., pp. 88–89.
313. Jñānagarbha, *Distinction between the Two Truths,* introduction, v. 2.
314. Not yet located. See Longchen Rabjam, *White Lotus,* vol. 2, p. 123.
315. Śāntideva, *Introduction to the Conduct of a Bodhisattva,* ch. 9, v. 35.
316. Ibid., v. 33.
317. *Verse Summation of the Transcendent Perfection of Discriminative Awareness,* ch. 2, v. 11; KPD, vol. 34, p. 8.
318. Candrakīrti, *Introduction to the Middle Way,* ch. 11, v. 16.
319. Ibid., v. 17.
320. See above, p. 149.
321. Candrakīrti, *Clear Word Commentary,* TPD, vol. 60, p. 398.
322. Candrakīrti, *Autocommentary on the Introduction to the Middle Way.* Not yet located. See Longchen Rabjam, *White Lotus,* vol. 2, p. 127.
323. *DGD* (p. 756) reads *brtsad pa po* for *gtsang ba.* See Longchen Rabjam, *White Lotus,* vol. 2, p. 127.
324. The lives of the eighty-four great accomplished masters of India are recounted in Abhayadattaśrī, *Biographies of the Eighty-Four Great Accomplished Masters.*

See the translation in Robinson 1979. The activities of the twenty-five disciples of Padmasambhava in Tibet, including King Trisong Detsen and his subjects, are described in the various editions of the *Injunctions of Padma.* See, e.g., Orgyan Lingpa, *Injunctions of Padma Discovered at Crystal Rock*; also Dudjom Rinpoche 1991, 1:512–21 and 1:534–37.

325. In Part 4, the primary source is Longchen Rabjam, *Treasury of Philosophical Systems.*
326. *Tantra of Inconceivable Rali Cakrasaṃvara.* This passage is also cited in *Treasury of Philosophical Systems,* p. 214. See the translation in Barron 2007, 242–43, also Dudjom Rinpoche 1991, 1:248.
327. *DGD* (p. 761) reads *lha dang snags kyis rang bzhin* instead of *lha dang sngags kyi rang bzhin.* See Longchen Rabjam, *Treasury of Philosophical Systems,* p. 214.
328. Buddhaguhya, *Sequence of the Path of Magical Emanation,* TPD, vol. 43, pp. 959–1041. The verse *don dam kun rdzob dbyer med pa* occurs in ch. 2 of that work, on p. 973, but without the following line.
329. Tib. *phung po lnga lhar dag pa yang.* This reading follows Longchen Rabjam, *Treasury of Philosophical Systems,* p. 215, whereas *DGD* (p. 761) reads *phung po lnga lhar grub pa yab.*
330. This source has not yet been identified.
331. Longchen Rabjam, *Treasury of Philosophical Systems,* p. 215, reads *sangs rgyas zhing,* whereas *DGD* (p. 761) reads *sangs rgyas zhes.*
332. *Tantra of the Secret Nucleus,* ch. 2, v. 4.
333. Ibid., ch. 12, v. 12.
334. One "countless" aeon (*asaṃkhyakalpa, grangs med bskal pa*) is quantified at ten to the power of fifty-nine.
335. *Prophetic Declaration of Enlightened Intention,* KPD, vol. 81, p. 616. This passage is also cited in Dudjom Rinpoche 1991, 1:256.
336. The reading *smad gyur pa'i* ("debasing") is based on the 1999 Chengdu imprint of Longchen Rabjam, *Treasury of Philosophical Systems.* In contrast, *DGD* (p. 762) and *Treasury of Philosophical Systems,* p. 217, both read *rmad du gyur pa* ("astonishing").
337. This is an alternative title of the *Sūtra That Gathers All Enlightened Intentions,* KPD, vol. 101, pp. 219–672. However, the original quotation is as yet unidentified.
338. *Tantra of the Indestructible Peak,* TPD, vol. 84, p. 464. Note that there are minor variants.
339. These words are found in Tripiṭakamāla, *Lamp of the Three Ways.* See also Dudjom Rinpoche 1991, 1:246.
340. Tib. *thabs des.* See Longchen Rabjam, *Treasury of Philosophical Systems,* p. 218. *DGD* (p. 763) reads *thabs res* ("by each skillful means").
341. The source for this and the following paragraphs is Longchen Rabjam, *White Lotus,* vol. 2, p. 128.
342. *DGD* (p. 763) reads *yon tan brgyad chas,* but see ibid.: *yon tan rgya chen.*
343. Snellgrove 1959, ch. 4, v. 69.

344. These words paraphrase the following verses from Maitreya, *Ornament of the Sūtras of the Great Vehicle,* ch. 10, v. 22: *snga ma phyi mar khyad med kyang* and v. 37: *de bzhin nyid ni thams cad la| khyad par med kyang dag gyur pa.* See *Five Treatises of Maitreya,* pp. 74 and 76, and the translation in Jamspal et al., 2004, 81 and 87. The latter also highlights parallel passages in Maitreya, *Supreme Continuum of the Great Vehicle.*
345. *DGD* (p. 764) and Longchen Rabjam, *White Lotus,* vol. 2, p. 129, both read *bdag nyid* for *dkyil 'khor.*
346. Note the missing verses in *DGD* (p. 764).
347. *Tantra of the Secret Nucleus,* ch. 2, v. 2.
348. The *Tantra of the Presence of Pristine Cognition* has not yet been identified. The immediate source for this quotation is Longchen Rabjam, *Treasury of Philosophical Systems,* p. 218.
349. The three kinds of dairy product (*dkar gsum*) are curd, milk, and butter. Changing of the three kinds of attire (*gos gsum brje ba*) implies wearing new clothes outwardly, guarding one's vows inwardly, and meditating on the deity secretly. See Nyima and Dorje 2001, 496.
350. Symbolic maṇḍalas are consecrated by visualizing the form of the deity, known as the "being of meditative commitment" (*samayasattva, dam tshig sems dpa'*), after which an invitation is made to the actual deity, known as the "being of pristine cognition" (*jñānasattva, ye shes sems dpa'*) to enter, and these two are then indivisibly absorbed. See Dorje 2016, 342.
351. On these five awakenings (*pañcābhisambodhi, mngon byang lnga*)—the throne with lotus and moon cushion, the seed syllable of buddha speech, the emblem symbolic of buddha mind, the fully formed body of the deity, and the presence of the being of pristine cognition—see also Dudjom Rinpoche 1991, 1:279–81.
352. Our text reads *chos gang.* See Longchen Rabjam, *White Lotus,* vol. 2, p. 133, for the correct reading *cho ga.*
353. The three empowerments of profundity—namely, those of secrecy (*gsang dbang*), discriminating pristine cognition (*shes rab ye shes kyi dbang*), and word and meaning (*tshig don gyi dbang*)—are conferred once the initial purificatory empowerments of the vase (*bum dbang*) have been conferred. Their fruition matures respectively as the buddha bodies of emanation, perfect resource, reality, and essentiality. For a detailed account, see Guarisco and McLeod 2005.
354. *DGD* (p. 766) reads *phyir* for *phyi bar.* See Longchen Rabjam, *White Lotus,* vol. 2, p. 134.
355. Indrabhūti, *Presence of Pristine Cognition,* TPD, vol. 26, p. 106. Note that our text refers to this as *rgyud* ("tantra") rather than *sgrub thabs* ("sādhana").
356. These comprise crystalized sugar, molasses, and honey. See Nyima and Dorje 2001, 915.
357. There are varying enumerations of the five meats. See Nordrang Orgyan, *Compendium of Buddhist Numeric Terms,* p. 1282. In general, they comprise the flesh of cattle, dogs, horses, elephants, and humans. The five nectars comprise excrement, urine, human flesh, blood, and semen.

358. This passage has not yet been identified in the *Tantra of the Indestructible Tent.* The immediate source for this and the following paragraphs is Longchen Rabjam, *White Lotus,* vol. 2, pp. 146–47.
359. The source for this and the following paragraphs on the Great Perfection is Longchen Rabjam, *Treasury of Philosophical Systems,* pp. 266ff.
360. *Tantra of the All-Accomplishing King,* ch. 38, vv. 2–9, Valby 2008–14, vol. 3, pp. 269–77.
361. Maitreya, *Supreme Continuum of the Great Vehicle,* ch. 1, v. 51. *DGD* (p. 768) and Longchen Rabjam, *Treasury of Philosophical Systems,* p. 267, both attribute this and the following quotation to the *Tantra of the All-Accomplishing King,* where they are not found. The source is accurately identified in Dudjom Rinpoche 1991, 1:298.
362. Maitreya, *Supreme Continuum of the Great Vehicle,* ch. 1, v. 5.
363. *DGD* (p. 768) reads *phyogs chad,* but see Longchen Rabjam, *Treasury of Philosophical Systems,* p. 268, which reads *phyang chad.*
364. *DGD* (p. 768) omits *zhes* after *dbyings,* while adding *ye shes.* See Longchen Rabjam, *Treasury of Philosophical Systems,* p. 268.
365. This line is omitted in *DGD* (p. 760) and Longchen Rabjam, *Treasury of Philosophical Systems,* p. 268. See Valby's edition, and the translation in Valby 2008–14, vol. 3, p. 278, which shows that the line is omitted in only two of the seven sources that he edits.
366. *DGD* (p. 769) and Longchen Rabjam, *Treasury of Philosophical Systems,* p. 268, both read *byang chub nam mkha' des mi 'grub,* but all seven sources edited by Valby have *byang chub nam mkha' de mi 'grub.*
367. In this and the three immediately following verses, *DGD* (p. 769) reads *byang chub nam mkha' des mi 'grub.* Longchen Rabjam, *Treasury of Philosophical Systems,* p. 268, correctly reads *byang chub nam mkha' de mi 'grub.*
368. This phrase is missing in our text and Longchen Rabjam, *Treasury of Philosophical Systems,* but found in four of the seven versions edited by Valby.
369. *Tantra of the All-Accomplishing King,* ch. 38, vv. 11–16. See the translation in Valby 2008–14, vol. 3, pp. 278–282.
370. *Tantra of the All-Accomplishing King,* ch. 9, v. 19. See Valby 2008–14, vol. 1, pp. 213–14. Only the first two and a half lines are found in extant versions of the text.
371. *Tantra of the All-Accomplishing King,* ch. 44, vv. 10–11. See Valby 2008–14, vol. 4, pp. 94–96.
372. *Tantra of the All-Accomplishing King,* ch. 42, vv. 2–4. See Valby 2008–14, vol. 4, pp. 60–61.
373. *Tantra of the Secret Nucleus,* ch. 12, v. 14.
374. Ibid., ch. 13, v. 20.
375. *DGD* (p. 770) and Longchen Rabjam, *Treasury of Philosophical Systems,* p. 270, both read *dngos po* ("entity") for *ngo bo* ("essential nature"), which is found in all seven versions edited by Valby.
376. *Tantra of the All-Accomplishing King,* ch. 37, v. 9. See Valby 2008–14, vol. 3, pp. 263–64.

377. This citation is not found in the extant versions of the *Tantra of the All-Accomplishing King,* but resembles the verses found in ch. 7, v. 23, lines 120–24. See Valby 2008–14, vol. 1, p. 176.

378. *DGD* (p. 771) reads *la,* whereas Longchen Rabjam, *Treasury of Philosophical Systems,* p. 274, reads *las.*

379. *DGD* (p. 772) reads *zhen,* whereas Longchen Rabjam, *Treasury of Philosophical Systems,* p. 275, reads *zhes.*

380. *DGD* (p. 772) and the Root Verses both read *brtan pa'i chos* ("supported phenomena") whereas Longchen Rabjam, *Treasury of Philosophical Systems,* p. 275, reads *brtags pa'i chos* ("imputed phenomena").

381. *DGD* (p. 773) reads *blos* for *chos.* See Longchen Rabjam, *Treasury of Philosophical Systems,* p. 276.

382. *DGD* (p. 773) reads *chos sku* for *chos su.* See Longchen Rabjam, *Treasury of Philosophical Systems,* p. 277.

383. *DGD* (p. 773) reads *shar ba* for *shar sa.* See Longchen Rabjam, *Treasury of Philosophical Systems,* p. 277.

384. At this point Longchen Rabjam, *Treasury of Philosophical Systems,* p. 277, includes a short section on the literature of the mind class of the Great Perfection, which is omitted in our text. On this, see Barron 2007, 315.

385. With regard to the axiom of equanimity concerning standpoints of being and nonbeing (*yin min phyogs mnyam gyi gtan tshigs*), *DGD* (p. 774) reads *phyogs nyal* for *phyogs mnyam,* but see Longchen Rabjam, *Treasury of Philosophical Systems,* p. 278.

386. In the axiom of natural purity with regard to common appearances (*mthun snang rang dag gi gtan tshigs*), *DGD* (p. 774) omits *dag.* See Longchen Rabjam, *Treasury of Philosophical Systems,* p. 279.

387. Tib. *'khrul sems la bzla ba'i gtan tshigs.*

388. From this point on, several subcategories of the class of space and the class of esoteric instruction are distinctively presented in terms of their essential nature (*ngo bo*), natural expression (*rang bzhin*), and defining characteristic (*mtshan nyid*). These three terms denote the buddha body of reality, the buddha body of perfect resource, and the buddha body of emanation, respectively.

389. Tib. *gyu ba stong yal gyi gtan tshigs.*

390. The latter is not discussed in Longchen Rabjam, *Treasury of Philosophical Systems,* and consequently it is not discussed in *DGD* (p. 776).

391. Tib. *rang gzhag.* Note that *DGD* (p. 777) reads *rang gzhan* for *rang gzhag.* See Longchen Rabjam, *Treasury of Philosophical Systems,* p. 283.

392. At this point, Longchen Rabjam, *Treasury of Philosophical Systems,* pp. 284–86, includes further classifications of the teachings of the space class of the Great Perfection, which are omitted in *DGD.* See Barron 2007, 323–24.

393. *DGD* (p. 779) follows Longchen Rabjam, *Treasury of Philosophical Systems,* p. 286, in reading *chos nyid* ("reality") for *mtshan nyid* ("defining characteristics"), but see Dudjom Rinpoche 1991, 1:351.

394. *DGD* (p. 779) reads *grol ba'i* ("liberated") for *thob pa'i* ("acquired"). See Longchen Rabjam, *Treasury of Philosophical Systems,* p. 287.

395. *DGD* (p. 781) reads *dngos zin pa* for *ngos sin pa* ("recognition"). See Longchen Rabjam, *Treasury of Philosophical Systems,* p. 290.
396. *DGD* (p. 781) reads *rgyud* ("tantra") for *rgyu* ("causal basis"). See Longchen Rabjam, *Treasury of Philosophical Systems,* p. 290.
397. These four visionary appearances (*snang ba bzhi*), experienced through the all-surpassing realization of the Great Perfection (*rdzogs chen thod rgal*), are described as follows: (1) The visionary appearance of actual reality (*chos nyid mngon sum gyi snang ba*) occurs at the time when an [awareness holder] with power over the life span first perceives the pristine cognition of inner radiance as smoke and so forth. (2) The visionary appearance of ever-increasing experience (*nyams gong du 'phel ba'i snang ba*) occurs when that diffusion intensifies so that outer and inner signs are perceived. Then (3) the visionary appearance that reaches the limit of awareness (*rig pa tshad phebs kyi snang ba*) occurs when the field of the buddha body of perfect resource is perceived; and (4) the visionary appearance of the cessation [of cyclic existence in] actual reality (*chos nyid zad pa'i snang ba*) occurs when that too becomes inward quiescence, so that there is no subjective apprehension. For a more detailed account, see Longchen Rabjam's explanation in Dorje 1987.
398. At this point, Longchen Rabjam, *Treasury of Philosophical Systems,* pp. 292–95, enumerates the texts pertaining to the three classes of the Great Perfection, but this has been omitted in our text. See Barron 2007, 333–36, and Dudjom Rinpoche 1991, 1:332–33.
399. Vimalamitra, *Illuminating Lamp, Collected Works of Longchen Rabjam,* vol. 2, p. 65.
400. Nowadays the three districts of Ngari (*mnga' ris skor gsum*) are considered to have a narrower geographical range, including Maryul (Rutok, Ladakh, and Zangskar), Guge (Zhangzhung and the upper Sutlej area), and Purang. Traditionally, however, at the height of the Tibetan empire in Central Asia, these enclaves were all included within the first district of Ngari, while the second extended north and west to Khotan, Gilgit, and Baltistan, and the third south to Khri-te or Spiti and its adjacent enclaves in present-day Himachal Pradesh. There are several modern Tibetan-language publications on Ngari, including Guge Tsewang Gyalpo, *Religious History of Ngari: Beauteous Ornament of the Land of Snows,* and Gangriwa Choying Dorje, *Ancient History of Ngari Korsum: The Undying Drumbeat.* See also Beckwith 1987; Vitali 1996; Dorje 2009, 399–454; and Namkhai Norbu 2013.
401. In the Tibetan heartlands of Utsang (*dbus gtsang*), the province of U traditionally comprised two "horns": Uru (*dbus ru*), corresponding to the upper Kyichu region, and Yoru (*g.yo ru*), corresponding to the Yarlung Tsangpo basin of Lhokha. Tsang (*gtsang*) included Yeru (*g.yas ru,* the Zhigatse region) and Rulak (*ru lag,* the highland region of the upper Brahmaputra and Gangetic basins). See, e.g., Ferrari 1958; Aris 1979, 8–39; Mills 2007; and Dorje 2009, 71–386.

402. There are corruptions in the text here. For the correct reading, see Konchok Tenpa Rabgye, *Doctrinal History of Amdo,* p. 1. The vast area of eastern and far eastern Tibet defined by the upper reaches of the Salween, Mekong, Yangtze, and Yellow rivers with their tributaries is according to one tradition divided into three regions—namely, Dokham (*mdo khams*) or Markham (*smar khams*); Do-me (*mdo smad*) or Yarmotang (*dbyar mo thang*); and Tsongkha (*gtsong kha*) or Gyitang (*gyi thang*).

403. Among these six upland ranges of low-lying Dokham, (1) Nguldza Zelmogang divides the Salween and Yangtze headwaters from the Yalong; (2) Tsawagang divides the Salween from the Mekong; (3) Markhamgang divides the Mekong from the Yangtze; (4) Poborgang divides the southern Yangtze from the Yalong; (5) Mardzagang divides the upper Yalong from the Yellow River; and (6) Minyak Rabgang divides the lower Yalong from the Gyarong. See Dorje 2009, 456–842.

404. Khitan (*khri ten*) is the name of a nomadic people originally inhabiting Mongolia and Manchuria from the fourth to the thirteenth centuries. In the time of Choying Tobden Dorje, this term would denote Manchuria itself. The name Khrom (*khrom*), which is considered cognate with Rome (see Beyer 1992, 140–41), may in the past have denoted Byzantium and by extension the Ottoman Empire that occupied Byzantium from the fifteenth century, hence Turkestan. Gesar (*ge sar*) is cognate with the names *cesar* and *czar,* hence Tartary.

405. There are various enumerations of the early Tibetan kings, on which see Haarh 1969, 33–71, and also the tables in Namkhai Norbu 2013, 133–54. The primary source for the present passage is Orgyan Lingpa's revelation entitled *Injunction of the King,* pp. 113–15. I have added the commonly accepted regnal numbers in parentheses, from the first king Nyatri Tsenpo through to the forty-second and last king of unified Tibet, Lang Darma. For recent research on the period of the Tibetan monarchy, based on ancient chronicles from Dunhuang, see Dotson 2009 and van Schaik 2011.

406. Orgyan Lingpa, *Injunction of the King,* p. 113. This succession also accords with the account found in most of the other historical sources including Sonam Gyaltsen, *Mirror Illuminating Royal Genealogies,* p. 55, and Dudjom Rinpoche, *Concise Political History of Tibet,* pp. 16–17. These seven kings are said to have been immortal beings who ascended to the heavens after fulfilling their reigns. Their succession was matriarchal, the names of their respective mothers being indicated in the legendary accounts. The first of them, Nyatri Tsenpo, is associated with the construction of the Yumbu Lagang or Yumbu Lakhar palace.

407. On these two kings, see Sonam Gyaltsen, *Mirror Illuminating Royal Genealogies,* pp. 55–58, and Dudjom Rinpoche, *Concise Political History of Tibet,* pp. 17–23. Among them, Drigum Tsenpo was the first "mortal" king in this line. He had three sons of whom the second, Chatri Tsenpo, was his successor, also known as Pude Gungyal. He hailed from Kanam and is revered as a cul-

ture hero who reputedly introduced base metals and agriculture and built the Chingwa Taktse castle in Chongye.

408. This listing accords with Orgyan Lingpa, *Injunction of the King*, p. 114, but for the second who is named as Lisho Lek rather than Desho Lek. Among the various alternative lists, Sonam Gyaltsen, *Mirror Illuminating Royal Genealogies,* p. 58, enumerates the patrilineal succession of these six kings as Asho Lek, Desho Lek, Tisho Lek, Guru Lek, Drongzher Lek, and Isho Lek. Dudjom Rinpoche, *Concise Political History of Tibet,* pp. 23–24, reads Esho Lek, Desho Lek, Tisho Lek, Gongru Lek, Drongzher Lek, and Isho Lek. It is said that during this period animals were domesticated and that irrigation and taxation developed. Following Orgyan Lingpa, *DGD* presents Zanam Lek as the last of this line, when, in other sources, he is usually considered to be the first king of the De dynasty.

409. This listing accords with Orgyan Lingpa, *Injunction of the King,* p. 114, although there are some variants in spelling. Most sources suggest that these seven kings of sundry succession (*rgyal rabs sil ma bdun*) follow De Zanam Zin. Thus, Sonam Gyaltsen, *Mirror Illuminating Royal Genealogies,* p. 59, lists all eight of them as follows: Zanam Zin-de, De Trulnam Zhungtsen, Senol Nam-de, Se Nolpo De, De Nolnam, De Nolpo, De Gyalpo, and De Trintsen. Dudjom Rinpoche, *Concise Political History of Tibet,* p. 24, concurs. This succession is also known as the "eight kings of intervening succession called De" (*bar la lde brgyad*). It was during this period that Tibetan trade with the Chinese Shu Han dynasty prospered, Tibetan horses being particularly valued.

410. Orgyan Lingpa, *Injunction of the King,* p. 114. These "five kings of connected succession called Tsen" (*tshigs la btsan lnga*) are elsewhere listed as Tore Longtsen (also known as Tongri Tongtsen?), Tri Tsen-nam, Tri Dra Pungtsen, Tri Tokje Tok-tsen, and Lhatotori Nyentsen, the last of whom is usually considered to have been the twenty-eighth king of Tibet. See Dudjom Rinpoche, *Concise Political History of Tibet,* pp. 24–25. Sonam Gyaltsen, *Mirror Illuminating Royal Genealogies,* pp. 59–60, omits the first named. The Tibetan folkloric traditions were established through the activities of Bon priests during this period, and it is said that during the reign of the last of these kings Buddhism made its initial appearance in Tibet.

411. Orgyan Lingpa, *Injunction of the King,* pp. 114–15. The thirteen imperial kings of Tibet are generally listed as Trinyen Zungtsen, Drong Nyenderu, Takri Nyenzik, Namri Songtsen, Songtsen Gampo, Gungri Gungtsen, Mangsong Mangtsen, Dusong Mangpoje (also known as Lung Namtrulgyi Gyalpo), Tri-de Tsukten Me Agtsom, Trisong Detsen, Mune Tsepo, Mutik Tsepo, and Tri Relpachen. Usually, Trinyen Zungtsen is regarded as the twenty-ninth king and Tri Relpachen as the forty-first king. In this imperial period, Tibet reached the zenith of its political and military power in Central Asia, and Buddhism was officially established by Padmasambhava, Śāntarakṣita, King Trisong Detsen, Vimalamitra, and others.

412. *DGD* (p. 786) includes the words *khri ral pa chen gyi sras glang dar,* which is a corrupt interpolation.

413. Following the assassination of Tri Relpachen, Buddhism appears to have undergone persecution in the central parts of Tibet at the hands of his usurper and elder brother, Lang Darma, who is usually regarded as the forty-second and last king of unified Tibet. Following his assassination in turn (ca. 846), the dominion that passed from his son, Nam-de Osung (840–893), through Pelkhortsen (881–910), and his son Kyide Nyima Gon was reestablished in Ngari. The latter's son was Tashi Gon, his son Lha Lama Yeshe-o, the latter's younger brother Jangchub-o, his son Lha-de, his son O-de, and his son Tsen-de. On this succession, see Vitali 1996.

414. The early shamanic rites and funerary liturgies are said to have reached Tibet from the Iranian world (*stag gzigs*) in the west and the steppes around the Yellow River basin of Ningxia (*'a zha*) in the northeast. On the advent of Bon in Tibet during the reign of Nyatri Tsenpo and the "immortal" monarchs who followed him, see Karmay (1972) 2001, 31–34; Namkhai Norbu 2013, 121–32. Readily accessible works on Bon in English include Kvaerne 1995; Karmay (1972) 2001; Namkhai Norbu 2009, 2013, 2015; Tenzin Wangyal Rinpoche 2004; Baumer 2002; and Snellgrove 1967.

415. An elaborate account of the life and teaching of Shenrab Miwoche is found in the eleventh-century revelation of Drangje Tsunpa Sermik, entitled *Nailing Discourse.* On this and other versions, see also Baumer 2002, 85–92; Namkhai Norbu 2009; and the illustrations in Kvaerne 1995, 48–51. The enumeration of eighty-four thousand doctrines parallels the classical Buddhist conception of eighty-four thousand sections of the sacred doctrine as the antidote for eighty-four thousand afflicted mental states.

416. As indicated in Dondrub Lhagyal et al., *Dictionary of Bon Culture,* p. 126, the four transmissions of causal Bon (*rgyu'i bon bzhi*) refer to the first four of the nine ways of Bon, and the four transmissions of fruitional Bon (*'bras bu'i bon bzhi*) denote the higher ways, on all of which see also the next note.

417. This enumeration of the nine ways of Bon is taken from Orgyan Lingpa, *Injunction of the Minister,* contained in the *Five Injunctions,* p. 496. Therefore, any unidentified or unsourced technical terms in this passage can at the very least be traced back to Orgyan Lingpa. These nine ways (*theg pa dgu*) comprise (1) the way of the priests of prediction, which is achieved by inspecting impediments and disease-causing obstacles on an oracular mirror (*bgegs dang nad kyi bar chod la sogs kyi pra brtag pas phya gshen gyi theg pa*); (2) the way of the priests of the visible world, which is achieved by preliminary practices such as ritual ransom, torma casting, and the attaining of long life and prosperity (*sngon 'gro glud gtor btang zhing tshe g.yang bsgrubs pas snang gshen gyi theg pa*); (3) the way of the priests of miraculous power, which is achieved by engaging Bon rites of protection, aversion, and killing (*bsrung bzlog gsad dbab kyi las la 'jug pas 'phrul gshen kyi theg pa*); (4) the way of the priests of the rebirth process, which is achieved by transferring the life force and liberating it into the expanse of space

(through funerary rites) (*tshe 'phos dbyings su sgrol bas srid gshen kyi theg pa*); (5) the way of lay practitioners, which is achieved by making extensive offerings and donations (through the observance of ten virtuous actions) (*mchod sbyin rgyas par 'bul bas dge bsnyen gyi theg pa*); (6) the way of ordained renunciants, which is achieved by acquiring the empowerments and commitments (*dbang bskur dam tshig ldan pas drang srong kyi theg pa*); (7) the way of the white syllable A, which is achieved by the emanation and absorption of the deities in union and the attainment of medicinal nectar (in the context of rites of approach and attainment) (*lha yab yum gyi 'phro 'du bdud rtsi sman du bsgrub pas a dkar theg pa*); (8) the way of the primordial priests, which is achieved by experientially cultivating methods based on the *Tantra of the Nine Vital Essences* (concerning pristine cognition and the expanse) and the meaning of the nine keys (of meditative stability) (*thig le dgu'i rgyud la brten nas thabs dang lde mig dgu'i don nyams su len pas ye gshen gyi theg pa*); and (9) the way of the extraordinary [Great Perfection], which is achieved by disclosing the inner content of the supreme view of the *Tantra of Quiescence* (concerning spontaneous perfection that transcends the intellect) (*zhi rgyud kyi lta ba chen po'i khog dbub nas ston pas khyad par chen po*). I am grateful to Dan Martin for rectifying the misspelled names in this section and for providing this commentary based on the writings of Gyermi Nyi'o (*gyer mi nyi 'od*) and Azha Lodro Gyaltsen. This enumeration of the nine vehicles accords with the "southern treasure" tradition of Bon (*lho gter gyi theg pa dgu*). On the distinction between this and the vehicles as outlined in the central tradition (*dbus gnyer gyi theg pa dgu*) and the northern treasure tradition (*byang gter gyi theg pa dgu*), see Dondrub Lhagyal et al., *Dictionary of Bon Culture,* p. 259. On all nine vehicles of the southern treasure tradition, see also Snellgrove 1967 and Baumer 2002, 159–60. The first four are said to constitute the causal Bon and the next four the fruitional Bon. The entire passage that follows has been commented on by Chogyal Namkhai Norbu in *Light of Kailash,* pp. 389–96. See also the translation of that work by Donatella Rossi, in Namkhai Norbu 2015, 54–68.

418. The four portals of ritual chanting (*gyer sgo bzhi*) comprise (1) the portal of offerings to the gods (*lha gsas mchod pa'i sgo*); (2) the portal of exorcism and ablution (*sel dang khrus kyi sgo*); (3) the portal of liberation and ritual ransom (*thar dang glud kyi sgo*); and (4) the portal of the rites of good fortune, prosperity, and appeasment of plague-causing Nyen spirits (*phya g.yang gnyan gyi sgo*). See Pasar Tsultrim Tenzin et al., *A Lexicon of Zhangzhung and Bonpo Terms,* p. 39. Cf. Snellgrove 1967, 43–97, and Tenzin Wangyal 2004, 202–3. Chogyal Namkhai Norbu, *Light of Kailash,* p. 390, provides an alternative enumeration from a Bon text entitled *Auspicious Neck Ornament of Eloquence* (*Legs bshad skal bzang mgrin rgyan*).

419. The thirteen miraculous powers by Wel-se Ngampa (*dbal gsas rngam pa,* here misspelled as *sbas gsas rngam pa*) comprise the attainment of the ritual objective (*don gyi sgrub pa*); dominion over the environment and its inhabitants (*snod

bcud dbang bsgyur); the perfect body of a spiritual being (*sems dpa' sku rdzogs*); the display of the conduct of desire (*'dod spyod rol pa*); the perfect body of the *mudrā* (*phyag rgya sku rdzogs*); the swift attainment of the vital essence (*thig le myur mgyogs*); the enchanted blood of insanity/intoxication (*myos pa'i khrag thun*); the enchanted arrow that is targeted (*gzir ba'i mda' thun*); the enchanted poison that separates the life force (*srog dang phral byed dug thun*); miscellaneous rites (*sna tshogs pa'i las*); refinement of first offerings (*phud sbyangs*); the red path (of death) (*dmar lam*); and oaths (*bro*). See Dondrub Lhagyal et al., *Dictionary of Bon Culture,* p. 553. An alternative listing of the thirteen miraculous powers of commitment (*dam tshig rdzu 'phrul bcu gsum*) include things not to be forsaken—namely, the sacraments of meat, blood, and torma offerings, nectar that should not dry up, retreat sessions, and the times for ritual practices. It also includes things not to be renounced. See Peltsul, *Anthology of the Doctrinal History of Yungdrung Bon,* p. 170, and Chogyal Namkhai Norbu, *Light of Kailash,* p. 390. Note that our text misreads *sku 'phrul bcu gsum.*

As for the six great methods (*thabs chen drug/ thabs chen sde drug*), these include the great method (*thabs che ba*), whereby all sentient beings arise from emptiness, abide as reflections of emptiness, and are finally absorbed into emptiness; the skilled method (*thabs mkhas pa*) by means of which a hundred thousand disciples may be granted transmission, perfect communion, and realization by a single teacher; the profound method (*thabs zab pa*) by means of which one recognizes one's own true nature based on the oral teachings, or one knows the reflections of emptiness to arise from emptiness; the auspicious method (*thabs bzang ba*), whereby experiences and realizations are actualized when the mother tantras are practiced; the manifold method (*thabs mang ba*), whereby a hundred thousand fortunate beings who experientially cultivate the supreme secret path without distinction share in the provision of pristine cognition; and the enhancing method (*thabs 'phel ba*), whereby a multitude of wisdom arises from a single attainment of genuine wisdom, so that inconceivable great benefits come about. See Dondrub Lhagyal et al., *Dictionary of Bon Culture,* pp. 249–50.

420. The 360 funerary rites (*shi thabs sum brgya drug cu*) by Durshen Mawo (*'dur gshen rma bo*, here misspelled *'dur gsas sba po*), comprise 120 funerary rites for the aged (*rgan rabs shi rkyen brgya nyi shu*), 60 funerary rites for the young (*gzhon rabs shi rkyen drug cu*), 60 funerary rites for children (*byis pa shi rkyen drug cu*), and 120 funerary rites for those who have died a terrifying, violent death (*nyam mnga gri rgod brgya nyi shu*). See Dondrub Lhagyal et al., *Dictionary of Bon Culture,* p. 654; also Peltsul, *Anthology of the Doctrinal History of Yungdrung Bon,* p. 170.

The four portals of the funeral rites (*'dur sgo bzhi*) comprise "splendid" funerals for old people (*bkra rgas pa'i 'dur*), "slightly splendid" funerals for young adults (*bkre'u gzhon pa'i 'dur*), "sword" funerals for people who die violently (*gri gri shi song ba'i 'dur*), and "ancestral" funerals for the young or small children (*mtshun chung 'dur ram byis pa'i 'dur*). See Pasar Tsultrim Tenzin et al., *A Lexicon of Zhangzhung and Bonpo Terms,* p. 122; also Tenzin Wangyal 2004, 204.

421. The four delights (*dga' ba bzhi*) may comprise the yogic experiences of delight (*dga' ba*), supreme delight (*mchog dga'*), particular delight (*khyad par gyi dga' ba*), and coemergent delight (*lhan skyes dga' ba*). See Dondrub Lhagyal et al., *Dictionary of Bon Culture,* p. 107. The two purities (*dag pa gnyis*) could imply purity of the environment and its inhabitants, or, according to Chogyal Namkhai Norbu, *Light of Kailash,* p. 391, the purity of ultimate and relative aspects of meditation. The three severities (*gnyan po gsum*) have not yet been identified but may possibly denote injunctions of body, speech, and mind that are not to be transgressed. In Orgyan Lingpa's *Injunctions of the Minister,* this term is given as *gnyen po gsum* ("three antidotes"), which Chogyal Namkhai Norbu, *Light of Kailash,* p. 392, equates with three supreme powers of enlightened activity (*phrin las stobs mchog gsum*). This approach was established by Yekhyen Trulgyal (*ye mkhyen 'phrul rgyal,* here misspelled as *ye mkhyen 'phrul rgyam*).

422. The ten constraints (*sbad pas bcu*) have not yet been sourced, but probably parallel the avoidances of the ten nonvirtuous actions mentioned in Buddhist texts. The term *sbas pas bcu* appears to be corrupt. Chogyal Namkhai Norbu, *Light of Kailash,* p. 392, equates it with the ten modes of conduct (*spyod pa bcu*) implied in the avoidances of the ten nonvirtuous actions. The two models (*mtshon pa gnyis*) have not yet been identified, but may be equivalent to the external protection rites (*phyi yi tshul*) and the inner ordination rules (*nang gi khrims*) prescribed for males and for females, on which see Dondrub Lhagyal et al., *Dictionary of Bon Culture,* pp. 283–84. The two refinements (*sbyangs pa gnyis*) have not yet been identified, but may denote the refinement of ultimate and relative conceptions (*don dam pa'am kun rdzob kyi rtog pa'i blo sbyong ba*), as suggested by Chogyal Namkhai Norbu, *Light of Kailash,* p. 393. The three attainments (*sgrub pa gsum*), though not yet sourced, may possibly imply the three levels of ordination paralleling the renunciant, novitiate, and full-fledged ordinations of the Buddhist tradition. Chogyal Namkhai Norbu, *Light of Kailash,* p. 393, suggests a more esoteric explanation, equating them with the generation, perfection, and nondual stages of meditation (*bskyed rdzogs gnyis med gsum*). This approach was established by Yungdrung Chayi Gyalpo (*g.yung drung phya'i rgyal po,* here misspelled as *g.yung drung cha yi rgyal po*).

423. The eighteen branches of attainment (*sgrub pa'i yan lag bco brgyad*) include six attainments of the ground pertaining to the maṇḍala (*dkyil 'khor gzhi yi sgrub pa drug*), six attainments of the path that are wondrous (*ngo mtshar lam gyi sgrub pa drug*), and six attainments of the result that are conclusive (*mthar phyin 'bras bu'i sgrub pa drug*). For the complete enumeration, see Dondrub Lhagyal et al., *Dictionary of Bon Culture,* pp. 140–41. The nine approaches to ritual service (*bsnyen pa'i [zhi ma] sgo dgu*) comprise the three preliminary ritual services associated with teachers and deities (*dpon gsas lha la bsnyen pa*), friends with the appropriate characteristics (*mtshan ldan grogs la bsnyen pa*),

and with those belonging to the same enlightened heritage (*rigs ldan gnas la bsnyen pa*); the three subsidiary ritual services associated with implements and sacraments (*yo byad rdzas la bsnyen pa*), the fulfillment of ritual ransom (*thar glud bskang la bsnyen pa*), and the appointment of external supports (*phyi rten skos la bsnyen pa*); and the three ritual services associated with establishing the protective boundary (*srung ba mtshams kyi bsnyen pa*), with establishing the maṇḍala (*dkyil 'khor bca' gzhi'i bsnyen pa*), and with inaugural preparations, induction into the maṇḍala, and supplementary rituals such as replenishing of the commitments (*sgo dbye bsre snon gyi bsnyen pa*). See Dondrub Lhagyal et al., *Dictionary of Bon Culture,* p. 197; see also Snellgrove 1967, 185–89. Note that our text (p. 789) misreads *gnyen po* for *bsnyen pa.*

424. The four entrances (*'jug pa rnam pa bzhi*) to this vehicle have not yet been identified, but may possibly denote four aspects of empowerment. Chogyal Namkhai Norbu, *Light of Kailash,* p. 394, suggests that they may comprise the symbolic method, the nonsymbolic method, the generation stage of meditation, and the perfection stage of meditation, in accordance with the *Immaculate Splendor* (*Dri med gzi brjid*). The sixty aspects of meditative stability (*ting 'dzin yan lag drug cu*) have not yet been sourced, although they are probably included among the eighty-two aspects of meditative stability listed in Dondrub Lhagyal et al., *Dictionary of Bon Culture,* p. 199. The latter comprise sixteen aspects of the meditative stability of nothing at all (*ci yang ma yin pa'i ting nge 'dzin la bcu drug*), sixteen aspects of the meditative stability of the real nature (*de bzhin nyid kyi ting nge 'dzin la bcu drug*), sixteen aspects of the meditative stability of complete perfection (*yongs su rdzogs pa'i ting nge 'dzin la bcu drug*), sixteen aspects of the meditative stability of total illumination (*kun tu snang gi ting nge 'dzin la bcu drug*), and sixteen aspects of the meditative stability of emanational basis (*sprul pa rgyu yi ting nge 'dzin la bcu drug*), with the addition of the unimpeded meditative stability (*thogs pa med pa'i ting nge 'dzin*) and the nonapprehending meditative stability (*ma dmigs pa'i ting nge 'dzin*). According to Chogyal Namkhai Norbu, *Light of Kailash,* p. 394, the *Immaculate Splendor* does refer to the "sixty aspects of meditative stability," without listing them.

The sixteen signs (*rtags bcu drug*) have not yet been sourced, but may possibly parallel the sixteen signs of success on the Buddhist path of insight (*mthong lam gyi rtags bcu drug*), otherwise known as the sixteen moments of cognition and receptiveness on the path of insight (*mthong lam shes bzod skad cig bcu drug*). Alternatively, they may be conflated with the signs of meditative realization, outlined in the Buddhist tantras (fireflies, smoke, etc.). Chogyal Namkhai Norbu, *Light of Kailash,* pp. 394–95, cites the *Immaculate Splendor,* suggesting that these may denote the feeling of warmth and reaching the limit in the experience of emptiness (*stong pa'i nyams la drod dang tshad 'byung*), and supernormal mastery over the four elements. This approach was established by Yewang Gyalpo (*ye dbang rgyal po*).

425. The three perspectives (*lta gsum*) comprise the nature of phenomena (*bon*), reality (*bon nyid*), and awareness (*rig pa*). See Achard 2005–2010, vol. 4, p. 108.

Our text misreads *lha gsum* ("three deities"). Chogyal Namkhai Norbu, *Light of Kailash,* p. 395, suggests that the alternative reading *lha gsum* could denote deities propitiated in the three lower vehicles who are here perfected in ultimate reality.

426. Tse-me Oden (*tshad med 'od ldan*) and Trulshen Nangden (*'phrul gshen snang ldan*) are the fourth and fifth lineage holders of the Aural Lineage of Zhang-zhung (*zhang zhung snyan brgyud*), immediately following Shenrab Miwoche. See Tenzin Wangyal 2004, 210.

427. According to Jowo Lhundrub Tashi and Menrampa Lobzang Chodrak, *Biographies of Yutokpa the Younger and the Older,* pp. 58–65, the Indian physicians Biji Gaje (*bi byi*) and Bilhama Gadze (*bi lha ma*) were born to the ruler of Padmagarbha and his two wives, who were a drum maker and a bell maker. Their mothers offered ten drums and ten bells to the Mahābodhi Stūpa at Vajrāsana. After studying medicine in Takṣaśīla under the renowned physician Atreya, they themselves became known as the king and queen of medicine. They then journeyed through India, China, Nepal, and Central Asia, visiting Tibet during the reign of Lhatotori Nyentsen. The narrative is also found in Sangye Gyatso, *Survey of the Medical Tradition,* on which, see Kilty 2010, 193–98; also Gyatso and Havnevik 2005, 170. The son of Biji and princess Lhacham Yidkyi Rolcha was Dungi Torchokchen, who is said to have mastered pulse palpation, pharmacology, moxibustion, bloodletting, and the treatment of wounds, and who served as a royal physician for two reigns. His descendants, in turn, formed both a familial "son" lineage (*bu rgyud*) and a "royal" lineage (*rgyal rgyud*), maintaining the role of royal physician for four generations.

428. Yutok Yonten Gonpo the Elder (708–833) was born at Tolung Kyina as the son of Yutok Khyungpo Dorje and Gyapa Chokyi Dolma, within the line descended from Dungi Torchokchen. During the reign of Me Agtsom, he became supreme among the nine eminent physicians of Tibet, and he maintained this role during the reign of King Trisong Detsen. Tibet's first medical institute, Sudarśana (*lta na sdug*), was founded by him at Menlung in 763. See Jowo Lhundrub Tashi and Menrampa Lobzang Chodrak, *Biographies of Yutokpa the Younger and the Older,* pp. 66–315.

429. The traditional account of the translation and concealment of the *Four Tantras* by Vairotsana and their discovery at Samye by Drapa Ngonshe in 1038 is recounted in several sources, e.g., Dudjom Rinpoche 1991, 1:753–54. Contemporary scholars recognize that the *Four Tantras* were redacted in their present form by Yutok Yonten Gonpo the Younger (c. 1128–1201). On this see Yang Ga 2014, 154–77.

430. On the descendants of Yutok Yonten Gonpo the Elder, including his son Bumseng, see Jowo Lhundrub Tashi and Menrampa Lobzang Chodrak, *Biographies of Yutokpa the Younger and the Older,* pp. 307ff.

431. This is the *Eighteen Branches of Medical Science,* composed by Yutok Yonten Gonpo the Younger, concerning the *Four Tantras.*

432. See above, *DGD* (p. 565).

433. Douglas and Bays 1978, pt. 2, canto 85, pp. 511–12.
434. These works are listed and elucidated in ibid., pt. 1, pp. 227–30. On the transmission and content of elemental divination in particular, see Dorje 2001.
435. See the traditional account in Dudjom Rinpoche 1991, 1:508–9.
436. On the legacy of Thonmi Sambhoṭa, see Jamgon Kongtrul's comments in Dorje 2012, 120, 251–53, and 782n472. Only two of his eight grammatical treatises are extant, the *Thirty Verses* and the *Introduction to Gender.*
437. The construction, history, and layout of the Rasa Trulnang Temple, along with the diverse anecdotes associated with the two highly revered images of Jowo Śākyamuni, is detailed in Dorje, Tsering, Stoddard, and Alexander 2010.
438. The construction and enumeration of the twelve main geomantic temples and the 108 subsidiary temples of the "district controlling" class (*ru gnon*), the "border taming" class (*mtha' 'dul*) and the "further taming" class (*yang 'dul*) are discussed in Aris 1979, 3–41; Sorensen 1994; Hazod, Sorensen, and Sensen 2005; and Mills 2007.
439. A traditional account of Songtsen Gampo's reign can be found in Shakabpa 1967, 25–29. On the legal system introduced by King Songtsen Gampo and his adroit minister Gar, see Uray 1972 and Kapstein 2006, 60–61. The ten virtuous actions (*dge bcu'i khrims*) include physical actions of abstention from killing, stealing, and sexual misconduct; verbal actions of abstention from falsehood, slander, irresponsible chatter, and verbal abuse; and the mental actions of abstention from covetousness, vindictiveness, and wrong views.
440. On the composition and anachronisms of the *Collected Words of the King concerning the Mantra* OṂ MAṆI PADME HŪṂ, see Martin 1997, no. 16; see also Kapstein 1992; Mills 2007. The work has been translated in Trizin Tsering Rinpoche 2007.
441. The establishment of Buddhism in Tibet and the translation activities undertaken during the reign of Trisong Detsen by all the renowned figures mentioned here are outlined in Dudjom Rinpoche 1991, 1:512–29, 533–40, 554–56, 601–6. See also Shakabpa 1967, 34–46; Kapstein 2006, 66–75.
442. For a description of Samye Monastery and the adjacent hermitages of Chimphu, see Dorje 2009, 208–18.
443. That is to say, the early translations are divided according to the ancient tripiṭaka division of the texts on monastic discipline (*vinaya, 'dul ba*), phenomenology (*abhidharma, mngon pa*), and discourses (*sūtra, mdo sde*), the last of which, by extension, includes the tantras (*rgyud sde*).
444. Dudjom Rinpoche 1991, 1:515.
445. Ibid., 1:524–25. For a contemporary description of Achung Namdzong, see Dorje 2009, 721–23.
446. The transmission of these distinct vinaya lineages is recounted in Roerich 1949, 74–101.
447. Dudjom Rinpoche 1991, 1:526.
448. Concerning the distinctions between the "higher" phenomenology of Asaṅga,

Compendium, and the "lower" phenomenology of Vasubandhu, *Treasury,* see Jamgon Kongtrul's convenient presentation in Dorje 2012, 476–548.

449. It is generally held that fewer first-turning sūtras were translated into Tibetan, with the focus of early and later translators being on the sūtras of the intermediate promulgation that emphasize emptiness and those of the third promulgation that emphasize the development of enlightened attributes. According to Pekar Zangpo, *Structure of the Sūtras,* this distinction may be based on volume rather than the precise number of texts; for there are 83 first-turning sūtras listed, in contrast to the 33 extensive second-turning sūtras, and 153 third-turning sūtras (plus the eight chapters of the *Great Bounteousness of the Buddhas* and the fifty chapters of the *Pagoda of Precious Gems*).
450. Dudjom Rinpoche 1991, 1:526–27.
451. Unfortunately, it appears that none of these manuscripts are extant at the present day, although they may have been formerly preserved in Lhasa and at Chimphu, as stated here.
452. *DGD* (p. 790) refers to this treatise as the *Nyi snang ba,* but see Zhuchen Tsultrim Rinchen, *Catalogue of the Tengyur,* p. 775, where the correct title is given as *Nyi khri snang ba.*
453. The seventeen "mother and child" discourses of this genre are discussed in Conze 1960.
454. On this composition of Śāntarakṣita, see Dorje 2014, 136–40.
455. See Dudjom Rinpoche 1991, 1:513ff.; on the various listings of the eight classes of Tibetan gods and demons (*bod kyi lha srin sde brgyad*), see ibid., 2:158–59.
456. Ibid., 1:534–37.
457. The eighteen tantra sections of Mahāyoga are all contained in Dg. NGB vols. 9–14, and the texts representing the classes of means for attainment (*sgrub sde brgyad*) pertaining to the eight meditational deities—namely, Yamāntaka, Hayagrīva, Viśuddha, Vajrāmṛta, Vajrakīla, Mātaraḥ, Lokastotrapūja, and Vajramantrabhiru, are contained in vols. 14–25.
458. These texts are similarly contained in Dg. NGB, those representing Anuyoga in vols. 7–8 and those representing Atiyoga in vols. 1–6.
459. These are the particular ceremonies commemorating the deeds of Guru Padmākara, held on the tenth day of each lunar month.
460. Douglas and Bays 1978, pt. 2, canto 84, p. 517.
461. On these activities of King Mutri Tsenpo, also known as Tri Desongtsen, see Shakabpa 1967, 46–49; Kapstein 2006, 75–77.
462. On the reign of Tri Relpachen, see Shakabpa 1967, 49–51; Kapstein 2006, 76–80.
463. Smṛtijñānakīrti was active in Tibet during the late tenth and early eleventh centuries, prior to Rinchen Zangpo. See Dudjom Rinpoche 1991, 1:11.
464. Dragyur Ling in Samye, on which see Dorje 2009, 214.
465. *DGD* (p. 792) reads Dharmaśīla again.
466. On these seventeen primary and secondary texts of definitive meaning (*nges don yab sras bdu bdun*), see above n. 453.

467. *DGD* (p. 793) here reads *'dul ba lung bzhi* for *'dul ba lung gzhi.*
468. *DGD* (p. 793) here reads *lung bzhi'i stod cha* for *lung gzhi'i stod cha.*
469. Orgyan Lingpa, *Injunction of the Minister,* p. 503, reads *mdo bzhi dems dang lnga bka' bstsal nas,* and then proceeds to list these texts as Dg. NGB vol. 7, nos. 1 and 3, and vol. 8, nos. 1–2, along with the key text Dg. NGB. vol. 7, no. 2. However, the translators of these texts are usually named as Vimalamitra, Chokrolui Gyaltsen, Dharmabodhi, Chetsenkye, and Vairotsana.
470. Douglas and Bays 1978, pt. 2, canto 84, pp. 503–4.
471. Ibid., canto 87, pp. 532–34.
472. *DGD* (p. 796) misreads Śāntideva.
473. It is unclear to me what the *Three Vows* (*trisaṃvara, sdom gsum*) would suggest in the context of the treatises of Asaṅga, other than being a reference to the divisions of the *Yogacaryā Level.* Extant commentaries on the three vows (*prātimokṣa, bodhisattva,* and *mantra*) in the Tengyur appear to have been composed after the early translation period, judging by the dates of their authors. Nor is it likely to refer to the first sūtra of the *Ratnakūṭa* (T 45)—the *Trisaṃvaranirdeśaparivarta.*
474. Douglas and Bays 1978, pt. 2, canto 88, pp. 535–38.
475. The mnemonic incantations of awareness (*vidyādhāraṇī, rig pa'i gzungs sngags*) are contained in the section of the Tibetan canon, known as the *Compilation of Mnemonic Incantations* (*gZungs 'dus*), T 846–1107.
476. According to Mahāyoga (Jamgon Mipham Gyatso, *Nucleus of Inner Radiance,* pp. 204–6, and Dharmachakra Translation Committee 2009, 124–26), there are outer offerings consisting of songs of praise, dance, desirable resources, sacramental substances, burnt offerings, and the like. Inner offerings comprise the specific sacraments of nectar, blood, and torma cakes (*sman rak gtor ma*), as well as the subtle body with its network of energy channels, winds, and generative essences. The secret offerings are those associated with the rites of union and liberation (*sbyor sgrol*), as well as the transformations of the five poisons into the five pristine cognitions. Rites of union generate the experience of the four delights in their causal and fruitional phase when in union with a yogic partner. Rites of liberation compassionately transfer the consciousness of hostile beings to a higher realm in order to eliminate negative karma. See Dorje 2016, 430–36 on the rites of union and 436–40 on the rites of liberation.
477. On these subdivisions of the esoteric instructional class of the Great Perfection, including the cycle of the most secret vital essence (*yang gsang thig le'i skor*), see above, pp. 197–226.
478. Douglas and Bays 1978, pt. 2, canto 70, p. 415.
479. Dudjom Rinpoche 1991, 1:538–40.
480. These lineages of the mind class and space class of the Great Perfection are recounted in ibid., 1:540–53.
481. Ibid., 1:555–56.
482. The lives of the lineage holders of the *Innermost Spirituality of Vimalamitra,*

including Longchen Rabjam and his predecessors, are recounted in Dudjom Rinpoche 1991, 1:556–96.

483. On the life of Nyak Jñānakumāra, see ibid., 1:601–5.

484. Concerning this succession of Nub Sangye Senge, see ibid., 1:607–16.

485. The hagiographical accounts of the lives of the three generations of the Zur family, from Zurpoche through Zurchungpa and Drophukpa are presented in ibid., 1:617–49.

486. This transmission of the Nyingma oral teachings, otherwise known as the Rong tradition, is contrasted with the Kham tradition outlined in the next paragraph. For the biographies of these lineage holders, see ibid., 1:650–84.

487. Padmakara Translation Group 1999, 197. On the Kham tradition of the Nyingma oral teachings, which evolved at Katok Monastery, see Dudjom Rinpoche 1991, 1:688–99.

488. For a contemporary description of Katok Monastery, see Dorje 2009, 576–79.

489. The precise source of this passage is as yet unidentified.

490. There is a well-known listing of "nine treasure finders who were Lingpas" (*gter ston gling pa dgu*) that comprises Sangye Lingpa (center), Dorje Lingpa (east), Ratna Lingpa (south), Pema Lingpa (west), Karma Lingpa (north), and Orgyan Lingpa (southeast), along with Dezhin Samten Lingpa, Zhikpo Lingpa, and Kunkyong Lingpa, also known as Rinchen Ter-nying Lingpa. See Dungkar Lobzang Trinle, *Great Dictionary of Dungkar,* p. 968. I have not been able to determine the enumeration of the eleven authentic Lingpas (*yid dril gling pa bcu gcig/'khrul med gling pa bcu gcig*), but it does appear to include these nine; extant sources specify that Sangye Lingpa, Pema Lingpa, and Orgyan Zhikpo Lingpa belong to this group.

491. The five immaculate ones (*dri med lnga*) are known as the "heart sons of Guru Padmākara" (*padma'i thugs sras*)—namely, the treasure finders Drime Kunga, Drime Lhunpo, Drime Ozer, Drime Dorje, and Drime Tsultrim. See ibid., p. 1110.

492. The lives of these treasure finders (*gter ston*) are recounted by Jamgon Kongtrul in Yeshe Gyamtso 2011. See also Dudjom Rinpoche 1991, 1:750—881.

493. Both the oral teachings of the commentarial tradition (*bka' ma*) and the spiritual revelations (*gter ma*) are continuously expanding. The most extensive version of the former is compiled in 120 vols. by Khenpo Munsel and Khenpo Jamyang of Katok (NK). The latter is exemplified by Jamgon Kongtrul, *Anthology of Precious Revelations* (72 vols.).

494. See Jamgon Kongtrul's account of the transmission of the action and conduct tantras in Zangpo 2010, 272–73; see also Guarisco and McLeod 2005, 99–125.

495. For Jamgon Kongtrul's account of the transmission of the union tantras, see Zangpo 2010, 273–75; see also Guarisco and McLeod 2005, 127–40.

496. Zangpo 2010, 275.

497. Ibid.; see also Roerich 1949, 355.

498. The distinct traditions of Nāgārjuna and Jñānapāda are discussed in Roerich

1949, 356–74; Zangpo 2010, 276–89; and also Guarisco and McLeod 2008, 138–48.

499. Regarding the tradition of Go (*'gos lugs*), see Zangpo 2010, 277–78.
500. The tradition of Marpa (*mar lugs*) is mentioned in ibid., 277.
501. Concerning the tradition of Jowo (*jo bo'i lugs*), see ibid., 278.
502. On the tradition of Chak (*chags lugs*), see ibid.
503. Concerning the tradition of Paṇchen Śākyaśrī (*paṇ chen gyi lugs*), see ibid.
504. For these four traditions of Kham (*khams lugs*), Sakya (*sa lugs*), Ra Lotsawa (*rva lugs*), and Nyo Lotsāwa (*gnyos lugs*) that descend from Jñānapāda, see ibid. and Dudjom Rinpoche 1991, 1:464–66.
505. The transmission of the Yamāri tantras in Tibet is outlined in Roerich 1949, 374–80; see also Zangpo 2010, 289–92, and Guarisco and McLeod 2008, 148–52.
506. On the translation activity of Chokdru Lotsāwa Sherab Lama, see Zangpo 2010, 291.
507. The activity of Nagtsho Lotsāwa in translating these commentaries is mentioned in Roerich 1949, 373, and Zangpo 2010, 291.
508. The life of Rongzom Chozang is presented in Dudjom Rinpoche 1991, 1:703–9.
509. A similar passage is found in Zangpo 2010, 281. Among them, the group of four included Chel Lotsāwa (*dpyal lo*), Chopel Zangpo, Dānaśīla, Chak Lotsāwa, and Lobo Lotsāwa.
510. Roerich 1949, 374–79, emphasizes the contributions of Ra Lotsāwa to this transmission.
511. The traditions of Kyo (*skyo*) and Zhang (*zhang*) are mentioned in Zangpo 2010, 291.
512. On the tradition of Nyo (*gnyos*), see ibid., 292.
513. See Roerich 1949, 204–10; see also Guarisco and McLeod 2005, 179–82.
514. Guarisco and McLeod 2005, 183–87.
515. On the transmission of this cycle, see Roerich 1949, 380–90; Zangpo 2010, 286–300; Guarisco and McLeod 2005, 167–78.
516. Zangpo 2010, 296; Roerich 1949, 380–82.
517. On the activities of Marpa in relation to this cycle, see Zangpo 2010, 296; Roerich 1949, 382–86.
518. Zangpo 2010, 296.
519. Roerich 1949, 390–94; see also Zangpo 2010, 297.
520. On the transmission of the Vajravārāhī cycle, see Roerich 1949, 389–96.
521. Concerning these transmissions of the *Tantra of Hevajra* through the Sakya and Kagyu lineages, see Zangpo 2010, 301–3; Guarisco and McLeod 2008, 161–66.
522. The various transmissions of the *Tantra of the Wheel of Time* are discussed extensively in Roerich 1949, 753–838, and summarized in Zangpo 2010, 305–8. On its content, see Guarisco and McLeod 2008, 154–61. Specifically on the tradition of Gyijo (*gyi jo lugs*), see Roerich 1949, 755; Zangpo 2010, 305.

523. On the tradition of Dro Lotsāwa (*'bro lugs*), see Roerich 1949, 755–56; Zangpo 2010, 305–6.
524. On the tradition of Tsami (*rtsa mi'i lugs*), see Zangpo 2010, 305; Roerich 1949, 795–96.
525. On the tradition of Ra (*rva lugs*), see Roerich 1949, 789; Zangpo 2010, 305.
526. The traditions of Paṇchen Śākyaśrī (*paṇ chen lugs*), Chak Drachom (*chag lugs*), and Shawaripa are mentioned in Zangpo 2010, 306.
527. On this distinction, see Guarisco and McLeod 2008, 153–66.
528. Zangpo 2010, 306–7.
529. Most of the prophecies attributed to Padmasambhava that now follow may have derived originally from Ratna Lingpa's *Prophetic Declarations*. However, the language is rarely identical, suggesting an intermediate source, as yet unidentified. Other examples of this genre (*bstan pa'i spyi lung*) revealed by Namcho Migyur Dorje and Dudul Dorje are quite dissimilar. On this specific prediction pertaining to Atiśa, cf. Ratna Lingpa, *Prophetic Declarations,* p. 585, lines 5–6. The teachings of the Kadampa tradition are detailed in Jinpa 2008 and Jinpa 2013.
530. Presently unidentified.
531. Padmakara Translation Group 1999, 188–89.
532. This quotation is as yet unidentified.
533. For Jamgon Kongtrul's account of the Kadampa lineage, see Harding 2007, 97–111. Also see Jinpa 2008 and Jinpa 2013.
534. Padmakara Translation Group 1999, 189.
535. Cf. Ratna Lingpa, *Prophetic Declarations,* p. 586, lines 4–5.
536. This quotation is as yet unidentified.
537. Cf. the prophecy on Phagmodrupa in Ratna Lingpa, *Prophetic Declarations,* p. 586, line 5.
538. This quotation is as yet unidentified.
539. Compare this to the shorter prophecy in ibid., p. 587, lines 1–2.
540. Cf. the dissimilar prophecy on Tsangpa Gyare in ibid., p. 567, lines 3–4.
541. Cf. the prophecy on Karmapa Dusum Khyenpa in ibid., p. 586, line 6.
542. On the prophecies pertaining to Taklung Tangpa, Zhang Yudrakpa, Lingje Repa, cf. ibid., p. 587, lines 2–3. The prophecy pertaining to Gotsangpa has not yet been identified. On those pertaining to Karmapa Rangjung Dorje and the thirteen successors, cf. ibid., p. 594, line 6 and p. 596, lines 3–4, respectively.
543. The "four great pillars" (*ka chen bzhi*) who extensively propagated Marpa's teachings are Mila Repa, Ngoton Chodor of Zhung, Tsurton Wang-nge of Dol, and Meton Tsonpo of Tsangrong.
544. The three men from Kham (*khams pa mi gsum*) who were the foremost disciples of Gampopa are Phakmodrupa Dorje Gyalpo, Karmapa Dusum Khyenpa, and Selton Shogom. The first of these founded eight distinct lineages including those of Drigung, Druk, and Taklung; the second is the fountainhead of the Karma Kagyu; and the third founded the hermitage of Lho Miyel in Nangchen.

545. For Jamgon Kongtrul's account of the various Kagyu lineages, see Harding 2007, 137–231.
546. See ibid., 230–31.
547. Cf. the prophecy on Khyungpo Neljor and Mokchokpa in Ratna Lingpa, *Prophetic Declarations,* p. 587, line 4.
548. For Jamgon Kongtrul's account of the Shangpa Kagyu lineage, see Harding 2007, 233–58.
549. Cf. the shorter prophecy on Phadampa Sangye and Machik Labdron in Ratna Lingpa, *Prophetic Declarations,* p. 586, lines 2–3.
550. The four "lion" disciples to whom the lineage descended (*bka' babs seng bu bzhi*) appear to be the lineage holders of Machik Labdron bearing the name Senge ("lion"). They include Khugom Cho-seng, Senge Dorje, Yeshe Senge, and Punyon Senge, on whom see Harding 2003, 208–10.
551. On Pacification and Severance, see Harding 2007, 255–88; Harding 2016; Roerich 1949, 867–999.
552. On Drokmi Śākya Yeshe, cf. the terse prophecy found in Ratna Lingpa, *Prophetic Declarations,* p. 596, line 3.
553. Padmakara Translation Group 1999, 189.
554. Cf. the prophecy in Ratna Lingpa, *Prophetic Declarations,* p. 588, line 1.
555. The text here reads *bdun rgyud* ("sevenfold lineage") but could it not be *gdung brgyud* ("familial lineage")?
556. On the five founders of Sakya and their lineages, see Harding 2007, 113–35.
557. Cf. the prophecies on Zangkar Lotsāwa, Trophu Lotsāwa, Yagde Paṇchen, Orgyanpa, and Ngok in Ratna Lingpa, *Prophetic Declarations,* p. 595, line 6–p. 596, line 3; and on Bodongpa, p. 596, lines 5–6.
558. Cf. the Jonangpa prophecy in ibid., p. 597, line 1.
559. Padmakara Translation Group 1999, 190.
560. This quotation is as yet unidentified.
561. This oft-cited prediction is found in the *Collected Works of Jowoje Palden Atiśa,* vol. 1, p. 296.
562. This prophetic dialogue is found in the *Secret Biography Entitled Dispelling the Darkness of Misconceptions,* in the *Collected Works of Lhodrak Namkha Gyaltsen,* vol. 1, p. 141.
563. For a description of the Great Prayer Festival of Lhasa (*lha sa'i smon lam chen mo*), see Dorje, Tsering, Stoddard, and Alexander 2010, 15–17.
564. A narrative recounting the history of Ganden, commencing with Gyaltsab and Khedrub, can be found in Jarigpa Lobzang Namgyal, *Concise Biographies of the Successive Throneholders of Ganden.* For a contemporary description of Ganden, see Dorje 2009, 170–73.
565. The seminal history of the Geluk tradition is contained in Sangye Gyatso, *Yellow Beryl.* On the lives of the successive Dalai Lamas, see Mullin 2001.
566. Padmakara Translation Group 1999, 190.
567. The discussion presented in this chapter accords with the Fifth Dalai Lama,

Precious Chariot Steering the Treasury of Phenomenology, which is contained in his *Collected Works,* vol. 17, pp. 393–663. This specific paragraph derives verbatim from that work, pp. 401–2.

568. Tib. *mtshan nyid der thal| mtshon bya de'i phyir|*. The expression "taking x as the subject for discussion" (*chos can*) is a stock phrase that introduces any logical argument. In the pages that follow, the most commonplace example is "taking knowable phenomena as the subject for discussion" (*shes bya chos can*).
569. The ten material elements (*gzugs can khams bcu po*) comprise the sense organ of the eye and sights, the sense organ of the ear and sounds, the sense organ of the nose and odors, the sense organ of the tongue and tastes, and the sense organ of the body (or genitalia) and tangibles. The five elements of consciousness (*rnam shes kyi khams lnga*) comprise visual, auditory, olfactory, gustatory, and tactile consciousness.
570. Vasubandhu, *Treasury of Phenomenology,* ch. 1, v. 40; TPD, vol. 79, p. 7. See the translation in Pruden 1988–90, 112.
571. Vasubandhu, *Autocommentary on the Treasury of Phenomenology,* ch. 1, v. 4; TPD, vol. 79, p. 69, lines 3–4. See Pruden 1988–90, 58–59.
572. On the distinctions between these three sorts of unconditioned phenomena, see Jamgon Kongtrul's explanation in Dorje 2012, 536.
573. The four aspects of renunciation (*spangs pa bzhi po*) are those that arise through seeing the four noble truths. If they were all substantially identical, they would all be obtained simultaneously when renunciation occurs through seeing the truth of suffering and there would be no need to cultivate the others. The *Autocommentary on the Treasury of Phenomenology* (Pruden 1988–90, 59–60) emphasizes that each instance of this cessation is substantially distinct, and that there are a multiplicity of such instances.
574. Jamgon Kongtrul points out (Dorje 2012, 536) that this may be exemplified by the nonarising of other modes of consciousness when visual consciousness is distracted by sights. The foregoing paragraphs derive verbatim from the Fifth Dalai Lama, *Precious Chariot Steering the Treasury of Phenomenology,* pp. 402–43.
575. The structure presented here and the logical examinations that follow derive verbatim from *Precious Chariot Steering the Treasury of Phenomenology,* pp. 404ff. However, only the first of these two topics is discussed in Choying Tobden Dorje's extract.
576. The latter is not discussed in Choying Tobden Dorje's extract.
577. The latter is not discussed in Choying Tobden Dorje's extract.
578. Vasubandhu, *Treasury of Phenomenology,* ch. 1, v. 28; TPD, vol. 79, p. 4. See Pruden 1988–90, 61.
579. Only sights are said to be visibly revealed (*sanidarśana, bstan yod*), whereas sounds are classed as unrevealed, or not visibly revealed. See Dorje 2012, 852n57.
580. Vasubandhu, *Treasury of Phenomenology,* ch. 1, v. 28; TPD, vol. 79, p. 6. See Pruden 1988–90, 90.

581. The vows of individual liberation (*so thar gyi sdom pa*) are said to derive from some of the primary elements. On this see Pruden 1988–90, 570.
582. Vasubandhu, *Treasury of Phenomenology,* ch. 1, v. 14; TPD, vol. 79, p. 4. See Pruden 1988–90, 72. The ten material sense fields include five inner sense fields (*nang gi skye mched lnga*)—namely, those of the eye, ear, nose, tongue, and body, and five outer sense fields (*phyi'i skye mched lnga*)—namely, those of sights, sounds, odors, tastes, and tangibles. The nonmaterial sense fields of the mental faculty (*yid kyi skye mched*) and of mental phenomena (*chos kyi skye mched*) are excluded. Similarly, the ten material sensory elements (*gzugs can gyi khams bcu*) include those of the five material sense organs (*dbang po gzugs can lnga'i khams*) and those of the five physical sense objects (*yul gzugs can lnga'i khams*).
583. The eighteen sensory elements (*aṣṭadaśadhātu, khams bco brgyad*) comprise the six internal sensory elements (*nang gi khams drug*), from the eyes to the mental faculty; the six external sensory elements (*phyi'i khams drug*), from sights to mental phenomena; and the six cognizant sensory elements (*rnam par shes pa'i khams drug*), from visual consciousness to mental consciousness.
584. This reading follows the *Precious Chariot Steering the Treasury of Phenomenology,* p. 405, line 1, whereas our text reads *de mtshungs kyi dbang po,* suggesting a form resembling one with a shared support. On this distinction, see Dorje 2012, 484, and 852n59.
585. Vasubandhu, *Treasury of Phenomenology,* ch. 1, v. 30; TPD, vol. 79, p. 6. See Pruden 1988–90, 93–95.
586. See Engle 2009, 258–59, especially n. 90. Sounds produced from organically retained elements include human language and the clapping of hands. Sounds produced from elements that are not organically retained include the whistling of the wind, the rustling of trees, and the flowing of water. Sounds produced from both elements that are organically retained and unretained include the sound of a musical instrument.
587. The sensory element of mental phenomena (*dharmadhātu, chos kyi khams*) has two parts—one comprising mental states (*sems byung*) that are in association with mind and have an object and the other mental states that are not in association with mind and do not have an object. See Pruden 1988–90, 98.
588. Vasubandhu, *Treasury of Phenomenology,* ch. 1, v. 34; TPD, vol. 79, p. 6. See Pruden 1988–90, 98–99. The nine material elements that may be either organically retained or unretained include the eye, ear, nose, tongue, body, sights, odors, tastes, and tangibles. This is because, in terms of the present, they are retained as a support by mind and mental states, and in terms of the past and future, they are unretained.
589. On form that is nonapperceived (*rnam par rig byed ma yin pa'i gzugs*), see above p. 88.
590. Vasubandhu, *Treasury of Phenomenology,* ch. 4, v. 13; TPD, vol. 79, p. 25. See Pruden 1988–90, 580.

591. Vasubandhu, *Treasury of Phenomenology,* ch. 1, v. 15; TPD, vol. 79, pp. 4–5. See Pruden 1988–90, 73–74.
592. On this hierarchy concerning the sensory elements in relation to the four meditative concentrations, see the fuller discussion in Pruden 1988–90, 125–29, based on Vasubandhu, *Treasury of Phenomenology,* ch. 1, v. 15; TPD, vol. 79, p. 7.
593. *DGD* (p. 816) and the *Precious Chariot Steering the Treasury of Phenomenology,* p. 405, line 1, both read *dus* ("temporal") for *'dus* ("conditioned"), purposefully conflating disparate etymologies.
594. Vasubandhu, *Treasury of Phenomenology,* ch. 1, v. 15; TPD, vol. 79, p. 4. See the discussion in Pruden 1988–90, 62.
595. Pruden 1988–90, 62.
596. The three modes of suffering (*sdug bsngal gsum po*) are suffering due to change (*'gyur ba'i sdug bsngal*), suffering due to past propensities (*'du byed kyi sdug bsngal*), and suffering due to pain itself (*sdug bsngal gyi sdug bsngal*).
597. Pruden 1988–90, 62–63.
598. Ibid., 63.
599. Ibid.
600. Yaśomitra, *Commentary on the Treasury of Phenomenology,* TPD, vol. 80, p. 55.
601. On all these five categories of sense object, see the discussion in Pruden 1988–90, 64–67.
602. Ibid., 67–68.
603. *DGD* (p. 819) reads *dgos dpyod* for *dogs dpyod*, but see the *Precious Chariot Steering the Treasury of Phenomenology,* p. 410.
604. Pruden 1988–90, 69–70.
605. This rule concerning elision of the technical marker *-ḍu* to form the particular inflection (*khyad par gyi don*) *-ṭu* is found in Nandakīrti, *Elucidation of Words with Terminations such as –ti,* TPD, vol. 120, p. 986. On the application of elision in Sanskrit, see Jamyang Gyatso, *Explanation of Elision.*
606. This rule concerning elision of the technical marker *-ñ* to form a dual termination occurs in Nandakīrti, *Elucidation of Words with Terminations such as –ti,* TPD, vol. 120, p. 984.
607. This rule is found in Pāṇini, *Uṇādi-sūtra* 1.69; see also Trorum Tsenam, *Tsandra byā ka ra ṇṇ'i uṇ'i mdo,* in *Commentary on the Grammar of Sārasvata,* p. 343.
608. This rule is similar in function to Pāṇini 3.1.134.
609. Pruden 1988–90, 69–70.
610. Ibid., 154–59.
611. The point here (ibid., 72) is that feelings of happiness, unhappiness, and neutrality are not inherent in the sense organs but arise from contact with the sense organs. There are also those that arise from contact with the mental faculty.
612. Faith may or may not coincide with the path.
613. On the aggregate of feelings, see Engle 2009, 267–71 and Dorje 2012, 485–86.
614. On the aggregate of perceptions, see Engle 2009, 271–72 and Dorje 2012, 486–88.

615. On the aggregate of formative predispositions, see Engle 2009, 273–326 and Dorje 2012, 488–511.
616. Vasubandhu, *Treasury of Phenomenology,* TPD, vol. 79, pp. 4–5. See Pruden 1988–90, 73–74.
617. Vasubandhu, *Treasury of Phenomenology,* TPD, vol. 79, p. 5. See Pruden 1988–90, 74–75. On the aggregate of consciousness, see Engle 2009, 327–46 and Dorje 2012, 511–30.
618. Vasubandhu, *Treasury of Phenomenology,* TPD, vol. 79, p. 5. See Pruden 1988–90, 74–75.
619. Vasubandhu, *Treasury of Phenomenology,* TPD, vol. 79, p. 5. See Pruden 1988–90, 75.
620. Vasubandhu, *Treasury of Phenomenology,* TPD, vol. 79, p. 5. See Pruden 1988–90, 75.
621. Vasubandhu, *Treasury of Phenomenology,* TPD, vol. 79, p. 5. See Pruden 1988–90, 76.
622. Vasubandhu, *Treasury of Phenomenology,* TPD, vol. 79, p. 5. See Pruden 1988–90, 76–77.
623. Vasubandhu, *Treasury of Phenomenology,* TPD, vol. 79, p. 5. See Pruden 1988–90, 77–80.
624. *DGD* (p. 822) again reads *dgos dpyod* for *dogs dpyod.*
625. That is to say, mental states are most elaborately elucidated in the context of the aggregates, material phenomena in the context of the sense fields, and both mind and matter in the context of the sensory elements.
626. The aggregates are explained for those of superior acumen, the sense fields for those of mediocre acumen, and the sensory elements for those of lesser acumen. Vasubandhu, *Treasury of Phenomenology,* TPD, vol. 79, p. 5. See Pruden 1988–90, 80.
627. Vasubandhu, *Treasury of Phenomenology,* TPD, vol. 79, p. 5. See Pruden 1988–90, 81.
628. Vasubandhu, *Treasury of Phenomenology,* TPD, vol. 79, p. 5. See Pruden 1988–90, 81–82.
629. Vasubandhu, *Treasury of Phenomenology,* TPD, vol. 79, p. 5. See Pruden 1988–90, 82–83.
630. Vasubandhu, *Treasury of Phenomenology,* TPD, vol. 79, p. 5. See Pruden 1988–90, 83.
631. Vasubandhu, *Treasury of Phenomenology,* TPD, vol. 79, p. 5. See Pruden 1988–90, 84.
632. Vasubandhu, *Treasury of Phenomenology,* TPD, vol. 79, p. 5. See Pruden 1988–90, 84–85.
633. Vasubandhu, *Treasury of Phenomenology,* TPD, vol. 79, p. 5. See Pruden 1988–90, 85.
634. Vasubandhu, *Treasury of Phenomenology,* TPD, vol. 79, p. 5. See Pruden 1988–90, 86.

635. Vasubandhu, *Treasury of Phenomenology,* TPD, vol. 79, p. 5. See Pruden 1988–90, 86.
636. Vasubandhu, *Treasury of Phenomenology,* TPD, vol. 79, p. 5. See Pruden 1988–90, 86–87.
637. Vasubandhu, *Treasury of Phenomenology,* TPD, vol. 79, p. 6. See Pruden 1988–90, 87–88.
638. Vasubandhu, *Treasury of Phenomenology,* TPD, vol. 79, p. 6. See Pruden 1988–90, 88–89.
639. Vasubandhu, *Treasury of Phenomenology,* TPD, vol. 79, p. 6. See Pruden 1988–90, 90.
640. Vasubandhu, *Treasury of Phenomenology,* TPD, vol. 79, p. 6. See Pruden 1988–90, 90–91.
641. Vasubandhu, *Treasury of Phenomenology,* TPD, vol. 79, p. 6. See Pruden 1988–90, 90.
642. Vasubandhu, *Treasury of Phenomenology,* TPD, vol. 79, p. 8. See Pruden 1988–90, 90–91 and 102–3.
643. Vasubandhu, *Treasury of Phenomenology,* TPD, vol. 79, p. 6. See Pruden 1988–90, 90.
644. Vasubandhu, *Treasury of Phenomenology,* TPD, vol. 79, p. 6. See Pruden 1988–90, 92.
645. Vasubandhu, *Treasury of Phenomenology,* TPD, vol. 79, p. 6. See Pruden 1988–90, 92–95.
646. Vasubandhu, *Treasury of Phenomenology,* TPD, vol. 79, p. 6. See Pruden 1988–90, 95–96.
647. Vasubandhu, *Treasury of Phenomenology,* TPD, vol. 79, p. 6. See Pruden 1988–90, 96–97.
648. Although frequently quoted, the exact source has not yet been identified.
649. Vasubandhu, *Treasury of Phenomenology,* TPD, vol. 79, p. 6. See Pruden 1988–90, 97–98.
650. Vasubandhu, *Treasury of Phenomenology,* TPD, vol. 79, p. 6. See Pruden 1988–90, 98.
651. Vasubandhu, *Treasury of Phenomenology,* TPD, vol. 79, p. 6. See Pruden 1988–90, 98–99.
652. Vasubandhu, *Treasury of Phenomenology,* TPD, vol. 79, p. 6. See Pruden 1988–90, 99–101.
653. Vasubandhu, *Autocommentary on the Treasury of Phenomenology,* TPD, vol. 79, p. 157. See Pruden 1988–90, 185.
654. The eight substances (*rdzas brgyad*) comprise sights, sounds, tastes, tangibles, earth, water, fire, and wind.
655. Pūrṇavardhana, *Pursuit of Defining Characteristics,* TPD, vol. 81, p. 335, where the same verses refer to the world system of desire (*'dod na*) instead of the world system of form (*gzugs na*), as indicated in the *Treasury of Phenomenology,* TPD, vol. 79, p. 10; Pruden 1988–90, 185.

656. Vasubandhu, *Treasury of Phenomenology,* TPD, vol. 79, p. 7. See Pruden 1988–90, 102–3.
657. Vasubandhu, *Treasury of Phenomenology,* TPD, vol. 79, p. 7. See Pruden 1988–90, 103.
658. Vasubandhu, *Treasury of Phenomenology,* TPD, vol. 79, p. 7. See Pruden 1988–90, 103.
659. Vasubandhu, *Treasury of Phenomenology,* TPD, vol. 79, p. 7. See Pruden 1988–90, 104.
660. Vasubandhu, *Treasury of Phenomenology,* TPD, vol. 79, p. 7. See Pruden 1988–90, 103–5.
661. Vasubandhu, *Treasury of Phenomenology,* TPD, vol. 79, p. 7. See Pruden 1988–90, 105.
662. Vasubandhu, *Treasury of Phenomenology,* TPD, vol. 79, p. 7. See Pruden 1988–90, 105.
663. On this discussion, see Vasubandhu, *Treasury of Phenomenology,* TPD, vol. 79, p. 7; Pruden 1988–90, 106–7.
664. Vasubandhu, *Treasury of Phenomenology,* TPD, vol. 79, p. 7. See Pruden 1988–90, 107–8.
665. Vasubandhu, *Treasury of Phenomenology,* TPD, vol. 79, p. 7. See Pruden 1988–90, 108–11.
666. Vasubandhu, *Treasury of Phenomenology,* TPD, vol. 79, p. 7. See Pruden 1988–90, 111–13.
667. The eight sorts of vision therefore include the five erroneous views (*lta ba lnga*), namely (1) the notional view of the self; (2) the view of eternalism and nihilism; (3) the view that denigrates the noble truths; (4) the view that overesteems lower views; and (5) the view that upholds false causes or paths. See Pruden 1988–90, 776ff. In addition, there are (6) the genuine view of mundane beings (*'jig rten pa'i yang dag pa'i lta ba*) or ordinary persons who employ discernment, though impure; (7) the view associated with the paths of learning (*slob pa'i lta ba*); and (8) the view associated with the path of no-more-learning (*mi slob pa'i lta ba*), which is that of an arhat. See Pruden 1988–90, 113–14.
668. This is because they are bare sense consciousnesses (*dbang shes*).
669. Vasubandhu, *Treasury of Phenomenology,* TPD, vol. 79, p. 7. See Pruden 1988–90, 114–18.
670. Vasubandhu, *Treasury of Phenomenology,* TPD, vol. 79, p. 7. See Pruden 1988–90, 118–22.
671. Vasubandhu, *Treasury of Phenomenology,* TPD, vol. 79, p. 7. See Pruden 1988–90, 124–26.
672. Vasubandhu, *Treasury of Phenomenology,* TPD, vol. 79, p. 7. See Pruden 1988–90, 126–29.
673. Vasubandhu, *Treasury of Phenomenology,* TPD, vol. 79, p. 8. See Pruden 1988–90, 129.

674. Vasubandhu, *Treasury of Phenomenology,* TPD, vol. 79, p. 8. See Pruden 1988–90, 130.
675. Vasubandhu, *Treasury of Phenomenology,* TPD, vol. 79, p. 8. See Pruden 1988–90, 130–31. The five feelings comprise happiness, unhappiness, satisfaction, dissatisfaction, and indifference. The five faculties comprise faith, perseverance, recollection, meditative stability, and discriminative awareness. The three powers of purification (*rnam byang gi dbang po gsum*) comprise the power of comprehending the unknown (*anājñātamājñāsyāmīndriya, mi shes pa kun shes par byed pa'i dbang po*), the power of comprehension (*ājñendriya, kun shes pa'i dbang po*), and the power endowed with comprehension (*ājñātāvindriya, kun shes pa dang ldan pa'i dbang po*).
676. *DGD* (p. 772) reads *ldog pa* ("counterpart") for *rtogs pa* ("realization").
677. *DGD* (p. 772) and the Root Verses both read "supported phenomena" (*brtan pa'i chos*), whereas Longchen Rabjam, *Treasury of Philosophical Systems,* p. 275, reads "imputed phenomena" (*brtags pa'i chos*).
678. *DGD* (p. 779), follows Longchen Rabjam, *Treasury of Philosophical Systems,* p. 286, in reading "reality" (*chos nyid*) for "defining characteristic" (*mtshan nyid*), but see Dudjom Rinpoche 1991, 1:351.
679. See *DGD,* p. 565.

Bibliography

Bibliographical references for this volume are presented in seven alphabetically arranged sections: (1) Vinaya Scriptures; (2) Sūtra and Tantra; (3) Indic Treatises; (4) Tibetan Treatises and Spiritual Revelations; (5) Chinese Divination Texts; (6) Non-Buddhist Indic Sources; and (7) Works in Other Languages.

1. Vinaya Scriptures

Analysis [of Monastic Discipline for Monks]
Vinayavibhaṅga
['Dul ba] rnam 'byed
Dg.K. 'Dul ba vols. CA, f. 21a–NYA, f. 269a; KPD, vol. 5, p. 62–vol. 8, p. 634; T 3.

Analysis [of Monastic Discipline for Nuns]
Bhikṣuṇīvinayavibhaṅga
['Dul ba] rnam 'byed
Dg.K. 'Dul ba vols. TA, ff. 25b–328a; KPD, vol. 9, pp. 72–784; T 5.

Four Great Scriptural Transmissions of Monastic Discipline
'Dul ba lung chen sde bzhi
Dg.K. 'Dul ba vols. KA–PA (1–13); KPD, vols. 1–13; T 1–7.

Ground Rules of Monastic Discipline
Vinayavastu
'Dul ba gzhi
Dg.K. 'Dul ba vols. KA–NGA; KPD, vols. 1–4; T 1.

Minor Transmissions [of Monastic Discipline]
Vinayakṣudrakavastu (also: Kṣudrāgama)
'Dul ba lung phreng tshegs kyi gzhi
Dg.K. 'Dul ba vols. THA–DA; KPD, vol. 10, p. 3–vol. 11, p. 805; T 6.

Supreme Scripture [of Monastic Discipline]
Vinayottaragrantha
['Dul ba'i lung] gzhung bla ma
Dg.K. 'Dul ba vols. NA, f. 1b–BA, f. 313a; KPD, vol. 12, p. 3–vol. 13, p. 733; T 7.

Sūtra of the Vows of Individual Liberation [for Monks]
Prātimokṣasūtra
So sor thar pa'i mdo
Dg.K. 'Dul ba vol. CA, ff. 1b–20b; KPD, vol. 5, pp. 3–60; T 2.

Sūtra of the Vows of Individual Liberation [for Nuns]
Bhikṣuṇīprātimokṣasūtra
dGe slong ma'i so sor thar pa'i mdo
Dg.K. 'Dul ba vol. TA, ff. 1b–25a; KPD, vol. 9, pp. 3–61; T 4.

2. Sūtra and Tantra

Array of Indestructible Reality
rDo rje bkod pa
See *Sūtra That Gathers All Enlightened Intentions*

Attainment of the Single Hero
Siddhaikavīra nāma-mahātantra
dPa' bo gcig bu sgrub pa zhes bya ba'i rgyud
Dg.K. rGyud vol. PA, ff.1b–13a; KPD, vol. 89, pp. 3–44; T 544.

Burning Mass of Flames
Me dpung 'bar ba
NL

Chiti [Yoga]
sPyi ti [yo ga]
A collective name for the second tier of tantras belonging to the Esoteric Instructional Class (*man ngag gi sde*) of the Great Perfection, which are contained in Dg. NGB vol. 2, nos. 12–22, and vol. 3, nos. 1–4.

Collection of Aphorisms [of the Arhat Dharmatrāta]
Udānavarga
Ched du brjod pa'i tshoms
Dg.K. mDo sde vol. SA, ff. 209a–253a; KPD, vol. 72, pp. 602–704; T 326.
Summarized in PZ, pp. 491–92. See Brough 2001.

Cycle of the All-Accomplishing King

Kun byed rgyal po'i skor

A collective name for the foremost tantras belonging to the Mind Class (*sems kyi sde*) of the Great Perfection, exemplified by *the Tantra of the All-Accomplishing King,* which are contained in Dg. NGB vol. 5, no. 24, and vol. 6, nos. 1–17.

Description of Transformations due to Past Actions

Karmavibhaṅga-nāma-dharmagrantha

Las kyi rnam par 'gyur ba zhes ba ba'i chos kyi gzhung (also known as Las rnams brjod pa)

Dg.K. mDo sde vol. SA, ff. 298b–310a; KPD, vol. 72, pp. 867–94; T 339.

Summarized in PZ, pp. 504–6.

Diamond Cutter

Āryavajracchedikā-nāma-prajñāpāramitāmahāyānasūtra

'Phags pa shes rab kyi pha rol tu phyin pa rdo rje gcod pa shes bya ba theg pa chen po'i mdo [short title: rDo rje gcod pa]

Dg.K. Shes phyin vol. KA, ff. 121a–132b; KPD, vol. 34, pp. 327–57; T 16.

Summarized in PZ, pp. 415–18. Translated in Red Pine 2001.

Distinction of Emptiness of Kāśyapa

'Od srungs stong pa rab 'byed

NL Cf. Dg.K. dKon brtsegs vol. CHA, ff. 119b–151b; KPD, vol. 44, pp. 332–409; T 87.

Eight Classes of Means for Attainment of Mahāyoga

Ma hā yo ga'i sgrub sde brgyad

These comprise (i) the cycle of Yamāntaka (*'Jam dpal gzhin rje gshad pa'i rgyud skor,* Dg. NGB vols. 15–17, Tingkye NGB vols. 20–22, T 838) also known as "Mañjuśrī, Indicative of Buddha Body" (*'Jam dpal sku*); (ii) the cycle of Hayagrīva/Aśvottama (*dPal rta mgrin padma dbang chen rta mchog rol pa'i rgyud sde rnams,* Dg. NGB vols. 17–18, Tingkye NGB vols. 23–24), also known as "Padma, Indicative of Buddha Speech" (*Padma gsung*); (iii) the cycle of Śrīheruka (*dPal yang dag thugs kyi rgyud sde rnams,* Dg. NGB vols. 18–19, Tingkye NGB vol. 25), also known as "Viśuddha, Indicative of Buddha Mind" (*Yang dag thugs*); (iv) the cycle of Vajrāmṛta (*'Chi med bdud rtsi yon tan gyi rgyud sde rnams,* Dg. NGB vols. 19–20, Tingkye NGB vol. 26, T 841), also known as "Amṛta, Indicative of Buddha Attributes" (*bDud rtsi yon tan*); (v) the cycle of Vajrakīla/Vajrakumāra (*bCom ldan 'das dpal rdo rje phur pa'i rgyud sde rnams,* Dg. NGB vols. 20–22, Tingkye NGB vols. 27–29), also known as "Kīla, Indicative of Buddha Activities" (*Phur pa phrin las*); (vi) the cycle of Mātaraḥ (*Ma mo srid pa'i dzong lung chen mo yum bzung ma'i dngos grub chen mo'i rgyud rnams dang ma mo rtsa rgyud 'bum tig gi skor,* Dg. NGB vols. 22–23, Tingkye NGB vols. 30–31, vol. 33, T 842), also known as "Mātaraḥ, Indicative of Imprecation" (*Ma mo rbod gtong*); (vii) the cycle of the protectors Lokastotrapūjā (*bsTan srung 'jig rten mchod bstod,* Dg. NGB vol. 24, Tingkye NGB vol. 32, T 844); and (viii) the cycle of Vajramantrabhīru (*rMod pa drag sngags,* Dg. NGB vol. 24, Tingkye NGB vol. 32, T 843).

Eight Transmitted Teachings: [*Means for Attainment*]
[sGrub pa] bka' brgyad
A collective name for the eight classes of means for attainment of Mahāyoga contained in Dg. NGB vols. 15–24; and Tingkye NGB vols. 20–33, especially vols. 31–32, which contain the general tantras (*spyi rgyud*) and the particular tantras (*sgos rgyud*) associated with the original Indian revelation of the *Tantra of the Gathering of the Sugatas of the Eight Transmitted Teachings* (*sGrub chen bka' brgyad dbe 'dus kyi rgyud*). This is the Mahāyoga source from which the subsequent Tibetan revelations (*gter ma*) of the Eight Transmitted Teachings *(bka' brgyad*) derive. The principal Tibetan revelations of this genre include (i) the *Eight Transmitted Teachings: Gathering of the Sugatas* (*bKa' brgyad bde gshegs 'dus pa*) discovered by Nyangrel Nyima Ozer; (ii) the *Eight Transmitted Teachings: Consummation of Secrets* (*bKa' brgyad gsang ba yongs rdzogs*), discovered by Guru Chowang; and (iii) the *Eight Transmitted Teachings: Natural Arising* (*bKa' brgyad rang shar*), discovered by Rigdzin Godemchen, which are all contained in the Anthology of the Eight Transmitted Teachings (*bKa' brgyad phyogs sgrigs*), 20 vols. Chengdu: Thubten Nyima, 2000.

Eighteen Lower Tantras of the Mind Class of the Great Perfection
rDzogs pa chen po sems smad bco brgyad
A collective name for the lower tantras belonging to the Mind Class (*sems kyi sde*) of the Great Perfection, some of which are contained in Dg. NGB vol. 6, nos. 18–27. The full listing is also given in Dudjom Rinpoche 1991, vol. 2, p. 221. Among the eighteen, the five earlier translations (*snga 'gyur lnga*) are attributed to Vairocana and the thirteen later translations (*phyi 'gyur bcu gsum*) to Vimalamitra, Nyak Jñānakumāra, and Yudra Nyingpo.

Eighteen Tantras of Mahāyoga
Ma hā yo ga'i rgyud sde bco brgyad
These comprise (i) *Guhyagarbha* (Dg. NGB vols. 9–11, Tingkye NGB vols. 14–16, T 832–37); (ii) *Buddhasamāyoga* (Dg. NGB vols. 11–12, Tingkye NGB vol. 16, T 366–67); (iii) *Candraguhyatilaka* (Dg. NGB vol. 12, Tingkye NGB vol. 16, T 477); (iv) *Guhyasamāja* (Dg. NGB vol. 12, Tingkye NGB vol. 17, T 442–43); (v) *Śrīparamādya* (Dg. NGB vol. 12, Tingkye vol. 17, T 487); (vi) *Karmamāla* (Dg. NGB vol. 12, Tingkye NGB vol. 17); (vii) *Heruka rol pa* (Dg. NGB vol. 13, Tingkye NGB vol. 18); (viii) *rTa mchog rol pa* (Dg. NGB vol. 13, Tingkye NGB vol. 18, T 839); (ix) *sNying rje rol pa* (Dg. NGB vol. 13, Tingkye NGB vol. 18,

T 840); (x) *bDud rtsi rol pa* (Dg. NGB vol. 13, Tingkye NGB vol. 18); (xi) *Phur pa bcu gnyis pa* (Dg. NGB vol. 13, Tingkye NGB vol. 19); (xii) *Ri bo brtsegs pa* (Tingkye NGB vol. 6); (xiii) *Ye shes rngam glog* (Dg. NGB vol. 7, Tingkye NGB vol. 12, T 830); (xiv) *Dam tshig bkod pa* (Dg. NGB vol. 5, Tingkye NGB vol. 12); (xv) *Ting 'dzin rtse gcig* (Dg. NGB vol. 2, Tingkye NGB vol. 8); (xvi) *Glang chen rab 'bog* (Dg. NGB vol. 13, Tingkye NGB vol. 19); (xvii) *rNam snang sgyu 'phrul drva ba* (Tingkye NGB vol. 19, T 466); and (xviii) *Thabs kyi zhags pa* (Dg. NGB vol. 13, Tingkye NGB vol. 19, T 835).

[*Eulogy to*] *Mañjuśrītīkṣṇa*
Wen shu shi li rui li zan tan
[bCom ldan 'das kyis 'jam dpal] rnon po [la bstod pa]
Dg.K rGyud vol. PA ff. 15a–15b; KPD, vol. 89, pp. 61–63; T 551.

Exegetical Tantra Entitled Splendor of the Sun
bShad pa'i rgyud chen nyi ma gzi brjid
Including root tantra, subsequent tantra, and further subsequent tantra
rTsa rgyud dang phyi ma phyi ma'i rgyud
NL

[*Exegetical*] *Tantra of Amoghapāśa*
Āryāmoghapāśakalpatantra
'Phags pa don yod zhags pa'i [cho ga zhib mo'i rgyal po] (also known as *Tantra of Buddha Speech: Amoghapāśa*, gSung rgyud don zhags)
Dg.K rGyud vol. MA ff. 1b–316a and TSA ff. 1b–57b; KPD, vol. 92 and vol. 93, pp. 3–150; T 686.

Expanse of Indestructible Reality
rDor dbyings
See *Tantra Entitled Summation of the Real*

Five Protective Mnemonic Incantations
Pañcarakṣā
gZungs grva lnga
A collective title for T 558–59 and T 561–63; KPD, vol. 90, pp. 176–351 and pp. 355–476. See also Dudjom Rinpoche 1991, vol. 2, p. 228.

Fivefold Nectar of Viśvabhuk
bSod skyabs bdud rtsi lnga pa
NL

Flash of the Splendor of Pristine Cognition
Sarvatathāgataguhyamahāguhyakośakṣayanidhidīpamahāpratapasādhanatantra-jñānāścaryadyuticakra-nāma-mahāyānasūtra
Ye shes rngam glog (also known as De bzhin gshegs pa thams cad kyi gsang ba gsang ba'i mdzod chen po mi zad pa gter gyi sgron ma brtul zhugs chen po bsgrub pa'i rgyud ye shes rngam pa glog gi 'khor lo zhes bya ba theg pa chen po'i mdo)
Dg. NGB vol. 7, no. 3; Dg.K. rNying rgyud vol. KA, ff. 290b–358a; KPD, vol. 101, pp. 749–end; T 830.

Four Sūtras [of Anuyoga]
[Anu yo ga'i] mdo bzhi
A collective name for the four Anuyoga texts contained in Dg. NGB vol. 7, nos. 1 and 3, and vol. 8, nos. 1–2, to which the key *Sūtra That Gathers All Enlightened Intentions* (Dg. NGB vol. 7, no. 2) is added.

Further Subsequent Tantra of Fierce Vajrapāṇi
Śrīvajracaṇḍacittaguhyatantrottarottara
dPal rdo rje gtum po thugs gsang ba'i rgyud phyi ma'i phyi ma
Dg.K. rGyud vol. JA, ff. 36b–39b; KPD, vol. 93, pp. 126–37; T 459.

Gathering of Enlightened Intentions
dGongs 'dus
See *Sūtra That Gathers All Enlightened Intentions*

General Cycle of the Mind Class
Sems sde spyi'i skor
A collective name for the general tantras belonging to the Mind Class (*sems kyi sde*) of the Great Perfection, some of which are contained in Dg. NGB vol. 6, nos. 28–53.

General Tantra Entitled Ornament of Emptiness
sPyi rgyud [khrag 'thung] stong gi brgyan pa
NL

[Heruka] Galpoche
[Khrag 'thung] gal po che
Tingkye NGB vol. 25, pp. 119.5–337.7.

Hundred Narratives of Pūrṇa and so Forth
Pūrṇapramukhāvadānaśataka
Gang po [la sogs pa]'i rtogs brjod [brgya pa]
Dg.K. mDo sde vol. AṂ, ff. 1b–286b; KPD, vol. 75, pp. 3–780; T 343.
Summarized in PZ, pp. 512–13.

Hundred Parables on Deeds
Karmaśataka
Las brgya tham pa
Dg.K. mDo sde vols. HA–A; KPD, vols. 73–74; T 340.
Summarized in PZ, pp. 506–7.

Hundred Thousand Marks of the Mātaraḥ
[Thugs kyi yang snying] ma mo 'bum tig gi rgyud
Dg. NGB vol. 23, no. 10.

Indestructible Nucleus: [Blazing Flames of Indestructible Reality]
Vajrahṛdayavajrajihvānala-nāma-dhāraṇī
rDo rje snying po [rdo rje lce 'bar ba zhes bya ba'i gzungs]
Dg.K. rGyud vol. JA, ff. 65b–68a; KPD, vol. 82, pp. 218–25; T 462.

Indestructible Stacked Mansions of Sumeru
Āryamahāvajrameruśikharakūṭāgāra-dhāraṇī
['Phags pa] rdo rje' ri rab [chen po'i rtse mo'i] khang bu brtsegs pa'i gzungs
Dg.K. rGyud vol. DZA, ff. 267a–295a; KPD, vol. 95, pp. 692–end; T 751.

Jewel Crest of the Assembly
Āryamahāsannipātaratnaketudhāraṇī-nāma-mahāyānasūtra
['Phags pa] 'dus pa [chen po] rin chen tog [gi gzungs]
Dg.K. mDo sde vol. NA, ff. 187b–277b; KPD, vol. 56, pp. 509–767; T 138.
Summarized in PZ, pp. 195–96.

Kingly Array of the Three Commitments
Trisamayavyūharāja-nāma-tantra
Dam tshig gsum bkod pa'i rgyal po zhes bya ba'i rgyud
Dg.K. rGyud vol. DA, ff. 181a–247a; KPD, vol. 87, pp. 543–742; T 502.

Lion's Roar of Śrīmālādevī
Āryaśrīmālādevīsiṃhanāda-nāma-mahāyānasūtra
'Phags pa lha mo dpal phreng gi seng ge'i sgra zhes bya ba theg pa chen po'i mdo
Dg.K. dKon brtsegs vol. CHA, ff. 255a–277b; KPD, vol. 44, pp. 712–75; T 92.
Summarized in PZ, pp. 137–41. Translated in Wayman and Hideko 1974.

Long Mnemonic Incantation
gZungs ring
NL

Mirror of the Sacred Doctrine of Vipaśyin
rNam gzigs chos kyi me long
NL

Mnemonic Incantation of the Thousand-Armed and Thousand-Eyed One
Qian shou qian yan you guan zi zai pu sa wu ai da bei xin tuo luo ni
['Phags pa spyan ras gzigs dbang phyug] phyag stong spyan stong gi gzungs
Dg.K. rGyud vol. TSA, ff. 94a–129b; KPD, vol. 93, pp. 251–54; T 691.

Mnemonic Incantation of the Wish-Fulfilling Gem
Cintāmaṇidhāraṇī
['Phags pa spyan ras gzigs dbang phyug gi gsang mdzod thogs pa med pa'i] yid bzhin 'khor lo['i snying po zhes bya ba'i gzungs]
Dg.K. rGyud vol. TSA, ff. 129b–137a; KPD, vol. 93, pp. 355–78; T 692.

Mother and Child Cycles pertaining to the White, Black, and Variegated Sections of the Class of Space
Klong sde dkar nag khra gsum ma bu'i skor
A collective name for the tantras belonging to the Space Class (*klong gi sde*) of the Great Perfection, which are contained in Dg. NGB vol. 5, nos. 12–23.

Ocean from the Exegetical Tantra Entitled Array of Letters
bShad rgyud yi ge bkod pa las rgya mtsho
NL

Outer Cycle and Inner Cycle
Phyi skor dang nang skor
A collective name for the fifth and sixth tiers of tantras belonging to the Esoteric Instructional Class (*man ngag gi sde*) of the Great Perfection, which are contained in Dg. NGB vol. 4, nos. 22–24; and vol. 5, nos. 1–11.

Pact of the Nine Offspring of the Emaciating Black [Slayer of Death]
Das chad nag po sras dgu kha thun (also known as gShin rje nag po'i kha thun)
Dg. NGB vol. 17, nos. 2–3.

Pagoda of Precious Gems
Ratnakūṭa
dKon brtsegs
Section of the Kangyur, comprising the sūtras T 45–93; KPD, vols. 39–44.
Summarized in PZ, pp. 24–144. Selected translations in Chang 1983.

Prophetic Declaration of Enlightened Intention
Sandhivyākarana-nāma-tantra
dGongs pa lung stan pa zhes bya ba'i rgyud
Dg.K. rGyud vol. CA, ff. 158a–207b; KPD, vol. 81, pp. 612–751; T 444.

Rite of the Informative Tantra [of Vajrabhairava]
Shuo hua da te luo yi gui
gTam rgyud kyi rtog pa
Dg.K. rGyud vol. JA, ff. 173b–174a. KPD, vol. 83, pp. 560–63; T 471.

Root Tantra Entitled Sūtra of the Emanational Play of the Seal of Pristine Cognition
rTsa rgyud ye shes phyag rgya rol ba'i mdo
NL

[*Root Tantra of Avalokiteśvara Entitled*] *Lotus Net*
Āryāvalokiteśvarapadmajāla-mūlatantrarāja
['Phags pa spyan ras gzigs dbang phyug gi rtsa ba'i rgyud kyi rgyal po] padma dra ba
Dg.K. rGyud vol. BA, ff. 224b–278a; KPD, vol. 91, pp. 826–1001; T 681.

Root Tantra of Fierce Vajrapāṇi
Śrīvajracaṇḍacitta-guhyatantra
dPal rdo rje gtum po [thugs gsang ba'i] rtsa ba'i rgyud
Dg.K. rGyud vol. JA, ff. 15a–30a; KPD, vol. 83, pp. 53–102; T 458.

Root Tantra of Mañjuśrī
Āryamañjuśrī-mūlatantra
'Phags pa 'jam dpal rtsa rgyud
Dg.K. rGyud vol. NA, ff. 105a–351a; KPD, vol. 88, pp. 354–end; T 543.

Root Tantra of the Awakening of Vairocana
Mahāvairocanābhisambodhivikurvitādhiṣṭhānavaipulya-sūtrendrarāja
rTsa rgyud rnam snang mngon par byang chub pa
Dg.K. rGyud vol. THA, ff. 151b–260a; KPD, vol. 86, pp. 436–756; T 494.
Translated in Hodge 2003.

[*Root Tantra of the*] *Indestructible Subjugator*
Vajravidāraṇa-nāma-dhāraṇī
rDo rje rnam par 'joms pa [zhes bya ba'i rtsa ba'i rgyud] (also known as *Sūtra of Ablution through the Indestructible Subjugator,* rDo rje rnam par 'joms pa khrus pa'i mdo)
Dg.K. rGyud vol. DZA, ff. 265b–266b; KPD, vol. 95, pp. 785–91; T 750.

Secret Cycle
gSang skor
A collective name for the fourth tier of tantras belonging to the Esoteric Instructional Class (*man ngag gi sde*) of the Great Perfection, which are contained in Dg. NGB vol. 4, nos. 12–21.

Seventeen "Mother and Child" Sūtras of the Transcendent Perfection [of Discriminative Awareness]
Pha rol phyin pa yum sras bcu bdun
These comprise the longer versions known as the "six mothers" (*yum drug*) and the shorter texts known as the "eleven children" (*bu bcu gcig*), on all of which, see Conze 1960.

Songs of Praise
bsTod pa glu blangs
NL

Subsequent Tantra of Fierce Vajrapāṇi
Śrīvajracaṇḍacittaguhyatantrottara
dPal rdo rje gtum po thugs gsang ba'i rgyud phyi ma
Dg.K. rGyud vol. JA, ff. 30b–36b; KPD, vol. 83, pp. 103–5; T 459.

Subsequent Tantra That Reveals the Secrets of Mañjuśrī
Phyi ma 'jam dpal gsang ba bstan pa'i rgyud (also known as 'Jam dpal gsang ba'i rgyud phyi ma)
Dg. NGB vol. 17, no. 14.

Supplementary Fragment of the Paramādya
Śrīparamādyamantrakalpakhaṇḍa
dPal mchog dang po['i sngags kyi rtog pa'i dum bu] hor kong bsabs
Dg.K. rGyud vol. TA, ff. 173a–265b; KPD, vol. 85, pp. 514–800; T 488.

Sūtra Elucidating the Secret Gate
gSang sgo 'grel pa'i mdo
NL

Sūtra of All-Gathering Awareness
Sarvatathāgatacittaguhyajñānārthagarbha-krodhavajrakulatantrapiṇḍārtha-vidyāyogasiddha-nāma-mahāyānasūtra
Kun 'dus rig pa (also known as De bzhin gshegs pa thams cad kyi thugs gsang ba'i ye shes don gyi snying po khro bo rdo rje'i rigs kun 'dus rig pa'i mdo rnal 'byor grub pa'i rgyud theg pa chen po'i mdo)
Dg. NGB. vol. 7, no. 1; Dg.K. rNying rgyud vol. KHA, ff. 1b–110a; KPD, vol. 102, pp. 3–266; T 831.

Sūtra of Diffusion from a Single Source
Ekottarikasūtra
gCig las 'phros pa
NL, but there is an extant eulogy entitled *Ekottarikastava,* by Maticitra, contained in Dg.T. bstod tshogs vol. KA, ff. 102a–102b.

Sūtra of Final Nirvāṇa
Mahāparinirvāṇasūtra
Myang ngan las 'das pa'i [chen po'i] mdo
Dg.K. mDo sde vols. NYA, f. 1b–THA, f. 152b; KPD, vol. 52, p. 3–vol. 54, p. 383; T 119–21.
Summarized in PZ, pp. 170–75. Translated in Yamamoto 1999–2000.

Sūtra of Indestructible Reality, Free from Deviations
rDo rje ma gol
NL

Sūtra of Protection through the Blue Clad Lord of Secrets
gSang bdag gos sngon can bsrung ba'i mdo
Cf. Bhagavatnīlāmbaradharavajrapāṇitantra
bCom ldan 'das phyag na rdo rje gos sngon can gyi rgyud
Dg.K. rGyud vol. DA, ff. 158a–167a; KPD, vol. 87, pp. 469–96; T 498.

Sūtra of Reversal Entitled Sitātapatrā Originating from the Protuberance [of All the Tathāgatas]
Āryasarvatathāgatoṣṇīṣasitātapatrā-nāma [aparājita] pratyaṅgira
gTsug gtor las byung gdugs dkar zlog pa
Dg.K. rGyud vol. PHA, ff. 205a–212b; KPD, vol. 90, pp. 676–701; T 590.

Sūtra of Supreme Golden Light
Āryasuvarṇaprabhāsottamasūtrendrarāja-nāma-mahāyānasūtra
'Phags pa gser 'od dam pa mdo sde'i dbang po'i rgyal po zhes bya ba theg pa chen po'i mdo
Dg.K. rGyud 'bum vol. PA, ff. 151b–273a; KPD, vol. 89, pp. 460–end; T 556.

Sūtra of Supreme Meditative Stability
[rGyud kyi rgyal po] ting nge 'dzin mchog [gi mdo/rgyud]
Dg. NGB vol. 8, no. 5.

Sūtra of the Applications of Mindfulness
Āryasaddharmasmṛtyupasthāna
'Phags pa dam pa'i chos dran pa'i nye bar gzhag pa
Dg.K. mDo sde vol. YA, f. 82a–vol. SHA, f. 229b (4 vols.); KPD, vol. 68, p. 238–vol. 71, p. 541; T 287.
Summarized in PZ, pp. 462–65.

Sūtra of the Bounteous Array
Āryaghanavyūha-nāma-mahāyānasūtra
'Phags pa rgyan stug po bkod pa zhes bya ba theg pa chen po'i mdo
Dg.K. mDo sde vol. CHA, ff. 1b–55b; KPD, vol. 50, pp. 2–127; T 110.
Summarized in PZ, pp. 163–65.

Sūtra of the Buddhas of Medicine in Eight Hundred Verses
Āryasaptatathāgatapūrvapraṇidhānaviśeṣavistāra-nāma-mahāyānasūtra
'Phags pa de bzhin gshegs pa bdun gyi sngon gyi smon lam gyi khyad par rgyas pa zhes bya ba theg pa chen po'i mdo (also known as sMan mdo brgyad brgya pa)
Dg.K. rGyud 'bum vol. DA, ff. 248b–273b; KPD, vol. 87, pp. 743–802; T 503.
Translated in Birnbaum 1979, 173–217.

Sūtra of the Cloud of Precious Jewels
Āryaratnamegha-nāma-mahāyānasūtra
'Phags pa dkon mchog sprin zhes bya ba theg pa chen po'i mdo
Dg.K. mDo sde vol. WA, ff. 1b–112b; KPD, vol. 64, pp. 3–63; T 231.
Summarized in PZ, pp. 309–17.

Sūtra of the Confession of Obscurations from the Confession of Downfalls on the Way to Enlightenment
Byang chub ltung bshags las sgrib bshags pa'i mdo
NL, but perhaps related to 'Phags pa sgrub pa rnam mpar dag pa zhes bya ba theg pa chen po'i mdo, contained in Dg.K. mDo sde vol. TSHA, ff. 284a–297b; KPD, vol. 62, pp. 760–99; T 218.

Sūtra of the Cornucopia of Avalokiteśvara's Attributes
Āryakaraṇḍavyūha-nāma-mahāyānasūtra
'Phags pa za ma tog bkod pa zhes bya ba theg pa chen po'i mdo
Dg.K. mDo sde vol. JA, ff. 200a–247b; KPD, vol. 51, pp. 529–640; T 116.
Translated by Peter Roberts, available online at 84000: Translating the Words of the Buddha, http://read.84000.co/#UT22084-051-004/title.

Sūtra of the Cuckoo's Emanational Play
Khu byug rol pa'i mdo (also known as De bzhin gshegs pa thams cad kyi sku dang gsung dang thugs kyi gsang ba dur khrod khu byug rol pa'i rgyud ces bya ba theg pa chen po'i mdo)
Dg. NGB vol. 8, no. 1.

Sūtra of the Cultivation of the Definitive Meaning of Pristine Cognition at the Moment of Death
Āryātajñāna-nāma-mahāyānasūtra
'Phags pa 'da' ka ye shes [nges don sgom pa] zhes bya ba theg pa chen po'i mdo
Dg.K. mDo sde vol. THA, ff. 153a–153b; KPD, vol. 54, pp. 384–86; T 122.
Summarized in PZ, p. 175.

Sūtra of the Descent to Laṅkā
Laṅkāvatārasūtra
mDo sde laṅkar gshegs pa

Dg.K. mDo sde vol. CA, ff. 56a–191b; KPD, vol. 49, pp. 141–506; T 107. Summarized in PZ, pp. 159–63. Translated in Suzuki 1932.

Sūtra of the Distinct Details of the Five Aspects of Buddha Speech
gSung lnga bye brag ma 'dres pa yi mdo
NL

Sūtra of the Elucidation of Enlightened Intention
Āryasandhinirmocana-nāma-mahāyānasūtra
'Phags pa dgongs pa nges par 'grel pa zhes bya ba theg pa chen po'i mdo
Dg.K. mDo sde vol. CA, ff. 1b–55b; KPD, vol. 49, pp. 3–140; T 106.
Summarized in PZ, pp. 152–59.

Sūtra of the Enlightened Attributes of Ten-Wheeled Kṣitigarbha
Daśacakrakṣitigarbhasūtra
Sa'i snying po'i 'khor lo bcu pa yon tan gyi mdo
Dg.K. mDo sde vol. ZHA, ff. 100a–241b; KPD, vol. 65, pp. 251–621; T 239.
Summarized in PZ, pp. 332–36.

Sūtra of the Essential Single Syllable
Ekākṣara-[mātā-nāma-sarvatathāgataprajñāpāramitā]
[De bzhin gshegs pa thams cad kyi yum shes rab kyi pha rol tu phyin ma] yi ge gcig ma snying po'i mdo
Dg.K. Shes phyin vol. KA, f. 147b; KPD, vol. 34, pp. 414–16; T 23.
Summarized in PZ, p. 420.

Sūtra of the Extensive Aspiration Prayer for Good Conduct
Bhadracaryāpraṇidhānarāja
bZang po spyod pa'i [rgya chen] smon lam gyi mdo
Dg.K. gZungs 'dus vol. VAṂ, ff. 262b–266a; KPD, vol. 98, pp. 921–30; T 1095 (also T 44, part 4).

Sūtra of the Five Gateways to Pure Pristine Cognition Forming the Five Aspects of Buddha Mind
Thugs lnga ye shes dag pa sgo lnga'i mdo
NL

Sūtra of the Gathering of All That Is Woven
Āryasarvavaidalyasamgraha-nāma-mahāyānasūtra
rNam par 'thag pa [thams cad bsdus pa] zhes bya theg pa chen po'i mdo
Dg.K. mDo sde vol. DZA, ff. 177a–188b; KPD, vol. 63, pp. 484–516; T 227.
Summarized in PZ, pp. 307–9.

Sūtra of the Great Bounteousness of the Buddhas
Buddhāvataṃsaka-nāma-mahāvaipulyasūtra
Sangs rgyas phal po che zhes bya ba shin tu rgyas pa chen po'i mdo
Dg.K. Phal chen vols. KA–A (1–4); KPD, vols. 35–38; T 44.
Summarized in PZ, pp. 6–23. Translated in Cleary 1993.
Chinese version: *Phal chen rgya nag ma.*

Sūtra of the Great Drumbeat
Mahābherihārakasūtra
rNga bo che chen po'i mdo
Dg.K. mDo sde vol. DZA, ff. 84b–126b; KPD, vol. 63, pp. 227–342; T 222.
Summarized in PZ, pp. 300–303.

Sūtra of the Great Mind Transmission
Sems lung chen mo'i mdo (also known as Byang chub kyi sems lung rnal 'byor chen po'i rgyud theg pa chen po'i mdo)
Dg. NGB vol. 8, no. 2.

Sūtra of the Hundredfold Homage of Renunciation and Fulfillment
Bai chan hui
sPang skong phyag brgya pa'i mdo
Dg.K. mDo sde vol. YA, ff. 1b–5b; KPD, vol. 68, pp. 3–12; T 267.
Summarized in PZ, p. 368.

Sūtra of the King of Meditative Stability
Āryasarvadharmasvabhāvasamatāvipañcita-samādhirāja-nāma-mahāyānasūtra
'Phags pa chos thams cad kyi rang bzhin mnyam pa nyid rnam par spros pa ting nge 'dzin gyi rgyal po shes bya ba theg pa chen po'i mdo
Dg.K. mDo sde vol. DA, ff. 1b–170b; KPD, vol. 55, pp. 3–411; T 127.
Summarized in PZ, pp. 177–79.
Partially translated in Gomez and Silk 1989 and Rockwell 1980.

Sūtra of the King on Whom Oral Instructions Are Conferred
mDo sde gdams ngag 'bogs pa'i rgyal po
NL. Cf. Dg.K. mDo sde vol. TSHA, ff. 207a–211b; KPD, vol. 62, pp. 550–65; T 214–15.

Sūtra of the Meeting of Father and Son
Āryapitāputrasamāgamana-nāma-mahāyānasūtra
'Phags pa yab dang sras mjal ba zhes bya ba theg pa chen po'i mdo
Dg.K. dKon brtsegs vol. NGA, ff. 1b–168a; KPD, vol. 42, pp. 3–495; T 60.
Summarized in PZ, pp. 58–61.

Sūtra of the Mount of Tārā
sGrol ma brtsegs pa'i mdo
NL

Sūtra of the Net of Brahmā
Brahmajālasūtra
Tshangs pa'i dra ba'i mdo
Dg.K. mDo sde vol. ĀḤ, ff. 70b–86a; KPD, vol. 76, pp. 205–49; T 352.
Summarized in PZ, pp. 521–24. Translated from Pali in Bodhi 1978 and Walshe 1987.

Sūtra of the Nondistinction between the Five Buddha Bodies
sKu lnga mi 'byed pa yi mdo
NL

Sūtra of the Profound View: The Heart of Discriminative Awareness
Bhagavatīprajñāpāramitāhṛdaya
bCom ldan 'das ma shes rab kyi pha rol tu phyin pa'i snying po [zab mo lta ba'i mdo]
Dg.K. Shes phyin vol. KA, ff. 144b–146a; KPD, vol. 34, pp. 402–7; T 21.
Translated in Red Pine 2004.

Sūtra of the Repayment of Kindness with Gratitude
Da shan qiao fang bian
[Thabs mkhas pa chen po sangs rgyas] drin lan bsab pa'i mdo
Dg.K. mDo sde vol. ĀḤ, ff. 86a–198b; KPD, vol. 76, pp. 250–563; T 353.
Summarized in PZ, pp. 520–21.

Sūtra of the Six Awareness Holders
Rig 'dzin drug gi mdo
NL

Sūtra of the Supramundane
'Jig rten las 'das pa'i mdo
Tingkye NGB vol. 13, pp. 498.7–591.6.

Sūtra of the Ten Levels
Daśabhūmikasūtra
Sa bcu pa'i mdo
Dg.K. Phal chen vol. KHA; KPD, vol. 36, pp. 355–603; T 44.
Summarized in PZ, pp. 12–14. Translated in Cleary 1993.

Sūtra of the White Lotus
Saddharmapuṇḍarīkasūtra
[Dam chos] pad ma dkar po
Dg.K. mDo sde vol. JA, ff. 1b–180b; KPD, vol. 51, pp. 3–476; T 113.
Summarized in PZ, pp. 167–69.
Translated in Kern (1884) 1968; Kato et al. 1975.
The abridged Tibetan title may also denote T 111–12.

Sūtra of the Wise and Foolish
Xian yu jing
mDzangs blun zhes bya ba'i mdo
Dg.K. mDo sde vol. A, ff. 129a–298b; KPD, vol. 74, pp. 399–995; T 341.
Summarized in PZ, pp. 507–10.

Sūtra Revealing Positive and Negative [Causes and Results]
Sheng shan e yin guo shuo da cheng jing
'Phags pa legs nyes [kyi rgyu dang 'bras bu] bstan pa zhes bya ba theg pa chen po'i mdo
Dg.K. mDo sde vol. ĀḤ, ff. 199a–208b; KPD, vol. 76, pp. 564–75; T 354.
Summarized in PZ, pp. 524–25.

Sūtra That Analyzes Past Actions
Karmavibhaṅgasūtra
Las rnam par 'byed pa
Dg.K. mDo sde vol. SA, ff. 277a–298b; KPD, vol. 72, pp. 808–66; T 338.
Summarized in PZ, pp. 501–4.

Sūtra That Appoints the Executors of the Rites
Las byed las la bkol ba'i mdo
NL

Sūtra That Ascertains the Enumeration of the Five Aspects of Buddha Activities
'Phrin las lnga'i rnam grangs nges pa'i mdo
NL

Sūtra That Demonstrates the Roots of the Three Codes of Ethical Discipline
Khrims gsum rtsa ba rab tu bstan pa'i mdo
NL

Sūtra That Eliminates Mistaken Views concerning the Five Aspects of Buddha Attributes
Yon tan rnam lnga gol sa bcad pa'i mdo
NL

Sūtra That Eradicates Immorality
[Buddhapiṭaka] duḥśīlanigraha-nāma-mahāyānasūtra
[Sangs rgyas kyi sde snod] tshul khrims ngan pa tshar gcod pa yi mdo
Dg.K. mDo sde vol. DZA, ff. 1b–77b; T 220.
Summarized in PZ, pp. 297–98.

Sūtra That Gathers All Enlightened Intentions [of All the Buddhas]
Sarvatathāgatacittajñānaguhyārthagarbhavyūhavajratantrasiddhiyogāgamasamājasarvavidyāsūtra-mahāyānābhisamayadharmaparyāyavyūha-nāma-sūtra
De bzhin gshegs pa thams cad kyi thugs gsang ba'i ye shes don gyi snying po rdo rje bkod pa'i rgyud rnal 'byor grub pa'i lung kun 'dus rig pa'i mdo theg pa chen po mngon par rtogs pa chos kyi rnam grangs rnam par bkod pa zhes bya ba'i mdo (short titles: mDo dgongs pa 'dus pa, and rDo rje bkod pa)
Dg. NGB vol. 7, no. 1 (ff. 1–110a); Dg.K. rNying rgyud vol. KHA, ff. 86b–290a; KPD, vol. 101, pp. 219–672; T 829.

Sūtra That Increases Resources through Vasudhārā
Nor gyi rgyun ma longs spyod spel ba'i mdo
Cf. Āryavasudhārā-nāma-dhāraṇī
'Phags pa nor gyi rgyun zhes bya ba'i gzungs
Dg.K. rGyud vol. BA, ff. 186a–190a; KPD, vol. 91, pp. 678–710; T 662.

Sūtra That Prolongs Life through Lord Amitāyus
Āryāparimitāyurjñāna-nāma-mahāyānasūtra
'Phags pa tshe dang ye shes dpag tu med pa zhes bya ba theg pa chen po'i mDo (also known as mGon po tshe dpag med pa tshe bsring mdo)
Dg.K. rGyud vol. BA, ff. 211b–220b; KPD, vol. 91, pp. 776–815; T 674–75.

Tantra Elucidating the Final Stage of Meditative Concentration
Dhyānottarapaṭalakrama
bSam gtan gyi phyi ma['i rim par phye ba'i rgyud]
Dg.K. rGyud vol. WA, ff. 223a–225b; KPD, vol. 96, pp. 738–47; T 808.

Tantra Entitled Summation of the Real
Tattvasaṃgrahatantra
De kho na nyid bsdus pa (also known as rtsa ba'i rgyud chen ta ttva saṃ ga ha)
Dg.K. rGyud 'bum vol. NYA, ff. 1b–142a; KPD, vol. 84, pp. 3–432; T 479.
Sanskrit version edited in Yamada 1981; also in Chandra and Snellgrove 1981.

Tantra of Acala
Āryācalakalpatantrarāja
Mi g.yo ba'i rgyud
Dg.K. rGyud vol. CA, ff. 1b–12a; KPD, vol. 81, pp. 3–39; T 432.

Also possibly equivalent to Dg.K. rGyud vol. THA, ff. 261b–22a; KPD, vol. 86, pp. 757–end; T 495.

Tantra of Buddha Body: Victorious Protuberance [of All the Buddhas]
Sarvatathāgatoṣṇīṣavijaya-nāma-dhāraṇīkalpasahita
[De bzhin gshegs pa thams cad kyi] sku rgyud gtsug tor [rnam par rgyal ba zhes bya ba'i gzungs rtog dang bcas pa]
Dg.K. rGyud vol. PHA, ff. 230a–243b; KPD, vol. 90, pp. 759–803; T 594–96.

Tantra of Buddhakapāla
Śrībuddhakapāla-nāma-yoginītantrarāja
[dPal] sangs rgyas thod pa [zhes bya ba'i rnal 'byor ma'i rgyud kyi rgyal po]
Dg.K. rGyud vol. NGA, ff. 143a–167a; KPD, vol. 80, pp. 434–505; T 424.

Tantra of Cakrasaṃvara
Tantrarājaśrīlaghusaṃvara-nāma
rGyud kyi rgyal po dpal bde mchog nyung ngu zhes bya ba
Dg.K. rGyud vol. KA, ff. 213b–246b; KPD, vol. 77, pp. 604–89; T 368.
Translated in Gray 2007, critical edition of Sanskrit and Tibetan in Gray 2012.
There is also said to be a nonextant and untranslated version entitled *Hundred Thousand Verses of Cakrasaṃvara* (bDe mchog 'bum).

Tantra of Cuṇḍa
Tsuṇḍa'i rgyud
NL

Tantra of Great Magical Emanation
Śrīmahāmāyātantrarāja
[dPal] sgyu 'phrul chen mo [zhes bya ba'i rgyud kyi rgyal po]
Dg.K. rGyud vol. NGA, ff.167a–171a; KPD, vol. 80, pp. 505–17; T 425.

Tantra of Heruka Galpo from the Viśuddha Class, Indicative of Buddha Mind
Yang dag thugs rgyud he ru ka gal po
Dg. NGB vol. 18, nos. 15–16 and vol. 19, no. 1.

Tantra of Hevajra
Hevajratantrarāja
Kye'i rdo rje zhes bya ba rgyud kyi rgyal po (short title: brTag gnyis pa, *Two Part Tantra of Hevajra*)
Dg.K. rGyud vol. NGA, ff. 1b–30a; KPD, vol. 80, pp. 3–92; T 417.
Edited and translated in Snellgrove 1959.
There is also said to have been a nonextant and untranslated version entitled *Five Hundred Thousand Verses of Hevajra* (dGyes rdor 'bum lnga).

Tantra of Inconceivable Rali Cakrasaṃvara
Śrīcakrasaṃvaraguhyacintyatantrarāja
Ra li bsam gyis mi khyab pa'i rgyud
Dg.K. rGyud vol. GA, ff. 196a–199a; KPD, vol. 79, pp. 561–71; T 385.

Tantra of Indestructible Wrathful Bliss
Vajrasukhakrodhatantrarāja
rDo rje bde khros [rgyud kyi rgyal po]
Dg.K. rGyud vol. JA, ff. 90b–93b; KPD, vol. 83, pp. 296–307; T 465.

Tantra of Mañjuśrī Yamāntaka Entitled Dark Secret Moon [Indicative of Buddha Body]
'Jam dpal gzhin rje [sku rgyud] zla gsang nag po'i rgyud
Dg. NGB. vol. 15, nos. 11–12.

Tantra of Paramādya
Śrīparamādya-nāma-mahāyānakalparāja
dPal chog dang po [zhes bya ba theg pa chen po'i rtog pa'i rgyal po]
Dg.K. rGyud vol. TA, ff. 150b–173a; KPD, vol. 85, pp. 447–513; T 487.

Tantra of Siṃhanāda
Siṃhanādatantra
Seng ge'i sgra'i rgyud
Dg.K. rGyud vol. TSA, ff. 164b–165b; KPD, vol. 93, pp. 478–82; T 702.

Tantra of Supreme Awareness
Āryavidyottama-mahātantra
'Phags pa rig pa mchog gi rgyud chen po (also known as *Tantra of Buddha Mind: Supreme Awareness:* Thugs rgyud rig pa mchog)
Dg.K. rGyud vol. DZA, ff. 1b–237b; KPD, vol. 95, pp. 3–694; T 746.

Tantra of Supreme Secret Conduct
gSang ba spyod pa mchog gi rgyud
NL

Tantra of Tārā [Blazing with Splendor]
Sarvatathāgatamātṛtārā-viśvakarmabhavatantra
[gZi ldan] sgrol ma'i ['bar ba'i] rgyud
Dg.K. rGyud vol. TSHA, ff. 202a–217a; KPD, vol. 94, pp. 516–72; T 726.
Cf. also T 724 and T 727–31.

Tantra of the Aeon Blazing like Fire, Indicative of Supreme Buddha Body
[sKu mchog rdo rje phur pa] bskal pa me ltar 'bar ba'i rgyud
mTshams brag NGB vol. 23, pp. 2.1–39.4.

Tantra of the All-Accomplishing King [the Enlightened Mind, the View Equal to Space]
Sarvadharmamahāsandhibodhicittakūlayarāja
Chos thams cad rdzogs pa chen po byang chub kyi sems kun byed rgyal po
(also known as Byang chub kyi sems kun byed rgyal po lta ba nam mkha' dang mnyam pa'i rgyud)
Dg.K. rNying rgyud vol. KA, ff. 1b–86a; KPD, vol. 101, pp. 3–189; T 828.
Also in various recensions of Collected Tantras of the Nyingmapa and NK.
The first sixty-nine chapters, along with the commentary of Khenpo Zhenphen Ozer, have been collated and translated in Valby 2008–14.

Tantra of the Assembly of the Mighty Wrathful King, Indicative of Melodious Buddha Speech
gSung dbyangs khro rgyal dbang chen 'dus pa'i rgyud
Dg. NGB. vol. 18, nos. 5–7.

Tantra of the Black Slayer of Death
Śrīkṛṣṇayamāri-tantrarāja-trikalpa
dPal gshin rje'i gshed nag po'i rgyud kyi rgyal po rtog pa gsum pa shes bya ba
Dg.K. rGyud 'bum vol. JA, ff. 164a–167b; KPD, vol. 83, pp. 522–31; T 469.
Also: Sarvatathāgatakāyavākcittakṛṣṇayamāri-nāma-tantra
De bzhin gshegs pa thams cad kyi sku gsung thugs gshin rje gshed nag po shes bya ba'i rgyud
Dg.K. rGyud vol. JA, ff. 134b–151b; KPD, vol. 83, pp. 429–84; T 467.

Tantra of the Dark Amulet
Ga'u nag po'i rgyud
NL

Tantra of the Deities
Lha rgyud
NL

[*Tantra of*] *the Descent of* [*Indestructible*] *Flames*
[Nīlāmbaradharavajrapāṇiyakṣamahārudra] vajrānalajīhvā-tantra
[Lag na rdo rje gos sngon can gnod sbyin drag po chen po] rdo rje me lce dbab pa'i rgyud
Dg.K. rGyud vol. JA, ff. 40a–65b; KPD, vol. 83, pp. 218–21; T 461.

Tantra of the Diffusion of Light Rays
'Od zer 'phro rgyud
NL

Tantra of the Emanational Play of Aśvottama, from the Lotus Class, Indicative of Buddha Speech
Sarvatathāgatabuddhānuttaraguhyāśvottamavīṇāsamata-mahātantra
[Padma gsung las de bzhin gshegs pa thams cad kyi dgongs pa bla na med pa gsang ba] rta mchog rol pa'i rgyud [chen po]
Dg. NGB vol. 13, no. 1; also Dg.K. rNying rgyud vol. GA, ff. 77a–129b; KPD, vol. 103, pp. 208–354; T 839.

Tantra of the Emanational Play of Nectar, from the Nectar Class, Indicative of Buddha Attributes
bDud rtsi yon tan rol ba che chung
Dg. NGB vol. 13, no. 3, and the related tantras in vol. 19, nos. 5–6, and vol. 20, nos. 1–9; also Dg.K. rNying rgyud vol. GA, ff. 202a–230a; KPD, vol. 102, pp. 559–625; T 841.

Tantra of the Empowerment of Vajrapāṇi
Āryavajrapāṇyabhiṣeka-mahātantra
['Phags pa] lag na rdo rje dbang bskur ba'i rgyud [chen po]
Dg.K. rGyud vol. DA, ff. 1b–156b; KPD, vol. 87, pp. 3–463; T 496.

Tantra of the Four [Indestructible] Seats
Śrīcatuḥpīthamahāyoginītantrarāja
rNal 'byor ma rgyud kyi rgyal po chen po dpal gdan bzhi pa
Dg.K. rGyud 'bum vol. NGA, ff. 181a–231b; KPD, vol. 80, pp. 549–685; T 428.
Edited with partial translation in Szántó 2012.

Tantra of the Gathering of the Transmitted Precepts of the Great Perfection
rDzogs chen bka' 'dus rgyud
Perhaps equivalent to rDzogs pa chen po nges don 'dus pa'i rgyud
Dg. NGB vol. 1, no. 17.

Tantra of the General Secrets [of All Maṇḍalas]
[Sarvamaṇḍala] sāmānyavidhīnām-guhyatantra
[dKyil 'khor thams cad kyi] spyi'i [cho ga] gsang ba'i rgyud
Dg.K. rGyud vol. WA, ff. 141a–167b; KPD, vol. 96, pp. 509–82; T 806.

Tantra of the Great Assembly of Vajrapāṇi
Phyag na rdo rje 'khor chen rgyud
GDKT vol. 8, no. 46.

Tantra of the Indestructible Cobra Hood
[Nīlāmbaradharavajrapāṇi]vajraphaṇakatantra [trilokavijaya-nāma]
[Lag na rdo rje gos sngon can] rdo rje gdengs pa'i rgyud
Dg.K. rGyud vol. JA, ff. 12a–15a; KPD, vol. 83, pp. 43–52; T 457.

Tantra of the Indestructible Peak
Vajraśekharamahāyogaguhyatantra
gSang ba rnal 'byor chen po'i rgyud rdo rje rtse mo
Dg.K. rGyud vol. NYA, ff. 142b–274a; KPD, vol. 84, pp. 432–740; T 480.
Translated from the Chinese in Giebel 2001.

Tantra of the Indestructible Subduer of the Three Spheres of Existence
Āryavajrapāṇinīlāmbaradharatrilokavinaya-nāma-tantra
['Phags pa lag na rdo rje gos sngon can] 'jig rten/sa gsum 'dul ba'i rgyud
Dg.K. rGyud vol. DA, ff. 177a–181a; KPD, vol. 97, pp. 530–42; T 501.

Tantra of the Indestructible Tent
Ḍākinīvajrapañjarāmahātantra
[mKha' 'gro ma rdo rje] gur gyi rgyud
Dg.K. rGyud 'bum vol. NGA, ff. 30a–65b; KPD, vol. 80, pp. 93–207; T 419.

Tantra of the King of Empowered Conception
dBang bskur rtog pa rgyal po'i rgyud
NL

Tantra of the King of Empowerment
dBang bskur rgyal po'i rgyud
Dg. NGB vol. 8, no. 4.

Tantra of the Litany of the Names of Mañjuśrī
Mañjuśrījñānasattvasyaparamārtha-nāma-saṅgīti
'Jam dpal [gyi] mtshan [yang dag par] brjod [pa] (also known as *Net of the Magical Emanation of Mañjuśrī,* 'Jam dpal sgyu 'phrul drva ba)
Dg. NGB vol. THA, ff. 123a–135b; Tingkye NGB vol. 15, pp. 97–118; Dg.K. rGyud vol. KA, ff. 1b–13b; KPD, vol. 77, pp. 3–31; T 360.
Translated in Dorje 2016, Wayman 1983, and Davidson 1981.
There is also said to have been a nonextant and untranslated version entitled *Litany of the Names of Mañjuśrī in Sixty Thousand Chapters* ('Jam dpal mtshan brjod le'u khri drug stong).

Tantra of the Lotus Crown
Padmamukuṭatantra
Padma cod pan rgyud
Dg.K. rGyud vol. TSA, ff. 157b–164b; KPD, vol. 93, pp. 451–77; T 701.

Tantra of the Net of Magical Emanation
Māyājālatantra
sGyu 'phrul dra ba'i rgyud

The *Four Sections of the Net of Magical Emanation* (sGyu 'phrul sde bzhi) comprise (i) *Tantra of the Secret Nucleus in Twenty-Two Chapters, from the Net of Magical Emanation of Vajrasattva* (rDo rje sems dpa' sgyu 'phrul dra ba las rgyud gsang ba snying po, Dg. NGB vol. 9, no. 1; Tingkye NGB vol. 14; T 832); (ii) *Tantra of Vairocana from the Net of Magical Emanation* (sGyu 'phrul rnam snang, Tingkye NGB vol. 19; T 466); (iii) *Tantra of the Goddess from the Net of Magical Emanation* (Lha mo sgyu 'phrul dra ba, Dg. NGB vol. 11, no. 1; Tingkye NGB vol. 15; T 836); and (iv) *Tantra of Mañjuśrī from the Net of Magical Emanation* ('Jam dpal sgyu 'phrul dra ba, aka *Tantra of the Litany of the Names of Mañjuśrī*, Dg. NGB vol. 10, no. 3; Tingkye NGB vol. 15; T 360).

The eight additional sections of the *Net of Magical Emanation of Secret Vajrasattva* (gSang ba rdor sems sgyu 'phrul sde tshan brgyad/sgyu 'phrul sde brgyad) altogether comprise (i) *Tantra of the Net of Magical Emanation, in Eight Chapters* (sGyu 'phrul brgyad pa, Dg. NGB vol. 10, no. 2; Tingkye NGB vol. 14); (ii) *Tantra of the Supreme Spiritual Teacher, in Thirteen Chapters* (sGyu 'phrul bla ma, Dg. NGB. vol. 11, no. 2; Tingkye NGB vol. 14; T 837); (iii) *Tantra of Supplementary Points from the Net of Magical Emanation, in Thirty-Three Chapters* (sGyu 'phrul le lag, Dg. NGB vol. 10, no. 5; Tingkye NGB vol. 14); (iv) *Tantra of the Ocean from the Net of Magical Emanation, in Twenty-Two Chapters* (sGyu 'phrul rgya mtsho, Dg. NGB vol. 10, no. 7; Tingkye NGB vol. 15); (v) *Tantra of the Mirror of Vajrasattva, in Thirteen Chapters* (sGyu 'phrul me long, Dg. NGB vol. 11, no. 4; Tingkye NGB vol. 15; T 833); (vi) *Tantra of the Net of Magical Emanation, in Eighty-Two Chapters* (sGyu 'phrul brgyad cu pa, Dg. NGB vol. 11, no. 5; Tingkye NGB vol. 14; T 834); (vii) *Tantra of the Net of Magical Emanation, in Forty-Six Chapters* (sGyu 'phrul bzhi bcu pa, Dg. NGB vol. 10, no. 4; Tingkye NGB vol. 14); and (viii) *Tantra of Penetration from the Net of Magical Emanation, in Twenty-Six Chapters* (sGyu 'phrul thal ba, Dg. NGB vol. 11, no. 6; Tingkye NGB vol. 15).

Tantra of the Ocean of Sky-Farers [of Cakrasaṃvara]
Ḍākārṇavamahāyoginītantrarāja
[bDe mchog] mKha 'gro rgya mtsho [rnal 'byor ma'i] rgyud
Dg.K. rGyud 'bum vol. KHA, ff. 137a–264b; KPD, vol. 78, pp. 404–773; T 372.

Tantra of the Ornament of the Indestructible Nucleus
Śrīvajramaṇḍalālaṃkāra-nāma-mahātantrarāja
[dPal] rdo rje snying po rgyan gyi rgyud
Dg.K. rGyud vol. THA, ff. 1b–82a; KPD, vol. 86, pp. 3–232; T 490.

Tantra of the Presence of Pristine Cognition
Ye shes grub pa'i rgyud
NL

Tantra of the Pure White Lotus, Indicative of Supreme Buddha Mind
[rDo rje rigs kyi sgrub lugs khro bo] thugs mchog rnam dag puṇḍa ri ka'i rgyud
Dg. NGB. vol. 19, no. 3.

Tantra of the Purification of All Lower Realms
Āryasarvadurgatipariśodhanatejorājakalpa
'Phags pa ngan song thams cad yongs su sbyong ba gzi brjid kyi rgyal po'i brtag pa
Dg.K. rGyud vol. TA, ff. 58b–96a; KPD, vol. 85, pp. 164–254; T 483.
Translated in Skorupski 1983.

Tantra of the Red Slayer of Death
Śrīmadraktayamāritantrarāja
dPal ldan gshin rje gshed dmar po'i rgyud kyi rgyal po
Dg.K. rGyud vol. JA, ff. 215a–244b; KPD, vol. 83, pp. 756–829; T 475.

Tantra of the Rites of Lokeśvara
Lokeśvarakalpa
'Jig rten dbang phyug gi rtog pa
Dg.K. rGyud vol. TSA, ff.151b–157b; KPD, vol. 93, pp. 434–77; T 700.

Tantra of the Rites of Vajrabhairava
Śrīvajrabhairavakalpatantra
'Jigs byed kyi rtog pa'i rgyud
Dg.K. rGyud vol. JA, ff. 167b–173b; KPD, vol. 83, pp. 537–59; T 470.

Tantra of the Secret Assembly
[Sarvatathāgatakāyavākcittarahasya] Guhyasamāja-nāma-mahākalparāja
De bzhin gshegs pa thams cad kyi sku gsung thugs kyi gsang chen gsang ba 'dus pa zhes bya ba brtag pa'i rgyal po chen po [short title: gSang ba 'dus pa]
Dg. NGB vol. NA, no. 3, ff. 89a–147a; Dg.K. rGyud 'bum vol. CA, ff. 90a–148a; KPD, vol. 81, pp. 442–578; T 442.
Translated in Fremantle 1971.

Tantra of the Secret [Enlightened] Mind [of the Mātaraḥ]
[Ma mo byang chub kyi] tsitta gsang rgyud
Dg. NGB vol. 23, no. 11.

Tantra of the Secret Nucleus
Guhyagarbhatattvaviniścayamahātantra
dPal [rtsa ba'i] rgyud gsang ba'i snying po de kho na nyid nges pa
Dg. NGB vol. TA, ff. 1–31b; Dg. NGB vol. DA, ff. 60a–82a (22 chs.); Tingkye NGB vol. 14, pp. 1–61; Dg.K. rNying rgyud vol. KHA, ff. 110b–132a; KPD, vol. 102, pp. 287–338; T 832.

Edited and translated in Dorje 1987; also translated in Dorje 2016 and Chonam and Khandro 2011.

Tantra of the Secret Zombie [*Marutse*]
[gNod sbyin ma ru tse'i] ro langs gsang ba'i rgyud
Dg. NGB vol. 17, no. 16.

Tantra of the Secrets of Mañjuśrī
['Phags pa] 'jam dpal [las bzhi 'khor lo] gsang ba'i rgyud
Dg.K. rNying rgyud vol. GA, ff. 60a–77a; KPD, vol. 102, pp. 159–207; T 838; also Dg. NGB vol. 16, no. 13.

Tantra of the Six Points of Meditation, Indicative of Perfected Buddha Activities
[Byang chub kyi sems] 'phrin las mthar phyin sgom don drug pa'i rgyud
Contained with commentary in NK vol. 98, pp. 125–58.
Cf. also Dg. NGB vol. 6, nos. 50 and 52.

Tantra of the Supreme Awareness of Vajrakīla in One Hundred Thousand Verses
Phur ba bidyottama 'bum sde'i rgyud
This is the title of the complete and not fully translated *Tantra of Vajrakīla*, parts of which are represented in Dg. NGB vol. 13, no. 4, vol. 20, nos. 10–13, vol. 21, nos. 1–28, and vol. 22, nos. 1–7 (also known as *Tantra of Supreme Awareness from the Vajrakīla Class, Indicative of Buddha Activity*: Phur ba phrin las kyi bidyottamala).

Tantra of the Unerring Goddess, Indicative of Spontaneously Perfect Buddha Attributes
Yon tan lhun rdzogs lha mo ma gol rgyud
NL

Tantra of the Wheel of Time
[Paramādibuddhoddhṛtaśrī] kālacakra-tantrarāja
[mChog gi dang po'i sangs rgyas las phyung ba] rgyud kyi rgyal po dpal dus kyi 'khor lo
Dg.K. rGyud vol. KA, ff. 22b–128b; KPD, vol. 77, pp. 57–311; T 362.
Partially translated in Newman 1987, ch. 1, and Wallace 2001, 2004, ch. 2, and 2010, ch. 4.
There is also said to have been a nonextant and untranslated version entitled *Root Tantra of the Wheel of Time in Twelve Thousand Verses* (Dus 'khor rtsa rgyud stong phrag bcu gnyis).

Tantra of Trailokyavijaya That Shines Within the Child
Khams gsum rnam rgyal sras khog snang ba'i rgyud
NL

Tantra of Ucchuṣmakrodha, Blazing like Fire
Khro bo sme brtsegs me ltar 'bar ba'i rgyud (also known as *Mantra of Eulogy to Ucchuṣmakrodha*: Krodhabhurkumkūṭarājastotramantra)
Khro bo rgyal po sme brtsegs la bstod pa'i sngags
Dg.K. rGyud 'bum vol. WA, ff. 7b–8a; KPD, vol. 96, pp. 30–32; T 756.

Tantra of Vairocana [from the Net of Magical Emanation]
[sGyu 'phrul] rnam snang
Tingkye NGB vol. 19; retranslated by Rinchen Zangpo in Dg.K. rGyud 'bum vol. JA, ff. 94b–134a; KPD, vol. 83, pp. 308–428; T 466.

Tantra of Vajrabhairava
Śrīvajramahābhairava-nāma-tantra
dPal rdo rje 'jigs byed chen po'i rgyud (also known as *Seven Rites of Vajrabhairava,* 'Jigs byed rtog bdun)
Dg.K. rGyud vol. JA, ff. 151b–164a; KPD, vol. 83, pp. 485–521; T 468.
There is also said to have been a nonextant and untranslated version entitled *Three Hundred Rites of Bhairava* ('Jigs byed rtog pa sum brgya).

Tantra of Vajramantrabhīru
Vajramantrabhīrusandhi-mūlatantra
Drag sngags
Dg.K. rNying rgyud vol. GA, ff. 253a–267b; KPD, vol. 103, pp. 726–73; T 843; also Dg. NGB vol. 24, no. 2.

Tantra of Vajrapātāla: [The Blue Clad Vajrapāṇi]
Āryavajrapāṇinīlāmbaradharavajrapātāla-nāma-tantra
['Phags pa lag na rdo rje gos sngon can] rdo rje sa 'og zhes bya ba'i rgyud
Dg.K. rGyud vol. DA, ff. 167a–172a; KPD, vol. 87, pp. 497–513; T 499.

Tantra Requested by Subāhu
Āryasubāhuparipṛcchā-nāma-tantra
'Phags pa dpung bzang gis zhus pa zhes bya ba'i rgyud (also known as *Exegetical Tantra Originating from the Buddha's Shoulders Entitled Subāhu*, dPung pa las byung bshad rgyud dpung pa bzang)
Dg.K rGyud vol. WA ff.118a–140b; KPD vol. 96, pp. 434–508; T 805.

Tantra That Achieves Excellent Accomplishment [Originating from the Buddha's Navel]
Susiddhikara-mahātantra
Legs par grub par byed pa'i rgyud chen po (also known as lTe ba dag las su ti ka ra'i rgyud)
Dg.K rGyud vol. WA ff. 168a–222b; KPD vol. 96, pp. 583–737; T 807.

Tantra That Gathers Perfect Unsurpassed Meaning
Bla med don rdzogs 'dus pa'i rgyud
NL

Tantra That Minutely Reveals the Rites
Āryamahāmaṇivipulavimānasupratiṣṭhitaguhyaparamarahasya-kalparāja
['Phags pa nor bu chen po rgyas pa'i gzhal med khang shin tu rab tu gnas pa gsang ba dam pa'i gsang ba'i] cho ga zhib mor ston pa'i rgyud
Dg.K rGyud vol. DA, ff. 286b–309a; KPD vol. 87, pp. 852–end; T 506.

Tantras of Mātaraḥ
Ma mo
Here used as a generic title for the texts contained in Dg. NGB vol. 22, nos. 8–11, and vol. 23, nos. 1–25; also Dg.K. rNying rgyud vol. GA, ff. 223b–253a; T 842.

Tantras of Vajrakīla
rDo rje phur pa
Here used as a generic title for the texts contained in Dg. NGB vol. 13, no. 4, vol. 20, nos. 10–13, vol. 21, nos. 1–28, vol, 22, nos. 1–7, and the fragment contained in Dg.K. rGyud vol. CA, ff. 43b–45b; T 439. The last of these is translated along with extensive commentary in Boord 2002.
These are all contained, along with extensive commentarial literature, in the *Anthology of Vajrakīla* (Phur pa phyogs sgrigs), 45 vols. Chengdu 2002 and 2011: Thubten Nyima.

Tantras of Vajravārāhī
rDo rje phag mo
A collective name for the tantras contained in Dg.K. rGyud vol. GA, ff. 32b–72b; KPD, vol. 79, pp. 154–211; T 377–79.

Tantras of Viśuddha
Yang dag
Here used as a generic title for the texts contained in Dg. NGB vol. 13, no. 2, vol. 18, nos. 15–16, and vol. 17, nos. 1–4.

Tantras of Yamāntaka
gShin rje bshed
Here used as a generic title for the texts contained in Dg. NGB vol. 15, nos. 11–13, vol. 16, nos. 1–13, and vol. 17, nos. 1–18.

Transcendent Perfection of Discriminative Awareness in Eight Thousand Lines
Aṣṭasāhasrikāprajñāpāramitā
Shes rab kyi pha rol tu phyin pa brgyad stong pa

Dg.K. Shes phyin vol. KA, ff. 1b–286a; KPD, vol. 33; T 12.
Summarized in PZ, pp. 402–6. Translated in Conze 1973.

Transcendent Perfection of Discriminative Awareness in One Hundred Thousand Lines (also known as *Long Mother,* Yum rgyas pa)
Śatasāhasrikāprajñāpāramitā
Shes rab kyi pha rol tu phyin pa stong phrag brgya pa
Dg.K. Shes phyin vols. KA, f. 1b–A, f. 395a; KPD, vols. 14–25; T 8.
Summarized in PZ, pp. 395–99.

Transcendent Perfection of Discriminative Awareness in Twenty-Five Thousand Lines (also known as *Intermediate Mother,* Yum 'bring po)
Pañcaviṃśatisāhasrikāprajñāpāramitā
Shes rab kyi pha rol tu phyin pa stong pa nyi shu lnga pa
Dg.K. Shes phyin vols. KA–GA; KPD, vols. 26–28; T 9.
Summarized in PZ, pp. 399–402. Translated in Conze 1975.

Unsurpassed [Secret] Cycle
[gSang ba] bla na med pa'i skor
A collective name for the third tier of tantras belonging to the Esoteric Instructional Class (*man ngag gi sde*) of the Great Perfection, which are contained in Dg. NGB vol. 3, nos. 5–11, and vol. 4, nos. 1–11.

Various Recensions of the Inspection of Great Mystery
gSang ba chen po brtag sna
NL. Cf. Dg. NGB vol. 16, nos. 6–7.

Verse Summation [of the Transcendent Perfection of Discriminative Awareness]
Prajñāpāramitāsañcayagāthā
Shes rab kyi pha rol tu phyin pa sdud pa tshigs su bcad pa
Dg.K. Shes phyin vol. KA, ff. 1b–10b; KPD, vol. 34, pp. 3–53; T 13.
Summarized in PZ, p. 412. Translated in Conze 1973.

Victory over the Three World Systems
Trailokyavijaya-mahākalparāja
'Jig rten gsum las rnam par rgyal ba [rtog pa'i rgyal po chen po]
Dg.K. rGyud vol. TA, ff. 10a–58a; KPD, vol. 85, pp. 26–163; T 482.

Wish-Fulfilling Gem: A Cornucopia Array
Za ma tog bkod cintāmaṇi
See *Sūtra of the Cornucopia of Avalokiteśvara's Attributes*; also 'Phags pa spyan ras gzigs dbang phyug gi gsang ba'i mdzod thogs pa med pa'i yid bzhin gyi 'khor lo'i snying po zhes bya ba'i gzungs
Dg.K. rGyud vol. TSA, ff. 129b–137a; KPD, vol. 93, pp. 355–78; T 692.

Yangti
Yang ti
A collective name for the first tier of tantras belonging to the Esoteric Instructional Class (*man ngag gi sde*) of the Great Perfection, which are contained in Dg. NGB vol. 1, nos. 1–23, and vol. 2, nos. 1–11.

3. Indic Treatises

Abhayadattaśrī
Biographies of the Eighty-Four Great Accomplished Masters
Caturaśītisiddhapravṛtti
Grub chen brgyad cu rtsa bzhi'i rnam thar/lo rgyus
TPD vol. 48, pp. 413–556. Translated in Robinson 1979.

Advayavajra
Precious Garland of the Real Nature
Tattvaratnāvali
De kho na nyid rin po che'i phreng ba
Dg.T. rGyud vol. WI, ff. 115a–120a; TPD, vol. 26, pp. 335–48; T 2240.

Ānandagarbha
Commentary [Illuminating the Summation of the Real]
Tattvālokakari
De nyid snang ba
Dg.T. rGyud vol. LI, ff. 1b–352a, and vol. SHI, ff. 1b–317a; TPD, vol. 29; T 2510.

Anon
Ordination Rite of the Novitiate
[Sarvāstivāda] śrāmaṇerakaraṇa
[Thams cad yod par sma ba rnams kyi] dge tshul gyi bya ba'i las
Dg.T. 'Dul ba vol. SU, ff. 28b–45a; TPD, vol. 93, pp. 800–847; T 4129.

Anon
Questions concerning Age Applicable for Novices
Śrāmaṇeravarśāgrapṛcchā
dGe tshul gi dang po'i lo dri ba
Dg.T. 'Dul ba vol. SU, ff. 64a–66a; TPD, vol. 93, pp. 885–903; T 4132.

Āryadeva
Autocommentary on the Forty Verses, Entitled Proof of Reasoning That Destroys Defects
Skhalitapramardanayuktihetusiddhi
'Khrul pa bzlog pa'i rigs pa gtan tshigs grub pa
Dg.T. dBu ma vol. TSHA, ff. 19b–22b; TPD, vol. 57, pp. 826–35; T 3847.

Compendium of the Nucleus of Pristine Cognition
Jñānasārasamuccaya
Ye shes snying po kun las btus pa
Dg.T. dBu ma vol. TSHA, ff. 26b–28a; TPD, vol. 57, pp. 851–55; T 3851.

Four Hundred Verses [of the Middle Way]
Catuḥśatakakārikā
bsTan bcos bzhi brgya pa
Dg.T. dBu ma vol. TSHA, ff. 1b–18a; TPD, vol. 57, pp. 783–825; T 3846.
Translated in Lang 1986.

Asaṅga
Commentary on the Elucidation of Enlightened Intention
Āryasandhinirmocanabhāṣya
['Phags pa] dgongs pa nges par 'grel pa'i rnam par bshad pa
[also known as dGongs 'grel ṭī ka bam po drug cu]
Dg.T. mDo 'grel vol. NGI, ff. 1b–11b; TPD, vol. 65, pp. 725–52; T 3981.

Compendium of Phenomenology [according to the Great Vehicle]
Abhidharmasamuccaya
Chos mngon pa kun las btus pa
Dg.T. Sems tsam vol. RI, ff. 44b–120a; TPD, vol. 76, pp. 116–313; T 4049.
Translated from French in Boin-Webb 2001.

Five Sections of the [Yogacaryā] Level
Yogacaryābhūmipañcavarga
[rNal 'byor spyod pa'i] sa sde lnga
Dg.T. Sems tsam vols. TSHI–'I; TPD, vol. 72, p. 671–vol. 75, p. 608; T 4035–42, comprising the three treatises of the *Actual Foundation of the Yogacaryā Level* (Yogācāryabhūmivastu)—namely, *Yogacaryā Level* (Yogacaryābhūmi, T 4035), the *Level of the Pious Attendants* (Śrāvakabhūmi, T 4036), and the *Level of the Bodhisattvas* (Bodhisattvabhūmi, T 4037, translated in Engle 2016), along with the *Summation of Ascertainment* (Yogacaryābhūmiviniścayasaṃgrahaṇī, T 4038), the *Summation of the Ground* (Yogacaryābhūmivastusaṃgrahaṇī, T 4039), the *Summation of Training Based on the [Yogacaryā] Levels* (Yogacaryābhūmivinayasaṃgrahaṇī, T 4040), the *Summation of Enumerated Categories Derived from the [Yogacaryā] Levels* (Yogacaryābhūmiparyāyasaṃgrahaṇī, T 4041), and the *Summation of Exegeses Based on the [Yogacaryā] Levels* (Yogacaryābhūmivivaraṇasaṃgrahaṇī, T 4042).

Summation of Ascertainment from the Yogacaryā Level
Yogacaryābhūmiviniścayasaṃgrahaṇī
rNal 'byor spyod pa'i sa rnam par gtan la dbab pa bsdu ba
Dg.T. Sems tsam vols. ZHI–ZI (2 vols.); TPD, vol. 74, pp. 3–1065; T 4038.

Yogacaryā Level
Yogacaryābhūmi
[rNal 'byor spyod pa'i] sa sde
Dg.T. Sems tsam vol. TSHI; TPD, vol. 72, pp. 671–end; T 4035.

Asvabhāva
Combined Commentary on the Summary of the Greater Vehicle
Mahāyānasaṃgrahapanibandhana
Theg pa chen po bsdus pa'i bshad sbyar
Dg.T. Sems tsam vol. RI, ff. 190b–296a; TPD, vol. 76, pp. 503–781; T 4051.

Aśvaghoṣa
Epic of the Deeds of the Buddha
Buddhacaritamahākāvya
Sangs rgyas kyi spyod pa zhes bya ba'i snyan dngags
Dg.T. sKyes rabs vol. GE, ff. 1b–103b; TPD, vol. 96, pp. 3–287; T 4156.
Edited and translated in Johnson (1936) 1972.

Atiśa
Collected Works of Jowoje Palden Atiśa
Jo bo rje dpal ldan a ti śa'i gsung 'bum
Beijing: Krung go bod rig pa dpe skrun khang, 2006.

Introduction to the Two Truths
Satyadvayāvatāra
bDen pa gnyis la 'jug pa
Dg.T. dBu ma vol. A, ff. 72a–75a; TPD, vol. 63, pp. 1050–54; T 3902.
Translated in Sherbourne 2000, 352–59.

Lamp of the Path of Enlightenment
Bodhipathapradīpa
Byang chub lam gyi sgron ma
Dg.T. Jo bo'i chos 'byung, ff. 1b–4b; TPD, vol. 64, pp. 1641–49; T 4465.
Translated in Sherbourne 2000, 328–45.

Avalokitavrata
Extensive Commentary on the Lamp of Discriminative Awareness
Prajñāpradīpaṭīkā
Shes rab sgron ma rgya cher 'grel pa
Dg.T. dBu ma vols. WA–ZA (3 vols.); TPD, vol. 58, p. 859–vol. 59, end; T 3859.

Bhāvaviveka
Flame of Dialectics
[Madhyamakahṛdayavṛtti] tarkajvālā

[dBu ma'i snying po'i 'grel pa] rtog ge 'bar ba
Dg.T. dBu ma vol. DZA, ff. 40b–329b; TPD, vol. 58, pp. 104–850; T 3856.
Partial translation (ch. 3) in Iida 1980.

Heart of the Middle Way
Madhyamakahṛdayakārikā
dBu ma'i snying po'i tshig le'ur byas pa
Dg.T. dBu ma vol. DZA, ff. 1b–40b; TPD, vol. 58, pp. 3–103; T 3855.
Edited and translated in Lindtner 2001a.

Lamp of Discriminative Awareness: [A Commentary on the Fundamental Stanzas of the Middle Way]
Prajñāpradīpa-[mūlamadhyamakakārikāvṛtti]
dBu ma'i rtsa ba'i 'grel pa shes rab sgron ma
Dg.T. dBu ma vol. TSHA, ff. 45b–259b; TPD, vol. 57, pp. 905–1486; T 3853.

Precious Lamp of the Middle Way
Madhyamakaratnapradīpa
dBu ma rin po che'i sgron ma
Dg.T. dBu ma vol. TSHA, ff. 259b–289a; TPD, vol. 57, pp. 1487–end; T 3854.

Buddhaguhya
Sequence of the Path of Magical Emanation
Māyājālapathakrama
sGyu 'phrul lam rim
P 4736; rGyud 'grel vol. BU, ff. 465b–506b; TPD, vol. 43, pp. 959–1041.

Buddhapālita
Commentary on the Fundamental Stanzas of the Middle Way
Buddhapālitamūlamadhyamakavṛtti
dBu ma rtsa ba'i 'grel pa bu ddha pa li ta
Dg.T. dBu ma vol. TSA, ff. 158a–281a; TPD, vol. 57, pp. 443–764; T 3842.

Candrakīrti
Autocommentary on the Introduction to the Middle Way
Madhyamakāvatārabhāṣya
dBu ma la 'jug pa'i bshad pa
Dg.T. dBu ma vol. 'A, ff. 220b–348a; TPD, vol. 60, pp. 600–928; T 3862.

Clarifying Lamp: [An Extensive Exegesis of the Tantra of the Secret Assembly]
Pradīpodyotana-nāma-ṭīkā
sGron ma gsal bar byed pa zhes bya ba'i rgya cher bshad pa
Dg.T. rGyud, vol. HA, ff. 1b–201b; TPD, vol. 15, pp. 3–676; T 1785.

Clear Word Commentary [on the Fundamental Stanzas of the Middle Way]
Mūlamadhyamakavṛttiprasannapadā
dBu ma rtsa ba'i 'grel pa tshig gsal ba
Dg.T. dBu ma vol. 'A, ff. 1b–200a; TPD, vol. 60, pp. 3–512; T 3860.
Translated in Sprung 1979.

Introduction to the Middle Way
Madhyamakāvatāra
dBu ma la 'jug pa
Dg.T. dBu ma vol. 'A, ff. 201b–219a; TPD, vol. 60, pp. 513–99; T 3861.
Translated in Huntington and Wangchen 1989; also in Padmakara Translation Group 2002.

Seventy Verses on Going for Refuge
Triśaraṇagamanasaptati
gSum la skyabs su 'gro ba bdun cu pa
Dg.T. dBu ma vol. GI, ff. 251a–253b; TPD, vol. 65, pp. 685–91; T 3971.
Translated in Sørensen 1986

Candranandana

Heart Commentary on the Eight Branches [of Medical Science]
Vaidyāṣṭāṅgahṛdayavṛtti
[sMan spyad] yan lag brgyad pa['i snying po'i 'grel pa]
Dg.T. gSo rig pa vol. HE, ff. 13b–44a; TPD, vol. 111, pp. 39–142; T 4309.

Daṃṣṭrasena

Extensive Commentary on the Transcendent Perfection of Discriminative Awareness in One Hundred Thousand Lines
Śatasāhasrikāprajñāpāramitābṛhaṭṭīkā
'Phags pa shes rab kyi pha rol tu phyin pa 'bum pa rgya cher 'grel pa (short title: 'Bum ṭīk)
Dg.T. Shes phyin vol. NA, ff. 1b–331a; TPD, vol. 54, pp. 627–end; T 3807.

Devaśarman

Collection of Consciousness
Vijñānakāya
rNam par shes pa'i tshogs
Extant in Chinese: Taisho 1539.

Dharmakīrti

Ascertainment of Valid Cognition
Pramāṇaviniścaya
Tshad ma rnam par nges pa
Dg.T. Tshad ma vol. CE, ff. 152b–230a; TPD, vol. 97, pp. 614–811; T 4211.

Exposition of Valid Cognition
Pramāṇavārttika[kārikā]
Tshad ma rnam 'grel gyi tshig le'u byas pa
Dg.T. Tshad ma vol. CE, ff. 94b–151a; TPD, vol. 97, pp. 469–613; T 4210.
English translation in Nagatomi 1957, ch. 2.

Seven Commentaries
Saptavṛtti
'Grel pa bdun (also known as Tshad ma sde bdun)
A collective name for the seven principal logical treatises of Dharmakīrti, comprising *Ascertainment of Valid Cognition* (Pramāṇaviniścaya, Dg.T. Tshad ma vol. CE, ff. 152b–230a; T 4211); *Exposition of Valid Cognition* (Pramāṇavārttika, Dg.T. Tshad ma vol. CE, ff. 94b–151a; T 4210); *Inquiry into Relations* (Sambandhaparīkṣā, Dg.T. Tshad ma vol. CE, ff. 255a–256a; T 4214); *Point of the Axioms* (Hetubindu, Dg.T. Tshad ma vol. CE, ff. 238a–255a; T 4213); *Point of Reason* (Nyāyabindu, Dg.T. Tshad ma vol. CE, ff. 231b–238a; T 4212); *Proof of Other Minds* (Santānāntarasiddhi-nāma-prakaraṇa, Dg.T. Tshad ma vol. CHE, ff. 355b–359a; T 4219); and *Reasoning of Polemics* (Vādanyāya, Dg.T. Tshad ma vol. CHE, ff. 326b–355b; T 4218).

Dignāga
Dissertation Entitled Compendium of Valid Cognition
Pramāṇasamuccaya-nāma-prakaraṇa
Tshad ma kun las btus pa zhes bya ba'i rab tu byed pa
Dg.T. Tshad ma vol. CE, ff. 1b–13a; TPD, vol. 97, pp. 3–30; T 4203.

Hundred Eight Dissertations of Dignāga
Rab byed brgya rtsa brgyad
A collective title for the works of Dignāga, especially the *Dissertation Entitled Compendium of Valid Cognition* and its commentaries.

Guṇaprabha
Ordination Rite
Ekottarakarmaśataka
Las chog karma sha dam (also known as Las brgya rtsa gcig pa)
Dg.T. 'Dul ba vol. WU, ff. 100b–259a; TPD, vol. 88, pp. 1105–end; T 4118.

Root Sūtra of Monastic Discipline
Vinayamūlasūtra
'Dul ba mdo rtsa
Dg.T. 'Dul ba vol. WU, ff. 1b–100a; TPD, vol. 88, pp. 837–1082; T 4117.

Haribhadra
Commentary on the Ornament of Clear Realization: An Instructional Treatise on the Transcendent Perfection of Discriminative Awareness (also known as *Short Commentary*)

Abhisamayālaṃkāra-nāma-prajñāpāramitopadeśasāstravṛtti
Shes rab kyi pha rol tu phyin pa'i man ngag gi bstan bcos mngon par rtogs pa'i rgyan zhes bya ba'i 'grel pa (also known as 'Grel chung)
Dg.T. Shes phyin vol. JA, ff. 78b–140b; TPD, vol. 52, pp. 205–361; T 3793.

Light for the Ornament of Emergent Realization: [An Exegesis of the Transcendent Perfection of Discriminative Awareness in Eight Thousand Lines] (also known as *Great Commentary on the Transcendent Perfection of Discriminative Awareness in Eight Thousand Lines*)
[Āryāṣṭasāhasrikāprajñāpāramitāvyākhyā] abhisamayālaṃkārāloka
[Shes rab kyi pha rol tu phyin pa brgyad stong pa'i bshad pa] mngon rtogs rgyan gyi snang ba (also known as brGya stong 'grel chen)
Dg.T. Shes phyin vol. CHA, ff. 1b–341a; TPD, vol. 51, pp. 891–1728; T 3791.
Translated in Sparham 2006–12.

Indrabhūti
[Means for Attainment Entitled] Presence of Pristine Cognition
Jñānasiddhi-nāma-sādhana
Ye shes grub pa [zhes bya ba'i sgrub pa'i thabs]
Dg.T. rGyud vol. WI, ff. 36b–60b; TPD, vol. 26, pp. 98–160; T 2219.

Indrasena
Analytical Reasoning
Rab tu 'byed pa'i gtan tshigs
NL

Jayānanda
Exegetical Commentary on the Introduction to the Middle Way
Madhyamakāvatāraṭīkā
dBu ma la 'jug pa'i 'grel bshad
Dg.T. dBu ma vol. RA, ff. 1b–365a; TPD, vol. 61, pp. 3–950; T 3870.

Jñānabhadra
Commentary on the Sūtra of the Descent to Laṅkā
Āryalaṅkāvatāravṛtti
'Phags pa lang kar gshegs pa'i 'grel pa
Dg.T. mDo 'grel vol. NI, ff. 1b–262a; TPD, vol. 70, pp. 3–804; T 4018.

Jñānagarbha
[Commentary on the] Distinction between the Two Truths
Satyadvayavibhaṅgavṛtti
bDen gnyis rnam par 'byed pa'i 'grel pa
Dg.T. dBu ma vol. SA, ff. 3b–15b; TPD, vol. 62, pp. 755–59; T 3882.
Translated in Eckel 1987.

Kamalaśīla
Lamp of the Middle Way
Madhyamakāloka
dBu ma snang ba
Dg.T. dBu ma vol. SA, ff. 133b–244b; TPD, vol. 62, pp. 1114–1403; T 3887.

Karo
Compendium of Discourses on the Stages of Meditation
Bhāvanākramasūtrasamuccaya
bsGom pa'i rim pa mdo kun las btus pa
Dg.T. dBu ma vol. KI, ff. 125b–148a; TPD, vol. 64, pp. 372–432; T 3933.

Katyāyanīputra
Introduction to Knowledge
Jñānaprasthāna
Ye shes la 'jug pa
Extant in Chinese: Taisho 1543–44.

Kumāralāta
Seventy Stanzas on Suffering
Duḥkhasaptati
sDug bsngal bdun cu pa
Not extant.

Lalitavajra
Means for Attainment of the Forty-Nine Deity Bhairava
Śrīvajrabhairavasādhana
dPal rdo rje 'jigs byed [zhe dgu pa'i] sgrub thabs
Dg.T. rGyud vol. MI, ff. 196b–201a; TPD, vol. 24, pp. 637–50; T 1998.

Mahākoṣṭhila
Enumeration of Classes
Saṃgītiparyāya
[Yang dag] 'gro ba'i rnam grangs
Extant in Chinese: Taisho 1536.

Maitreya
Distinction between Phenomena and Actual Reality
Dharmadharmatāvibhāga
Chos dang chos nyid rnam par 'byed pa
Dg.T. Sems tsam vol. PHI, ff. 46b–49a; TPD, vol. 70, pp. 916–34; T 4022.
Translated in Scott 2004.

Distinction between the Middle and Extremes
Madhyāntavibhāga
dBu mtha' rnam par 'byed pa'i tshig le'u byas pa
Dg.T. Sems tsam vol. PHI, ff. 40b–45a; TPD, vol. 70, pp. 902–13; T 4021.
Translated in Dharmachakra Translation Committee 2006.

Five Treatises of Maitreya
Byams chos sde lnga
Comprises the five individual works of Maitreya listed here.
Beijing: mi rigs dpe skrun khang, 1991; also Sichuan mi rigs dpe skrun khang, 1992.

Ornament of Clear Realization
Abhisamayālaṃkāra-[nāma-prajñāpāramitopadeśaśāstrakārikā]
[Shes rab kyi pha rol tu phyin pa'i man ngag gi bstan bcos] mngon par rtogs pa'i rgyan
Dg.T. Shes phyin vol. KA, ff. 1b–13a; TPD, vol. 49, pp. 3–30; T 3786.
Translated in Conze 1954 and Thrangu Rinpoche 2004.

Ornament of the Sūtras of the Great Vehicle
[Mahāyāna]sūtrālaṃkārakārikā
[Theg pa chen po] mdo sde'i rgyan zhes bya ba'i tshig le'ur byas pa
Dg.T. Sems tsam vol. PHI, ff. 1b–39a; TPD, vol. 70, pp. 805–90; T 4020.
Translated in Jamspal et al. 2004.

Supreme Continuum of the Great Vehicle
Mahāyānottaratantraśāstra
Theg pa chen po rgyud bla ma'i bstan bcos
Dg.T. Sems tsam vol. PHI, ff. 54b–73a; TPD, vol. 70, pp. 935–79; T 4024.
Translated in Takasaki 1966; Holmes and Holmes 1985.

Maitripa
Dispelling of Negative Views
Kudṛṣṭinirghāta
lTa ba ngan pa sel ba
Dg.T. rGyud vol. WI, ff. 104b–110a; TPD, vol. 26, pp. 288–302; T 2229.

Maudgalyāyana
Treatise on Designation
Prajñaptiśāstra
gDags pa'i bstan bcos
This treatise is extant in three parts: *Designation of the Mundane* (Lokaprajñapti, 'Jig rten gdags pa), *Designation of Causes* (Kāraṇaprajñapti, rGyu gdags pa), and *Designation of Actions* (Karmaprajñapti, Las gdags pa). It is the only one of the

seven sections of phenomenology (*sde bdun*) extant in Tibetan translation. Also in Chinese: Taisho 1538.
Dg.T. mNgon vol. 1, ff. 1b–229a; TPD, vol. 78, pp. 629–end; T 4086–88.

Miscellaneous Authorship
Eight Great Grammatical Texts of India
'Phags yul du brda sprod kyi bstan bcos brgyad
Those of Indra, Candra, Kāśakṛtsna, Āpiśali, Śākaṭāyana, Pāṇini, Amara, and Jinendra. See Dudjom Rinpoche 1991, vol. 2, pp. 157–58.

Six Texts on Vārāhī
Phag mo gzhung drug
Identified in Roerich 1949, 390, as the treatises contained in Dg.T, vol. ZA, ff. 199a–208b; TPD, vol. 12, pp. 587–623; T 1551–56.

Nāgārjuna
Autocommentary on the Fundamental Stanzas of the Middle Way [Entitled Fearlessness in All Respects]
Mūlamadhyamakavṛttyakutobhaya
dBu ma rtsa ba'i 'grel pa ga las 'jigs med
Dg.T. dBu ma vol. TSA, ff. 29b–99a; TPD, vol. 57, pp. 83–269; T 3829.

Collection of Eulogies
Stavakāya
bsTod pa'i tshogs
A collection of nineteen or twenty eulogies.
Dg.T. bstod tshogs vol. KA, ff. 63b–84a; TPD, vol. 1, p. 181–266; T 1118–37.

Collection of Reasoning [of the Middle Way]
[Madhyamaka] yuktikāya
[dBu ma] rigs tshogs
Comprises (i) *Fundamental Stanzas of the Middle Way Entitled Discriminative Awareness* (Prajñā-nāma-mūlamadhyamakakārikā, T 3824); (ii) *Sixty Verses on Reason* (Yuktiṣaṣṭikā, T 3827); (iii) *Seventy Verses on Emptiness* (Śūnyatāsaptati, T 3827); (iv) *Refutation of Disputed Topics* (Vigrahavyāvartanī, T 3828); (v) *Technique of Pulverization* (Vaidalyasūtra, T 3826); and (vi) *Precious Garland* (Ratnāvalī, T 4158, in lieu of the nonextant Vyavahārasiddhi).
Tibetan edition: *dBu ma rigs tshogs drug.* Gansu Tibetology Research Institute 1996.

Collection of Tales
Parikathākāya
gTam tshogs
Comprises epistles (*sprin yig,* T 4158, 4160–61), along with certain treatises on common ethical customs (*Thun mong ba lugs kyi bstan bcos,* T 4328–30) and so forth.

Fundamental Stanzas of the Middle Way [Entitled Discriminative Awareness]
Prajñā-nāma-mūlamadhyamakakārikā
dBu ma rtsa ba'i tshig le'u byas pa
Dg.T. dBu ma vol. TSA, ff. 1b–19a; TPD, vol. 57, pp. 3–46; T 3824.
Translated in Padmakara Translation Group 2016.

Precious Garland
[Rājaparikathā] ratnāvalī
[rGyal po la gtam bya ba] rin chen phreng ba
Dg.T. sPrin yig vol. GE, ff. 107a–126a; TPD, vol. 96, pp. 288–334; T 4158.
Translated in Hopkins 1998.

Refutation of Disputed Topics
Vigrahavyāvartanī
rTsod pa zlog pa'i tshig le'ur byas pa
Dg.T. dBu ma vol. TSA, ff. 27a–29a; TPD, vol. 57, pp. 74–82; T 3828.

Nandakīrti
Elucidation of Words with Terminations such as -Ti
Tyādyantakriyāpadarohaṇa
Ti la sogs pa'i mtha'i bya ba'i tshig gsal ba
Dg.T. sNa tshogs vol. PO, ff. 265a–270a; TPD, vol. 120, pp. 975–1138; T 4458.

Pāṇini
Uṇādi-sūtra
Edited by Aufrecht. Bonn: Adolf Marcus, 1859.

Prajñākaragupta
Ornament of the Exposition of Valid Cognition
Pramāṇavārttikālaṃkāra
Tshad ma rnam 'grel kyi rgyan
Dg.T. Tshad ma vol. TE, ff. 1b–308a, and vol. THE, ff. 1b–282a; TPD, vol. 99, p. 769–vol. 100, p. 758; T 4221.

Pṛthivībandhu
Commentary on the White Lotus
Miao fa lian hua zhu
Pad dkar 'grel pa (also known as Dam pa'i chos puṇḍa ri ka'i 'grel pa)
Dg.T. mDo 'grel vol. DI, ff. 175b–302a; TPD, vol. 69, pp. 476–828; T 4017.

Puṇḍarīka
Great Commentary [Entitled Taintless Light]
Vimalaprabhā-nāma-mūlatantrānusāriṇī-dvādaśasāhasrikā-laghukālacakra-tantra-rājaṭīkā

bsDus pa'i rgyud kyi rgyal po dus kyi 'khor lo'i 'grel bshad rtsa ba'i rgyud kyi rjes su 'jug pa stong phrag bcu gnyis pa dri ma med pa'i 'od (also known as Dus 'khor 'grel chen, or 'Grel chen)
Dg.K. Dus 'khor 'grel bshad vol. ŚRĪ, ff. 1b–469a; KPD, vol. 99, pp. 3–815; T 845.
Skt. ed. in Jagannatha Upadhyaya, Bibliotheca Indo-Tibetica, vols. 11–13. Sarnath: Central Institute of Higher Tibetan Studies, 1986. See Kilty 2004.

Pūrṇa
Collection of Sensory Elements
Dhātukāya
Khams kyi tshogs
Extant in Chinese: Taisho 1540.

Pūrṇavardhana
Pursuit of Defining Characteristics: [An Exegetical Commentary on the Treasury of Phenomenology]
Abhidharmakośaṭīkā-lakṣaṇānuśariṇī
Chos mngon pa'i mdzod kyi 'grel bshad mtshan nyid kyi rjes su 'brang ba
Dg.T. mNgon pa vol. CU, ff. 1b–347a; TPD, vol. 81, pp. 3–918; T 4093.

Rāhula
Eulogy of the Mother
Yum la bstod pa
Contained in Ratnakīrti's *Eulogy to the Deities of Fourfold Union.*

Ratnakīrti
Eulogy to the Deities of Fourfold Union
Yogacaturdevastotra
sByor bzhi'i lha la bstod pa
Dg.T. bsTod tshogs vol. KA, ff. 246b–249a; TPD, vol. 1, pp. 738–46; T 1770.

Śākyaprabha
Stanzas on the Novitiate of the Mūlasarvāstivāda Order
Āryamūlasarvāstivādaśrāmaṇerakārikā
['Phags pa gzhi thams cad yod par smra ba'i dge tshul gyi] tshig le'ur byas pa
Dg.T. 'Dul ba vol. SHU, ff. 63a–74a; TPD, vol. 93, pp. 167–99; T 4124.

Samudramegha
Exegesis of the Bodhisattva Level
Yogacaryābhūmau bodhisattvabhūmivyākhyā
rNal 'byor spyod pa'i sa las byang chub sems dpa'i sa'i rnam par bshad pa
Dg.T. Sems tsam vol. YI, ff. 1b–338a; TPD, vol. 75, pp. 609–1443; T 4047.

Śaṅkarānanda

Proof of Elimination
Apohasiddhi
Sel ba grub pa
Dg.T. Tshad ma vol. ZHE, ff. 281a–302b; TPD, vol. 106, pp. 769–820; T 4256.

Śāntarakṣita

Autocommentary on the Ornament of the Middle Way
Madhyamakālaṃkāravṛtti
dBu ma rgyan gyi 'grel pa
Dg.T. dBu ma vol. SA, ff. 56b–84a; TPD, vol. 62, pp. 906–80; T 3885.
Edited and translated in Ichigo 1985.

Ornament of the Middle Way
Madhyamakālaṃkāra
dBu ma rgyan gyi tshig le'u byas pa
Dg.T. dBu ma vol. SA, ff. 53a–56b; TPD, vol. 62, pp. 895–905; T 3884.
Translated with commentary in Padmakara Translation Group 2005; also Blumenthal 2004, and Doctor 2004.

Rite according to the Discourse of Bhaiṣajyaguru
sMan bla'i mdo chog
Long title: *Sequential Recitations Compiled from the Discourse of the Particularly Extensive Former Aspirations of the Seven Sugatas along with the Discourse That Presents the Offerings and Rites of Aspiration Associated with the Seven Tathāgatas*
Qi ru lai wang xi shi yuan shu sheng guang da
De bzhin gshegs pa bdun gyi sngon gyi smon lam gyi khyad par rgyas pa'i mdo sde bklag cing de bzhin gshegs pa bdun mchod de smon lam gdab pa'i cho ga mdo sde las btus te rim par bklag pa
Dg.T. rGyud vol. PU, ff. 295b–301b; TPD, vol. 38, pp. 918–34; T 3134.

Śāntideva

Compendium of Lessons
Śikṣāsamuccaya
bSlab pa kun las btus pa
Dg.T. dBu ma vol. KHI, ff. 3a–194b; TPD, vol. 64, pp. 1009–1519; T 3940.
Translated in Bendall and Rouse 1971.

Introduction to the Conduct of a Bodhisattva
Bodhisattvacaryāvatāra
Byang chub sems dpa'i spyod pa la 'jug pa
Dg.T. dBu ma vol. LA, ff. 1b–40a; TPD, vol. 61, pp. 951–1048; T 3871.
Translated in Padmakara Translation Group 1997; commentary in Padmakara Translation Group 2007.

Stanzas of the Compendium of Lessons
Śikṣāsamuccayakārikā
bSlab pa kun las btus pa'i tshig le'u byas pa
Dg.T. dBu ma vol. KHI, ff. 1b–3a; TPD, vol. 64, pp. 1005–8; T 3939.

Saraha
Treasury of Spiritual Songs
Dohākoṣagīti
Do ha mdzod kyi glu
Dg.T. rGyud vol. WI, ff. 70b–77a; TPD, vol. 26, pp. 193–210; T 2224.
Translated in Guenther 1993.

Śāriputra
Sections of the Sacred Doctrine
Dharmaskandha
Chos kyi phung po
Extant in Chinese: Taisho 1537.

Smṛtijñānakīrti
Sword at the Gateway to Language
Vacanamukhāyudhopama
sMra sgo mtshon cha [lta bu]
Dg.T. sGra mdo vol. SHE, ff. 277b–281b; TPD, vol. 109, pp. 1827–40; T 4295.
Beijing: Mi rigs dpe skrun khang, 1980.

Śrīlāta
Seventy Stanzas on Particles
*Rajusaptati
rDul bdun cu pa
No longer extant.

Sthiramati
Commentary on the Thirty Verses
Triṃśikābhāṣya
Sum cu pa'i bshad pa
Dg.T. Sems tsam vol. SHI, ff. 146b–171b; TPD, vol. 77, pp. 389–456; T 4064.

Śūra
Garland of Birth Stories
Jātakamālā
sKyes pa'i rabs [kyi rgyud]
Dg.T. sKyes rabs vol. HU, ff. 1b–135a; TPD, vol. 94, pp. 3–385; T 4150.
Translated in Speyer 1895.

Sūryasiddhi
Exegesis of the Exegesis of the Ten Levels
Daśabhūmivyākhyānavyākhyāna
Sa bcu'i rnam par bshad pa'i rnam par bshad pa (also known as *Branch Commentary of the Ten Levels,* Sa bcu pa'i yang lag gi 'grel pa)
Dg.T. mDo 'grel vol. JI, ff. 1b–119b; TPD, vol. 67, pp. 3–308; T 3998.

Tilopa and Nāropā
Six Doctrines [of Nāropā]
Ṣaḍdharmopadeśa
Nā ro chos drug [gi man ngag]
Dg.T. rGyud vol. ZHI, ff. 270a–271a; TPD, vol. 26, pp. 1725–29; T 2330.

Tripiṭakamāla
Lamp of the Three Ways
Nayatrayapradīpa
Tshul gsum sgron ma
Dg.T. rGyud vol. TSU, ff. 6b–26b; TPD, rGyud vol. 41, pp. 19–70; T 3707.

Vasubandhu
Autocommentary on the Treasury of Phenomenology
Abhidharmakośabhāṣya
Chos mngon pa'i mdzod kyi bshad pa
Dg.T. mNgon pa vol. KU, ff. 26b–258a; TPD, vol. 79, pp. 65–630; T 4090.
Translated from the French in Pruden 1988–90.

Commentary on the Distinction between the Middle and Extremes
Madhyāntavibhāgaṭīkā
dBu dang mtha' rnam par 'byed pa'i 'grel pa
Dg.T. Sems tsam vol. BI, ff. 1b–27a; TPD, vol. 71, pp. 3–70; T 4027.
Translated in Anacker 1984, 211–86.

Commentary on the Three Mothers Entitled Subduer of Harm
Yum gsum gi gnod 'joms (also known as *Great Commentary on the Transcendent Perfection of Discriminative Awareness in One Hundred Thousand, Twenty-Five Thousand, and Eighteen Thousand Lines*)
Śatasāhasrikāpañcaviṃśatisāhasrikāṣṭādaśasāhasrikāprajñāpāramitā-bṛhaṭṭīkā
'Phags pa shes rab kyi pha rol tu phyin pa 'bum pa dang nyi khri lnga stong pa dang khri brgyad stong pa'i rgya cher bshad pa
Dg.T. Shes phyin vol. PHA, ff. 1b–292b; TPD, vol. 55, pp. 645–1376; T 3808.
Note that the authorship of this text is also attributed to Daṃṣṭrasena.

[Dissertation in] Thirty Verses
Triṃśikā [kārikāprakaraṇa]

Sum cu pa'i tshig le'u byas pa
Dg.T. Sems tsam vol. SHI, ff. 1b–3a; TPD, vol. 77, pp. 3–7; T 4055.
Translated from the Chinese in Cook 1999; also Anacker 1984, Kochumuttom 1982.

Dissertation in Twenty Verses
Viṃśakaprakaraṇa (also known as Viṃśakakārikā)
Nyi shu pa'i rab byed (also known as Nyi shu pa'i tshig le'ur byas pa)
Dg.T. Sems tsam vol. SHI, ff. 3a–4a; TPD, vol. 77, pp. 8–11; T 4056.

Dissertation on the Five Aggregates
Pañcaskandhaprakaraṇa
Phung po lnga'i rab tu byed pa
Dg.T. Sems tsam vol. SHI, ff. 11b–17a; TPD, vol. 77, pp. 35–40; T 4059.
Translated, along with Tibetan and reconstructed Sanskrit editions, in Engle 2009; also Anacker 1984.

Dissertation on the Proof of Past Actions
Karmasiddhiprakaraṇa
Las grub pa'i rab tu byed pa
Dg.T. Sems tsam vol. SHI, ff. 134b–145a; TPD, vol. 77, pp. 355–83; T 4062.

Exegesis of the Ten Levels
Āryadaśabhūmivyākhyāna
['Phags pa] sa bcu pa'i rnam par bshad pa (also known as *Root Commentary of the Ten Levels,* Sa bcu pa'i rtsa 'grel)
Dg.T. mDo 'grel vol. NGI, ff. 103b–266a; TPD, vol. 65, pp. 1020–end; T 3993.

Exposition of the Three Natures
Trisvabhāvanirdeśa
Rang bzhin gsum nges par bstan pa
Dg.T. Sems tsam vol. SHI, ff. 10a–11b; TPD, vol. 77, pp. 29–34; T 4058.

Rational System of Exposition
Vyākhyāyukti
rNam par bshad pa'i rigs pa
Dg.T. Sems tsam vol. SHI, ff. 29a–134b; TPD, vol. 77, pp. 81–354; T 4061.

[*Stanzas of the*] *Treasury of Phenomenology*
Abhidharmakośakārikā
Chos mngon pa'i mdzod kyi tshig le'ur byas pa
Dg.T. mNgon pa vol. KU, ff. 1b–25a; TPD, vol. 79, pp. 3–59; T 4089.

Vasumitra
[*Great*] *Treasury of Detailed Exposition*
[Mahā]vibhāṣakośa

Bye brag bshad mdzod [chen mo]
Extant in Chinese: Taisho 1545.
Tibetan translation by Lobzang Chophak (10 vols.). Beijing: Krung go'i bod rigs dpe skrun khang, 2011.

Vasumitra, arhat
Dissertation
Prakaraṇapāda
Rab tu byed pa
Extant in Chinese: Taisho 1541–42.

Vimalamitra
Illuminating Lamp
[Dung yig can rgyud kyi khong don bsdus pa] sgron ma snang byed
Contained in the *Collected Works of Longchen Rabjam, Bi ma snying thig,* vol. 2 (series no. 107), pp. 63–115. dPal brtsegs bod yig dpe rnying series, 4 vols. (nos. 106–9). Beijing: Krung go bod rig pa dpe skrun khang, 2009.

Vimuktisena
Commentary on the Ornament of Emergent Realization
Āryapañcaviṃśatisāhasrikāprajñāpāramitopadeśaśāstrābhisamayālaṃkāravṛtti
'Phags pa shes rab kyi pha rol tu phyin pa stong phrag nyi shu lnga pa'i man ngag gi bstan bcos mngon par rtogs pa'i rgyan gyi 'grel pa (short title: mNgon rtogs rgyan gyi 'grel pa)
Dg.T. Shes phyin vol. KA, ff. 14b–212a; TPD, vol. 49, pp. 33–500; T 3787.
Translated in Sparham 2006–12.

Illuminating Commentary on the Transcendent Perfection of Discriminative Awareness in Twenty-Five Thousand Lines
Nyi khri snang ba
See previous entry.

Yaśomitra
Commentary on the Treasury of Phenomenology
Abhidharmakośaṭīkā
Chos mngon pa'i mdzod kyi 'grel bshad
Dg.T. mNgon pa vols. GU–NGU; TPD, vol. 80; T 4092.

4. Tibetan Treatises and Spiritual Revelations

Anon
Phangtang Catalogue
dKar chag 'phang thang ma
Beijing: Mi rigs dpe skrung khang, 2003.

Chenak Hūṃchen and Yeshe Ozer Dolma
An Historical Anthology of the Mantrin Communities of Repkong
Reb kong sngags mang gi lo rgyus phyogs bsgrigs
sNgags mang dpe tshogs series. Beijing: Mi rigs dpe skrun khang, 2004.

Chogyal Namkhai Norbu
The Light of Kailash: A History of Zhangzhung and Tibet
Zhang bod lo rgyus ti se'i 'od
Beijing: Krung go'i bod kyi shes rig dpe skrun khang, 1996.
Translated in Namkhai Norbu 2009, 2013, and 2015.

Choying Tobden Dorje
Treasury of Sūtra and Tantra
mDo rgyud mdzod (5 vols., 25 books)
Chengdu: Sichuan mi rigs dpe skrun khang, 2000.
Books 1–10 translated in Zangpo 2015, Books 15–17 translated in Dorje 2016.

Dalai Lama V
Precious Chariot [*Steering the Treasury of Phenomenology*]
Chos mngon rin chen 'dren pa'i shing rta
Collected Works of Dalai Lama V, vol. 17, pp. 393–663.
Gangtok: Sikkim Research Institute of Tibetology, 1991–95.

Dampa Gyagarwa (Phadampa Sangye)
Cycles of the Sacred Doctrine: Pacification of Suffering
Dam chos sdug bsngal zhi byed kyi skor rnams
Selected texts of this cycle are contained in Jamgon Kongtrul, *gDams ngag mdzod,* vol. 13, and in *Zhid byed dang shangs pa'i chos skor,* pp. 1–37.
dPal brtsegs bod yig dpe rnying zhib 'jug khang series. Lhasa: Bod ljongs mi dmangs dpe skrun khang, 2010.

Dondrub Lhagyal et al.
Dictionary of Bon Culture
Bon gyi shes rig tshig mdzod
Lhasa: Bon ljongs mi dmangs dpe krun khang, 2012.

Dragon Konchok Tenpa Rabgye
Doctrinal History of Amdo
mDo smad chos 'byung (also known as *The Ocean Annals of Amdo,* Deb ther rgya mtsho)
3 vols. Delhi: Lokesh Chandra, 1973; Lanzhou: Gansu mi rigs dpe skrun khang, 1982.

Drangje Tsunpa Sermik (disc.)
Nailing Discourse
mDo zer mig
Ziling: Krung go'i bod kyi shes rig dpe skrun khang, 1991.

Dromtonpa Gyalwa Jungne et al.
Father and Child Teachings of the Kadam School
bKa' gdams pha chos bu chos (also known as the *Book of Kadam,* bKa' gdams legs 'bam)
2 vols. Ziling: Qinghai mi rigs dpe skrun khang, 1994.
See Martin 1997, no. 69. Translated in Jinpa 2008, also Jinpa 2013.

Drubthob Ngodrub et al. (disc.)
Collected Words of the King concerning the Mantra OṂ MAṆI PADME HŪṂ
Ma ṇi bka' 'bum
On this work, which may not have reached its final form until the fifteenth century, see Martin 1997, no. 16, p. 30. Translated in Trizin Tsering Rinpoche 2007.

Drungchen Ngodrub Gyatso
Exegesis of the Treasury of Phenomenology: Intelligence That Opens the Lotus of the Mind
mDzod kyi rnam bshad blo gsal blo'i pad mo kha 'byed
Beijing: Krung go'i bod rig pa'i dpe skrun khang, 2008.

Dudjom Jigdrel Yeshe Dorje
Concise Political History of Tibet: An Unprecedented Mirror of Clear Crystal
Gangs can bod chen po'i rgyal rabs bsdus gsal du bkod pa sngon med dvangs shel 'phrul gyi me long (short title: bDud 'joms rgyal rabs)
Delhi 1978. Contained in the *Collected Works of Dudjom Jigdrel Yeshe Dorje,* vol. 3. See Martin 1997, no. 510.

History of the Nyingma School of Tibetan Buddhism
Gangs ljongs rgyal bstan yongs rdzogs kyi phyi mo snga' 'gyur rdo rje theg pa'i bstan pa rin po che ji ltar byung ba'i tshul dag cing gsal bar brjod pa lha dbang g.yul las rgyal ba'i rnga bo che'i sgra dbyangs (short title: bDud 'joms chos 'byung)
Kalimpong 1967. Contained in the *Collected Works of Dudjom Jigdrel Yeshe Dorje,* vol. 1.
See Martin 1997, no. 471. Translated in Dudjom Rinpoche 1991 by Gyurme Dorje and Matthew Kapstein.

Dudul Dorje (disc.)
General Prophetic Declarations concerning the Buddhist Teaching
[rDzogs pa chen po dam chos dgongs pa yongs 'dus las] bstan pa spyi'i lung bstan ['od kyi dra ba]

Contained in the *Collected Revelations of Powo Terton Dudul Dorje,* vol. 1, pp. 45–84.
Darjeeling: Kargyud sungrab nyamso khang, 1997.

Dungkar Lobzang Trinle
Great Dictionary of Dungkar
Dung dkar tshig mdzod chen mo
Beijing: Krung go'i bod rig pa dpe skrun khang, 2002.

Gangriwa Choying Dorje
Ancient History of Ngari Korsum: The Undying Drumbeat
Gangs can bod kyi nub ngos mnga' ris skor gsum gyi sngon byung lo rgyus 'chi med rnga sgra
Lhasa: Bod ljongs mi rigs dpe skrun khang, 1996.

Guge Tsewang Gyalpo
Religious History of Ngari: Beauteous Ornament of the Land of Snows
mNga' ris chos 'byung gangs ljongs mdzes rgyan
Lhasa: Bod ljongs mi rigs dpe skrun khang, 2006.

Jamgon Kongtrul
Anthology of Precious Revelations
Rin chen gter mdzod
Compiled by Jamgon Kongtrul. Palpung edition, republished in 72 vols. and held at sDe dge spar khang.

Jamgon Mipham Gyatso
Nucleus of Inner Radiance: [An Overview of the Tantra of the Secret Nucleus]
[gSang snying spyi don] 'od gsal snying po
NK vol. 69; also in *Collected Works,* vol. 23, pp. 97–320.
Chengdu: Sichuan mi rigs dpe skrun khang, 2000.
Translated in Dharmachakra Translation Committee 2009.

Jamyang Gyatso
Explanation of Elision [of Anubandhas]
rJes 'brel sogs dbyi tshul bshad pa
In *Extensive Exegesis of the Sārasvata Grammar,* edited by Kelzang Ngawang Damcho, pp. 619–27.

Jarigpa Lobzang Namgyal
Concise Biographies of the Successive Throneholders of Ganden
dGa' ldan khri pa rim byon gyi mdzad rnam mdor bsdus
Lhasa: Bod ljongs mi dmangs dpe skrun khang, 2008.

Jigme Chokyi Dorje
Great Anthology of Buddhist Icons according to the Tibetan Lineages
Bod brgyud nang bstan lha tshogs chen mo
Ziling: Qinghai mi rigs dpe skrun khang, 2001.

Jigme Tekchok
Successive Hierarchs of Rongpo Gonchen
Rong bo dgon chen gyi gdan rabs rdzogs ldan gtam gyi rang sgra
Ziling: Qinghai mi rigs dpe skrun khang, 1988.

Jowo Lhundrub Tashi and Menrampa Lobzang Chodrak
Biographies of Yutokpa the Younger and the Older
g.Yu thog gsar rnying gi rnam thar
Beijing: Mi rigs dpe skrun khang, 1982.

Khenpo Munsel and Khenpo Jamyang of Katok
Collected Transmitted Teachings of the Nyingmapa [NK]
rNying ma'i bka' ma shin tu rgyas pa
120 vols. Chengdu 1999.

Khepei Deu
Extensive Religious History of India and Tibet
rGya bod kyi chos 'byung rgyas pa
Lhasa: Bod ljogs mi rigs dpe skrun khang, 1987.

Khyungpo Neljor
Six Doctrines of Niguma
Ni gu'i chos drug
Contained in Jamgon Kongtrul, *gDams ngag mdzod,* vol. 11, pp. 1–27. The tracts of guidance are contained in vol. 12.

Six Yogas of Esoteric Instruction
Man ngag sbyor drug
Contained in Jamgon Kongtrul, *gDams ngag mdzod,* vol. 15, pp. 6–13.

Lhodrak Namkha Gyaltsen
Secret Biography Entitled Dispelling the Darkness of Misconceptions
gSang ba'i rnam thar log rtog mun sel
Collected Works of Lhodrak Namkha Gyaltsen, vol. 1, pp. 135–53.
Lhasa: Bod ljongs bod yig dpe rnying dpe skrun khang, 2004.

Longchen Rabjam
Dispelling All Mental Darkness with the Light of Eloquence: An Overview of the Glorious Tantra of the Secret Nucleus

dPal gsang ba'i snying po'i spyi don legs par bshad pa'i snang bas yid kyi mun pa thams cad sel ba
dPal brtsegs bod yig dpe rnying series, vol. 130, pp. 52–183. Beijing: Krung go bod rig pa dpe skrun khang, 2009.

Dispelling the Darkness of the Ten Directions
[dPal gsang snying gi rgyud gyi 'grel pa] phyogs bcu mun sel
dPal brtsegs bod yig dpe rnying series, vol. 128. Beijing: Krung go bod rig pa dpe skrun khang, 2009; also NK vol. 68.
Translated in Dorje 1987 and in Chonam and Khandro 2011.

Great Array of the Highest (revelation)
Ati bkod pa chen po
An alternative title of the *Innermost Spirituality of Vimalamitra.*

Innermost Spirituality of Vimalamitra (revelation)
Bi ma'i snying thig
dPal brtsegs bod yig dpe rnying series, vols. 106–9. Beijing: Krung go bod rig pa dpe skrun khang, 2009.

Treasury of Philosophical Systems
[Theg pa mtha' dag gi don gsal bar byed pa] grub pa'i mtha' rin po che'i mdzod (short title: Grub mtha' mdzod)
dPal brtsegs bod yig dpe rnying series, vol. 120, pp. 1–336. Beijing: Krung go bod rig pa dpe skrun khang, 2009.
Translated in Barron 2007.

White Lotus [Autocommentary on the Treasury of Wish-Fulfilling Gems: A Treatise of the Pith Instructions of the Great Vehicle]
[Theg pa chen po'i man ngag gi bstan bcos yid bzhin rin po che'i mdzod kyi 'grel pa] padma dkar po
dPal brtsegs bod yig dpe rnying zhib 'jug khang, 2 vols., 118–19. Beijing: Krung go bod rig pa dpe skrun khang, 2009; also Potala edition, vol. 1 (312 ff.); Gangtok: Dodrupchen Rinpoche, n.d. (I–Tib–143); Chengdu: Adzom Chogar, 1999.

Namcho Migyur Dorje (disc.)
General Prophetic Declarations concerning the Buddhist Teaching
bsTan pa'i spyi lung
In *Collected Revelations of Namcho Migyur Dorje,* vol. 1, ff. 69a–70b. Paro: Dilgo Khyentse Rinpoche, 1983.

Ngendzongpa
Aural Lineage of Ngendzong
Ngan rdzong snyan brgyud

In the *Great Anthology of Drigung Kagyu Doctrines,* 'Bri gung bka' brgyud chos mdzod chen mo, vols. 63–64.
151 vols. Edited by Agon Rinpoche. Lhasa 2004.

Nordrang Orgyan
Compendium of Buddhist Numeric Terms
Chos rnam kun btus
3 vols. Beijing: Krung go'i bod rig pa dpe skrun khang, 2008.

Nyangrel Nyima Ozer (disc.)
[*Eight Transmitted Teachings*]: *Gathering of the Sugatas*
[bKa' brgyad] bde gshegs 'dus pa
Comprises five general root tantras (*rtsa ba'i spyi rgyud lnga*) and ten particular tantras (*sgos rgyud bcu*), which are all contained in Dg. NGB vols. 14–15; also Tingkye NGB vols. 31–32; bKa' brgyad phyogs bsgrigs. 12 vols. Chengdu: Thubten Nyima, 2000; and Tsamdrak ms. edition, 13 vols. Paro: Lama Ngodup, 1979–1980.

Orgyan Lingpa (disc.)
Gathering of the Transmitted Teachings: Ocean of the Sacred Doctrine
bKa' 'dus [chos kyi rgya mtsho]
Comprises ten general tantras (*bka' 'dus spyi rgyud bcu*) and twenty-one particular tantras (*sgos rgyud nyer gcig*).
Rediscovered by Jamyang Khyentse Wangpo.
Contained in RTD vol. 23, pp. 209–429. Xylo. Kalimpong, West Bengal, India: Zangs mdog dpal ri, n.d.

Injunction of the King
rGyal po bka' thang
Contained in the *Five Injunctions,* bKa' thang sde lnga, pp. 227–302.
Beijing: Mi rigs dpe skrun khang, 1988.

Injunction of the Minister
Blon po bka'i thang yig
Contained in the *Five Injunctions,* bKa' thang sde lnga, pp. 425–539.
Beijing: Mi rigs dpe skrun khang, 1988.

Injunctions of Padma [*Discovered at Crystal Rock*]
Padma'i bka' thang [shel brag ma]
Chengdu: Sichuan mi rigs dpe skrun khang, 1987.

Pasar Tsultrim Tenzin et al.
A Lexicon of Zhangzhung and Bonpo Terms
Osaka: National Museum of Ethnology, 2008.

Pekar Zangpo
Structure of the Sūtras
mDo sde spyi'i rnam gzhag
Beijing: Mi rigs dpe skrun khang, 2006.

Peltsul
Anthology of the Doctrinal History of Yungdrung Bon
g.Yung drung bon gyi bstan 'byung phyogs bstus
Lhasa: Bod ljongs mi rigs dpe skrun khang, 1988.

Ratna Lingpa (disc.)
Prophetic Declarations
Zab mo klong gsal skor gsum las ma 'ongs lung bstan pa spyi lung| gang zag sgos pa'i lung| mtha' dmag 'khrugs pa'i lung bstan rnams
Contained in the *Collected Works of Ratna Lingpa,* vol. 17, pp. 575–616.
21 vols. Serta Nubzur Gon (gSer rta nub zur mgon): sNga 'gyur rnying ma dpal bla med gsang chen gnubs zur dgon, 2014.

Rechungpa
Aural Lineage of Rechung
Ras chung snyan brgyud
In the *Great Anthology of Drigung Kagyu Doctrines,* 'Bri gung bka' brgyud chos mdzod chen mo, vols. 58–62.
151 vols. Edited by Agon Rinpoche. Lhasa 2004.

Śākya Chokden
Exegesis on Difficult Points in the Treasury of Phenomenology: Great Lake of the Treatise of Detailed Exposition
Chos mngon pa'i mdzod kyi dka' ba'i gnas rnam par bshad pa'i bstan bcos bye brag tu bshad pa'i mtsho chen
In the *Collected Works of gSer mDog Paṇ chen Śākya mChog ldan,* vol. 21 (ZHA).
24 vols. Beijing: Krung go'i bod rig pa dpe skrun khang, 2013.

Sangye Gyatso
Survey of the Medical Tradition
[gSo dpyad] sman gyi khog 'bubs
Bod kyi gso ba rig pa'i gna' dpe phyogs bsgrigs dpe tshogs series 8. Beijing: Mi rigs dpe skrun khang, 2004.
Translated in Kilty 2010.

Yellow Beryl
[dGa' ldan chos 'byung] bai ḍūrya ser po
Ziling: Qinghai mi rigs dpe skrun khang, 1991.

Sonam Gyaltsen
Mirror Illuminating Royal Genealogies
rGyal rabs gsal ba'i me long
Beijing: Mi rigs dpe skrun khang, 1981.
See also Martin 1997, no. 94, pp. 60–61, and Sørensen 1994.

Takzham Nuden Dorje (disc.)
Biography of Tsogyal
mKha 'gro ye shes mtsho rgyal gyi rnam thar
Chengdu: Sichuan mi rigs dpe skrun khang, 1989.
Translated in Padmakara Translation Group 2002.

Tavihrica and Pongyal Tsenpo
Aural Lineage of Zhangzhung
Zhang zhung snyan brgyud
See Dondrub Lhagyal et al. 2012, 30–31.
Translated in Achard 2005–10 (4 vols.).

Thonmi Sambhoṭa
Introduction to Gender
[Lung du ston pa] rtags kyi 'jug pa
Dg.T. sNa tshogs vol. co, ff. 161b–162b; TPD, vol. 115, pp. 402–6; T 4349.
See also references in next entry.

Thirty Verses
[Lung du ston pa'i rtsa ba] sum cu pa
Dg.T. sNa tshogs vol. co, ff. 160b–161b; TPD, vol. 115, pp. 397–401; T 4348.
Tibetan text also in *Sum rtags rtsa ba phyogs sgrig,* Chengdu: Sichuan mi rigs dpe skrun khang, 1992; and in *dKyil grva dka' chen padma'i brda dag phyogs bsgrigs*, pp. 240–48, Lhasa: Bod ljongs bod yig dpe rnying dpe skrun khang, 2001.

Trorum Tsenam
Commentary on the Grammar of Sārasvata: A Slight Clarification
brDa sprod pa dbyangs can gyi mdo'i 'grel pa nyung ngu rnam gsal
Beijing: Krung go bod kyi shes rig dpe skrun khang, in collaboration with Qinghai Xinhua Bookstore, 1998.

Yutok Yonten Gonpo, Drapa Ngonshe et al.
Four Medical Tantras [of Dratang]
[Grva thang] sman gyi rgyud bzhi
Beijing: Mi rigs dpe skrun khang, 2005.

Eighteen Branches of Medical Science
Cha lag bco brgyad
2 vols. Gansu: Gansu mi rigs dpe skrun khang, 1999.

Zhabkar Tsokdruk Rangdrol
Autobiography of Zhabkar Tsokdruk Rangdrol
Zhabs dkar tshogs drug rang grol gyi rang rnam
Ziling: Qinghai mi rigs dpe skrun khang, 1985.
Translated in Ricard 1994.

Zhuchen Tsultrim Rinchen
Catalogue of the Tengyur
bsTan 'gyur dkar chag
Lhasa: Bod ljongs mi rigs dpe skrun khang, 1985.

5. Chinese Divination Texts

Most of the treatises on elemental divination that are considered to be Chinese in origin are no longer extant. However, their titles, content, and occasional excerpts are known from later Tibetan commentaries, such as Sangye Gyatso's *White Beryl.*

Disclosure of the Hidden
Gab pa mngon phyung
NL

Divination Science of Pang-gyen Lama
sPang rgyan bla ma'i gtsug lag
NL

Fivefold Mother and Child of the Clarifying Lamp
sNang gsal ma bu cha lnga
NL

Gathering of Four Brahmā Divinations
Tshangs bzhi 'dus pa
NL

Gathering of the Nine Branches
sDong po dgu 'dus
NL

Tantra Comprising the Divisions
sDe ru longs pa'i rgyud
NL

Tantra of Utterly Secret Mind
Yang gsang dag thugs rgyud
NL

6. Non-Buddhist Indic Sources

Anon

Cycle of Training That Effects Recollection
Dran par byed pa bslab pa'i 'khor lo
NA

Fifty Defining Characteristics
mTshan nyid lnga bcu pa (Sāṃkhya)
NA

Bṛhaspati

Essence of the View That Refutes Everything
Thams cad la skur ba 'debs pa la lta ba'i snying po (Bāhaspatya)
NA

Six Tantras of Bṛhaspati
Phur bu'i rgyud sde drug (Bārhaspatya)
NA

Īśvarakṛṣṇa

Stanzas on Sāṃkhya
Sāṃkhyakārikā (Sāṃkhya)
dBang phyug nag po'i gzhung
Translated from Sanskrit in Sinha 1915. Edited and translated in Suryanarayana Sastri 1935. Extracts also in Radhakrishnan and Moore 1957.

Jaina Canon

gZhung rgyal byed
Comprises forty-five works that include (i) eleven main texts (*aṅga*); (ii) twelve subsidiary texts (*upāṅga*); (iii) ten miscellaneous texts (*prakīrṇaka*); (iv) six discourses on ascetic practice (*chedasūtra*); (v) two texts on epistemology (*cūlikāsūtra*); and (vi) four root sūtras (*mūlasūtra*).

Janaka

School of the Sage [King] Janaka
Ṛṣijānakaśākhā
Drang srong skyed byed kyi yal ga
The school of Vedic lore associated with the Kingly Sage Janaka who is mentioned in the *Bṛhadāraṇyaka Upaniṣad*.

Jayanta
Flower Cluster of Reason
Nyāyamañjarī
Sanskrit edition in two parts by Gaṅgadhara Śāstrī Tailaṅga. Vizianagaram Sanskrit Series No. 10. Benares: E. J. Lazarus, 1895, 1896.

Kapila
Sixty Chapter Tantra
Saṣṭitantraśāstra (Sāṃkhya)
rGyud drug cu pa
NA

Miscellaneous
Esoteric Words
Upaniṣad
gSang tshig
A corpus of fifty or one hundred eight esoteric texts revered by the various schools of Vedic lore that espouse different Vedic arrangements, Brāhmaṇas, and Āraṇyakas.

[*Teachings of the*] *Schools Espousing Rituals and Vedic Arrangements*
Kalpasaṃhitāśākhā
rTog pa la phan pa'i yal ga
These are the teachings of the diverse schools of Vedic lore that espouse distinctive compilations of the Vedas with their corresponding rituals (Brāhmaṇas) and esoteric texts (Āraṇyakas and Upaniṣads).

Rāṇāyana
Esoteric Words of the Rāṇāyanīya
Lo ma can gyi gsang tshig
Name of a hermit sage embodying the lifestyle of the forest-dwelling practitioners of the Āraṇyakas.

Uddalaka Aruni, hermit sage of Pañcāla
Gateways to Ablution
Snānadvāra
Khrus kyi sgo
NA

Tantras of Śiva
Zhi ba'i rgyud (Śaiva)
A collective name for the ninety-two Shaivite tantras, which are said to include (i) sixty-four "monistic" (*abheda*) Bhairava tantras; (ii) eighteen "monistic or dualistic" (*bhedābheda*) Rudra tantras; and (iii) ten "dualistic" (*bheda*) Śiva Tantras.

Tantra of the Quiescence of Viṣṇu
Khyab 'jug zhi ba'i rgyud
NA

Vālmīki
Esoteric Words of Vālmīki
Grog mkhar gyi gsang tshig

Vyāsa (diffuser/redactor, dates uncertain)
Anthology of Bharata
Bharatasaṃhitā
Bha ra ta ka'i dum bu

Four Vedas
Caturveda
Rig byed bzhi
The primary source texts or divine revelations of the Brāhmaṇical tradition of Hinduism, comprising the Ṛgveda (*nges brjod kyi rig byed*), Atharvaveda (*srid srungs kyi rig byed*), Sāmaveda (*snyan tshig gi rig byed*), and Yajurveda (*mchod sbyin gyi rig byed*). See Gonda 1975, chs. 3–7. Among them, the Ṛgveda includes the renowned *Puruṣasūkta* hymn (10:90).

Yajñāvalkya
Bṛhadāraṇyaka Upaniṣad
One of esoteric instructions pertaining to the White Yajurveda. Translated in Radhakrishnan 1953, pp. 147–333.

7. Works in Other Languages

Achard, Jean-Luc, trans. 2005–2010. *The Oral Lineage of Zhangzhung*. 4 vols. (*Three Precepts,* 2005; *The Dawn of Awareness,* 2006; *The Four Lamps,* 2007; *The Precepts in Eight Chapters,* 2010). Paris: Zhangzhung Nyengyu Studies, Naldjor Institute for Movement and Tibetan Yoga.
Anacker, Stefan. 1984. *Seven Works of Vasubandhu*. Delhi: Motilal Banarsidass.
Aris, Michael. 1979. *Bhutan: The Early History of a Himalayan Kingdom*. Warminster: Aris and Phillips.
Barron, Richard, trans. 2005. *A Marvelous Garland of Rare Gems*. Junction City, Calif.: Padma Publishing.
———, trans. 2007. *The Precious Treasury of Philosophical Systems*. By Longchen Rabjam. Junction City, Calif.: Padma Publishing.
Basham, A. L. 1951. *History and Doctrine of the Ājīvikas*. London: Luzac.
Baumer, Christoph. 2002. *Bon: Tibet's Ancient Religion*. Translated from the German by Michael Kohn. Bangkok: Orchid Press.

Beckwith, Christopher L. 1987. *The Tibetan Empire in Central Asia.* Princeton, N.J.: Princeton University Press.

Bendall, Cecil, and W. H. D. Rouse, trans. (1922) 1971. *Śikṣā Samuccaya.* Delhi: Motilal Banarsidass.

Beyer, Stephan V. 1992. *The Classical Tibetan Language.* Albany: State University of New York Press.

Birnbaum, R. 1979. *The Healing Buddha.* Boston: Shambhala Publications.

Blumenthal, James. 2004. *The Ornament of the Middle Way: A Study of the Madhyamaka Thought of Śāntarakṣita.* Ithaca, N.Y.: Snow Lion Publications.

Bodhi, Bhikkhu, trans. 1978. *The Discourse on the All-Embracing Net of Views.* Kandy: Buddhist Publication Society.

Boin-Webb, Sara, trans. 2001. *Abhidharmasamuccaya: The Compendium of the Higher Teaching (Philosophy).* By Asaṅga. Translated into French by Walpola Rahula. Fremont, Calif.: Asian Humanities Press.

Boord, Martin J., trans. 2002. *A Bolt of Lightning from the Blue.* Berlin: edition khordong.

Brough, John. 2001. *The Gandhari Dharmapada.* Delhi: Motilal Banarsidass.

Cabezón, José I. 2013. *The Buddha's Doctrine and the Nine Vehicles.* New York: Oxford University Press.

Chandra, Lokesh, and David L. Snellgrove. 1981. *Sarvatathāgata-tattva-saṃgraha: Facsimile Reproduction of a Tenth-Century Sanskrit Manuscript from Nepal.* New Delhi: Sharada Rani.

Chang, Garma C. C., ed. 1983. *A Treasury of Mahāyāna Sūtras.* Delhi: Motilal Banarsidass.

Chonam, Lama, and Sangye Khandro, trans. 2011. *The Guhyagarbha Tantra: Secret Essence Definitive Just as It Is.* Ithaca, N.Y.: Snow Lion Publications.

Cleary, Thomas, trans. 1993. *The Flower Ornament Scripture.* Boston: Shambhala Publications.

Conze, Edward, trans. 1954. *Abhisamayālaṅkāra.* Serie Orientale Roma 6. Rome: Istituto Italiano per il Medio ed Estremo Oriente.

———. 1960. *The Prajñāpāramitā Literature.* New Delhi: Munishiram Manoharlal.

———, trans. 1973. *The Perfection of Wisdom in Eight Thousand Lines and Its Verse Summary.* Bolinas, Calif.: Four Seasons Foundation.

———, trans. 1975. *The Large Sutra on Perfect Wisdom.* Berkeley and Los Angeles: University of California Press.

Cook, Francis H., trans. 1999. *Three Texts on Consciousness Only.* Berkeley: Numata Center for Buddhist Translation and Research.

Davidson, Ronald M., trans. 1981. "The Litany of Names of Manjushri: Text and Translation of the Manjushri-nama-samgiti." In Michel Strickmann, ed. *Tantric and Taoist Studies, in Honour of R. A. Stein,* 1–69. Mélanges Chinoises et Bouddhiques, vol. 20. Brussels: Institut Belge des Hautes Études Chinoises.

Dharmachakra Translation Committee, trans. 2006. *Middle beyond Extremes: Maitreya's Madhyāntavibhāga with Commentaries by Khenpo Shenga and Ju Mipham.* Ithaca, N.Y.: Snow Lion Publications.

———, trans. 2009. *Luminous Essence: A Guide to the Guhyagarbha Tantra.* Ithaca, N.Y.: Snow Lion Publications.

Doctor, Thomas, trans. 2004. *Speech of Delight: Mipham's Commentary on Śāntarakṣita's "Ornament of the Middle Way."* By Ju Mipham. Ithaca, N.Y.: Snow Lion Publications.

Dorje, Gyurme, trans. 1987. "The Guhyagarbhatantra and Its XIVth Century Tibetan Commentary Phyogs bcu mun sel." 3 vols. PhD diss., University of London, School of Oriental and African Studies. Revised introduction available at Wisdom Books online reading room, www.wisdom-books.com.

———. 2001. *Tibetan Elemental Divination Paintings.* London: Eskenazi and Fogg.

———. 2009. *Tibet.* 4th ed. Bath: Footprint.

———, trans. 2012. *The Treasury of Knowledge: Book Six, Parts One and Two: Indo-Tibetan Classical Learning and Buddhist Phenomenology.* By Jamgön Kongtrul. Boston: Snow Lion.

———. 2014. "The Buddhas of Medicine." In Theresia Hofer, ed. *Bodies in Balance: The Art of Tibetan Medicine,* 128–53. Seattle: University of Washington Press.

———, trans. 2016. *The Complete Nyingma Tradition from Sutra to Tantra, Books 15–17: The Essential Tantras of Mahayoga.* By Choying Tobden Dorje. Boulder, Colo.: Snow Lion.

Dorje, Gyurme, with Tashi Tsering, Heather Stoddard, and Andre Alexander. 2010. *Jokhang: Tibet's Most Sacred Buddhist Temple.* London and Bangkok: Edition Hansjorg Mayer.

Dotson, Brandon. 2009. *The Old Tibetan Annals: An Annotated Translation of Tibet's First History.* Vienna: Austrian Academy of Sciences Press.

Douglas, Kenneth, and Gwendolyn Bays, trans. 1978. *The Life and Liberation of Padmasambhava.* Translated from the French translation of Gustave-Charles Touissant entitled *Le Dict de Padma.* Berkeley: Dharma Publishing.

Dudjom Rinpoche. 1991. *The Nyingma School of Tibetan Buddhism: Its Fundamentals and History.* 2 vols. Translated by Gyurme Dorje with Matthew Kapstein. Boston: Wisdom Publications.

Eckel, Malcolm D. 1987. *Jñānagarbha's Commentary on the Distinction between the Two Truths.* Albany: State University of New York Press.

Engle, Artemis B., trans. 2009. *The Inner Science of Buddhist Practice.* By Vasubandhu. Ithaca, N.Y.: Snow Lion Publications.

———, trans. 2016. *The Bodhisattva Path to Unsurpassed Enlightenment.* By Ārya Asaṅga. Boulder, Colo.: Snow Lion.

Ferrari, A. 1958. *Mk'yen brtse's Guide to the Holy Places of Central Tibet.* Serie Orientale Roma 16. Rome: Istituto Italiano per il Medio ed Estremo Oriente.

Folkert, Kendall W., and J. E. Cort. 1993. *Scripture and Community: Collected Essays on the Jains.* Atlanta: Scholars Press.

Fremantle, Francesca. 1971. "A Critical Study of the Guhyasamāja Tantra." PhD diss., University of London, School of Oriental and African Studies.

Giebel, Rolf. W., trans. 2001. *Two Esoteric Sutras.* Berkeley: Numata Center for Buddhist Translation and Research.

Gomez, L. O., and J. A. Silk, eds. 1989. "The Sutra of the King of Samādhis, Chapters I–IV." In *Studies in the Literature of the Great Vehicle,* 11–88. Ann Arbor: University of Michigan.

Gonda, J. 1975. *Vedic Literature.* History of Indian Literature series, vol. 1, fasc. 1. Wiesbaden: Otto Harrassowitz.

Gray, David B., trans. 2007. *The Cakrasaṃvara Tantra.* New York: American Institute of Buddhist Studies at Columbia University.

———. 2012. *The Cakrasamvara Tantra: Editions of the Sanskrit and Tibetan Texts.* New York: American Institute of Buddhist Studies at Columbia University.

Gruschke, Andreas. 2001. *The Cultural Monuments of Tibet's Outer Provinces: Amdo. Volume 1: The Qinghai Part of Amdo.* Bangkok: White Lotus.

Guarisco, Elio, and Ingrid McLeod, trans. 2005. *The Treasury of Knowledge: Book Six, Part Four: Systems of Buddhist Tantra.* By Jamgön Kongtrul. Ithaca, N.Y.: Snow Lion Publications.

———, trans. 2008. *The Treasury of Knowledge: Book Eight, Part Three: The Elements of Tantric Practice.* By Jamgön Kongtrul. Ithaca, N.Y.: Snow Lion Publications.

Guenther, Herbert, trans. 1971. *Buddhist Philosophy in Theory and Practice.* Boulder, Colo. and London: Shambhala Publications.

———, trans. 1993. *Ecstatic Spontaneity: Saraha's Three Cycles of Dohā.* Berkeley: Asian Humanities Press.

Gyatso, Janet, and Hanna Havnevik. 2005. *Women in Tibet.* London: C. Hurst.

Haarh, Eric. 1969. *The Yar-luṅ Dynasty.* Copenhagen: G. E. C. Gad's Forlag.

Harding, Sarah, trans. 2003. *Machik's Complete Explanation.* Ithaca, N.Y.: Snow Lion Publications.

———, trans. 2007. *The Treasury of Knowledge: Book Eight, Part Four: Esoteric Instructions.* By Jamgön Kongtrul. Ithaca, N.Y.: Snow Lion Publications.

———, trans. 2016. *The Treasury of Precious Instructions.* Vol. 14, *Chöd.* Compiled by Jamgön Kongtrul. Boulder, Colo.: Snow Lion.

Hazod, G., P. Sorensen, and P. Sensen. 2005. *Thundering Falcon.* Vienna: Österreichisch Akademie der Wissenschaften.

Hodge, Stephen, trans. 2003. *The Mahā-Vairocana-Abhisaṃbodhi Tantra with Buddhaguhya's Commentary.* London: RoutledgeCurzon.

Holmes, Kenneth, and Katia Holmes, trans. 1985. *The Changeless Nature.* Eskdalemuir: Karma Drubgyud Darjay Ling.

Hopkins, Jeffrey, trans. 1998. *Buddhist Advice for Living and Liberation: Nāgārjuna's Precious Garland.* Ithaca, N.Y.: Snow Lion Publications.

Huntington, C. W., and Geshe Namgyal Wangchen. 1989. *The Emptiness of Emptiness.* Honolulu: University of Hawaii Press.

Ichigo, M. trans. 1985. *Madhyamakālaṃkāra of Śāntarakṣita with His Own Commentary or Vṛtti, and with the Subcommentary or Pañjikā of Kamalaśīla.* Kyoto: Buneido.

Iida, Shotaro. 1980. *Reason and Emptiness.* Tokyo: Hokuseido Press.

Jaini, Padmannabh S. 1979. *The Jaina Path of Purification.* Delhi: Motilal Banarsidass.

Jamspal, Lobzang et al., trans. 2004. *The Universal Vehicle Discourse Literature*. New York: American Institute of Buddhist Studies at Columbia University.

Jinpa, Thupten, trans. 2008. *The Book of Kadam: The Core Texts*. Boston: Wisdom Publications.

———, trans. 2013. *Wisdom of the Kadam Masters*. Boston: Wisdom Publications.

Johnson, E. H. (1936) 1972. *Aśvaghoṣa's Buddhacarita or Acts of the Buddha*. Part I, Sanskrit text; Part II, translation, cantos I–XIV. Reprint, Delhi: Motilal Banarsidass.

Kapstein, Matthew T. 1992. "Remarks on the Maṇi bKa'-'bum and the Cult of Avalokiteśvara in Tibet." In S. D. Goodman and R. M. Davidson, ed. *Tibetan Buddhism: Reason and Revelation*, 79–93. Albany: State University of New York Press.

———. 2006. *The Tibetans*. Oxford: Blackwell Publishing.

Karmay, Samten G., trans. (1972) 2001. *The Treasury of Good Sayings*. London: Oxford University Press. Reprint, Delhi: Motilal Banarsidass.

Kato, Bunno et al., trans. 1975. *The Threefold Lotus Sutra*. Tokyo: Kosei Publishing.

Kato, Junsho. 1980. " Notes sur les deux maîtres bouddhiques Kumāralāta et Śrīlāta." In *Indianisme et Bouddhisme: Mélanges offerts à Mgr. Étienne Lamotte*, 197–213. Publications de l'Institut orientaliste de Louvain 23. Louvain-la-Neuve: Université catholique de Louvain, Institut orientaliste.

Kern, H., trans. (1884) 1968. *Saddharma-Puṇḍarīka or the Lotus of the True Law*. Oxford: Oxford University Press. Reprint, Delhi: Motilal Banarsidass.

Kilty, Gavin, trans. 2004. *Ornament of Stainless Light*. Boston: Wisdom Publications.

———, trans. 2010. *Mirror of Beryl*. Boston: Wisdom Publications.

Kochumuttom, T., trans. 1982. *A Buddhist Doctrine of Experience*. Delhi: Motilal Banarsidass.

Kvaerne, Per. 1995. *The Bon Religion of Tibet*. London: Serindia Publications.

Lang, Karen, trans. 1986. *Āryadeva's Catuḥśataka: On the Bodhisattva's Cultivation of Merit and Knowledge*. Copenhagen: Akademisk Forlag.

Lindtner, Christian. 2001a. *Madhyamakahṛdayam of Bhavya*. Chennai: The Adyar Library and Research Centre.

———, trans. 2001b. *Chapter on Mimāṃsa of Madyamakahṛdaya*. Chennai: The Adyar Library and Research Centre.

Martin, Dan. 1997. *Tibetan Histories*. London: Serindia Publications.

Mills, Martin A. 2007. "Re-Assessing the Supine Demoness: Royal Buddhist Geomancy in the Srong btsan sgam po Mythology." *Journal of the International Association of Tibetan Studies*, no. 3.

Mullin, Glenn H. 2001. *The Fourteen Dalai Lamas: A Sacred Legacy of Reincarnation*. Santa Fe: Clear Light Books.

Nagatomi, Masatoshi. 1957. "A Study of Dharmakīrti's *Pramāṇavārttika*: An English Translation and Annotation of the *Pramāṇavārttika* Book I." PhD diss., Harvard University.

Namkhai Norbu, Chogyal. 2009. *The Light of Kailash*. Vol. 1, *The Early Period*.

Translated from the Tibetan and edited by Donatella Rossi. Merigar: Shangshung Publications.

———. 2013. *The Light of Kailash*. Vol. 2, *The Intermediate Period*. Translated from the Tibetan and edited by Donatella Rossi. Merigar: Shangshung Publications.

———. 2015. *The Light of Kailash*. Vol. 3, *The History of the Later Period*. Translated from the Tibetan and edited by Donatella Rossi. Merigar: Shangshung Publications.

Newman, John. 1987. "The Outer Wheel of Time: Vajrayāna Buddhist Cosmology in the Kālacakra Tantra." PhD diss., University of Wisconsin–Madison.

Nyima, Tudeng, and Gyurme Dorje, trans. 2001. *An Encyclopaedic Tibetan-English Dictionary*. Vol. 1. Beijing and London: Nationalities Publishing House/SOAS.

Padmakara Translation Group, trans. 1997. *The Way of the Bodhisattva: A Translation of the Bodhicharyāvatāra*. By Shantideva. Boston: Shambhala Publications.

———, trans. 1999. *Lady of the Lotus-Born: The Life and Enlightenment of Yeshe Tsogyal*. By Gyalwa Changchub and Namkhai Nyingpo. Boston: Shambhala Publications.

———, trans. 2002. *Introduction to the Middle Way: Candrakirti's Madhyamakavatara with Commentary by Jamgön Mipham*. Boston: Shambhala Publications.

———, trans. 2005. *The Adornment of the Middle Way: Shantarakshita's Madhyamakalankara with Commentary by Jamgön Mipham*. Boston: Shambhala Publications.

———, trans. 2007. *The Nectar of Manjushri's Speech: A Detailed Commentary on Shantideva's "Way of the Bodhisattva."* By Kunzang Pelden. Boston: Shambhala Publications.

———, trans. 2016. *The Root Stanzas on the Middle Way: The "Mulamadhyamakakarika."* By Nagarjuna. Boulder, Colo.: Shambhala Publications.

Pruden, Leo M., trans. 1988–90. *Abhidharmakośabhāṣyaṃ*. By Vasubandhu. Translated into French by Louis de La Vallée Poussin. English translation by Leo M. Pruden. 4 vols. Berkeley: Asian Humanities Press.

Pu Wencheng. 1993. *Gang Qing Zangchuan Fajiao Siyuan* [Tibetan Buddhist Monasteries of Gansu and Qinghai]. Ziling: Qinghai Peoples' Publishing House.

Radhakrishnan, S., trans. 1953. *The Principal Upaniṣads*. London: Allen and Unwin.

Radhakrishnan, S., and Charles A. Moore, eds. 1957. *A Source Book in Indian Philosophy*. Princeton, N.J.: Princeton University Press.

Red Pine, trans. 2001. *The Diamond Sutra: The Perfection of Wisdom; Text and Commentaries Translated from Sanskrit and Chinese*. Berkeley: Counterpoint.

———, trans. 2004. *The Heart Sutra: The Womb of Buddhas*. Berkeley: Counterpoint.

Ricard, Matthieu, trans. 1994. *The Life of Shabkar*. Albany: State University of New York Press.

Robinson, James B. 1979. *Buddha's Lions: The Lives of the Eighty-Four Siddhas*. Berkeley: Dharma Publishing.

Rockwell, John, Jr. 1980. "Samadhi and Patient Acceptance: Four Chapters of the *Samadhiraja-sutra*." MA thesis, The Naropa Institute, Boulder, Colo.

Roerich, George, trans. 1949. *The Blue Annals*. 1st ed. Delhi: Motilal Banarsidass.

van Schaik, Sam. 2011. *Tibet: A History*. New Haven, Conn.: Yale University Press.

Scott, Jim, trans. 2004. *Maitreya's Distinguishing Phenomena and Pure Being*. Ithaca, N.Y.: Snow Lion Publications.

Shakabpa, Wangchuk D. 1967. *Tibet: A Political History*. New Haven, Conn.: Yale University Press.

Sherbourne, Richard, trans. 2000. *The Complete Works of Atiśa*. Delhi: Aditya Prakashan.

Sen, Prabal Kumar. 1983. "Śrīlāta: A Pre-Vasubandhu Philosopher." *Journal of the Department of Philosophy, University of Calcutta* 1: 119–31.

Sinha, Nandalal, trans. 1915. *The Samkhya Philosophy. Containing the "Tattvasamāsa" and "Sāṃkhyākārikā" with Other Texts*. Allahabad: Panini Office.

Skorupski, Tadeusz. 1983. *The Sarvadurgatipariśodhanatantra: Elimination of All Evil Destinies*. Delhi: Motilal Banarsidass.

Snellgrove, David L., trans. 1959. *The Hevajra Tantra*. Two Parts. London: Oxford University Press.

———. 1967. *The Nine Ways of Bon*. London Oriental Series 18. London: Oxford University Press.

Sørensen, Per K., trans. 1986. *Candrakīrti: Triśaraṇasaptati, The Septuagint on the Three Refuges*. Vienna: Arbeitskreis für Tibetische und Buddhistische Studien Universität Wien.

———. 1994. *Tibetan Buddhist Historiography: The Mirror Illuminating the Royal Genealogies*. Wiesbaden: Harrassowitz Verlag.

Sparham, Gareth, trans. 2006–12. *Abhisamayālaṃkāra with Vṛtti and Ālokā*. *Vṛtti* by Ārya Vimuktisena. *Ālokā* by Haribhadra. 4 vols. Fremont, Calif.: Jain Publishing.

Speyer, J. S., trans. 1895. *The Jātakamālā of Āryasūra*. London: The Pali Text Society.

Sprung, Mervyn, trans. 1979. *Lucid Exposition of the Middle Way*. London: Routledge and Kegan Paul.

Suryanarayana Sastri, S. S., ed. and trans. 1935. *The Sāṅkhyakārikā of Īśvara Kṛṣṇa*. Madras: University of Madras.

Suzuki, Daisetz T. 1932. *The Laṅkāvatārasūtra*. London: Routledge and Kegan Paul.

Szántó, Péter-Dániel. 2012. "Selected Chapters from the *Catuṣpīṭhatantra*." 2 vols. DPhil diss., Oxford University.

Takasaki, Jikido. 1966. *A Study on the Ratnagotravibhāga (Uttaratantra)*. Serie Orientale Roma 33. Rome: Istituto Italiano per il Medio ed Estremo Oriente.

Tenzin Wangyal Rinpoche. 2004. *Wonders of the Natural Mind*. Delhi: New Age Books.

Thondup, Tulku. 1999. *Masters of Meditation and Miracles*. Boston: Shambhala Publications.

Thrangu Rinpoche, Khenchen, et al., trans. 2004. *The Ornament of Clear Realization*. Auckland: Zhyisil Chokyi Ghatsal Charitable Trust Publications.

Trizin Tsering Rinpoche, trans. 2007. *The Mani Kabum.* Singapore: Evergreen Buddhist Culture Service.

Uray, Geza. 1972. "The Narrative of Legislation and Organization of the Mkhas pa'i Dga' ston: The Origins of the Traditions concerning Sroṅ brcan Sgam po as First Legislator and Organizer of Tibet." *Acta Orientali* 26: 11–68.

Valby, Jim, trans. 2008–14. *Ornament of the State of Samantabhadra: Commentary on the All-Creating King of the Pure Perfect Presence of the Great Perfection of All Phenomena.* 6 vols. Shelburne Falls, Mass.: Jim Valby Publications.

Vitali, R. 1996. *The Kingdoms of Gu.ge Pu.hrang.* Dharamsala: Tho ling dpe med lhun gyis grub pa'i gtsug lag khang lo 1000 'khor ba'i rjes dran mdzad sgo'i sgrig tshogs chung.

Wallace, Vesna A. 2001. *The Inner Kālacakratantra: A Buddhist Tantric View of the Individual.* New York: Oxford University Press.

———, trans. 2004. *The Chapter on the Individual together with the Vimalaprabhā.* New York: American Institute of Buddhist Studies at Columbia University.

———, trans. 2010. *The Kālacakratantra: The Chapter on Sādhanā together with the Vimalaprabhā Commentary.* New York: American Institute of Buddhist Studies at Columbia University.

Walshe, Maurice, trans. 1987. *The Long Discourses of the Buddha.* Boston: Wisdom Publications.

Wayman, Alex, trans. 1983. *Chanting the Names of Mañjuśrī: The Mañjuśrī-Nāma-Saṃgīti Sanskrit and Tibetan Texts.* Delhi: Motilal Banarsidass.

Wayman, Alex, and Hideko Wayman, trans. 1974. *The Lion's Roar of Queen Śrīmālā.* New York: Columbia University Press.

Yamada, Isshi. 1981. *Sarva-tathāgata-tattva-saṃgraha nāma mahāyāna-sūtra: A Critical Edition Based on the Sanskrit Manuscript and Chinese and Tibetan Translations.* New Delhi: Sharada Rani.

Yamamoto, Kosho, trans. 1999–2000. *The Mahāyāna Mahāparinirvāṇa Sūtra.* 12 vols. Edited by Tony Page. London: Nirvana Publications.

Yang Ga. 2014. "The Origins of the *Four Tantras* and an Account of Its Author, Yuthog Yonten Gonpo." In Theresia Hofer, ed. *Bodies in Balance: The Art of Tibetan Medicine,* 154–77. Seattle: University of Washington Press.

Yeshe Gyamtso, trans. 2011. *The Hundred Tertöns.* By Jamgön Kongtrul. Woodstock, N.Y.: KTD Publications.

Zangpo, Ngawang, trans. 2010. *The Treasury of Knowledge: Books Two, Three, and Four: Buddhism's Journey to Tibet.* By Jamgön Kongtrul. Ithaca, N.Y.: Snow Lion Publications.

Index

Ekajaṭī